IN THE EYE OF THE STORM

GEORGE V AND THE GREAT WAR

Alexandra Churchill

Helion & Company Limited
Unit 8 Amherst Business Centre
Budbrooke Road
Warwick
CV34 5WE
England
Tel. 01926 499 619
Fax 0121 711 4075
Email: info@helion.co.uk
Website: www.helion.co.uk
Twitter: @helionbooks
Visit our blog http://blog.helion.co.uk/

Published by Helion & Company 2018
Designed and typeset by Battlefield Design, Gloucester (www.battlefield-design.co.uk)
Cover designed by Paul Hewitt, Battlefield Design (www.battlefield-design.co.uk)
Printed by Short Run Press, Exeter, Devon

Text © Alexandra Churchill 2018
Images © as individually credited
Map drawn by George Anderson © Helion & Company 2018

ISBN 978-1-911628-26-2

British Library Cataloguing-in-Publication Data.
A catalogue record for this book is available from the British Library.

For details of other military history titles published by Helion & Company Limited contact the above address, or visit our website: http://www.helion.co.uk.

We always welcome receiving book proposals from prospective authors.

Contents

List of Photographs

Dedication

In grateful memory of Neville, Lord Wigram, Godson of King George V, who died before he could see the result of his contribution to this book.

For Garry Brown, with love.

And for Phineas Potts of Gallipoli and Mile End.

Acknowledgements

Her Majesty Queen Elizabeth II. At the Royal Archives Laura Hobbs, who has put nearly as many hours into this book as I have; also Lynne, Allison and Julie. The State Archives of the Russian Federation, the Bodleian Library, Oxford, the Imperial War Museum and The National Archives for their flexibility with Lord Kitchener's papers. Duncan Rogers and Andy Miles at Helion Publishing, Paul Hewitt and Mary Woolley at Battlefield Design.

Special thanks to Lord Astor of Hever and the late Lord Wigram and family. Also, Charlie, for taking pity on a nerd, without your generosity this book would absolutely not exist,

Thank you to Andrew Holmes, Eric Sauder, Carolyn Day, Dee and Steve Prior, and Anne, for providing a home away from home in Windsor, Rob Hildyard, my Assistant Historian. Paul Hildyard: the Prince of Power, James Thompson, Research Assistant, Gary Bain, Bryn Hammond, Peter Hart, Andy Tonge, Gary Sheffield and John Bourne.

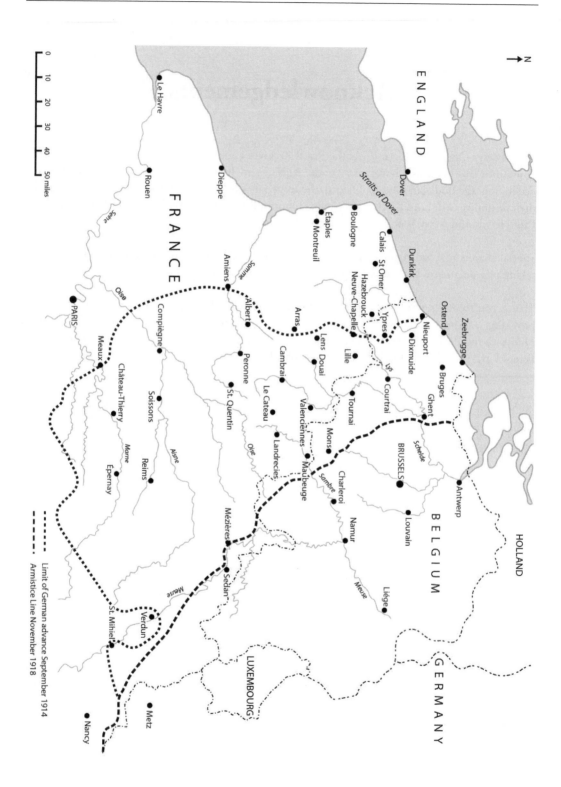

Introduction

"This Mighty Pilgrimage"

The English approach two things with unparalleled stoicism: rain, and queues. It is a matter of national pride to greet both with a stiff upper lip. And this is patriotic, English rain; a light, persistent drizzle that can scarcely be felt, but soaks everything it touches as it falls through a thick veil of city fog on a mild January day. But Londoners bundle themselves up warmly in their clutch coats, their bowler hats and their fur wraps. They seize their trusty umbrellas and they make for the heart of the capital. They climb out onto the street from the stifling, muggy Underground at Westminster to find Big Ben swathed in mist, and clamber down from sleek, wet buses and trams into puddles in front of the Houses of Parliament. They search for the back of a thick, uncomplaining, very British queue that already snakes all the way from Westminster, across Vauxhall Bridge; highlighted by black armbands, black caps, jet trinkets. After hours of waiting they enter the south door of Westminster Hall and pass under a triumphant medieval roof that has sheltered centuries of seismic events in British history. The chill hits them. It is no warmer than outside, but it is at least dry. The pilgrims pause at the top of a flight of stone steps and gaze down at the spectacle in the middle of the otherwise empty floor.

The endless procession divides and the lines move parallel, two or three abreast, keeping a slow, steady pace along a grey carpet that has been laid on the stone floor to muffle their footsteps. None of them speak. "During the slow passage of this mighty pilgrimage…how sharply the silence [is] broken by the cry of an infant carried in its mother's arms or by the occasional sound of a motor-horn in the streets outside."[1] All eyes are on the lit catafalque, upon the Imperial Crown resting atop the thick folds of a Royal Standard; draped over a coffin and on the golden cross that surmounts it all. Still figures surround this small display in this enormous space. They wear scarlet tunics, black boots, white gauntlets and lean silently on their swords. The whole solemn journey through Westminster Hall takes less than three minutes, then the pilgrims are back outside in the rain. And yet people are not deterred. As the grey light fades, newcomers emerge. Darkness falls and still they come. At half past nine some 20,000 visitors still await the short honour of entering the Palace of Westminster underneath wet, heavy flags, slapping loudly in the wind at half-mast aloft, and solemnly proceeding past the coffin.

All scheduling is disregarded as the week wears on. There are so many people waiting that there is nothing for the authorities to do but to continue to let the public in. At night the King's crown sparkles in the glare of six grand candles that surround his coffin. Amid the grandeur, cleaners arrive and silently sweep the carpet ready for when the doors open again. Notices are pasted up at Underground stations, urging the converging masses to walk to Westminster, as the nearby station cannot cope with the influx of arrivals. When Lambeth Bridge is closed to traffic it is estimated that the line of Britons waiting to pay their respects is nearly three miles long. A police car with a loud speaker mounted on the roof cruises slowly up and down outside Westminster Hall, directing new arrivals down the banks of the Thames to the end of the waiting masses. In a display of organisation

---

1   *The Times: Hail and Farewell: The Passing of King George V*, pp.60-8.

and discipline wholly characteristic of his people, three queues have evolved just for His Majesty's subjects to join the dense main procession; from Lambeth, from Vauxhall and from over the bridge at Westminster. On the last day of his lying in state, the dead King's subjects wait upwards of seven hours to see him.

All of this fuss would have astonished the deceased. On Monday his widow comes. She wants to see the crowds for herself, wants to see the scale of respect for her late husband. "A few minutes before the change of the guard at 6 o'clock, five cars drive into New Palace Yard."[2] In the first is Queen Mary, heavily veiled, accompanied by the Princess Elizabeth. But for those who have waited for hours for their turn to pass the coffin, the arrival of the Royal Family is unobtrusive. Slowly heads turn towards them, then they resume their procession. It is estimated that in four days, nearly 800,000 men, women and children have journeyed to Westminster to see the King. The night before his funeral, the queue is still halfway across Vauxhall Bridge, and thousands stubbornly await their turn.

"The Squire of Sandringham"

In January 1936 a hush had begun to fall over London. King George V greets the New Year a tired man. During the first days of January he plods about the Sandringham estate on his white pony, Jock, but by the middle of the month he is confined indoors. Snowflakes drift past the windows of the house as he sits by the fire in his dressing gown. Queen Mary is concerned, and on 17th January she sends for his doctors. Their prognosis distresses her greatly. Their children arrive almost immediately and the Queen walks in the gardens with her eldest sons. "A very sad day,"[3] she records, for her beloved husband's heart is beginning to fail.

On Monday it rains in his capital. Every now and again the clouds part, and streaks of bright sunshine gleam off of wet pavements. The population wavers between hope and the sad expectation that an era is coming to an end. By evening, London is stilled. Music and dancing in public places has ceased; the streets are deserted. Outside the palace, despite the frequent downpours, people abandon their routine and stand together. In homes across the country, wireless sets are tuned in to wait for news. Hearts sink at 5:30pm: *The condition of His Majesty the King shows diminishing strength. The King is dying; there is no more to be done, or feared, or wished, but only a vigil to be kept."* Four hours later comes the solemn announcement from Sandringham: "*The King's life is moving peacefully towards its close."* BBC programming is stopped as the nation holds its breath. The wireless forms a tie between home and palace "and listeners feel in the presence of a loved friend on the confines of the next world... At 10 o'clock the haunting phrase: '*The King's life is moving peacefully towards its close,'* again came through the air." At Sandringham, Queen Mary sits down to make an entry in her diary. "Am brokenhearted," she begins. "At five to twelve my darling husband passed peacefully away."[4]

Known as *the Squire of Sandringham* on account of his preference for the life of a country gentleman, as word of his death begins to radiate across the globe, the world begins to react. In Ottawa additional staff are called in to all the telephone exchanges to cope with the influx of calls regarding the King's death. On the other side of the world, it is just about lunchtime. In Australia, newspapers begin churning out special editions. Flags are pulled down to half mast, public offices closed, and sports cancelled. In South Africa, the King's death had occurred in the small hours, but

2   Ibid.
3   RA PRIV/QMD/1936 (17/1).
4   Ibid., (20/1).

when the Dominion awakes to the news on 21st January, the country spontaneously observes it as a day of mourning. Day was just breaking in India, where tidings of the King's death spread like wildfire. The remotest parts of the country are aware of his passing within an hour. "Men told the news to crowds coming out into the grey, rain-flecked morning from mosques and temples."[5] But it is not just by his own people that His Majesty's death is met with immediate tribute. In Italy, the papal court holds a service of intercession, and Mussolini attends another at the Anglican church in Rome. In Madrid the former King attends one of four consecutive services at the English church that have to be held to accommodate all of the mourners. President Roosevelt sends a telegram to the new King, Edward VIII. So does the Emperor of Japan, who has never forgotten King George's kindness to him.

But what is truly touching about the death of the Sovereign is that the outpouring of sorrow at his passing is not confined to the public platitudes of statesmen. People are genuinely moved the world over. 50,000 assemble in Melbourne in the height of an Australian summer to mourn him. In Canada, guns are hauled through the snow to the top of Mount Royal to salute the dead King, and in Newfoundland, thousands walk through a blizzard to attend a service. Bombay spends a day in solemn mourning, whilst the English in Kenya embark upon a pilgrimage to a hillside outside Nairobi, where they fashion a great crown of stone and flowers.

In France it is as if they mourn one of their own, with spontaneous outbursts of grief for a fallen ally. Italian wireless stations suspend their programming, whilst in Tokyo the streets are full of runners with bells proclaiming news of the King's death. There are tributes to His Majesty at Lisbon, Cairo, Montevideo, Jerusalem, Tunis, Warsaw and Prague. In China, guns sound and flags fly at half-mast. There is a service in Washington Cathedral. The solemn proceedings are not confined to Britain's friends and allies. Former enemies also mourn. In Vienna, Constantinople and Budapest flags are lowered and services held. In Germany, famous soldiers who have opposed his troops in years past pay tribute. *The Times* reports that Adolf Hitler has the Nazi flag hauled down and replaced by a Union Jack in every ship of the German Navy.

The morning after the King's death, Queen Mary goes to his room. He looks peaceful, younger; as if all of the frailty and pain of his last weeks have left him. At 5:00pm his coffin, made of Sandringham oak, is closed. As twilight begins to absorb the last of the short, winter afternoon, the Queen follows on foot as men of the Grenadier Guards carry her husband away to the little church nearby. There is a short service, which is a comfort to her. The only mourners present are from the estate, "our own, kind people."[6] Then the time for private mourning is over. Crowds watch from platforms along the main Cambridge line as the train carrying the King's coffin rattles south, removing their hats as it speeds past. By Thursday evening he lies in state in Westminster Hall.

There remains one final act of pageantry before the King can be laid to rest: a procession through the streets of London to Paddington Station for his final journey to Windsor. People begin to reserve their spot along the route days in advance. They gather in their thousands, braving the damp January chill and collecting on kerbs along St. James's Street, Piccadilly and Edgware Road; clustering thickly in the neighbourhood of Westminster and along Whitehall. They wander up and down in the middle of the night, choosing their vantage points. They sit on kerbs, lean on pavement guard rails. Some lie down to sleep wrapped in newspapers or rugs. Before dawn trains begin to converge at London stations, bringing mourners from all across Britain. Whole families arrive, some of them dragging with them their kitchen chairs to rest on until the procession begins.

---

5   *The Times: Hail and Farewell: The Passing of King George V,* pp.60-8.
6   RA PRIV/QMD/1936 (21/1).

The centre of London grinds to a halt. An unprecedented crowd watches in hushed silence as the gun carriage emerges with the coffin of His Majesty atop, draped in the Royal Standard. The sailor King is led home by naval bluejackets as the procession leaves Westminster. Behind him walk his sons, extended members of the Royal Family and foreign dignitaries. Queen Mary and her female relatives follow in carriages as under leaden, sad skies the procession moves slowly towards Paddington. Policemen and soldiers vainly try to control the dense crowds as they begin to encroach on the route. Piccadilly and Marble Arch are at a standstill as tens of thousands of Britons watch their King leave his capital for the last time, and as the gun carriage passes over darkened streets, slick with rain from morning showers, pipes plays a lament, drums throb, spectators hang from every window. The late King's subjects cling to every available viewpoint. "Railings and trees were perched upon by late-comers, some of the trees in Hyde Park looked like rookeries; and almost every roof thrust up an irregular line of silhouettes against the slowly paling sky." But the tens of thousands who crowd onto the streets of London, they make hardly a sound. Instead the air is filled with "the mingling of bells, the solemn strokes of Big Ben… and the peals that speak from the new tower of Westminster Abbey."[7] Gloomy London is ablaze with colour. Black and purple flutter from balconies, flashes of scarlet uniforms accompany the royal carriages. There is the metallic glare cast by the ceremonial costume of cavalrymen, by the bandsmen brandishing their instruments as they march past. And everywhere there is an assortment of khaki and blue uniforms.

A steam engine pulls out of Paddington shortly after 12:30pm. Now it is time for his family to say goodbye. The town has turned out in force and every available patch of grass in the Lower Ward at Windsor is arranged with floral tributes as the procession arrives at St. George's Chapel. "The wreaths looked too lovely… then the beautiful service in the chapel and we left him sadly, lying for the present with his ancestors in the vaults."[8]

"Simplicity is Strength"

The Times tries to sum up for its readers why they are witnessing such an immense outpouring of sorrow at the death of His Majesty, not only amongst his own people, but amongst those much further afield who have come into contact with him throughout the course of his reign: "Gratitude for a life spent in service, sorrow for the loss of one who had, time and time again, proved himself a true friend of his subjects of every class and creed." No man is universally loved, and nobody claimed that the King was perfect. In fact, many writers were at pains to point out that he was simply an ordinary man. In fact, this is what has made him popular. Understated, not one to show off or make a scene, he was handed a difficult role in life. To be King of the United Kingdom and the British Dominions, and Emperor of India was a relentless job, all encompassing, and one that only ended with death. It was not the role that he was born for, not the role in life that he had foreseen or wanted for himself, but as far as his people were concerned, when it fell to him he had overcome the adversity of not having been prepared for it, and for a quarter of a century he had not failed them. For precisely the reasons that have since drawn ambivalence, disdain or even mockery as the context of his reign has been lost, His Majesty was loved by his people. "In taking up the heavy burden of his office," wrote one contemporary, "Cleverer men, in easier times, had worn the crown before him, and had shown themselves overburdened by it. King George, armed only with the powers of an averagely gifted individual, had to stand at the head of his people in crisis after

---

7   *The Times: Hail and Farewell: The Passing of King George V,* pp.60-8.
8   RA PRIV/QMD/1936 (28/1).

crisis… There he remained, undefeated by them all."[9] So to his contemporaries, then, the King was an example to his subjects of what an ordinary man could do if he applied himself to the best of his ability. Across the board, those who are required to put pen to paper at the beginning of 1936 in order to commemorate his reign are also unanimous in their praise when it comes to His Majesty's work ethic; as it is put in very Victorian terms: *his sense of duty*. This is a trait held in hugely high esteem by any true British patriot of the age. Largely as a result of simple hard work, the King had repackaged the monarchy, rebranded it, and made it viable in a world that ended up crumbling about the other crowned heads in Europe.

Such a legacy required professional integrity, but that was not all. His Majesty had lived through an era which not only saw the growth of the popular, pictorial press but also the birth of defined concepts of image and public relations. Previously unprecedented coverage meant that the personal life of a King was open to more scrutiny than ever before. There were few places to hide for a public figure, but His Majesty's reign was able to stand up to such close attention on his death because in the eyes of his subjects, he presented an example of personal morality that the nation could be proud of. On his death, the King was regarded by huge swathes of his people not only as an industrious man, but a respectable one, a cornerstone of both public and private integrity for his subjects to aspire to.

When he ascended the throne, many doubted him. On his death, they believe that he had proved them wrong. His Majesty had cousins who were testament, in part, as to what could happen if the wrong man wore a crown. They were dead at the hands of their own people or living out long and lonely years in exile. In 1936, many Britons believe that the King had not only been a successful monarch, but that he has left the monarchy stronger and more credible in the eyes of the modern world than when he succeeded his father. His reign is described using lofty words such as *honour* and *dignity*. "None could foresee how this simplest… of men would so round out the idea of Kingship as to leave it, [in a world gone mad] a nobler ideal than he found it. He made a good King indeed; but that was not all. Kingship itself is the higher for his example."[10]

The Good Pilot

The element of stability and credibility that radiated from Buckingham Palace might not be so precious to the people of Britain, but for the fact that in recent years the world has changed beyond all recognition. When the King was born, Britain sat atop a world that had just borne witness to the industrial revolution. The first steam locomotives and the first cameras were still in living memory. He died on the eve of World War Two. To the vast crowds that mourn him, King George stands pertinaciously, resolutely for tradition in a frightening, rapidly advancing world. This is no mean feat for a man who felt threatened by the quickening pace of life in the twentieth century, during his advancing years. In his quasi-Edwardian attire and in upholding his hard-working, moral standards, he stands for something comprehensible in a world that no longer makes sense. The people of Britain believe that his reign, which had begun in 1910, has ushered in more change than one might expect in twice as many years. "Men still short of middle age can say that they have witnessed the work of more than a generation. They have seen the dynastic diplomacy of the old century spend itself in blood on the battlefields of the new." His Majesty was forced to serve his people at what felt like breakneck speed. A journalist surmised broad social feeling amongst the King's

9   *The Times: Hail and Farewell: The Passing of King George V,* pp.60-8.
10   Ibid.

subjects. "For a hundred reasons our modern life is becoming increasingly complicated, tangled, confused." If only they could recover and cling to the virtues that were attributed to His Majesty.

In the midst of the whirl of amusements, keep a steadying rule of duty... let service come before self. While marriage is being treated with so much recklessness and frivolity, remember the home life of King George... When a hundred voices... in the Press, and in talk are muddling and confusing conscience, set before yourselves some fixed standard of personal integrity and honour below which you will scorn to fall. Prove in your own lives what King George proved in his: that simplicity is strength.[11]

By the time of his death, the King was a father figure to his people. He had managed not only to survive the advancements that threatened to engulf them all, but he had on occasion turned them to his advantage. His Majesty was the first monarch to broadcast on the radio, including the introduction of the Sovereign's Christmas message, meaning that people all over the world had experienced the revelation of having him speak in their own homes. "He used it supremely well, not because of any special gift of oratory, but just by his simple sincerity. In his Christmas broadcast... His voice was clear and strong, his words - perfectly spoken - were unaffected, admirable in dignity and gravity, without a touch of pompous or autocratic self importance." The King's determination to be amongst his people from the first made him more accessible than any British monarch before him. His people felt that they knew their King. In the House of Lords it was said that "there was no home under the British flag that did not feel his death as a personal loss. The first gentleman in the land, he taught that only he who served could rightly claim that title." And now he was gone. "In the reawakening of barbaric thoughts over so large a part of Europe, he who was passing stood for the good pilot who steers in the storm, symbol of our guard against the traps and entanglements of social change, the stability of achievements hard won and cherished, the proof and touchstone of our hopes for the world."[12]

The seismic event that stood out above all others and with which, as they mourn him, the nation associates their King, is the Great War. Hardly a testimony penned on his death fails to mention what His Majesty had meant to his people and his Allies in the years 1914-1918. Hundreds of thousands of his subjects had personally witnessed him in some capacity as he worked as hard as any of them during the most horrific war that the world had ever seen. "The truth is that the King was head and front of our whole war effort," claimed Churchill in later years. "Certainly, he had none of the clear-cut duties which fall to the lot of Ministers or heads of departments. His labours were all the more exacting for being ill-defined, for while these distinguished functionaries had the worry and strain of a circumscribed set of duties, the King had to bear the whole burden of care." Ministers came and went, officials stepped down or were removed. There was no escape for the King. "His Majesty was on duty the whole time. Day in and day out during those four frightful years he was the repository of doubts and anxieties of them all... Everything concerning the conduct of the war was known to him, he insisted upon being told everything about our disasters as well as our victories."[13] He might not have known where to begin on the outbreak of war, but in the end, to the detriment of his own health, His Majesty did not know where to stop. And unlike appointed officials, he was in it until the bitter end.

Of course, his legacy was helped by the fact that he was on the winning side, but the effusion of affection towards the Sovereign, who became a focal point for the manifestation of patriotism

11   Ibid.
12   Ibid.
13   Churchill: *Great Contemporaries,* pp.14-15.

heightened by the war, was quite astonishing; even when acknowledging all of the energy he put into the nation's war effort.

> Why did he take hold of his People's heart so strongly?… In that time of great ordeal he had revealed himself as a man of courage, of faith, and of sympathy… He never lost his nerve or his confidence in pulling through. He did his duty - a hard duty - through those years of tragic sacrifice. The people remembered that.[14]

The impression of serenity and confidence projected by the King was all the more impressive because it by no means reflected his inner feelings. He was a worrier and for more than four years he was burdened with crisis after crisis. No matter how terrified he was, exposed as he was to all facets of the war's progress, he had to remain outwardly unflinching. One of the King's ADCs said that: "the war aged him, for he was subjected to a big, unremitting strain. He knew that every day, everyone he encountered expected to leave the King's presence with a lighter heart and more determined to win the war."[15] The public mask of confidence that he needed to show his public never slipped to reveal the sleepless nights and potentially cataclysmic concerns underneath. For a man that was not sure of himself in public and not attracted to the constant glare of attention, this was all the more a remarkable achievement. Whilst monarchies fell, crowned heads were murdered, and whole nations fell into disarray and revolution, the exhausting four years of the Great War were the making of King George V and the House of Windsor.

---

14   Gibbs: *George the Faithful: The Life & Times of George V "The People's King" 1865-1936*, pp.5-6.
15   Anon: *The Life of King George V: The Life and Work of a Monarch Beloved of his Peoples*, pp.6-8.

1865 - 1914

Disparity

"Georgie"

Before the Great War, Kings and Queens are thick on the ground. There are only three Republican governments on the continent. Europe glitters with crowns and Britain's Royal Family is one of the oldest of them all, predating both her courts of law and her Parliament by centuries. With the exception of the interregnum between 1649 and 1660, an unbroken line of the King's ancestors have occupied the throne for a thousand years.

Thanks to events in the seventeenth century, His Majesty is a constitutional monarch; one who reigns, but does not rule. In the one hundred years or so before the accession of his grandmother, Queen Victoria, the growth of party politics and the individuals who inherited the throne conspired, some of them unwittingly, to reduce the monarchy in both power and esteem. It began when George I declined his right to sit in on Cabinet meetings. The absence of the Sovereign went from habitual, to accepted and then the norm. George II "was a coarse and selfish debauchee, lost to every sense of decency and dignity."[1] George III ruled for an age, fighting against the decline of the power of the Crown and his own declining faculties. When his son, George IV, died in 1830, *The Times* claimed that "there never was an individual less regretted by his fellow creatures than this deceased King."[2] William IV was better, popular, but unprepared to rule; referred to as "a bluff sailor, knowing very little more of statesmanship than a horse knows of trigonometry."[3] The organised political party was on the rise, and as the electorate also expanded, the monarch was less able to intervene in policy by manipulating individuals and was instead reduced to the ability to use the sovereign's *influence* to try and sell a point of view instead of hoping to go and effect change personally by taking part in the process.

In truth, nobody expected much of the diminutive girl who ascended the throne on the death of her uncle. The year was 1837, and she was eighteen years old. Nonetheless, her reign was to revolutionise the role of the sovereign. The reinvention which gave birth to the modern concept of monarchy in Britain began in 1840 when the young Queen Victoria wedded Prince Albert. It was a dubious age in which to be a crowned head of state in Europe. Revolution was rife, but Prince Albert recognised that he could not combat the insult that he received tens of thousands of pounds for doing nothing if he was not visible in his work. Royal philanthropy was not a new concept, but Victoria and Albert elevated it to prominence. Thanks to the advent of the railways, they took the royal message to the deepest corners of the realm with a fearless vitality and genuine sincerity. At the same time, Queen Victoria set about giving birth to nine children, and the virtue of the royal couple only enhanced the prestige of the monarchy. To be perceived as morally unimpeachable,

---

1   RA PS/PSO/GV/C/O/1106/39.
2   Bogdanor: *The Monarchy and the Constitution*, p.36.
3   RA PS/PSO/GV/C/O/1106/39.

an exemplary family, when so many of her immediate predecessors had proved incapable of such modest behaviour, was another protective layer than went hand in hand with her sex and a relentless work ethic to shield the monarchy from criticism as Victoria's reign progressed.

This, then, is the family that Prince George Frederick Ernest Albert is born into at 1:18am on 3rd June 1865. He arrives early, which is completely out of character. His grandmother is four years into a dramatic widowhood, withdrawing from public life after Prince Albert's untimely death from typhoid at the age of 42. The baby's father, Edward, Prince of Wales has a perennially troubled relationship with the Queen, who doesn't often bother to hide variously her disappointment, irritation and even contempt for her heir. After his parents caught wind of an early introduction to theatres, dancing, casinos and prostitutes in London, Prince Albert had started scheming for a wedding for the wayward 'Bertie' before he was even twenty. After a search for a potential German bride, his eye settled on Princess Alexandra of Denmark; beautiful, gentle and of virtuous upbringing. His father's death should have been the catalyst for the Prince of Wales to step up, to fill the void left by the industrious Prince Albert, but despite the fact that the Queen was under pressure to let him take on more responsibility, she pushed him away. He was an engaging hulk of a man; no genius, but not incapable; and completely underestimated by his mother. Yet she went so far as to say at about the time of Prince George's birth that the Prince of Wales was "Totally, totally unfit for ever becoming King."[4] Away from her prying eye, the Prince began to establish a social presence for himself that was the antithesis of his mother's stilted court. And she didn't like that either.

Nobody is anticipating that little Prince George will ever be a King. The Princess of Wales had already given birth to another son prematurely the previous year, so that it is Albert Victor; *Eddy,* who will have to grow up with a crushing realisation of what his future will entail. The two boys are followed by three sisters: Louise, 'Toria' and Maud. The Prince of Wales utterly refuses to repeat the relentless upbringing that so harrowed him as a child. Thus, his own parental errors are completely the opposite of the ones he suffered; instead of inflicting oppressive, discipline is lacking in his childrens' development.

Prince George is more robust than any of his siblings, who are a sickly bunch. He is lively and immediately more promising than Eddy in particular, who as they grow continues to be oddly listless and backward. Eddy is not unlikeable by any means, but being charming and sweet alone does not make a king. He is self-indulgent and lacks any sort of drive. George's influence on his elder brother is deemed to be important, and the two are paired together in everything. He is forever aware of not exciting his sibling, or making him anxious. He becomes Eddy's protector. Himself, he is prone to bad tempered outbursts and a little too much confidence, but gives his parents no particular concerns. In 1877 it is decided that Prince George should embark upon a career in the Royal Navy, joining the training ship *Britannia.* Ordinarily, an heir such as Eddy would not have gone with him, but his lack of progress and the want of any vitality is of such concern to family and tutors alike, that the idea of separating him from his younger brother proves to be unthinkable. Unfortunately, two years of training does nothing to improve Eddy's countenance. It has already been decided that George will spend a prolonged spell cruising around the world to prepare him for his future career, and despite reservations about an accident befalling them both at sea, the Queen decides that they can travel together in the *Bacchante.* They return with memories of Gibraltar, Italy and Greece; the West Indies, Buenos Aires, New Zealand and Australia, China and Singapore to name but a few destinations.

4   Ridley: *Bertie: A Life of Edward VII,* p.79.

In 1883 Prince George is posted to his first ship, HMS *Canada,* and six years later he receives his first command, a tiny torpedo boat. Life gets more complicated when he is given HMS *Thrush* in 1890. On arrival he is given "an enormous sackful of official papers and correspondence." It is too much, as he later recalls. "I fished out the ship's log and one or two other things. All the rest I threw overboard."[5] In the meantime, Eddy is still failing to progress in his preparation to one day take the throne. He has been sent to Cambridge, and to the army, but still he seems to have no gravitas about him at all. Worse, newly created as the Duke of Clarence and Avondale, Eddy has inherited his father's penchant for delinquent behaviour. The worst incident comes in 1889, when Eddy is linked, whether honestly or spitefully, with the Cleveland Street Scandal; his name allegedly appearing on a list of patrons of a male brothel. The Queen and his parents consider a number of options to settle the future King and decide to try to find Eddy a wife, in the hope that a new bride at home will put the breakers on any distasteful conduct. None of Eddy's own inclinations are suitable, and in the end, the Royal Family begin conspiring to pass the hopeless Duke onto Princess May of Teck. "I do not anticipate any real opposition on Prince Eddy's part if he is properly managed and is told he *must* do it," says his father's Private Secretary. "That it is for the good of the country etc. etc."[6] Eddy obediently proposes and the wedding is planned for the following February, the quicker the better. But Princess May and her parents are at Sandringham to celebrate his birthday with the family in the New Year when tragedy strikes. Prince Eddy dies. Returning to the house from shooting he feels unwell. The following day, his birthday, he is almost crippled with influenza and the illness begins to affect his lungs. He dies on 14th January 1892, at the age of twenty eight.

Prince George is not in a fit state to be dealing with the consequences of his brother's death. Aside from the shock of Eddy's demise, the previous November he had contracted typhoid. The same ailment had killed his grandfather Prince Albert thirty years before, and he is still in a weakened state having survived his ordeal. Now, at the age of 26, he has to come to terms with the fact that he has been thrust to the forefront of the line of succession, and that one day he will reign. The Prince has no taste for entertaining or for ceremonial duties, which will now be the mainstay of his responsibilities one day. In fact, they terrify him. He has not inherited his father's confidence in the slightest, he has never had a particular personal interest that would have caused him to pursue a knowledge of politics, science, or the arts, and he has had no urgent need for foreign languages, so the fact that any cursory attempts to instil French or German in him as part of the Wales childrens' haphazard education yielded no immediate success was not pursued.

Prince George is created Duke of York in May 1892. These are worrying times for the future prospects of the monarchy. A lack of discipline with Prince Eddy had resulted in disaster, and George is prepared for nothing but his naval career. The Duke appears to lack both the temperament and the experience to make a promising sovereign, and nobody is more aware of this than he. Immediately the family begins to address his shortfalls as a future sovereign. A Cambridge professor is brought in to instil in him the finer points of the constitution. Never one to give up flogging a dead horse, the Queen raises the lack of linguistic ability again. After summer naval manoeuvres, during which the Duke spends the entirety of the time suffering from crippling seasickness, he is sent to a fussy professor in Heidelberg to try and finally master German. He finds it next to impossible, not to mention boring. He is more concerned with the fact that the trip is robbing him of valuable shooting time at home. Nonetheless, while abroad, he carries out one of his first engagements in his new role when he represents the Queen at celebrations to mark the golden wedding anniversary

5   Rose: *King George V,* p.18.
6   Ibid., p.23.

of the Grand Duke of Saxe-Weimar. Required to wear a uniform that has been gifted to him along with honorary command of a regiment, his Danish mother, who is vehemently anti-Prussian, is enraged. "And so my Georgie boy has become a real live, filthy, blue-coated Pickelhaube German soldier!! Well, I never thought I would live to see *that!*"[7] Queen Victoria, though, is thrilled with the impression that he has made on his continental relatives.

"A Widow Before She is a Wife"

Eddy's unfortunate fiancée, Princess May of Teck, had been brought up at at White Lodge in Richmond Park and at Kensington Palace, and despite her title thinks of herself as English. In her own right she is a great granddaughter of George III and her mother is Queen Victoria's cousin. There is one sticking point which mars her suitability as a royal bride. She is of morganatic blood, which explains why she is still unmarried at 24, as does the lack of a promising dowry on account of her family's eternal financial troubles. Fortunately for May, Queen Victoria doesn't care about either so far as this promising young woman is concerned. May is tall, fair; handsome. She fills her days with reading, in fact she is passionate about learning, about expanding her mind. Besides challenging her obvious intellect, she spends long hours doing charitable work with her mother too. Philanthropy has been instilled in her from an early age and social responsibility is something that the Princess takes extremely seriously. She wants to be of use, to spend her time constructively. She is a sensible young woman, and that is why she has caught Queen Victoria's ailing eye. The Queen and her son did not need a swooning bride, caught in the throes of passion and potentially helping Eddy down a heady path to ruin. He had needed a wife to effectively save him from himself, keep him in line, and May had seemed like an ideal bride for the wayward young man.

Now, following his sudden death, the nation is in shock. Princess May returns to her home at White Lodge with her future in tatters. Her almost-in-laws grieve for her. "It is hard," the Prince of Wales writes. "that poor little May should virtually become a widow before she is a wife."[8] Thin and pale; Prince George convalesced. Slowly. The gravity of Eddy's sudden death has stunned him. "No two brothers could have loved each other more than we did," he writes to the Queen in the week following the tragedy. "Alas! It is only now that I have found out how deeply I did love him; and I remember with pain nearly every hard word and little quarrel I had with him and I long to ask his forgiveness, but… it is too late now!"[9] He cannot sleep; devastated not only by his brother's death but stunned by the idea that now, one day, he will be King. Everything that he thought he was, everything that defines him, defined what his future would be, has been snatched away and replaced with a truly terrifying prospect. This fragile young man recovering from his own life-threatening illness is the last surviving son of the Prince of Wales, all that stands in the way of complete calamity for the Royal Family. The Queen and his parents resolve to marry him off as soon as possible and ensure that Victoria's dynasty is safe.

Prince George cannot abide the idea of marrying someone who does not care for him. "I should be miserable for the rest of my life."[10] But Queen Victoria is determined that Georgie should marry May. There is precedent for such a match. In Russia, the Princess of Wales's sister had taken the next brother in line for her husband when her intended died. But there is the difficulty in Mays' mind that, by marrying Prince George, it will seem that she never cared for Eddy at all. She has gone abroad with her family to get over her loss, and puts off returning home a number of times

7   Massie: *Nicholas and Alexandra,* p.87.
8   Rose: *King George V,* pp.24-5.
9   Nicolson: *King George V: His Life and Reign,* p.96.
10   Pope-Hennessy: *Queen Mary, 1867-1953,* p.249.

because of the rumours of a new engagement to her dead fiancé's brother. Eventually though, the matter can be put off no longer, and the pair began to spend time together. Their first meetings are awkward, more so because neither is any good at expressing themselves face to face. Then slowly the ice begins to break, and a genuine fondness develops, despite May's shyness and the Prince's inability to articulate himself. Some fifteen months elapses before the pair become engaged on 3rd May 1893, by which time they have managed to give voice to their feelings at least on paper. "I am very sorry I am still so shy with you," May tells him. "I tried not to be the other day, but alas failed… It is stupid to be so stiff together and really there is nothing I would not tell you, except that I love you more than anybody in the world." The wedding takes place in the Chapel Royal at St. James's Palace and the Duke pours his heart out to his new bride: "I know I am, at least I am vain enough to think that I am capable of loving anybody (who returns my love) with all my heart and soul, and I am sure I have found that person in my sweet little May… I do love you darling girl with all my heart, and I am simply devoted to you."[11]

"Ich Dien"

Dynastic matters are taken care of swiftly, beginning with the arrival of a son in 1894. The Duke spurns the diktat issued by his grandmother, that all male heirs should be named after her beloved Prince Consort and names his son Edward, after the baby's grandfather. But to his family he will always be known by one of his numerous middle names: David. A second son, Bertie is born the next year, followed by a daughter, Mary, in 1897 before the arrival of three more boys at regular intervals. Duties are light. Even in London, life ambles along: the theatre, billiards and his beloved stamps; the occasional dinner party at York House. There are occasional state requirements, such as journeying to Russia for the funeral of the Tsar, but so infrequent are the commitments required of him, that the Duke of York also continues to serve in the Royal Navy.

But then life becomes eminently more serious in January 1901 when an era comes to an end after nearly sixty five years. "Our beloved Queen and Grandmamma, one of the greatest women that ever lived, passed peacefully away."[12] George, Duke of York, is now next in line to the throne. Work intensifies. His father, crowned Edward VII, is of a much less jealous disposition than Queen Victoria had been when he was the heir-apparent. The Duke begins reading Cabinet papers and Foreign Office documents made available to him at the King's command, attends debates in the House of Lords and even sits on a Royal Commission investigating the intricacies of food supplies coming into the country during times of war. In the months leading to his grandmother's death, plans were being made to send the Duke and Duchess abroad to open the first Parliament in the Commonwealth of Australia. The whole idea stalls on the death of the Queen, for Edward VII is reluctant to lose his son for so long a period, but the heir himself is far from opposed to the trip. Arduous as it would be; he wants to include Canada as well as Australia, New Zealand and South Africa; lest any jealousy ensue if a Dominion was left out. During more than seven months on tour, the Duke and Duchess receive a brutal introduction to the kind of pressure both might expect in future years. The Duke diligently notes that they are away for 231 days and that in that time they have travelled 45,000 miles, presented 4,329 addresses and received 544 more. 62,000 troops have been inspected, and he has officially shaken hands with 24,855 people. His mother is concerned that it is too much, but her Georgie is determined to fulfil his duty. "It is all very well for you and Papa to say we mustn't do too much but it is impossible to help it. Our stay at each place is so

11   Ibid., p.280.
12   Rose: *King George V*, p.43.

short that everything has to be crammed into it, otherwise people would be offended and our great object is to please as many people as possible."[13] In 1905, now as Prince and Princess of Wales, the royal couple find their passions stirred by a second tour. They land at Bombay in November for a four month trip through India that to be proves life-changing. After nine thousand miles by train, carriage and motor, both are effected greatly by the trip.

In the spring of 1910, King Edward begins to feel ill. He has some inclination of his prognosis, but stubbornly, he refuses to cancel his engagements. "I shall not give in,' he replies to a visitor who remonstrated with him. "I shall work to the end."[14] On the morning of 6th May, he doggedly gets dressed but collapses in the middle of the day. He is able enough in the late afternoon to have a brief conversation with the Prince of Wales about the racing at Kempton Park, but the words prove to be the last coherent ones that he will ever manage. "At 11:45 beloved Papa passed peacefully away," writes the Prince, "and I have lost my best friend and the best of fathers… I am heartbroken and overwhelmed with grief but God will help me in my responsibilities and darling May will be my comfort as she always has been."[15] The new Queen feels much the same, overwhelmed with feelings of panic and awe. Within a week her husband has been proclaimed King George V. Her first name is Victoria, and it is unthinkable that there should be another Queen of that name so soon; and so May is proclaimed Queen Mary. She is bemused. "It strikes me as curious to be rechristened at the age of 43."[16]

"I Move with the Times"

And so, His Most Excellent Majesty George the Fifth, by the Grace of God, of Great Britain, Ireland, and the British Dominions beyond the seas, King, Defender of the Faith, Emperor of India, comes to the throne a few weeks short of his forty-fifth birthday. He is physically the opposite of his imposing father; five and a half feet tall and slight in build. His light brown hair is always meticulously neat; his Van Dyke beard carefully anointed with lavender water, and he views the world through large, watery blue eyes. Until the end of his days, though his sleeves conceal elaborate red and blue dragon tattoos from his days as a seaman, his is impeccably turned out in proper attire, the epitome of a British gentleman. His modest appearance matches his personality. He is a simple man, not stupid, but uncomplicated in interpreting his role is as a new King. And above everything else he is wholly dedicated to it. He is hard working, conscientious and has an innate sense of responsibility. He may not be as clever as some of his ministers, but "he knew what was going on in politics, and in economic and international affairs, in considerable detail and he often expressed firm opinions on such matters bluntly, in a loud voice and at some length."[17] He may not be an academic, or a classical scholar, but the King's adequate intelligence, common sense and a keen interest in his work carry him a long way. Generally, for his ministers, the King's opinions are a good measure of what the general public are thinking. He is more articulate on paper than he is in voice, when he has a tendency to waffle or lose track of the subject. If His Majesty looks old-fashioned, in some ways he is ahead of his time. There is no hint of snobbery about the King, nor any discrimination on the base of age, gender, class, or ethnicity.

The new King is also approachable. One-time Prime Minister Arthur Balfour lists two royal princes with whom he thinks he can converse man to man, and His Majesty is one of them.

---

13   Ibid., p.45.
14   Ibid., p.74-6.
15   Ibid.
16   Ibid.
17   Marie Louise, Princess: *My Memories of Six Reigns*, p.52.

One acquaintance gave his first thoughts on the King a few years before he was crowned: "My impression of him… was that he was a very cheery, talkative young sailor and just a little bit too outspoken."[18] His Majesty is indeed candid. He encourages those around him to be so too; to tell him the bad, as well as the good. Accordingly, he says what he thinks. In private, he is prone to the odd burst of a fiery temper inherited from his father, when his face flushes bright red, and he loves to gossip. His language has about it "the tang and exuberance of the salt sea waves."[19] His naval life has also indentured him to banter. He has the kind of sense of humour where he freely mocks and chafes his friends, and expects the same in return. Sometimes he comes across as boorish and rather loud, but His Majesty has not an intentionally spiteful bone in his body. "How many woodcock did you shoot today?' he asks a guest once, and then, quick as a flash: 'And how many did you miss?"[20] Later in life, despite the anxiety that the rise of the Labour Party gives him, the King is still able to joke about it. When asked how he is getting on with his new Government, His Majesty will reply: "Very well. My grandmother would have hated it; my father would have tolerated it; but I move with the times."[21]

If he can be severe, the King can also be remarkably sensitive. As a man who finds showing affection very difficult indeed, he will forever try to make it up to Queen Mary with his writing. His letters overflow with sentiment. "I fear, darling, my nature is not demonstrative," he writes soon after his accession, "but… My love grows stronger for you every day, mixed with admiration and I thank God every day that he has given me such a darling devoted wife as you are."[22] A relative says that His Majesty is "one of the kindest and most generous men you can imagine. Under that rather gruff manner was the most considerate of hearts… His generosity, unknown to the outside world, was perfectly wonderful."[23] Perhaps it is this sensitive side of his nature that explains the King's tendency to slip towards fits of melancholy and worry. Following his father's death and his accession, he suffers many a sleepless night. "He told me he cannot sleep," writes one confidant. "He wakes about five and finds himself making notes of things which lie before him in his day's work." His Majesty refers to such concerns as his 'anxieties.' He finds himself sick with nerves over public engagements, especially if they contain any element of public speaking. He refers to opening Parliament for the first time, when he is required to give a speech, as "the most terrible ordeal I have ever gone through."[24] With all of his concerns and all of the state and public requirements that he is now expected to fulfil, it is unsurprising that out of the spotlight, the King prefers to continue to live as simply as possible. He likes to relax with his two passions in life: his stamps and his shooting. With regard to the former, he amasses an incredible collection, and as to the latter, His Majesty is one of the best shots in the country.

Life as King quickly assumes a routine, devoutly adhered to as if His Majesty were still commanding a ship at sea. He rises early, reads the newspapers and then devotes his time to reading Government documents that arrive relentlessly in red boxes for him to digest and sign. In this endeavour he will be assisted by his able Private Secretary. In Victorian Britain, courtiers usually came from an aristocratic background. This was not so in the case of Arthur Bigge, who was one of a dozen children born to a vicar in Northumberland. After training at Woolwich he became an officer in the Royal Artillery. He was later introduced to Queen Victoria, who was so taken with Bigge that

18   Rose: *King George V,* p.64.
19   Nicolson: *King George V: His Life and Reign,* p.249.
20   *The Times: Hail and Farewell: The Passing of King George V,* p.43.
21   Anon: *The Life of King George V: The Life and Work of a Monarch Beloved of his Peoples,* p.21.
22   Pope-Hennessy: *Queen Mary, 1867-1953,* p.426.
23   Marie Louise, Princess: *My Memories of Six Reigns,* p.191.
24   Rose: *King George V,* p.100.

she appointed him to her own household. A slight, serious-looking man with thinning hair and an inquisitive face like a bird, he would remain in royal service for over half a century. He began with a fifteen year stint assisting the Queen's Private Secretary, before he assumed the senior role during her difficult, final years. On her death in 1901, Bigge agreed to work with George, Duke of York. In a strictly hierarchical sense his appointment was a demotion, but selfless as he was, he accepted the role.

The Private Secretary is the most important colleague that a British sovereign has, and the job requires a superhuman feat of juggling everything at once and employing complete discretion. Bigge will serve King George tirelessly, faithfully, for three decades. He makes a tribute to his predecessor that encompasses what he thinks the role should entail: "The absolute non-existence of conceit, side or pose; the charming courtesy to strangers old, young, high, low, rich, poor… enormous powers of work - too much - it killed him, but I never heard him say he was hard-worked or had too much to do."[25] In his turn, Bigge is meticulous and industrious to a fault, always putting the King's interests before his own. "He taught me how to be a King," His Majesty later says.[26] Bigge is no mere assistant. He is friend, confidante, advisor and mentor. And crucially, he is the gatekeeper. To get to the King, one has to get past his secretary, and so it is a role that requires quick-thinking, deft diplomacy and tact in order to restrict the flow of those looking for royal favour and influence from overburdening the Sovereign with their demands. A lesser man might only let His Majesty see the positive, keep him shielded from anything disappointing or insulting; but Bigge is utterly determined that his King will know all, no matter how difficult it might be to accept. To be able to do this, he invites a network of sources: peers, politicians, army officers, clergy, businessmen, to write to him and keep him, and therefore the His Majesty, fully informed of both social and political matters. He takes care of the broad strokes, but also of the minute detail in helping the King to establish himself in his new position. He cautions him on not looking bored at functions, tries to get him to look like he is enjoying himself in public and not on duty like the naval officer that he no longer is. Bigge is not without fault, but his contribution to the reign of King George V is as vital as that of the monarch himself. "Fancy how quickly time flies," His Majesty writes a few years before being crowned. "What would have happened to me if you had not been there to prepare and help me with my speeches, I can hardly write a letter of importance without your assistance." Working so closely, of course there are tense moments. "I fear sometimes," wrote the then Prince of Wales,

> I have lost my temper with you and often been very rude but I am sure that you know me well enough by now to know that I did not mean it. I offer you my thanks from the bottom of my heart. I am a bad hand at saying what I feel, but I thank God that I have a friend like you, in whom I have the fullest confidence and from whom I know on all occasions I shall get the best and soundest advice whenever I seek it.[27]

"Fritz" Ponsonby is another key member of the King's household. The son of Queen Victoria's long-serving Private Secretary, and a former Guards officer who had served in South Africa, he is tall, thin, elegant and if possible, more obsessed with sartorial propriety than the King. In his spare time he liked to paint, attempting to copy old masters from the royal collection. The King used to joke that he replaced the originals with his own and made off with them. "Loyal and industrious," he is an unrivalled authority on "all the litter miseries of etiquette… yet he was too outspoken to

25   Rose: *King George V*, pp.48-9.
26   Nicolson: *King George V: His Life and Reign*, p.64.
27   Rose: *King George V*, p.49.

be the perfect courtier, and his long career was punctuated by differences with three successive sovereigns." Somewhat ornery, he wrote a little unfairly of His Majesty that he "hated all insincerity and flattery, but after a time he got so accustomed to people agreeing with him that he resented the candid friend business. At one time he took a dislike to me as he thought I invariably disagreed with any views he happened to express, but after a time regarded me as an unavoidable critic."[28] The King had more than one openly candid friend. Ponsonby was, however, of a perfect, sharp-tongued character to take on niggly or temperamental issues with a firm, even bullish hand, but of all the King's advisors, Clive Wigram, His Majesty's Assistant Private Secretary is the closest in temperament to the Sovereign. The Queen and Princess Mary, who is especially fond of him, refer to him as Wiggie. The son of a member of the Indian Civil Service, an accomplished sportsman and officer in the Indian Army, Wigram had fought on the Northwest Frontier and in South Africa before serving temporarily on His Majesty's staff during his trip to India as Prince of Wales. When he joined the King permanently in 1910, Ponsonby was not a little jealous, and said that Wigram was a man of limited horizons. He lacked experience of foreign languages and the elder man criticised the fact that his political views were like an ordinary officer at Aldershot. But then the same could be said of the King, who saw Wigram as a breath of fresh air, unfettered by decades of courtly ties. His Majesty said that he was "indeed lucky in having found a man like him." Stamfordham wrote to Wigram's mother: "His natural power of looking ahead, his common sense, his patient temper, his untiring energy and industry have enable him to achieve successfully what would have baffled not one man but several."[29] Of all the King's men, Wigram is the reformer, the fresh eyes. He had not the pedigree of Ponsonby, and he was not the intellectual equal of Stamfordham, but neither was His Majesty, who appreciated his company in times in stress.

Edward VII was quite cavalier about his red boxes, but his son, aided by Bigge, who is quickly created Lord Stamfordham, follows his grandmother's example. "Except on those rare occasions when he was seriously incapacitate by illness, no day ever passed without the King studying the contents."[30] The boxes arrive from Government departments on behalf of the Ministers who oversee them and Stamfordham organises what needs a signature or consent. There is also a nightly red box from him, containing anything that he thinks of particular interest. After dealing with these, the rest of the King's morning is devoted to receiving dignitaries and Ministers, investitures, or more work with his secretaries. More boxes accumulate throughout the day, and these claim His Majesty's time until dinner. His preference is a quiet, yet formal meal with his family before more reading until he took to his bed before midnight. Windsor is a more peaceful environment. The household are permitted to dress down to a certain extent; even if the boxes still lurk in the background and claim his time. They even follow him to Sandringham, which is much more homely. The King leaves his mother to inhabit the big house, whilst he prefers to remain tightly ensconced in the muddle of haphazard York Cottage. This concept is slightly ridiculous, as it can barely contain his large family, but the Sovereign is insistent. When asked where on earth the servants sleep, he quips that they nest in the trees outside. Stamfordham has to work in his bedroom and making a telephone call involves standing in the middle of a corridor. Sir Charles Cust, who is on ancient and friendly enough terms to question the arrangement, tells the King that it is ridiculous that an old lady and her unmarried daughter have the run of the main house, whilst the King of England and his Queen, five princes and a princess are squashed into a cottage. His Majesty tells him to mind his own business. Those who had enjoyed the commanding personality and glittering intensity of life in the company of

28   Rose: *Kings, Queens & Courtiers*, p.242.
29   Ibid.
30   Hardinge, Lady: *Loyal to Three Kings*, p.52.

Edward VII are apt to be rather bored by the pace of things under the new regime. The established court routine of blackmail, intrigue, meddling and scandal holds no interest for the King. Contrary to his father, he once famously says that he has no interest in anyone's wife but his own. At Balmoral in 1911, a friend comments that the strange "electric element" that seemed to fizz around King Edward is gone, "Yet everything is very charming and wholesome and sweet. The house is a home for children, six of them at luncheon the youngest running round the table all the while."[31]

Though guilty of crassness and speaking out of turn as a younger man; from the moment that he assumes the office, His Majesty never speaks publicly without the dignity befitting his crown. This is no small thing for a man who is known to be opinionated, and has put his foot in his mouth on many an occasion before coming to the throne. He takes great pains to try to be an exemplary exponent of a sovereign's neutrality and no scandal or disaster arises from him speaking out of turn. He cannot abide showing off. As his reign progresses the lack of flamboyance will not harm his subjects' opinion of him. In fact, it is the quiet and very traditional way he goes about his business that appeals to them. The King's occasionally booming voice masks his nerves and Court officials plead with him to expose some of his personality, to show the public the warmth that his friends see, but before the war, this is mostly in vain. As straightforward as he is, His Majesty is a King, and people will try to make scandal. One accusation levelled at him is that he is a bigamist; that he has a wife squirrelled away in America. Charles Cust hears alternatively that she lives in Plymouth. "Why there, I wonder?" The King had pondered. Whilst engaged to Queen Mary he even joked that "we can't get married after all. I hear I have got a wife and three children."[32]

"The Secret of Life"

His Majesty, like his predecessors, bases his royal conduct on a seminal work about *the English Constitution* written in the 1860s. The King has inherited certain responsibilities and ceremonial duties. Only he can summon a session of, or dissolve Parliament. Likewise, only he can appoint or dismiss a Prime Minister. His Majesty is the sole person in the Kingdom that can pardon one of his subjects, or bestow honours and peerages. He is also the titular head of both the Army and of the Royal Navy, roles which he takes extremely seriously. There are things he could do without any input from a Minister of his Government, such as issuing a proclamation to the people and finally no Bill can pass into Law until it has received Royal Assent from the King.

In reality, by law and by precedent, the Sovereign is not quite so independent as it might seem. Responsible government has evolved and curtailed the actual power of the King, so that he is obliged to follow the advice of his Ministers. If he were to reject their advice, it could mean disaster. The Government could tender their resignations on the basis of his lack of trust in them, forcing a general election. In this scenario His Majesty could put himself in an extremely awkward situation with his subjects. It has become unheard of. When the King took the throne, it had been more than 200 years since a British monarch had exercised their right to veto a Bill that had successfully passed first through the House of Commons, then the House of Lords before landing on Queen Anne's desk to be given Royal Assent to become law.

There are positive aspects to this way of doing things. Constitutional monarchy separates the Sovereign from the messiness of party politics. With his neutral stance, the King can stand above all of their squabbles. According to Bagehot, then, His Majesty is left with three things when it comes to the practicalities of governing. He has the right to be consulted by his Ministers; he has the right

31   Rose, p.90.
32   Rose: *King George V,* p.86.

to encourage them when he believes that they are following the right path and finally, much more difficult, he has the right to try and find an acceptable line when he thinks they are wrong between *warning* them as to their progress and actually interfering with the business of governance. With an unwritten constitution then, and a relatively new publication by Bagehot for guidance, how much influence the new King attempts to wield is a matter of his own work ethic, how he interprets his role, how much he chooses to take interest in and to what extent. His Government will govern regardless, but Queen Victoria has left a daunting precedent. On the advice of Prince Albert, she vowed never to put her signature on anything until she had read and understood it. This could be a frustration to her ministers, but it was within the prerogative of the sovereign and perfectly valid.

In 1890, whilst he commanded HMS *Thrush* in the West Indies, Prince George, as he then was, wrote in a bible on board: *"The secret of life is not to do what one likes, but to try to like what one has to do."*[33] Armed with this sentiment, the King also has six maxims printed and hung on the walls of his study in Buckingham Palace:

Teach me to be obedient to the rules of the game.

Teach me to distinguish between sentiment and sentimentality, admiring one and despising the other.

Teach me neither to proffer, nor to receive, cheap praise.

If I am called upon to suffer, let me be like a well-bred beast that goes away to suffer in silence.

Teach me to win, if I may; if I may not, teach me to be a good loser.

Teach me neither to cry for the moon, nor to cry over spilt milk.[34]

The King is aware of his own limitations. He has been educated for a life in the senior service, not extensively like those he will likely encounter in Government. But he is far from dimwitted and makes a point of reading and digesting the piles of documents he is sent by his Ministers with an attention to detail that would make his grandmother proud. But Bagehot did not have all of the answers, and as His Majesty finds out immediately on his accession, there are grey areas, and he will have to navigate his way through them during unprecedented crises in the opening years of his reign.

"Baptism of Fire"

In the years before the war, the overwhelmingly Conservative House of Lords had a habit of exercising its right to reject or amend legislation passed up from the elected House of Commons, which at the time of Edward VII's death and George V's accession was populated by a majority of liberals with whom they most often disagree with. For legislation to be passed up, only to be knocked back at the next stage of the political process because it is coming up against the Conservative members of the House of Lords, effectively makes a mockery of the democracy that has populated the House of Commons with a liberal majority in the first place.

33   Anon: *The Life of King George V: The Life and Work of a Monarch Beloved of his Peoples*, p.9.
34   Ibid., p.10-11.

It had been several hundred years since the Upper House had declined to pass a financial Bill into law. After the 1909 Budget they did, leaving the country to function without any money, and so triggering a General Election. One solution pursued after the election had been fought and the Budget finally, grudgingly passed, was whether or not King Edward would agree to create enough Liberal peers, and it would need to be in their hundreds, to level the playing field in the House of Lords. The King died before the matter could be settled, and the whole mess dropped into his son's lap and left him in an awful position.

His Majesty's Prime Minister is the Liberal Party's Herbert Asquith, who has held the position since 1908. The King had committed another of his verbal faux pas before coming to the throne, remarking to Churchill that he thought Asquith was trustworthy, but "not quite a gentleman." The Prime Minister was not impressed, and His Majesty later admits that he could not hold it against him. "I ought not to have said it, and it was a damned stupid thing to say; but Winston repeated it to Asquith, which was a monstrous thing to do, and made great mischief."[35] The Prime Minister exacts a revenge of sorts over the constitutional crisis involving the Lords. In the end, the King is humiliated at a meeting with Asquith and the Leader of the House of Lords, Lord Crewe, where they attempt to browbeat their inexperienced monarch into submission, and get him to agree to conferring a vast number of Liberal peerages if they win the next election. When the King asks them what will happen if he refuses, the Prime Minister says he will resign, triggering an election and then tell everyone that His Majesty has sided with the Peers against the bulk of his people. The bullying lasts for an hour and a half. At one point the King walks to the fireplace and he hears one of them say to the other: "I can do nothing with him. You have a go." Finally, His Majesty relents. The new King thinks that both men have "behaved appallingly," and that they have instigated "a dirty low-down trick."[36] He will never forget the incident, but his mother has wise words for him. "I know for certain Papa would have been obliged to act exactly in the same way. It was unavoidable and the only course open to you so although a bitter pill for you to swallow do not worry about the step you were obliged to take."[37] In the event, the King is never required to confer a bulk of peerages on Liberals, but he is still smarting from the affair in the 1930s.

The opening years of His Majesty's reign are fraught with industrial unrest too. There are strikes with a spate of violence in South Wales at the end of 1910 and the Metropolitan Police are sent to keep the peace. Throughout the King's coronation summer the country repeatedly suffers at the hands of strikes. There are nearly 900 of them, nearly a million workers are involved and at one point troops have to converge on Manchester. To say that His Majesty is concerned is an understatement. He absolutely believes that if the strikes continue, they will become political by nature and that the crown will be under threat. Far from feeling browbeaten and powerless, the King feels that he could actually help to avert further trouble. It is his belief anyway, that a Sovereign should get out and show himself to his people. London may be the centre of his Empire, but he recognises that by going further afield he can do good. Queen Mary has had it ingrained in her by her mother that you help people who are less fortunate than yourself. This is not a constitutional endeavour, it is a symbolic effort to present the King and Queen as the head of the nation, dignified and moving amongst their subjects, showing interest and concern that they genuinely feel.

And it works. People respond to the very genuine, empathic way that King George and Queen Mary conduct themselves; humble and at ease with people of all classes. In June 1912 they go off the beaten track in South Wales for three days, including into Keir Hardie's constituency in the

35   Rose: *King George V,* p.71.
36   Ibid., p.125.
37   Battiscombe, Georgina: *Queen Alexandra,* pp.277-8.

mining areas of Glamorgan and the Merthyr Valley. This is no easy gesture, considering that the man himself, the former Labour Party leader and a vehement anti-monarchist, has referred to the tour as a sham. It pleases the Queen immensely to think of what he will make of the visit when it turns out to be a success. The King too, cannot not quite believe the "extraordinary welcome"[38] that he receives. He ventures underground, and the Queen accompanies him to pit-heads, "riding in the colliery trams and chatting with the men and boys as they emerge grimy from beneath ground."[39] Her Majesty even sends their tour guides into a panic when she suddenly demands to see the inside of a miner's cottage for herself. Mrs Thomas Jones happily welcomes her royal visitor, who explores the cottage, drinks tea with the lady of the house and commends her on her excellent housekeeping. News of this spontaneous, natural behaviour spread through the valley. Then it is on to Yorkshire. The King remains deep inside the bowels of the earth for more than half an hour examining working conditions and talking to miners about their concerns and about the need to find an end to industrial unrest, and an estimated three million subjects turn out to catch a glimpse of the royal couple on their tour of the north. Their Majesties return home one evening in time to receive the tragic news that an explosion has occurred in the main pit at Cadeby since their departure. Dozens have been killed and mortally wounded. Worse still, as a rescue party tries to get to them, a second explosion occurs killing more than 50 more men. The King immediately orders everybody back into their cars and returns to Cadeby late into the evening, meeting a large, panicked crowd outside the site offices. "We went to enquire and to express our sympathy with those who had lost their dear ones."[40] Their Majesties remain, talking to families and colleagues of the victims throughout the night. As Queen Mary stands talking to the bereaved, she is trying to maintain her composure with tears flooding down her cheeks.

For their people, this behaviour by the King and Queen is a revelation. The difference between these visits and those made by their predecessors is a complete lack of formality, and a complete lack of condescension or patronising sentiment. The people who come into contact with them recognise the sincerity with which they show their concern, and the genuine interest in what they have to say. The royal couple feel more at ease with British working people than they ever will with members of high society or with foreign royalty. However much His Majesty is denigrated by his own class for being dull in comparison to his father, the country at large begins to find common ground with the new Sovereign.

If the 1910 constitutional crisis was inherited from his father, the Irish question that simmers for the two years leading up to the summer of 1914 and threatens Britain with civil war belongs wholly to King George. He becomes almost consumed by his efforts to prevent such a disaster, and pushes his mandate as a constitutional monarch to the limit in order to help broker an agreement between warring political parties.

As soon as the House of Lords loses their right to veto bills being passed up from the Commons, it becomes inevitable that Asquith will take advantage of this to try and push legislation through bestowing some measure of home rule on Ireland. His Bill is put into play in 1912. His Majesty is not against the idea of Home Rule. He believes that it can be accorded, and that if it is done properly, there is no reason that Ireland cannot become a loyal, self-governing Dominion in the same vein as Australia or Canada and maintain her loyalty to the Crown. In hindsight the Bill is extremely tame, and has so many exceptions as to what will remain the prerogative of Westminster, that it "virtually

---

38   Nicolson, Harold: *King George V: His Life and Reign,* p.196
39   Ibid.
40   Ibid.

reduced the Irish National Parliament to the status of a glorified County Council."[41] Yet at the time it is an immense undertaking, and the key point is that overwhelming Protestant Ulster could find themselves sitting in an assembly utterly dominated by Catholics in the south.

By mid-January 1913, the Bill has gone through three readings and is passed up to the House of Lords. Predictably, it is rejected. From the King's perspective, the most terrifying aspect is that now, when the Lords run out of rejections and the Bill automatically passes to him for Royal Assent to become law, the Unionists are relying on him to veto it. "I shall then be face to face with a serious dilemma," he frets. "If I assent, half the people of this country will rightly or wrongly consider that I have not been faithful to my trust, while the people of Ulster will declare that I have deserted them." The alternative was no more appealing. "On the other hand, if I withhold my assent, my Government would resign, the other half of the people would condemn my action and the whole of Ireland except Ulster would be indignant against me… In either case I should not be able to put my foot in Ireland again, a position of affairs which would be intolerable."[42]

Abusive letters arrive in large numbers at Buckingham Palace. Stamfordham tells the King to ignore these cowardly and unsigned diatribes, but it is in his nature to worry. In addition, His Majesty grows more and more frustrated by the way the Liberal Government seems to be ambling through the crisis. "I have in these days come to greatly admire the King," says the Lord Chancellor. "He has shown himself to have far more of his father's qualities of tact and judgement than I supposed. He is being bombarded by the Tory extremists with all sorts of suggestions… He remains quite calm, is sure of his constitutional position and is being of real service in seeking a way out."[43] His Majesty summons Asquith to Buckingham Palace. Fully cognisant of the fact that his strength does not lie in attempting to argue his position face to face with him, he instead presents him with a carefully prepared written memorandum, constructed with Stamfordham, that successfully articulates his thoughts.

Time and time again, the King has warned Asquith against the use of the army to coerce Ulster into submission, and he, as he was wont do to when His Majesty pressed him on numerous matters, has dismissed his sovereign's apprehension as mild hysteria. But there is a real danger concerning what will happen if the army becomes involved in any situation where they might be expected to fire on their own countrymen, and when, at the end of March 1914 the situation comes to a head, His Majesty's name is dragged into the controversy when army officers are given a mistaken ultimatum between assenting to operations in Ireland or resigning. Dozens of officers are poised to do the latter.

The King is completely unaware that any of this is happening. His Majesty does not learn that anything is amiss until he opens a newspaper one morning. It is not only humiliating on a personal level, but it is of dire embarrassment to his troops, *his* army. "I am grieved beyond words at this disastrous… catastrophe which has befallen my army," he writes personally to the Prime Minister. "I must complain that I was left in complete ignorance of yesterday's unhappy occurrences or of the circumstances which led up to them."[44] However merely symbolic his role as the head of the army is, he takes it very seriously. Loud protestations are made against him, questioning why he has not prevented such a dire situation. According to Stamfordham, radicals are denouncing all of the evil coming from within "Buckingham Palace." This is a blatant attempt at attributing this evil to the King, and the fact that it is hidden behind the name of his residence angers him even more. "What do they mean by saying that Buckingham Palace is not me?' His Majesty exclaims. 'Who else is

41   Ibid., p.198.
42   Ibid., p.139.
43   Ibid.
44   BD: MS Asquith A.1 3 21/3/1914.

there, I should like to know? Do they mean the footmen?"[45] Though it was over quickly, the events among officers at the Curragh belittle the Government, resignations follow, and the Prime Minister has to take up the duties of the Secretary of State for War in addition to his own.

45   Rose: *King George V,* p.156.

1914

Descent

King George knows Franz Ferdinand. On Sunday 28th June 1914, the day that the heir to the Austrian throne died, London is bathed in glorious sunshine and His Majesty has been to tea with two of his aunts. They sit in the garden at Kensington all afternoon, until the sun finally dips behind the trees and the fading light motivates his return to Buckingham Palace. News of an outrage in Sarajevo awaits him, for a Bosnian-Serb nationalist has shot and killed the Archduke and his wife. The murder is likened, dynastically, to a Prince of Wales being murdered in Ireland. The King's first reaction is one of shock and sorrow, in particular for the elderly Austrian Emperor, the victim's uncle. But that is as close as he feels to the assassination. Although "regrettable and sad,"[1] it is not an intensely personal loss for him. His Majesty is a spectator, not a participant in this far-off tragedy. And besides, trouble exudes from the Balkans, weeps like a menacing contagion infecting the far reaches of the continent. That such events should have transpired seems grimly inevitable. The King dines alone with Queen Mary and then retires to mark a new stamp catalogue. He is in bed by 11:30. The following day he does break with protocol to visit the Austrian Embassy and give his condolences in person to Albert, Count Mensdorff. His actions are more for this man than for the dead royal couple, for His Majesty thinks highly of this distant cousin; a popular diplomat and anglophile who has been his country's Ambassador in London since 1904.

The odd newspaper speculates that complications might lead to a more general war, but there is no sustained concern in Britain throughout most of July. If anyone is paying much attention to events transpiring in Vienna or Belgrade, they expect at most a localised clash that will not concern them. Aside from the Home Rule saga and attempting to fashion an amendment, the Cabinet occupy themselves with discussions on India, Persian bases at the mouth of the Gulf and finance matters. Like everyone else, the King moves on. If he expects anything to give him sleepless nights this summer, it is Ireland. He is still intent on securing a peaceful settlement over the Home Rule Bill. In April he had told Asquith that time was "slipping away."[2] In mid-June His Majesty again warns his Prime Minister that letting the matter drift could result in disaster. The King's only hope, in trying to avoid being placed in an impossible position between a veto and a dissolution, is to get the politicians to compromise. Protestants and Catholics are smuggling rifles into Ireland and stockpiling ammunition in anticipation of violent scenes. As early as 1st May His Majesty had approached a member of the Government and asked if he would be willing to preside over a conference on the dispute. Twice the King urges Asquith to seek a resolution in this way, but his Prime Minister continues to refuse.

In July His Majesty boards a train with Asquith and sets off for Portsmouth to review the fleet; an ironically timed show of Britain's naval supremacy. The King has requested that the visit be kept business-like, with a minimum of elaborate ceremony, but crowds accumulate for hours outside

1   RA GV/PRIV/GVD/1914 (28/6).
2   Nicolson, Harold: *King George V: His Life and Reign*, p.240.

the station at Portsmouth Harbour and at Portsea, from where they can watch the royal train pass slowly over the viaduct to the dockyard. The water is crammed with every imaginable craft: small steamers, tugs and ferry boats, overflowing with spectators anxious to get even a momentary glimpse of the Sovereign. The King stands at the window of his saloon and acknowledges them with a wave as the engine pulls into the station.

The sight awaiting him off the coast is breath-taking: endless silhouettes of ships standing boldly upon grey waters. The foreshore and promenade are packed with locals and holiday makers along the coast, watching, mesmerised by the might of Britain's seapower. "Dark visaged torpedo destroyers ploughed along within a stone's throw of the water's edge, and excursion steamers packed with passengers steaming up and down outside the lines of leviathans which lay stretching from Southsea Castle to beyond East Cowes, a distance of some seven miles." At nightfall the fleet looks like a city afloat. "For miles the waters across to the Isle of Wight were dotted with thousands of glimmering spots of light." A single rocket soars aloft from HMS *Iron Duke*. This is a signal for all of the battleships and cruisers to ignite their searchlights, "mingling with the clouds in a curious and wonderful manner." As the display continues, the beams are lowered in tandem to light up the surface of the Solent. So bright is the spectacle that it is possible to read a newspaper on the beach. Then the searchlight beams begin to dance. "The most pretty and kaleidoscope effects were produced when the beams were swept and waved both horizontally and vertically. At one minute a break in the clouds would be suddenly revealed, at the next the sails of a yacht, then one of the forts would be lighted and so on."[3] Spectators along the shoreline are awestruck. It makes the King immensely proud to see such a magnificent display. He is so impressed by the evening's entertainment that when it finishes, he asks if they wouldn't mind start again at the beginning.

"The Summit of a Volcano"

It is a twin tragedy in Europe's history that Kaiser Wilhelm II's grandfather lived for so long, and that his father died so young. The eldest son of Edward VII's sister Vicky, the German Sovereign is the King's first cousin. He had taken the throne in 1888; grabbed it rather distastefully in fact, considering his father had just succumbed to a brutal cancer, equipped with a vastly over-inflated opinion of his own capabilities.

He was a complicated individual from birth. Queen Victoria's first grandchild: Wilhelm, 'Willy' or often just plain William to his British relatives, was born after a complicated labour that left one arm permanently damaged. He underwent all kinds of emotionally scarring, tortuous procedures including electric shock and stretching regimes, but it never grew properly. He could not even cut up his dinner without help, and the upshot was that he would never be the perfect specimen of Prussian manhood that he so admired. In addition to his physical affliction he suffered in much the same way as his uncle, Edward VII, in that his mother's parenting regime was suffocating. She veered between passionate love and a panic about his potential inadequacies. Her perennial disappointment took its toll. She could not stand the famous Prussian militarism either. In his miniature uniform as a child she said that Willy looked like an organ grinder's unfortunate little monkey. Wilhelm though, was in love with all things military from the first. As he grew up he embraced everything about it: the uniforms, the camaraderie, the pageantry; his obsession with this masculine world had almost a homoerotic edge to it. To their dismay, he grew away from his liberal parents and instead fell into the arms of the Emperor, his grandfather and namesake, who was militaristic to the core and scorned his parents' liberal ideals for their son's education.

3   *The Times* 20/7/1914.

The new Reich was less than twenty years old when Crown Prince became the Kaiser. The constitution of 1871 was vague, described as "not so much a contribution in the traditional sense as a *treaty* among the sovereignties that had agreed to form the German Empire;"[4] a not wholly efficient attempt to combine the priorities and ambitions of a number of different small monarchies in one piece of legislation. Nobody was really in any doubt that the Hohenzollerns' Prussia, Wilhelm's house, was the dominant force. Prussia accounted for 65% of the surface area in the new German state, 62% of the population was within its borders and the Prussian military code was also to be disseminated as soon as possible throughout Germany. Prussian bureaucracy was more powerful than that of the broader Reich and this was still the case before the First World War.

Wilhelm wields formidable power; including supreme command of both the army and navy. He has the power to declare war, to end it, to represent the German Empire abroad, organise alliances and treaties and to appoint ambassadors. But to Wilhelm his role is intrinsically ceremonial too. The imperial monarchy was still a flexible concept. It was not a focus of public life, such as in Britain. Any precedent from the Middle Ages had been forgotten and so even a coronation that would have been taken for granted elsewhere was absent. Wilhelm wanted to change this. He was free to try and mould his monarchy into what he saw fit. He wanted to be visible, adored, a figurehead. He created public holidays, travelled extensively among his people, he appeared dynamic and vivacious. He wanted a lifestyle and an image that befitted the monarchy and veered away from sparse, Prussian tradition. In short, Wilhelm promised greatness for his country, stemming from his own person. He even dabbled with Divine Right, proclaiming himself as having been established in his office to fulfil God's plan for the new Germany.

And so with good reason, the nation looked upon his accession as the possible foundation of a shining new era. To some extent he began to deliver. Naval tradition amongst society in Germany was non-existent on his accession. The service was closer to a laughing stock than to the prestige of Britain's senior service. It is Wilhelm who drives this development forward, but there is another side to the Kaiser. If Britain's constitution bears a likeness to an adult that has reached full maturity, Germany at the advent of the Great War is an unwieldy adolescent, still trying to find her way in the world. In the hands of a different individual, this need not have presented a concerning diplomatic issue, but Wilhelm's personality epitomises the restless nature of his young nation: desperate to catch up, to place itself at the forefront of European affairs. In appraising him many years later, Churchill will surmise that Wilhelm strutted, posed, rattled the undrawn sword. He thought that the Kaiser wished above all else to be Napoleon reincarnated, without having to fight any of his battles. "If you are the summit of a volcano, the least you can do is to smoke."[5] And smoke Wilhelm does. Endlessly. For much of his reign he prefers to speak of his own accord, without the input of writers. He can command an audience with ease, but it is the content of such performances that is "often catastrophic,"[6] especially when they are reproduced in printed format. All of the nuances of speech and magnetism of his manner is lost, and by the time that the press have finished applying his diatribes to the political context of the day and analysing them, he is left open to criticism and ridicule. "I wish," his mother once said, "I could put a padlock on his mouth for all occasions where speeches are made in public."[7] The smoke became overwhelming as the years went by, until his people began to choke on it. Wilhelm veers between interests and preoccupations at an alarming rate, which is of huge concern when married with the influence he wields. "Today one thing and

4   *Clark: Iron Kingdom*, p.557.
5   Churchill: *Great Contemporaries*, p.27.
6   Clark, Christopher: *Kaiser Wilhelm II, A Life in Power*, p.222.
7   Ibid., p.230.

tomorrow the next and after a few days something completely different."[8] The Kaiser is allergic to criticism of any kind, and those around him quickly learn the art of flattery. Because he claims credit for everything, when it goes wrong, Wilhelm is left in an uncomfortable position that makes him culpable in a way that his British cousin never experiences. Nervous, emotional meltdowns are the usual outlet for his anxiety.

Most significantly, in pre-war Europe there is much prestige attached to the political art of diplomacy. Sadly for Wilhelm, he is largely a failure at it. He attempts to stamp the German monarchy with his own brand of personal diplomacy, which frequently ends badly. His efforts, which are often clumsy and cause offence, result once in his indomitable grandmother in England declaring that he needs a good flogging. The crises that occur during his reign and bear his fingerprints, at the very least, are plenty before the war. At times, he is quite simply bonkers. He has offended just about every crowned head in Europe with his rude or inappropriate behaviour, which has included spanking the King of Bulgaria's backside during a state visit and telling the King of Italy that he is a dwarf.

As the Great War approaches, the sheer amount of rhetoric that Wilhelm has produced, combined with the blunders and his lack of focus has eroded the worth of utterances coming from his personage. It is commonplace for his Government to just disassociate themselves from the things that he has said. Kaiser Wilhelm II is not a warmonger. He is, though, a volatile, bombastic, essentially well-meaning, but nonetheless potentially dangerous individual; and one severely out of his depth. He has not made good on the promises of his early reign, and he has caused Germany embarrassment on the international stage. He has exhausted his family, his ministers and his people. For all of his articulate speeches about his role as Germany's saviour, the Kaiser has demonstrated many times over that, despite his rhetoric, he lacks the ability to live up to his own press.

But even for someone devoid of Wilhelm's natural paranoia, Germany's pre-war position is concerning. France and Russia have concluded an alliance and their cooperation has been long established. Conversely, German alliances with fellow powers have been allowed to lapse, or have been circumvented, and the Kaiser has witnessed the growing diplomatic isolation of his country. He believes that his mother's homeland has set out to cut Germany off, to encircle her with those hostile to her ambitions, to hold her back. The King finds his cousin's constant suspicion about Britain amusing. After Queen Victoria's death in 1901 the Kaiser considers himself the preeminent royal voice in Europe and his ego swells accordingly. This was the least of the reasons that his uncle, Edward VII had no time for him. He was sickened by the way that Wilhelm had treated his sister Vicky, who died the same year as their mother and he sarcastically referred to his brash nephew as "Wilhelm the Great"[9] For his part, true to form, Wilhelm's attitude towards his uncle alternated from one extreme to the other, bending over backwards to impress him and gain his approval at one moment, petty slights and violent rages condemning him and waxing lyrical about how his lifestyle disgusted him the next. One courtier remarked that meetings became a farcical performance of congeniality between the pair in the years before the King's death in 1910. Georgie and Willy spent little time together in their youth, but they get along well enough. In the four years of His Majesty's reign that lead to the outbreak of the Great War, there is enough domestic angst to ensure that the King is less focused on foreign affairs than his father had been. Though he was aware of developments, the passion for the continent displayed by Edward VII, his son displayed for the British Empire instead. Before he was even crowned, His Majesty had had a taste of the pitfalls and risks associated with even a casual conversation with Wilhelm. Things have a tendency to get

---

8   Carter: *The Three Emperors*, p.155.
9   St. Aubyn, Giles: *Edward VII: Prince and King*, pp.278-9.

twisted and manipulated to suit the Kaiser's aims and erroneous quotes are levelled publicly in the King's direction. Unsurprisingly, given his parents' distaste, George refers to his cousin in mocking tones, referring to him as things like William the Fidgety, but he is a less dominant personality than his father, and is largely willing to let Wilhelm bluster without putting up any opposition to his ego. His approach is to smile politely and say as little as possible. And Wilhelm does have his moments. He might not have been able to stand Edward VII, but he clasped the King's hand at the head of his coffin in 1910.

"The Principle of Autocracy"

Like the German Emperor, Nicholas II, Tsar of All the Russias, is completely unsuited for the hand that life has dealt him. Nicholas is the wrong man, in temperament and ability; in the wrong place, an ungovernable state such as Russia was; at the wrong time, at a point in history where the concept of limitless, unquestionable power in the hands of an autocrat has fully outstayed its welcome in Europe.

Nicholas was born three years after the King in St Petersburg. His father, fated to be Tsar Alexander III, sobbed as he was brought into the world. He was a bear of a man. Once, at the dinner table an Austrian ambassador suggested that his country might mobilise two or three army corps against Russian interests. Nicky's father picked up a silver fork, bent it into a knot and tossed it into the ambassador's plate. "That," he said quite calmly, "is what I am going to do to your two or three Army corps."[10] Like His Majesty, the Tsar shares a deep bond with his mother. Marie, as she had come to be known on her conversion to Orthodoxy, is Queen Alexandra's younger sister. In total contrast to her gruff husband, Minny, as she was known to her family, was petite, dazzlingly stylish and blessed with a sparkling personality which she used to charm the Russian court on his behalf.

From the outset, Nicky's was a life of extremes. Extreme power, extreme wealth and extreme isolation. At home, at best he viewed the outside world through the palace gates, observing gleefully the populace going about their business. The Princess of Wales adored her sister, and there was much contact with the Romanovs when the King was a boy. They met often on Danish summer holidays, when the boys would roam free and Prince George referred to Nicky's giant father as "dear old fatty."[11] For all of the Romanovs present, including the entertaining, free-spirited Alexander, who played endlessly with the children, it was freedom personified after the cloistered life of the Tsar's court.

In March 1881 Nicky was twelve. His grandfather, Alexander II was reigning as a liberal minded Tsar, and had just signed a new constitution when he was ripped apart in a bombing attack. Nicky saw him grotesquely maimed and watched him bleed to death. Alexander III withdrew his family even further from the rest of the world, and so ended the Romanov dynasty's voluntary liberal experimentation. These two factors then, have combined to help shape Tsar Nicholas's view of the world. He would try and follow his father's example in all things when he came to the throne. His complete isolation from other boys, from the people, indeed from reality has left him unable to make educated decisions that affect a gigantic Empire. Liberalism to him is gruesome in its consequences. Liberalism equalled a bloody, violent death; stability, peace he associates with his father's subsequent, reactionary rule. And in 1894 Nicholas's time came. Still only in his forties, Alexander III succumbed suddenly and unexpectedly to kidney failure and his devastated son

10   Massie: *Nicholas and Alexandra*, p.9.
11   Ibid., p.76.

ascended the throne in abject terror, convinced that he was unready and unable to rule, and referring to his new role as: "the awful job I have feared all my life."[12]

The new Tsar prided himself in living like a Russian, wearing simple, peasant dress. Unlike his court, who favour French, he prefers to speak in Russian. He reads Russian literature, watches Russian opera. He rules over a frightening proportion of the globe, a vast Empire with an archaic, inefficient administration that stretches from Poland in the west all the way to the Pacific. Like Wilhelm, when Nicholas took the throne the world seemed full of promise. But any hopes of welcoming a new, liberal reign have come to nothing by 1914. "I shall maintain," Tsar Nicholas has said, "the principle of autocracy just as firmly and unflinchingly as it was preserved by my unforgettable dead father."[13]

But the fatal flaw in the Tsar's intentions is that he is a terrible autocrat. Had he been required to rule as a constitutional monarch in the style of the King, he could have been an unqualified success. He is a good man, a kind individual, and he loves his country and his people, but if, constitutionally speaking, Britain has the most stable system, and Germany's is youthful and untried, then Russia's is withering, decrepit and not fit for purpose. Tsar Nicholas theoretically wields limitless power. Hundreds of years after Divine Right was severed in Britain by the axe that struck off Charles I's head, it still holds sway in Russia. As Romanovs have done for generations before him, the Tsar appoints and sacks ministers as he sees fit, and is under no obligation to listen to anything they tell him. Along with apparently unquestionable authority, Tsar Nicholas bears full responsibility for his country's fortunes. But his management style is flawed. Instead of conducting himself strongly, he avoids all confrontation. He is so charming that it disarms people, and with his impeccable manners he tries to paper the cracks in both his authority and in his strength as a ruler. One Courtier describes him as "exasperatingly polite."[14]

The Tsar was the antithesis of Wilhelm; a largely invisible figure. He contradicts himself. One cannot simultaneously be an effective autocrat whilst trying to put oneself in a sphere of blissful, domestic isolation. As his reign progressed, Tsar Nicholas put less stock in the word of his ministers. Civilian strife had gained momentum since the turn of the century and following military disaster, humiliation even, at the hands of Japan, by 1905 Russia was in the midst of a revolutionary crisis. Demands were made for freedoms and representation. Perhaps it needn't have been, but the October Manifesto was cataclysmic for Tsardom and signalled the beginning of the end for the Romanov dynasty. Russia went from autocracy to halfway constitutional monarchy, on paper at least, with a flourish of Nicholas's hand. By the outbreak of the Great War, essentially a representative body is allowed to exist in Russia, and after a traumatic experience, the Tsar has begun to work with it, but his endeavours will prove too little too late.

Tsar Nicholas bears a stark resemblance to King George, so much so that when the former was in London for his cousin's wedding in 1893, someone mistook the then Duke of York for the Emperor and gave him an invitation to his own nuptials. A French minister said on meeting the King for the first time: "I was immediately struck by his resemblance to his cousin… Yet his colour was not so pale, his expression less dreamy, his smile less melancholy and his gestures less timid."[15] But the similarities extend far beyond mere physical traits. The nature of both men is full of parallels: domesticity, love of their families, a passion for the countryside, dislike of courtly responsibilities, fear of public speaking. Private men, both are worriers, and neither is perfectly suited to their role in life, but their sense of duty and their work ethic are unimpeachable.

12   Massie: *Nicholas and Alexandra,* p.62.
13   Ibid., p.67.
14   Massie: *Nicholas and Alexandra,* p. 179.
15   Nicolson, Harold: *King George V: His Life and Reign,* p.217.

Whilst His Majesty keeps the Kaiser at arms-length, Nicholas had initially enjoyed good relations with his German cousin, had confided in him on occasion. But their relationship has soured since the turn of the century. Wilhelm, still regarding himself as Europe's senior royal, attempts to manipulate his younger cousin; and Nicholas's response it to charmingly evade him.

On only two occasions were the three together as Sovereigns. On the last, the wedding of Wilhelm's daughter in 1913, he tried fruitlessly to use the event to his own diplomatic ends. He was jealous of the easy and affectionate friendship between King and Tsar, and their proximity to each other right under his nose sent his paranoid tendencies into overdrive. No plotting took place. The affair was deemed purely personal and as a result the King did not even take a Minister with him to Germany. Nonetheless, when he and the Tsar were alone, His Majesty quipped that "William's ear was glued to the keyhole."[16] The three cousins will never see each other again. In a little over a year they would be trying to prevent an international catastrophe. By the end of 1918, one will have been murdered by his own people, another will have fled his country and the last will be the only one still with a throne to occupy.

"Within Measurable Distance of a Real Armageddon"

In Britain, eyes are still turned inward as July progresses. A brief mention of the European situation and Austria's reaction to the assassination of the Archduke in the Cabinet does not even make it into the written summary of political deliberations that Asquith provides daily for the King. *The Times* believes that Austria-Hungary will remain relatively contrite, lest she appear to bully Serbia; a scenario that will inevitably anger Russia, who sees herself as a defender of Slavs. Conversely, it still seems highly possible that the Irish situation could come to a bloody head. A confidant has told the King that he is doing no good by worrying himself to death over the Home Rule Bill, but His Majesty despairs. And Asquith too is panicking; he is not so dismissive of his Sovereign now that he is facing potential political ruin. For his part, the King is accused of sitting in Buckingham Palace, his mind made up and determined to use the royal veto for the first time in two centuries to deny home rule. He continually presses Asquith for a resolution to the embittered discussions. He repeats more than once his offer to political leaders to sit down together and come to a solution, offering Buckingham Palace as a venue. No party wants to lose face, and so it would have to be orchestrated by His Majesty. He will take the lead, for then they can be seen to be meeting out of obligation to the Sovereign. It is a move that would be frowned upon in plenty of quarters, perceived as the King over-reaching his constitutional powers, but that he can live with, for this last resort, if something could come of it, would be worth the trouble. Any irritation engendered by appearing to command the presence of political leaders at Buckingham Palace is far more preferable than facing the impossibility of having to either refuse Royal Assent or let the Home Rule Bill pass.

Finally, on 17th July, Asquith accepts that he can get no further and calls upon His Majesty. As far as the Sovereign is concerned, whilst the politicians are still talking, there is hope of averting a constitutional crisis and civil war. On 21st July the delegates arrive and are settled in the 1844 Room at Buckingham Palace. His Majesty makes a short speech, which the Prime Minister chastises as "a truly artless performance,"[17] and then after a meeting with his dentist he sits in the garden and wills the politicians to resolve their differences. A section of the press foams at the mouth at the King having the cheek to gather politicians under his own roof. "All the radical papers are furious with one for calling the conference," the King muses in his diary. "It is difficult to please anybody

---

16   Rose: *King George V,* p.166.
17   (ed.) Brock: *H.H. Asquith: Letters to Venetia Stanley,* p.109.

in this world."[18] But on 24th the conference collapses. "I am sorry to say they could come to no settlement," writes His Majesty. "I am greatly worried by [the] political situation which is now becoming very grave."[19] The day had dawned under a threatening, tumultuous cloud moving in from Ireland, but despite the failure of the conference at the Palace, by the end of it, this issue will have already begun receding rapidly out of the limelight; when the simmering Austro-Hungarian reaction to the assassination of their Emperor's heir finally begins to boil over.

The Hapsburgs are one of Europe's longest reigning houses. Their Austro-Hungarian Empire dominates the centre of the continent, but is a rapidly decaying conglomerate of fifty million people. At the advent of the twentieth century this unwieldy population, a bewildering array of nationalist and ethnic entities, was threatening to rip it apart from within. Notable among the protagonists in its demise are the Serbs, who yearn for independence. Quite understandably then, after one of their number fired the shots that killed Archduke Ferdinand and his wife, as far as Imperial interests are concerned, the door is open for the Dual Monarchy to put these troublesome subjects in their place.

If the rest of Europe is guilty of antipathy after the death of the Archduke, they are no more so than the Austrians themselves. One witness raged at the "third class burial" of the royal couple. Allegedly, during a requiem the elderly Emperor glanced around the chapel "with complete indifference and the same unmoving, glacial expression he showed towards his subjects on other occasions."[20] Franz Josef has been on the throne for nearly half a century. He is old, he is tired and he is barely on the periphery of the decision making process as, despite the lack of emotion displayed over the Archduke's murder, tension escalates between Austria-Hungary and Serbia in the first three weeks of July. Instead of stamping his autocratic authority, the Emperor goes on holiday. Suspicious of such new-fangled things, he even refuses to keep in touch with his Government by telephone. And so, his two Prime Ministers, in Vienna and Budapest, find themselves in a position of worrying power.

The Kaiser is satisfied that there will be no "serious complications"[21] but crucially, Wilhelm consents for a telegram to be sent to Vienna, saying that although it is not his place to intervene, as per their alliance he will support the Austrian Emperor in whatever resolution he thinks necessary. Vienna now believes that they have a license to take any action against Serbia, with the promise of the backing of Germany. They have what becomes referred to as a 'blank cheque' when formulating an ultimatum for Serbia. When a draft of said ultimatum is handed to Franz Josef for approval, he is surprised at the severity of it and the potential connotations with Russia, but he does nothing to have it reworded. One of his aides will claim that the Austrian Emperor regards it as a diplomatic bluff, only to be "deeply shaken"[22] when he realises the potential consequences. The list of demands that his Ministers deliver to Serbia on 23rd July, whilst the King is engrossed in the Irish conference at Buckingham Palace, almost reduce it "to an Austro-Hungarian dependency."[23] The Foreign Minister, Sir Edward Grey says that he has never seen one nation present such a document to another. But although the Austro-Hungarians know that it will rile Russia, with the promise of German support, they have issued it with damning confidence.

18   RA GV/PRIV/GVD/1914 (22/7).
19   RA GV/PRIV/GVD/1914 (24/7).
20   Palmer: *Twilight of the Hapsburgs*, pp.325-6.
21   Clark, Christopher: *Kaiser Wilhelm II, A Life in Power*, p.286.
22   Ibid., pp.199-200.
23   Palmer, Alan: *Twilight of the Hapsburgs*, p.330.

Tsar Nicholas is on his yacht as the crisis deepens. As well as the Slavic connection between herself and the tiny nation, threatening Serbia also threatens Russia's influence in the Balkans. Serbia will obviously, immediately, appeal to their powerful ally for support. But despite the Tsar's determination to support Serbia, he is confident that the situation can be worked out diplomatically. "Notwithstanding appearances," he says, "the Emperor William is too cautious to launch his country on some wild adventure and… Franz Josef's only wish is to die in peace."[24]

As Serbia reels in the face of Vienna's impossible demands, finally, the gravity of the situation on the continent begins to take shape in the eyes of the British Government. The Prime Minister goes from pining for his mistress, like "a man who is being sucked away from his life buoy,"[25] to the reality of an impending European war in a matter of hours. A Cabinet meeting is held. As the Ministers assembled might have expected, talk was of Ulster; but then, in his quiet manner, Sir Edward Grey reads the text of the ultimatum and reveals the connotations of it. If Austria fight Serbia, Russia will defend them, Germany have already effectively told Austria that they will side with them, which will then bring France in as Russia's ally. A chill descends on the room. "We are within measurable distance of a real Armageddon," writes Asquith.[26] The King may well have been a beat ahead of his Government, for on 21st, when he opened the Irish conference, he made a "very bloodcurdling reference to foreign affairs"[27] that was not properly recorded. On the morning of 25th, Sir Edward Grey arrives at Buckingham Palace to speak with His Majesty. "It looks as if we are on the verge of a general European war… very serious state of affairs."[28] The Irish situation had threatened to drive him to distraction, threatened to pull down the Government, provoke civil war and damage the monarchy, and yet now an eventuality even more frightening has emerged.

In the course of Britain's descent into war, the King will find himself at the very centre of events, with almost no power to affect them personally. Nonetheless he has no intention of leaving London. One thing that the Government can do to try and help avert war is to attempt to utilise his family connections with Europe's other crowned heads to combat the darkening landscape of international affairs. Of course, when suddenly national boundaries conflict with bloodlines, this is a minefield of differing perspectives and potential misunderstandings amongst relatives. On Sunday 26th, "another nasty, cold day, blowing hard, not much like July,"[29] Prince Henry of Prussia, the Kaiser's brother, stops in at Buckingham Palace to bid farewell to his English cousin before he hurriedly returns to Germany. After a brief conversation in which the King says that his country will do all they can to avert war, the Prince departs for Germany. Somehow, taking into account Henry's interpretation of this conversation and Wilhelm being Wilhelm, the Kaiser believes that His Majesty has assured him of Britain's neutrality. Wilhelm says he has the word of a King, and that is enough for him. Although the Germans' selective hearing might have given the Kaiser the idea that he did not have to concern himself with potential British intervention, this does not bring about war. It does, however, leave the Kaiser bitter and complaining to neutral countries later on that His Majesty has duped him.

On 28th July, regardless of Serbian contrition, Austria-Hungary declares war on the tiny nation. "I have done my best," is Franz Josef's slightly bizarre response, "but now it is the end."[30] Finally, the

24   Massie: *Nicholas and Alexandra,* p.262.
25   (ed.) Brock: *H.H. Asquith: Letters to Venetia Stanley,* p.122.
26   Asquith: *Memories and Reflections Vol. II,* p.5.
27   Beaverbrook: *Politicians & the War 1914-1916,* p.31.
28   RA GV/PRIV/GVD/1914 (25/7).
29   Ibid., 26/7.
30   Palmer, Alan: *Twilight of the Hapsburgs,* p.331.

following day, he returns to Vienna. In Russia, the declaration of war against Serbia proves to be the turning point in the crisis, as the bullying of their fellow Slavs fills Ministers with resolve. If the King was under any illusions as to the severity of the situation, Churchill visits the palace to assure His Majesty that the Royal Navy is in a state of readiness. "Where will it end?" The King writes in his diary. "These are very anxious days we live in."[31] He has already begun cancelling his summer engagements. In Germany there is concern. When Wilhelm sees the telegram sent to Serbia by Austria he is said to be "terribly upset."[32] After all, has Austria-Hungary not been told that they can count on Berlin's unconditional support? The German ambassador in Vienna has questioned "whether it pays to bind ourselves so tightly to this phantasm of a state which is cracking in every direction."[33] The same realisation is dawning on the Kaiser, who arrives at Potsdam on 27th July and begins to make frenzied attempts to mediate between Vienna and St. Petersburg before Russia sides with Serbia and declares war on Austria-Hungary. Hang the blank cheque issued to Austria, he'd rather keep the peace. He spends the day making it clear to Ministers that even if it is seen as leaving Franz Josef in the lurch, he means to avoid war. But his Government has other ideas. "I pointed out," says the war minster, "that he no longer has control over the situation."[34]

Both Russia and Germany have already taken precautionary military action. The peaceful intentions of the two Emperors are at odds with the grim preparations of their Governments. Although the German Chancellor is now seeking to mediate with Vienna, on 29th Wilhelm is under pressure to raise his country's preparations for war another notch. The *State of Impending War* is the last step before full mobilisation, and the Kaiser resists putting it into action. At Buckingham Palace, the King is buried beneath an increasing pile of panicked correspondence, including a communication from the Tsar, deploring Austria's actions and how recklessly they have pushed Europe to the brink of war. "It is awful!" He writes. Russia, he insists, is confident not only of her strength but in her position as defender of a weaker nation being bullied by a significant power. Austria will not listen. And now, as Nicholas puts it, his country is compelled to beginning full mobilisation as an emergency measure for her own defence along the common border with Hapsburg territory. "As a last resort I have written to William to ask him to bear strong pressure upon Austria so as to enable us to discuss matters with her. He has promised to be mediator between us... I do hope this may still save matters as a war at this precise moment would be a dreadful calamity."[35]

The Tsar's hopes are in vain. When he reads a note from the Nicholas, saying "we need your strong pressure on Austria to come to an understanding with us," Wilhelm flies into a rage and scrawls "No, there is no thought of anything of that sort!"[36] On the document. He is furious that Russia has partially mobilised, regardless of whether they believe it to be a means of defending their own borders. He takes it as a slight upon him, a betrayal by Nicholas.

His Majesty, meanwhile, is increasingly anxious. On 30th July, the Tsar meets with his War Minister, who tells him that he does not believe that they can hold off giving the order for the Russian Army to fully mobilise for much longer. Nicholas chokes on his response. "Think of the responsibility you are advising me to take. Remember it would mean sending hundreds of thousands of Russian people to their deaths." But from Government's point of view, what more can they do? There is the moral question of supporting Serbia as well as the political issue of letting Germany and

31   RA GV/PRIV/GVD/1914 (29/7).
32   Marie Louise, Princess: *My Memories of Six Reigns*, p.178.
33   Massie: *Nicholas and Alexandra*, p.368.
34   Stibbe: *Kaiser Wilhelm II: The Hohenzollerns at War*, pp.267-9.
35   RA PS/PSO/GV/C/Q/1549/1.
36   Massie: *Nicholas and Alexandra*, p.271.

Austria-Hungary combine to dominate the Balkans on their doorstep. "The Tsar remained silent and his face showed the traces of a terrible inner struggle. At last, speaking with difficulty, he [says]: "You are right. There is nothing left for us to do but get ready for an attack upon us. Give… my order for general mobilisation."[37] But before the news arrives in Berlin, Nicholas sends one more communication to Wilhelm; telling him that he cannot stop mobilisation, but that he gives his word of honour that while Austria are still taking part in diplomatic discussions his troops will not cross the frontier.

Wilhelm responds by saying that it will be the Tsar's fault and nobody else's if Europe goes to war. It is now inevitable that his own forces will scale up their existing military preparations. "So the celebrated encirclement of Germany has finally become an established fact," he writes bitterly. He blames Britain, as usual giving his mother's homeland far too much credit for her hold on Europe's affairs; though the King is safe from his wrath. Of all people, he holds His Majesty's father responsible, like a spectre from beyond the grave attempting to drag him spitefully into oblivion. "Even after his death Edward VII is stronger than I," he complains.[38] The consequences seem to multiply by the hour. Wilhelm is shocked to find out from his Ambassador in London that British neutrality might not be a given if the conflict escalates out of the Balkans. The Kaiser denounces the English as scoundrels and mean shopkeepers. What else is this nightmare, in the Kaiser's mind at any rate, than a blatant opportunity for Britain to play the puppet master of Europe, to turn the rest of the continent against his country?

But though Wilhelm might still hope to avoid all out war, his army chief thinks very differently. "This gave rise to an extremely lively and dramatic dispute." The Kaiser wants to stop his troops readying for war, whilst his advisor thinks that to abandon mobilisation whilst potential enemies continue to prepare is suicide. "Moltke had become almost hysterical. In a private aside to Falkenhayn, the war minister, he confided, close to tears "that he was now a totally broken man, because this decision by the Kaiser demonstrated to him that [Wilhelm] still hoped for peace."[39]

His Majesty is deftly poised between his cousins, and tells the Tsar that he is glad to hear that Wilhelm is making efforts to cooperate with Nicholas to maintain widespread peace.

> Indeed I am earnestly desirous that such an irreparable disaster as a European War should be averted… Trust William will use his great influence to induce Austria to accept this proposal thus proving Germany and England are working together to prevent what would be an international catastrophe. Pray assure William I am doing and shall continue to do all that is in my power to preserve peace of Europe.[40]

For now the King's Government remains split on whether Britain should intervene, but His Majesty fears the worst. "Everything, alas, looks very bad," he frets. "Russia and Germany mobilising, almost impossible not to prevent a general European war."[41] On 31st July Wilhelm complains to the King about Russian mobilisation. "He has not even awaited the results of the mediation I am working at and [has] left me without any news. I am off for Berlin to take measures for ensuring safety of my Eastern Frontiers where strong Russian troops are already posted."[42] Later in the day a lengthy and effusive plea for assistance arrives at the palace from the President of the French Republic. For all of

37   Ibid.
38   Rose: *King George V*, pp.162-3.
39   Clark, Christopher: *Kaiser Wilhelm II, A Life in Power*, pp.297-8.
40   RA PS/PSO/C/Q/1549/6a.
41   RA GV/PRIV/GVD/1914 (31/7).
42   RA/PS/PSO/C/Q/1549/8.

Wilhelm's complaints about Russian mobilisation, France has garnered terrifying news from their own frontier about the gathering of the Kaiser's own forces.

As King George readies for bed after a long and worrying day, the German Ambassador in St. Petersburg presents an ultimatum. Berlin has given Russia twelve hours to cease military preparations. A mile away from Buckingham Palace, the Prime Minister has sat down with colleagues. Together they draw up a telegram from the King to the Tsar; a strong personal appeal to stop Europe's great powers plunging into war. His Majesty is already asleep when a member of his household appears to say that Asquith is in the Palace and asking to see him. Having hurried up The Mall in a taxi, the Prime Minister is waiting in an audience room with the telegram he wants the King to send in his name. "One of my strangest experiences was sitting with him," writes Asquith, "clad in a dressing gown, while I read the message and the proposed answer."[43] His Majesty agrees to send the message at once and in the early hours of 1st August an order is despatched to the British ambassador in St. Petersburg. Sir George Buchanan is to apply for an audience with the Tsar at once, in order to read the King's telegram. It begins by outlining Germany's accusation, that Nicholas has mobilised his forces whilst the Kaiser and his ministers were still attempting to mediate between the Russian capital and Vienna. The Germans consider that in their approaches to Austria, they have "gone to the furthest limit of what can be suggested to a sovereign state which is the ally of Germany." Thanks to the timely arrival of the news of the Tsar's army mobilising, Austria will no longer listen to diplomacy regarding Russia. Furthermore, the German Government have stated to their British counterparts that "this action on the part of Russia is also directed against Germany." In their opinion, they had been backed into a corner, and if Russia do not stop the movement of her troops, they will match it and there will be war.

The ambassador was then to convey to Nicholas that the King could not help thinking "that some misunderstanding" was responsible. This is certainly the case as far as Nicholas is concerned. Had he not told Wilhelm that his hand had been forced, that he had no choice but to mobilise with Austria doing the same? Had he not also told his German cousin that upon his word, his troops would not cross the border whilst diplomacy prevailed? His Majesty's official message continues:

> I am most anxious not to miss any possibility of avoiding the terrible calamity which at present threatens the whole world. I therefore make a personal appeal to you to remove the misapprehension which I feel must have occurred, and to leave still open grounds for negotiation, and possible peace. If you think I can in any way contribute to that all important purpose, I will do everything in my power to assist in re-opening the interrupted conversations between the powers concerned.[44]

As Germany prepares to declare war on Russia, the King takes his work out into the garden at Buckingham Palace, where he has a large tent into which has been carried a desk and his parrot, Charlotte. "George received any number of telegrams with war news," remarks the Queen, "which were not satisfactory."[45] In response to the French plea, His Majesty is to reply that he is committed to using all of his influence to help Russia and Germany find a solution that does not include immediate military operations. "I intend to prosecute these efforts without intermission so long as any hope remains of an amicable settlement."[46] The reply steers clear of committing Britain to any course of action, but assures the President that his Ministers will continue to converse freely with

43   Asquith: *Memories and Reflections Vol. II*, p.7.
44   RA PS/PSO/C/Q/1549/11.
45   RA PRIV/QMD/1914 (1/8).
46   RA PS/PSO/C/Q/1549/10.

them on any point in which the fates of their nations are both concerned.

But Germany has declared war on Russia and the Tsar's ambassador has already left St. Petersburg. Dinner is delayed till after nine, when the King updates his family on the situation. Germany want the French to declare their neutrality and stay out of their fight with Russia, and for Britain to guarantee that they will threaten their allies with force to maintain their neutrality. This is unacceptable. And, Britain will have to operate at sea in this war, to help her neighbour defend her coastline at the very least, even if she declines to send troops. It is a solemn meal. Afterwards His Majesty sits with the Prince of Wales, answering telegrams as the clock ticks on. "France is begging us to come to their assistance. At this moment public opinion here is dead against our joining in the war," he notes, "but I think it will be impossible to keep out of it as we can not allow France to be smashed."[47]

That night, as the Tsar tries to absorb the reality of being at war with Germany, the magnitude of the situation he now faces, a delayed telegram arrives from Wilhelm. Essentially, it was still promising hopes of peace, at a time which Nicholas now knows Germany was in the midst of declaring war on his country. He is livid, and it proves the final break between he and the Kaiser. "He was never sincere, not a moment," fumes Nicholas. "In the end, he was hopelessly entangled in his own net of perfidy and lies."[48] He despairs at the cheek of Wilhelm's attempts to blame him outright and awakes the next morning resolved. "I felt as if a weight had fallen from my mind. My responsibility to God and my people was still enormous, but at least I knew what I had to do."[49] The Tsar believes that he has done all he could, and now that this war had been thrust unwillingly upon him, he intends to win it.

In London the Cabinet are at each others' throats. In essence, everything now rests on Belgium. France, Russia's ally has begun to mobilise, and the issue at hand is whether German troops will violate Belgian soil as they march on Paris. She is an ally of Britain, but the question is, by existing treaties, is Britain legally bound to go to her defence? The answer is no, but there is the question of a moral obligation in defending a small nation against unwarranted aggression. Bleary-eyed, the King awakes on Sunday morning to find a response from Nicholas to the telegram for which he had been dragged out of bed a little over 24 hours before. "I would have gladly accepted your proposals had not German Ambassador... presented a note to my Government declaring war," his cousin begins. The Tsar believes that since the moment that Serbia had been presented with an impossible ultimatum, he had devoted himself to peace. Russia simply could not stand by and watch a great power crush her weak friends. Germany did nothing to rein in Austria until it was too late. He had been forced to mobilise his forces along Russia's Galician border to offset both the fact that Austrian troops were concentrating in the area, and that they had already begun bombarding Russia's Serbian allies. "I had given most categorical assurance to the Emperor William that my troops would not move so long as negotiations continued." It is, of course, in the Tsar's interests that as his existing ally, Britain joins Russia in fighting Germany. "In this solemn hour I wish to assure you once more that I have done all in my power to avert war. Now that it has been forced on me, I trust your country will not fail to support France and Russia in fighting to maintain balance of power in Europe." Sir George Buchanan, Britain's ambassador in St. Petersburg, adds a note of his own before he submits this to London. "If we do not respond to Emperor's appeal for our support, we shall... at the end of the war... find ourselves without a friend in Europe while our Indian empire will no longer be secure from attack from Russia."[50]

47   RA GV/PRIV/GVD/1914 (1/8).
48   Massie: *Nicholas and Alexandra,* p.273.
49   Ibid., p.276.
50   RA PS/PSO/C/Q/1549/15.

That Sunday, 2nd August, German troops march into Luxembourg as they attempt to swing in an arc through the Low Countries, down into France, seize Paris, and knock the Republic out of the game, thus enabling them to turn their whole strength against the seemingly infinite manpower of Russia. Everything now hinges on whether the German Army will violate Belgian soil to effect this. Inside Buckingham Palace a mood of depression hangs over the Royal Family at this prospect. Outside, public opinion is beginning to swing away from neutrality. Large crowds are gathering at Downing Street. At the end of The Mall up to 6,000 people assemble and well into the night they sing *God Save the King* and *Rule Britannia*.

On Bank Holiday Monday the King receives a desperate plea from Albert, King of the Belgians; "a supreme appeal to the diplomatic intervention of Your Majesty's government for the safeguard of the neutrality of Belgium." Germany issues a demand: stand aside and let us through. His Majesty's approved response is swift. His Foreign Secretary is about to make a speech in Parliament that will prove his and his country's "desire and intention to do all in our power to respect and secure the integrity, independence and neutrality of Belgium."[51] When Sir Edward Grey speaks, his performance is remarkable; "almost an hour long, for the most part almost conversational in tone and with some of his usual ragged ends, but extraordinarily well reasoned and tactful and really cogent, so much so that our extreme peace-lovers were for the moment reduced to silence."[52] That evening His Majesty holds his second council of the day to issue an order of general mobilisation for the army, to commence at midnight. France has declared war on Germany. And "public opinion," writes the King, "since Grey made his statement in the House today, has entirely changed... now everyone is for war and our helping our friends."[53] That night the crowds are so dense outside Buckingham Palace that the Prince of Wales has to squeeze in through the garden when he comes back from an evening walk. "Oh!! God," he writes, "the whole thing is too big to comprehend!!"[54]

On 4th August the King breaks away from work only to walk in the garden. He sends a response to the Tsar's emotional message, which reveals just how close Britain is to declaring war on Germany. "We both have serious and grave times before us and my earnest prayer is that both our countries may meet them with calm and with trust in divine Providence."[55] The Kaiser's troops have entered Belgium. "This simplifies matters, writes the Prime Minister. "We sent the Germans an ultimatum to expire at midnight requesting them to give a reassurance... that they would respect Belgian neutrality."[56] It is Churchill who arrives at the Palace with this news. The King works with one eye on the clock, convinced that it is only a matter of time until his assent will be required to send his country to war. Half an hour before Britain's ultimatum to Germany is due to expire, the Prime Minister telephones the Palace to say that the British Ambassador to Berlin has been handed his passport. The King presides over a Privy Council meeting to declare war on Germany. "It is a terrible catastrophe," he writes shortly afterwards, "but it is not our fault."[57]

Throughout the day, the crowd outside His Majesty's windows has been swelling. On the preceding three nights the King and Queen have stepped out onto the balcony to acknowledge the cheers of the crowd as thousands of subjects wave miniature Union Flags and French Tricolours. When they go back inside, an estimated 10,000 people begin chanting *We Want King George* to the tune of the chimes at Westminster. The effect of the now hysterical patriotism on his doorstep is a moving

51   RA PS/PSO/C/Q/1549/19.
52   Asquith: *Memories and Reflections Vol. II*, p.20.
53   RA GV/PRIV/GVD/1914 (3/8).
54   RA EDW/PRIV/DIARY/1914 (3/8).
55   RA PS/PSO/C/Q/1549/23.
56   Asquith: *Memories and Reflections Vol. II*, p.21.
57   RA GV/PRIV/GVD/1914 (4/8).

spectacle for the King. "The enormous crowd collected outside the Palace... When they heard that war had been declared the excitement increased and it was a never to be forgotten night when May and I with David went on to the balcony, the cheering was terrific."[58] Patriotic airs give way to hymns, started off by individuals, picked up by those about them and then carried further afield until the huge ensemble forms a powerful choir surrounding the new Victoria Memorial and away down The Mall. The Prince of Wales lies in bed and listens to the noise go on throughout the night.

The likelihood that any single Sovereign could have averted war in August 1914 is slim. Of all of them, perhaps Franz Josef could have had a crucial impact on events had he intervened before Austria's ultimatum was sent to Serbia. But that is not to say that the others do not try. Ultimately, though, for all Nicholas tried to limit the effects of the Russian Army's mobilisation, he knew it was a highly provocative move. The same is true for Wilhelm, as Germany declared war on France and decided to violate the neutrality of smaller nations caught up in their advance. Of all of Europe's participating monarchs, perhaps King George is the one who could ask what more he could have done. He had pleaded with his cousins, and carried out all that his Government had asked of him.

The outbreak of the Great War has an instantly unifying effect on nations struggling to come to terms with the world at the beginning of the twentieth century. Wilhelm's popularity was on the wane in the years before 1914. "In the struggle that is before us," he declares in the Reichstag on 4th August, "I recognise no more parties among my people. There are only Germans."[59] In response, his subjects galvanise themselves at his side. Despite revolutionary sentiment, when the Tsar returns to St. Petersburg by boat and issues a formal proclamation at the Winter Palace on a sweltering hot, summers' day, the enormous square outside is filled with singing, cheering crowds waving flags and banners. In Britain, Herbert Asquith regards the outbreak of the Great War at the greatest stroke of luck in his political career. He was within an inch of political ruin at the hands of the crisis brought about by his Home Rule Bill, and then suddenly he was regarded as having delivered a masterstroke, bringing Britain united into the war.

For the rest of his life, the King will be irrevocably associated with the coming great struggle. A lack of direct power by no means intimates that His Majesty must remain idle. For an industrious constitutional monarch in a changing world, as well as forming the most testing time of his reign, the war will also present the King with an opportunity to shape the monarchy for the modern age. Whether in victory or defeat, there is hardship and tragedy to come, and much work to be done. In the words of Winston Churchill: "The ungovernable passions of nations had broken loose. Death for millions stalked upon the scene. And all the cannons began to roar."[60]

"Clean Consciences"

In the summer of 2014, a national newspaper published a letter that they claimed proved that the King was in favour of war. Taken 100 years after the fact, based on hindsight applied decades later, the evidence was used to make a snappy headline that contorted historical fact. The King did not want war, far from it; but once a general European conflict became inevitable and Britain began to swing slowly, like the bow of one her great ships, towards the conflict breaking out on the continent; he was all in, determined that his country and her Allies would prevail. As such, the King concurs with the actions of his Ministers in July and August. As he writes to the Tsar:

58   Ibid.
59   Clark, Christopher: *Kaiser Wilhelm II, A Life in Power,* p.239.
60   Churchill, Sir Winston: *The World Crisis 1911-1918,* pp.28-30.

Both you and I did all in our power to prevent war, but alas, we were frustrated and this terrible war which we have all dreaded for so many years has come upon us. Anyhow Russia, England and France have clean consciences and are fighting for justice and right… I trust that for all our sakes that this horrible war will soon be over and peace once more exist in Europe.[61]

When the US Ambassador arrives at the Palace for an audience, the King just puts his hands in the air. "My God, Mr Page, what else could we do?"[62]

His Majesty's presence is required three separate times on the balcony on 5th August, "wonderful as it was raining."[63] But he does it, day after day. He bears the crowds and their military ardour graciously for nearly a week after war is declared, which is more than could be said for David, who is tired of trying to sneak in and out of the palace unnoticed and labels them as "intolerable."[64] After a huge display of patriotism on 9th August, when the King estimates that 50,000 people are gathered down The Mall, the crowds finally drift away. The following days bring tales of early naval activity, but there is a strange lull as most of the nation waits for war-like things to happen. The British Expeditionary Force, comprised of some 100,000 regular soldiers and reservists, who are now being recalled to the colours, need a fortnight or so to execute their departure plan and make their way to a pre-planned assembly point near the Franco-Belgian border designated for the event of a European war. There are tales of woe from the British Ambassador to Berlin, who arrives home and reports personally to his Sovereign; regaling him with dramatic accounts of mobs smashing the windows of the Embassy, "and the many insults he and his staff had to put up with during his journey to the Dutch frontier."[65] The Prime Minister finds King George fussy and anxious, but really just relieved that the endless, uncertain days running up to Britain's ultimatum to Germany are behind them. At least now the situation is clear and he knows what he must do. "He really is a good deal relieved that war has come. He could not stand the tension of last week."[66]

As a man, the King deplores the notion of abandoning a friend, an officer or a minister who has done him good service; and the biggest personal wrench of the opening weeks of war is the loss of the Austro-Hungarian Ambassador. Albert Mensdorff stays in Britain for eight days after war is declared on Germany, dimly hopeful that Britain and France will not commence hostilities on his own country. On 9th, the King, who could have, probably should have limited his communications with this probable enemy to curt politeness, invites Mensdorff to tea in the garden at the palace. Arriving via a side entrance to avoid the press, he finds that His Majesty's attitude towards him has not changed at all. "He said that England had gone to war about the neutrality of Belgium and the protection of the French frontiers, not about Serbia and the Balkan question."[67] But within days the Cabinet have decided that they will follow France as soon as she makes her declaration against Austria-Hungary, and so with great sadness, King George is forced to hold a council at Buckingham Palace to follow suit. "I am too sorry for poor Albert Mensdorff," he mourns, "who will have to take leave at once."[68] Within an hour he has despatched a letter to his distant cousin to assure him that his feelings have not change towards him, and that he looks forward to the day when he will be able to welcome him back to London. Mensdorff is overwhelmed. "It must indeed be without

61   RA GV/ADD/COPY/174.
62   Nicolson, Harold: *King George V: His Life and Reign,* p.247.
63   RA GV/PRIV/GVD/1914 (5/8).
64   RA EDW/PRIV/DIARY/1914 (4/8).
65   RA GV/PRIV/GVD/1914 (6/8?).
66   (ed.) Brock: *H.H. Asquith: Letters to Venetia Stanley,* p.157.
67   Rose: *King George V,* p.170.
68   RA GV/PRIV/GVD/1914 (12/8).

precedent in history that at the same time as the declaration of war the sovereign writes such a letter to the ambassador beginning: "My dear Albert" and ending "ever your devoted friends and cousins George and Mary."[69]

In private, to anyone that will listen, the King expresses his anger at Germany; but he is not especially visible in public circles. His behaviour in the opening days of the war is far subtler than that of his cousin. "The Kaiser was making the world ring," says one journalist. "A persistent claque filled two hemispheres with tales of what he was doing and what he was about to do. Even the date of his promised entry into Paris as victor was told, and his menu at the triumphal dinner detailed. His speeches, his threats, his promises, his unending journeys, and his intrigues filled many columns." There is certainly something to be said for the German Emperor's publicity in the opening weeks of war, even if in true Wilhelmine fashion his efforts are embarrassingly over the top. After the war, it is suggested that the King's advisers might not have "acted more wisely had they planned more display for him. This was an hour when the very pomp of Kingship could be wisely employed."[70] But for now, beyond constitutional obligations, His Majesty remains in the background. This is made possible, perhaps even acceptable, because instead of the Sovereign, an immense figure, one that the King trusts implicitly, steps into the spotlight and acts as a rallying point for the early war effort.

Late on 3rd August, Asquith had dashed off a note. "I was very sorry to interrupt your journey today, and I fear I caused you inconvenience. But with matters in their present critical position I was anxious that you should not get beyond reach of personal consultation and assistance."[71] The recipient was Field Marshal Lord Kitchener, who had made it as far as Dover in anticipation of returning to his work in Egypt after being home for some Imperial discussions and a spot of leave. Ever since the Curragh debacle the previous March, which resulted in the resignation of the Secretary of State for War, Asquith has been filling the empty role himself. Now, with war looming he realises that he cannot continue to shoulder the burden of two jobs at once. On 5th August he convinces Kitchener to step into the breach. "It requires the undivided time and thought of any man to do the job properly... [He] was, to do him justice, not at all anxious to come in, but clearly understood... and... his place at Cairo is kept open so that he can return to it when peace comes back."[72] The post has been sold to the famous soldier as his duty to King and Country, which is something he has taken very seriously throughout a very long and illustrious career.

It is a move on the part of the Government that comes as an immense relief to the King, whose friendship with Kitchener spans three decades. Invariably known as 'Lord K', or just 'K', this towering, enigmatic figure that inspires devoted faith in the hearts and minds of Britons has spent little time living there. Soldier, adventurer, explorer, even spy, he was part of the failed rescue expedition sent to extricate General Gordon from his folly at Khartoum before he took up the rather lofty sounding post of "Governor of the Egyptian Provinces of Eastern Sudan and Red Sea Littoral," which was not as impressive as the length of the title implied. Early battles made him a household name, but it was Omdurman that elevated him to even dizzier heights when General Gordon was avenged. Here, in 1898, Kitchener commanded a British advance that decisively defeated the Mahdist forces and secured British control of the Sudan. Two years later Kitchener served as Chief of Staff to Field Marshal Lord Roberts, who took over the ailing campaign in South Africa. More honours followed the end of that difficult war, and once again Britain celebrated Horatio Herbert

69   Rose: *King George V,* p.170.
70   (ed.) Hammerton & Wilson: *The Great War Vol?,* p.9.
71   TNA: PRO 30/57/76 (3/8).
72   Asquith: *Memories and Reflections. Vol. II,* p.24.

Kitchener. Soon the hero was on the move again, this time to India, where he took up the matter of reforming the army there with vigour. Kitchener remained a firm royal favourite after the death of Queen Victoria. Edward VII wanted him to become Commander-in-Chief in the Mediterranean, but it was hardly the most taxing of posts. He would much rather have been Viceroy of India when that job became available, but his ambitions were left unfulfilled and so he was offered a senior post in Egypt, as Consul-General.

The Field Marshal's fearsome reputation is enhanced by his appearance. He is comfortably over six feet tall, but at 64, bears the scars of a lifetime spent travelling the globe. Above his world famous moustache he assumes a penetrating glare caused in part by damage to his eyes sustained during a spell in the desert. He had once left the Prime Minister of South Africa trembling and in 1912, an Egyptian nationalist had tried to assassinate him. In Cairo he broke through a crowd wielding a gun. Kitchener apparently walked steadily towards the man and asked what he wanted and the offender ended up grovelling on his knees.

But this loyal servant to the King is far from a simple, dedicated soldier driven forward on an outstandingly ambitious career trajectory. He shares many characteristics with His Majesty. Both are outwardly gruff, but surprisingly sensitive when an acquaintance manages to crack their awkward exterior. Clive Wigram's new wife admits during the war that she takes quite a fancy to him, despite his funny ways. "Lord Kitchener has a funny abrupt way of hurling things at ones head," she writes. The first time she met him "he suddenly said "FINE FELLOW YOUR HUSBAND.""[73] Both men are only really comfortable with a small circle of friends and are largely unskilled at getting their point across vocally or addressing a crowd. Neither displays any semblance of the prejudices of race, colour or class typical of their contemporaries. Both regard their duty as paramount, and devote themselves wholly to it; but in the course of doing so, both, despite their lofty positions they can be thoughtful and approachable.

After Omdurman, Kitchener supervised the evacuation of the wounded and then organised a memorial service for General Gordon outside the ruined palace in Khartoum. "Gordon's favourite hymn had been 'Abide with Me', and after this had been sung Kitchener was heard sobbing audibly with tears running down his cheeks… In a quiet and hesitant voice he explained how much it meant to him to have avenged Gordon who had done so much for Britain"[74] An aide wrote to his father at the turn of the century from South Africa about the future Field Marshal and his love of animals. "The other morning we found him darting about his room in his early morning attire (tousled hair, short dressing gown etc.) trying to catch a couple of young starlings that had fallen down his chimney." Once he had rescued them, Kitchener was besotted. "There was much fuss all day about their food; and the good man would leave his important duties every half hour to see if I had given them meat, or procured succulent worms, and bustle in and say they were starving." Kitchener was so entranced watching the mother bird feed her chicks that he all but forgot about the war in hand. "The operations in South Africa received no attention most of… the day… the [man responsible for] some 200,000 men at war spends half his day watching it "fluffing" worms, and chirping at it through the wires."[75]

Popular acclaim is never something that Kitchener courts, but it is near impossible to overstate just how highly he is regarded by the public. As far as Britons are concerned, in four decades of service, he has never failed in anything that he has attempted to do in the name of their country. And all that he has achieved, he is perceived as having done out of duty, not for personal gain. As such he was incapable of delegation, so he has plenty of traits that have rubbed colleagues the

73   PP: NW 6/4/1915.
74   Warner: *Kitchener: The Man Behind the Legend,* p.99.
75   Ibid., pp.130-131.

wrong way over the years, as has his rapid promotion and the accolades that have come with it. Inside Whitehall, Kitchener's appointment as Secretary of State for War is not a wholly welcome decision. He is not a politician, and Asquith does not expect him to be. He is, and remains, a military man to the bone. The Prime Minister is under no illusions about the abrasive Cabinet member he is assuming, but it is worth the risk. He is getting an icon, one that is willing to slot into his Government in Britain's best interests. Asquith's action is shrewd, for he is projecting the image of national unity with this non-partisan appointment. But his actions are honest too. At this time of crisis he does not reach out to Kitchener for the sake of his Government's image alone. "It is a hazardous experiment," he writes, "but the best in the circumstances, I think."[76] The Prime Minister accepts that it is going to be a bumpy ride. The first active soldier to sit in the Cabinet since the days of the Charles II, Kitchener remarks over breakfast the day after his appointment: "May God preserve me from the politicians."[77]

The Field Marshal believes in brief discussions, and makes them "hot" while they last.[78] He has no tolerance for time-wasting. His first Army Council meeting at the War Office is described by the officers in the Finance Division as ""hell with the lid off."[79] Within a week he has so bludgeoned the existing setup at the ministry that it is reeling. Asquith sent in a mediator in the form of Lord Haldane, a Cabinet colleague, "and… there is a perceptible lowering of the temperature."[80] But the rest of the Government accept that this man knows more than the rest of them combined about the military matters that now supersede all others, and this knowledge allied with his self-assurance means Kitchener quickly becomes a dominant personality in the Cabinet. David Lloyd George, the Chancellor of the Exchequer, later records that the room is in complete awe of him. On 11th August, the Prime Minster writes cheerfully that the large part of Governmental dialogue that day had been between Churchill and Kitchener, "the former posing as an expert on strategy, and the latter as an expert on Irish politics!"[81]

The new War Minister's opinion that the war will last for years is one that is shared by the King, though it is decidedly unpopular amongst his colleagues. This belief, combined with the fact that he insists that Britain will have to contribute huge forces to the field leads to his insistence that he must raise an immense new army. The opening days of war are dominated by a virile recruitment campaign and an ensuing rush to the colours. It is not His Majesty whose face adorns the posters, it is his trusted friend orchestrating this outpouring of enlistment in his name. The message about what these volunteers will be fighting for is articulate and clear. They will be fighting for their King and their country. Likewise, those already in uniform, six divisions that await their imminent departure in August 1914, are issued with a message from the War Minister. "You are ordered abroad as a soldier of the King to help our French comrades against the invasion of a common enemy. You have to perform a task which will need your courage, your energy, your patience." It is signed: "Do your duty bravely, Fear God, Honour the King, Kitchener."[82]

"Before the war," writes one journalist, "there were many men, some in the British Isles and some abroad, who spoke as if the old spirit of Britain were dead… they lamented or they sneered at the decay into which they believed the British people had fallen." The population are thought to be "supine, easy-going, pleasure-loving, unorganised and un-disciplined. The women are "giddy and

76   Asquith: *Memories and Reflections. Vol. II*, p.24.
77   Cassar: *Kitchener: Architect of Victory*, p.177.
78   Warner: *Kitchener: The Man Behind the Legend*, p.13.
79   Cassar: *Kitchener: Architect of Victory*, p.169.
80   Ibid., p.168.
81   (ed.) Brock: *H.H. Asquith: Letters to Venetia Stanley*, p.165.
82   Warner: *Kitchener: The Man Behind the Legend*, pp.176-177.

incapable of serious thought or effort, except a few unbalanced fanatics who smash windows and horse-whipped Ministers. The men were "flanneled fools…" content to idle away their time in theatres, clubs, on the river or in a… football crowd."[83] But the war has awakened the population. The people of Britain are flinging themselves into action. At Buckingham Palace members of the Royal Household enlist, carriage horses are taken from the Royal Stables and sent to do ambulance work and the carriages themselves are set aside for the business of taking wounded men from railway stations to hospitals on their arrival in London. It is a surreal, ominous experience, waiting for the storm to break. The King has resolved not to leave his capital until the situation becomes clearer, for the Battle of the Frontiers is already raging. France, attempting to take the initiative, will suffer nearly a quarter of a million casualties during this August fight as they take on Germany's numerically superior force. It is a national catastrophe. Storming through Belgium, the Kaiser's troops have their sights set on Paris. King Albert's tiny army faces annihilation in trying to repel the German invaders.

In London, the King is taking leave of those preparing to depart with the British Expeditionary Force. One of their leading officers is General Sir Douglas Haig, who will command one of the two corps going to France. His Majesty is reasonably well acquainted with him, but he had been more of a favourite of the King's father, having married one of Queen Alexandra's Maids of Honour. The army man does not think that His Majesty quite grasps the severity of what his country has become embroiled in. "The King seemed anxious, but he did not give me the impression that he fully realised the grave issues both for our country as well as for his own house… nor did he really comprehend the uncertainty of the result of all wars between great nations… no matter how well prepared one may think one is."[84] Kitchener arrives at the palace to inform the King that in just a few days in mid-August, the entire BEF, some 100,000 men, has been landed safely in France. They have begun to creep into Belgium, and by 23rd August they reach the grimy little Belgian industrial town of Mons. Shortly after dawn, the BEF fight their opening battle of the Great War. Within hours, German pressure forces the British troops back, signifying the beginning of a tense fortnight in which it looks like the war might be over as soon as it has begun, and with devastating results for the Allies.

Kitchener informs the King that both the British and the French are retiring out of Belgium. Like the Prime Minister, His Majesty baulks at the thought of the casualties. No list of the fallen has arrived, but it is bound to include a slew of familiar names, friends. There are rumours that the Germans are executing the wounded as they are left behind in the haste of withdrawal. Unless the French can turn and fight, Kitchener, who does not have a particularly high opinion of the French Army, having seen it in action first hand, fears that the British force might cave in on its flanks. His Majesty receives an early account of the fighting Mons when his cousin Leopold arrives home on 25th August with a leg wound, but for nearly two weeks, like his ministers, he is largely left to ponder the very worst as he relies on snippets of information that filter through to the War Office or into the newspapers. The Royal Family cling to the hope that all of those "missing" might yet turn up when the situation calms down, that all is not lost, but the Cabinet have begun sketching plans to help evacuate the French gold reserve to London to keep it from the enemy.

Sir John French, the commander of the BEF and Haig's direct superior, shows signs of cracking. By the end of August his headquarters has reached Compiegne some fifty miles north of Paris. From there he informs Kitchener in a rambling telegram that his men have had enough and that he proposes to withdraw them to behind the River Seine, leaving the French to fend for themselves.

83   (ed.) Hammerton & Wilson *vol.XII*, p.417.

84   (ed.) Sheffield & Bourne: *Douglas Haig: War Diaries and Letters 1914-1918*, p.56.

Asquith and his Cabinet colleagues are horrified. Kitchener replies, "expressing his own surprise and asking Sir John French for his reasons for the contemplated movement."[85] An unsatisfactory response results in a hurried sit down at Downing Street, led by the Prime Minister, Kitchener and Churchill. "We came to the… conclusion that the only thing to be done was for K to go there without delay and unravel the situation. He is a real sportsman [in an emergency] and went straight home to change his clothes." A train pulls out of Charing Cross shortly after 1:00am on 1st September and makes for Dover, where Churchill has ordered a fast cruiser to take the War Minister to the front. "Hardly a dozen people realise that he is not at the War Office today,"[86] boasts Asquith.

The King is informed in the morning, and throughout the course of the day is in disturbed consultation about the conduct of the war with Churchill and the Prime Minister. When Sir John French appears in front of him, Kitchener, though calm, absolutely squashes the concept of a British removal. The BEF's commander is "sour, impetuous… sullen and ill tempered in expression," as he sulks about the fact that the Secretary of State for War is wearing his Field Marshal's uniform. As far as French is concerned, this is an effort to undermine him, but in London, news reaches the Palace that Kitchener has averted a possible disaster. He departs France less than 24 hours after he has arrived, much to Asquith's relief, as he has envisaged a nightmare scenario in which the enemy seizes a member of his Cabinet. "You never know how far the German cavalry may have penetrated, and he would be the best bag they could secure."[87] Almost as soon as he arrives in London, Kitchener goes to see the King, who is emphatically relieved that his old friend's flying visit to France has been a success.

For now, the German tide is stemmed. "The terrible period of retirement is ended,"[88] Sir John French writes to his Sovereign. By 9th September, the tables have turned and the enemy is retreating away from Paris again. The situation is still uncertain, and fraught with terrifying possibilities, but suddenly turning the German Army on its heels has a galvanising effect on the exhausted BEF. Not only has disaster been averted, but Kitchener has called upon the King to tell him that projected casualties were much, much lower than had originally been feared. Seven weeks of anticipation, and then panic and anxiety are at an end. King George receives word that more men are being despatched to make good British losses, and the Germans suddenly look less than invincible.

But the King is still anxious, as a thousand and one other fledgling problems relating to the war have to be thrashed out. How will Britain administer the influx of Belgian and French refugees coming across the Channel? The Belgian military authorities are desperately appealing for assistance in the defence of Antwerp as the Kaiser's forces continued to plough across her territory; and the King himself will become deeply concerned with the question of the machinations of separation allowances and military and naval pensions for dependants, widows, and orphans. British merchant ships in the South Atlantic are being hunted by the enemy, and war is already being waged with force in East Africa.

For most people, once their friends, neighbours and loved ones leave for war, they vanish "behind a veil of secrecy. They were fighting or watching "somewhere in France" or "somewhere in the North Sea."[89] No such censorship restrictions apply to the King and his immediate family. The ordinary subject will have to rely on newspapers, from tales that came from the lips of those who come home wounded or on leave. His Majesty will receive a constant flow of detailed information, and not just personal correspondence from relatives who have gone straight to the front. The contents of papers

85   RA PS/PSO/GV/C/R/175.
86   Asquith: *Memories and Reflections. Vol. II,* p.29-30.
87   Ibid.
88   Nicolson, Harold: *King George V: His Life and Reign,* p.259.
89   (ed.) Hammerton & Wilson: *The Great War Vol. XII,* pp.421-422.

from Cabinet Ministers will ensure throughout the war that the King is, for better or for worse, uniquely informed on a staggering array of subjects. His Majesty's knowledge of naval and military affairs is so good thanks to the connections of his secretaries too, that Asquith complains that he lacks a good civilian to balance out this close group. But though Stamfordham, Clive Wigram and Fritz Ponsonby have ensured that there will be continuous information coming into the Palace from those quarters, the King also receives reports from British representatives across the globe; from the Viceroy in India, Governors, consular officials and ambassadors to church, newspaper and business men.

From the Western Front after the Great Retreat, letters gain in momentum. Smith-Dorrien, in command of II Corps, had sent reports to His Majesty of a similar fashion in years gone by and so it is unsurprising that the King has asked it of him again. Sir John French is of a jealous disposition, and resents his direct subordinate's contact with the Sovereign, but he does not help himself in that regard. He too has been invited to write to the Palace but he often delegates this to a member of his staff. He even selects "Billy" Lambton for the job, an officer whom the King describes as "a charming man and an old friend of mine."[90] Thus he fuels his own insecurities about what His Majesty is being told. The accounts that arrive at the palace do not only contain sweeping updates on the British war effort, but the minutiae of life at the front: a trench raid here, capture of a machine gun post there. It is Clive Wigram who suggests to Haig's wife that he should send his diary direct to Buckingham Palace and that once the King has read it can be forwarded to her to keep. "I have not had a regular 'diary," Haig replies, worried that his contributions might not be up to scratch. "I have, however… noted on some of the more important events in which I have been concerned."[91] As soon the wounded begin to return home to convalesce, and leave begins, a stream of visitors passes through the palace gates to converse with His Majesty and provide even more insight as to the fighting. Naval officers, many of them old friends are always on hand with letters. There are also more specialist visitors, such as Havelock Charles, who returns from France with news of the establishment of base hospitals.

In mid-September, the Prince of Wales gloats in a letter to his aunt that Germany has overreached. "It really looks as if the allies are getting a proper grip of the situation and that the German downfall has commenced, the brutes seem to be returning in a muddled state."[92] But those who think that any swift end is in sight to hostilities are about to receive a rude awakening, for the war is about to take a very unexpected turn. In France, the Kaiser's retiring forces come to a halt on the heights of the Chemin des Dames, which sits on a ridge overlooking the River Aisne. By the time that the French and British catch up with them, they have begun furiously digging trenches to prevent themselves from being pushed further back. Any attempts to dislodge them fail, and so the Allies dig-in opposite them. The result is static lines that will take years to overcome. "The Battle of the Aisne," Sir John French informs the King, "is very typical of what battles in the future are mostly likely to resemble, Siege operations will enter largely into tactical problems and the spade will be as great a necessity as the rifle."[93] The Western Front has been born.

"Write and Tell me All About It"

Over the years, the image of George V as a Dickensian villain has been adopted in terms of his role as a father. He has been described as a thoughtless bully; and Queen Mary as a cold and unfeeling

90   RA EDW/PRIV/MAIN/A/1415.
91   RA PS/PSO/GV/C/Q/832/111
92   RA QM/PRIV/CC50/1099.
93   Nicolson, Harold: *King George V: His Life and Reign,* p.259.

mother. Nothing could be further from the truth. It is important to consider the pitfalls of applying universal distaste for Victorian parenting methodology solely at the feet of the King and Queen, and indeed to recognise that for people of their class and of their time, Their Majesties played more of a hands-on role with their children than most of their contemporaries.

The King is not perfect. As a boy, his naval service had instilled in him an obedience to authority which in turn, he expected to receive. He can be loud, brusque, and he has a short temper. And so to his small children, yes, he could be formidable. He could also be a little thoughtless as far as their sensitive young minds were concerned. When Prince Henry was born, David, who was five or so at the time, asked some awkward questions about where he had come from. "I told him that the baby had flown in at the window during the night,"[94] he recalled. When David asked where his wings were, his father left him mortified when he joked with his little boy that they had been cut off. His dry sense of humour could come off as more insulting than was intended. On one occasion, Prince Harry and a friend had decided that they would build an aeroplane. He confessed to his father that he was not sure if it would work, and the King, who did not like aeroplanes in the first place, informed him that "neither of you will attempt to fly in it, as I am sure you would both come to grief."[95] This chaffing was part of King George's own upbringing, the inevitable result of a youth spent in service of the Royal Navy. Once, on a shooting excursion at Sandringham, a local boy was given the King's snack by mistake, and he forever mocked him as "The Boy Who Ate My Sandwiches."[96]

The King's struggle to show his feelings applied to his offspring as well as his Queen. But despite his personality ticks and his awkwardness, the King adores their children, as does Queen Mary. They saw more of them than most of their class could boast, indeed this was an inevitability for part of the year when they insisted on occupying York Cottage, which was hardly big enough to contain their large family. But it was not merely a physical manifestation of their chosen residence that produced an intimate family setting. Simple domesticity was a marked, undisputed feature of King George's reign, and this could hardly be achieved in the absence of their children. One of The Queen's ladies-in-waiting wrote that although the King and Queen had been depicted as distant parents, "this they most certainly were not... I believe that they were more conscientious and more truly devoted to their children than the majority of parents in that era."[97] Contrasted with the Kaiser, this would certainly seem to be the case. King George's children remained at home longer than Wilhelm's and never did they have to apply for an appointment to see him, unlike their princely German counterparts. In fact, the harshest criticism that Clive Wigram can make in 1918 is that His Majesty needs to let go more; for it would seem that his assistant saw parallels with the King's own upbringing. "He does not mean [to] but he was treated like a baby and he thinks he must do likewise."[98]

The King took pains to try to be more demonstrative with his children. In 1912, faced with the terrifying prospect of a teenage daughter, he didn't quite know what to do to improve his relationship with shy Princess Mary. When the two found themselves without the rest of the family for a snatched few days at York Cottage, Queen Mary was quick to orchestrate a way for them to spend some time together. "I have written to Mary and begged her to... ask you whether she may sit in your room if she will not be in your way. She would never dream of doing such a thing of her own accord."[99] The King was extremely proud of the result. "I have invited her to come and sit in my room while I write, she is just coming now, and seems pleased at the idea, although, she doesn't talk much, at least to me, but that will come I hope."[100]

Of course there were unique pressures and anxieties to which each family member was exposed as a result of being born into the Royal Family, and some of King George's children dealt with them better than others. The eldest, David and Bertie were undoubtedly scrutinised more closely, and the King never forgot his responsibility in terms of preparing the next generation of royals. "I trust that you will always remember," he wrote to David when his eldest son became Prince of Wales, "that now you must always set a good example to the others by being very obedient, respectful to your seniors and kind to everyone."[101] The King was devoted to his duty, and expected the same of his family, especially his heir, to whom he would bequeath an Empire, but he did not bully his children into submission. A direct comparison would be the brutal regime that his father was subjected to. Edward VII and his siblings, thanks to a programme designed by Prince Albert, were constantly harangued, and thanks to Queen Victoria they were constantly reminded of their flaws and inadequacies. Her husband once told her that the origin of her any problematic relations with her children lay "in the mistaken notion that the function of a mother is always to be correcting, scolding, ordering them about and organising their activities."[102] King George was a moderate blend of both his grandmother's severity and his father's reactionary parenting, which instilled almost no discipline at all, yet with similar results.

Much of what David wrote about the flaws in his upbringing, which forms the bulk of the evidence against the King and Queen, was penned half a century later. In the interim, much troubled water had passed beneath that particular bridge, including his abdication, exile and his dissatisfaction about his subsequent settlement. Even then, he admitted he had never wanted for affection, and that he had not had it so bad. He wrote that Sandringham had been idyllic. The Prince of Wales, as the King then was, taught his sons to shoot when they were thirteen. "He laughed and joked," David recalled, "and those 'small days' at Sandringham provided some of my happiest memories of him."[103] Though the children were encouraged to be modest and thoughtful, they were not denied. Christmas and birthday presents were lavish. When Prince Harry advised his parents that he would need to adhere to a school tradition and provide a birthday cake on his special day to be shared among the boys at his table, a cake arrived "which happened to be so big," Harry wrote to the King and Queen, "that I had to give it to the whole school instead of one table otherwise I would not have finished it at the end of term."[104] All of King George's sons were pranksters as children and they harboured no fears about making their father one of their victims. One day they watched, apoplectic with glee as he began stirring his tea and the spoon simply dissolved in the cup. Obtained from a joke shop and made of an alloy with a low melting point, antics like these do not suggest oppressed children under a terrifying yoke. Neither do children who live in fear of their father engage in full-blown food fights in front of him. King George had longed for a girl after David's birth and was particularly fond of Princess Mary, his only daughter. The image of her mother in looks, kindness and her shyness, he was far less stern with her. By 1914 the two could regularly be seen riding together in the mornings, and when David teased his sister about being necessarily stuck with their parents as a young girl while he and the rest of her brothers

99   RA QM/PRIV/CC08/159.
100   RA QM/PRIV/CC04/10.
101   Ziegler, p.30.
102   Ridley: *Bertie: A Life of Edward VII*, p.34.
103   Rose: *King George V*, p.53.
104   Frankland: *Prince Henry, Duke of Gloucester*, p.23.

were out in the world, she replied: "You need not feel so sorry for me."[105] The only thing she minded were dull dinners on occasion when the King would sit and read his paper and there would be no conversation.

Unlike his two elder brothers, Prince Henry was sent away to school and this filled the King with interest, for it was a world that he had never experienced. Harry was not simply packed off. After attending a reputable preparatory school as a day boy by way of an experiment, it was decided to send him as a boarder, to his apparent joy. The King longed to know all about it and complained that his letters were not detailed enough. He wanted this insight to his son's school life: "What you do, the people you meet and who your friends are and who do you fag for?"[106] Prince George is a live-wire; confident, the brightest of all the children and a charmer. One member of the Household is invited out on a family afternoon at Windsor in 1915 and they motor over to Swinley Woods for a walk. She is much amused as the whole party, which includes the Queen, Mary, Harry and Georgie, make their way along, singing Tipperary at the top of their voices: "Prince George slithering down trunks of trees getting the seat of his trousers impossibly green." The Queen laughs as she vainly shakes her umbrella at his head saying: "Come off that at once. Papa hates you spoiling your clothes!!"[107]

His Majesty is immensely proud of both his children's looks and their achievements. Bertie is an excellent shot, and their shooting was a bond between them. When Harry too began to show promise, the King was thrilled to receive a letter saying that he had shot his first stag. "I hope it was a good one, write and tell me all about it." They spent an afternoon at Sandringham together soon afterwards and His Majesty was "frightfully pleased"[108] to be shooting side by side with his improving son. When the King could be unforgiving, it was arguably because he did not want his children to encounter the same difficulties that he had had to contend with. His Majesty was somewhat knock-kneed, and he went to extreme-sounding lengths to try and make sure that his sons did not grow to adulthood with the same affliction. Both Bertie and Harry were obliged to spend portions of their childhood sleeping with leg splints on and wearing them for spells during the day too. It made them miserable, but the King was unmoved. On one occasion he found that the boys' personal attendant had given in to Bertie and removed them. His Majesty promptly sent for the servant. "Drawing his trousers tightly against his legs to display his own knock knees, he said sternly: "Look at me. If that boy grows up to look like this, it will be your fault."[109] Both boys adhered to the regime and neither grew up with their father's affliction.

The King is even more determined that when his children become of an appropriate age, they will be ready for the public life and the duty that awaits them. They will, after all, become part of a unique family business. He had been expected to prop up his weak elder brother Eddy throughout his entire youth, and that left a mark. He himself was not educated or prepared to rule when his brother died and elevated Prince George to the direct line of succession and he was, understandably, insistent that this would not be the case for his own heir. When the King and Queen settled on Eton for Harry, he had to undergo rigorous schooling in Latin verse to gain admission, because until then His Majesty had been insistent instead that he, along with his siblings would be able to speak French and German, which he was not able to do with any fluency because modern languages had been neglected in his own schoolroom.

105   Ziegler: *King Edward VIII: The Official Biography,* p.80.
106   Frankland: *Prince Henry, Duke of Gloucester,* pp.30-31.
107   PP: CW April 1915.
108   Frankland: *Prince Henry, Duke of Gloucester,* pp.37-39.
109   Rose: *King George V,* p.54.

But even though the King was firm in respect of what he wanted to prescribe for his children, his rebukes when they failed him were by no means as harsh as has been implied. Once, when Harry missed the train back to school he simply remarked that it was because he was "always so vague about everything."[110] When George managed to dislocate his knee playing French cricket at school, his father's only criticism was that he had never heard of such a thing, and that he "thought it was bound to be a silly game."[111] Far from being over-demanding in respect of his children's abilities, mediocrity is enough as far as His Majesty is concerned. Queen Victoria's offspring had been subjected to an endless barrage of criticism, but as long as his children try, he is satisfied. When Bertie did badly, the King's preoccupation was not that he was not the brightest boy in his class, it was that he had been informed that his son did not take his work seriously. Praise was forthcoming when he pulled himself together. "We are glad to hear that you have done well in French lately," Queen Mary wrote to him in 1909, "and on other subjects too, this is a great thing and shows you are taking more trouble with your work."[112] At the time he was still practically bottom of his class. When Harry finished halfway down his division at Eton, his father was pleased, because it "was quite credible and shows what you can do if you like."[113] To Prince George he once wrote: "So your exams begin today, I hope you will do well in them and gain some places in the order."[114]

More than anything the King wants his children to be good people. Their Majesties ensure that they are both polite, and that they lack any semblance of arrogance given their privileged circumstances. Once, when he was riding with two of his sons in Windsor Great Park, the boys over-exuberantly cantered past two labourers on the side of the road, who had stopped to salute the royal riders, without returning the courtesy. "At once their father halted them, wheeled them round, and made them return to the two astonished men, who received elaborate apologies from the boys for their unintentional rudeness."[115] The King is also the complete opposite of Edward VII in terms of his extra-marital behaviour, his scandals; and a lack of discipline had resulted in disaster with Prince Eddy. His Majesty is not puritanical, but his father and his brother had been amorous or rakish, and the King will be damned if his boys were going to succumb to the same temptation whilst he has any influence over matters.

"Slipped from the Leash"

When war breaks out, the King's two eldest sons are both of an age to contribute to the coming struggle. Prince Albert is easy to deal with. He had received his first commission on HMS *Collingwood* in 1913. "Johnson" as he is known to his shipmates, does not expect to be treated unlike any other man on board, and his father had confirmed as much on 28th July. His Majesty had last seen his second son at the naval review at Portsmouth in mid-July and Bertie was expecting leave at the beginning of August. "I have just heard from your Captain that for the moment all leave is stopped on account of the European situation." The King was asked if he had any special instructions regarding his son and he declined to interfere. "I am sure you would be the last to wish to be treated differently to anybody else," he wrote.[116] On the same day Queen Mary anxiously wrote to her aunt. "If we have to go to war; I suppose it means... that Bertie will have to go...

110   Frankland: *Prince Henry, Duke of Gloucester.*, p.36.
111   Ibid., pp.37-9.
112   RA GVI/PRIV/RF/11/051.
113   Frankland: *Prince Henry, Duke of Gloucester*, pp.37-39.
114   RA GV/PRIV/AA60/336.
115   Anon: *The Life of King George V: The Life and Work of a Monarch Beloved of his Peoples*, p.19.
116   Bradford: *George VI* p.77.

not an agreeable thought, but I am not going to make difficulties and he must go to fight for his country."[117] On 31st July *Collingwood* anchored at Scapa Flow in the early evening. Prince Albert kept watch, helped to sight turrets and put on old clothes for an eight hour coaling stint. Four days later, owing to his watch pattern, he slept through the expiry of the German ultimatum and the British declaration of war, but before he went to bed, His Majesty had written a prayer for his son in his diary.

Bertie has lived much of his life so far in David's shadow, and is plagued with an inferiority complex; the upshot of everyone he has ever met inevitably comparing him to his brother. As children they were always paired together, and Bertie grew to resent not only his brother's obvious importance, but being stage-managed by him. With David at Oxford, he remained at Dartmouth where he began to do better without the Prince of Wales's presence, and of late the two have grown apart. Prince Albert is well thought of. Clive Wigram's wife writes that Bertie is "extraordinarily attractive"[118] with a charming smile and easy to get along with. Asquith met him at the naval review in July 1914 and thought him a nice, handsome boy. Straight, honourable, kind-hearted are some of the other adjectives expended on Prince Albert.

"Papa sent a most interesting telegram to the fleet," records Bertie when he wakes up to find that he is at war with Germany. "At this grave moment in our National history I send to you and through you (i.e. Sir John Jellicoe) to the officers and men of the fleets of which you have assumed command, the assurance of my confidence that under your direction they will revise and renew the old glories of the Royal Navy, and prove once again the sure shield of Britain and of her Empire in the hour of trial."[119] Bertie is so taken with his father's words that he copies them into his diary. For his part, the King cannot quite comprehend that it has been a mere three weeks since he saw his boy at work in the fore turret of *Collingwood* at the review. The life of a sailor is a life that he knows, and he muses about what his son might be up to. "I suppose you have to go back to Scapa Flow every now and then to fill up with coal. I wonder if you have landed all your boats, tables, chairs and all woodwork. It must be very uncomfortable without them, but that can't be helped." After all, when the German shells flew, if they were still aboard they would be plaqued with threatening splinters. Like any father with a son about to board a transport, or take to the seas, more than anything he wants his child to be safe. "May God bless and protect you my dear boy. Those are the "earnest prayers of your devoted Papa. Write a line when you can as I want to know how you are," he pleads. Afterwards he goes back and scrawls, a reminder in between two lines. "Always do your duty."[120]

But Bertie's first war outing lasts a little over a fortnight. He had had bouts of gastric trouble at Dartmouth that he kept quiet. On the day of the Battle of Mons he is crippled with violent stomach pains and has trouble breathing. Two days later he is diagnosed with appendicitis and has to be craned ashore at Aberdeen to have the offending organ removed. The King sympathises with his sailor son. "The poor boy will despair of having to leave the *Collingwood*," but for now he is safe. Bertie arrives back in London at the beginning of October, and when a chill interrupts his convalescence, the King, who is away, rues his bad luck and with the Queen sees to it that he is at least put to work in the War Room at the Admiralty so that he might feel useful.

What to do with the Prince of Wales is far more problematic. As soon as the war begins David is climbing the walls at Buckingham Palace, agonising over the thought of being held back on account of his dynastic importance. The real decline in David's relationship with his father has

117   RA QM/PRIV/CC26/95.
118   PP: NW 16/4/15.
119   RA GVI/PRIV/DIARY/1914 (5/8).
120   RA GV/PRIV/AA59/290.

not yet begun. The signs are there, but in 1914 the relationship is firmly that of parent and child. The Prince is immature. More than one observer remarks upon the fact that David, although he is twenty, is much younger than his years. He is a popular young man with his peers, but Clive Wigram's wife found him the only member of the family that she could not forge any sort of easy acquaintance with. She found him difficult to talk to in comparison with his siblings. "I don't know if it was shyness, or what it was."[121] David is bright, and given a task he is a hard worker, conscientious; always eager to please. But much like his father in his youth he is prone to be indiscrete, and unhappiness about his station in life already chips away at his countenance.

It is difficult to judge a child. Hindsight is a temperamental business, but even as a boy David's reluctance to acknowledge that he would one day be King was discernible. One of the children's nurses remembered his boyhood protestations about taking the throne. As he grew older he hated to stick out, to be set apart from other boys. He just wanted to be like everybody else. As soon as he reached 18 and assumed increased public duties he singled out the most ceremonious and official of them as being deplorable. His father doesn't particularly like this aspect of his role as Sovereign either, the attention or the expectation, but David lacks his father's pragmatism. He is by nature a sulker, and while His Majesty places his duty above his personal desires, David kicks against his fate and what people expect of him as the heir to the throne more and more as the years pass. The crown will drive a wedge between father and son before long. When during the war, a military acquaintance of his father's comments that he should devote more of his time to world affairs, David says: "Of course he is right really and I don't attempt to be a Prince of Wales or prepare for being so… but how I hate all that sort of thing and how unsuited I am for the job!!"[122] On his 21st Birthday, one of David's dearest friends will write that he cannot think of any present that will please him. "The only thing I know of that you would really like, I cannot give you, and that is that you would become an ordinary person."[123]

So when in August 1914 David's resignation about his future is combined with the fact that that role stops him carrying out the desire being exercised by thousands of young men across Britain and going to war, the Prince is stroppy and utterly depressed. "This is just about the mightiest calamity that has ever or will ever befall mankind," he tells Bertie, for David has a flair for drama. "England at war with Germany!!' That seems a sentence which would appear nowhere but in a mad novel." He envies his brother. "I am as good as heartbroken to think I am totally devoid of any job whatsoever and have not the faintest chance of being able to serve my country. I have to stay at home with the women and children, a passenger of the worst description!!"[124]

A vast charitable undertaking is begun in David's name; *The Prince of Wales's Relief Fund*, for those suffering hardship as a result of the war. The King is happy enough to give it a home at York House, and for David to attach his name to it, but he wants it stressed clearly that the Prince has nothing to do with administering the money. It was the truth, but he did not want David embroiled in arguments with applicants who were rejected. Operations begin on 6th August and within 48 hours, the fund has received an unfathomably vast sum. When his Aunt sends him £1,000, David thanks her for her generosity: "I am so pleased to be taking some part in the defence of the country."[125] But after an inaugural meeting he complains that "It's such a rotten show for me; just a mere figurehead with the name Prince of Wales as usual!"[126] In a matter of days the fund

121   PP: NW 16/4/15.
122   Ziegler: *King Edward VIII: The Official Biography,* pp.74-75.
123   Ibid., p.57.
124   Ibid., p.49.
125   [ed.] Longford: *Darling Loos: Letters to Princess Louise 1856-1939,* p.286.
126   Ziegler: *King Edward VIII: The Official Biography,* p.52.

swells to a million pounds, "and no one seems to have the least idea what exactly it is for, or how or by whom it is going to be spent," complains the Prime Minister.[127]

The Prince is lonely and frustrated, and the King is sympathetic, but the fact is that nobody is going to let the heir to the throne stare down the barrel of a German rifle. David meets with his father about the fund, and blurts out that he cannot tolerate being a civilian. He must serve his country. He asks for a commission in the Grenadier Guards, "and dear Papa never hesitated a moment."[128] His Majesty has David attached to the King's Company. "It was a happy moment for me," the Prince writes, "and now I am an officer in the army and am going to do some active service! I get away from this awful palace where I have had the worst weeks of my life!"[129] Early on he is stationed at Warley in Essex with fat reservists who need beating back into shape. He feels that this is a stepping stone to better things, and he is not idle. Soon he is back in London. The battalion sends out guards to various places, including Olympia, where prisoners of war are being held, "so there is plenty of work, and it is such a joy to me to have a grand job like this."[130] The King is proud to have his son serving on his doorstep. "David came on guard today," he records, "and carried the colours, I should think it is the first time a Prince of Wales has ever carried the colours on a King's Guard."[131]

But the thing about David, is that it is in his nature to yearn for something, like his commission; to wholeheartedly ache for it; but then when he has it, it is not enough, and he immediately begins to yearn for something else. It means he is never happy. He has been to see the newly arrived German prisoners of war at Olympia, "the wretched brutes."[132] He has sat at the dinner table at home and listened to stories from the front. Members of his father's household on active service have brought home despatches and stopped at the Palace to regale the Royal Family with adventurous tales. David listens to it all, rapt. Being in uniform is not enough anymore. He must get to the front with his battalion, who are preparing to leave for France. But on 8th September the King sits him down and tells him that he will not be going with them. Instead, the Prince will be transferred to another outfit of the Grenadier Guards which will remain at home. "All my best friends in the regiment are going… while I have [to] stick here… It is a bitter disappointment and has broken my heart!!"[133]

Evidently the King cannot console him, nor the Queen. David argues that he is expendable, that he has plenty of brothers behind him in the line of succession, which of course makes no impression on his parents. The King does waver about the possibility of him serving at some headquarters on the staff, in relative safety from the enemy, but ultimately it is not his father standing the way of David's crossing to the front in this capacity, but Kitchener, who has told the King that he will not sanction it. It's the War Secretary's job to envisage a worse scenario than a martyr Prince dead on the battlefield and a blow to the succession: a worldwide propaganda coup for the pugnacious Kaiser and the German war effort. And so, when he complains to his parents, he is sent to the War Office to see the man himself. Kitchener fixes young David with that famous stare and says drily: "What if you were not killed, but taken prisoner?'"[134]

The fact is too, that David is not prepared for life in the firing line, however much he wants to be there. By standards at the beginning of the war, any training that he has had is not sufficient

127   (ed.) Brock: *H.H. Asquith: Letters to Venetia Stanley,* p.175.
128   RA EDW/PRIV/DIARY/1914 (6/8).
129   Ibid.
130   RA GV/PRIV/AA68/198.
131   RA GV/PRIV/GVD/1914 (17/9).
132   RA EDW/PRIV/DIARY/1914 (25/8).
133   RA EDW/PRIV/DIARY/1914 (11-13/9).
134   Ziegler: *King Edward VIII: The Official Biography,* p.51.

to warrant it. Both his parents and the authorities would have been remiss in allowing him to be sent into action in September 1914. The heir to the throne would have been undertrained and ill-experienced going into the 1st Battle of Ypres, as his battalion did; which would not only have put him at risk, but the men under his command. Even if they had let him, and he had astounded everyone with his capabilities as a very junior infantry officer, given the fate of the 1st Grenadier Guards and the officers that did depart for the front, it is wholly likely that he would have been dead or at the very least wounded or captured.

Not only that, but his parents are constantly anxious about David's health, with good reason. He does not look after himself. He operates on very little sleep, they don't know how, but most worrying are his eating habits, or lack of them. David displays symptoms of some form of eating disorder. He is thin, note those who meet him, too thin, but he is also preoccupied with fat on himself and others. He obsesses over what he eats, and then he obsesses about exercising like a madman to work the food off. He eats frugally, and thinks that people are gluttons, and that they eat more than they need to. He is up with the lark, running. Before breakfast he plays squash too, then he runs more. The thought of loose flesh on his body terrifies him, notes one peer. When circumstances prevent him from exercising, or when he does not have control over what he eats, he is bereft. The King has been preaching on deaf ears for some time by 1914. "You are just at the critical age from now till you are 21," he has told his son, "and it is most necessary that you should develop properly, both in mind and body. It all depends…whether you develop into a strong, healthy man or remain a sort of puny, half grown boy." It puzzles the King and Queen that something so obvious, that one must eat to live, is incomprehensible to their nearly grown boy. For the King, the worry manifests itself further, for this boy will succeed him. If he cannot manage his own diet, how will he manage as King? As an Emperor? "I am only telling you these things for your own good," he pleads, "and because I am so devoted to you and take such an interest in everything."[135]

Matters come to a head, again, when the Prince is told that he will not be going to the front with his battalion in September. It prompts a downturn in his mood. "Another 'health flap' has started," he complains. "Bloody nuisance: the usual thing, not enough food and sleep, too much exercise etc. I am more than fit so why the hell can't they leave me alone!!"[136] He is summoned to his father for "a hot telling off… Bloody, it was and it made me wild! He has spies who watch me!!"[137] The King and Queen send for an Oxford specialist, and he has a proper talk with David and introduces some guidelines so that he will not fade away to nothing. Depressed, by October the random obscenities and fits of despair in the Prince's diary are more frequent, but luckily for David, the King hates to say no to him. Throughout the war he will indulge almost his every whim to make up for the heartache that his boy suffers from not being allowed to go into action. He battles Kitchener to get the Prince onto Sir John French's staff at GHQ. He argues that this presents a unique opportunity for the future king to learn about the army first hand. "Of course it would have been impossible for you to have gone with your battalion, but on the Commander in Chief's staff [is] quite another thing,"[138] is His Majesty's reasoning. But Kitchener says no, and not even the King can get a word in edgeways when his old friend is resolved. The Prime Minister tells his wife that His Majesty has literally begged for David to be allowed to go to France.

But His Majesty is determined and so for now he works around his war minister, who is unmoved by his appeals. In mid-October the King has Stamfordham meet with Billy Lambton to devise a plan for David to serve at the front, so that this is no vague conception fraught with risk being

135   Ibid., p.31.
136   RA EDW/PRIV/DIARY/1914 19/9.
137   Ibid., 21/9.
138   RA EDW/PRIV/MAIN/A/1415.

presented to Kitchener. Not only does it plan an insight in to all branches of army administration, of Generals commanding troops, it would be his first prolonged exposure to Imperial subjects, as Indians are due to arrive on the Western Front imminently. The Prince would have a man attached to him too, a babysitter, though of course it will not be phrased thus and armed with this scheme Lambton goes to see Sir John French, who proposes that David is appointed as an aide to him for the sake of formality, and that the Prince live with him.

And yet more than a fortnight later Kitchener remains the sole obstacle to David's deployment abroad. Finally, he relents and tells the Prince that he can go, but he will have to wait a month. "I can't use any language strong enough for the bugger!"[139] Fumes David. But Kitchener's stubbornness is justified, for throughout all of this planning the war has been in the balance, the Germans have almost beaten a way through to the Channel coast and at the beginning of November, fighting has continued to rage. The War Secretary is more than happy to play the villain.

When the battle in question does finally tail off, Kitchener immediately relents. The King sits down with Stamfordham to issue a letter of thanks to the Commander in Chief for his willingness to receive the Prince of Wales and to make it very clear to French what he would like done with his son. Always accepting that Sir John had many responsibilities already, which superseded educating David, His Majesty would like him to gain a full and practical understanding of all that is required to orchestrate a vast campaign. He would like the Prince to be successively attached to different departments at GHQ. The King hopes, too, that it will prove possible to send David out along the lines of communication, behind the fighting, to observe how troops arrived and departed, how they received ammunition, food and stores. Indeed, this could prove to be a unique and invaluable military education. The Prince is expected to work, and it is imperative for his father that he be assigned his own duties. The King reminds Sir John that his son speaks both French and German, and concludes by giving instructions that the officer attached to David should accompany his son at all times when is not with the Commander in Chief or a member of his staff. The King is shrewd. After all, as David has crowed, once he is at the front anything is possible, and His Majesty knows that his son will push the boundaries and attempt to get as close to the fighting as possible.

On 16th November the King rises early to take leave of his son. "I never saw anyone so happy as he was when he was slipped from the leash," Stamfordham tells a friend.[140] "I am sure you will find plenty of interesting work," His Majesty writes to David on his arrival. He is just relieved that all of the Palace's efforts to get him there have paid off. "Of course I know how keen you have been to go to the front ever since the war began," he tells his son. "I miss you very much, but at the same time I am glad you have gone as every young man ought to be serving his country at such a time as the present." He'd like David to write when he can, and number his letters so that he can keep them as a diary. "Take care, sleep enough, eat enough and keep warm… God bless you. Ever my dear boy, your devoted Papa."[141]

"Duty is your Watchword"

At the onset of war, as a constitutional monarch, King George has no definable job. Although there are obvious state duties to perform, it is up to he and his advisors to shape a role according to his constitutional prerogative. With tens of thousands of his subjects dedicating themselves to the war effort, it is clear that he must do *something* tangible that presents him as the symbolic leader of the

139   RA EDW/PRIV/DIARY/1914 (10/11).
140   PA: S/13/15/14 18/11/14.
141   RA EDW/PRIV/MAIN/A/1415.

British Empire at war. To begin with, as titular head of the army, the King would be remiss if he did not show a concerted interested in his troops. There is plenty to see in the immediate vicinity as far as preparations are concerned. Soldiers march constantly through London: regulars in their uniforms and new recruits in civvies. Before the Battle of Mons the King rides one morning in Hyde Park with Princess Mary. They watch hundreds of recruits who all eagerly stop to salute when they spy him watching them. Scores of remounts were being broken in and father and daughter were keenly interested by the process. Kitchener has already issued a detailed message those in the army, with an emphasis on discipline and the dangers of wine and women. The Palace issued the King's own address too: "You are leaving home to fight for the safety and honour of my Empire," it began. "I have complicit confidence in you, my soldiers. Duty is your watchword and I know your duty will be nobly done. I shall follow your every movement with deepest interest… indeed your welfare will never be absent from my thoughts. I pray to God to bless you and guard you and bring you back victorious."[142]

The King does all he can to see individual divisions off to join the war effort. "It became a tradition with the British Army that "first you're trained; then you're polished up; then the King comes; and then you're off."[143] Civilian volunteers claim to feel like real soldiers once they have been looked at by His Majesty. As early as the 11th August, the King dons his Field Marshal's uniform and with the Queen, he motors down to Aldershot to see Sir Douglas Haig. The General's two divisions are lined up on either side of the road and the King shakes hands with the officers. The Garrison do not know the first thing about the royal visit until Their Majesties have all but left Buckingham Palace, sending a message ahead. Troops are engaged on routine work when they are hurriedly drawn in and assembled in lines. His Majesty does this on purpose, because he prefers to see people about their work than standing woodenly in front of him. The King is never one to restrict himself to greeting the higher ups. To him this is a complete waste of time. As he makes his way around the army establishment in Surrey, he stops constantly to speak to enthusiastic troops; buoyed by the sight of the enthusiastic new volunteers who hold the fate of his realm in their hands. "The men looked splendid and are well up to war strength, they have the right spirit and are tremendously keen."[144] Some inspections require much greater effort on the part of the troops. "Clean up, take your cleaning gear with you in your pack… everything had to shine, even the tips on your boots," writes an underage recruit "And we set off from Codford to Stonehenge where King George was on his horse and on a dais he took the salute… When the inspection was over we returned again on foot to the camp having completed 30 odd miles in the day."[145]

The King shows none of the scorn for the territorial force that his friend Kitchener does. Organised on county lines, these volunteer soldiers who train in their spare time, as well as a huge influx of new recruits, have agreed to serve abroad in their thousands at the onset of war. One day the King motors out to Horley to see Londoners on the march, at Luton Hoo there are North Midland men. With the situation at the front so uncertain, His Majesty doesn't stray too far from his capital; St. Albans for more Londoners, Huntingdon for the Highland Brigade. No plans are made too far in advance, either. The King decides to visit one or two days prior to his departure. The relative informality of his inspections surprises the soldiers as much as the press, who commend "our very human King"[146] and are charmed by the sight of His Majesty feeding his charger with a lump of sugar from his own hand.

142   Telegraph 18/8/14.
143   (ed.) Hammerton & Wilson: *The Great War Vol?*, p.20.
144   RA GV/PRIV/GVD/1914 (11/8).
145   IMW Sound: Thomas McIndoe: Catalogue #568, Reel 3, 1975.
146   *The Times* 9/10/14.

For these early units, they mostly get one glimpse of the Sovereign and then they are off, but the relationship that the King forges with Kitchener's New Army formations is more intimate because he sees them develop from civilian volunteers without a rifle to their name in the early weeks of the war, to the finished article ready to depart for the front the following year. It is part of the King's established routine to adjourn with Queen Mary for a little quiet time at Aldershot in the summer months. Their residence for these visits was the Royal Pavilion, a simple bungalow on the edge of a long valley; surrounded by a single white fence, some trees and flowering shrubs. They arrive in September 1914 and spend almost a week amongst these patriotic enlistees, the biggest swathe of lunteers that Britain has ever seen; young men swept up by recruitment fervour at the beginning of the war. Very few of the men have ever laid eyes on royalty before. They bunch towards the front to get a better look. The Garrison straddles Surrey and Hampshire, and from the pavilion the King and Queen go to all of the outlying stations at Camberley, Frensham, Chobham, Witley and the like. On one hot day the King drops in on men from four divisions of Kitchener's army, accompanied by the man himself. "Altogether we saw 82,000 men, very fine material. Most of them have not got uniforms yet, but they are tremendously keen and training very hard."[147] He stops on Tweseldown Racecourse to watch various detachments of artillery, cavalry and other branches at drill in the long valley, approaching them to observe their work more closely. The appearance of these vast new formations amuses Queen Mary. The men present "a somewhat motley appearance, some in kilts, some in trews and some in Khaki."[148] On Sunday there is a huge inspection, which "would have shocked the disciplinarian of the older school." The men are "in every garb, from the Navy's fustian to the Harris tweeds of the Bank Clerk."[149] "Never," boasts one newspaper, "in the history of the British Army has a sovereign seen such a cosmopolitan gathering of troops."[150]

The appearance of the troops is not the only thing that is surprising. The weather is blazing hot, but leaving their motor car at the end of the long lines of men, it is estimated that the King, accompanied by the Queen and Princess Mary, walk five miles in intense heat in reviewing them. The abandonment of formality is taken to an entirely new level. As soon as Their Majesties pass a unit, the men are permitted to relax and sit, or lie on the ground in the sunshine if they so wish.

In the ensuing weeks the country begins to notice the effort being made in royal quarters: "a source of infinite pleasure to the recruits."[151] His Majesty's interest is quite obviously genuine. He is touted as the travelling King. Aside from the military encampments in West Surrey and Hampshire, His Majesty visits Sittingbourne, Chatham, Epsom, Leatherhead and Ashtead, Bedford, Canterbury, Winchester and Woolwich to name but a few destinations. The mileage ebbs with the downturn in fortunes at the front, but by mid-November The King begins to return to familiar units. "They have come on wonderfully well in their training since I saw them six weeks ago."[152]

"Pilgrimage of Pity"

Where there is war, there is suffering. At the end of August the wounded begin to return to hospitals at home, and His Majesty throws himself into visiting them wholeheartedly. On 31st August the King Edward VII hospital in Grosvenor Gardens receives 30 officer patients, and Their Majesties arrive the next day. The wounds are slight, mostly from shrapnel and the men are cheerful at

147   RA GV/PRIV/GVD/1914 (26/9).
148   *The Times* 28/9/14.
149   *Daily News* 28/9/14.
150   *Morning Advertiser* 26/9/14.
151   *Daily Call* 9/10/14.
152   RA GV/PRIV/GVD/1914 (12/11).

being home again. The ladies of this, London's most affluent area, are following the Queen's lead in plunging themselves into war work, and many quickly establish "hospitals" under their own roofs; setting rooms aside for convalescent men and caring for them. The King and Queen begin making short forays from the palace nearby and stopping by each day after lunch, arriving quietly and unattended and scorning all formality and etiquette so as not to inconvenience patients or staff. The King's aunts immediately give over part of their own houses. Beatrice has three officers at Hill Street, in a borrowed house, and Louise has two more under her care at Kensington Palace. The houses, the Queen observes, are all very well arranged, and in many instances, where space was available civilian cases are being moved into grand house establishments to make valuable space in London's hospitals for the more seriously wounded arriving from France.

The rank and file begin to arrive at the capital's hospitals too. The King and Queen put as much effort into visiting the men as they do the officer class. In the first week they see more than a thousand at ten different institutions; again turning up without ceremony so as not to disturb the routine. The only indication that anyone is expected at the London Hospital comes with the hoisting of the Union Jack and the Red Cross flag. As soon as His Majesty enters the first ward the men attempt to stand to attention. "The King indicated that he did not wish them to try, but they made the effort all the same."[153] Some convalescents who are well enough have insisted on 'doing something to help.' When Their Majesties appear in the doorway, they are armed with brooms and sweeping the floors. One soldier, "in a tone indicative of his astonishment exclaimed, "The King!"" The men instantly draw up in close formation, each of them presenting a broom instead of a rifle. So spontaneous is the comical salute, so serious the faces of the men, that after a brief silence everyone in the room collapses into fits of laughter, Their Majesties included.[154] They stop at every bedside in ten wards to converse with each patient and share a word of sympathy. They read the cards with their names and their nature of their injuries. The army is not yet the gargantuan machine that it becomes later in the war, but a familiar institution, especially for one as well acquainted with it as the King. His knowledge of their units and their officers stuns the men. One soldier is sitting up in a kilt. "Hello," says His Majesty. "Seaforth; or are you a Cameron?" Then he answers his own question. "Ah I see now you are a Cameron; the plaids are similar." The patient is delighted.[155] The men are so quickly placed at their ease that they begin chattering excitedly with their King and Queen about their experiences at the front and the injuries that have brought them home. One man has had a bullet pass through his nose and out through his throat, resulting in no more damage than a lost tooth. Another walked sixty miles on the retreat barefoot. his feet were so swollen that he could not get his boots on. From underneath their pillows soldiers proudly produce morbid, precious relics; bullets and shrapnel that have been extracted from their bodies. They tell the King that they intend to have them mounted in scarf pins and brooches for their wives and mothers, and he is fascinated by X-Ray images that show the bullets in situ before their extraction. Outside word has spread through East London that Their Majesties are present, and traffic has been stopped. When they leave, they are cheered by a raucous crowd of thousands who have flocked to the hospital gates.

A week later the King and Queen are south of the river at St. Thomas's to see almost 150 more men from the front in wards lent to the War Office. They arrive just as lunch is being served, and the King orders that the midday meal should be neither interrupted nor delayed on his account. There is already a system in place to ensure that every patient is accounted for by Their Majesties. They move down opposite sides of the wards, before swapping at the far end of the room and returning along the opposite row of beds. The King asks incessant questions. He wants to know about the

---

153   *The Times* 4/9/14.
154   *Daily Telegraph* 4/9/14.
155   Ibid.

nature of the fighting, did their boots stand up to the long marching? How was their equipment? He is particularly concerned about the Royal Scots and the protection that their headgear provides in the hot summer months. The men don't like to complain. They tactfully reply that it would have been nice on the retreat if "something had kept more sun off."[156] When His Majesty stops at one bedside where a man tells his Sovereign about his unfortunate wound. He was lying down on a grassy slope, "well removed, as he thought, from the passing convoys." Then someone drove a cart over his foot as he reclined and crushed it, "Oh! Hard Luck!" Exclaims the King.[157] Men speak with pride of the day that His Majesty came and sat at their bedside; "how he had used their slang to them, and how his quiet remarks showed that he knew the British sailor and soldier."[158] Journalists stare open mouthed as the men fire back questions at the King and he obliges them. They ask him for news of their officers, and quite often he able to furnish them with details. One giant Guardsman is left speechless when His Majesty recites the names of his officers back to him. "He seemed to carry the blinking army list in his 'ead!"[159]

After what may be considered a gentle introduction, the King and Queen are soon exposed to the very worst that war can inflict on the human body; victims of the *Amphion,* which has been blown up by a mine and from the *Hogue, Aboukir* and *Cressy,* all sunk on one morning by a German submarine. At the beginning of October it is revealed that Their Majesties will visit naval hospitals on the Kent coast and meet the wounded from these incidents. The newspapers plead for privacy. "There are to be no guards of honour, no receptions and no formalities."[160] But where royalty is concerned, the requests fall on deaf ears. Crowds line the streets and string bunting from their houses. The hospital at Chatham is filled with dozens of men from the four ships recovering there, some of them suffering from hideous burns.

As the weeks go by casualties at the front mount. As of mid-September more organised forays are made to hospitals further afield. At Netley, the King's arrival is delayed because a hospital train is in front of his, but His Majesty insists that under no circumstances are they to interfere with the work of unloading patients, or hurry on his account. The wounded, friend and foe, come first. The King sees almost 500 men individually inside, including some 70 Germans, half of whom were seriously wounded. He speaks to them as much as he can in their own language, and they seem pleased to be in England, because it is better than being at the front. The prisoners are deeply touched by the sympathy of this enemy King, as he asks if they are comfortable, if they have everything they need. Their Majesties find both the volume of these visits, which are dubbed a "pilgrimage of pity"[161] by the press, strenuous and emotionally disturbing, as they are forced sometimes daily to look upon the cost of war. "You can't conceive what I suffered going round those hospitals in the war,"[162] the King says years later. But they are determined to sit side by side with the crippled and the maimed, the shell-shocked and the diseased. If Queen Mary suspects that they are being introduced to more palatable cases, she marches off on her own to find the most cruelly afflicted. The men have not been spared the worst of it, and neither shall they be. Autograph hunters are obliged, His Majesty fusses over whether the patients have enough jam for tea, at Isleworth the Queen even asks a man to unbutton his shirt so that she might see the spot from which a bullet was extracted. The King has an eye for an interesting patient. In one hospital he sees a boy who cannot be more than sixteen lying wounded in bed.

156   *Daily Telegraph* 8/9/14.
157   *Daily News* 26/9/14.
158   (ed.) Hammerton & Wilson: *The Great War Vol. V,* pp.10-15.
159   *The Telegraph* 8/9/14.
160   *Daily Mirror* 3/10/14.
161   *The Daily Mail* 11/1/15.
162   Pope-Hennessy: Queen Mary, p.498.

"Well, my lad," he says, "how old are you?" He claims to be nineteen. "Yes, I know that is your military age," says His Majesty with a smile, "but what is your real age?"[163] He finds a man a year his senior in a hospital and says: "Bravo! You beat me by just a few months!"[164] At one establishment he notices a white-haired soldier sitting on his bed. "You are a reservist are you not?" He asks. "No, Sir," the man replies. "I enlisted again for the war; I wanted to have a whack at the Germans." The King glances at his arm, swathed in bandages. "It seems to me that these Germans have had a whack at you. How old are you?" The man glances quickly at the card above his bed to check. "I'm forty-five, your Majesty." There is a twinkle in both men's eyes. 'And how old are you, really?" Asks the King. 'I'm sixty-two, sir," the patient admits.[165]

But sometimes it isn't laughter that the men need. His Majesty visits a Colonel severely wounded and unable to get out of bed. The man is in obvious pain, and the King leans over him and gently provides a few words of appreciation as to his heroism and self-sacrifice. The man is lost for words to express his gratitude. At one particular hospital, an ordinary soldier on the danger list begs to see the Queen in particular. She arrives at his bedside, but he is unable to speak. She sits by his bedside and comforts him for a time. "The Royal Touch"[166] is defined by genuine interest, warmth and a meticulous determination to see as many wounded men as possible and hear from their own lips their tales of war and of woe; share their laughter and their pain. One journalist asks a ward full of soldiers what they have made of their Sovereign's visit. The King, they reply, has made them feel as if they are his old friends. "He's real human, that's what he is," says a spokesman.[167]

"One Did Think That One Had Seen the Last of Him"

On the Western Front, changes are afoot. On the one hand, British troops are besieged, embroiled in a doomed fight to save Antwerp. However, the main bulk of the Expeditionary Force is about to leave the banks of the Aisne. Kitchener informs the King that his troops will soon be concentrated on the left flank of the French, much further north closer to the Channel and supply lines from home, but it is His Majesty's own service that is causing him more anxiety in October. Prince Louis of Battenburg is the brother in law of the King's youngest aunt, Princess Beatrice. Thus both an uncle and a cousin to His Majesty in the complicated network of European royal houses; he is in fact only a decade or so older than the Sovereign. Austrian by birth, the Prince had become a naturalised British subject at the age of fourteen and joined the Royal Navy before marrying a granddaughter of Queen Victoria. He has dedicated half a century to his career, and by the onset of the war is the First Sea Lord, the officer at the head of the Royal Navy alongside the service's civilian chief and Cabinet representative, the First Lord of the Admiralty, Winston Churchill. Prince Louis is hard-working and diligent, which makes up for a certain lack of creativity, and the mobilisation of the Royal Navy and her part in transporting troops to France has been carried out admirably; but this matters little to a large public contingent that seize upon the Prince's name, his accent and his heritage and bludgeon him with all three. *John Bull* christens him "the Germhun."[168] For a populace terrified of spies at every turn, the threat of invasion and the enemy within, he is a miscast symbol of Teutonism amidst a storm of hysteria. The King declares himself "much worried"[169]

163   (ed.) Hammerton & Wilson: *The Great War Vol V,* pp.10-15.
164   *The Graphic* 29/3/16.
165   (ed.) Hammerton & Wilson: *The Great War Vol V,* pp.10-15.
166   *Daily Mirror* 10/10/14.
167   Ibid.
168   John Bull 3/10/14.
169   RA GV/PRIV/GVD/1914 (28/10).

about the situation at the Admiralty. "He is of noble character," fumes Queen Alexandra, "and has sacrificed himself to the country he has served so well and [which] has now treated him so abominably.'[170] The pressures of his post in wartime, combined with anonymous, abusive, even threatening correspondence and a public outpouring of hatred in his direction take its toll. His son, a naval cadet at Osborne, even has to endure rumours that the Prince has been frogmarched to the Tower of London, charged with being a German spy and that he is imprisoned there, guarded by Beefeaters.

Finally, Prince Louis can take no more. "Our poor blue-eyed German will have to go," Asquith tells his mistress[171] With a dignified letter to Churchill, the First Sea Lord steps down, "driven to the painful conclusion that at this juncture my birth and parentage have the effect of impairing in some respects my usefulness on the Board of Admiralty."[172] The King is mortified for him, appalled by the treatment that he has received. "I feel deeply for him," he writes; "there is no more loyal man in the country."[173] He has not retired, and His Majesty hopes that perhaps he can serve again when the war is over. He is determined to show his support, and as empty a gesture as it must feel to all involved, he tells everyone that will listen that he is making the Prince a Privy Councillor, so that all may observe the trust that he places in his relative. But the King agrees with Prince Louis, that matters had effected him and his work to such an extent that his only option had been to withdraw from the Admiralty.

Worse still for His Majesty than Prince Louis's resignation is his proposed replacement. Admiral Sir John Fisher is one of the foremost reformers in the history of the Royal Navy, having "enjoyed remarkable success in covering with charm an unusual mixture of eccentricity, insolence and solid administrative drive"[174] throughout a long and industrious career that came to a close with his retirement in 1911. He had been a great favourite of both Queen Victoria and Edward VII, not to mention Queen Alexandra, whom he would seize by the waist and swing about the dance floor, but he enjoys no such lofty patronage by 1914. The King has known Jacky Fisher since he was but a lowly Midshipman in 1882, with no thoughts of the throne. Their relations had once been cordial, with exchanges of private correspondence, but as Fisher rose to the rank of First Sea Lord initially, the future Sovereign no longer trusted him. He also disagreed with Fisher's reduction of British force in the Mediterranean and was not discreet enough in his opinions. A violent conflict amongst Admirals sealed the tone of their relationship. His Majesty had supported Lord Charles Beresford, a sworn enemy of Fisher, and he had supported him loudly, publicly, unwisely given his position by then as Prince of Wales. He had told people that Fisher would be the ruin of the Navy and lost all respect for the Admiral when he found out that he had employed underhand methods to keep watch on his rival. For his part, Fisher, who misses the favour he once courted in royal circles, is scathing of the King and calls those in the His Majesty's favour 'the Royal Pimps."[175]

His Majesty finds out about a proposed move to reinstate Fisher at the head of the navy when Churchill visits the palace on 27th October. The King does not dislike Churchill, but he is wary of him, and with good reason; for he is a wily politician. Dominating personalities, men who wage Machiavellian war with an abundance of words make him uneasy. "Almost more of a cad in office than he was in opposition,"[176] his father had once said, and this opinion of Churchill has

170   Battiscombe: *Queen Alexandra,* p.284.
171   Rose: *King George V,* pp.170-172.
172   Ibid.
173   Ibid.
174   Jenkins: *Churchill,* p.257.
175   Rose: *King George V,* p.159.
176   Ibid., p.110.

stuck with His Majesty. He can see both his minister's faults and his virtues; and both agreed and disagreed with elements of his policy after he took charge of the Admiralty in 1911. The fallout was limited, though. Churchill accused the King of "talking stupidly," and labelled the Sovereign's opinions on one occasion as "cheap and silly drivel.'[177] For his part, His Majesty had been annoyed with the First Lord too. Churchill didn't do himself any favours in repeatedly pressing the King to name a ship HMS *Oliver Cromwell*, after a regicide. He got no joy either in attempting to call one HMS *Pitt*. 'His Majesty," wrote Stamfordham, "is inclined to think that the name… is neither euphonious or dignified… There is moreover always the danger of the men giving the ship nicknames of ill-conditioned words rhyming with it."[178]

When Churchill brings up Fisher's name as a prospect for Prince Louis's replacement, His Majesty is mortified. He cannot block his appointment, but he can certainly try and induce his Prime Minister not to make what he sees as a horrific error. Churchill maintained even in hindsight that Fisher was "the most distinguished British Naval officer since Nelson," but acknowledged that at 74 he was "a weather beaten sea-dog."[179] The King protests the appointment vehemently. Surely Fisher is too old, he says; and the navy has no confidence in him. Yes, of course in his first spell in the post he did much for the Royal Navy, but his feats were only achieved whilst alienating officers and creating a feeling of great unrest. This, the country does not need in wartime. Churchill asks who else is suitable, and shoots down each of His Majesty's suggestions. The decision ultimately rests with Churchill, for he will have to answer for it in Parliament, but though his agreement should be a constitutional formality, the King tells his minister that he cannot consent to Fisher's appointment until he has spoken to Asquith. The following day, Stamfordham is despatched to see the Prime Minister, who supports Churchill's choice. His Majesty, he tells Asquith, is appealing to him not to make the appointment for all of the reasons he had already urged. The Prime Minister says that there is nobody else suitable for the post. The Board at the Admiralty, he claims, is weak, shows no initiative, and the navy had failed to live up to the country's expectations thus far in the war. The Prime Minister thinks that the country will welcome the return of Lord Fisher, and that the King's suggestions are "nonsense."[180]

His Majesty remains fully determined to employ his right to council, and in this case warn his Government against what he is convinced is a grave mistake. He feels that if he does not, he would not be doing his duty. He argues his case again, this time to Asquith's face. "He gave me an exhaustive and really eloquent catalogue of the old man's crimes and defects," the Prime Minister wrote that evening, "and thought that his appointment would be very badly received by the bulk of the navy and that he would be almost certain to get on badly with Winston." Asquith didn't necessarily disagree with the King's last point. Two such overwhelming personalities were bound to rile each other. "I have some misgivings of my own, but Winston won't have anybody else, and there is no one among the available admirals in whom I have sufficient confidence to force him upon him."[181] The conversation is cordial, but Asquith holds firm and His Majesty is forced to concede that he has done all he can. Fisher has been preparing to spend the winter abroad, claiming that it was pointless to remain in the country when the King has it in for him and the Prime Minister kow-tows to him. Now, he is suddenly called out of retirement.

177   Ibid., p.160.
178   Ibid., p.161.
179   Churchill: *The World Crisis 1911-1918*, p.220.
180   Rose: *King George V*, pp.186-187.
181   (ed.) Brock: *H.H. Asquith: Letters to Venetia Stanley*, pp.295-296.

His Sovereign signs the appointment, noting: "I did all I could to prevent it." The document is accompanied by a letter expressing once again his anxious misgivings about Fisher's return. "I readily acknowledge his great ability and administrative power," he tells Asquith, "but at the same time I cannot help feeling that his presence at the admiralty will not inspire the Navy with that confidence which it ought to… especially when we are engaged in so momentous a war, I hope that my fears prove to be groundless."[182] Though a bitter pill to swallow, some of Fisher's most fierce critics accept the appointment without too much fuss, because if he was riddled with faults, he could at least be relied upon to keep Churchill, whose position has been weakened in the opening weeks of war after successive failures, in check. The King's friend, Admiral Sir David Beatty, searches for the positives. "As far as the Navy is concerned, we want a Kitchener at the head. We are only playing at war. We are all as nervous as cats, afraid of losing lives, losing ships, and running risks. We are ruled by panic law, and until we risk something shall never gain anything."[183] But Churchill too covets absolute power, and His Majesty isn't the only one thinking that the Navy will totter precariously under their joint influence. "[They] cannot work together; they cannot both run the show."[184]

Fisher is no victim. It is probably Churchill that tells him of the King's opposition to his appointment and he combats His Majesty's "unconquerable aversion" to him "salvo for salvo." He blames the Sovereign for a myriad supposed indiscretions, including, ludicrously, the loss of ships off the coast of Chile at the Battle of Coronel in the opening weeks of the war. Visiting the palace fills him with as much disgust as the King suffers on receiving him. "I spent a maudlin hour yesterday," Fisher tells Churchill a few weeks after his appointment. "I won't go anymore, *I'll be sick*."[185] For His Majesty's part, had he carried out this threat, the King would be entirely satisfied never to have to deal with the Admiral again.

"Sickening Anxiety"

At the outbreak of the war His Majesty's relatives occupy thrones across Europe and throughout a vast, extended Royal Family, loyalties are divided. Queen Victoria and Prince Albert had courted unions for their children with German spouses and six of their offspring had been wedded thus. Across the continent, their descendants now find themselves on opposite sides of the divide or resident in neutral countries. Princess Beatrice, the King's youngest aunt, married a Battenburg but her three sons were serving in the British Army. On the other hand, His Majesty's cousin Charlie had succeeded as Duke of Saxe-Coburg and Gotha and is disliked both in his native England and in Germany because of his split connections. As an officer in the Kaiser's army, he is stranded when war begins, though Wilhelm excuses him from physically taking up arms against his country. The King's aunt Helena had lost one of her sons during the Boer War. The other had been sent to manage the family estates in Silesia and had joined the Wilhelm's army. "Our only boy is with the German army on the wrong side!!" His mother writes in despair. "Oh, the sickening anxiety, for so many dear ones out on the front, on <u>both sides</u>."[186] Sometimes it is difficult for His Majesty to separate these familial connections from the conflict that his country is now embroiled in. "Even Asquith looked askance when the King explained to him that his cousin… was 'not really fighting on the side of the Germans,' but had only been put in charge of a camp of English prisoners near

182   Rose: *King George V,* pp.186-187.
183   Chalmers: *The Life & Letters of David Beatty, Admiral of the Fleet,* pp.160-161.
184   (ed.) Brock: *H.H. Asquith: Letters to Venetia Stanley,* p.294.
185   Rose: *King George V,* pp.186-187.
186   Wake: *Princess Louise,* p.396.

Berlin. "A nice distinction," the Prime Minister quips to his mistress.[187] Queen Mary's brothers were all on active service during the Boer War too. Their letters had been read to the King's children, their exploits shown to them using pictorial magazines. Now they too have gone to France. 'Dolly' arrives at Princess Beatrice's hospital on Hill Street, ignominiously struck down with gastritis after one day of fighting and terribly disappointed at having had to return home; whilst 'Alge' is wounded by a shell in mid-October.

Of Beatrice's three sons, two are wounded early, but by far the heaviest blow of the opening weeks of war so far as the Royal Family is concerned comes on 28th October 1914.

The town of Ypres, dominated by a cathedral and a medieval cloth hall, is no strategic prize. Its misfortune is to lie in the path of the German advance to the Channel, and beyond that, England. The Kaiser's men begin their endeavours to turn the BEF out of it on 20th October, and a bloody battle commences, in which British and German artillerymen alike take on an unheralded role as they pour shells into each other's lines. It is a baptism of fire for the infantry too, and Prince Maurice, Princess Beatrice's youngest, favourite son, is in the thick of it.

He had come near to the fighting at Mons. His feet had stood up to the long hours of march on the retreat, before his first fight came on 10th September.

> We were going advanced guard when we suddenly came upon a retiring German column, which we immediately attacked… after 2.5 hours fighting they surrendered… I had a very lucky escape, as I had a bullet through my cap and you know how small they are. How on earth it did not touch me I cannot think, of the two men who were lying on either side of me one was killed outright and the other seriously wounded.[188]

Then Maurice witnessed the onset of trench warfare and artillery duels on the Aisne. "A shell from one of the big German guns pitched right on the roof of the barn, where all my company was lying resting. The havoc it created was terrible." By chance, Maurice was across the road, but fifteen of his men were killed and 40 injured. "Never have I seen such a ghastly sight as the inside of that shed. Some of the wretched men were literally blown to pieces. It is hateful to lose men in that way."[189] Trenches were dug, "so deep, that one lies underground like a rabbit."[190] Then came the BEF's move north, when Maurice had responded to a letter from his cousin, the King. "It will be a great relief to get away, as we are all heartily sick of sitting here in trenches… There has been very little actual fighting, but we are continually under shellfire. This does really very little harm, but gets terribly on one's nerves after a bit."[191] Three days later he was on his way to do battle at Ypres, ensconced in a cattle truck with his fellow officers, making themselves as comfortable as possible by piling straw on the floor.

On 27th October, Maurice's battalion is ordered to advance east of Ypres, keeping touch with the French on their left. Their path led them across farmland, "the only cover being a few scattered farms and houses running along the top of the ridge on each side of the road." The terrain is covered with shallow trenches, hastily dug by both German and French troops as the latter had tried to advance. "While we were there the ridge," wrote Maurice's battalion adjutant, "was getting terrific shelling and one [shell] came right into our trench… During the eastward advance from

187   Rose: *King George V*, pp.173-4.
188   RA PS/PSO/GV/C/Q/832/32.
189   RA PS/PSO/GV/C/Q/832/33.
190   RA PS/PSO/GV/C/Q/832/37.
191   RA PS/PSO/GV/C/Q/832/39.

the ridge, the battalion came under a terrific shell fire as well as rifle fire and… lost very heavily." In all, Prince Maurice's battalion suffers nearly 200 casualties and on 28th October His Majesty receives word from Alge that Maurice is dead. His brother in law is desperately trying to find more information, but the addition of this sudden personal shock, the loss of this charming, likeable boy, this promising soldier compounds all the existing anxiety the King feels in his lonely, exalted position. At noon Their Majesties leave for Kensington Palace and find there both of Maurice's wounded brothers, Leopold and Drino, with Princess Beatrice. "She was very brave, but feels it terribly, poor thing,"[192] writes the King.

It transpires that Maurice was killed outright on the ridge from which his battalion advanced. The Royal Family exchange sorrowful letters about their loss. "Poor sweet Beatrice!"[193] His Majesty's uncle, Arthur, Duke of Connaught writes. "My heart bleeds for poor Beatrice, what a terrible blow for her, he ever was her favourite son."[194] On 5th November the family gather for a memorial service. The Princess is beside herself, desperately trying to remain stoic. 'It is one of those losses one can never get over," she told one correspondent,

> and it is so terribly hard to sit quietly and resignedly realising that one's dear child, who was like a ray of sunshine in the house, will never be amongst us again in this world. In the midst of all I have much to be thankful for, in that he died a noble soldier's death and without, as I am assured, suffering, and I have two dear sons still spared to me, when so many poor mothers have lost their one and only one.[195]

Prince Maurice has been killed as the fighting at Ypres is still escalating, but his body is barely in the ground when the entire war hangs in the balance for the Allies. Bit by bit Sir John French's men are being pushed back, exhausted; their formations hugely depleted and lacking in reinforcements to press up and fill the line. The fate of His Majesty's realm sways precariously as the battered BEF resist the German onslaught at Gheluvelt, to the east of Ypres. The tiny hamlet falls on 31st October, and for a moment the path for the Kaiser's men lies open to the Channel and beyond that, England. Then troops rally and seize it back. The King is informed that Wilhelm is lurking at Courtrai, waiting to make a triumphant entry into Ypres, but on 4th November the Prime Minister delivers the best news for some time to the palace. The German attack is waning, and for now Calais, and England, appear to be safe from the Kaiser's clutches. The battle winds down with the full onset of winter and leaves a jagged line of trenches stretching from the North Sea all the way to the Swiss border.

For the King, bad news continues to arrive. Charlie Fitzmaurice; "for many years an equerry and personal friend,"[196] was killed two days after Prince Maurice. His Majesty is mortified at his loss. "I shall miss him greatly. I felt very depressed,"[197] he laments. "I know how well you deplore it," writes Queen Alexandra to her son, "as I know how much you liked [him] and he will be such a loss to you."[198] The King and Queen visit his widow and his family. "They were very brave but they feel his death terribly."[199] By the end of November he is also mourning Willy Cadogan, a long-time friend and equerry to the Prince of Wales. Having died as a result of a gunshot wound to the groin, he

192   RA GV/PRIV/GVD/1914 (28/10).
193   RA GV/PRIV/AA42/1.
194   RA VIC/ADDL/MSS/A/17/1212.
195   RA VIC/ADDA/A25/877.
196   Gore: *King George V, A Personal Memoir*, p.294.
197   RA GV/PRIV/GVD/1914 (31/10).
198   RA GV/PRIV/AA34/41.
199   RA GV/PRIV/GVD/1914 (8/11).

is laid to rest in the same cemetery as Prince Maurice. "Such a loss to us," grieves the Queen, "too sad."[200] His Majesty despairs. "All the best officers and our friends are going in this horrible war."[201]

"I Am Doing What I Consider Is My Duty"

The one thing that cheers David up as his role develops early on in France and fails to meet his expectations, is the sudden news that his father is about to pay a visit to GHQ. It will bear no resemblance at all to the time that Wilhelm has thus far spent on the German front; where he had established himself with a huge train of Ministers and hangers-on in anticipation of a victorious entry into Paris.

At this point the King's outlook is bleak. He is in a pessimistic frame of mind after the conclusion of the fighting at Ypres. His Majesty has decided that he must view the situation for himself; not from an interactive strategical or tactical perspective, and not just to ensconce himself at GHQ with senior generals, but because he thinks it will be a good use of his time to go and see for himself the shattered units of the BEF; some of whom have been through hell at Ypres and are facing a miserable winter. They might feel buoyed by the sight of their Sovereign actively checking on their wellbeing and congratulating them on all they have achieved in stemming the German tide.

No British sovereign has led his soldiers in the field since George II fought at Dettingen in 1743, and so Clive Wigram approaches Billy Lambton. "His Majesty's idea, as far as I know, is to go over and visit the different army corps and divisional headquarters and see as many of the troops as he can, but he does not wish to interfere in any way with the work of Sir John French and the General Headquarters staff." In no way does King George want to resemble his bombastic cousin. "The King would probably only come over with two or three of his household and not in any way ape the German Emperor with a full military staff and large escort."[202]

First there are obvious questions to consider. Where will the King sleep, will he need to provide his own transport in the shape of horses and motors, where and what will he eat? At headquarters, Lambton begins to plot a possible itinerary that will provide a glimpse of the King for as many men as possible, whilst keeping His Majesty out of harm's way. By the middle of November the situation has calmed enough, and Lambton informs the palace that now is as good a time as any, and that GHQ will only require a few hours' notice. The visit is viewed as a purely military one, so while the King will happily receive General Joffre, the French commander, if he cares to see him, he does not want to waste time organising functions with the President. The King and his representatives will spend nearly five years avoiding unnecessary, official contact with French politicians whilst walking on their soil, simply because time spent with them is time not spent with British troops, which is the express purpose of his visits. This feat of diplomacy falls to the Foreign Office, who are left to advise when to inform Britain's allies that the trip is to take place. The King of the Belgians, ensconced on Belgium's Channel coast and refusing to leave his country, is viewed as an entirely different matter, and the King is determined to see him.

His Majesty is asked to state if there if are any particular things he wishes to see. Lambton is also on the lookout for any key medal recipients that might cross the Sovereign's path, and any French officers who had been cooperating closely with British troops that might warrant royal recognition. Lambton thinks that the visit is going to be hugely beneficial.

---

200   Ibid.
201   Ibis (13/11).
202   RA PS/PSO/GV/PS/WAR/QQ7/4745.

I am sure that a sight of the King and a few words from him will do a world of good, and will delight the troops… A lot of nearly 50 officers who have been recommended for the DSO has been sent home to the War Office. They are all good cases, if the King will sanction these and present them the effect would be good.[203]

Official correspondence needs to be maintained when His Majesty is away. Messengers are arranged to collect special bags from both the War Office and the Privy Purse Door at the palace. One was to leave in the morning and one at lunchtime, mirrored by two more making the four and a half hour journey between GHQ at St Omer and Victoria Station in the opposite direction. A team of Metropolitan Police officers has to be arranged too. Whilst the army will take care of safety in a military sense, these plain-clothes men will be in attendance throughout the trip as personal security, led by Superintendent Patrick Quinn of New Scotland Yard; a cheerful man who isn't one to grumble when forced to improvise and who will make the lot of both the King and his retinue much easier on the road. One of the last headaches fell on Stamfordham with regard to secrecy. He recommends to Asquith that the Press Censor is prevented from publishing the landing place of His Majesty, as it could tip off the enemy as to his method of return. The Court Circular, which reports the Kings movements in the press is not to refer to the journey. With tongue firmly in cheek, Stamfordham declares that if the British people, who are shaken enough, cannot trust the veracity of the Court Circular, they will have nothing left to believe in. It is kept deliberately vague, "like George Washington: it could not tell a lie!"[204] In the end it simply declined to mention the King at all from November 30th to 5th December. It was known that His Majesty intended to go abroad, but his arrival at the front does not become public knowledge until he reaches St. Omer. Then there is the packing. "It is awfully muddy, you want big boots, almost waders at times, or else galoshes to put over your boots."[205] A well protected box is included in the baggage that contains fifteen Victoria Crosses, thirteen engraved for the recipients and two spare for anyone else His Majesty may come across on his travels. The box also contains 100 Distinguished Service Orders, engraved Distinguished Conduct Medals and a vast array of brooches and ribbons that can be cut and sewn as required.

On 29th November, the day of the King's departure, a last minute telegram is sent to the British Ambassador in Paris so that he might inform the French, casually bringing the visit to the attention of the President and his ministers. "The time of the King will be entirely occupied with visits to the various units of his troops and the hospitals etc." Lord Bertie is informed. "He hopes he may see General Joffre; but it is his particular desire that neither the President nor any member of Government should give themselves the trouble to meet him as his time is short and every minute will be occupied. I have no doubt you will be able to explain this."[206] All that is left for the King is to placate his mother. Queen Alexandra does not approve of the risk at all. "My ever darling Georgie! If you are really going off… I must see you!"[207] Queen Mary was just as pained to see him depart, but because she cannot go with him. "For all these years I have, thank God been able to accompany you on all important journeys during our married life, so I feel it rather having to stay at home." She does, however, completely support his decision to go. "It will be such a help and encouragement to officers and men in their arduous work."[208] "I felt very low at leaving you yesterday," the King says

---

203   Ibid.
204   Ibid.
205   Ibid.
206   Ibid.
207   RA GV/PRIV/AA34/42.
208   Pope-Hennessy: *Queen Mary, 1867-1953*, p.496.

to her on arrival in France, "especially so under the depressing influences of this awful wicked war. You have always accompanied me on my voyages and expeditions, ever since we were married but this is one that of course it was impossible for you to do so."[209]

David is waiting for his father at Dieppe, and as the King, Stamfordham and Wigram disembark from the *Brighton* they all look wretched and seasick after a terrible, rough crossing; a heavy gale whipping up the sea and tossing the little boat back and forth. "It is like a bad nightmare to think of it now," the King writes to Queen Mary.

> It was blowing a whole gale with a heavy sea and we knocked about like anything, the worst passage possible… I was deadly ill the whole time. I remained on deck as long as possible, until I was drenched by the sea. We only reached Dieppe at 8:45… went to bed as early as possible but slept badly, as there was no bed. I slept on a sofa, sirens made an awful noise all night.[210]

It is still windy the following morning, as the group rises early and leaves for Boulogne with the rain coming down in sheets. The King's visit is in no way to be elitist. He has no interest in pouring over maps and sipping tea with the army's hierarchy, he wants to devote more time to junior officers and the ordinary rank and file. His Majesty begins his tour at a casino that has been converted into a hospital. Some of the patients are laid up with frostbite after spells in the burgeoning trench system further forward, but what is more noticeable to their Sovereign is that at home, he has met the more stable cases, those who were well enough to be safely transported across the Channel. Here, as he visits the 500 wounded men at the casino, he sees harrowing injuries; visits the lost causes "which can't recover, alas;"[211] men shot through the head and waiting to expire, spinal injuries. After a quick lunch at the Hotel de Folkestone, the King is conducted through two more base hospitals; including one for Indians housed in a Jesuit College; where His Majesty finds 400 patients. The weather has not improved; and as the King's car makes the 30 mile journey along broken roads to St Omer it is jostled by fierce wind and soaked with rain. The royal party is received by Sir John French, the whole of his staff, Indian princes and a guard of honour of the Royal Irish Regiment before finally His Majesty can settle into a house directly opposite the Commander in Chief's.

The contrast during and after dinner between the optimists at the front and those that have come out from England is marked, and highlighted by the observations of the King and of his eldest son. "Had a talk with French,"[212] His Majesty records in his diary. "He is optimistic as they all are out here." The Prince of Wales notes that, "it was curious to notice how pessimistic people are at home with serious thought of German invasion and the view that the war will be a very long one. Here we are optimistic!!"[213] The Prince is young, and is quick to assume passionately the opinions of those more experienced officers he meets. After less than a fortnight at the front he knows that Sir John French is strained, paranoid about his position. He also knows that the King is not the Commander in Chief's staunchest supporter. David watches shrewdly a frosty conversation between his father and the Field Marshal; "on the subject of some appointment or other: no doubt he was very worried!!"[214]

209   RA QM/PRIV/CC04/121.
210   Ibid.
211   RA GV/PRIV/GVD/1914 (30/11).
212   Ibid.
213   RA EDW/PRIV/DIARY/1914 (30/11).
214   Ibid.

The first three days of the King's tour are devoted entirely to achieving the feat of visiting representative troops of every division at the front, with an attention to detail and a level of interest that presents itself to those who meet him as "almost insatiable."[215] "After various flaps,"[216] His Majesty gets away at 9:00am on 1st December, the convoy led by the Prince of Wales driving his own car. The King is thrilled to be spending time with his eldest son. "David is with me all day. I am glad to say he is very popular with everyone and is tremendously keen to do anything he can,"[217] His Majesty proudly writes to the Queen. In wind and heavy rain, a ceaseless procession continues. The King presents medals, acknowledges guards of honour drawn up for his arrival. Everywhere he goes men are collected at junctions, in fields, in the middle of villages and at railway stations. He visits artillerymen in orchards with their guns; successfully hidden from their enemy counterparts and almost impervious to their shellfire. At Estaires, a village full of bullet ridden, half-destroyed houses, men are lined up at the side of the road, loud and enthusiastic as the car bearing a little tin Royal Standard bumps by. Sometimes the enemy troops ensconced on the other side of the lines can hear the commotion. The King's soldiers wear all manner of strange, innovative garb to keep out the cold: fur jackets and coats courtesy of every dead animal from foxes to badgers; and thick socks stuffed with straw. The guns boom in the background; an aeroplane winds and twists lazily above; easily dodging German anti-aircraft shells. He drives on, past guns being dragged along the road. "You must have been thrilled," writes Queen Mary, "and have felt so proud of being their King! I know I should be."[218]

In one sodden neighbourhood, word has spread that His Majesty is at the front. An anonymous officer in the Royal Engineers had been ordered off, with six of his men in tow, on an important mission: to construct a bridge over a field that has become a veritable swamp to conduct his Sovereign to a point where he will present several medals. Punctually at 1:30 the sounds of cheering approaches like a breaking wave. The royal party rumbles across his bridge and then gets out of their cars, the King and his heir included. If he thought that his bridge had been ordered to protect His Majesty's shoes, the officer is wrong; for the King promptly ignores the vile conditions and begins to wade a complete circuit of the field through mud and slush to see all of the assembled men face to face. "It was really a most impressive sight, one of those showery days, with spells of beautiful weather and blue sky, all round the field warriors with fixed bayonets and drawn swords. in the centre, the King and his suite." Highlighted against the temporarily bright winter sky, there are two British aeroplanes, "purring away," ready to fend off any enemy counterparts. It occurs to the officers and he watches proceedings atop his horse, that it would be some bag for the German guns if they had known where to point them at that precise moment. The men come up and His Majesty pins medals on each and says a few words to each a smile. "They did look proud as they went away." Then the officer watches as the King traverses his bridge again and went on with his tour. "Meanwhile I had galloped back to my billet some two miles away, and was in time to see the King pass on his way back… He is most thoughtful, even took the trouble to acknowledge my humble salute. I had a better view of royalty that day than I am ever likely to get again."[219]

There is little high ground from which to observe the battlefield generally. His Majesty walks to the top of a rare hill in the vicinity of the British lines.

215   (ed.) Hammerton & Wilson: *The Great War Vol. IV*, pp.211-214.
216   RA EDW/PRIV/DIARY/1914 (1/12).
217   RA QM/PRIV/CC4/129.
218   RA QM/PRIV/CC8/175.
219   *Madras Times* 7/1/15.

Luckily it was so bright this afternoon that I was able to get an excellent view from the top of a hill about three miles from the German trenches and out artillery were shelling them all the time, so it was very interesting to see the shells bursting all about them. I also saw the enemy's shells bursting on a hill not far from us.

With binoculars he observes all of those little Belgian hamlets whose names have become so familiar to him in past weeks: and Ypres. "I saw the cathedral and celebrated hall quite plainly, all in ruins."[220] There too are Gheluvelt, Wytschaete, Messines. Woods have been ripped down by artillery fire and villages lie black, smoking and ruined. Away to the right is France; the towns of Lille and Roubaix both occupied by the enemy, with smoke rising lazily from their chimneys.

Special Attention is paid to certain troops along the way. The King is always looking for ways to pay due respects to his Indian soldiers, and then there are Britain's French allies. His Majesty tells Queen Mary that he is not surprised when official meetings prove unavoidable. In the event he is not really so very sorry when the President appears alongside General Joffre and accompanies King George in his open car for the afternoon, past both French and British soldiery and back to St. Omer. "Had a long talk with him, he made himself very agreeable and is very optimistic about the war."[221] He thinks it is very civil that Monsieur Poincaré has made the effort to come such a long way to meet with him, and not in any way that ruin his schedule. His only criticism is that he thinks the French politician might be a little over optimistic about the Allied prospects for imminently winning the war. The Prince of Wales is not so impressed. He thinks the President a "pompous little ass" in a mad suit and "such a civilian."[222] The French party remain for dinner, and the King has a long yarn with Joffre afterwards. He thinks the joint visit will have done much good and even David thinks that although a bore, it has been useful to the war effort.

A visit to a fellow monarch deposed from his capital by German occupation was always marked down as an essential part of His Majesty's visit, and the King travels north to the Belgian coast to see stern King Albert and his vivacious, flirtatious Bavarian Queen, Elizabeth. Passing through Dunkirk, at the Hotel de Ville The King appoints the Belgian Sovereign to the Order of the Garter, with which he is delighted. There is also the opportunity for His Majesty to meet with his brother in law, Alge, who is part of the British Mission liaising with the Belgian Army. The Queen lays on an excellent lunch for her British visitors by the dunes at La Panne, where the Royal Family have settled in semi-exile by the sea; determined to share the lot of the Belgian people. At nightfall the British party leaves, buffeted by gale force winds and torrential rain all the way back to St. Omer. "It was blowing very hard and we had an awful drive home as it was pouring in sheets beside and quite dark," writes the King. "Once or twice, I thought the car would be blown over, as the road was very exposed, the country being so flat."[223]

His Majesty is careful to include units in his schedule that are just as important to the war effort as those rotating in and out of the trenches. The second half of his visit is dedicated to medical establishments and the lines of communication, all of the supplementary troops that make it possible for the army to fight in front of them. He is introduced to signallers, men ferrying about supplies and ordnance by lorry or by horse and cart, veterinary units, and even army postmen delivering letters and parcels up and down the line. At one stop, the King even observes a unique unit of the Army Service Corps whose job it is to make charcoal for use in the trenches. He sees medical units all along the chain of evacuation; dressing stations further forward, large field

220   RA QM/PRIV/CC04/129.
221   RA GV/PRIV/GVD/1914 (1/12).
222   RA EDW/PRIV/DIARY/1914 (2/12).
223   RA QM/PRIV/CC04/ 130.

ambulances and a convalescent home that manages to stop the equivalent of a battalion a month from evaporating into the bureaucracy and red tape of recovery that keeps men from re-joining their units efficiently. His Majesty also spends a full day observing the complicated and multi-faceted work of General Headquarters at St. Omer. He attends one of Sir John French's conferences with his intelligence officers, then he is introduced to the various subsections in charge of all facets of the BEFs war effort; he evens watches maps being printed. The King moves through this network of administration slowly and purposefully, taking it all in. He stops in at the central signal office, where the staff claim that their room is the nerve centre of the British Expeditionary Force, "for into it radiate the tentacles along which flash messages from every part of the field of operations [and] from England,"[224] they tell their Sovereign. The room pulsates with the tick, tick, tick of different machinery. In one room His Majesty watches as the operators perforate long strips of paper. Then they are sent off by a high-speed bit of kit that he is told can transmit up to 600 words a minute.

All in all, at the end of his week in France and Belgium, the King is pleased to find the army in better spirits than his own glum mood had predicted, but Haig still thinks his view is too rosy. He sits next to His Majesty at dinner before his departure.

> The King seemed very cheery but inclined to think that all our troops are by nature brave and is ignorant of all the efforts which a Commander must make to keep up the morale of their men in war, and of all the training which is necessary in peace in order to enable a company for instance to go forward as an organised unit in the face of almost certain death. I told him of the crowds of fugitives who came back down from the Menin Road from time to time during the Ypres battle having thrown everything they could, including their rifles and packs, in order to escape, with a look of absolute terror on their faces, such as I have never seen before on any human being's face.[225]

The trip is rounded off with a long, private talk between King George and Sir John French about the campaign so far and the future of the BEF in this war. His Majesty comes away relatively satisfied. A special order of the day is issued to his troops; from the highest rank to the lowest:

> I am very glad to have been able to see my army in the field... I wish I could have spoken to you all, to express my admiration of the splendid manner in which you have fought, and are still fighting against a relentless enemy... I cannot share in your trials, dangers and successes, but I can assure you of the proud confidence and gratitude of myself and your fellow countrymen. We follow you in our daily thoughts on your certain road to victory.[226]

From all the King has seen in the newspapers, his visit has done good; "[they] seem to approve of my having come out here. I don't really care if they don't as I am doing what I consider is my duty."[227] Now he just wants to get home to the Queen. "I am certainly looking forward to seeing you darling... more than I can say." He feels better for having seen the front himself, and is optimistic. "I feel almost confident that the Germans will not break through our lines now, however many fresh troops they may bring up, as we are so strongly entrenched."[228]

224   *Daily Telegraph* 6/12/14.
225   (ed.) Sheffield & Bourne: *Douglas Haig: War Diaries and Letters 1914-1918*, pp.82-83.
226   *The Times* 5/12/14.
227   RA QM/PRIV/CC04/ 127.
228   RA QM/PRIV/CC04/ 130.

David is miserable to see his father go, but proud of his achievement in seeing so many of the men in such a short time. The King has already told Queen Mary how pleased he is that their son is so popular at the front; but his old problem is surfacing again. "I am pleased with him except he eats practically nothing, everyone tells me the same thing, what a curious thing it is."[229] Mother takes it up again with son with as much tact as she can muster. "I have heard most flattering accounts of you from various people, the only fault they find is that you neither eat nor drink, always the same old story, and it surprises them how you are able to keep on doing so much on so little food - How I wish you would try and eat more really nourishing things."[230]

As soon as his father leaves, David sits down and draws him a meticulous map illustrated with coloured lines that show the routes that they have travelled on each day together "I have put it in my journal," the King assures him,

> and it will be most useful when I want to refer to the places I went to. It was so nice seeing you and having you with me during the week I spent in France, and I was so delighted to see how keen and interested you were in everything and how well informed you were about people and all that was going on, I know you are very observant. But what pleased me most was to hear how popular you have made yourself, not only without our troops but also with the French. Everyone told me so and it gives both Mama and me much pleasure to hear it. I was much interested in hearing about what you have been doing... I quite understand that at GHQ you don't meet anyone of your own age, but as I hope you will visit the different Divisional Commanders from time to time, they will enable you to be brought into contact with younger officers. I was very sorry to say goodbye to you at Boulogne on Saturday afternoon.[231]

Presents are distributed to all those who have contributed to a successful endeavour. A tie pin for the man who piloted the *Brighton* from Newhaven to Dieppe, similar mementoes such as cigarette cases, brooches and cufflinks for officers who have accompanied and commanded escorts of guards, security men, chauffeurs, chefs, the housekeeper, and the maid at St Omer. A press communique issued on 6th December outlines all that has been done during the King's week in France and the editor of *The Spectator* dashes off a note to Stamfordham: "a line to congratulate you most heartily upon the splendid success of the King's visit... I did not realise how great that effect would be. You must feel very happy about it all."[232]

Germany has not managed to effect a quick and decisive victory over the Allies in 1914. The conflict has reached a deadlock on the Western Front that it will take years to break. As the festive season approaches it is clear that celebrations will be almost non-existent. The Royal Family usually retire to Sandringham for a number of weeks, but the Queen admits that "we can have no real festival this year, only do what we can to make others as comfortable as possible under the sad circumstances."[233] They leave for a much curtailed period in Norfolk the day before Christmas Eve, where the only concessions to any normal celebrations is a 27 foot tree. And the King has not broken with tradition when it comes to his workers' families. Half a dozen bullocks are slaughtered on the estate and butchered into joints; each tagged and laid out on white tablecloths in the coach

229   RA QM/PRIV/CC04/ 128.
230   RA EDW/MAIN/A/1433.
231   RA EDW/PRIV/MAIN/A/1415.
232   PA: S/13/15/15 8/12/14.
233   RA PRIV/QMD/1914 (10/12).

house for them to collect. Those who have a family member absent at the front are given special attention; gifts of warm clothing are purchased, and treats are baked in the royal kitchens for the elderly and infirm in the villages surrounding Sandringham. The King crams in as much shooting as possible in an attempt to relax. Christmas Day is blissfully quiet. "No newspapers published today," he notes in his diary.[234] He is a thoughtful man; and he doesn't put his feelings to one side easily. Though he has implicit faith in Kitchener, the King is "a man of peace, a very sensitive, highly strung nature…. With none of his father's power to divert his thoughts, into easier channels, with only a little of his… elasticity and joie de vivre."[235] The glory of war is non existent for His Majesty. Every bit of the suffering and waste that he has seen weighs upon him, depresses him a little more and not to have to read about it all; even for a single day, is a blessing. The King sees out the year going over trench maps which David has brought home from France with his son. "This has been a sad year for us all," he writes on New Year's Eve. "May 1915 be happier one and may it bring peace."[236] He is in bed by 11:30.

234   RA GV/PRIV/GVD/1914 (25/12).
235   Gore: *King George V, A Personal Memoir,* pp.291-293.
236   RA GV/PRIV/GVD/1914 (31/12).

1915

Disarray

The Unknown Officer

Throughout 1915, the country's effort to galvanise itself for the continuation of an incomprehensible war will be mirrored by the endeavours of her Sovereign as he approaches all facets of his war work with vigour and determination. A relentless, disorganised approach will exhaust him, but no matter where he goes and what he does, as he unknowingly begins establishing himself as a symbolic figurehead for Britain's war effort, the King returns to his red boxes; piles of papers that require his signature, his deliberation, his decision and his comments each and every day. He analyses them with Stamfordham without fail; on the telephone if he is absent, and never affords himself a complete day off from his work. In the course of the war, His Majesty will take less 'leave,' that is fewer days away from the business of State and of war, than an ordinary private soldier that survives the entire conflict.

Throughout 1915, inspections of men prior to their departure for the front continue. The King is determined to try to see each division off personally. The types of troops that march past him change as the year goes on. After bidding farewell to the first divisions, he sees a host of troops that have returned from stations across the globe and are now being sent to war. Then it is the turn of territorial divisions; Britain's existing part time soldiery. There are inspections at Blandford, Banbury, and on Parker's Piece at Cambridge, where whilst walking up and down lines of Welsh troops, His Majesty is told that there is an old soldier wearing the Kandahar ribbon present. A memento of a battle fought as long ago as 1880, the King insists of retracing his steps through black mud to find him. At Aldershot in the first week of March it is bitterly cold and snow flurries cast an icy veil upon his inspections. He visits a training camp for ambulances, watches tactical exercises, route marches, artillery practice, new recruits getting to grips with their rifles. He spends hours out riding with his daughter, and even officially starts a divisional cross-country race; more than 500 runners contesting a seven mile course. He tells Stamfordham that he is impressed "with the great progress made in the practical training of the troops."[1] Encounters are not necessarily planned. From a train in Scotland one Saturday morning, the King notices a small group of soldiers near a station. He jumps down from his carriage, climbs the embankment and hurdles several other obstacles on his way to where men are washing from buckets. One of them swiftly recognises His Majesty's uniform and stands to attention for this unknown officer. The King slips into easy conversation with them remains for about a quarter of an hour and then departs again. Only then do the men realise who the officer was.

Inspections are not limited in 1915 to fighting troops. A smile and a wave from the King is an glowing acknowledgement of all facets of war work. His Majesty meets a Scottish branch of the Red Cross; who despite persistent rain, park their ambulances the length of The Mall from the

---

1   PA S/14/3/2: Lytton Strachey.

Victoria Memorial all the way to Admiralty Arch ready for a brief royal ceremony. The vehicles are named after the districts and towns that have funded them. The *County of Fife, Edinburgh, Dundee;* all operated by Scottish drivers, move slowly through the Garden Gate into the grounds of Buckingham Palace and past the terrace steps. The King approves greatly of their endeavours, the quality of the vehicles and of their smart appearance on parade. He also pays tribute "to the great public generosity, which was providing so many ambulances for the use of British and French forces, and said that he was glad to see that Scotland was well to the fore in this work."[2] Vehicles of all types pass through the same gates in 1915. On 20th March they receive a fleet of motor kitchen cars provided by the Church Army. "Built on a lorry chassis, the cars have the outward appearance of motor ambulances... and they bear the sign of the Red Cross." This deception was so that they might stay as close to the front line as possible without drawing fire, "to supply men going to, or coming from the firing line with steaming hot tea, coffee, cocoa and meat essences." The three vehicles so far have cost the princely sum of £1,200. His Majesty looks them over in great detail. One fitting that draws his particular attention is a box tucked away in the corner of the cab, "containing all the requisites for communion: portable altar, chalice, cassock, surplice and stole." Having not long returned from the front himself, the King declares it a capital idea, and that "he knew many officers and men were glad of an opportunity of communion on before taking their turns in the firing line."[3] Volunteerism is celebrated in a royal setting too. The City of London National Guard pass through the palace grounds on foot. More than 2,000 men, most of them past military age march from Mansion House and through Hyde Park on their way to Buckingham Palace. Clad in a mixture of khaki-grey uniforms and civilian attire, these volunteer clerks, accountants, merchants, businessmen, bankers and traders are escorted by four recruiting bands. His Majesty is much interested in their appearance, calling them "a fine body of men,"[4] and approves of their energetic contribution to the war effort; asking all sorts of questions about how they fit their duties around their existing work.

A few days later it is the turn of the recruiting bands, who play all over the city to boost the numbers enlisting at various offices. "While the long vista of The Mall was thickly veiled in a morning mist," they set out for Buckingham Palace, "each of the bands taking its turn in playing a brisk march as the little column, some 300 strong, made its way along The Mall, and so within the palace gates." Led by the Lord Mayor they march into the Quadrangle and swing left in order to line up facing the King and Queen, who have been joined by the Prime Minister. His Majesty descends the steps as all together the musicians crash out the National Anthem. "Played by so many instrumentalists, the magnificent volume of the music was most inspiring as it reached the large crowd of spectators gathered outside the palace." The King is interested in every detail of the bands' formation. He wants to know what the pay is like, about the design of the uniforms, and what their work entails. "It was explained to His Majesty that the bands were distributed... from Stratford in the East to Hammersmith and Chelsea in the West, and from the heart of the metropolis to Battersea, Camberwell, Deptford and Woolwich, on the south side of the river."[5] They explain to him that they play recruits to railway stations as they depart for training, that they accompany route marches, of which there are plenty, through the street. The King, who thinks that they play "extremely well."[6] He summons the conductor because he has noticed medals on his breast. He wishes to know at length of Mr Conquer's 26 years of service; including seventeen years as bandmaster of the Territorial London Irish Rifles. "The bands proceeded to take their departure

---

2   *Daily Telegraph* 18/2/15.
3   *Daily Telegraph* 20/3/15.
4   RA GV/PRIV/GVD/1915 (20/3).
5   *Daily Telegraph* 25/3/15.
6   RA GV/PRIV/GVD/1915 (24/3).

one by one, each playing its own selected music… past the King, and finally emerged from the quadrangle by the northernmost archway in the main facade of the palace."[7]

In 1915 His Majesty will also attempt to present as many decorations to individual recipients as possible. On 13th January, the first large-scale investiture is held in the 1844 Room at Buckingham Palace. The occasion is dubbed 'Heroes Day' by the press, for the King distributes nine Victoria Crosses, won at Le Cateau, Zillebeke, Néry, and on the Aisne. He also presents 34 Distinguished Service Orders and 34 medals to naval men from the action at Heligoland. It is a damp, misty morning, and a brave crowd stares through the railings; many of them watching friends and relatives disappear inside to receive their medals. A representative from the War Office stands beside the King, and as each man approaches the Sovereign he reads a brief record of service that has led to his award. They salute; His Majesty pins the medal to their tunic, shakes his hand and whilst congratulating him, says what a pleasure it is for him to be able to confer the prize in person. One of the Victoria Cross recipients is Spencer Bent, a sturdy young man, but shy. He takes the medal straight off and puts it into his pocket in the hope of avoiding waiting newspaper men outside. He is met by his proud father and other relatives and begins to slip through the crowd. "It was not until a group of photographers had persuaded him again to put on the cross on his breast for the purposes of a picture that his identity was revealed."[8] The crowd lift him onto their shoulders to be photographed. Frederick Holmes also collects his VC that day. His wife is outside and more excited that she has given birth to their son a mere 48 hours before. Journalists ask her what she intends to call the baby. "Mrs Holmes…Speaking with her pretty Irish brogue, said "I must wait and ask my husband, It will have to be something out of the way under such circumstances - something to remind him of the war?"[9] Her mother in law, when reminded what an honour it is to be awarded the Victoria Cross, replies that she is more thankful of her son's safety than anything else.

Though men come to organised ceremonies, others arrive on any given day of the week, often just one or two at a time. Palace officials are diligent in rooting out those who have received awards, or those who might have interesting tales to tell as they pass through London; coming or going from leave, which had begun soon after the fighting at Ypres died down, or having been sent home wounded. At the beginning of the year Fred Dobson, who has been awarded the Victoria Cross for dragging wounded comrades to safety on the Aisne, is discovered in London. He is run to ground, but officials find him in mufti, which won't do for an investiture. He is rushed off to the Coldstream Guards' Headquarters, stuffed into an available dress uniform and conducted to Buckingham Palace accompanied by two officers of his regiment.

Abide With Me

At the beginning of 1915 a craze has emerged through which the King can continue to expand his war work. There are constant revues and stage performances in aid of various war charities; and His Majesty sits through a diverse array of entertainment; from army quadrilles, to choral efforts, an entire concert given by military bands, to a whimsical interpretation of Tipperary by the Coldstream Guards on bassoon and piccolo. The Queen attends far more of these galas than the King, some of which are true feats of endurance in their longevity, but His Majesty's two favourite performances come in the middle of May.

7   Daily Telegraph 25/3/15.
8   Ibid., 14/1/15.
9   The Times 14/1/15.

"The Man Who Stayed At Home" is moved to the Palace Theatre in order to allow a bigger audience to attend a special matinee in honour of the Officer's Families Fund. "Priding themselves on a lack of formality and promptness,"[10] the group helps dependants of officers who require money, hospitality, medical assistance, education and advice. It is a necessarily discreet venture, as these are not a class who are normally reliant on charity. One box at The Palace is priced at a hefty £200, and the performance had already sold out with a week to go. The Queen herself has purchased 400 seats in the gallery for wounded soldiers from London hospitals; and two anonymous ladies have purchased these men's programmes, which are dispensed by famous actresses. The Royal Box is decked in red and white tulips when the King, Queen and Princess Mary arrive. "First the audience clapped its hands, then it waited a moment as if reflecting that clapping was after all but a poor, inadequate welcome and then, overcoming its shyness, it burst their acknowledgments to all parts of the house, and in particular to the gallery." His Majesty is between the Queen and the Princess, looking cheerful but perhaps a little weary, with a white flower in his buttonhole. One wounded man missing an arm decides to mount the ledge of the gallery and call for three cheers for Their Majesties, before he and his injured comrades join the rest of the audience in singing the National Anthem. All stand, if they are able, but many have to be helped. "After that came the play, and there could surely be no better one for the occasion. Very amusing, it is blood curdling in its excitement."[11] Dennis Eadie stars as a Secret Service agent. "It is essentially a war play, of which the theme is the German system of espionage here at home." The audience are fixated in the "thrall which the action and reaction of plot and counter-plot exerts at every turn." The King is excited and thinks the piece very well acted, but more than one newspaper man notices that he keeps glancing at the wounded, his large blue eyes lifting towards the gallery. The rest of the audience, too, recognise that these 400 men are the afternoon's greatest spectacle. "In their hundreds… they swarmed round to the gallery exit and sympathetically cheered the men as they descended into the street." They climb and are carried back into waiting omnibuses to be taken back to hospital. "The impressions these men made upon the spectators were stirring, Women were moved to tears; men were on the verge of them. Here was one of the few glimpses which have been permitted to the Londoner of the stern realities of war." The crowd spontaneously begins throwing gifts. "People flung cigarettes, singly and in packets to the soldiers occupying the outside seats… until cigarettes fairly rained on them. Are we downhearted? Shouted a young fellow from the top of an omnibus as it moved off: the answer "NO!" of the crowd might almost have been heard at Charing Cross."[12]

Clara Butt, the famous contralto, has also used all of her celebrity pull to organise a huge concert at the Royal Albert Hall in aid of the Red Cross. £5,000 has been raised before the curtain goes up, many boxes and seats having been purchased for the wounded, with one Cardiff gentleman paying £1,000 after the King orders the Prince of Wales's box to be offered for the evening. "Under the organ the massed bands of the Guards, blazing with gold and the light glinting on their instruments, made a gorgeous splash of colour. So did a box full of wounded soldiers in their blue clothes, and whole rows of nurses in their trim blue and white."[13] Sitting above the band are 250 singers, many of them stars in their own right, who have lent their services for a good cause. 10,000 little white satin flags, mounted on miniature poles and bearing images of the King and Queen are handed out on arrival to each member of the audience. The crowd sits with them fluttering gently in their hands, waiting for the arrival of the royal party. Amidst a buzz of expectation and excitement, at exactly half past eight His Majesty enters his box with Queen Mary and their daughter. The whole

10   Ibid., 23/4/15.
11   Ibid., 12/5/15.
12   *Daily Telegraph* 12/5/15.
13   *The Times* 14/5/15.

audience stands to greet them, flags in hand, and an enthusiastic programme is begun in stirring, enthralling style. The large choir sings the first verse of God Save the King, and Clara Butt sings the second as a solo before all join together, with the band too in the third. "And then, as the last note died away the house burst simultaneously into cheering and waving of flags, till from the gallery to the arena the air seemed thick with snowflakes."[14] Clara Butt performs more solos, as does her baritone husband, who has been given special leave from the War Office to take a break from his role stimulating recruitment. The massed bands of Brigade of Guards play, and the Queen has requested *Land of Hope and Glory* and her favourite hymn: *Abide With Me*.

Though there are certainly themes that emerge, such as entertainment benefits and investitures, a huge amount of ad hoc work is also undertaken by His Majesty in 1915. The King hears of a free military buffet at one of London's large railway termini and decides he must see it, arriving within three days of its opening. Some thoughtful ladies and gentlemen have decided that there is a need for reviving military passengers, giving soldiers and sailors a place to set down as they arrive and depart the capital. The Great Eastern Railway provides a large room for their use, "which they fitted up as a restaurant, and decorated with flags, flowers, and palms." On the table they have placed newspapers and magazines. They begin work with a teapot and loaves of bread, and feed 400 men on the first day. By the time His Majesty arrives, 2,000 servicemen have taken advantage of their service already. The King questions the staff on every aspect of their operation, approving of it all. "Not a point was missed, His Majesty going behind the counter and making inquiries." The King is offered a cup of tea, and he smiles and nods, "whereupon the ladies began to make a fresh infusion. But just at that moment the obstinate geyser refused to work. Not a drop of water was forthcoming… His Majesty did not allow anyone to be disconcerted and appeared thoroughly to have enjoyed the incident." He laughs heartily. "Your arrangements are excellent," he says on departure, leaving Major Lennox hopeful that the publicity from the royal visit will lead to many more donations and that they will be able to expand their operation to other stations."[15]

The King also plays a part in the founding of the Welsh Guards in 1915. After their inception he talks to the Colonel raising the regiment in detail, and helps with critical little details like an appropriate cap badge. After only a short period of recruiting the first battalion is already at full strength in mid-1915, and in the summer he presents the regiment with their colours. A huge crowd gathers outside the palace on the steps of the Queen Victoria memorial just to see the troops disappear into the grounds and then wait for them to emerge again. The new regiment lines up on the lawn facing the western terrace underneath threatening black clouds. The King is wearing the Welsh Guards' service uniform, and does a double take at the sight of the Prince of Wales's Company in the centre of the line, composed of the most impressive recruits, who all tower above him. *Land of My Fathers* is sung. The men are about to commence their march past when a violent thunderstorm erupts, and all are caught in the downpour. One journalist with a vivid imagination sees the rain as a divine intervention, a baptism for the new regiment. The King and Lord Kitchener do not flee. Neither wear overcoats, for the regiment do not, and so they too get a soaking. His Majesty is determined to remain until the end of the proceedings, and he gives a speech, an expression of pride at the formation of a new regiment of foot guards; anticipation of the loyal and gallant days to come, before wishing them all possible success in their endeavours. The National Anthem is played again, and then the men march away in the streaming rain, fife and drums playing the *March of the Men of Harlech*, new colours dripping wet. "All the more casual

14   Ibid., 12/5/15.
15   *Daily Telegraph* 26/3/15.

spectators outside the palace drifted off at the sound of the first thunderclap, but many hundreds remained to cheer the Guards as, drenched to the skin, they marched back to the barracks"[16]

Then there is inertia verging on the bizarre that the palace fight to keep off of the King's desk. One day in 1915 the Provost Marshal in London arrives at Buckingham Palace and presents himself to Fritz Ponsonby. In dramatic fashion he declares that he wants to obtain His Majesty's permission to take a German spy named Captain Lodi into the ditch at the Tower of London and shoot him. "I was considerably startled by such a curious request," writes Ponsonby later on, "but merely asked why the King's permission was necessary. He said that as the Tower of London was a Royal Palace, the King's Coroner would have to sign the death certificate and he could not do this without the King's permission." Ponsonby has no intention of letting His Majesty be dragged into the matter of executing Germans. He fobs the official off for a few hours and frantically telephones the Lord Chancellor's Secretary to ask for help. "I [said] that it would be well if the law officers of the Crown could think of some way of preventing the King's name being used in connection with this."[17] Happily, he receives a message to the effect that technically, the ditch is outside the Tower of London, therefore it is not part of a Royal Palace and His Majesty's permission is not necessary. Ponsonby breathes a huge sigh of relief.

"United, Calm, Resolute, Trusting in God"

With an adventurous trail blazed across the globe by characters such as Drake, Captain Cook and Cecil Rhodes; defended by the likes of Nelson, the Duke of Wellington and Lord Kitchener, if there is one aspect of his birthright that the King understands implicitly it is that which makes him the head of his country's vast empire. At the beginning of the nineteenth century "Britain appeared as a colossus astride the world. Britain dominated every field of human activity and its people seemed to possess an almost demonic energy."[18] She was marketed from within as strong; Britain was purposeful, Britain had integrity, a moral compass and a work ethic that drove forward the human race. This was the world that the King was born into. and since then, though perceptions have evolved, the importance of Empire has not died in the minds of the British people. "At the turn of the twentieth century a whole generation of boys had been bred to go out into the world and administer it; bombarded by popular magazines written especially for them and steeped in the ideas of the new imperialism."[19] Britain still has no rival in terms of imperial territory in 1914, nor in population and this is a source of immense pride. In the words of Baden-Powell: "Your forefathers worked hard, fought hard, and died hard to make this Empire for you. Don't let them look down from heaven, and see you loafing about with your hands in your pockets, doing nothing to keep it up."[20] "The King is no longer merely King of Great Britain and Ireland," writes one former Prime Minister.

> He is now the greatest constitutional bond uniting together in a single Empire, communities of free men separated by half the circumference of the Globe. All the patriotic sentiment which makes such an Empire possible centres in him… and everything which emphasises his personality to our kinsmen across the seas must be a gain to the Monarchy and the Empire.

16   Ibid., 4/8.
17   Syonsby: *Recollections of Three Reigns*, p.327.
18   James: *The Rise and Fall of the British Empire*, pp.169-170.
19   Ibid., pp.206-209.
20   Ibid., p.330.

He is under no illusion. "Our people overseas do not care a rush for Asquith and me. They hardly know our names. For them, the symbol of the Empire is the King."[21]

By the advent of the Great War, Canada, Newfoundland, South Africa, Australia, New Zealand were all self-governing Dominions. Britain is reliant on their cooperation for manpower in August 1914, for nearly one third of the Empire's white population lives in them. Technical training and staff cooperation is supervised by the Imperial General Staff, and all have made contributions in ships or money to the strength of the Royal Navy, which benefits the security of all. With the outbreak of war, all pledge support. The same sentiments of adventure and patriotism that cause a flood of enlistees across Britain drive men to recruiting stations in her Dominions, and King George becomes "the rallying war-point for the Empire."[22] "I desire to express to my people of the overseas Dominions," he says in a statement on the outbreak of war, "that with appreciation and pride I have received the messages from their respective Governments during the last few days. These spontaneous assurances of their fullest support call to me the generous, self-sacrificing help given to them by the confident belief that in this time of trial my empire will stand united, calm, resolute, trusting in God."[23] He also addresses further, separate messages to each country, thanking them for their early commitment to Britain's fight, and emphasising "the importance of the unity of Empire in face of this "unparalleled assault upon the continuity of civilisation and the peace of mankind."[24] The response is positive. One Australian newspaper says that: "besides being appreciated at its full value from end to end of the Empire, [it] will convey to the rest of the world a powerful impression of British solidarity."[25] In Wellington, it is surmised that much of the unity on display is in no small measure attributable to the Royal Family. "The British monarchy has greatly strengthened its hold upon the affections of the nation… respect… has steadily increased with the spread of diplomatic principles and the happy relations of mutual trust."[26]

There is no choice for colonies and dependencies, bound to enter the war with Britain as soon as it has been declared. Many air the same sentiments as the Dominions. With indignance, the Chief of the Basuto in southern Africa indignantly asks "why he, the King's servant should stand idle when his King was fighting his enemies."[27] African colonies would supply 57,000 fighting men and 932,000 labourers and porters in the conflict, with Nyasaland contributing two thirds of its adult male population, but the most significant of all Imperial contributions in terms of numbers were the 1.4m Indians who participated in the Great War.

It is impossible to underestimate the pride with which Imperialists viewed India, led by a perception that British rule had wholly bettered the lot of her subjects. But with betterment came a desire to become part of the decision making process. Before the advent of the 20th Century, thousands of Indians had earned degrees and hundreds of thousands had graduated from secondary schools; taught in English and exposed to British political ideology. Unsurprisingly, these men wanted a say in their own futures. In 1885 the Indian National Congress was founded, the Muslim League followed in 1906. All across India by the outbreak of the Great War are scattered and increasingly organised spectres of nationalism, but the upper echelons of Indian society stand to lose if British rule is terminated, and the declaration of war sees India rally to Britain's cause. The

21   Bogdanor: *The Monarchy and the Constitution,* pp.18-19.
22   Hammerton: *Our King & Queen: A Pictorial Record of Their Lives,* p.1.
23   Ibid., p.14.
24   (ed.) Hammerton & Wilson: *The Great War Vol. II,* pp.237-254.
25   *Sydney Daily Telegraph* 11/9/14.
26   *Dominion (Wellington)* 11/9/14.
27   (ed.) Hammerton & Wilson: *The Great War Vol. II,* pp.237-254.

King has journeyed throughout his Empire more than any of his ancestors, with an attitude that is enlightened at the time. He does not judge a man by the colour of his skin. On his tour of India he realised that the British were wont to look down their noses at the natives, and that as they became more and more educated, Indians realised this fact. He lamented prejudicial customs, but more importantly he clearly didn't believe that British control over her Indian subjects was necessarily permanent. "We must either trust the natives more and give them a greater share in the government," he recorded, "or anyhow allow them to express their views." As a Prince he recognised that some form of self-government could not be withheld, "that the people of India must be encouraged to mould their own political destiny."[28]

The outpouring of support from India in August 1914 is a huge boon to the British war effort, for the enemy had hoped that the upheaval of war would destroy Britain's empire. "In Germany reports are being circulated to the effect that the overseas dominions are preparing to seize the opportunity afforded by the war for what is called: "throwing off the British yoke."[29] But whilst it is true that the Himalayan frontier presents difficulties, Germany's hopes that "the great Mutiny would be surpassed in horror by the upheaval that would inevitably follow the entanglement of Britain in a great war,"[30] will be frustrated. Artwork showing His Majesty in the garb of an Indian prince is produced to stimulate recruitment, but blind obedience is not the sole motivation driving Indians to enlist. Many hope that contributing to the war will provide them with opportunities in the future. And so come forth Sikhs, Pathan Muslims, Baluchis and those from the Punjab. Then are the Hindus: Brahmans, Rajputs, Mahrattas and Dogras; all of them the first Imperial troops to take to the Western Front.

With action comes casualties, and the King immediately seeks out injured Indian soldiers. Whilst it does of course make His Majesty look better in the eyes of his people if he makes such visits, especially throughout the Empire; it would be unfair to say that he only shows an interest in his Imperial soldiers as a public relations exercise. He cares deeply about those men who have travelled thousands of miles to fight in his name; especially those from his beloved India who find themselves in an alien and cold country suffering from wounds.

On hearing that locations are needed to treat them, the town of Brighton leaps into action; offering a workhouse, a school and the Corn Exchange, but the Mayor and the Corporation really catch the world's attention when they put the Royal Pavilion at the disposal of the hospital authorities. A seaside palace, the Pavilion sits by the busy waterfront like a miniature Taj Mahal; "All minarets and cupolas, with pillars and ornaments,"[31] it is hoped that it will appeal to the imaginations of Indian patients, and remind them of home whilst exposing them to the healthy sea air. The King issues a telegram thanking the town for both its public spirit and good will, and the Pavilion is ready to begin accepting patients in December 1914. The novelty of both the building and the patients ensures that the Indian exhibitionists are never in want of attention. In January 1915, rainclouds that have dogged Brighton since Christmas part just long enough to accommodate a visit from Their Majesties; their first to the seaside town since the time of their coronation. Ordinarily Brighton "would have been a blaze of colour and the visit would have been known weeks, perhaps months beforehand."[32] But as is becoming their habit, the King and Queen desire no special effort be made on their behalf, and so rumours about their impending arrival only begin to whip through the town when their train has already left London. "So informal was the

28   Nicolson: *King George V: His Life and Reign,* p.66.
29   *Daily Telegraph* 11/9/14.
30   (ed.) Hammerton & Wilson: *The Great War Vol. I,* p.153.
31   Churchill, Alexandra: *Britain at War Magazine,* August 2016
32   Ibid.

visit that outside the railway station the royal car was delayed for a few moments by a number of Kitchener's men on a route march."[33]

At the pavilion there are now nearly 600 beds available. With sunlight pouring through open doors and windows, Their Majesties pass through the dome, where concentric circles of white beds fan out, divided into caste sections, lighting up "in the richest hues the golden colouring of the Saracenic pillars and arches, the panelled mosaics of roof and walls." The King surveys every feature of the Dome with absorbed interest, repeatedly inquiring about the working of this and that contrivance, "expressing his amazement at the perfection of the equipment for hospital purposes."[34] Other wards open out onto comfortable verandas, or large balconies on the upper floors. The state apartments have been converted into different wards decorated with palms, sunshine streaming in through the ornate windows. There are young boys and grey bearded veterans. Those that can stand proudly to attention by their beds either in khaki or light blue suits beneath their pristine white turbans. Other dark-skinned patients are propped up on pillows. More, severely injured, have to lie prone as the King passes among them. His Majesty even visits the kitchens which are on a very elaborate scale on account of caste distinctions. One supplies the wants of the vegetarians, another caters for the Hindus, Gurkhas, or Dogras and a third is dedicated to the Muslims.

The King greets patients warmly and sympathetically, and although he moves through the Pavilion with an interpreter, the patients are thrilled to discover that he knows enough of their native tongue to converse with them about where they are from, what has happened to them, who their officers are. His Majesty asks a Gurkha what he thinks of the Germans. They are no good when we can get at them with the knives in the trenches, was the reply. As for the German armoured motor cars, says another soldier, they are the inventions of the devil.[35] Men are asked what their understanding is of why they are fighting a war. Many simply reply that it is because the Raj has asked it of them. Another explains that the Emperor of Australia has been murdered in the country of the Emperor of Serbia, the latter has shrugged off responsibility, saying that it was not his army it was dacoits; armed robbers. "The Emperor of the Australians then replied, never mind, I choose to fight you, and I will fight you, and so he did."[36]

The excitement at seeing Their Majesties in person is evident. Some of the men have spent hours grooming themselves fastidiously for this honour and "evinced rapturous delight"[37] when they were all given new turbans for the occasion. One man with a wounded hand had enlisted a friend to spend hours grooming his beard and his hair for when he meets the King. His Majesty notices that he also sports a miniature of Kitchener worn proudly on his uniform. The King reaches out to touch it, makes a comment and the patient beams. As usual, the King also picks out men wearing tokens of meritorious service and questions several of these men as to how they got them. He laughs outright when one invalid tells him that his only grievance is that someone has 'pinched' the precious, coveted bullet which has been extracted from the wound in his leg.

But there is pain and suffering in abundance, too. As the King and Queen progress through the pavilion they are visibly distressed at some of the cases that they encounter. The King ventures into a private side room to see the second Indian recipient of the Victoria Cross. Darwin Singh Negi is a powerfully built man, enormous; the gymnastics instructor of his regiment. But he has been struck down by three bullets and another has carved a groove in the top of his skull. At Brighton

33   *Daily Mirror* 11/1/15.
34   Churchill, Alexandra: *Britain at War Magazine*, August 2016
35   *Daily Mail* 11/1/15.
36   Ibid.
37   Churchill, Alexandra: *Britain at War Magazine*, August 2016

he is in a serious condition, and there are fears that he may not recover. The King speaks quietly with him for a time. There is a young Gurkha who has been shot in the jaw and has lost his tongue; the Queen has tears in her eyes when Their Majesties sit with another man blinded in both eyes by shrapnel. His head is swathed in bandages. The Queen has to look away and she says: "poor fellow, how sad."[38] For Her Majesty though, the case of two brothers is too much. Bal and Pim are 17 and 18 and in adjoining beds. One shell has ripped into Pim's leg and torn off his arm, and Bal has lost a leg. The Queen gives them a flower she has to hand and they salute the King when he has finished talking with them and wishes them a safe journey home. Queen Alexandra will meet the brothers too. They are redoubtable. She asks them if they can talk with her in English and they are crushed that they cannot, but they quickly pipe up that they can sing instead, before belting out *Tipperary* for the King's Mother.

The Dominions' speedy rush to Britain's side is as much about self-interest as it is about imperial devotion. New Zealand quickly offers 8,000 men and drafts to keep up that number. Hospitals are quickly established dedicated to each self-governing Dominion, and the New Zealanders are cared for a smart establishment at Walton on Thames; which will be visited by the King and Queen on several occasions. Newfoundland, the oldest of Britain's colonies nobly offers 500 men from her tiny population, to go with all of her seamen.

With her much larger population, Canada pledges 20,000 men, and promptly recruits 100,000 volunteers. The King is privy to all that transpires in that Dominion thanks to the presence of his uncle as Governor General. The Duke of Connaught is the seventh of Queen Victoria's nine children, and some fifteen years the King's senior. Immediately he assures his nephew that "Canada stands united from the Pacific to the Atlantic in her determination to uphold the honour and traditions of her Empire." The Prime Minister, Robert Borden, says that "so long as we are able to raise a man to stand by the guns or a dollar to carry on the fight we shall go on until the oppressor is subdued." Canada's outpouring of support does not end with Government promises of troops. Anticipating hardships in Europe, donations begin. A million bags of flour are promised, Alberta pledges 500,000 bushels of oats; Quebec offers nearly 400,000 pounds of cheese, Saskatchewan 1,500 horses, British Columbia 25,000 cases of tinned salmon. Nova Scotia pledges £100,000, while the Women of Canada donate £60,000 for hospitals and equip a hospital ship for the navy. Eighteen cities between them raise another million pounds in ten weeks. Even Berlin, Ontario, whose population of 18,000 is two thirds German, or of German descent, pledges £15,000 to Kitchener "to see militarism in Germany smashed for good."[39]

By the end of October 1914, transport after transport had begun to dock on Britain's south coast in front of dense crowds. Thousands of Canadians are then sent on to Salisbury Plain for training. The Duke of Connaught is immensely proud of this swift mobilisation. "I am most anxious you should see them," he tells his nephew, "and … think that it would be a great disappointment to this large and patriotic body of Canadians were they not to be inspected by their Sovereign."[40] The King concurs. A fortnight before their arrival, he had already been to Bulford to inspect 3,500 huts being built to house Canadians. He is back almost as soon as they arrive, side by side with Lord Kitchener. "We saw over 30,000 very fine men, but they require more training before they can go to the front."[41] When he returns twelve weeks later, His Majesty is hugely impressed. They don't

38   Ibid.
39   (ed.) Hammerton & Wilson: *The Great War Vol. II*, pp.237-254.
40   RA GV/PRIV/AA41/51.
41   RA GV/PRIV/GVD/1914 (4/11).

know it, but they are about to depart for France. "They are now fully trained and are a splendid lot of men and will I am sure give a very good account of themselves at the front."[42]

The King's presence is a huge hint as to their imminent departure and the Canadians are "red-hot"[43] to get at the enemy. In the early months of 1915, brave Canadian troops are taxed to the limit, and the Dominion suffers more than 6,000 casualties. A memorial gathering is held at St. Paul's "and hours before the service commenced, not only were the great aisles of the cathedral itself thronged, but thousands waited outside, anxious to show their presence,"[44] The Canadian Prime Minister visits Britain to discuss detailed questions of administration and cooperation. The King is thrilled with the idea and most impressed with Mr Borden, whom he finds extremely easy to talk to; and hopes that the visit will become an important precedent.

But each Dominion brings with it its own separate issues that cause the King anxiety. In the case of Canada, whilst his close links with the Governor General promise detailed knowledge of all that is happening there, the Duke of Connaught's own personal dislike of the Minister of Militia causes untold difficulties for his nephew. From his first days in Canada, His Majesty's uncle had clashed with Sam Hughes. Not only does he think that this longstanding politician is a bounder, but having been personally besieged by Hughes when he badgered the British authorities to give him a Victoria Cross, twice, based on some far fetched and fantastical interpretations of events during the Boer War, he also characterised him as a madman who refused to listen to counsel. Any antagonism he harbours towards Britain on account of this, Hughes finds an outlet for it when it came to Connaught, who by the Great War has come to see the minister as a source of constant frustration and alarming behaviour. He wants him gone, but admits to the King that he has little say in the matter.

The involvement of Canadian forces in the war brings Hughes directly into His Majesty's sphere of activity and never in a good way. "I fear that there will be considerable confusion and delay in disembarking the force as they were very badly embarked, owing to the action of the Minister of Militia," wrote Connaught in October 1914. Hughes has he says, "although supremely ignorant in all military matters, upset all the arrangements… and insisted on running the embarkation himself with the most <u>ghastly</u> results," The King is now directly caught up in the personal enmity between his uncle and the politician. "He is quite mad with conceit and insults everybody right and left," complains the Duke. "He has the greatest contempt for me and makes a point of never doing anything I suggest."[45] Hughes manages to get himself to Europe, and Connaught is furious that his concerns have been ignored. He says that the Canadian Government lacked the moral courage to tell him to stay behind. "Considering my social position and that as a British Field Marshal I think that the Government might have shown me a little more consideration after all I have done for them."[46] At the beginning of 1915, there are issues concerning Hughes's refusal to acknowledge that a 66 year old General was not suitable to command one of the Canadian divisions in the field. His Majesty sides with his uncle and forwards on Connaught's concerns to Kitchener. The War Minister sends back telegrams that had already been exchanged with Hughes in the matter and the King is astonished by the latter's stance. "It seems incredible that anyone holding an important office could lower himself to use the arguments and expressions employed by… General Hughes."[47]

---

42   RA GV/PRIV/GVD/1915 (4/2).
43   *Daily Chronicle* 17/3/15.
44   (ed.) Hammerton & Wilson: *The Great War Vol. V,* pp.201-222.
45   RA GV/PRIV/AA42/52.
46   RA GV/PRIV/AA2/53.
47   TNA: PRO 30/57/56.

The Canadian will receive a knighthood before his departure home, much to His Majesty's disgust, as he had been railroaded on the matter by his own ministers. He is also apoplectic with rage when it transpires that Hughes has been offered a military promotion without his having been consulted. "I am sure you will understand when I say that the King is surprised and annoyed," writes Stamfordham to Asquith. The offer is made "not only without his Majesty's approval, but in the face of his strong opposition to the appointment."[48] As it stands, he "vows he will not sign"[49] any document to this effect. Once again, the King has been backed into a corner, as Hughes has already been told about his promotion.

> His Majesty recognises that in these circumstances he has been committed to consenting to an appointment which he feels should not be made and he therefore records his objections. At the same time the King appeals to you to make it clear to ministers that they have no authority to approach anyone on the question of their acceptance of any post or honour dependent upon the sovereign's approval without having previously [sought his permission].[50]

Australia matched Canada's offer of troops, immediately surpassed that number and began raising money too, a large portion of which is meant for the purchase of food supplies for the British Isles. In terms of worries, the discipline of the Australian troops gives the King headaches early on. News arrives from Egypt at the beginning of 1915 to say that parts of the force are terrorising the locals. "At Christmas they made a raid from Mena and painted Cairo red."[51] On Good Friday there is a riot in which a man is killed by military police. They are splendid looking, brave specimens of potential soldiery early on, impressive on the eye; but one witness notes that though they look magnificent, as a group "they are universally loathed for their wealth, insolence, crudity, and lack of any sort of discipline, manners or consideration."[52]

Based on her population, South Africa pledges to release 6,000 Imperial troops currently engaged on defensive duties there, and there were offers from all parts of the Union to serve in other contingents. At the beginning of the war though, South Africa had severe security concerns much closer to home. The declaration of war exacerbates existing friction amongst an anti-British faction, especially when the Union undertakes to march on German South West Africa. Rebellion breaks out, aided by the Germans and though the Government acts quickly to suppress it, is yet another worry on the King's shoulders. But though there are concerns to be addressed, in the opening months of the year, King George is genuinely overwhelmed by the outpouring of support throughout his Empire and the commitment of tens of thousands of men who have pledged to fight in his name from across the globe. He stands next to General Monash, an Australian commander on Salisbury Plain and says: "Look at these fine troops. The Germans started out to smash the British Empire, smash it to pieces, and look, just look; see what they have really done. They have made an Empire of us… It makes a lump come into my throat to think of all these splendid fellows coming all these many thousands of miles, and what they have come for."[53]

48   BD: MS Asquith A.1 4 #221.
49   BD: MS Asquith A.1 4 #233.
50   BD: MS Asquith A.1 4 #235.
51   (ed.) Brock: *H.H. Asquith: Letters to Venetia Stanley,* p.399.
52   Ibid., p.401.
53   Hammerton: *Our King & Queen: A Pictorial Record of Their Lives,* p.12.

Two Fatal Things in War

But while thousands of Kitchener's men are in training, and tens of thousands more are en route to Europe to join the fray, Britain must decide what to do with them. This proves to be a supremely difficult task throughout the year, as civilian, naval and military authorities discover that Britain is in no way equipped to fight an industrial war on an unprecedented scale. "The year 1915," comments Churchill later on, "was disastrous to the cause of the Allies and the whole world."[54] For a start, nobody can agree on how long the war will last. The King still believes that it will go on for years. As does Kitchener who claims that the war will only be beginning at Easter. Sir Edward Grey optimistically thinks that the Germans will collapse in June. The Prince of Wales predicts that however long it lasts, they will all be sitting in exactly the same positions when the war ends.

One thing that should have been clear is that the Government needs to seize matters by the scruff of the neck. The King considers that the military power of Germany must be broken: her army reduced, her navy abolished, the Kiel Canal nationalised and her forts taken down. Alas, his Government fails to drive the country forward with anything like this severity. The War Committee has only met three times since its inception by the turn of the year, and Lloyd George feels compelled to raise the matter with the Prime Minister. "Occasional meetings will end in nothing... I feel that a continuation of the present deadlock is full of danger."[55] And yet the drifting approach of the Government will continue.

On the Western Front, His Majesty fears that his troops are not in the best hands. On paper at least, General Smith-Dorrien is the only highly placed figure there not telling the King that Sir John French is out of his depth at the end of 1914. But French is not enamoured of this comrade and his belligerence towards his subordinate, who is liked by His Majesty, will not improve the King's opinion of him. The two Generals had got on reasonably well in the past, but Smith-Dorrien found French's philandering distasteful, and French was a jealous man, who resented that Smith-Dorrien had succeeded him in a previous post and promptly changed what he had done during his own tenure. By March 1915 Sir John French has decided that Smith-Dorrien's performance in the war is not up to scratch. French subsequently declared that he had "failed to get a real grasp of the situation." His messages were "wordy," "windy" and "unintelligible," while his "pessimistic attitude has the worst effective on his commanders and their troops."[56] On 6th May Smith-Dorrien is removed from his command on the flimsiest evidence. The King has been aware that the situation is troubled for some weeks, but nonetheless, when Smith-Dorrien is sent home, His Majesty is thoroughly unimpressed.

But far more harmful for French as far as the King's opinion of him is concerned is his inability to get on with Kitchener. To align oneself against the Secretary of State for War and make it personal is tantamount to taking up a position against the Sovereign. His Majesty does underestimate French, but the General harms his own position by over-egging his campaign prospects when he meets with the King, who projects a long war. Added to this, French is insecure, as well as paranoid, and requires constant reassurances about his position. His Sovereign has no time for this type of vanity.

By the beginning of 1915 the strain of French's command is beginning to show already. His physical and mental condition has started to fray. Haig says that he looks rather "pulled down,"[57] and Sir John tells him that he might have had a heart attack, and that his doctors have ordered him to rest. Kitchener and French cling to cordial professionalism, but their ability to work together

54   Nicolson: *King George V: His Life and Reign*, p.265.
55   Grigg: *Lloyd George, From Peace to War 1912-1916*, pp.192-193.
56   Holmes: *The Little Field Marshal: A Life of Sir John French*, p.284.
57   Ibid., pp.255-256.

is starting to disintegrate, taking with it any good opinion that His Majesty has left of the BEF's Commander in Chief. Kitchener has no inherent belief in French's ability to command the largest force Britain has ever put into the field. Margot Asquith claims that over dinner she asks him what he thinks of Sir John. "He said that he had great intuition and courage. If you say "mass your men up there" or "take this or that position," he will carry out your orders better than anyone; but he is the worst organiser, and a stupid man. He can't make a plan of any kind, he is bad at staff work, and has a bad staff."[58] French doesn't help himself with the men he chooses to surround him, either. His military secretary, Billy Lambton, is well thought of the palace, but the others are not. Margot Asquith warns French that his private secretary, Brinsley Fitzgerald, and an aide, Freddie Guest go "backward and forward making mischief like old women between you and K and all the generals."[59] Lord Esher also tells French that his team requires strengthening, and that the King regards the Commander-in-Chief's advisers as trouble-makers. Other generals are expressing concerns about his command to the palace in mid-January. "Nothing we could do out here will, I fear, put sense into the head of [French]," writes one, "and I should not be in the least bit surprised if he repeated his performance of last summer, only with more disastrous results to himself. The state of affairs is to my mind a positive danger to the Empire."[60]

French finds more ways to denigrate His Majesty's opinion of him. He keeps up what is perceived as a skulduggerous correspondence with Winston Churchill, whom the King thinks highly competent, but capable of behaving like a blackguard. In addition to the letters, Churchill visits French in France throughout 1915, which undermines Kitchener, who has already had clashes with the irascible Winston in years gone by. In the end the naval minister is told to put a stop to these continental excursions. "These meetings," Asquith wrote to Churchill, "have in K's opinion already produced profound friction between French and himself and between French's staff and his staff, which it is most desirable to avoid."[61] As for Kitchener, he is even more blunt. He writes to Churchill and suggests that he might like to replace him as War Minister and have done with it.

Then there is the meddlesome influence of General Sir Henry Wilson, whom the King has no time for at all, thinking him devious. He is an experienced staff officer, close to French, and an enemy of Kitchener. "In front of even junior officers he poured ridicule on Kitchener as well as on any of his schemes with which he did not agree, and did his best to poison the mind of the temperamentally suspicious and excitable Commander in Chief."[62] Kitchener reviles him as: "arrogant, presumptuous, impatient, giving to scheming."[63] French knows that Wilson is trouble, but thinks in his current position on his own staff, he is harmless.

Amidst all of this turmoil, most of Belgium is in enemy hands, as are vital industrial towns in northern France. Not to mention, parts of the front line are uncomfortably close to Paris, Calais and the English Channel. The Allies have got to try and evict the German Army, and they have got to defeat it decisively, otherwise the Kaiser's men might live to fight another day. For His Majesty's troops, what transpires in March 1915 to this end is a plan to attack at Neuve Chapelle; Britain's first attempt to dislodge the Kaiser's men from their now entrenched positions by breaching his lines and sending men flooding into the gap to overcome them. Due to the friction between them, Kitchener makes little attempt to intervene with French's tactical planning. Through a third party

58   Asquith: *The Autobiography of Margot Asquith,* p.127.
59   Holmes: *The Little Field Marshal: A Life of Sir John French,* p.255.
60   RA/PS/PS/GV/C/Q/2522/2/17.
61   Jenkins: *Churchill,* p.262.
62   Cassar: *Kitchener: Architect of Victory,* p.265.
63   Ibid., p.229.

he makes certain suggestions, but Sir John says in response that he would like to put the War Minister up against a wall and shoot him.

The outcome of the fighting in France in 1915 does nothing to salvage the King's opinion of Sir John French. The initial bombardment of artillery shells at Neuve Chapelle is like nothing previously seen in the history of warfare. It paves the way for the infantry to carry German trenches and the village itself, but they are unable to exploit initial success. Any further attempts to displace the enemy fail. Within a week Asquith has told the King "that there was evidence of a regrettable want of cooperation between the French and British armies."[64] Sir John French claims a victory, which it is not, and so he looks foolish when the truth emerges. At Aubers Ridge a few weeks later the infantry fail to take their allotted objectives. Another attempt, at Festubert, follows and is disastrous. As well as these offensive failures, at Ypres the Germans are causing heavy casualties and introducing new horrors such as gas warfare to the Western Front. And the French are no better off. Costly attacks up and down their front cause tens of thousands of wasteful casualties by the middle of 1915 with paltry gains to show for them.

There are seemingly other options as to how best to conduct the war in 1915, and two clearly divergent opinions emerge. One, with which the King concurs, is that the war will only be won on the Western Front. The other is that the issue should be forced somewhere else. As the year unfolds, the King becomes more and more an avid Westerner. "I consider this war will be lost or won in the main theatres of war," he writes to his uncle in Canada.

> I mean in France, in Russia and in Italy, and the British Empire must make haste and concentrate all our strength and energy to produce as strong an army as possible to take the offensive in France… and the Allies must deliver their attacks simultaneously and… the Central Powers I am sure will not be able to stand the strain.[65]

An additional option is championed by the likes of Churchill and Lloyd George; and Asquith is not completely opposed to this, but he makes a prophetic statement: "There are two fatal things in war; one is to push blindly against a stone wall, the other is to scatter and divide your forces in a number of separate and disconnected operations. We are in great danger of committing both blunders."[66] There are several suggestions: attacks via Dalmatia, Syria, Borkum or Schleswig; but the one that prevails is an attempt to strike for Constantinople, via the Dardanelles and a peninsula named Gallipoli. Endeavours begin as a naval operation, for if seapower alone can secure a gateway to Constantinople, this will be a much cheaper victory. At this early stage the King monitors events keenly. "The *Ocean, Irresistible* have been sunk by floating mines… but crews were saved," he writes in his diary. "The French lost the Bouvet with all hands.[sic] We shall go on till we do get through whatever the losses may be."[67] But he observes the combined allied effort to force the Dardanelles fail, and so it is decided to commit further and land an army force there. In mid-March, the King bids an official farewell to Sir Ian Hamilton, who is to command it.

From France, Sir Douglas Haig will come to refer to the campaign as "almost like the canker of the Peninsula to Napoleon's armies."[68] An exhibition in tactical buffoonery, instead of pursuing one decisive scheme with which to land on the peninsula, conflicting ones are cobbled together so that the hastily envisaged Mediterranean Expeditionary Force attempts to carry out multiple, disjointed

64   RA PS/PSO/GV/C/R/213.
65   Rose: *King George V*, p.190.
66   (ed.) Brock: *H.H. Asquith: Letters to Venetia Stanley*, p.389.
67   RA GV/PRIV/GVD/1915 (20/3).
68   RA PS/PS/GV/C/Q/2521/V/131.

attacks at the same time. The lack of cohesion means that the Gallipoli landings at the end of April are a predictable disaster. "Every time Allied reserves arrived they were soon matched by Turkish reinforcements and swiftly frittered away in attacks that had little or no military justification."[69]

But though the King does not approve of unfolding events in the Dardanelles, he displays far more disgust at the prospect of yet another front opening up in the east. He will never be as irate about Gallipoli as he is about the possibility of Britain's involvement in the Balkans. The idea of a Salonika expedition provokes hot, even violent debate in 1915. "To many it seemed the key which would unlock central Europe to the liberating armies of the Entente powers."[70] Others, including His Majesty, consider it a waste of resources and an unnecessary risk. On 28th January a War Council discusses sending a British force to the Balkans, assuming that Greece could thus be tempted to abandon her neutrality, therefore removing any objections to such a landing. In the Cabinet tensions flare. Lloyd George, who "without doubt… began the year with an over simplified view of Balkan politics,"[71] is adamant that Britain must stop Serbia being annihilated. Kitchener says that there are no men available and has no way of knowing whether a landing at Salonika would induce even one Balkan state to side with the Entente. Men could end up isolated, and heaven forbid, a further relief force may even have to go and get them. With the Western Front, Britain's safety and the defence of the Suez Canal in Egypt to consider, he was unwilling at that stage to commit to yet another force. His Majesty would rather offer possession of Cyprus to secure Greece as an ally. The idea has been raised by Asquith in his routine correspondence as having been discussed at some length by the Cabinet, and the King thinks it a far more sensible suggestion than sending troops. His Majesty wishes Asquith to know that despite Kitchener's opposition to such a scheme, he hopes "earnestly" that this possibility be examined further. "Strategically considered, His Majesty understands [Cyprus] is a failure: harbours impracticable and ships obliged to lie off six miles from the coast."[72] Asquith agrees that the transfer of the island to Greece may be the best all round solution if it gained Britain another ally

However, not to be dissuaded from sending troops, Lloyd George visits France. "His excuse for going to Paris was that he had to confer with his French and Russian opposite numbers… But he had no intention of confining himself to financial business, and much of his time was spent discussing grand strategy with leading French politicians."[73] After a subsequent conference with Grey and Asquith, a loose agreement has occurred between the three to the effect that they advocate the sending of a British force to Greece. The King is openly "rather startled by the idea of sending a British Army Corps to that country!" He raises a number of pertinent questions, already sure of the answers: "Have we got one ready and thoroughly equipped? Would not its transport and maintenance with a long line of communication be a serious undertaking? Is it strategically sound to employ 'detachments' unless it can be shown that they will be of greater use so employed than in operating in the main theatre of war? Is it certain that sending this force would bring in Greece and Romania?[74] In the end, the idea of giving away Cyprus comes to nothing, and when it transpires that the contemplated expedition will not induce Greece to enter the war on the side of the Allies, much to the King's relief, the idea of sending a force to the Balkans is shelved for now, but it is not the last that His Majesty will hear of Salonika.

69   Hart: *The Great War*, pp.173-174.
70   (ed.) Hammerton & Wilson: *The Great War Vol.II,* pp.1-2.
71   Grigg: *Lloyd George, From Peace to War 1912-1916*, p.209.
72   RA PS/PS/GV/C//838/2.
73   Grigg: *Lloyd George, From Peace to War 1912-1916*, pp.204-205.
74   RA PS/PS/GV/C/Q/838/4.

The truth is, that across the board Britain's leaders lack collectively the drive, or an appropriate sense of urgency with regard to the war. As well as watching the faltering campaigns across Europe play out, the King observes his ailing Government in a state moderate despair in the opening months of 1915. A typically petty scene occurs at a meeting in January. Churchill and Fisher have become embroiled in an argument over the possibility of an attack at Zeebrugge. At one point Fisher storms away from the table and stands with his back to his colleagues, refusing to return. Kitchener tries to appease him by joining him at the window and asking him what he is doing. Fisher says that he is going to resign, and Kitchener has to dash off a note to Asquith who has to come and mediate.

Kitchener himself comes under an increasing volley of fire. Though it would be wrong to say that all of the aggravation in the Cabinet is caused by the War Minister, much of the antagonism involves the Field Marshal in some capacity. Nobody can deny his achievement in bringing into existence the new armies, but "his vast stature, the slow congested movements of his body, face and mind, suggested an enormous and resplendent monolith… Even the least impressionable of Ministers could be cowed by the stare of affronted anger, or incomprehension, in those blue but disparate eyes."[75] He cannot delegate, and he is secretive, withholding information lest it leak and giving his colleagues the impression that he does not trust them. Lloyd George compares him to Herod, but Kitchener's opinion of his Cabinet colleagues isn't much better. "The blatant selfishness and intrigue of people whom he regarded as political lightweights appalled him."[76] In turn, his attitude irritated them, and he lacked the flair or coherency to rival them in debate. Like Fisher, Kitchener threatens them all with several resignations. "Some were provoked by unjust criticism or by exasperation when he failed to get his way; some were tactical devices for overcoming opposition."[77] He feels somewhat at ease with Asquith, who shows little of the increasing contempt for the War Minister that other Cabinet men do. But the only other individual with whom Kitchener is comfortable in discussion is the King, who he regards "as his liege lord to whom not only loyalty and honour were due but devotion and reverence." He considered His Majesty's friendship an honour, and visited the Palace repeatedly during any given week. "There, in the presence of congenial company, he found temporary relief from the suffocating atmosphere of political intrigue."[78]

And the King remains determined to stand by his War Minister. In London, Kitchener has been living in a borrowed house. Though it is beautiful, with a chronically bad leg he finds the stairs there extremely difficult to deal with. His Majesty decides that he wants to lend him York House, which is eminently more suitable. The idea had a dual appeal, as it would give the King a method to distance the Royal family from the cumbersome relief fund, which was currently installed there, if it was needed for another purpose. Ponsonby is against the idea, not only because Kitchener receives a £5,000 salary, but as it would suggest favouritism for this Minister. The Lord Chamberlain's office completely disagrees. Had Kitchener not willingly given up his job and his official residence, including his furniture, in Egypt the instant his country required it of him and taken a job he did not want? Also, "K is no parliamentary hack, he hates and despises all politics and politicians of all creeds. The offer to him could never be construed into a precedent for hereafter, for he is apart from party and all normal position."[79] Stamfordham thinks there is no harm in it under these circumstances. "It would be a gracious act of the Sovereign to place at his disposal during his tenure of office unoccupied rooms in St. James's Palace. It would be a recognition of what he has done and is doing, it would rather enable him to live close to his work and within handy reach of

75   Nicolson: *King George V: His Life and Reign,* p.260.
76   Cassar: *Kitchener: Architect of Victory,* p.141.
77   Ibid., p.256.
78   Ibid., p.190.
79   RA PPTO/PP/GV/PP4/67/20.

Buckingham Palace… I should like HM to do what would be a gracious and popular act and one which need create no precedent for the conditions will, please God, not arise again.[80] The offer is made, and Kitchener gratefully accepts. His Sovereign's support is everything to him. His private secretary writes later to the King of how often he has heard Kitchener say "that the King's unstinted and unswerving support enabled him (and perhaps alone enabled him) to achieve what he did during the Great War."[81]

No nation expected to fire as many shells they were forced to in the opening months of the war. In Britain, the Boer War provides no precedent, "for during the whole of the two and three quarters years for which it lasted the amount of ammunition used was not much more than was spent by our artillery alone in a fortnight in and around Neuve Chapelle." The expenditure, according to all existing expertise, is lunacy; and yet spend it armies do, because warfare is changing before their eyes and the rules that armies have lived by no longer apply.

The War Office call in the great British armament firms and introduce a system of sub-contracting, involving nearly 3000 companies, but the deliveries do not come in on time. It can be argued that Sir John French exaggerates the shell shortage "to shift attention away from his own tactical shortcomings,"[82] but others at GHQ are left genuinely exasperated over War Office pledges to supply a certain amount of ammunition and their failure to keep their promises. "The ball is at our feet and we are unable to kick it," writes one officer. "And it is a disgrace for a large industrial country like England that it cannot do as well as France does. The ammunition supply required is not in my opinion in excess of what could be done if the country chooses to do it. If the country does not choose to do it then it does not deserve to win."[83]

The Government, and Kitchener in particular, is not oblivious to their plight. Asquith establishes that whilst the army in the field had multiplied four to five times in numbers, the supply of ammunition has increased nineteen-fold. He argues that there is a difference in negligently failing to produce munitions and failing to keep up with a wholly unprecedented trend in warfare taking place in front of their very eyes. The types of shells required are changing too, to add to difficulties, but, he says, his Government has engaged more firms, diluted the skilled workforce, brought women into industry and placed orders abroad. Britain had produced 3,000 heavy shells a month in July 1914, and by spring 1915, that number had risen to 400,000. But Asquith's arguments fail to comprehend the requirements of prolonged, static warfare on an immense scale such as that which his country is facing. In short, though production of shells has been massively increased, Britain is still utterly failing to exploit her industrial capability to supply the war effort abroad.

And so tensions rise within the Cabinet. Huge responsibilities for negotiating and placing contracts, inspecting firms, quality control and researching new avenues for supply have been placed on the War Office, and it is failing to keep up. In March, Lloyd George threatens to resign unless control of munitions is taken out of Kitchener's hands. Despite the fact that in peace-time he had "done his best to starve [the Army] of equipment and material essential to victory,"[84] he believes that it is Kitchener's neglect that has failed to create enough ammunition with dire consequences for the man in the front line. He had a stick with which to beat the Secretary of State for War and he fully employed it to his own ends. The prestige of Kitchener's position far outweighs that of his

80   RA PPTO/PP/GV/PP4/67/3.
81   Cassar: *Kitchener: Architect of Victory,* p.261.
82   Simkins: *Kitchener's Army: The Raising of the New Armies 1914-1916,* p.133.
83   RA PS/PS/GV/C/Q/2522/3/172.
84   Cassar: *Kitchener: Architect of Victory,* p.341.

as Chancellor of the Exchequer. Any ambitious politician will quite rightly aspire to higher office, "but in the process of advancing his political career he showed himself to be destitute of all moral qualities. He not only resorted to methods of chicanery without parallel in the recent annals of British politics, but placed his own interests, ahead of those of the nation."[85] The Leader of the Opposition remarked that "in matters of office and power, Lloyd George was a self-seeker and a man who considered no interests except his own."[86] "He couldn't see a belt without hitting below it," comments Margot Asquith."[87]

There is no doubt that Lloyd George is genuinely disillusioned with Asquith's war leadership. It cannot be denied that at this juncture, his unparalleled energy and determination is something that the British war effort desperately needs, or that his output in 1915 will be of huge benefit in bridging the gap between the improvements already made in ammunition manufacture and that which still needed to be accomplished to render the British Army an effective fighting machine. But initial attempts to address the issue at the beginning of April lead to a "royal row" between Lloyd George and Kitchener with both threatening to quit their Cabinet posts. Lloyd George is apt to get personal and says things "that Kitchener will be more than human to forget"[88] At one point the Postmaster-General has to fling himself in front of the door to prevent the War Minister from walking out through it. "In his customary fashion, Asquith… tried to avert a head-on clash in the Cabinet by effecting a compromise but succeeded only in adding to the confusion, since, under the new system, neither Lloyd George nor Kitchener was wholly in control of munitions output."[89]

Colonel Repington is a complicated character with little regard for the Royal Family and vice versa. He had had more than one run in with Edward VII. After a high profile affair with a married woman he was forced to leave the army, and after King George's father refused twice to reinstate him, a venomous article subsequently appeared in The Times - where he found employment as a military correspondent - about the King, that had his fingerprints all over it. In the middle of May 1915, Repington produces a damning piece about the shell shortage. The King is furious. Worse, it appears that Sir John French has helped him produce it.

The Commander in Chief had already angered His Majesty in March, with a press interview in which he made inappropriate military disclosures. Stamfordham interviews Asquith in an attempt to find out who is culpable for this new article, without much success. French has undoubtedly provided Repington with information, as well as various politicians. He certainly wouldn't be sorry to see the back of Kitchener, and he is not above scheming; but it appears in this case that his involvement was probably more misguided and hapless than vindictive. The problem is that The Times, as well as the Daily Mail, are owned by Lord Northcliffe, who "was disturbingly powerful." One critic has described him as "the victim of megalomania… unscrupulous, dictatorial, capricious and opinionated."[90] He is egged on by Lloyd George, who is attempting to use the shell shortage and oratory condemning the War Office to press his own case to take control of munitions. Northcliffe also has his own axe to grind so far as Kitchener is concerned and the matter quickly escapes French's amateur attempts at intrigue and spirals out of his control. From a piece condemning the shell shortage grows a press vendetta against Lord Kitchener in which he is embroiled. Both of Northcliffe's newspapers run editorials damning the Government for a lack of shells, and there is a piece advocating Kitchener's removal from the Cabinet. One acquaintance claims that he sees

85   Ibid., p.343.
86   Ibid., p.344.
87   Ibid., p.344.
88   Asquith: Memories and Reflections. Vol. II, pp.73-74.
89   (ed.) Hammerton & Wilson: The Great War Vol. V, p.131.
90   Cassar: Kitchener: Architect of Victory, p.351.

Northcliffe at the Ritz one afternoon and that he told him that he meant to "go on attacking Lord Kitchener day in, day out, until he had driven him from office,"[91] and the King declares that he is now holds *The Times* in great contempt.

French comes off worst, with some Cabinet Ministers suggesting that he be recalled in disgrace for his part in this press campaign. But Northcliffe suffers too. Certain clubs in London banish his publications, the circulation of one fell by 200,000. "3,000 members of the Stock Exchange assembled and, following a bonfire of the Northcliffe papers, gave three cheers for Kitchener.[92] Northcliffe abandons his smear campaign, Lloyd George publicly disassociates himself from the whole affair, and Kitchener remains silent. The King responds by appointing his friend a Knight of the Order of the Garter.

"Roses at Richmond"

At the same time as the shell crisis, and as the Repington article makes its appearance, the King is also dealing with critical fallout at the Admiralty. "Mount Fisher, from whom… dangerous rumblings and puffs of smoke had been emerging for several months, finally went into full operation on Saturday, May 15th."[93] The only surprising thing is that the matter has not come to a head before now. Fisher has at last met his match, and having verbally crushed his assailants for decades, he cannot stand up to Churchill. "He is always *convincing* me,"[94] he complains. "They were like a husband and wife who could not live without each other but who could not live together either."[95] The King has of course anticipated this, but he finds these two flogging each other horribly distasteful. The Admiral is always threatening to quit the Admiralty for some reason. "Old Jack Fisher seriously proposed… to shoot all the German prisoners here, and when Winston refused to embrace this statesmanlike suggestion (which would have led in turn to the massacre of all our poor men in Germany) sent in a formal written resignation of his office."[96] At the end of January both men sat in front of the Prime Minister like naughty schoolboys and aired their mutual grievances. Fisher is exhausted. He has been discovered sleeping in his office. He writes daily to Churchill, expressing his desire to return to the cultivation of his roses at Richmond. He becomes increasingly irate about the Dardanelles, but just how much of his final hysteria is genuinely down to this, or whether it is an excuse for him to get out of the Admiralty is open to interpretation. In April his protestations get louder. "You are just simply eaten up with the Dardanelles and can't think of anything else," he writes to Churchill. "Damn the Dardanelles! They'll be our grave!"[97] He then sends Asquith a note on 12th May, saying that he should have resigned when the Dardanelles first came up and that he is being dragged through the campaign against his will. Two days later he announces that he was against it from the beginning, though evidence for this is scant. The following day, Churchill is walking past Whitehall when he is accosted by a secretary who tells him that Fisher has resigned. Again. He adds: "I think he means it this time."[98]

The letter that accompanies this revelation is bizarre. "I have come to the regretted conclusion I am unable to remain any longer as your colleague. It is undesirable in the public interests to go into details… I am off to Scotland at once so as to avoid all questionings." But Fisher does not go

91   Beaverbrook: *Politicians & the War 1914-1916,* pp.95-96.
92   Cassar: *Kitchener: Architect of Victory,* p.356.
93   Jenkins: *Churchill,* p.269.
94   Ibid., p.260.
95   Ibid., p.256.
96   (ed.) Brock: *H.H. Asquith: Letters to Venetia Stanley,* p.359.
97   Jenkins: *Churchill,* p.263.
98   Ibid., pp.270-272.

to Scotland. He occupies a room at the Charing Cross Hotel, some 300 yards from the Admiralty, and hides. Churchill is not inclined to take him entirely seriously, but Asquith orders a search. Continental boat trains are checked, his wife is contacted in Norfolk. The Prime Minister issues a handwritten note "commanding Fisher, in the name of the King, to return to his duty." He is run to ground that afternoon, "carried in in one of the retrievers' mouths and dropped bloodshot and panting at the door of the Cabinet Room."[99] He seems calm enough, but he utterly refuses to work with Churchill again.

His Majesty finds out all that has happened the following day, and he is mortified. The situation only becomes more ridiculous. Fisher, it seems, has gone barking mad. He wants to be on a similar footing to Kitchener at the War Office and so he issues a set of demands. "If the following conditions are agreed to," he begins, "I can guarantee the successful termination of the war." He insists that Churchill is put out of the Cabinet. He wants an entirely new board at the Admiralty too. He also requires "complete professional charge of the war at sea, with the absolute disposal of the fleet and the appointment of all officers of all ranks whatsoever," and "that I should have the sole absolute authority for all new constructional and dockyard work of whatever sort whatsoever, and complete control of the civil establishments of the Navy."[100]

Stamfordham is keeping the King updated for he is away attending to war work. As to the demands, he says that: "the Prime Minister thinks this paper indicates signs of mental aberration!"[101] His Majesty is livid that an Admiral would run away in a time of war, or pretend to. After some investigation, it is postulated at the palace that the First Sea Lord is appointed by patent, that nobody new will assume the post until one is issued, and so it follows that Fisher is illegally absent from his post. "The King thinks it important that Lord Fisher's resignation should be accepted before the new First Lord is appointed." Otherwise His Majesty thinks that it will fall on the new incumbent, as his first act, to get rid of Fisher, which the old sea dog "would not fail to make use of in the press and elsewhere."[102]

The resignation is finally accepted, for nobody is going to entertain Fisher's demands for a moment. By this point he is genuinely in Scotland. From there, he attempts shamelessly to get into the King's good graces, first arguing that he took the only course of action available to him, but asking His Majesty to treat his letter as secret. The King agrees, and politely thanks Fisher for "the great services which you have rendered to the navy while you have been at the Admiralty."[103] After all he has gone, that is all that matters. But taking this as an invitation to continue the correspondence, Fisher sends the King a lengthy account of all that he has contributed since his return, including a list of almost 600 ships. "Such an Armada, a veritable armada it is has never in the memory of man of the annals of the world been devised and constructed in so short a time as they will all be fighting next spring."[104] By 4th July he was asking for an audience with His Majesty for some other matter in which he wished to press his opinion, but for the King, Fisher's outrageous behaviour at a moment when it was thought that the German Fleet was about to put to sea was unforgivable. In future he will flush red and fly into a rage when speaking of the incident. "If I had been in London when Fisher was found," he later says, "I should have told him that he should have been hanged at the yardarm for desertion of his post in the face of the enemy." Publicly, the King was too much of a gentleman to make derisive comments about his enemy. Fisher was not so gracious, and did so

99   Ibid.
100   Churchill: The World Crisis, p.468.
101   RA PS/PSO/GV/C/K/770/3.
102   BD: MS Asquith A.1 4 #118.
103   RA PS/PSO/GV/C/G/775/11.
104   RA PS/PSO/GV/C/G/775/12.

at every opportunity. In December 1916 he wrote that "Kings will be cheap soon!" And he would continue to refer to the King and Queen as "Futile and Fertile."[105]

In the spring of 1915, the shell crisis and Fisher's resignation help generate a complete political crisis that leaves the King staring into the oblivion as far as his Government is concerned, in the midst of what is turning out to be a year of constant failure. The Cabinet is too large to be efficient in the midst of a war, with 22 cumbersome opinions vying for attention at every turn, incapable of swift decision. Lord Esher, a long time royal confidant, comments that if the country was being slow to realise just what is required of a nation embroiled in a modern war, they are taking their lead from the Prime Minister. Asquith largely maintains his pre-war schedule, retreating to the country for long weekends to escape the pressures of Westminster. He is at a wedding whilst the search is on for Lord Fisher and before the situation at the Admiralty was resolved he was again away from town. "If I live to write the history of this war!!" Rants Lord Esher, "I shall point to… 10th May, a day when we were fighting for our existence in Flanders. When the coming of Italy hung in the balance, when the Board of the Admiralty was crumbling to pieces. When the biggest soldier of the Emperor was hesitating whether he could carry on. And the King's Prime Minister was out of town playing golf."[106]

The public has begun to realise that the war is not being conducted effectively. The shell crisis, the disarray in dealing with interning enemy aliens, the failure of the Gallipoli campaign, a lack of progress on the Western Front, all appear to highlight mismanagement at the highest levels. Not only among the opposition but also amongst political supporters of the Cabinet, there is "a growing feeling that the time had come for the constitution of a Government of Public Safety which should combine the best brains of both political parties."[107] Within seven days, Asquith has to go from disregarding the idea of a coalition, to accepting that the shell scandal and Fisher's resignation have made his Government untenable. On 17th May, the Prime Minister announces in the House that he is considering reconstructing the Government on a broader basis. On the same day he tells Stamfordham that this is a necessity, a conclusion that His Majesty has already mooted with Asquith's assistant the week before.

By Saturday the King returns to London and Asquith arrives at the palace to bring him up to speed with the formation of his coalition. Kitchener looks set to remain, and the King sincerely hopes that former Prime Minister Arthur Balfour will take the reins at the Admiralty, in place of Churchill, who he would like to see the back of, and "who has become impossible."[108] He also urges the Prime Minister to form a new Ministry of Munitions to spare Kitchener some of his terrifying workload. He wants Lloyd George to be put in charge of it, as he thinks him in 1915 as "most sensible on things in general."[109] "He spoke strongly to the Prime Minister in favour of giving the fullest support to Lord Kitchener: also with regard to friction with GHQ and declared his determination to support Lord Kitchener to the utmost of his powers."[110] Asquith remains to go into fine detail as to the various appointments, and why each man has been selected for each post. The King is generally approves, especially when he learns that Churchill will be given a minor Cabinet role, as he considers him far less dangerous inside the Government than scheming against it. Churchill, unimpressed, writes in later years that "Asquith did not hesitate to break his cabinet

105   Rose: *King George V,* pp.187-189.
106   RA PS/PS/GV/C/Q/724/25.
107   (ed.) Hammerton & Wilson: *The Great War Vol V,* pp.311-312.
108   RA GV/PRIV/GVD/1915 (22/5).
109   Ibid., 20/9.
110   RA PS/PSO/GV/C/K/770/11.

up… end the political lives of half his colleagues… and sail on victoriously at the head of a coalition government. Not all done by kindness! Not all by rosewater! These were the convulsive struggles of a man of action and of ambition at death grips with events."[111] He also claimed that Asquith had thrown the Lord Chancellor, Haldane, to the wolves. This did stick in the Prime Minister's throat, but Haldane had once referred to Germany as his spiritual home and he had been suffering a similar maniacal campaign of hate as that endured by Louis of Battenburg prior to his stepping down at the Admiralty. Sir Edward Grey remained at the Foreign Office, but was disgusted by Haldane's removal, and the King takes it badly too.

Kultur

When His Majesty has time to contemplate the enemy in 1915, as opposed to warring factions at home, he finds it extremely hard to stomach the manner in which the Great War begins to abandon all semblance of humanity and decency, of what is deemed acceptable between warring nations. In July 1900, the Kaiser had addressed German troops and said that: "whoever falls into your hands is forfeit to you, just as 1,000 years ago the Huns under King Attila made a name for themselves which is still mighty in tradition and story."[112] Hence the Germans are referred to as Huns. The term *Kultur* mocks a German ideal, that Germanic civilisation is superior, and therefore it is the duty of the Kaiser and his realm to bring it to the rest of the world. It becomes a term used to represent what the Allies, and the King, consider to be acts of atrocity.

What was referred to as the Rape of Belgium in 1914 was epitomised by events at Louvain some 30 miles to the southeast of Antwerp. It was the Belgian equivalent of Oxford, with magnificent gothic churches stuffed with priceless art, a beautiful medieval town hall that was an architectural wonder, and its University. The priceless library, frequented by the likes of Erasmus and Sir Thomas More was the jewel in its crown. The King hears first-hand descriptions of how Louvain was brutally destroyed by shellfire, how the town's inhabitants cowered in their cellars as it burned. Witnesses claim that bodies of those murdered were strewn throughout the smoke-filled streets. There are tales of executions, of piles of furniture that were torched. Though certain German soldiers are said to have helped to protect the town hall from the flames, the library, filled with irreplaceable manuscripts and volumes, was destroyed. A professor of the university, standing in his garden, saw charred fragments of priceless illuminated manuscripts floating past him on a summer breeze.

In Spring 1915, the Germans also unleash poisonous gas onto the Western Front. As General Rawlinson points out in a letter to the palace, "its effect is no doubt cruel to the last degree… but I am not sure that it has been yet proved to be a weapon of great military value." Its use is regarded as spiteful as more than anything else. "It is a horrible weapon. The results of which are agony and torture."[113] The King sees this terror for himself. On 31st May Their Majesties visit the Cambridge Hospital, where victims of gas are housed in a surgical ward, giving them "an opportunity off seeing the terrible suffering caused."[114] They spend an hour and a half talking to these men about what they have endured; agonising pain, wet lungs, the feeling of drowning on dry land.

But what the King finds utterly incomprehensible is the encroachment of the war on the Home Front, something that Britain has not suffered since the 17th Century; the threat to civilian life and property away from the battlefields. The sight of German prisoners of war brings home to His Majesty the human aspect of the conflict as much as his visits to hospitals, and his sympathy extends

111   Churchill: *Great Contemporaries*, p.122.
112   (ed.) Hammerton & Wilson: *The Great War Vol V,* p.401.
113   RA PS/PS/GV/C/Q/2522/30.
114   The Standard 1/6/15.

to those interned as well as those recovering from wounds. He has a preoccupation throughout the entirety of the war with prisoners of war, whatever nationality and wherever they are detained. He is not in favour of the initial suggestion in the Cabinet that German prisoners be brought to Britain instead of being handed over to the French for internment there. Asquith argues that as a matter of international law, it is doubtful that Britain could wash their hands of their custodial obligations, or those they had assumed for their treatment by capturing them in the first place. "But," he tells the palace, "further, as a matter of policy, the knowledge that German prisoners will be retained by us will greatly facility exchanges, and will safeguard the peoples' treatment of our prisoners in Germany."[115] The King relents.

The internment of now enemy civilians in Britain who happened to reside in the country when war was declared was a highly charged issue in early 1915. The indiscriminate rounding up of aliens had been approached without proper attention to planning or continuing logistics. Asquith's report to His Majesty in November 1914 stated that there were 12,000 men interned in Britain. The King was alarmed by seeming lack of attention being paid to their welfare, for wives and children had been disregarded, many of whom were British by birth. It has thus been decided that unless there was actual suspicion on an individual, they would be left at large for now, whilst Local Government Boards were to attend to the relief of the families of those interned.

When it comes to those that find themselves in German captivity, His Majesty spends the war obsessively gathering information as to their treatment and protesting to all who might listen when it comes to trying to intervene on their behalf. In December 1914 he rants at the dinner table about the plight of his interned troops. This outburst was likely fuelled by a report that compiled multiple sources claiming that British prisoners are singled out for brutal treatment above their French counterparts. A French priest says that he saw German soldiers kicking prisoners in the stomachs and hitting them over the back when they were on the ground. "The British are almost starved and such have been their tortures that thirty of them asked to be shot."[116]

The King speaks up for German prisoners as much as British. He sees men behind barbed wire at Frimley and has Stamfordham write a firm letter to the Prime Minister after he is told that they will live in tents throughout the winter. "His Majesty can hardly believe that such an arrangement is contemplated, for it would inevitably arouse public feeling in German if not in this country and probably react upon our prisoners [there]."[117] The King wants reassurances that this will not happen, and Kitchener is reminded of the principle too, that Britain should treat German prisoners as she would wish her own to be treated. This attitude extends to His Majesty's own family too. Prince Henry is invited to Camberley to see German prisoners who have arrived in Britain and he is keen. The King squashes the idea flat. He thinks the notion is in incredibly poor taste. How would you like it, he asks his son, "if you were a prisoner for people to come to stare at you as if you were a wild beast."[118]

His Majesty insists that two unfortunate members of Gottlieb's Band are released from internment, but he is far more concerned about the issue that arises over the captured crew of a German submarine in April 1915. His own Government have declared that given the unsavoury nature of their work, such prisoners are to be treated differently from other interned Germans. The King thought that a public announcement to this effect was an unsuitable course of action, "and fears that the German Government will be only too glad to have this excuse to make reprisals upon our officers and men imprisoned in Germany, whose lot in any case, judging from recent

---

115   RA PS/PSO/GV/C/ Q/870/2.
116   RA PS/PSO/GV/C/Q/989/6.
117   BD: MS Asquith A.1 4 #28.
118   Frankland: *Prince Henry, Duke of Gloucester,* p.35.

reports, is hard if not cruel."[119] His Majesty wants specifics as to how treatment will differ from ordinary prisoners. The men are split between detention quarters at Devonport and Chatham, and apparently well fed and provided for, but he is not placated. "In the King's opinion they have but obeyed orders, brutal and inhuman though those orders may be. In any case either they are criminals and should be tried and punished as such: or they are prisoners of war and ought to be treated accordingly." He disagrees with the principle that the Admiralty wants to decide their punishment based on their appraisal of their actions; and thinks that the regime is severe. "The King yields to no one in abominating the general conduct of the Germans throughout this war [but] deprecates the idea of reprisals and retaliation: he has always hoped that at the end of the war we shall as a nation stand before the world as having conducted it as far as possible with humanity and like gentlemen."[120] His Majesty has suggested that the American Embassy be invited to provide a report on the crew's treatment for the Germans, who are seething, but Churchill refuses.

The situations escalates exactly as His Majesty fears when 39 British officers in captivity are withdrawn from their quarters and incarcerated in a fortress. "We are now locked day and night in separate cells," one of them writes to the palace in an appeal for intervention, "except for one hour's walk round a small yard. We are not allowed to speak to each other, and are treated in every way like criminals… I hope you will forgive me bothering you… It is very hard for officers who have only done their duty and no criminal act to be treated in this way."[121] The King, with individual officers now appealing directly to him for assistance, despairs. "His Majesty appeals to you," Stamfordham now writes to Balfour, who has replaced Churchill as First Lord of the Admiral, "The King knows how difficult it is to give in, but we are dealing with people who have no regard for justice, mercy, or righteousness, and for the sake of humanity and pity upon our gallant soldiers His Majesty hopes that the German conditions - unfair, unjust and unreasonable though they may be - may be compiled with."[122]

Asquith is now aware of how strongly the King feels, and reports on 5th June that the Cabinet has discussed the matter of the German submariners at some length. "The balance of opinion was that their separate treatment should be discontinued."[123] When 25 new members of a submarine crew are captured, to the King's relief, it forces the Government's hand. "Differential Treatment Abandoned," reads one headline. Balfour rises in the House of Commons to give his maiden speech as First Lord of the Admiralty and the Government backs down. "There has not been any substantial difference between the treatment of German submarine prisoners and that of other prisoners of war. As there seems, however, to be some doubt in the public mind on the subject… arrangements are being made under which the treatment will… be… absolutely identical."[124] His speech is cheered.

The first successful attacks on British soil in the Great War do not come from the air. The German Navy opt for sending fast cruisers the short distance to Britain's east coast under cover of fog. "They could set out at six in the evening, arrive off our coast at seven in the morning, open fire as soon as dawn showed them their target and retire at full speed at the first sign of danger."[125] On 16th December 1914 they did just this with devastating effect. It was the first time that Britons had been attacked by an enemy on their own soil since the mid-seventeenth century. "Yesterday morning,"

119   BD: MS Asquith A.1. 4 #100-101.
120   BD: MS Asquith A.1. 4 #94-6.
121   BD: MS Asquith A.1. 4 #109.
122   RA PS/PSO/GV/C/Q/760/31.
123   RA PS/PSO/GV/C/R/226.
124   RA PS/PSO/GV/C/Q/760/35.
125   (ed.) Hammerton & Wilson: *The Great War Vol. VII*, pp.357-358.

the King wrote in his diary, "four large German cruisers… appeared off the east coast of Yorkshire about 8 o'clock and shelled Hartlepool and Scarborough for forty minutes, doing considerable damage." He has been told that there are about 100 victims; men, women and children, and he is outraged. "This," he fumes, "is German "Kultur."[126] Hartlepool had awoken to the sound of shells and watched as three ships came within two miles of the shore and opened fire. Women ran into the streets in their nightgowns, a dense crowd of barefooted civilians rushed about in disarray.

> One sad case was that of the wife of a soldier, who sought to make her escape with her six children. A shell burst nearby, three of the children were killed… two of the other children were injured and the mother was maimed. She was carried to hospital, where she lay for weeks before she was told of her children's deaths.[127]

Scarborough was hit too. The upper floors of the Grand Hotel were decimated, as was the suburb of Falsgrave. Then the perpetrators moved on to Whitby before escaping into the fog. The crews responsible are dubbed *Baby Killers,* and Britain is plunged into a state of shock and outrage. The attack boosted recruiting. "Men of Yorkshire were urged to "Shew the enemy that Yorkshire will exact a full penalty for this COWARDLY SLAUGHTER."[128] Neutral countries think that Germany owes an explanation for bombarding undefended seaside towns such as Scarborough and Whitby, but German newspapers are defiant. "We think we may say that - the English part of the world apart - people everywhere will have heard with satisfaction and just Schadenfreude of this… punishment of the great sea robber who oppresses the whole world."[129]

As if this was not disgusting enough, the King is then utterly repulsed by the ensuing air war conducted by Germany over British soil. Asquith warns him as early as September 1914 that there is a danger of enemy airships losing projectiles on targets at home. Germany was known to have more than a dozen on the outbreak of war, and the location of their apparent construction was only 280 miles from Yarmouth. "It was obvious that, given suitable weather conditions, a Zeppelin could not only cross to our coast and return, but could sail over large areas of England unless we had some means to check it."[130]

The first bomb ever to be dropped on Britain fell on Dover on Christmas Eve, 1914. "It was taken for granted that the main purpose… would be to attempt to drop explosives on harbours, docks, ships and military positions." And London has plenty of targets. Paris has already been raided and it only follows that England might be next. In 1915 the Kaiser's airships are ready to start raiding Great Britain in force, and they begin by edging their way towards the east coast. After a quiet period, a party of two appear, looking like two drifting, bright stars, dropping nearly twenty bombs near Sandringham. At Yarmouth the quick-thinking authorities hear the mayhem and cut the electricity supply at the mains, but an elderly lady and a middle-aged shoemaker become the first two Britons killed by an aerial attack. The King and Queen arrive at York Cottage a week later to find safety measures being enacted. Two naval officers and 19 men now constitute an aerial defence detachment at Sandringham, armed with two searchlights and two guns. They are to be present whenever Their Majesties are in residence. Before shooting one morning, the King also visits three officers and 133 men of the Grenadier Guards quartered nearby. Afterwards His Majesty goes to see more local guns and searchlights. On 29th January the alarm is raised and these arrangements

126   RA GV/PRIV/GVD/1914 17/11.
127   (ed.) Hammerton & Wilson: *The Great War Vol. VII*, pp.378-389.
128   Ibid., p.384.
129   Ibid., pp.389-396.
130   Ibid., p.360.

are first put to the test. Aircraft have been spotted heading north, and officers and men run to their posts. "About nine we heard that the noise of a motor boat had been taken for aircraft!" Exclaimed Queen Mary. "So peace reigned again."[131] To the King, it all seems rather an overreaction. Ponsonby has protested on His Majesty's behalf at what he is concerned is a waste of the country's resources, but on the advice of the naval authorities, who have been placed in charge of the country's aerial defence, the King backs down. When he arrives at Windsor for Easter Court some weeks later he inspects another detachment, "a section of the Naval anti-aircraft guns in motor cars, which have come here to protect us from Zeppelins."[132]

Whilst raids creep closer to London, the enemy's press boasts that the capital has "not yet felt the power of the German air menace."[133] In an outburst, the Kaiser has declared, "that there would be no peace before England is defeated and destroyed. Only amidst the ruins of London will I forgive Georgie."[134] One faction is concerned about how such a campaign might look to neutral countries, but many Germans concur with bombing Britain's cities. The idea that civilian targets might escape is fading, and a mixture of naval men, Special Constables and Boy Scouts are to protect and warn the capital's population. There are anti-aircraft personnel at Tower Bridge and Regent's Park. The nearest guns to the Palace sit at Green Park, Marble Arch, the Foreign Office, but they are inadequate to combat airships and their falling shells threaten to do as much damage to London as they do to protect it. Museums remain open, but valuable pieces are placed in the cellars. A special plan is worked out to protect Buckingham Palace in the event of an air raid and is sanctioned by the Office of Works. "The street lights of London were subdued, sky signs were obliterated, and householders were ordered to darken the windows of their lighted rooms a night time. The rays of searchlights wheeled over the London sky."[135] One slightly misguided minister has remarked to the King that if Buckingham Palace were hit it would have a stimulating effect on the people. "Yes," the King quips, "but rather a depressing effect on me."[136]

The King is paying another visit to Aldershot when the capital suffers its first air raid on 31st May and five people are killed in East London. The casualties may be few, but a hundred bombs demonstrate that after centuries of isolation, safe behind the screen of the Royal Navy, Britain is now vulnerable. Like something from a science fiction novel, death rains from above. "Suddenly you realise that the biggest city in the world has become the night battlefield in which seven million harmless men, women and children live." Writes one newspaper. "Here is war at the very heart of civilisation threatening all the millions of things that human hearts and human minds have created.... If the men up there in the sky think they are terrifying London they are wrong. They are only making England white-hot mad"[137] Londoners are determined not to be beaten, but Germany rejoices. Britain, the newspapers say, have forced them to fight for their lives. "We shall not allow these wonderful weapons, which German intelligence invented, to grow rusty," says the *Cologne Gazette*.[138]

The King's first experience of an air raid comes on 13th October when at about half past nine bombs begin to fall on the West End, along with water ballast that causes a light, misty spray on London's streets. Shows are mid-performance in theatres.

131   RA PRIV/QMD/1915 (27-31/1).
132   RA GV/PRIV/GVD/1915 (3/4).
133   (ed.) Hammerton & Wilson: *The Great War Vol.VII*, p.10.
134   Stibbe: in Leadership in Conflict, p.272.
135   (ed.) Hammerton & Wilson: *The Great War Vol.VII*, p.2.
136   Ibid., p.178.
137   Ibid., pp.27-28.
138   Ibid., p.5-7.

There was a sudden crackle of anti-aircraft gunfire, and simultaneously a dreadful sound…a sound like no other on earth…the mournful wail created by the velocity of a descending bomb… The streets were pandemonium… There was a ring of ambulance bells and the imperious clang of fire alarms - and above it all, a terrible, insistent thudding; more bombs, death, destruction… They held every card up there. It was so easy for them.[139]

The Royal Household have been instructed to get away from the windows in the event of a raid, but this does nothing to suppress the King's enthusiasm for observing a Zeppelin first hand. With the Queen he rushes onto a balcony at the palace. He can hear the Green Park anti-aircraft gun firing at it, can see the beams of the searchlights playing across the sky; but any airship is on the wrong side of the palace to be observed. Their Majesties arrive at Charing Cross Hospital and the King is both saddened and livid to see the suffering caused to civilians. "A good many have died already, several have lost legs and arms, it is simple murder and the Germans are very proud of it."[140]

King George, a sailor, is no less disturbed by the use of the submarines. In 1915 Germany declares the waters around Britain a war zone, and threatens to sink whoever sails within it, including merchant ships. All of this flies in the face of centuries of maritime law. Captured vessels should be taken to port, crew and passengers are supposed to be safely removed before sinking their ship can be justified. "It is simply disgusting that Naval Officers could do such things," writes the King, but he is similarly unimpressed with the practices brought in to evade enemy submarines. One of these is removing the British ensign and flying a neutral flag instead. "He said he would rather be sunk under his own flag."[141] And His Majesty is determined to discount the policy of retaliation both at sea and in terms of civilian air raids. He wants Britain to emerge from this war with her head held high; a brave statement to make in the first half of 1915 and one that becomes increasingly difficult to believe in. At first the German submarine threat amounts to very little in the way of losses, but on 7th May *Lusitania* is torpedoed off of Kinsale, resulting in the deaths of almost 1,200 people, including some 100 children, more than two dozen of them infants. In Germany medals are struck commemorating the sinking. The King finds out the following morning and is stunned. "It is a most dastardly crime and has created a great sensation here."[142] Submarine warfare, alleged mistreatment of prisoners, gas, Zeppelins, conspired to prompt bouts of violence; a "sporadic and local spirit of lawlessness which showed itself in organised attacks on shops believed to be occupied by Germans. The whole country grew more and more anti-German as the war went on, and each successive outrage committed by the enemy on land or sea stirred the nation to a deeper detestation of Germany and everything German." After *Lusitania* "something like a pogrom" was instituted "against tradesmen with German names. Hundreds of so-called Hun-shops… were sacked by undiscerning mobs composed partly of honest people who could not restrain their anger and partly of hooligans who welcomed a pretext for looting." Violence does not go unpunished. "It should be added that both police and the local military authorities resisted and repressed these riots… and that the magistrates had no mercy on [those] who were brought before them after each outburst."[143]

139   Parker: *Gott Strafe England, Vol. I. 1914-1916,* pp.153-154.
140   RA GV/PRIV/GVD/1914 (16/10).
141   Rose: *King George V,* p.173.
142   RA GV/PRIV/GVD/1915 (8/5).
143   (ed.) Hammerton & Wilson: *The Great War Vol.XII,* pp.1-30.

Learning to Swim Without Getting Wet

One constant amongst continuing mayhem in 1915 for His Majesty are his more traditional, diplomatic functions, and there are new relationships to manage. When the war begins, the King and Queen are not particularly familiar with Belgian royalty, but now, not only are they Allies, but King Albert's heir, Prince Leopold has joined fifty or so Belgian boys at Eton College, refugees from prominent families; he is in the same house as Prince Henry, so that whenever Queen Elizabeth comes to England to see him, or bring him back to school, she stops by the palace on a social visit.

More important is the constant effort, canvassing even, that needs to be applied in pursuit of new Allies, and the King can play a significant role. It is a difficult game. Neutral nations are willing to exploit the desperation of those already embroiled in the war to extort the maximum benefits of participation for themselves, and this can count for more than which side they share most empathy with. His Majesty has little to do with attempting to effect the intervention of Bulgaria, save for monitoring the situation until she eventually sides with Germany and Austria-Hungary. He only hopes that Greece can be brought in on the side of the Allies to restore some kind of balance, and grows more anxious as situation in the Balkans becomes more complicated in 1915.

The most consistent canvassing action on His Majesty's part throughout the year concerns the prolonged, stressful attempts to help to secure Italy as an ally. Italy has an alliance with both Germany and Austria that goes back to 1882, but she is not good terms with either by 1914. She gets less out of the alliance than she puts in and there have been tense dealings with Austria over territorial questions. As for the question of the Balkans, "on this rock the leaking barque of the Triple Alliance was finally to split."[144] The Italian Government approaches Vienna with a list of demands in exchange for allying herself with the Central Powers, but the Austro-Hungarians decline. By March 1915, they have turned to Britain. At the end of the month the Cabinet spend "much of their time discussing how cheaply they can purchase the immediate intervention of that "most voracious, slippery, and perfidious power: Italy." Asquith thinks that the Italian territorial demands, which include almost the entirety of the Dalmatian coast in the event of victory, are greedy, but that it was a price worth paying.[145] By the end of the month the Italians "softened" their demands, but there is still resistance from Russia about terms and Asquith panics that timing is everything. "I think," he says on 31st, "that we may be driven to playing our last diplomatic card; a personal message from the King to the Tsar."[146] His Majesty sends a telegram to his cousin urging Russia to back down; and Asquith reports to the King that the Russian Foreign Minister has "withdrawn, rather pugnaciously, his remaining objections to the terms of the proposed agreement between Italy and the Allies."[147] Six days after the royal telegram, a document is signed in London, pledging that Italy join the Allies within a month. "It is to be kept a secret till she is ready,"[148] His Majesty records as he sends an appropriate message to the King of Italy. Finally, on 23rd May, Italy declares war on Austria. The Italian Ambassador is presented to the King at the palace. "I told him how pleased I was that Italy had joined the allies."[149]

One of Britain's most controversial measures in the Great War is the blockade of Germany. In 1914, Asquith reported to the King that a notable increase in shipments of wheat from New York

144   Ibid.
145   (ed.) Brock: *H.H. Asquith: Letters to Venetia Stanley,* pp.502-505.
146   Ibid., pp.518-524.
147   RA PS/PSO/GV/C/R/219.
148   RA PRIV/GVD/1915 (26/4).
149   Ibid., (23/5).

had been docking at Rotterdam, "undoubtedly having as their ultimate destination the German market."[150] A week later His Majesty learned that the Cabinet had been discussing how best to cut off the import of such food supplies to Germany as a means of weakening the enemy. On 20th August 1914, "it was resolved to treat as 'conditional contraband' and liable to seizure, food consigned through Dutch ports to a German destination."[151] After the onset of the enemy's submarine campaign in 1915, the King declares an Order of Council on 11th March that scales up seizure of contraband into a full blockade; "steps to prevent commodities of any sort from reaching or leaving Germany." It would take several months to get up to speed, but "no more food and goods for Germany will be allowed to pass," and nor will enemy reservists in neutral ships [be] permitted to return to the Fatherland."[152]

Such a move antagonises neutrals in Scandinavia who will spend the war complaining about these drastic British measures. They do, after all, have a direct economic impact on the trade of countries that might consider siding with Germany as a result. It becomes more and more difficult to stay in their good graces, and they put His Majesty in an awkward position personally too, though he does not condemn the measures as a result. His cousin is the Crown Princess of Sweden; his sister is the Queen of Norway; his mother's family occupy the Danish throne too and he is subjected to pressure from all of them on the matter. The foreign distaste over the blockade only increases as the war wears on, but Asquith has laid out his stance. "The Germans declare that they will sink every merchant ship they believe to be British, without regard to life, without regard to the ownership of the cargo, without any assurance that the vessel is not neutral, and without even the pretence of legal investigation." Britain is responding with the blockade. "This at least may be said in its favour. It cannot cause the death of a single innocent civilian; it cannot destroy neutral lives and neutral property… it cannot inflict injury upon neutral commerce."[153] Nonetheless, the blockade of Germany does harm to Britain's relations with neutral powers, including the most important of them: America. The sheer financial, industrial, agricultural power, not to mention the amount of men she could supply in the event of deciding to enter the war, means that it is absolutely imperative that she be convinced preferably to join the Allies and if not, to remain neutral. The King and his Government expend as much energy on the United States as a neutral power than they do on their Allies. Germany, too, is hard at work trying to secure her support. It is not to be taken for granted for the Allies. There are twelve million ethnic Germans in America, as well as a huge anti-British contingent dominated by Irish immigrants. The United States is determined to stay out of the war, but Germany is not subtle in trying to win her over. A lengthy transmission from the Kaiser to President Wilson is intercepted early on, attempting to clarify his innocence in events that have led to war. An *educational campaign* is also undertaken by Herr Dernberg, who arrived in America in August 1914 with the returning German Ambassador.

His Majesty is filled with anxiety. An article in *The Times* concerning Britain's attitude to neutrals sends him into a panic and he is also concerned when American correspondents are denied access to the British front, but the military authorities are adamant. Every effort at relief and charity relating to the war and conducted by the United States has to be acknowledged, and the King visits a "very comfortable and well run hospital"[154] at Highgate operated by Americans. The importance of not being outdone by the enemy in acknowledging their efforts reaches nonsensical levels at Christmas

---

150   RA PS/PSO/GV/C/R/165.
151   RA PS/PSO/GV/C/R/171.
152   (ed.) Hammerton & Wilson: *The Great War Vol.XIII*, p.41.
153   Ibid., p.42.
154   RA GV/PRIV/GVD/1915 (18/4).

1914. The British press gave "The Santa Claus Ship"[155] a lengthy write up: an American vessel packed with some five million presents to be distributed across war-torn Europe. The palace is drawn into a furore when it is wrongly suggested that there has been a "stirring difference" between Britain and Germany concerning the treatment of the party who brought over the *Jason.* The enemy sent a special party to Genoa to meet them, threw a party in Berlin and they were smothered with royal kindness. Apparently it was a stark affair when the same party arrived at Plymouth. "I was going to ask you," writes one of Stamfordham's correspondents, "whether the King would not perhaps send a letter… to signify his interest in the scheme… I do think that adequate recognition of American sympathy may become of great importance to us."[156] Stamfordham thinks that such action on the part of the King is overdoing it, but he thinks that His Majesty might be convinced to meet with the organiser as he passed back through London on his way home. "I suppose there is no doubt the Germans are leaving no stone unturned in their attempts to ingratiated themselves with American public opinion," he ponders.[157]

But Germany do not have it all their way. The Kaiser refuses to see the American Ambassador in Berlin, "on the grounds that the USA has not prohibited exports of contraband to the allies,"[158] but American officials in London are greeted with open arms, and what better way to make them feel special than with an audience with the King? His Majesty is fond of the Ambassador, Walter Page; a North Carolina native about to turn 60. He has been in London since the spring of 1913, and "from the first moment of their acquaintance, feelings of warm regard and confidence were established between these two men, who possessed many qualities in common." He believes that the English-speaking peoples of the world should be in harmony. "What I want… is to have the President of the United States and the King of England to stand up side by side and let the world take a good look at them,"[159] he says. But more important than Page is Colonel Edward House, of Texas. He was instrumental in getting Woodrow Wilson nominated in 1912 and as a close friend of the President, he roams Europe like an unofficial ambassador, "and owing to his discretion and sagacity exercised a great and beneficent influence in world affairs."[160] He has access both in Berlin and in London, but he is very much in favour of America joining the war on the side of the Allies. The King meets House in March 1915 and likes him immediately. "He told me the Americans are entirely with us in this war."[161]

Britain's Ambassador in Washington has already declared in April that: "The German submarine horrors are working here and have their effect," but not enough to reverse the general position, which is that America wants to stay out of the war. "They will do everything possible to keep out of it."[162] With the loss of 123 Americans aboard the *Lusitania* though, more than anything so far, the ocean liner's destruction appears to justify the United States changing her neutral stance. Both Page and House agree that America can only respond by declaring war on Germany. "The outrageous attack on the *Lusitania* is making the entry of America into the alliance possible," writes Stamfordham, "some think probable, and President Wilson must be in a very delicate and responsible position just now."[163] But Wilson begins trading notes with the Kaiser's Government which manage to drag out his response to the sinking of the *Lusitania* and the loss of American

155   *The Times* 31/12/14.
156   RA PS/PSO/GV/C/Q/709/1.
157   RA PS/PSO/GV/C/Q/709/4.
158   RA PS/PSO/GV/C//P/618/7.
159   Nicolson: *King George V: His Life and Reign,* p.218.
160   Ibid., p.29.
161   RA GV/PRIV/GVD/1915 1/3/15.
162   RA PS/PSO/GV/C/P/618/7.
163   RA PS/PSO/GV/C/P/284/32.

lives for months. At the beginning of June, House stops in at the palace on his way home to see the King and tells His Majesty that he considers war between America and Germany inevitable. It is a fine outlook, but House has got ahead of himself. The British Ambassador in Washington surmises that Wilson is following his people, not leading them. Page puts is succinctly: "The United States does not desire to fight... The United States does not desire to openly and publicly give way. The compromise is to assert American rights, but not in such a way as to involve a conflict. It is to learn to swim without getting wet." Too many American interests will not profit by entering the war, too many Americans are making money from the conflict, and added to this, some interests in America do not want Britain to win the war. The fact is, in Spring 1915, though "the great bulk of the American people sympathise with the allies,"[164] this sentiment, and outrage at the sinking of the *Lusitania* is not enough to bring America into the conflict. The mirage sketched for the King by Colonel House that shows a swift, decisive end to the war with the arrival of the United States vanishes.

"Dignified Without Being Dogmatic"

"The bells are ringing in London. Not for an English victory. Unlike Berlin, we want to make sure of our victories before we celebrate them... The cheerful sounds from the steeples have no relation to the war; they mark the fifth anniversary of King George's accession to the throne." The firing of the traditional salute in St James's Park caused excitement in Whitehall. "Old ladies looked anxiously at the sky and rushed for cover, and newspaper men... came running out of the Press Bureau."[165] A month later the King also marks his 50th birthday. Both events receive plenty of coverage, almost exclusively tied in some way to the war, but celebrations are muted. His Majesty's birthday dawns "dull, cold with a northwest wind, very depressing." He spends a quiet day with the Queen. She gives him his presents before breakfast and they sit in the tent answering telegrams and letters. At the King's command there are to be no festivities and no acknowledgements, save for the flying of flags if people so wished: no trooping the colour; there is a large marquee up on Horse Guards for recruitment instead. And there are to be no guns fired in salute this time. "There is too much thunder of guns elsewhere."[166]

Editorials commemorate the King's milestone by paying tribute to the "his inspiring example." His birthday has come, they say, "at an extraordinary time in British history... The kingdom at death-grips with a powerful and unscrupulous nation and involved in nearly a dozen wars besides in various parts of the world."[167] It has not gone unnoticed that he has travelled the length and breadth of the country. To his people, at this moment in time His Majesty represents what they think it is to be British: hard working, a gentleman, no desire to fuss or show off. "He is dignified without being dogmatic, and the Emperor Wilhelm is dogmatic without being dignified." He may not have been as popular as his father when he came to the throne, but after a year of war, they think that he is showing them different qualities, no less valuable. "His time, his energy, his brain, his sympathies are places absolutely at the disposal of his people."[168]

And yet the King does not agree with every patriotic appeal that arises. He has a particular issue with the rewriting of history. Lord Roberts had to be brought in to convince His Majesty that the Kaiser and his son should be stripped of honorary commands of British regiments. The King thinks

164   RA PS/PSO/GV/C/Q/1110/2.
165   *The Standard* 6/5/15.
166   *The Ladies Field* 5/6/15.
167   *Daily Mirror* 3/6/15.
168   The *Ladies Field* 5/6.

that they should have to resign themselves, but eventually agrees for their names to be omitted from the next edition of the Army List; but he will refuse to let any public statement be made to that effect. He disagrees even more with the cry that arises over banners hanging in St George's Chapel at Windsor, representing members of the Order of the Garter who now number amongst Britain's enemies. His Majesty believes that these banners are part of the order's history, and that they cannot now be pulled down as if they never existed. The situation can be reviewed again at the end of the war. Much is written on the matter, "and it was even suggested that the Chapel should be raided by patriots and the banners torn down by force." Eventually the King relents, and eight banners are quietly taken down. One publication reports that it is the first time since 1621 that there is a record of the degradation of a Knight of any order in Britain. And yet the Kaiser, the Emperor of Austria, the German Crown Prince, and five others are struck from the roll of the order. His Majesty, refuses, however, to take the brass name plates from their stalls. "They are," writes Lord Stamfordham, "historical records and His Majesty does not intend to have any of them removed."[169] However reluctant the King was to eradicate the banners from St. George's Chapel, the response to his action, which came a week after the sinking of the *Lusitania*, is positive. The Order of the Garter, one newspaper writes, has a long tradition of service and courage. "Its Knights are not only pledged by their profession not to do evil, but commanded by the order's motto not to think evil. What place can the Kaiser and his shameless heir have among such men. The King, it is said, "has redeemed the Garter from dishonour by contemptuously expelling Wilhelm of Hohenzollern."[170]

Headlines belong to His Majesty again a little over two weeks later when he appoints Lord Kitchener a Knight of the Garter. Not only does this replace one of the enemy incumbents on the roll, but it reaffirms publicly the King's determination to support the War Minister. He presents it to his friend on his own birthday. It is by far the most conspicuous feature of the honours list; "the Sovereign's reply… to the gross personal attacks made on a great soldier and a trusted public servant. The nation was stirred to wrath by the sneers, the taunts, and the venomous suggestions, and the King has associated himself with his peoples' resentment by giving Lord Kitchener the greatest honour he has in his power to bestow."[171] Senior army officers are satisfied, they are tired of "this wretched personal factor which creeps in everywhere;"[172] and Lord Esher tells Kitchener that he thinks it is "the best 'riposte' possible to the fools who thought to shake your authority."[173]

"The Third Enemy"

In the meantime, despite overhauling his Cabinet, and despite the institution of a Ministry of Munitions under Lloyd George, it is going to take a superhuman effort from Asquith and his Government to mobilise Britain's industry properly for war. One of the overwhelming problems affecting the country's ability to produce enough ammunition is the productivity of the workforce. Skilled men are earning such high wages that they hold all of the cards. Firms cannot compel them to work a full week if they don't want to, and union restrictions prevent employers from using less skilled replacements to try and keep pace with their contracts for the army. "No one realises the gravity of the situation better than the King,"[174] writes Wigram, and in mid-March a number of solutions are being examined by the Cabinet. They include having the Government take

169   Nicolson: *King George V: His Life and Reign,* pp.249-250.
170   *Daily Express* 14/5/15.
171   Ibid., 3/6/15.
172   RA/PS/PSO/GV/C/Q/832/276.
173   TNA: WO/57/111/3.
174   RA PS/PSO/GV/C/Q/2522/3/171.

over the armament business for the duration of the war, Government tribunals to arbitrate labour disputes over pay, and regulating opening hours for public houses. There is a direct link between workers spending business hours in pubs, making the most of their newfound wealth and a lack of productivity. The King is in favour of these restrictions. "His Majesty trusts that the Government will not hesitate to exercise to the full, if necessary, the powers given by the Defence of the Realm Act."[175]

Drink is but one issue of many, but thanks to Lloyd George it assumes a disproportionate prominence which sweeps the King along with it. As the Prime Minister puts it, no sooner has he settled one row in the Cabinet involving Lloyd George, than "this versatile and volatile personage goes off… on the question of drink, about which he has completely lost his head. His mind apparently oscillates from hour to hour between the two poles of absurdity: cutting off all drink from the working man… and replacing it by a huge state monopoly." Lloyd George approaches Asquith with a scheme "for buying out the drink trade at a cost of some 250 millions!"[176] The Prime Minister despairs, but Lloyd George has become fixated on the evils of alcohol. He says "that drink is doing us more damage in the war than all the Germany submarines put together."[177]

There is precedence of sorts, for in Russia, the Tsar has banned vodka for the duration of the war; but Britain is not governed by an autocracy, and if the Welshman wants to get anywhere at all he must gather support. He arrives at the palace to convince His Majesty of the perils of drink, and succeeds. Lloyd George says that employers have told him that they attribute all of their manufacturing woes to drink. He provides one alleged example from the northeast, when a battleship went in want of urgent repair because the men "were in an upper flat of a public house, having what they called a "sing-song," and no persuasion on the part of the yard management could induce those men to go to their work."[178] Such dramatic examples stir the King's imagination, and Stamfordham tells Lloyd George that His Majesty is deeply concerned, that he feels that nothing but the most vigorous measures will successfully cope with the grave situation now existing in armaments factories. "The King is willing to do whatever he can to help, and fears that if something is not done it will only prolong the war. I am to add that if it be deemed advisable, the King will be prepared to set the example by giving up all [alcohol] himself and issuing orders against its consumption in the Royal Household, so that no difference shall be made so far as His Majesty is concerned between the treatment of rich and poor in this question."[179] Lloyd George ignores the *if it be deemed advisable* inference, and immediately presents the King's abstinence to the Cabinet as a done deal. If the letter from the King could be published, he writes, "it would I feel certain have an extraordinary effect and all classes would hasten to follow the lead thus given by the Sovereign in the gravest emergency this country has ever been confronted with."[180] The letter is duly published and provokes a wealth of praise for His Majesty. "We have a King," says *The Times*, "who is ready, amid all the anxieties of his high calling… to share in the minor sacrifices by which the humblest of his subjects may set forward the common cause."[181] The act is referred to as "the King's example,"[182] and "His Majesty's call to arms against the third enemy."[183]

175   BD: MS Asquith A.1 4 #90.
176   (ed.) Brock: *H.H. Asquith: Letters to Venetia Stanley*, pp.525-527.
177   (ed.) Hammerton & Wilson: *The Great War Vol. V*, p.307.
178   PA: C/5/6/19: Lloyd George.
179   RA PS/PS/GV/C/Q/762/14.
180   PA C/5/6/19: Lloyd George.
181   *The Times* 1/4/15.
182   *Daily Telegraph* 1/4/15.
183   *Pall Mall Gazette* 1/4/15.

The King has somewhat unwittingly done his part to enable Lloyd George's scheme, but as the minister says himself to Stamfordham: "It must now be followed by declarations from judges, Cabinet Ministers, clergy, the medical profession, and the great manufacturers, and if possible the Trades Union leaders." Unfortunately for the palace, he also writes: "I am trying to find someone who will take this in hand,"[184] which sounds rather vague to Stamfordham, who has justifiably assumed, along with the King, that the country's abstinence pledge will be driven forward with all of the formidable enthusiasm that Lloyd George has a reputation for mustering. "You say you are trying to find someone who will take this in hand," he replies with trepidation. "Will you allow me to express a hope that you will not depute this delicate duty to anyone?"[185]

In the event, Lloyd George neither took the matter on himself nor assigned such a task to anyone else. His Majesty has been committed to abstention publicly, and the support he has been led to believe will be forthcoming does not materialise. Even in the Cabinet, only Kitchener pledges to follow the King's lead. This affair is characteristic of Lloyd George. His enthusiasm for solving a problem, for making a difference sometimes outruns a sufficient level of thought. He hadn't decided what he wanted; namely prohibition, government control of alcohol, or some other measure. "Moreover, if there was to be prohibition or a tough measure of State control, then why was it necessary for the King to start a movement of voluntary denial? Lloyd George seems not to have asked himself this question."[186] Neither is he sympathetic about the position he has placed His Majesty in. It rather looks not as if the King is following the advice of his ministers in abstaining from alcohol for the duration of the war, but that he is giving the order himself. Newspapers are advocating that their readers follow *The King's Pledge*. All the palace can do is accept what has transpired and tell Lloyd George that "the King now hopes the Government will take such measures as they consider indispensable to deal satisfactorily with the evil of drink in the present national crisis."[187] The Royal Household goes dry on 6th April 1915. "A beastly day," His Majesty records. "blowing hard… cold, damp with rain off and on… This morning we have all become teetotallers until end of the war, I have done it as an example, as there is a lot of drinking going on in the country, I hate doing it, but hope it will do good."[188]

Clive Wigram's wife Nora reports from Windsor later in the month that: "the only things I have seen being consumed are seltzer waters, home-made orange ale - very good - and lemonade. And then Caley's Ginger Ale. which seems to be the most in request amongst the gentlemen."[189] The King complains to his uncle that the whole affair is a great bore. His old friend and courtier Charles Cust is said to have fainted on the first night after dinner, and His Majesty tells Margot Asquith at Windsor that when the palace cellars were locked up, his servants "arranged a large wreath of empty bottles outside the door and put a crepe bow on them with a placard and the word 'dead' written on it. We both laughed." Asquith dined with Kitchener a mere 72 hours after the War Minister had followed the King's lead. "Neither the retreat… or Neuve Chapelle affected his spirits as badly as three days on lemonade."[190]

Compensation, the logistics that would be entailed in controlling the industry, and the likely response of the country to prohibition mean that the fierce legislation that His Majesty is waiting for does not come close to materialising. Even if he hates it, the King's abstention is a good exercise in public relations both at home and abroad, but Stamfordham will not let anyone railroad the

184   PA: C/5/6/19: Lloyd George.
185   PA: C/5/6/20: Lloyd George.
186   Grigg: *Lloyd George, From Peace to War 1912-1916*, p.231.
187   PA: C/5/6/19: Lloyd George.
188   RA GV/PRIV/GVD/1915 (6/4).
189   PP: NW 16/4/15.
190   Asquith: *The Autobiography of Margot Asquith*, pp.92-3.

Sovereign so easily again. As for Lloyd George, despite palace chagrin, Stamfordham at least credits him for attempting to take on a difficult issue, but his guard will be up in future.

"Flags and Flowers"

Whilst ministers attempt to tackle the problems of labour and production legislatively, the King assumes a more direct approach; he goes out to meet and encourage people, to show his support for those engaged in war industry. His first visit to a munitions establishment occurs just a week after the army attacks at Neuve Chapelle. He wants to see work at the Woolwich Arsenal; "to go without any special preparations merely in order to see the place at full work." Officialdom is to be scorned. "The work should be carried on as usual and there should be no red carpet or anything of that sort. In fact as little preparation as possible."[191] His Majesty spends "a most interesting" two hours immersing himself in all that is happening at this centre of war production. The workforce has nearly trebled to some 30,000. "They have several more workshops and they are working day and night with two shifts. They are turning out over 40,000 shells a week and 3,300,000 rifle cartridges from all sources in the country but it is not half enough."[192] Accompanied by Kitchener, the King visits almost every department "to try and buck up the men" who are getting a bad press.

His Majesty decides that he wants to visit industrial establishments further afield, and he has Stamfordham write to Kitchener requesting a list of the names of all principal munition factories. Kitchener thinks it a sound idea, and plans to join the King at as many of them as he can. His Majesty boards a sleeper with Wigram on 16th May and they are at Kirklee Station near Glasgow in time for breakfast, refreshed and ready to begin work. After quick receptions with local dignitaries, the King reaches his first shipyard at half past ten. Here, and at six more, including John Brown and Harland & Wolff, he spends the day conscientiously observing work being carried out on mines, gun equipment, submarines, aeroplanes, battleships, destroyers, cruisers, monitors, and patrol vessels. When he returns to Kirklee His Majesty is tired, but feeling accomplished. "I saw many thousands of men working in the yards, they seemed pleased to see me… There were large cheering crowds in the streets I passed through."[193] The following day, His Majesty is impressed by the men at Denny Brothers at Dumbarton. "First rate establishment and the men all working very well."[194] He watches the men at work, meets foremen and office staff and as he continues on he refuses to pass the Red Cross hospital on the High Street and stops in to talk with sixteen wounded men. He has "a kindly word of sympathy to each, and expressed to the matron his profound admiration for the excellence of the arrangements."[195] Then it is on to Scotstoun for a difficult meeting with the proprietor, Mr Yarrow, whose younger son Eric has just been killed near Ypres in a bout of heavy shellfire. The sad gentleman gives the King a tour; showing him gunboats for use in Mesopotamia and a dozen-more large river boats bound for the Danube. "Riveters in the yard entered into their work with extra zeal when His Majesty approached and the noise was so deafening that conversation was impossible for a time."[196] At Barclay Curle & Co in Whiteinch there is a Guard of Honour drawn up; many of them wounded men from the front. The King asks one of the foremen how they are getting on. "Your Majesty, they are working like heroes. There is not one of them in this department who would not work till he dropped for the sake of his King and Country." His Majesty was delighted

---

191 RA PS/PS/WAR/QQ3/1783.
192 RA GV/PRIV/GVD/1915 (17/3).
193 RA GV/PRIV/GVD/1915 (17/5).
194 RA GV/PRIV/GVD/1915 (18/5).
195 *Morning Post* 19/5.15.
196 Ibid.

with this little speech and smilingly assured the foremen that he believed every word of it."[197] The highlight of the visit for the city is an inspection and investiture on Glasgow Green. The King rides his black charger, Delhi, from the Nelson monument where there are 50,000 people present in fine weather. Private Tollerton and Drummer Kenny receive the Victoria Cross, and His Majesty thinks them both "splendid men."[198] He then watches the gathered troops march past, before proceedings are rounded off with the National Anthem.

Someone extremely bright has also suggested to Stamfordham that the King should receive men of the local armaments committees, after all what could be more motivational than a pep talk from the Sovereign? They have been asked to present themselves at Kirklee Station after tea, and His Majesty gives a short speech to a collection of representatives of employers, workmen and Government departments before sitting down to start work on his red boxes for the day. Wigram receives a letter lauding the reception. "The… representatives of our committee were delighted with their experience… and it is quite clear that His Majesty's visit to the Clyde has done an enormous amount of good."[199] His opinion is backed by the coverage of the visit given in the working man's paper, *The Daily Record and Mail*. Before leaving Scotland, the King also receives a resolution from the men of the Fairfield's shipyard; "that nothing will be lacking on their part to complete in the very shortest time possible every item of work entrusted to them by the Government in this time of extreme national need." This is music to His Majesty's ears. "It will indeed be a happy outcome of my visit to the Clyde if it has in any way conduced to this expression of patriotic resolve on the part of the men of one of the most important establishments in this renowned industrial centre."[200]

The royal approach on the Clyde has gone down extremely well. "The King has… the same outspoken, direct, human and hearty manner whether he is talking to the chairman of the company, to a discharged soldier among the employees or to a shop steward. He meets them all on the same level… plies them with questions." And he never appears to be in a hurry. He is not there to take a quick look around, he wants to enter every department, "to have the purpose of each machine and of each shop explained to him, to follow each process… to stop every now and then to engage one of the workers in animated conversation and to carry on a brisk and heavy fire of questions and observations." All this is done, says one observer during the war, "with new and unintelligible sights… beating upon ones eyes and brains, to keep up ones interest, and to show not a trace of fatigue, is no slight test of mental alertness and physical condition. Try it, if you doubt it." And yet the King never seems for one moment tired or bored. He is quite clearly genuinely interested. "he really wants to know. There was no pretence about it. The King, when he goes the round of a… factory, gives pleasure because he takes pleasure. The men and women enjoy his visits because he enjoys them himself."[201]

The royal train makes for Newcastle, for with the rivalry existing between the northeast ship workers and those on the Clyde, it won't do to visit one and not the other. His Majesty is ready to exploit the competition. He has a brief conversation with the Lord Mayor and tells him that he has been most impressed by what he has seen on the Clyde, and was much gratified by the loyalty of the workmen. The Lord Mayor assures the King that he will find the same enthusiasm on Tyneside. His Majesty observes construction at one yard and is satisfied to see work abandoned for now on two passenger steamers so that the whole workforce can contribute to the war effort. He says that clearly,

197 *Daily Chronicle* 19/5/15.
198 RA GV/PRIV/GVD/1915 (18/5).
199 RA PS/PS/GV/C/Q/2520/8.
200 *Daily Chronicle* 19/5/15.
201 Ibid., 16/3/15.

the Tyne is trying to do its best for the Admiralty. At Hawthorn Leslie's the King meets a foreman shipwright who has been 54 years with the firm and has launched and incredible 432 vessels. Then there is a worker who remembers meeting the King many years ago. "A've seen ye afore but you were only a bit lad," he says, making the King laugh heartily.[202] At Palmer's in Jarrow the King finds the mayor working as a joiner and tells him that he is proud to see him wearing his war service button.

The tour of Tyneside is proving every bit as successful as that on the Clyde, one newspaper claiming that it "will put heart into workmen who have been subjected to a great deal of unwanted abuse by people who have never driven a rivet."[203] Shipyard officials interviewed after his Majesty's departure say that "the workmen would undoubtedly be encouraged by the King coming amongst them."[204] Kitchener joins His Majesty on 20th May, they have a long talk over breakfast before leaving for the huge works at Elswick. Another inspection follows, this time on the Town Moor, and more hospital visits. The King meets representatives of the Northeast Armaments Committee too, and as he did on the Clyde he appeals for the men on the Tyne to work with the authorities to set aside restrictive rules and regulations for the duration of the war. It saddens the press in some quarters that this is necessary. "It is scandalous that it should be necessary for such an appeal to be made to any group of Englishmen after nine months of war; it is even more horrible to have to admit the possibility the appeal may be in vain."[205] There is a final stop, where in a gun-mounting shop, men working on each one of the big gun-turrets sang Rule Britannia, to the King's delight. He is also thrilled to see 500 women at work, mostly relatives of the workmen. He returns to Buckingham Palace in the hope that his work has done some good. "I think my tour of inspection has been a success, hope it will bear good fruit."[206]

In July, the King is escorted by Stamfordham and Wigram from Windsor Castle to Coventry. Crowds have gathered in pouring rain to see the King arrive, and they sing the National Anthem as he emerges from the train. He sees the biggest guns of all at the Ordnance Works, at Daimler they are making lorries, cars and tractors for the war effort, and at Rover there are a diverse array of cars, grenades and shells in the making. Once again he meets with local armaments committees before departing for Birmingham. The rain has stopped as the royal train pulls into New Street Station at three o'clock. The King's arrival comes as a complete surprise to the city. Shoppers have no idea that on the other side of the station the His Majesty is departing in an open motor car on his tour until they hear distant cheering. At the Birmingham Small Arms Company at Small Heath the King makes one of his speeches to the workers. "He had not come to criticise;" he said, "but to show his interest in the country's efforts to meet the heavy demands for the means of carrying on the war. He fully appreciated the end of zeal and cheerfulness… not only to maintain the present output, but to increase it. He was confident that this would be done and there would be but one certain result, victory."[207]

The King presses on. "Those who are privileged to know what goes on behind the scenes are amazed by His Majesty's *technical knowledge* on may branches of industry. At some of the centres visited the showrooms are elaborately prepared, but the King insists on a minute and patient inspection of the workshops themselves."[208] Ordinary workers are surprised to find that they receive as much attention as the company directors. The King is much pleased with all he has seen. "At each place I saw all the work, people who were most enthusiastic, a great many of them women,

202   *The Standard* 20/5/15.
203   *Westminster Gazette* 20/5/15.
204   *Daily Chronicle* 20/5/15.
205   *The Graphic* 21/5/15.
206   RA GV/PRIV/GVD/1915 (21/5).
207   *The Times* 24/7/15.
208   *Daily Sketch* 24/7/15.

and they had decorated their workshops and machines with flags and flowers in my honour. They are working splendidly at Birmingham."[209]

The last tour of the year takes His Majesty to Yorkshire. On the first day he ventures into Leeds, his first visit since 1894. He sees foundry works and a brand new National Shell Factory. "I walked through all the workshops, they are all making tools, shells, cartridge cases or turbines for the Government, saw many thousand of workers both men and women and they are working very hard."[210] At a foundry the elder workmen are presented to the King and he is interested in the oldest of all, Tom Adgie, *Tapper Tom* because he works on a tapping machine; a "white-whiskered veteran 80 years of age." He strikes up a conversation with His Majesty in a thick Yorkshire accent. "Eh! I am praed to see ye!" The King smiles. "And," he replies, "I am glad to see you, to see you looking so well. How are you? And aren't you tired of working yet?"

"Not I, came the reply. I think nowt about it, I may look old, but looks doesn't count, it's what one feels."

Another 75 year old workman name Alfred Wilson has worked at the foundry for 51 years. "He shook my hands right heartily," he tells newspaper men of His Majesty, "and my black oily hand left a lovely mark right across his glove, but he did not seem to care."[211] In fact the King laughs. His Majesty is keen on souvenirs and is presented with specially produced shell cases in the main, but he sources his own too. In one workroom he picks up a small handful of cartridges and, with a cheeky smile he drops them into his pocket.

The visit has brought Leeds to a standstill. Excited citizens line the streets with flags, and the King smiles and waves. Crowds are so dense at one point that the convoy of motor cars can barely progress along the street. After a final hospital visit to a former workhouse the following morning, His Majesty leaves for Sheffield and arrives in time for lunch. The usual round of cheering crowds, munitions committees and dignitaries begins. At the Atlas works, a man produces a photograph of the King as a midshipman, given to him by His Majesty when both were serving in the *Bacchante*. The King is astonished, because he remembers the photograph being taken in Athens in 1882. Later that afternoon the His Majesty meets three members of one family who have spent the whole of their lives working for one firm. Before he leaves he spots another elderly gentleman and says "why, you must have been working here years before I was born, and you look as if you have plenty of work left in you yet."[212] A final day in Rotherham on 29th September, and the King completes his exhausting motivational tour of the country for 1915. He has spoken to shipyard and munitions workers, met with production committees, not to mention visited thousands of troops in hospitals and on parade and given out hundreds of decorations. It is a simple formula, but one that has brought a British Sovereign closer to a wider cross-section of his people than ever before.

As the anniversary of the outbreak of war approaches, royal telegrams are exchanged with Britain's Allies. The completion of the first year of war is very much seen as a time for Britain to reaffirm her vows, her commitment to her cause. There is to be a large service at St. Paul's on 4th August; "to inaugurate the second year of the war by invoking God's help."[213] It is not a new concept. The Cathedral had seen Te Deums in Queen Anne's reign for Marlborough's victories, services for the peace that brought the Crimean War to a close in 1856, the suppression of the Indian Mutiny three years later, and then the end of the war in South Africa in 1902.

209   RA GV/PRIV/GVD/1915 (24/7).
210   RA GV/PRIV/GVD/1915 (27/9).
211   *Daily Telegraph* 28/9/15.
212   *Morning Post* 29/9/15.
213   *Evening News* 22/7/15.

"The King and Queen prefer than their arrival at the City's cathedral shall be as quiet as possible."[214] There is to be no state procession. Kitchener has done his utmost to try and make it a proud occasion for recruiting, with triumphant hymns, but he accuses the clergy of being "the most tiresome, unimaginative people in the world."[215] It is going to be a simple, solemn affair. The dome and transepts will be reserved for wounded sailors and soldiers, while the whole nave was to be open to the public on a first come, first served basis. The day before the service, the authorities are expecting such a crowd that "great wooden barricades are being placed across the streets leading to St Paul's churchyard."[216] Special regulations to deal with the traffic have been drawn up. The City of London Police Reserve, a thousand strong, will be in their ordinary clothes but will marshal the crowd in their red and white armlets and peaked caps bearing their special badge.

Their Majesties leave the palace in a Russian carriage half an hour before the service begins; in the King's own words, to "attend a service of humble prayer to Almighty God on behalf of the nation and Empire."[217] Inside St. Paul's, "a few shafts of light came piercing through the windows of the dome;"[218] "like the dusty beam of a searchlight."[219] The cathedral is full of wounded men. "Many had armless sleeves pinned to their tunics, others their arms in slings, and there were yet others who had lost a leg… One or two, as yet unused to crutches, preferred to hop the whole way upon their one sound leg." There are eye patches, swathed heads and men who are clearly suffering from wounds hidden somewhere beneath their uniforms. "An officer, himself partially crippled, could be seen helping a more severely injured comrade from the ranks."[220] The Prime Minister is there; and "Sir Edward Grey, his face keen and hawklike, Kitchener, towering, stout and well… contrary to legend, his face was wreathed in smiles" as he stopped to speak to the Canadian Prime Minister. Near him are two privates in shabby uniforms and the Tsar's brother, Grand Duke Michael, in light khaki. Cheering rises in the background, distant at first then becoming louder and louder until the north door opens and in comes the King, followed by Queen Mary and Queen Alexandra. His Majesty is satisfied with the tone. "The service was quite simple, very fine and most impressive."[221] "The hymns were hymns of petition, such as *Rock of Ages*," but there is no despondency; "it was rather the air of those who were only now recognising the magnitude of the task ahead, and who, having recognised it, were preparing themselves for the great fight."[222] The service ends with a vibrant rendition of *God Save the King*, for which thousands waiting outside the cathedral join in with the singing.

"The Dardanelles Sink"

At the end of June the King writes that the overall military situation, "is full of anxieties."[223] His diaries are rife with concern. On the Western Front he is losing faith in Sir John French's ability to command the BEF and now believes a change needs to be made. "Things in Russia are very serious, as they are steadily being driven back. Kovno and other fortresses have fallen… it makes

214   *Daily Telegraph* 23/7/15.
215   Asquith: *The Autobiography of Margot Asquith*, p.171.
216   *Daily Telegraph* 3/8/15.
217   RA GV/PRIV/GVD/1915 (4/8).
218   *Daily Telegraph* 5/8/15.
219   *Daily Graphic* 5/8/15.
220   *Daily Telegraph* 5/8/15.
221   RA GV/PRIV/GVD/1915 (4/8).
222   Hammerton: *Our King & Queen: A Pictorial Record of Their Lives,* p.21.
223   RA/PRIV/GVD/1915 (26/6).

one very anxious."[224] And continually draining British resources is the campaign at Gallipoli. "The Dardanelles is the blackest spot of all, and the annoying part of it is that in no circumstances could it even be expected to lead to our benefit," fumes Sir William Robertson to Stamfordham from GHQ. "Constantinople has been the chief bone of contention amongst the Balkan States for 2,000 years or more, and why it should ever have been thought that our possession of the Dardanelles or the Russian acquisition of Constantinople would… put the Balkan States in complete harmony and on our side I have never been able to imagine."[225] Haig is solicited for his opinion too. "I… think that it is _fatal_ to pour more troops and ammunition down the Dardanelles sink!"[226] He tells Wigram. Before the landings had even taken place, the King told Nora Wigram at Windsor that he feared some people had willed the campaign to fail just to be able to say "I told you so."[227] General Hamilton sends long letters to the palace about his campaign. They are colourful and descriptive, but wildly optimistic, verging on delusional. In May the King hears via Asquith that all is well on the Gallipoli Peninsula, then at the end of the month His Majesty receives claims of a "well-conceived and successful operation in the Dardanelles."[228] In hindsight these are difficult claims to swallow. By the beginning of August reinforcements have been sent east and a new landing is to be attempted at Suvla Bay on 6th. Yet again, attempts to kick-start the Gallipoli campaign fail. Hamilton writes to Kitchener telling him that he will need another 95,000 men if he is to have superiority. The Government is not impressed. "They had built high hopes on the landings because they had been led to believe that success was all but certain."[229] The British force is at a loss, and as the year wears on the King doubts any prospects of defeating the Turks. In October he learns of the possibility of "washing them out"[230] by means of powerful jets of water, a plan adopted during the construction of the Panama Canal for knocking down hills.

Worse than the prospects for the Gallipoli campaign so far as His Majesty is concerned, is the fact that the possibility of a largescale campaign in Salonika rears its head again, and he is determined to protest against it loudly. As soon as it becomes evident that Bulgaria is going to enter the war on the side of the Central Powers in October, the Allies believe that they can count on Greece coming onto their side. Indeed the Greek Prime Minister asks King Constantine for a general mobilisation immediately. He also appeals to France and Britain for 150,000 men. The French agree to send half and so it is unsurprising that the King hears that his Government intend to send two divisions from Gallipoli. "Is it wise to embark upon this second subsidiary theatre of war?" Stamfordham writes in a set of notes. "Shall we not weaken our position in the Dardanelles and give the enemy a chance of defeating [us] after the two divisions are withdrawn? Will the central powers plus Bulgaria attack Serbia before the Allies can send a man to Macedonia?"[231] His Majesty is mortified. "The news from Bulgaria is very serious," he writes to the Tsar, "…Unfortunately none of our allies can send troops to support Serbia. We want every man in France and in Gallipoli and in the latter our position is none too secure."[232]

Stamfordham reports to the King that "the politicians want to embark on this new campaign in Macedonia and Serbia, but… they… think they can put 150,000 in, knowing that once the

224   RA/PRIV/GVD/1915 (20/8).
225   RA/PS/PSO/GV/C/Q/832/276.
226   RA/PS/PS/GV/C/Q/2521/V/133.
227   PP: CW 16/4/15.
228   RA/PS/PSO/GV/C/R/233.
229   Cassar: _Kitchener: Architect of Victory,_ pp.383-390.
230   RA/PS/PS/GV/C/Q/838/16.
231   RA/PS/PSO/GV/C/O/2243/1.
232   RA GV/ADD/COPY/177.

campaign had begun it would need three times that."[233] But before that, Anglo-French contingents begin to disembark at Salonika. Unfortunately the Greeks have not yet declared war, and so despite the fact that he has asked for these men, their Prime Minister, Venizelos, is forced to issue a protest. The situation remains calm, but nobody has factored in King Constantine, the British Sovereign's first cousin on his mother's side, who disagrees with his Prime Minister with regard to joining the Allies. In the end, Venizelos has to resign, opposed to the King's neutrality. His replacement promises benevolence towards the Allied landing at Salonika, but there will be no Greek troops to put into the field to help save Serbia from the combined might of Germany, Austria, Hungary and now Bulgaria; "and the Anglo-French forces found themselves not a minute fraction, but the whole of the relieving army that was to save Serbia."[234] His Majesty's initial fears are confirmed. Men have been shed that Britain can ill-afford to spare from more important theatres of war. Lord Esher runs into Kitchener in Paris after he has discussed the matter with General Joffre. "He was particularly mental about the whole Salonika episode. I will tell you some day the message he wants me to deliver to Joffre!"[235]

By 9th October there are 20,000 Allied troops at Salonika, 25% of them British. Stamfordham writes to Asquith in the name of the King, who wants them removed again. "His Majesty desires me to let you know what a grave responsibility he considers would be incurred were we now to embark on a campaign in the Balkans. As His Majesty understands the question, our agreement with the French to send 150,000 men to Salonika was on the supposition that the Greek Army would cooperate with us in that theatre. Since however, we can apparently no longer count upon such cooperation, the French Government will surely appreciate the weighty reason why we must reconsider our position with regard to this compart."[236] No more troops are to be sent, but the King is only half satisfied, because the rest will remain. Asquith brushes this concept aside, but His Majesty continues to press his opinion. "We have become enmeshed by their blunder,"[237] Esher says of the French.

The situation on every front at the end of 1915 is rife with uncertainty. Russia has consumed vast resources; two million men and huge quantities or munitions. Early Italian endeavours have failed, and in Mesopotamia, although General Townshend has advanced almost far enough up the Tigris to reach Baghdad, by the end of the year he will have suffered a humiliation that will ruin his career. In France and Belgium, before the year is over, Britain's army will embark on the largest advance in her history, but to no avail. Kitchener wants to wait until 1916 to make another attack, when his new armies will be available in abundance and an offensive on the Western Front can perhaps be timed to coincide with one in the east. But the French are adamant; showing "a criminal disinclination to learn from the experience of repeated failures… [persisting] in directing offensives against an enemy which was protected by an elaborate trench system."[238] Billy Lambton tells the King from GHQ at the end of June that he thinks "that both Sir John and Joffre have come to the conclusion that some other plan will have to [be] tried, and I believe they are to confer this week and discuss some mutual operation on a big scale."[239]

Though it is not clear if it is sent, a letter is drafted by His Majesty to Asquith that clearly suggests that he thinks that the idea of trying to defeat the Germans on the Western Front in 1915

233   RA PSO/PSO/GV/C/Q/838/12.
234   (ed.) Hammerton & Wilson: *The Great War Vol.XII*, pp.2-3.
235   RA/PS/PS/GV/C/Q/724/49.
236   RA/PS/PS/GV/C/Q/838/17.
237   RA/PS/PS/GV/C/Q/838/61.
238   Cassar: *Kitchener: Architect of Victory*, pp.377-383.
239   RA PS/PS/GV/C/Q838/231.

should be carefully considered. "From what I hear I am afraid we have a great deal to learn from the Germans, whose trenches are so deep and their communications completely underground that they are practically immune from shellfire. I only wish ours were the same and they ought to be as we have plenty of troops behind our lines." When Sir John French comes home to discuss the future, the King would like to see the representation from GHQ bolstered. "I strongly urge the importance of Sir William Robertson also being asked to attend. I am sure this will be most helpful in the interests of everyone."[240]

Having discussed matters with both men, and Sir Henry Wilson, the Government then exhaustively discuss what is to be done, weighing up options against the pressures from France. The Cabinet regard the Western Front as the dominant theatre, but with artillery stocks such as they are, "it should be strongly represented to the French that they should defer any offensive operations." If, however they were insistent about making an attack in what remains of 1915, Sir John French has assured the Cabinet that he can do so without it being "unduly"[241] costly to his force. Joffre indeed continues to press for an offensive before the end of the year, with the British fighting at Loos, a mining region rife with villages, slag heaps and mines. French demurs, and Kitchener too thinks that though the prospects of a decisive military result are slim, "that we cannot, without serious and perhaps fatal injury to the alliance, refuse the cooperation."[242]

"Our troops and the French have made an attack on the German trenches today on the whole of our front," the King writes in his diary on 25th September. "I only pray that they may be successful."[243] But though it is the most powerful attack the British Army has ever put into place, it isn't powerful enough to combat extremely well entrenched German positions. British forces use gas for the first time, "to cover the gaping chasm between ambition and reality,"[244] Just as at Neuve Chapelle the enemy quickly brings up reserves and claims back lost ground, and French's men find themselves right back where they started from at a cost of almost 60,000 casualties. Four days later the King is conversing in a converted lunatic asylum in Sheffield with wounded evacuated from the battlefield, listening to grim tales of inevitable failure.

As for the French, they launch larger scale offensives on the 25th September, and like the British, they fail. France pays for her haste to take the offensive before the end of the year in blood, with almost 200,000 losses. His Majesty dutifully puts a positive spin on affairs in a letter to his cousin the Tsar.

Thank God we have had good news from your army lately, and I trust that you have almost arrested the enemy's advance. On the Western Side both the French and ourselves have gained decided successes as the Germans have lost considerably in both men and material. Progress of course against such strongly prepared positions must necessarily be slow, but our movement will undoubtedly draw troops from your front.[245]

The Allies are now united in looking to 1916 for a decisive end to the war.

240   RA PS/PSO/GV/C/Q/2517.
241   RA PS/PSO/GV/C/R/235.
242   RA PS/PSO/GV/C/R/244.
243   RA GV/PRIV/GVD/1915 (25/9).
244   Hart: *The Great War,*. p.153.
245   RA GV/ADD/COPY/177.

"May We Only Prove Ourselves Men"

By the end of September 1914, more than 60 members of staff at Buckingham Palace alone had joined the services. They began to die immediately. The first of the King's men to fall was John Robertson, a labourer in the woods on the Balmoral estate, during the retreat; and more followed at Ypres. In the first half of 1915, several men had already fallen on the Western Front in the Spring, including one of the cooks from Buckingham Palace who was serving on the Argonne with the French Army. The King regrets each and every one, but the most painful for His Majesty so far occurs in May.

Lord Stamfordham has one son. John Bigge is 27, a Captain in the King's Royal Rifle Corps. In the middle of May, Stamfordham's wife has not been well for some time and the Government is falling apart. On 19th, His Majesty's principal secretary spends much of the day with Asquith, fretting over the reconstruction of the Government. "And now I fear John is wounded," he writes to the King, who is away on his tour of Scotland, "but my daughter cannot get any particulars."[246] And so begin four days of torture. His Majesty is anxious for him, and replies immediately. "Thank you, Sir, from the depth of a very anxious heart," Stamfordham replies. "John is everything to us: but if it is God's will that he is to be taken we must be brave: and we shall only be like many, many others."[247] By 22nd May, with the Cabinet still being reformed, the worst possible outcome is emerging. "Poor old John Bigge is reported killed," writes David in his diary at the front.[248] "Things lately have been a bit depressing," the Queen writes to Bertie. "John Bigge is wounded and missing, not been seen since May 16th. Poor Lord S is in despair tho' we try to encourage him to hope John will still be heard of."[249] But by the following day it seems there is no longer any doubt. Billy Lambton dashes a letter off to the King. "I regret to say that the news about Lord Stamfordham's son is most unsatisfactory and I fear that there is no doubt that he has been killed, though it is curious that up to now no trace can be found of him; he has not been through any of the hospitals and one cannot hold out any hope now."[250] During the Battle of Festubert, after multiple delays and rescinded orders, anxious hours spent listening to the battle and sat under shellfire, John's battalion had finally been ordered to advance on 15th May. British and Indian troops made an attack on a moonlit night towards the German front line about 350 yards in front. Amidst flares, shells and sweeping machine gun fire, John Bigge vanished.

Devastated, Stamfordham breaks the news to His Majesty. "It is a terrible loss to his poor parents who were so devoted to him."[251] But Stamfordham stays at his post. The loss of his only son has come in the midst of the formation of the coalition, as Italy's joining the Allies hangs in the balance, whilst the King is busy with his tours to manufacturing centres, only a fortnight after the sinking of the *Lusitania* and some ten days after Repington's irresponsible despatch is printed in *The Times*. His Majesty needs him, and he is a faithful servant, as well as desperate to divert himself. "There is nothing to do but <u>work</u>," he writes to one acquaintance, "but it is heart breaking for my wife and daughter as he was everything for them."[252] It seems to him, too, churlish to forget that thousands are dying. But he is angry too. He says to the Prime Minister's wife: "Neither you nor I, Mrs Asquith, would mind our only sons dying in a Waterloo, but in this muddled, mis-managed war, everyone feels the uselessness of their losses."[253]

246   RA PS/PSO/GV/C/K/770/3.
247   RA PS/PSO/GV/C/K/770/8.
248   RA EDW/PRIV/DIARY/1915 (22/5).
249   RA GVI/PRIV/RF/11/204.
250   RA PS/PSO/GV/C/Q/832/228.
251   RA GV/PRIV/GVD/1915 (23/5).
252   PA: BL/50/3/49 26/5/15.
253   Asquith: *The Autobiography of Margot Asquith*, p.157.

One unit boasts more Royal Household men than any other in the army, a territorial battalion raised at Sandringham. In consultation with King Edward, in 1908 Frank Beck, His Majesty's land agent, the estate manager, went about forming a company from amongst workers and the surrounding area. The result was E Company of the 1/5th Norfolk Regiment, organised geographically and thus a close unit, full of colleagues, neighbours and relatives; with the local gentry as officers, senior workers as NCOs and their charges beneath them. For Frank Beck, now 53, and his men, the opening weeks of the war were a disappointment. By early December 1914 they were still no closer to leaving the country and Beck pleaded with the palace to help them. The King promptly instructed Fritz Ponsonby to move the matter on, but the War Office pleaded that it was no simple question of choosing the 5th Norfolks to go abroad above another battalion. "The Adjutant General hopes you will explain to His Majesty the reasons why it is hoped this question will not be pressed, for it might raise an awkward precedent."[254]

But by mid-February, still nothing has changed and Ponsonby is informed that there is still no chance of the men leaving England. The War Office suggests that if a division remains at home on the vulnerable east coast it is surely a place of honour. "The Adjutant General [also] asked me to bring to the King's notice that Norfolk is the best county for recruiting of which he knows."[255] But the King is no fool. He is extremely proud of the Sandringham men, of how quickly they answered the call to serve, and he desperately wants to help Beck and his men. And if anybody can turn the screw, it is Ponsonby. "It is naturally rather disappointing to His Majesty," he writes to the War Office, "after having allowed 120 men to join the forces as an example to other landowners, to find that they have got to further than Colchester." The King hopes that they will carefully look at whether anything can be done without upsetting bigger plans. Ponsonby is wary of His Majesty pressing too far for special treatment for his estate workers, but, "at the same time… cannot help feeling that the answer given by the Adjutant-General is absolute nonsense." After all, the Northumberland Yeomanry had gone abroad, and Sir John French had once been in that unit. The same with Oxfordshire Territorials, which had transpired to be a favour to Churchill. "Did the War Office attempt any logical excuse, or put forward reasons why these… regiments should not be selected on no particular principle? No, I am sure nothing of the sort happened. Now therefore when His Majesty makes for a comparatively simple matter the War Office becomes logical."[256]

The King thinks it would be best if Beck returns his work on the estate. "There are so many matters requiring decision at Sandringham that His Majesty thinks it would be well if you were to be obtain leave for a month or so."[257] Back returns to Norfolk until finally, in May the Norfolks are sent to St. Albans to prepare to go overseas. Beck immediately asks permission to join the rest of the estate men with the Norfolks. "His Majesty said," Ponsonby informs him, "that he quite understands your desire to go with the Sandringham Company… you should take steps to ensure that you are not left behind."[258] Fate has conspired to send the King's men to Gallipoli, and before their departure His Majesty writes to Beck: "My best wishes to you and to the Sandringham Company. I have known you all for many years, and am confident that the same spirit of loyalty and patriotism, in which you answered the call to arms, will inspire your deeds in face of the enemy. May God bless and protect you."[259]

---

254   RA PPTO/PP/SHM/MAIN/NS/70.
255   Ibid.
256   Ibid.
257   Ibid.
258   McCrery: *All the King's Men*, p.48.
259   RA PPTO/PP/SHM/MAIN/NS/86.

The Norfolk men board the *Aquitania*. She is palatial, one of the largest passenger liners afloat. Dolphins play alongside the ship, the weather gets hotter. Moved onto progressively smaller boats, finally they can see shells bursting on the peninsula. A year after the war began, they are almost a real part of it. Beck and the Sandringham contingent are to be part of the new landing at Suvla Bay, but the plan was terrible, the leadership flawed. The landing force became stuck looking up at their objectives from dubious positions. The East Anglian Territorials are sent to try and clear the area of Turkish snipers. As they approached Suvla Bay the Norfolk men were singing, laughing, cheering. Troops were identifiable on the shore line, they could heat the rattle of machine guns and the thud of shells. They anchored half a mile from shore in the early evening and watched smoke rising from the battle.

On 12th August the Sandringham men are told that they are to help make an advance late that afternoon. Sent out with two pints of water to last three days, they walk straight into heavy shellfire. They dutifully press on, the company being cut to ribbons around what looks like a farm; little fields dotted with stone buildings. Afterwards, there are less than 400 men left in the battalion. "Where the others are all gone no one knows. Some must be killed but I cannot believe all and I think they must have been taken prisoners," writes one of Beck's nephews. "The last I saw of Alec and Uncle Frank they were just one field behind me."[260] Attacking in broad daylight, over open ground, the Sandringham men never stood a chance of reaching their objectives. The advance had been so hurried that they didn't know where to find ammunition, where to send the wounded, or even where their own machine gunners were stationed. The maps they had covered the wrong area, and so in retrospect perhaps it is not surprising that Frank Beck and much of the Sandringham Company disappeared into the chaos of the battlefield. The whole affair is confused by constant speculation. The Turkish authorities are notoriously slow about relaying prisoner information, and this raised hopes. Surely they couldn't all be dead?

The King is quite naturally desperate for information. Arthur Beck telegraphs London to say that his brother is reported missing, and as soon as the message arrives the palace approaches the War Office for news. They cannot find anything more about Frank Beck's fate or his men, but they are told that "frequent instances have occurred in the Dardanelles of those reported as missing being ultimately found to be prisoners in the hands of the Turks." Arthur Beck is content to leave War Office communications in the hands of the palace. "I have no doubt you have arranged for any news of my brother to be reported direct to His Majesty." But he does not hold out much hope. "The fighting at Suvla Bay appears to have gone against us and I fear the slaughter has been terrible and that we must be prepared to face the worst. So far my brother's wife bears up well and bravely."[261]

But all across the Sandringham estate, families are in turmoil. Stamfordham sends a letter to Frank Beck's wife on 1st September. "[I] can fully sympathise with you in your anxiety having experienced much the same myself. Am doing everything I can."[262] The King makes a personal enquiry himself, a telegram to Hamilton in command of the Mediterranean Expeditionary Force. "I am most anxious to be informed as to the fate of the men... as they included the Sandringham Company and my agent Captain Frank Beck."[263] Hamilton is always anxious to please His Majesty, but he has nothing to add. "I greatly regret," he replies immediately, "... that up to the present I have no news... beyond the fact that 14 officers and about 250 men are missing." The division's commander had personally informed Hamilton "that the battalion and their leader were filled with

260   Ibid.
261   Ibid.
262   Ibid.
263   McCrery: *All the King's Men*, pp.88-89.

ardour and dash and on coming into contact with the enemy pressed ahead of the rest of the Brigade into close broken country when he entirely lost track of them."[264] The national press picks up on the story, before another titbit arrives from Hamilton: "A Turkish Prisoner has said that he saw seventy British prisoners near Bulair a few days ago so these *might* be some of the Norfolks."[265] As the occupant of the main house at Sandringham, Queen Alexandra is also bereft. She has her secretary go through Mr Page in London to the American Embassy in Constantinople, specifically for news of Frank Beck and his nephew, but the response from the Turks in December is that they have found no trace of either. The matter of the Sandringham men is even raised in the House of Commons.

At the beginning of September a letter from a Corporal Adams claims that Frank Beck is dead, "for it was like going into the gates of hell… it was just like running into a death trap; it was simply awful." The King is saddened with this news. He doesn't think that it really clarifies what has happened, but he is slowly beginning to accept that the likelihood of Beck being found alive now is diminishing. Their Majesties have sent letters to the families of the missing men, and he has sent a notice of support to Sandringham and it is posted all over the estate and the surrounding area. The Vicar of Dersingham is grateful for the thought. "Will you be so kind as to tell His Majesty how deeply grateful the relations and friends of the Dersingham men in that company are to His Majesty for his kindness."[266]

In the meantime the King exploits every avenue he can think of to try and ascertain what has happened. On his visit to Leeds at the end of September he hears of a Norfolk Regiment man wounded in the neck and back. "I see, said His Majesty, that you are a Norfolk man, like myself, and asked if he could enlighten him at all as to [Beck's] fate. The soldier could only reply that Captain Beck had probably been killed."[267] Appeals for information are put in newspapers, but no eyewitnesses come forward and eventually the War Office are forced to admit that those still unaccounted for have died on or since 12th August. More than fifty men from the Sandringham estate took part in the attack at Suvla. Sixteen were killed, 20 wounded and eighteen more survived. Of 22,000 graves on the Gallipoli Peninsula, only 9000 are identified. The remains of 14,000 men were never recovered. After the war the British Army arrived once more in the region and began to clear the battlefields. A Norfolk cap badge was kicked up in the vicinity of the Sandringham company's attack, and sent to a chaplain still searching for news of the battalion. He had advanced alongside the Norfolks, and after the failed attack on 12th August had gone out onto the battlefields under heavy fire to help the wounded.

In the area where the cap badge was found, a mass grave was unearthed. In a secret report sent on to the King, it was stated that "what are most certainly the remains of the officers and men of the 5th Norfolks who were missing after the action of the 12th August 1915 have now been discovered." The bodies were scattered, well behind what had been the Turkish front line, "and were lying most thickly round the ruins of a small farm." 180 bodies had so far been found, 122 of which have been identified by shoulder titles as belonging to the 5th Norfolks. Only two individual soldiers could be identified. The man who owned the land was interviewed, and "stated that when he returned to the ruins of his farm after the evacuation it was covered with decomposing bodies of British soldiers which he threw down a small ravine in the immediate neighbourhood. It was in this ravine that many of the bodies were found and it would appear from this that a portion of the battalion were surrounded in the farm and annihilated."[268] The farmer also said that other

264 RA PPTO/PP/SHM/MAIN/NS/86.
265 McCrery: *All the King's Men,* p.95.
266 RA PPTO/PP/SHM/MAIN/NS/86.
267 *Daily Telegraph* 29/9/15.
268 RA PPTO/PP/SHM/MAIN/NS/86: Report.

bodies had been thrown into a dry bed that became a stream in the rainy season and that these had been carried away. Most of the remains they had were simply bones. It was apparently a habit of the Turkish soldiers not only to loot the bodies but to collect identity discs, which accounted for their anonymity. A burial ceremony was held on 7th October 1919 and the unknown remains were interred in Azmak Cemetery; but not one of the fallen Sandringham men at Gallipoli: gardeners, farmers, gamekeepers, nor their leader Frank Beck has a marked grave. They are commemorated on the Helles Memorial.

"The Sternest Resolve"

"Recruits are coming in in embarrassing numbers," Asquith told the King in autumn 1914. "At present the average rate is about 30,000 a day."[269] But by the onset of the battle at Ypres, numbers had tailed off drastically. Hundreds of thousands of men simply didn't want to go to war. The rector of Stondon Massy in Essex said of one of his parishioners that he declared: "that he felt he owed a greater duty to his mother at home than to King George, for his mother had done much for him, whereas the King, so far as he knew, had not rendered him any service."[270]

The Government decided to launch a canvassing scheme at the end of the year to ascertain the country's resources and find out who might be willing to come forward. The response rate is slow, and by the beginning of 1915 there is widespread disapproval about the official response to a lack of volunteers coming forward. The distant threat of conscription is a huge issue in Britain, where the concept of volunteerism is sacred. After the forming of the Coalition Government, the King meets with Arthur Henderson, who has just been made the first Labour Cabinet Minister and immediately begins squeezing him for information. In June His Majesty writes to Asquith "I earnestly trust that the cabinet will agree without delay to registration being carried out… I trust we shall not be obliged to come to compulsion, but I am interested to see that it has been advocated in the House this evening by one of your late whips who has been at the front for ten months!!!"[271]

As the summer progresses, the new Coalition Cabinet procrastinates as much as its predecessor, and the calls for conscription get louder. The National Registration Bill is finally introduced at the end of June. It is about time. "The effects of… groping in the dark were notorious. Men had been recruited for the Army who should never have left the workshops, while many others who were well capable of serving the country in some efficient way were contributing nothing to the national effort, or were doing work which could equally well be done by women." The Bill will take stock of everyone, and whether they could be better utilised in different work,[272] but it edges closer to conscription that is palatable for some.

"It will have to come before next year,"[273] the King writes in his diary after conversations with Kitchener in August. The War Minister, Asquith, Sir Edward Grey and Balfour all met with His Majesty on 24th. The King does not care about the philosophical question of abandoning Britain's adherence to voluntary service, his outlook is practical. "We four sat in conclave with the Sovereign on the subject of compulsion for nearly two hours," wrote the Prime Minister, "a very unusual proceeding." What, of course, affects him the most is… the growing division of opinion, and the prospect of a possible political row."[274]

269   RA PS/PSO/GV/C/R/179.
270   Simkins: *Kitchener's Army: The Raising of the New Armies 1914-1916,* p.119.
271   RA PS/PSO/GV/C/Q/2517.
272   (ed.) Hammerton & Wilson: *The Great War Vol. V,* pp.317-318.
273   RA GV/PRIV/GVD/1915 (24/8).
274   Asquith: *Memories and Reflections. Vol. II,* p.109.

The National Register assesses every man and woman between the ages of 15 and 65 and reveals that more than five million men of age are not in the forces. Less than half of these are single and only 690,138 are in working in vital war industries. So, theoretically, that leaves the Government 1,489,093 single men who are available for service before they even touch the 2,832,210 married ones at large. All the while, casualties are accumulating at the various fronts and depleting units. In September 1915, only 71,617 men enlist, the lowest number since the war began. To keep units at existing strength, Kitchener says that the army needs an average of 35,000 a week.

In October 1915, Kitchener advocates at least some element of compulsory service, but the notion is rejected. The King is once again losing patience with Asquith and writes to him on 10th.

> Now that the results of the registration are known, I earnestly trust that when parliament reassembles you will make an explicit statement as to the future needs of the army. If, as I hope, we are going to get the necessary recruits under the voluntary system we must take the country into our confidence. Lord Kitchener should tell the government his estimate of 30,000 a week or whatever figure he and his experts decide upon, and then I beg you to announce it in parliament - the fact of your doing this will, I am certain, have a most [beneficial effect.] The country I know is waiting for a statement and now is the moment.[275]

Asquith's last attempt at maintaining voluntary service is to appoint Lord Derby Director-General of Recruiting, telling His Majesty's friend to make the best of the information gathered by the National Register. The day after meeting with the King at the palace to outline his plan, Derby announces it in public. Excluding Ireland, a canvas is to be done of men aged 18-41 based on the National Register. Men will be asked either to attest now, or express their willingness to do so when called upon. The latter category will be split between married and single men and then subdivided further, and the groups will be called up in strict order, beginning with 19 year old single men. The youngest married ones will not be called up until all single men have been worked through. The scheme starts well, but His Majesty still has grave concerns, for it looks like the Coalition is faltering already, and the last thing he, or his country can bear at this juncture is another change of Government. On 20th October, Stamfordham is informed by Sir Edward Grey that the Cabinet is in turmoil over the question of a compulsory service bill and that as many as eight ministers may defect. The press know that something is afoot. "The King summons a night council," says the *Daily Mirror*. "Privy Councillors called to Buckingham Palace... The business," says the Press Association, "was a suddenly arising matter connected with the war."[276]

His Majesty is attempting to support Derby's scheme as much as he can by making an appeal for men. It is postured that even if it fails, the King cannot now be culpable, as it will be on record that he has backed to the last the principle of voluntary service. His Majesty's plea is published on the 23rd October:

> At this grave moment... I appeal to you. I rejoice in my Empire's effort, and I feel pride in the voluntary response from my subjects all over the world who have sacrificed home, fortune, and life itself in order that another may not inherit the free Empire which their ancestors and mine have built. I ask you to make good these sacrifices. The end is not in sight. More men and yet more are wanted to keep my Armies in the field, and through them to secure victory and enduring peace. In ancient days the darkest moment has ever produced in men

275   RA PS/PSO/GV/C/Q/806/1.
276   RA GV/PRIV/GVD/1915 (21/10).

of our race the sternest resolve, I ask you, men of all classes, to come forward voluntarily and take your share in the fight.[277]

"I hope my appeal in the papers will have the desired effect of getting the recruits we want,"[278] the King writes to Queen Mary. Press reaction to his message is emphatic. One newspaper refers to it as "a noble document, inspired by a great and critical occasion and worthy of it… What is more, they come from a Sovereign who, from the anxious day when he ascended the throne of his ancestors, has never failed to present his subjects a shining example of duty well performed."[279] The mainstream press has no such sympathy for the Government; condemning the *Wait and See Party*. This is the last stand for Britain's proud voluntary position. "Once again the King has said just the right thing at the right time… We confess we much prefer the King to his Ministers, not only on the obvious ground of loyal duty, but because he sees facts and states them plainly."[280]

"Three Cheers for the King"

Fritz Ponsonby claimed that he spent most of 1915 urging His Majesty to go to the front, the more often the better. "I urged Bigge to advise the King to go in the spring and again in the summer, but he took the view that [he] was doing far better work at home."[281] Finally, it is fixed that His Majesty will cross the Channel at the end of October. The size of the BEF has expanded greatly, and there is much more for him to see. The *Victoria* sails into a light mist, but by the time she docks in France the sun has emerged. "I was very sorry to leave you this morning," the King writes to Queen Mary, "as I always hate being away from you and especially during these anxious times as you help to cheer me with all I have to do."[282] French is there to greet him, but "seemed rather shy and did not melt much."[283] His Majesty spends his first three days in France touring the British bases at Boulogne, Havre and Rouen. He sees troops at camps waiting to be sent forward, veterinary hospitals which have saved thousands of army horses and remount depots where thousands more wait to be claimed. He is hugely interested in the vast buildings packed with supplies; "several hundred thousand shells of all sizes and bombs and grenades and [some seven] million small arms cartridges, besides food of all kinds."[284] At Havre there is a shed half a mile long, "containing all the supplies, ammunition for 400,000 men… They employ over 5,000 labourers."[285] Ponsonby notes that they have enough rum to float a battleship. "One sees how the money is spent,"[286] writes the King. At Rouen there are bakeries that turn out 90,000 rations of bread every day. He sees repair shops too, where salvage men send mud encrusted items. "Everything possible is repaired: rifles, machine guns, bayonets, swords, boots, clothes, equipment, saddles and leather gear, a most useful and practical place."[287]

There are huge base hospitals too, and convalescent camps where the men are almost ready to return to duty. His Majesty sees the Quai d'Escale at Havre, "from where all the sick and wounded leave for England."[288] He returns to the converted casino that has now dealt with 80,000 cases.

277   Hammerton: *Our King & Queen: A Pictorial Record of Their Lives*, pp.21-22.
278   RA QM/PRIV/CC04/139.
279   *Daily Telegraph* 23/10/15.
280   *The Standard* 23/10/15.
281   Syonsby: *Recollections of Three Reigns*, pp.312-315.
282   RA QM/PRIV/CC04/133.
283   Syonsby: *Recollections of Three Reigns*, pp.316.
284   RA GV/PRIV/GVD/1915 (21/10).
285   RA GV/PRIV/GVD/1915 (22/10).
286   RA QM/PRIV/CC04/134.
287   RA GV/PRIV/GVD/1915 (22/10).
288   Ibid.

"Some of the men there had been gassed and it was painful to watch them," writes Ponsonby, "blue in the face and gasping for breath. I found one was a German and regretted the pity I had wasted on him; but the King rebuked me and said that after all he was only a poor dying human being, in no way responsible for the German horrors."[289] The visits run smoothly. His Majesty has learned a lot in this busy year, and finds it better to make few plans or timetables, because inevitably he lingers too long and things change, whence "there has been great disappointment when the King has not been able to visit some particular factory or hospital."[290]

His Majesty boards a train and leaves for Aire. "I own that… I was quite tired, but am all right today after a good night," he writes.[291] It is an odd house, higgledy piggledy and fashioned out of red brick; raised off the ground with ornate decoration about the windows. "I must prepare Your Majesty for the most awful decorations," a member of French's staff has warned the King. "It is full of what are - I believe - known in the trade as "Viennese novelties." But the house itself is as good as any house that I have seen in this part of France… where for people to have a bathroom is considered as great an eccentricity as to keep a giraffe."[292] But it is comfortable, with a nice little sitting room. But more importantly for His Majesty, there is room for another guest in the room next door, who is waiting for him on his arrival. "I had a grand bath and change to be ready for Papa's arrival," writes David. "Papa looks well, though of course he is a bit tired having had a very long day; we dined at 8:30 and… a damn good dinner it was too!!"[293]

Sunday morning is cold and foggy, and the King attends a church parade nearby; "a little old-fashioned town with a market place of the French description covered with cobblestones. Some 800 men were drawn up in the square and a band contributed to the solemnity of the occasion. There was a large attendance of Generals and staff officers," Ponsonby notes wryly. "In fact, there was quite an epidemic of religious fervour of the part of the staff."[294] The King and Queen of the Belgians arrive for lunch, along with Queen Mary's brother, Alge. "Of course I did not think him looking well," he writes to his sister of her husband a few days later. "I have no doubt all this worry has had something to do with it, but I think though this water diet is not particular good for him. I thought him looking thin and several persons said so also."[295]

"An awful morning pouring with rain… blowing hard from the east and cold, a jolly outlook,"[296] the King writes before departing for Ribemont to meet with French officials, including the President. His Majesty intends to take every opportunity to try and get to the bottom of the French Government's problems during his visit. "The train journey from Paris was badly delayed; with the result that the buggers didn't turn up till noon," writes David, "and we had a most bloody cold 45 minute wait."[297] The King wanders off to a nearby cottage, "where the woman, having no idea who he was, prattled away and told him about the German soldiers who had been there… She showed the King and Allenby the cupboards…which had been smashed in with a rifle butt."[298] When the French finally arrive, His Majesty bravely pins medals on French soldiers in a northeast gale and cold sleet and is thoroughly interested in a contingent of Algerian troops brought to meet him. On galloping away again, one of the men falls from his horse and at first it is feared that he has hurt

289   Syonsby: *Recollections of Three Reigns*, p.317.
290   RA PS/PSO/GV/PS/WAR/QQ6/3330.
291   RA QM/PRIV/CC04/139.
292   RA PS/PSO/GV/PS/WAR/QQ6/3330.
293   RA EDW/PRIV/DIARY/1915 (23/10).
294   Syonsby: *Recollections of Three Reigns*, p.318.
295   RA QM/PRIV/CC53/428.
296   RA EDW/PRIV/DIARY/1915 (25/10).
297   Ibid.
298   Syonsby: *Recollections of Three Reigns*, p.320.

himself badly. "It was amusing to see the difference between the behaviour of the King and the President," Ponsonby writes.

> The King, on seeing the man fall, at once went to see what had happened. This was the natural impulse; the President, on the other hand… remained where he was, uncertain whether it was the right thing for a President to get mixed up with an accident of this sort. However, when it came to the President and his staff remaining behind while everyone else went forward, he determined to follow the King and joined in with the others.[299]

The latter part of His Majesty's visit is to be dedicated to a systematic review of British troops, and he begins with a visit to inspect Australians in the town square at Steenvorde. One of the rare criticisms about the King's 1914 visit had been his visibility. The King moved about on foot or in a motor, and soldiers further back were disappointed that they could see nothing of him. "I therefore suggested," wrote Ponsonby, "that at all inspections of troops His Majesty should ride… The King approved of the idea and told me to make arrangements for a fresh horse at each inspection."[300] Ponsonby provides very particular criteria when liaising with GHQ to make sure that suitable mounts are found. He doesn't care what they look like, within reason. He doesn't think anyone will be paying much attention to the animal if the King is sitting on it. Ponsonby is more interested in the temperament. "Will you take every precaution to have a quiet horse… if the King was bucked off before his troops it would be disastrous. Horses generally quiet are apt to get frightened with much cheering, so one cannot be too careful."[301]

On 28th October the Royal party departs after breakfast to see troops from the First Army. They meet Sir Douglas Haig at a nearby crossroads and in wretched, gusty weather His Majesty mounts a chestnut mare belonging to the General. The animal has much experience with ceremonies in the heart of London, with loud music, and together with Haig. the King rides off towards Hesdigneul. The wet weather means that the ground is saturated, and it will be quite impossible for the men to march past. Instead, His Majesty will ride past them, and after he has passed by a sensible distance, they will be allowed to give three cheers.

Things begin well. "The King's horse behaved admirably and never took any notice of the cheering. His Majesty got so at home on the animal that he dropped the reins on the horse's neck and decorated Captain Foss with the VC, an operation which required both hands."[302] He then canters across the main road to Bethune to go and see a comparatively small party of Royal Flying Corps men, no more than fifty. His Majesty finishes his inspection and pauses to ask questions about new aeroplanes. "Seeing his superior engaged in conversation with the King, it occurred to the second in command, who apparently was ignorant of the instructions issued on the subject, that it devolved on him to call for three cheers."[303] "We were within 50 yards of the place at which he was to dismount and look round the aeroplanes on foot," writes Haig. "The mare was so quiet all through the day, too, but the waving caps and the sudden cheering would have upset any horse at such a close distance."[304]

The noise startles Haig's mare, and with the King still mounted, she rears up. She comes back down on her forefeet, but rears again and her hind legs buckle underneath her on the boggy ground.

299   Ibid., p.322.
300   Ibid., p.315.
301   RA PS/PSO/GV/PS/WAR/QQ6/3330.
302   Syonsby: *Recollections of Three Reigns*, pp.323-326.
303   Ibid., pp.323-326.
304   (ed.) Sheffield & Bourne,: *Douglas Haig: War Diaries and Letters 1914-1918*, p.167.

She falls backwards, right on top of His Majesty. The whole accident happens so quickly that there is no time for Ponsonby to reach him. "I at once jumped off and flung the reins to the nearest man. I ran up and knelt down by the King, who had had all the wind knocked out of him." For what seems like minutes, His Majesty lies completely still. His skin has turned "a fearful colour."[305] Then he finally opens his eyes. David has his back turned at the terrible moment, and the first thing he sees is his father being lifted to his feet. He rushes to him. Ponsonby's first thought is that the horse must have broken the King's pelvis, "but he suddenly expressed a wish to stand up and we supported him on each side." Relieved, Ponsonby believes that nothing can be broken after all; "a conclusion which I afterwards learned was absolutely wrong."[306] His Majesty simply asks for his cap and asks Ponsonby to look after his cane.

Haig asks what on earth they are going to do, and it is decided that the best course of action is to return the King to the chateau at Aire. The motor cars are sent for and Ponsonby asks for a telegram to be sent for a doctor. They carry him to his motor, bundle David in with him and set off.

"I suffered great agonies all the way,"[307] His Majesty has David record in his diary later. "That Papa was hurt and in pain was obvious," writes the Prince of Wales, "and I was very nervous as I drove with him in the car as he got so white: and breathing was an effort and his speech was slow and hard to understand. He complained of pains in his side and groin."[308]

As they speed along they see troops going up to assemble for the King's inspection of the new Guards Division. Troops he had already inspected hear the cheering further down the road and assume he is driving back past. The men were primed to raise their caps and cheer when a covered green motor "was seen tearing down the road at full tilt." A staff officer jumps out and forbids everyone from cheering as there had been an accident. Not everybody heard.

> It was a curious spectacle. Along one portion of the front the men stood silently to attention, while their comrades… further away down the road were raising their caps on their bayonets and cheering with true British lustiness. From where I stood at the edge of the roadside I caught just a glimpse of His Majesty as the car swept silently past. He was sitting half bent in the corner of the vehicle, and his face wore a faint smile of acknowledgment.[309]

It takes 45 minutes to reach Aire. The Prince of Wales and Charles Cust lift the King and carry him from the motor up the stone steps. His Majesty howls in pain as he is moved. With the help of servants, David and the others manage to get him up to his room, undress him and lay him on a sofa. It pains David to leave his father suffering, but although in agony, the King says that he refuses to be examined by every doctor that comes. He will wait for his own, Bertrand Dawson, or for Bowlby. But by extraordinary chance, Cust remembers that Sister Edith Ward is at the front and on a barge somewhere nearby. A veteran of the South African War, with thirty year's experience, Miss Ward had not only nursed His Majesty's brother Eddy, but also the King himself during his bout of typhoid in the 1890s. A car is sent for her and she rushes to Aire. "She turned up and had Papa in bed, and comfortable by 1:45," writes David. Miss Ward is joined by a nurse who is in charge of the Canadian Clearing Station that the King had visited earlier in the week and he is shooed from the room.

305   RA QM/PRIV/CC53/428.
306   Syonsby: *Recollections of Three Reigns,* pp.323-326.
307   RA GV/PRIV/GVD/1915 (28/10).
308   RA EDW/PRIV/DIARY/1915 (28/10).
309   *The Times* 30/10/15.

The King's doctors, Sir Bertrand Dawson and Sir Anthony Bowlby, both happen to be working at the front, and arrive from Bailleul. David waits anxiously downstairs as they assess his father's injuries. "By 3:30 they had come out of the room with the most joyful and satisfactory report that Papa had absolutely no injuries, either external or internal, but that he was suffering from the shock of the fall and was severely bruised about the groin."[310] If this is indeed the assessment that David is given, both men are lying. "The injuries were more serious than could then be disclosed," wrote Dawson years later, though it could be that the proper diagnosis is initially missed. "Besides widespread and severe bruising the pelvis was broken in at least two places and the pain was bad, the subsequent shock considerable."[311] Even the letter drafted to the Queen omits any written reference to skeletal injuries, though Ponsonby did manage to connect a telephone call to the palace on the same day as he husband's fall and may have said otherwise.

> The bruising is extensive and severe and is most pronounced on the right thigh, the right groin, the lower part of the back and round the waist. We have made a careful examination of the King and are glad to be able to state that we find no evidence of injury to the internal organs. There is pain in breathing deeply, which is due to the bruised muscles and not to any injury of the lungs. We are giving medicine to subdue the pain and inflammation.[312]

Queen Mary had been shopping and has just returned from having tea with Queen Alexandra when Stamfordham breaks the news. German newspapers will claim that the King's condition was so severe that she rushed to France, which makes Her Majesty most indignant. A few hours after the incident, the King is more comfortable, "but the slightest movement gave him untold agonies."[313] It is then that David suggests going home immediately to his mother to explain what has happened in person, and he writes that his father "jumped at this proposal." He stops in one final time to bid his father goodbye and "the change for the good in those three hours was remarkable!! His colour had returned and he was out of pain so long as he lay still on his back and he was altogether more cheery… thank God Papa is all right!"[314] He is back in London by lunchtime the following day, and goes straight to his mother and Stamfordham to bring them up to speed.

"I suffered great pain and hardly slept at all as I was so terribly bruised all over, and I also suffered much from shock,"[315] the King records later of the three days following the accident. He is continually probed by doctors. "Papa is getting on slowly," writes David on 30th October, "the pain is diminishing and he is depressed, but no wonder!"[316] Sir John French is anxious to get rid of His Majesty, terrified of Germans trying to bomb the King. He visits Aire and emerges from an audience to tell Ponsonby "that it would not be long before the whole incident reached the Germans through spies, and that the enemy's aeroplanes would buzz round and drop bombs on the villa. He said it was therefore necessary to move the King shortly, and argued that if the doctors were agreed there would be less risk in moving him than in bombs."[317] French sends additional anti-aircraft guns to Aire, and has the RFC make regular patrols of the chateau. Dawson and Bowlby concur with the Prince of Wales over concerns that His Majesty will be moved too soon.

310   RA EDW/PRIV/DIARY/1915 (28/10).
311   Watson: *Dawson of Penn*, pp.138-140.
312   RA/QM/PRIV/CC04/145.
313   Syonsby: *Recollections of Three Reigns*, pp.323-326.
314   RA EDW/PRIV/DIARY/1915 (28/10).
315   RA GV/PRIV/GVD/1915 29/10?
316   RA EDW/PRIV/DIARY/1915 (30/10).
317   Syonsby: *Recollections of Three Reigns*, pp.323-326.

How well I remember the insistent urging of GHQ that we should get the King to England before the Germans had time to bomb the house, indifferently sheltered in a small wood, and how we insisted we must wait till there had been some recovery from the shock and time enough to know that there were no hidden internal injuries... The bladder might easily have ruptured and the result have been fatal.[318]

The King has no intention of moving for any of them. "You can tell French from me to go to hell and stay there," he says to Ponsonby after he learns of the Commander in Chief's fears. "I don't intend to move for any bombs." Dawson, who happened to be at the door, heard these gracious words and repeated them to French, who was hugely amused."[319] He is more gracious with regard to Haig's horse. He sends the General a message expressing the hope that the horse was not hurt in the incident and assuring him that he is not to blame himself or the animal.

A public bulletin is issued at home to reassure the public, and it is reported that His Majesty is severely bruised and is to remain in bed. But nonetheless rumours spread that the situation is worse than assumed. "The King was already dead, said some. The accident was caused, not by a horse falling, said others; a German shell had very severely wounded him. It was recalled that not until almost the last moment had the physicians around the late King Edward taken the nation into their confidence about the real gravity of his illness."[320] His Majesty receives worldwide sympathy. India offers up her prayers, from Rome the King of Italy telegraphs for news, as does the Pope. People are stopping in to various British embassies for news. Naturally in Canada, the King's uncle is keen for information and other enquiries came from as far afield as Japan. Wishing His Majesty a speedy recovery is at least something that everyone could agree on. "We have talked less about politics, which may be a good thing."

Thank God it was no worse," writes Queen Mary, "the Doctors gave a fair report and if no complications set in we may hope for a good recovery before long, but it is very distressing and worrying... You can imagine my anxiety and this in addition to everything else we have to bear just now."[321] She assures the King that he "can't think how thankful we shall all be to get you back... every preparation is being made to make all as comfortable as is possible... nobody to meet you *anywhere* and I will wait in my room until *you* send for me, for I presume you would rather be settled in your bed before you see me."[322] At the chateau in Aire, they have to dismantle the balustrade to get His Majesty's stretcher down the stairs. The journey has been planned by the top medical officer in France. Accompanied by the doctors and his two nurses, the King is placed aboard a hospital train at the nearest station where French and Haig come to see him off. He is also determined to decorate a soldier of the Coldstream Guards who was to have received his Victoria Cross on the day of the King's accident. Sergeant Oliver Brooks is led to His Majesty's bedside. Cust reads the medal citation. "He knelt on the floor and bent over the bed. The King tried to fasten the cross on his coat, but it was soon evident that he had overrated his strength, and, someone had to come to his assistance to push the pin through the stiff khaki of the soldier's uniform."[323] His Majesty is placed carefully aboard the hospital ship *Anglia*. Ponsonby remains close by at all times with Superintendent Quinn of Scotland Yard, doing his best to keep people out of the way. "I thought the King would hate a crowd."[324]

318   Watson: *Dawson of Penn*, pp.138-140.
319   Syonsby: *Recollections of Three Reigns*, pp.323-326.
320   Hammerton: *Our King & Queen: A Pictorial Record of Their Lives*, pp.23-24.
321   RA QM/PRIV/CC26/101.
322   Pope-Hennessy: *Queen Mary, 1867-1953*, p.50.
323   Hammerton: *Our King & Queen: A Pictorial Record of Their Lives*, p.24.
324   Syonsby: *Recollections of Three Reigns*, pp.323-326.

The crossing is rough, high winds and a tumultuous sea. His Majesty suffers a great deal, along with fifty other wounded men tossed about on their way across the Channel. Seasickness adds to his other woes. Miss Ward and Miss Tremaine are rendered so ill themselves that two of the *Anglia's* nurses have to tend to the King. At Victoria Station he is bundled inside a motor ambulance by a specially selected party of bearers from the Red Cross to make the short journey to the palace. The vehicle travels at three miles an hour and even then His Majesty is in agony. As soon as he is settled the Queen rushes to see him. "Thought him looking thin and ill and he was very tired."[325] David is relieved. "I thought him looking much better than I expected, despite his [being] sick towards the end of a rather rough crossing… It's a great relief to get Papa home!"[326] The King is every bit as grateful. "I was indeed deeply thankful to find myself home again. Darling May, Mary, David and Mama and Toria came to see me and made me comfortable for the night."[327]

But it will be a slow road to recovery. "For the first fortnight I never remember having suffered so much pain."[328] His Majesty is not only suffering physically, but he cannot stand being idle. "He does so hate having to lay in bed and be inactive,"[329] remarks David. "The doctors visited me twice a day, suffered a good deal of pain and much discomfort, slept only with the aid of sleeping draughts."[330] The King is also instructed to take a small measure of alcohol every day during his convalescence, the fact of which has to be published lest the public get the wrong idea about his consumption. Family visit every day, but there is still work to be done too. Stamfordham arrives twice a day with red boxes, Kitchener stops by on his way to the Dardanelles to assess the prospects of that campaign; and the Prime Minister drops in to talk business. His Majesty has been extremely lucky. He will be confined to his room for more than a month and it is almost a fortnight before he can be sat up in a chair. "Not too comfortable."[331] The following day, the King holds a council, "but am still full of aches and pains and can't put my feet to the ground."[332] It will be a further week before he is strong enough to be able to have a proper bath and get dressed. The truth is that His Majesty will never be quite the same again. "The callus which formed at the sites of injury could be felt as irregular bony nodules for the remainder of the King's life, and his movements were henceforth somewhat limited and stiff and even at times painful."[333] His shooting also suffers. "Those best qualified to know - keepers, loaders, friends, have testified that in efficiency as a shot and in physical powers he was never the same man again after his accident."[334]

"You can see how inconvenient it is this accident coming when there is so much to be done, to see to, in every way," the Queen writes to her aunt."[335] She assumes some of His Majesty's engagements that can't be neglected; such as continuing to inspect divisions before their departures for the front. She sees one on Salisbury Plain, another featuring South African soldiers at Aldershot, "a fine looking lot of men who have been fighting in German West Africa lately."[336] At one review she walks more than five miles up and down the lines of soldiers, with her bad knee. "As the men

325   RA PRIV/QMD/1915 (1/11).
326   RA EDW/PRIV/DIARY/1915 (1/11).
327   RA GV/PRIV/GVD/1915 (1/11).
328   Rose: *King George V,* pp.180-182.
329   RA EDW/PRIV/DIARY/1915 (2/11).
330   RA GV/PRIV/GVD/1915 (2-8/11).
331   Ibid., 9/11.
332   Ibid., 10/11.
333   Watson: *Dawson of Penn,* pp.138-140.
334   Gore: *King George V, A Personal Memoir,* pp.279-278.
335   RA QM/PRIV/CC26/102.
336   RA PRIV/QMD/1915 (2/12).

inspected were delighted to testify, the inspections were carried out with as much thoroughness and attention to detail as though the King had been acting in person."[337]

"Can actually stand now and use a wheeled chair," His Majesty records on 14th November. He dresses for the first time a week later, and is able to walk a little, climb in and out of the bath, "but my ribs and side still hurt me a good deal."[338] He reads plenty of books before he is fit to venture across the palace to receive visitors, and spends an entire afternoon walking up and down the balcony outside his room. He feels stronger each day, and on the 1st December is able to leave the palace to have lunch with his mother. When eight recipients of the Victoria Cross visit Buckingham Palace to receive their medals a few days later, the *Pall Mall Gazette* reports that His Majesty still shows signs of weakness, but is able to remain on his feet. Sisters Ward and Tremaine leave the palace, and the doctors make their last examinations for now. On 13th December they issue a bulletin:

> We are happy to report that the King has so far recovered from the grave accident of October 28th as to be able to resume work with certain limitations.
>
> The King has lost seriously in weight, and until a normal state of health is attained it is essential that his Majesty should avoid any cause of fatigue.
>
> It has been necessary on medical grounds that the King should take a little stimulant daily during his convalescence.
>
> As soon as the King's health is quite restored, His Majesty will resume that total abstinence which he has imposed upon himself for public reasons.[339]

"A Source of Great Weakness"

In terms of bickering and conflict at home, it has been a terrible year in political circles and the Royal Navy has had its moments. But throughout the King's tough convalescence it is the army that gives him sleepless nights. By the beginning of October, Kitchener is miserable. The resignation threats that he makes whilst sitting with His Majesty at the palace alarm him, to say the least, and he tells his Minister that he simply won't allow it, and that he retains every confidence in him. Sir William Robertson is by now Chief of Staff at the front, and he is beside himself. "We are like a ship without a rudder," he tells Stamfordham in mid-November. "There is no controlling head at all. A certain amount of reorganisation is required in technical staff at the War Office in order to meet the great development of our army."[340] A nonsense suggestion had been made in September that His Majesty should take command of the army himself. Analysing the concept, Esher points out that he is just as qualified as the Tsar, who has done this in Russia, but nobody took the idea seriously, least of all the King.

His Majesty does, however, make a radical suggestion. "The King feels that the time has come when the general control of all military operations should be centred under one responsible authority," Stamfordham writes to Asquith. "There are evident signs of what can only be described as a lack of discipline in the relations between the Commander in Chief in France and the War Office; there is a need of one single dominating, directing mind not only in administration but in the strategy of the war. The King therefore asks the Prime Minister to consider the advisability of appointing Lord Kitchener Commander in Chief of all British forces at home and abroad and

337   *The Ladies Field* 21/9/18.
338   Ibid., 19/11.
339   Hammerton: *Our King & Queen: A Pictorial Record of Their Lives*, p.25.
340   RA PS/PS/GV/C/Q/939/1.

making him responsible for the conduct of the various campaigns to which we are now committed. The responsibility will be a heavy one: but His Majesty believes it will be easier borne on the shoulders of one man than as at present divided, and the best plan which suggests itself to His Majesty is to invest the Secretary of State for War with executive powers as commander in chief of the Imperial Forces."[341]

It is a suggestion that will not come to fruition, but the situation is no better in December. On a rainy, painful afternoon for the King during his convalescence, Kitchener visited the palace again. "Things are very difficult at present," writes His Majesty. "Some grave decisions will have to be come to."[342] After the meeting he sits and drafts a letter to Asquith with Stamfordham. The King has heard a notion that Sir William Robertson might be suitable for the post of Chief of the Imperial General Staff; the leading military advisor to the Government in London. It is a move Haig has already postured to His Majesty. The King had last seen Robertson at the palace in July and thought him very sensible. He trusts his judgement and agrees that it would be hugely beneficial if he and Kitchener can fathom a way to work alongside one another at the War Office. "His Majesty does believe that important advantages would be secured by the transfer of [Robertson] to the part of CIGS, making him responsible only to the War Council for whose information and advice he his staff would deal with all matters of strategy and conduct of war." By the King's reckoning, that would allow Kitchener, as a member of the War Council, to accept or debate Robertson's advice, but it would relieve him of a considerable amount of work and leave him free to better devote himself to the administration of the War Office, "especially with respect to finance upon which he has always been regarded as almost an expert authority." His Majesty had quite obviously discussed this eventuality with his friend during his visit to Buckingham Palace on 1st December. "The King has every reason to believe that an arrangement on the above lines would be acceptable to Lord Kitchener."[343]

Kitchener tells Robertson he ought to take the job in London, but the latter refuses, he does not think that the arrangement will work unless the War Secretary agrees to put some of his workload under someone else's authority, which is exactly what His Majesty has suggested. Robertson, however, does not want to go to the War Office if Kitchener is not there waiting for him either. Together, he thinks, they could be "a tower of strength against the politicians and the French… I most earnestly hope he will remain, and I have told him so. His removal would do more than anything to encourage the enemy. It is foolish to turn him into the street." Robertson pleads with Wigram. "Do all you can to keep him at the War Office. He and I will get on splendidly I am sure."[344] His Majesty is thoroughly satisfied with this arrangement, and once detailed discussions begin he only intervenes once. "The King hopes you will see Robertson before he actually takes up work at the War Office," Stamfordham tells Asquith, "and make certain that he and Kitchener are in complete agreement as to the future procedure and working relations between the CIGS and the Secretary of State. It is most important that all possible precaution should be taken to ensure success to this new combination."[345] The Prime Minister carries out this request two days later, on 18th December. Robertson agrees to return to London to take up the role, and the day before Christmas Eve he stops in at the palace for his first audience with the King in his new post. "If he and K will only work together," writes His Majesty, "all will be well."[346] But less harmonious is the question of

341 BD: MS Asquith A.1 4 #137.
342 RA PS/PS/GV/C/Q/838/49.
343 Ibid.
344 RA PS/PS/GV/C/Q/838/57.
345 RA PS/PS/GV/C/Q/838/66.
346 RA PRIV/GVD/1915 (23/12).

what to do with Sir John French, an issue which the King has placed himself in the very thick of, and despite his own broken pelvis, at the end of the year he is determined to ensure that the General is replaced as Commander in Chief.

Haig had expressed his concerns about French's suitability for commanding the BEF less than a week after Britain's declaration of war. If the King agreed, he did not articulate this opinion with any force at the time. After the retreat, however, when Kitchener was forced to race to France to convince Sir John not to remove his force from the line, His Majesty had begun to express his doubts. But after a difficult opening to the war, he had been sympathetic when David told him that the Commander in Chief was laid low. "I think it a very good thing that Sir John should go to bed for a few days, especially when there was a lull in the fighting, as the strain during the last three months has been very great."[347]

But since then, Sir John French has completely undermined his own position in the eyes of the King. There was the report after Neuve Chapelle in which a small amendment claimed credit that belonged to Haig. Then French gave his indiscreet interview with the press, which greatly astonished His Majesty. The article was wildly optimistic with regard to prospect of victory, too optimistic, and the King felt that it was "are apt to undo for this country what anyone with any influence is endeavouring to do, namely to persuade the masses to take their part in the war and to make them realise the work still to be accomplished."[348] French antagonised the King again by sending General Smith-Dorrien home. His Majesty thought that the Commander in Chief's treatment of his subordinate was appalling, and sent the latter a token gift. "Will you say," writes Smith-Dorrien, "that under existing circumstances I appreciate the King's thought more than words can express. You will understand that, hard as I try, it is not very east to keep cheerful just now, and that being remembered in this way by the King and Queen has acted as a powerful tonic."[349] But French's biggest faux pas in 1915 so far as His Majesty is concerned is his running feud with Lord Kitchener. "The fact is," writes Haig to Wigram, "that Sir John is of a jealous disposition, and is at the same time not quite sure in his own mind as to his fitness for his present position! Hence, imagine, all this anxiety to be puffed up in the press." Haig thinks that French is wasting his energies on intrigue. "Personally I have no time to spare to take part in these squabbles."[350]

As the summer approaches, the King believes that French is making no effort to improve relations with Kitchener. There is a constructive effort on the part of the palace to get Haig to try and mediate between the two Generals. He tries but to no avail. Additionally, members of French's staff are actively involved in publicly attacking Kitchener and intriguing in a way that is detrimental to the war effort. By the end of May, the King is extremely anxious. He has David reporting to him about infighting on the Western Front. "French may be a good soldier," he writes to his uncle in Canada, of course a senior army officer himself, "but I don't think he is particularly clever and he has an awful temper. Whether he is now suffering from the strain of campaign or from swollen head I don't know, but he is behaving in a very odd way, which adds to my many anxieties. I know you never had a very high opinion of him."[351]

By the beginning of July, the King has told Kitchener that he will support him, whatever he decides to do about French, but His Majesty also has a conversation with Robertson at Buckingham Palace. "I had a long talk with him about the position of affairs at the front. I am convinced it

347   RA EDW/PRIV/MAIN/A/1415.
348   RA PS/PSO/GV/C/Q/750/6.
349   RA PS/PSO/GV/C/Q/832/354.
350   RA PS/PS/GV/C/Q/2521/V/129.
351   Rose, Kenneth: *King George V,* pp.266-267.

would be better for all concerned if the Commander in Chief were changed."[352] All His Majesty wants is efficiency, to ensure that the army is in the best condition to win the war. When French visits him the day after his conversation with Robertson he is positive. The King says that he hopes now that the Commander in Chief's relations with both Kitchener and the French would be better now, but his optimism has faded somewhat when he sees Haig two weeks later when he is home on leave and brings up the subject of the bad blood between French and Lord Kitchener again. He remarks how unsavoury he finds French's dealings with the press; Repington and Northcliffe in particular. It is not, in His Majesty's opinion, behaviour befitting an officer in his army.

The nail in Sir John French's coffin, so far as his command is concerned, proves to be the Battle of Loos. Worryingly, after a conversation mid-battle with Haig, the latter makes the observation that "he seemed tired of the war, and said that in his opinion we ought to take the first opportunity of concluding peace otherwise England would be ruined!"[353] Things like this always get back to the King. When the offensive fails to break the German Army on the Western Front, the question of the deployment of the reserves in the midst of battle becomes a bitter issue. French attempts to place the blame for their tardy arrival squarely on Haig's shoulders, and Haig proves a lot less docile than during the minor controversy of the reports of Neuve Chapelle. A "fiery"[354] exchange of correspondence follows between the two, and Kitchener asks for a report from Haig on the matter. Haig's account is not without flaws, but he is not the only General venting his negative opinion of Sir John French. His Majesty amasses considerable documentation from different sources that supports Haig's version of events. Repington goes to work with his poison pen to try and support the Commander in Chief, but his opinion carries no weight with the King.

According to Robertson, who comes home to talk with the Cabinet, its members are turning away from supporting the Commander in Chief. His lack of ability to get along with his French counterparts is of huge concern. They ask Robertson for an opinion on the expediency of removing Sir John. Robertson defers answering until he has had a chance to discuss the matter with Haig back at the front. The latter is now void of any inclination to speak up for the Commander in Chief. "In view of what had happened in the recent battle over the reserves, and in view of the seriousness of the [military] situation, I have come to the conclusion that it is not fair to the Empire to retain French in command." In his diary, he adds that none of his subordinates commanding his corps have "any opinion of Sir John's military ability or military views: in fact, they find no confidence in him." According to Haig, "Robertson quite agreed, and left me saying "he knew how to act, and would report to Stamfordham."[355]

The King arrives in France a few days later for his visit, and makes a pointed attempt to glean as much information as possible about French's command. He talks to Generals Gough and Haking, who are less than complimentary. In the course of a "long talk... They pointed out that there was a great want of initiative, a fighting spirit and no proper plans made in high quarters and that everyone had lost confidence in the Commander in Chief. They had seen more fighting than anyone out here... and [said] that unless a change was made we should never win this war." Haig comes to dinner. "[He] was not very communicative, but he never shone much in conversation, although when he did speak it was sound stuff," wrote Ponsonby later. "After dinner he had a long talk to the King alone... I gathered from His Majesty that he spoke strongly about there being no proper plan of campaign. The King said he would repeat all he heard to Asquith, who intended

---

352   RA GV/PRIV/GVD/1915 (1/7).
353   (ed.) Sheffield & Bourne: *Douglas Haig: War Diaries and Letters 1914-1918*, p.159.
354   Ibid, p.162-163.
355   Duff Cooper: *Haig*, p.275.

discussing whether some change would not be advisable."[356] Haig has indeed spoken frankly. "He entirely corroborated what the other two had said," writes His Majesty, but went much further and said that the Commander in Chief was a source of great weakness to the army and no one had any confidence in him anymore… all these things add to my worries and anxieties."[357] The day before his accident. The King interviews Robertson too. "He is strongly of opinion that a change should be made here as soon as possible."[358] His Majesty's opinion with regard to French's capability for command had been further galvanised. "The troops here are all right," he writes home to Stamfordham from Aire, "but I find that several of the most important generals have entirely lost confidence in the Commander in Chief and they advised me that it was universal and that he must go, otherwise we shall never win this war. This has been my opinion for some time.[359]

French is not in great shape at the beginning of November. He returns home on leave and takes to his bed as criticism rains down about his despatch following the Battle of Loos. Haig postulates that his inert state is a result of his having been asked to correct this document. French is allegedly most anxious to tell Haig that he has had no part in Repington's latest effort. "I said that my only thought was how to win the war," writes Haig in his diary, "and that my duties [commanding] First Army took up all my time. I gather that no one of importance takes much notice of Sir John when he goes to London, and that he feels his loss of position."[360] The King is not sympathetic either. "He ought to come home."[361]

By mid-November, Asquith has discussed the matter fully with His Majesty, and has come to the conclusion that it is time for Sir John French to go. He despatches Lord Esher from Paris to tactfully convince him to depart quietly. French is aware that he is going to be removed from his post, and Esher reports that he is "in bed and in very low spirits!"[362] But he is also "inclined to show fight."[363] The King is already frustrated with how long the matter is taking to resolve itself, but French's acolytes are scurrying back and forth trying to illicit support for Sir John, who believes that with Kitchener out of the picture, assessing the position in the Dardanelles, he has support in the Cabinet that might win through. But he writes: "Such a fate has befallen much better and greater men than I am and I am only thankful to be able to know in my heart that the army I have commanded really saved the country from dire disaster. One never does look for much gratitude in this world."[364]

Thanks in large measure to His Majesty's machinations, Asquith's mind is made up. Esher does his best, and French is offered a peerage, money and a post as Commander in Chief Home Forces. Esher says: "It was a painful affair, and I do not wish to go through anything like it again… The Field Marshal went away immediately after my talk with him. He thought it desirable to see Asquith as soon as possible."[365]

Sir John arrives in London convinced that he still has a choice. He meets with the Prime Minister on 29th November and Asquith presses the matter, but French says he will not take the post at home if Kitchener remains at the War Office, and so he returns to France still having not given way. His Majesty has Stamfordham pen a letter to Asquith on 2nd December on the need for

356   Syonsby: *Recollections of Three Reigns*, p.320.
357   RA GV/PRIV/GVD/1915 (24/10).
358   RA GV/PRIV/GVD/1915 (27/10).
359   Nicolson: *King George V: His Life and Reign*, pp.266-267.
360   (ed.) Sheffield & Bourne: *Douglas Haig: War Diaries and Letters 1914-1918*, p.169.
361   RA GV/PRIV/GVD/1915 (15/11).
362   RA PS/PS/GV/C/Q/724/59.
363   RA PS/PS/GV/C/Q/838/47.
364   Holmes: *The Little Field Marshal: A Life of Sir John French*, pp.308-309.
365   RA PS/PS/GV/C/Q/724/60.

expediency: "The King thinks that you have shown him every consideration both in the manner by which you endeavoured to arrange his resignation and also respecting the conditions. You offered with a view of making the suggested course as easy and acceptable as possible to him. But in his opinion Sir John is not treating you with the same regard. He therefore hopes you will now ask Sir John to give effect to the suggestion conveyed to him nearly a week ago through [Esher] in which His Majesty understood he expressed his willingness to acquiesce... the King feels that GHQ should not be left much longer without a Commander in Chief."[366] A member of the Cabinet has a telephone conversation with him on 4th December and tells him that resignation is his only option and, finally, he gives way. "For three weeks no one has thought of the enemy,"[367] Churchill told his wife on the day that French finally resigned. "To cut a long story short," Robertson writes from the front on 5th December, "Sir John tells me that he sent in his resignation yesterday so the matter should now be definitely settled."[368] The news becomes public in mid-December. French will receive a peerage and command of the home forces, but he is left a sad, bitter man. Churchill was with him during his final day as Commander in Chief.

> He brought me back from the front, and we drove together during all the daylight hours, from army to army and from corps to corps. He went into the various headquarters and said goodbye to the generals... We lunched out of a hamper in a ruined cottage. His pain in giving up his great command was acute. He would much rather have given up his life... It poured with rain all day.[369]

366   Nicolson: *King George V: His Life and Reign*, p.269.
367   Rose: *King George V*, p.193.
368   RA PS/PS/GV/C/Q/838/50.
369   Churchill: *Great Contemporaries*, pp.76-77.

1916

Desecration

"A Time of Unusual Trouble"

The King departs for Sandringham with his family for Christmas. The estate is swathed in gloom, with many sad homes feeling the impact of the attack at Suvla in August, but Their Majesties do their best to keep up traditions. With Wigram the King works on his boxes, and he speaks to Stamfordham on the telephone from the hall at York Cottage. He also makes time to sit and write a letter to his faithful secretary.

> We have passed through another strenuous and anxious year and I don't deny that I have felt the strain of it, as have most people. It is not possible for me to find words to express how really deeply grateful I am to you for all your kind and helpful advice and the enormous amount of work you have done for me during these last twelve months. For you and Lady Stamfordham it has been a terrible year and I know what your sorrow is. I do indeed feel most deeply for you and have tried to show my sympathy. Only time, alas, can heal a wound like yours... The country is united and determined to win this war whatever the sacrifices are and, please God, 1916 may bring us victory and peace once more is the heartfelt prayer of your sincere and grateful friend.[1]

Gales and cold squalls sweep through Norfolk, but His Majesty is determined to get back to shooting, even though he will walk for a time with a stick. He is unable to keep to his usual program, so he comes home after lunch or spends time motoring on the estate when he finds himself in too much discomfort. He conceals his suffering greatly, but occasional bursts of temper reveal the strain. His mood is lightened by the presence of David and Bertie. They arrive from London in time for the news that the Gallipoli peninsula has been evacuated without the loss of a single man, "which is a great feat."[2] "Papa quite his old self again but for a certain lameness," writes David. "Terribly dull and quiet of an evening and the only subject of course is the war, which gets a bit monotonous being the only thing I don't want to talk about, but such is life and... it is really nice to get home to the peace and seclusion." The Royal Family sing in the billiards room after dinner, and the King stays up as late as his strength allows. "Too bloody it is my last night at this dear place after ten glorious days I've had with the parents, Mary and brothers," David writes before leaving for France. "It's done me the world of good!"[3]

Business compels His Majesty to return to London frequently in January. His most strenuous feat is to decorate 424 people in the ballroom, including six recipients of the Victoria Cross. There

1   Gore: *King George V His Life & Reign*, p.298.
2   RA GV/PRIV/GVD/1916 (10/1).
3   RA EDW/PRIV/DIARY/1916 (16/1).

are dignitaries and representatives to receive; French, Japanese, Russian; all of them are in the capital for an Allied conference. There is no escaping the war anymore. Back in Norfolk the King and Queen are required to step in with Mrs Beck, who is struggling to cope since the loss of her husband and whom His Majesty says is "in a very excitable state again."[4] They take walks down to her house to check in on her, and His Majesty monitors her situation with her brother-in-law Arthur, who has continued in Frank's post at Sandringham.

Their Majesties return to London properly on 2nd February, but the King is forced to give up the state opening of Parliament on the advice of his doctors. There is a full scale investiture at the palace, but Queen Mary is still helping to lighten his workload; receiving dignitaries and visitors to the palace, making hospital visits, meeting exchanged prisoners, soldiers, politicians, foreign representatives; even the captain of a ship that had been blown up in the channel 48 hours before. But his Majesty must continue his recovery, and it is announced that he will make his first public appearance since his accident, at the Royal Albert Hall "when the Royal Choral Society will sing the Requiem by Verdi in memory of those who have fallen in the war."

On the day of the concert the King throws himself into a full schedule that includes visiting wounded Indians, presenting a knighthood, reviewing the plans for a convalescent home in Richmond and then leaving for the Royal Albert Hall in a carriage with the Queen. The crowd gathering about the venue have enthusiastically welcomed ambassadors and dignitaries as they arrive, but there is a great cheer from the spectators thrilled to see His Majesty alive and well as he steps from his carriage at the royal entrance. He is rather surprised, and raises his hat in acknowledgement. "It was noticed that the King walked firmly, and appeared once again to be in good health. There is still a certain amount of stiffness but… was observed with obvious satisfaction and delight by the people assembled to greet Their Majesties."[5] Everyone is watching him for signs of weakness, but His Majesty seems to be enjoying himself. "The King…followed the performance with keen attention."[6] He enjoys it so much that after the performance, His Majesty sends a special message to the conductor to tell them how impressed he is. Days later the King's doctors approve of his resuming his visits to troops in training, and he travels to Hatfield to see "the caterpillar, which is an armoured motor car with guns which goes over trenches and through wire and with which we hope to attack the Germans." The King has seen one of the first tanks, and he is thrilled. "I hope we shall have a hundred of them."[7]

There is every reason to be hopeful for 1916. Britain's military machine is getting up to speed, and the results of Kitchener's vast recruiting, and Lloyd George's incessant effort at the Ministry of Munitions will be ready for action. There are accounts from behind enemy lines. Mr Andersen, a Danish agent sent the King's way by his royal relations there, "says the German position all round is worse than it was four months ago."[8] There is fresh impetus after the evacuation of Gallipoli, and the removal of Sir John French; a clean start. Lord Kitchener tells the King on his return from a visit to France that he is very pleased with Haig and all he showed him. His Majesty has already sent his new Commander in Chief a letter in his own hand:

> I take the earliest opportunity of expressing the great satisfaction with which I approved of your succeeding Sir John French as Commander in Chief of my army in France. I know

4   RA GV/PRIV/GVD/1918 (17/1).
5   *The People* 6/2/16.
6   *Daily Mirror* 7/2/16.
7   RA GV/PRIV/GVD/1916 (8/2).
8   Ibid., (12/2).

you will have the confidence of the troops serving under you and it is almost needless to assure you with what implicit trust I look forward to the successful conduct of the war at the Western Front under your able direction. Remember that it will always be a pleasure for me to help you in any way I can to carry out your heavy task and important responsibilities. I hope you will from time to time to write to me quite freely and tell me how matters are progressing.[9]

Though they are not intimate friends, the King likes Haig, who was on the fringes of his father's circle and it is undoubtedly going to be a much easier relationship than his rather distant and stilted communications with French. Haig is of a similar no-nonsense temperament as the Sovereign and to boot, he has immediately wired home to the Queen's brother, the Duke of Teck too, and asked him if he will be his Military Secretary. The omens are good. Just a few days after assuming command of the BEF Haig writes an informal letter to Wigram about a conference with the French. One Minister has told him, "If only we had had the present happy relations a year ago things would now be in a much better state. However it is not yet too late."[10]

But it is also clear that whilst His Majesty means to support Haig by any means he can, this does not run to blindly agreeing with his new chief. One of the first things that Haig has to deal with is a messy situation regarding two Guards officers that had been accused of fraternising with the enemy on Christmas Day 1915. Haig has come down hard on them, but the King counsels leniency, and suggests that surely it can be left in the hands of the divisional commander. Their sentences are quickly suspended and the men in question are sent back to the line. It is a brief affair but indicative of the fact that the King does not unquestioningly do Haig's bidding.

As Lord Derby's Scheme closes, men rush forward on the promise of being called up in a fair order. The scheme is extended three times to allow all who are willing to serve at some stage to attest, but there are simply too many men in Britain who still want no part in fighting. And elements of confusion have stopped the rest of those attesting who might have been willing. For instance, would a married man who has put his name down be sent to war ahead of all the single men who have refused to pledge their service? There are a lot of them. Nearly half of the single men on the National Register have not come forward and in fact the total response rate to Derby's scheme is only just over 50%.

Asquith cannot justify calling up married men ahead of those without families. Conscription is inevitable, and as a result, once again the King is threatened with a Cabinet crisis. His Majesty has to dash back to London from Sandringham, and Asquith tells him that the Home Secretary has resigned already, completely opposed to any form of compulsion. Two more are threatening to go because they dispute the size of the army Kitchener wants to maintain in the field and, most crushing of all for the Prime Minister, Sir Edward Grey says if these additional resignations follow, he will go too. Asquith is "naturally much hurt by what seemed to him desertion by one of his oldest friends and colleagues at a time of unusual trouble, if not danger." The Prime Minister responds to this threat by refusing to accept such a resignation, "adding that if Sir Edward Grey wished to do what would be regarded as a triumph and almost a victory by our enemies he would certainly do so by adhering to his expressed desire to leave the Government."[11] Asquith is hopeful that he can stop the exodus. "The King assured the Prime Minister of his absolute confidence in him and that he…

9   RA PS/PSO/GV/C/Q/832/112.
10   RA PS/PS/GV/C/Q/2521/V/136.
11   RA PS/PSO/GV/C/K/869/3.

would stand by and support even if all his colleagues were to leave him."[12] His Majesty thinks that men who have attested might wear an armlet over their sleeve to try and stimulate those who have not earned the right to own one. But at the turn of the year this does not stop the Cabinet having to draft the Military Service Bill.[13] Stamfordham admits to sympathising with McKenna and Runciman, the two ministers still threatening to resign. "Can we stand financing all our allies, maintaining the command of the sea, keeping up our export trade and at the same time supplying an army similar to which the other military nations of the world maintain, who have not the same responsibilities and commitments as we have undertaken?"[14] McKenna, the Chancellor of the Exchequer, makes his position clear: "I don't want to stop the supply of men for the army: but we must explain to our Allies that they can't have <u>both</u> men and <u>money</u>. Much better ask these frankly, what they will have."[15]

Under the Bill, all men between 18 and 41 will be required to attest. The only ones exempt are those employed on vital war work, those widowers who are supporting dependants alone, those who are unfit and conscientious objectors who have been approved by a tribunal. The Prime Minister is able to present himself at Buckingham Palace on 13th January and report to the King that yet another crisis has been calmed, that there have been no more resignations and that he believes the Military Service Bill "will pass with very little opposition."[16] It is as well, for letters from Haig to His Majesty that week claim that only 620 reinforcements are notified. A fortnight later, the Military Service Bill reaches the hands of the King. With Royal Assent, it becomes law and Britain breaks with her long established tradition of refusing to compel men to serve.

"Are We Downhearted?"

The people of Britain are beginning to realise the depth of commitment that it is going to take to win the war: every shell, every man, every penny. The nation will have to unite as one and put the country before personal considerations. This concept is embodied throughout the war by the sheer scope of the King's charitable endeavours. So far as cash donations are concerned, they seem endless. By the end of 1916 alone His Majesty will have donated £15,000 to the Red Cross and the Order of St. John of Jerusalem, almost a million pounds in 2018's money. But as well as a large regular donation to help care for the wounded, the King sends money to a vast array of diverse organisations; such as the Naval Employment Agency, which finds jobs for men who have left the senior service with reports of good character; the families of interned Belgian soldiers, *The Times* fund for sick and wounded, the Victoria Station free buffet, the army Christmas pudding fund, the Indian Soldiers fund, and the Church Army to name but a few.

Christmas inevitably reveals a natural spike in their endeavours. It is impossible to repeat the sending of royal tins containing gifts for soldiers in 1915. Their Majesties want to at least send cards, but they are asked not to do either by the military authorities. "They came to the conclusion that… it would be impossible to undertake the transport and distribution of the cards. Every bit of available space on board ship is required for hospital necessaries, ammunitions and other military supplies."[17] With reluctance, the King and Queen agree, but they find other ways to try and spread at least a modicum of Christmas cheer. His Majesty donates money to the *Daily Chronicle's* fund

12   Ibid.
13   RA PS/PSO/GV/C/K/869/3.
14   PA: S/13/15/24: Strachey.
15   RA PS/PSO/GV/C/K/869/3.
16   RA PRIV/GVD/1916 (13/1).
17   *The Times* 7/12/15.

for sending Christmas presents to soldiers. At the same time the *Daily Graphic* reports that he has subscribed to their fund to send fresh fruit and vegetables to the navy and more money for another effort to send hampers to prisoners of war. The King and Queen also arrange a Christmas tea at Windsor Castle. A thousand children from the town and surrounding areas with fathers on active service are invited to sit at dozens of tables. The room is dominated by a 30 foot tree sent by His Majesty and covered in gold baubles, snowflakes and Chinese lanterns. The Queen sends hand dressed dolls representing the countries of the Allies, Princess Mary sends a huge bin stuffed with crackers. After tea, the visitors are treated to a Punch and Judy show before the party is rounded off with the National Anthem.

The King spends the entirety of the war giving things away too, including properties. Having heard that the Canadians are looking for a house in the vicinity of London to serve as a convalescent home, he offers Upper Lodge on the Royal Estate at Bushey Park. Birds brought down during the King's shooting outings are distributed to those in need. Large quantities of game, principally pheasant, are sent from both Sandringham and Windsor to numerous causes, including the Docking Workhouse in Norfolk, Chichester Military Hospital and the Church Army. When the game is sold, the King refuses to pocket the profits. In 1917 he donates £430 to the Red Cross and Order of St. John of Jerusalem; all of it monies received for produce from his estates. It is reported in October 1915 that the King has given one of the most valuable stamps in his collection to the National War Fund; antiques and other valuables are also rooted out and gifted to various auctions, and 300 bottles of rare vintage wines in the royal cellars raise thousands. His Majesty also supports the Agricultural Relief of Allies Committee, who are trying to render assistance to French farmers whose livestock have been obliterated in battlefield regions, by donating Shearling rams that end up being sent to the Meuse region with other animals, tools and seeds. The King even gives away most of his civilian wardrobe, and the only new clothes he orders during the war are uniforms. One Welsh newspaper even claims that he is donating his father's walking sticks to the wounded.

> Many of these are special interest, having been presented to His Late Majesty by celebrities who knew of his fancy. But those collected by King Edward are of the greatest interest. Whenever he went for a holiday on a visit he bought a walking stick. In order to appeal to him it must have some peculiarity: and the odder and quainter it was the better.[18]

This is to say nothing of the sundry artificial limbs, items made by disabled men, coffee, chocolates, sweets, flowers, and anything else made by or requested by wounded men that the King and Queen meet on their travels. There are esoteric donations too. His Majesty hears that soldiers at the front are struggling to get hold of matches, for the Post Office refuses to carry them, and in France the state monopoly of them provided only "vile sulphurous things, and dear at that"[19] The King intervenes, and pushes through a scheme whereby the Post Office will forward them to Southampton from where they will be safely sent over. He starts the ball rolling by sending a huge consignment himself.

One contemporary newspaper's estimate of the King's total charitable contribution during the Great War equates in 2018 to £16.5 million pounds. It is also reported also that His Majesty declines the offer of a separate civil list for the Prince of Wales on the grounds that the £40,000 he receives from the Duchy of Cornwall is quite sufficient for his needs, but by far the largest donation made is a lump sum that the King wants to hand over to the Government in 1916. The task of how to go about this falls to Ponsonby. "I anticipate a bad time for the monarchy after the war

---

18   *Swansea & Cambria Daily Leader* 24/8/15.
19   *Daily Sketch* 5/10/15.

when the readjustments of the labour market must inevitably entail strikes and possibly anarchy,"[20] Ponsonby prophesises, and he is keen that His Majesty be able to make a public gesture such as this. Surprisingly he finds that the Prime Minister is opposed to the idea. He would rather that the King takes the responsibility of picking a worthy organisation and gives it to them himself. But not only is Ponsonby a formidable opponent, His Majesty is determined. The sum settled on is £100,000 and it will be placed at the disposal of the Treasury. As far as can be ascertained, the larger portion comes from the King's private funds, whilst the rest comprised money from the civil list that he had been given, but had managed to not spend through economising measures in the preceding year and wanted to return. The money is to be "applied in whatever manner is deemed in the opinion of His Majesty's Government."[21]

The gesture is lauded by the press as characteristic of a selfless monarch; the King sharing in the financial sacrifices imposed on his subjects by the war. "Such splendid munificence could not fail in any circumstances to impress the public mind,"[22] says one newspaper. The donation is used to articulate yet more frustration with Government indecision. "While Ministers have been content to preach economy and self denial this King himself has acted," says another. "They have lectured; His Majesty has led,"[23] says another publication. Northcliffe's *Daily Mail* is scathing. "Not many months ago the Chief Secretary for Ireland had declared in favour in a reduction of Minister's salaries. On December 15 Asquith replied that "I take my salary and I mean to continue to take it." and it all went quiet."[24] The Budget is about to be announced, and the country is expecting higher taxes. The press and public anxiously wait to see what will be done with money, and they are in favour of a symbolic gesture. An airship, one journalist claims, costs exactly £100,000.

In the middle of February, the King and Queen drop in at a tea party being given at Grosvenor Hall by various eminent ladies for wounded sailors and soldiers. His Majesty observes 100 men enjoying cakes and sandwiches before a concert is put on for them and he is most impressed with the arrangements. Less than two weeks later they have decided that they would like to do something similar in the Royal Mews at Buckingham Palace. Their Majesties have chosen three consecutive afternoons at the end of March and in all some 760 will be able to be catered for on each day. Interest is incessant. The press beg for admittance so that they might write about the royal tea parties, and in the meantime the King inspects preparations. The catering is to be done by Messrs. J Lyons and Co. Flowers are being ordered; His Majesty would prefer daffodils if they are ready; invitation cards are being sent out, and a programme of entertainment is published. Alfred Butt has amassed an impressive collection of stars from the West End and variety theatres across London to appear that week in the makeshift theatre in the Royal Riding School and everyone from Gerald du Maurier and Gladys Cooper to the Two Bobs and the Palace Dancing Girls are to be accompanied by a miniature orchestra. The glass porticos in the coach houses have been extended with huge marquees, wheelchairs and carrying chairs are ready for those who cannot walk; Special Constables organised to carry them.

In hospitals across London, preparations are as meticulous as at the palace. Men fuss with their hair and polish their boots. Every vehicle conceivable discharges the guests of the King and Queen: motor buses, ancient horse-drawn buses pulled back into service, cars, taxis. They are greeted by crowds peering through the palace gates, keen to see their heroes. There are blind men led along by

20   BD: MS Asquith A.1 4 #180-1.
21   *Daily Sketch* 3/4/16.
22   *Morning Post* 3/4/16.
23   *Morning Post* 3/4/16.
24   *Daily Mail* 3/4/16.

their comrades. "Here were one-legged men and one-armed men, and men with no legs and others with no arms at all. Here were some who hopped along, some still half covered with bandages, some whose eyes would never see the light of day again. The onlooker was hardened indeed who could watch them without emotion." The Guards Bands are playing popular music, and the crowd sings along with Tipperary and other favourites and call out : *"Are we downhearted?"* [25] They come from dozens of hospitals across London; Camberwell, Denmark Hill, Lewisham, Dulwich, men missing limbs from Roehampton, and Croydon; blinded men from St. Dunstan's, Wandsworth, Tooting, Epsom and Regent's Park, Fulham, Hampstead and Edmonton; Bethnal Green, Mile End, St Thomas's, and a dozen blinded naval officers. Their tables are decorated with great silver bowls overflowing with daffodils and at the buffet tables the silver urns were decorated with scores of pink azaleas. The men sit down somewhat nervously to bread and butter, potted meats, sandwiches and every kind of cake imaginable. When the Royal Family arrive each day they "at once set everyone at ease by moving from table to table and saying kindly words to every man." [26] In his uniform, "those who watched the King, who still used a stick in getting about, could see his face lighten with joy and pride, for he was among his own men again." [27] To one worn looking sailor who stands to greet him, His Majesty says: "Sit down my good fellow, don't stand to talk to me. You are wounded, and no doubt tired after your journey" and then, he glances around and tells him to help himself to as much as he can. "Mind you stock up well. That is very important." [28]

The series of royal tea parties is a huge effort not only on the part of the King and Queen but of their extended family, their friends and the Royal Household. Some 100 notable ladies and gentlemen present themselves in the Royal Mews to wait on wounded servicemen. Each table is colour coded, and the ladies wear a corresponding ribbon in their hair so that the guests might identify their waitresses. Throughout the week sections are supervised by Princess Beatrice, her daughter Princess Maud, and the Duchess of Teck. Waiters include Stamfordham, the Duchess of Devonshire and the Duchess of Sutherland. Princess Mary and Prince Albert ply men with more cake, and Admiral Lord Beresford endears himself to all of the sailors present. "Lord Beresford was to be seen wielding a teapot at the tables occupied by the naval men, and recalling old times with members of the senior service who had sailed with him." [29] He finds himself in huge demand and has a grand time parading back and forth with a silver teapot, spilling it all over the floor and causing laughter when he gallantly tried to bow to the Queen with it in hand. One naval man declines a cup of tea from a Duchess. "No thank you... I won't have any unless Admiral Beresford pours it out." [30] The Admiral obliges him with a big grin.

Queen Alexandra proves to be one of the most popular personages of the week. She tries to get men to stuff buns into their pockets; she worries that they have not had enough to eat. The second afternoon is to a large extent given over to soldiers from the Dominions. "One young Canadian, trust a Canadian to not lose anything by failing to ask for it, pulled out his fountain pen, presented his programme of the day... to Queen Alexandra, and asked her to autograph it." As soon as she has signed one with a smile, she is suddenly surrounded. She sits and signs every programme that is waved at her; "smiling, talking to the men... 'Gee!' said one lad... from Calgary. 'They would not believe out west that the King had asked me to tea if I had not something to show for it. I wouldn't trade Queen Alexandra's signature for a hundred dollars!" [31] Both Princess Beatrice and the Duke of

25   Hammerton: *Our King & Queen: A Pictorial Record of Their Lives*, p.12.
26   *Daily Telegraph* 22/3/16.
27   Hammerton: *Our King & Queen: A Pictorial Record of Their Lives*, p.12.
28   *Daily Graphic* 24/3/16.
29   *Morning Post* 22/3/16.
30   *Daily Graphic* 22/3/16.
31   Hammerton: *Our King & Queen: A Pictorial Record of Their Lives*, p.12.

Connaught come to her assistance, but she has no intention of going until every man waiting has his souvenir. The following day, word has got around that there are autographs to be had and she is again besieged, as are Princess Beatrice and Bertie.

After tea comes the entertainment. The stage is draped with blue, white and red facing; a deep blue curtain drawn across it. The footlights are hidden behind piles and piles of fresh cut floral arrangements. Each man is handed a pack of cigarettes for the show, and before the first act takes to the stage, the King wanders throughout the crowd, chatting to members of the audience and making sure that they are comfortable. Special attention is paid to those men with the worst wounds, those who are wheeled or carried into the auditorium with their doctors or nurses vigilantly keeping an eye on them. On one of the afternoons a string of blind men are led in by a nurse, each with a hand on the shoulder of the man in front.

Smoke begins to fill the room, and on the first afternoon the men are quite reserved until part-way through the performance. This is addressed on the following days by an announcement in the Royal Music Hall, as it has now been dubbed. "All are cordially invited to join in the choruses."[32] This breaks the ice. The men are also forbidden from rising when the Royal Family enters the rooms. The King does not want wounded men struggling to their feet on his account. It is a homely atmosphere, and Bertie stands to the side in his Midshipman's uniform chatting freely with the men in between turns. Throughout the week, the King and Queen's guests are treated to Harry Lauder and Miss Ethel Levery, George Grossmith, Arthur Playfair, Nelson Keyes and many others. Cornalia and Eddy displayed their shambolic acrobat tricks and the Palace Theatre girls acted as a chorus. There are rousing singalongs too; *Australia Will Be There, Oh Canada, Land of Hope and Glory*, and loudest and most emotional of all; *God Save the King,* all of which are followed by raucous cheering. The audience gets louder and more rowdy the more at ease they feel, till there is a rollicking atmosphere in the riding school. One Tommy says that he expected everything to be very formal and decorous, "at which it would be out of place to indulge in a hearty laugh." But he finds it is nothing of the kind. "Before the show had long been in progress, we were a roistering, almost raucous crowd of 'crocks'… we were the merriest crowd of invalids I have ever seen."[33]

"The King spoke to me as if I was his chum,"[34] says another wounded visitor. But nobody can fail to notice one particular soldier. The press man sitting behind him is mesmerised by Private Phineas Potts of Gallipoli and Mile End. "His laughter was infectious. So was his singing." He laughed "with falsetto notes embroidering a vast rolling bass." He is having the time of his life. The press man can see that there is something wrong with the soldier's right foot, "because it was supported by an elaborate kind of tape and wood sling." But it is not until he gets a glance of Potts side on that he realises the full extent of his injuries. "There was something wrong with the left side of his face, something that would hardly bear describing. A shell had been unkind. You would never have guessed it, but for that fleeting glimpse." Phineas Potts is determined to enjoy every moment of his afternoon. "Fred Emney 'fairly sent him off' as he confided breathlessly to the man with no fingers next door. George Graves's 'Duchess' kept him in happy chuckles for fifteen minutes, so that the vibration unsettled the bandage that made a sort of hero's nimbus round his stubbly bullet head. 'Strike me,'[35] he groaned."

At 6 o'clock the men file breathlessly out of the riding school, their pockets stuffed with fruit that the King and Queen have ordered brought out for them. A large crowd is gathered outside the palace to see them off. "I didn't think you did things like this in England," says one Australian on his

32   *Evening Standard* 26/3/16.
33   *Daily Sketch* 22/3/16.
34   *Daily Graphic* 22/3/16.
35   *Daily Mail* 24/3/16.

way out. "It will be something to tell them when I go back that I had a talk with the King."[36] Their Majesties are thrilled with the outcome of their endeavours. "For three days this week we have given entertainments to wounded soldiers and sailors in our riding school," the Queen proudly tells her aunt. "Over <u>2,000</u> have been able to come… I am glad to say, everything was very well organised and arranged for their comfort…. it was all so informal, friendly and nice."[37] A notice appears in the press on behalf of the Their Majesties; an "expression of gratitude to all those, in whatsoever capacity, who… generously placed their services at the disposal of the King and Queen."[38]

"My Glass Case"

In 1915 the Prince of Wales comes of age and it is important that he begins to take on a more defined role befitting an heir to the throne. The war provides ample opportunities for this and during his time in France, even allowing for certain amount of sycophancy, it is fair to say that his senior officers have been impressed with his efforts. That the Prince is keen, diligent, and industrious is the general appraisal. In particular, his knowledge of French and German has given him a chance to excel during his time with the intelligence branch at GHQ. Father and son have much to talk about when David is home on leave. They walk in the gardens at Windsor or at Buckingham Palace. "We had an excellent talk," the Prince writes of one visit, "and I was busy telling him all I could about the campaign in northern France."[39]

But though David is getting a unique and rapid education in certain aspects of military operations, there is little structure to his role. He is a supernumerary at French's Headquarters, and the King's request that he spends time with different sections and different units further afield, means that his work is rather ad hoc. "I practically spent the whole day doing odd jobs in the office and dodging generals," he writes, "Robinson was up in the front line reconnoitring all the morning and I should have been with him, but of course I couldn't come out of my f****** glass case."[40] He feels even worse in the midst of battle. "I bugger along all right out here while all is quiet, but it is so bloody when there is any fighting on." Stamfordham warns him not to go to His Majesty with his woes, for there is every likelihood the King will solve the problem by summoning him home.

The problem is that the Prince of Wales will never be happy until he is actively being shot at along with his friends and comrades. "His main desire appeared to be to get either killed or wounded," claimed one witness. "At intervals he had to be retrieved from advanced trenches and dugouts, whither he had escaped by one subterfuge or another."[41] He spends a night in the trenches in July, and the King is not best please to find out second hand. "My impressions that night were of constant close proximity to death, repugnance from the stink of the unburied corpses… and general gloom and apprehension," he subsequently writes to his father. The letter from David placated His Majesty, "which shows," Stamfordham tells the Prince hopefully, "that so long as the King hears of your doings direct from yourself it is all right."[42]

The Prince thinks he has come up with a solution to combat the fact that he is bored of his role in France, bored of inaction. He wants to go to the navy instead. He usually makes such approaches via Stamfordham, and he appears to have convinced French to speak up for him too, and returns

36   *The Times* 23/3/16.
37   RA QM/PRIV/CC26/106.
38   *The Times* 25/3/16.
39   RA GV/PRIV/GVD/1916 (10/4).
40   RA GV/PRIV/GVD/1916 (11/5).
41   Ziegler: *King Edward VIII: The Official Biography,* pp.57-58.
42   Ibid., p.60-61.

home brandishing a letter to that effect. But his hopes are soon dashed. "I had a talk with Papa on the subject of my going to see the Fleet and he strongly disapproved!!" He also saw Billy Lambton who came down specially from London and said it was to be 'off.' Damnable... Why Papa has taken this very strong line, God only knows, Mama is quite in favour."[43] It is the only instance in the Great War of David not getting his own way when he asks something of his father. The King does not articulate his reasons for opposing the scheme, but there a number of potential pitfalls. Not having his two eldest sons with the fleet should it become embroiled in a fight to the death with the enemy is one; or how it would look if his son left the army to go and do something else might have been another, for no other officer could hold up his hands and walk away from his duty at the front because it had become tiresome facing the Germans for prolonged stretches of inactivity. His Majesty does appease his son a little by sanctioning his request to go north to at least visit Bertie whilst he is with the fleet and then spend a few days relaxing at Abergeldie. "It is really good for Papa to let me go," he admits.[44]

But then back to France David goes, to join the new Guards Division. And he almost manages to get himself killed during the Battle of Loos. "This was my first real sight of war and it moved and impressed me enormously." However, as he is returning to his car one day, the little party comes under shrapnel fire. They fling themselves into a trench and avoid injury, but on returning to the car they find it damaged and the Prince's driver killed. "He was an exceptionally nice man, a beautiful driver and a first rate mechanic; it's an absolute tragedy and I can't yet realise that it has happened." Sir John French's reaction is to immediately summon David away from his division to a place of greater safety. He is mortified. "I can assure you it is one of the biggest blows I have ever had," he writes to the King. "My dearest Papa, I implore of you to have this most unfortunate and deplorable order from GHQ cancelled as soon as possible." French rescinds his order, but His Majesty sets out more stringent guidelines to protect both his son and the officers responsible for him. David still isn't satisfied. "If only I could spend 48 hours in the line I should get an idea of what trench life is like, which it is absolutely impossible to do otherwise... I suppose you wouldn't like to make permission for me to do this a form of Christmas present to me?"[45] The request is made with tongue firmly in cheek but the King placates his son by approving his son a spell of leave with time in London, and even sends Bertie to meet him. The Prince also manages to talk his father into letting Bertie pay a visit to the front. "I immediately broached the subject of B returning to Flanders with me to Mama, who approved and then to Papa!! He was furious at first and raised many objections but I was able to talk him round. A real triumph for me," writes David, "of course I had told Mama what to say."[46]

Little victories aside, David continues to be bored in France, and matters are made worse when he is told he will be removed from the Guards Division when it goes forward. His next scheme is an extended trip to Egypt, though at first Stamfordham warns him that the King is not keen on account of the danger from Submarines. "I wrote at length to Lord S. (Complaining that there are plenty of mines in the channel) What a wretched creature I am, and all on account of being a f****** bloody prince!!"[47] But Stamfordham does much to help him and His Majesty decides that the visit could have its benefits. It is a huge step for him to send one of his children out on his own tour for the first time, especially when taking into consideration the added dangers of travelling in wartime, and David's seemingly peculiar health problems. "I hope the Prince will not overdo his

43   RA EDW/PRIV/DIARY/1916 (11/4).
44   RA EDW/PRIV/DIARY/1916 (28/8).
45   Ziegler: *King Edward VIII: The Official Biography,* pp.60-61.
46   RA EDW/PRIV/DIARY/1916 (2/2).
47   Ibid., 12/2.

exercise," Stamfordham tells one of the officers who is to supervise him. "It is curious how he thinks that it is necessary to get rid of every superfluous bit of flesh on his bones."[48] David is to provide a report on the defences in Egypt and pay visits to troops that His Majesty will not be able to get to. "Egypt… will be a nice trip," David writes the day before leaving France, "but I shan't enjoy it and shall feel such a shit leaving the division."[49] The Prince is proving impossible to please.

Aspects of Egypt are a culture shock to David, such as the necessity to pay an official visit to the Sultan. He hates such formal occasions, but he plays up well at a luncheon, "and really did very well; and soon got over his shyness."[50] He moves on to the Suez Canal, where British troops are protecting this vital waterway from Ottoman attack. David looks at camps and infrastructure, even the officer's club, "which seems a most repulsive spot and no better than a glorified pub!"[51] He is not enjoying the process of compiling a report on the canal defences. It is detailed and meticulous, but he sulks about it: "life is absolutely bloody and f****** and bloody… what it is to be a prince!! How particularly odious!"[52] He visits wounded Australians, "I made fatuous remarks to the sick!"[53] The Prince's complaints in his diary are not reflected in his outward countenance. To others he talks with enthusiasm about his doings. He is warmly received by the British and Indian troops, from whom he picked up some Hindustani, but especially by the Australians. As he rides through their camp, observing them at work, "they would rush to across to wherever the Prince was coming up and make a line for him and cheer time after time" one witness tells the palace. "There was something very touching in seeing his young boy on his little Arab… It is the fact of his having come here to see them that they appreciate… the Prince was I think a little taken back by the reception he got, as of course he has never had anything of this kind to do before with soldiers."[54]

David becomes desperate to extend his tour down to Khartoum. British officials in the city concur that it is a good idea, as do the military authorities, who fear the troops in Sudan feel rather left out and forgotten. The King's first inclination is to say no, for he does not want anyone to think that his son is having a jolly time cruising the Nile, but Kitchener is keen, and Stamfordham agrees with him and together they convince His Majesty. "The King, reconsidering the proposal on Lord Kitchener's representation as to political advantage of visit, gives consent to it on condition that… His Royal Highness can stand the heat."[55] David is to provide another report, this time on the situation at Khartoum, "and by his presence give confidence to the population in the security of British rule. He should also see the British and native troops."[56]

Having pleaded to sail south, on the eve of his departure the Prince writes: "Well 'here goes' for this bloody trip to Khartoum which is going to be hellish official… Such a trip as this is wrong and unnecessary in wartime and is particularly odious to me just now."[57] His diary throughout the visit continues in the same vein, lashing out against his station in life and what it requires of him. The voyage back up the Nile is the only element of sightseeing, and it quickly bores the Prince. "I'm utterly fed up with visiting temples and never want to see another again!!" The King, however is enthusiastic about the successful outcome of David's travels, so much so that he allows Kitchener to convince him that the Prince might stop in Italy on the way home and visit some Allied troops.

48   RA PS/PSO/GV/C/O/910/20.
49   RA EDW/PRIV/DIARY/1916 (28/2).
50   RA PS/PSO/GV/C/O/910/9.
51   RA EDW/PRIV/DIARY/1916 (24/3).
52   Ibid., (25/3).
53   Ibid., (26/3).
54   RA PS/PSO/GV/C/O/910/9.
55   RA PS/PSO/GV/C/O/901/15.
56   RA PS/PSO/GV/C/O910/16.
57   RA EDW/PRIV/DIARY/1916 (4/4).

The King approves entirely of giving David another chance to impress, but specifies that his son's movements should be convenient to the King of Italy, who has already previously extended an invitation for a royal visit, and that he is not to go to Rome, for that would necessitate a visit to the Pope, which he did not want to inflict upon his inexperienced son as yet; for it would require an element of political manoeuvring of which as yet David has little experience.

"What a hateful life!"[58] Is the Prince's response to the tour, but when the Royal Navy ship carrying him passes through a gate in the boom and docks at Spezia on 4th May, for "this fearful Italian stunt,"[59] David he finds that the King of Italy is entirely to his liking. There is little fanfare about Victor Emmanuel III. "He is a simple, charming little man who drives about the front with a telescope mounted on a tripod in his car, stopping for sandwiches on the side of the road. His grasp of English is that of a native. When Asquith once told him that he was astounded by his vocabulary, idiom, and pronounciation, the Italian King laughed. "Well it would be a wonder if I couldn't speak English: my nurse was English, my governess was English, my tutor was English, and till was fourteen I rearely spoke any other language."[60] "All the meals are comic and we get a lot of fun out of the King's staff."[61] The Italian King is desperate for his guest to enjoy himself and proves very easy to get along with, but he is also wily in keeping the Prince of Wales out of danger and comes up with cunning ways to do so. "The King will not permit any risks to be taken and says he does not wish any "historical incidents" of an undesirable nature to take place while he is with him."[62] David knows when he is beaten, and takes it in good grace. "He is a dear and charming little man and I would never say anything against him!!"[63] The Prince returns to London having undergone a challenging introduction to adult royal life. The King is thrilled to see that David looks the picture of health on his return to Windsor; "better than I have ever seen him," Stamfordham writes."[64] Father and son sit down excitedly after dinner and David describes all he has seen.

On his return to France, there is a more concerted effort to give the Prince a definite position, this time at a corps headquarters under the Earl of Cavan. But by June he has had enough of his new job, and has lapsed back to his old pattern of not enough food or sleep. "It's a farce my being out here really; a f****** Prince of Wales is more of a passenger in war time than generally."[65] And in August he writes: "I couldn't face… any company: I wanted to be alone in my misery!! I feel quite ready to commit suicide and wouldn't if I didn't think it unfair on Papa, though of course most of this 'glass half full' balls is his fault!! I'd sooner get killed and be finished with it."[66] With no hope of leaving the Western Front, he makes the most derogatory comment that appears in his war-time diaries about his father: "Papa isn't always easy to tackle."[67] and as winter brings more enforced inaction, things become worse; culminating in an incident in which he is sent to bed by a general for smashing things. Nothing short of becoming an infantry officer in the fighting line is going to make David happy.

58   RA EDW/PRIV/DIARY/1916 (23/4).
59   RA EDW/PRIV/DIARY/1916 (4/5).
60   Asquith: *Memories and Reflections*, p.120.
61   RA EDW/PRIV/DIARY/1916 (7/5).
62   RA PS/PSO/GV/C/O/910/73.
63   RA EDW/PRIV/DIARY/1916 (7/5).
64   RA PS/PSO/GV/C/O/910/77.
65   RA EDW/PRIV/DIARY/1916 (28/6).
66   Ziegler: *King Edward VIII: The Official Biography*, p.75.
67   RA EDW/PRIV/DIARY/1916 (18/8).

"A Spinning Top Among a Pot of Ninepins"

Though the campaign in the Dardanelles has been shut down, the King's anxieties have not lessened. As 1916 began, in Mesopotamia troops were still under siege at Kut. From India, the Viceroy sends His Majesty anxious letters, for many of those trapped are Indian soldiers. "There is… no doubt that fighting against the Turks is very unpopular with our Mohammedan troops, especially with the Pathans and trans-border men, I am sorry to say that there have been some desertions from the latter, and we have in consequence given up recruiting them."[68] His Majesty sends a message of support to the garrison's chief, but there is nothing that he or anybody else can do for those in Kut, and in command, General Townshend submits to a humiliating surrender in April. Ireland occupies the King's thoughts again at Easter. In Dublin on Easter Monday, nationalists seize the Post Office, St Stephen's Green, the Four Courts and Jacob's biscuit factory. "Looting broke out in the city, British soldiers were murdered in the streets, and a great part of Sackville Street went up in flames."[69] Some 2,000 offenders are taken to England and incarcerated. Then there is the matter of former civil servant turned militant nationalist, Roger Casement. He is arrested having landed in County Kerry on his way back from trying to secure German military assistance for his cause. The King wants a trial as soon as possible, and is not impressed by calls for leniency. The final ruling is a medical report that classifies Casement as "Abnormal, but not certifiably insane."[70] In August His Majesty notes that he has been hanged for High Treason and says: "he thoroughly deserved it."[71]

Romania enters the war on the side of the Allies in August. "I rejoice that the valiant Romanian Army will now fight side by side with the armies of the Allies," says the King's telegram to their Sovereign;[72] but although this new, long sought-after ally brings hundreds of thousands of men into the fray, their introduction only comes after two months of procrastination. The moment when their addition to the field could have had its greatest impact was gone. Ill-equipped, her armies are annihilated in four months and the civilian population is subjected to ensuing famine. "Thus did Romania share in the end the hideous miseries of all the Balkan peoples."[73]

And Greece and her affairs will always be a disproportionate headache for the King when weighed up against her actual importance to the war. Until 1913 when he was assassinated, his mother's brother George had reigned there. Now His Majesty's cousin Constantine sits upon the throne and is causing no end of trouble. Still, to the King's chagrin, in 1916 the spectre of Salonika looms in the background, with the French hell bent on keeping a large force there. By the summer he fears that the Government might be bending to the will of the attacking whim of their French allies. "The King is concerned at the apparent relaxing of our hitherto firm opposition to any proposed offensive by the allies from Salonika… [He] trusts that there is no idea of increasing our force [there] and that our efforts will be confined to equipping the existing force which in itself will, His Majesty fears, make considerable demands upon our resources." Stamfordham points out to Asquith that the country is already enraged with failures at Gallipoli and in Mesopotamia, "and His Majesty earnestly entreats the Government not to embark upon another subsidiary campaign."[74]

In September, the King is still not happy and pens his own letter to Asquith:

68   RA PS/PSO/GV/C/P/522/83.
69   Nicolson: *King George V: His Life and Reign,* pp.275-276.
70   RA PS/PSO/GV/C/R/293.
71   RA GV/PRIV/GVD/1916 (3/8).
72   *Daily Mail* 30/8/16.
73   Churchill: *The World Crisis 1911-1918,* pp.669-683.
74   RA PS/PS/GV/C/Q/838/98.

I am anxious at the way matters appear to be drifting in Greece, where at the instigation of France, the Allies have agreed about certain action, which seems to me harsh and even open to question whether it is in accordance with international law. Are we justified in interfering to this extent in the internal Government of a neutral and friendly country, even though we be one of the guarantors to its constitution? I cannot help feeling that we have allowed France too much to dictate a policy and that as a republic, she may be somewhat intolerant of, if not anxious to abolish the monarchy in Greece. But this I am sure is not the policy of Government, nor is it that of the Emperor of Russia, who writing to me a few days ago said: *"I feel rather anxious about the internal affairs of Greece. It seems to me the protecting powers, in trying to safeguard our interests concerning Greece's neutrality, are gradually immersing themselves too much in her internal home affairs to the detriment of the King."* If the Allies would treat her kindly and not if I may say so, in a bullying spirit, she will in all probability join them. I do not wish to interfere with the action of my Government, but I regard it is my duty to place on record my views upon this question at the present moment."[75]

Asquith insists that "at every stage of the recent proceedings in Greece the British Government has sought to mitigate the severity and brusquerie of the French proposals."[76]

The King has to field frantic enquiries from his mother when it comes to Greece, her nephew and his throne. "Tino" as he is mockingly referred to, is regarded in Britain as weak and pro-German, which means that His Majesty is caught in an awkward position. "I can't make out what Tino is doing in Greece," he says to his uncle, "and why he has allowed the Bulgarians to occupy different ports… it places the allies in a very awkward position and we may have to take drastic steps although we have no wish to quarrel with Greece."[77] The fact is, that their shared blood taints the King and his endeavours on more than one occasion, though he tries to keep his cousin at arms' length.

Foreign concerns aside, spring 1916 brings yet another domestic crisis for His Majesty to weather. It is transpiring to be far more difficult to define the enemy in the political arena than it is at the front. There have been criticisms of the Coalition Government since its inception. "To the onlooker here there seems to be no supreme control exercised over the war as a whole,"[78] Haig writes to Wigram just a month after the formation of the Coalition. During the crisis over manpower at the end of the year, the *Daily News* declares that the Government is "incapable of arriving at any decision on the issues presented to it,"[79] Lord Esher is typically even more scathing in a letter to Stamfordham. "The Government is rather like a spinning top among a pot of ninepins. It knocks over one, bumps up against another and finally rolls over on its side inert!"[80] It is worse when Asquith is absent, as one witness explained after a Cabinet meeting:

Everyone seemed desirous to speak at the same moment. One would say, "Please allow me to finish was I am saying." Another would interrupt, and a third would shout from the far end of the table that he meant to have his say on the matter too. Poor Lord Crewe feebly rapped on the table, and said "Order please" in a disconsolate way! This sort of thing really makes one tremble for the Empire![81]

75   BD: MS Asquith A.1. 4 #224.
76   BD: MS Asquith A.1. 4 #226.
77   RA VIC/ADDA15/6596.
78   RA PS/PS/GV/C/Q/2521/V/133.
79   *Daily News* 23/10/16.
80   RA PS/PS/GV/C/Q/724/59.
81   Rose: *King George V,* pp.193-194.

In particular, the press is scathing over the King's £100,000 donation to the war effort. By May a dogged MP has made it his mission to find out what has become of the money. He asks in the House whether the Government has yet decided what they proposed to do with the royal gift. "We are now preparing a scheme to lay before His Majesty, and when his pleasure has been taken upon it it will be made public,"[82] he is told. Twelve weeks later he presses again and Asquith tells him that, "after a review of various other suggestions, the Government have come to the conclusion with His Majesty's approval, that his generous gift would be most appropriately devoted to the general purposes of the war."[83] This is interpreted as yet another example of a dithering Government. They King has handed over this money in the best spirit, and they have let the country down again. Instead of putting the money to a "patriotic purpose to stir the imagination of the people,"[84] it had simply been absorbed into the nation's funds.

But the question that threatens to bring down Asquith's Government in April 1916 is that of universal conscription. By March 1916 the War Office has been compelled to call upon the younger married men that attested under Derby's Scheme. The press are outraged that these volunteers are going to war whilst there were still single men refusing to come forward. If the country is to optimise its resources then the Coalition will have to instigate universal conscription. Kitchener has come around to this, as has Robertson, and their cause has support in the shape of another prominent member of the Cabinet.

On 15th April, the Lord Chief Justice pays an anxious, private visit to the palace and tells Stamfordham that another cabinet crisis is on the horizon. Lloyd George is threatening to resign unless universal conscription is implemented and every available man of military age forced to serve. If he steps down, he will do so claiming that the Government is not pressing the war with the utmost vigour, which would be a damning public indictment. This eventuality has more potentially dire consequences for Asquith and his Government. Firstly, he has only managed to pass the Military Service Act by making promises that he will not compel unwilling married men to serve. To go back on this promise will enrage the Labour Party and members of his own party. Secondly, Lloyd George's resignation will inevitably trigger an exodus from the Cabinet and a subsequent General Election, "with the consequent free speaking and necessary explanations for the views held by the various candidates. Thus laying bare to our enemies our demands, resources, economic situation, besides the strength of our forces at home and in the field. This would be disastrous to ourselves and to our allies, the neutrals and of the greatest value to our enemies."[85]

The situation is also rife with pitfalls for the King. Interference might be criticised as unconstitutional. His Majesty is asked if he might intervene in by talking with Lloyd George. This immediately seizes Stamfordham as a bad idea. The King might induce the parties involved to accommodate each other, but Lloyd George is hardly likely to do as His Majesty asks, and instead he could speak about how the King attempted to persuade him away from a course of action. Stamfordham's main worry is if the likes of Northcliffe are fed information, the King could be damned for overstepping the bounds of his role as a constitutional monarch. "Under no circumstances," writes Stamfordham, "must it be possible for him to say "I yielded to persuasion.""[86]

82   *Daily Telegraph* 5/5/16.
83   *Morning Post* 4/8/16.
84   RA PS/PSO/GV/C/O/1106/18.
85   RA PS/PSO/GV/C/K/951/1.
86   Ibid.

The King spends the following day listening to rain pound the windows of the palace and worrying about the possible collapse of his Government. Stamfordham does the rounds of the parties concerned. Bonar Andrew Law is worried about his own position and hopeful that this is simply another empty Lloyd George threat of resignation. Stamfordham makes a set of notes for the King in which he tells His Majesty: "I was struck with Mr Lloyd George's energy, keenness, earnest determination." He does not claim universal conscription for himself. The army have asked for men, not an excessive number, and he says that they should be providing them. "The Welshman says, and these words will come back to haunt him, that *the soldiers were the best judges and he accepted their figures. If the Government did not do so, he would resign and state to the country his reasons.*"[87]

But there is another school of thought that sees the threatened resignation as a power play, an attempt by Lloyd George to take Asquith's place. The Welshman is pugnacious when visited by Stamfordham. He tells him that he sees no issue with the collapse of the Government. "We politicians always imagine that no one can govern the country except ourselves."[88] He thinks it would have no impact on the war effort at all, and that it is his duty to carry this threat through if necessary. Despite being impressed with the zeal of Lloyd George, the way in which he brushes aside genuine concerns about how his actions might harm the war effort alarms the King's Private Secretary; because the potential ripples extending from Lloyd George's resignation, should he do it, are terrifying. Frantic meetings take place between War Office men with their manpower estimates and members of the Cabinet. More and more names are touted to follow Lloyd George from the Coalition Cabinet should he go. Lord Esher arrives at the palace with the horrifying prospect of both Kitchener and Robertson walking away from the War Office should they be starved of recruits. For several days the Government appears to be on the brink, but having reported that his Coalition was about to collapse, on 20th April, the King receives a letter from Asquith telling him that the crisis is over and that the Government have come to an agreement about recruiting; agreeing that universal conscription can no longer be held off. It is less an outright victory for Lloyd George than it is a necessity for Britain's war effort. Nonetheless His Majesty writes a thankful letter to his Prime Minister: "It is with greatest satisfaction that I learn… of the happy agreement arrived at by the Cabinet today. I do most heartily congratulate you on having by your patience and skill extricated the country from a position the dangers of which it was impossible to over-estimate."[89]

A second Military Service Bill is introduced at the beginning of May, extending service requirements in England, Wales and Scotland; and receives the King's assent on 25th. As of June, by default, every man aged between 18 and 41 is deemed to be in the army, to be called upon and compelled to serve by law when he is needed. All discharges are to be suspended. The only men exempt are clergymen, those not fit to serve, those with a tribunal certificate and any former prisoner of war. His Majesty is keen to let the country know how greatly he appreciates the efforts made under the voluntary system before compulsion has become inevitable. In a message to the nation outlining the need for universal conscription, he says: "I desire to take this opportunity of expressing to my people my recognition and appreciation of the splendid patriotism and self-sacrifice which they have displayed in raising by voluntary enlistment, since the commencement of the war, no less than 5,041,000 men… one which will be a lasting source of pride to future generations."[90]

87   Ibid.
88   Ibid.
89   RA PS/PSO/GV/C/K/951/10.
90   *The Times* 26/6/16.

"Deeds Not Words"

After his bout of appendicitis and his spell at the Admiralty, Prince Albert had re-joined HMS *Collingwood* in early 1915. "May God watch over him,"[91] His Majesty wrote in his diary. By July, when the King visited the fleet at Scapa, Bertie was once again confined to a hospital ship under observation with stomach trouble. David visits the fleet and watches uneasily as they wash his brother's insides out with a rubber tube, a torture the young Prince is put through again and again. He finds Bertie very low, frustrated at his health worries and his lack of a contribution to the war effort. A long period of inaction follows, before finally in May 1916 he is fit to return to the *Collingwood*. "We shall miss him very much,"[92] writes the Queen.

On his arrival the Prince finds the fleet much as he left it. "We have been leading the quiet life as usual, no excitement of any sort and still in the same old place." But a week after his arrival, on 30th May; the fleet, including *HMS Collingwood*, leaves for a cruise on hearing that the German counterparts have put to sea. By mid-afternoon, news has arrived of the enemy having been sighted and Admiral Beatty, who is on his way to join the main fleet, has given chase. He engages them a little over an hour later at long range, off the coast of Denmark and the Battle of Jutland commences. Early casualties are harrowing, especially among British battle-cruisers. At about 4pm *Indefatigable* explodes taking all but two of her 1,019 crew to their graves. Half an hour later *Queen Mary* is gone too, blown into oblivion with the loss of nearly 1,300 men. The light favours the German ships. Approaching the battle with his contingent from Scapa, Admiral Jellicoe's crews work like the devil to gain all possible speed. Thick mist descends by 5:30pm, limiting visibility to a mere five or six miles, but soon the men of the *Collingwood* begin to hear the sound of immense naval guns. Then the flashes of these monstrous weapons being set off begins to punctuate the murk across their narrow field of visibility, for the fog is so thick that Jellicoe struggles to make out exactly where the enemy ships are as he sails into battle. The King spends the day at Portsmouth in a downpour, doggedly carrying out his itinerary in spite of the weather. His Majesty has been warned that the enemy fleet has ventured out and he is anxiously awaiting news. As a naval man, there is pride that the Grand Fleet have finally taken their part in the struggle, for inaction was unbearable for them, but there are huge losses, and nobody can seem to indicate which fleet has won.

As parents, Their Majesties are sent into a panic. "You can imagine our feelings when we heard about the naval battle in the North Sea being in progress!" Queen Mary writes to Bertie afterwards. They know by 2nd June that their son is unscathed. The main danger to the *Collingwood* had come from torpedo boats, for mercifully the German battleships were never closer than to be the cause of distant orange flashes in the mist. "What an experience," writes the Queen, "we are longing to get a letter from you and to hear about your impressions. The loss of valuable lives and fine ships is indeed terrible, and ones heart bleeds for the awful sorrow this battle has brought to many hearts; for one fears but few are saved. The enemy must have suffered severely, much more than he will admit."[93] The Germans have proclaimed victory, but the King is keen to make it clear that he knows better. "I mourn the loss of brave men, many of them personal friends of my own," he telegraphs to Jellicoe, "Yet even more do I regret that the German High Seas Fleet, in spite of its heavy losses, was enabled by the misty weather to evade the full consequences of an encounter they have always professed to desire, but for which, when the opportunity arrived, they showed no inclination."[94]

The 3rd June is the King's birthday, but it is of course a gloomy affair. The sheer weight of almost

91   RA GV/PRIV/GVD/1915 (12/2).
92   RA QM/PRIV/CC26/109.
93   RA GVI/PRIV/RF/11/227.
94   (ed.) The Times: *Hail and Farewell: The Passing of King George V,* p.176.

7,000 casualties inevitably depresses him, makes him "miserable over the great loss of life;"[95] as does the sight of his friends' names on the list of those lost. In France, David has to make do with scant information until he receives a wire from his father; "saying he regretted the heavy losses in the naval battle, but that *Collingwood* had had no casualties which shows that she took part, and so old Bertie has been present at the biggest sea fight in history!! Lucky devil, though I'm awfully glad for his sake!"[96]

Three days after His Majesty receives the news of thousands of lives lost at Jutland, he sustains one of his biggest blows of the war. Lord Kitchener, his Secretary of State for War, his trusted advisor and his friend of thirty years, is dead.

By 1916 Kitchener had lost much of the confidence of his colleagues, but he had no intention of going anywhere, and whether they liked him or not, the Cabinet had to accept that for now at least, he was firmly ensconced at the War Office. Some of their criticisms were fair, and some, such as blaming the War Minister for the Salonika expedition, were not. Much of the blame levelled at the Field Marshal by his colleagues could have been levelled at Asquith's Government on a broader scale, and Robertson wrote to the palace at the end of 1915 and attempted to be reasonable: "Lord K is a great personality. He stands higher in public opinion than any other public servant to the King... We shall not win this great war without the support of the people, for the stress of war has been neglected by statesmen for years past. We are now paying the penalty, and stand in special need of a 'man' to give confidence. Lord K has the confidence of the people as a whole. He is a loyal and honest servant of His Majesty, which is more than we can say to the same extent of others. He has no axe of any kind to grind. He is objected to by the War Office because of his methods and by [Cabinet] colleagues. But think who some of these colleagues are!" Kitchener, he reasons, may not be perfect, but it must be considered that he is under immense strain. "It is going very far to lose him. He has no friends, no wife; no one to help or sympathise with him. He has had indifferent and weak assistants. Winston Churchill and others have been his better enemies from the start, he has been worked very hard. He needs more rest and more assistance, before he can be set aside as of no use!"[97]

In the meantime, Russia, "with the disadvantages of a backward industrial system and creaking bureaucracy," was suffering from "food shortages which sapped civilian morale; and a crippling lack of munitions and guns which accounted for her reverses in 1915." As 1916 dawned, "there were signs that Russia was drifting towards economic and psychological collapse."[98] To properly understand their needs, and the Tsar's requests for assistance, it seems that the best thing to do would be to send a worthy emissary there to observe the situation for himself. Kitchener has always been interested in Russian affairs, and the Tsar formally invites the Field Marshal to sail to Archangel with an appropriately knowledgeable party. Nicholas is desperately keen, excited even, for the visit to take place, not only on the subject of munitions. "He added that it would be most acceptable to him to hear personally from Lord Kitchener his views on railway and transportation matters, of which he had such wide and valuable experience, and that it would be so helpful to his ministers and... to have a straight and full discussion on all these and relative questions for which any amount of cabling or writing never gave such satisfactory results as a personal interview. "From what I have always heard," he added, "he is not a man who will hesitate to speak out and give us his views, even if they are not in entire accord with ours."[99]

95   RA GVI/PRIV/RF/11/227.
96   RA PS/PS/GV/C/Q/838/61.
97   RA PS/PS/GV/C/Q/838/61.
98   Gerwarth: *The Vanquished,* p.176.
99   Hanbury-Williams: *The Emperor Nicholas II As I Knew Him,* pp.95-97.

On 2nd June, Kitchener stops in at the palace to see the King before he departs, and two days later he has joined Jellicoe aboard his flagship at Scapa Flow. "He was spontaneously cheered by the sailors, who seemed delighted to have him on board." A northeasterly gale is howling about the Orkney Islands and the sea is rough as HMS *Hampshire* sets sail on the evening of 5th June. Jellicoe has recommended postponing the journey. "Had Kitchener been a bad sailor he probably would probably have agreed to this," opined a friend, "and his life might have been spared; but he was at home in the worst of weather and therefore decided to start."[100]

The ship's crew have no idea where they are taking their distinguished party. Tossed back and forth, the destroyers ordered to provide an escort are unable to keep up in the turbulent conditions. They almost disappear under tumultuous seas, pushed off course. Kitchener's transport has to slow down for them, but still they lag behind and so they turn back. The *Hampshire* is now completely alone, her hatches battened and giant waves crashing over her.

Owing to the weather, Jellicoe has ordered her captain to pass the rocky, western coast of the main island, as it "gave promise of shelter and a better opportunity for destroyers to screen [her] against submarine attack"[101] than sailing up the eastern route. The channel has not been swept for mines, because the Germans have never previously paid any attention to the area so far north. Merchant vessels have plied these waters without coming to grief. Jellicoe considers it perfectly safe, but he has no idea that on 28th May, a German submarine had laid a line of 22 mines off Mawick Head.

As she battles through heavy seas, suddenly an explosion all but tears the *Hampshire* in half. "A terrible draft came rushing along the mess deck, blowing all the men's caps off." She settles askew in the water, a hole ripped in her bottom. Kitchener emerges from the Captain's cabin into smoke and the fumes of high explosives and climbs a ladder onto the quarter deck. An officer leads him along shouting: "make way for Lord Kitchener!"[102] "The rudder would not respond to the helm. The power failed and the lights flickered out. No wireless communication was possible."[103] The Captain surveys this chaos and immediately gives the order to abandon ship. Kitchener is talking to two officers, wearing his uniform but no overcoat. There is no light, and no escape. The sea is so rough that there is no hope of launching the lifeboats properly. Those of them that are sent out are smashed up. The ship sinks by the head in ten minutes, performing an unwieldy somersault as she plunges to the bottom, dragging her boats with her. Ships are sent out to pick up survivors, all available motor vehicles in Stromness to search the coast; but out of 600 crew, a dozen have survived, washed off the ship aboard rafts as she sank. "Lord Kitchener went down with the ship," one of them tells the newspapers. Every member of his party has been lost. "He did not leave her."[104]

News of the loss of HMS *Hampshire*, and Kitchener with her, devastates the nation. "Many British people recalled that no event during the war produced more universal alarm and despair. A blanket of silence fell over London. The blinds were drawn in the War Office and in the Admiralty, and the principal stores closed for the rest of the day."[105] "People in the streets read the news of his death on the placards, and for a truth all the warmth went out of the sunshine, and no one had the heart to speak in more than a whisper."[106] Owing to the necessary secrecy, the public are not even aware that Kitchener had left London. Rumours are wildly postulated that he is a German prisoner, "that he had found refuge in a cave under those dark and threatening cliffs and in due

100   Birdwood: *Khaki and Gown*, p.305.
101   TNA: PRO 30/57/89.
102   Warner: *Kitchener: The Man Behind the Legend*, pp.198-200.
103   Cassar: *Kitchener: Architect of Victory*, pp.476-480.
104   Warner: *Kitchener: The Man Behind the Legend*, pp.198-200.
105   Cassar: *Kitchener: Architect of Victory*, p.480.
106   *Daily Telegraph* 13/6/16.

course would emerge like some Nordic God," that he was now in an enchanted sleep like heroes such as [King Arthur] or Sir Francis Drake, that when his country was in its hour of need he would awake and return."[107]

The King spends 6th June inspecting establishments in Suffolk in light showers. He is in the middle of the tour when the news is broken to him. "It is indeed a heavy blow to me and a great loss to the nation and the Allies. I had every confidence in him and he was a great personal friend."[108] He expands on his feelings of grief and shock further in a letter to his uncle: "I had the greatest admiration for him and absolute confidence in his judgement. I shall miss him terribly and his guiding hand. No man has worked harder or with more success during this war, having created our army of several million men… They hadn't a chance of being saved."[109] To Bertie, the King admits that "I had known him for 30 years and he always told me everything. He has left behind a terrible blank."[110] "Only… [last] week he was in my room," writes Stamfordham, "full of life, and keen at the prospect of his visit to Russia."[111]

It is a miserable evening at the palace. "All here are determined to carry on the work which he started," writes the Queen, "though with aching hearts for his loss - We had seen much of him during the last 22 months, he was a real friend, like a rock and always straight and full of confidence."[112] Queen Alexandra immediately cancels her engagements. She had told the King that she thought the Russian trip foolhardy, and when she hears of the loss of the *Hampshire*, she is stunned.

> What fearful news are these! …On his way to Russia! Which I felt and told you only last Sunday was unnecessary at this very important moment too. His loss, our greatest military man of the day will be a calamity in every sense of the word. And what will happen now! And who can ever replace him. He had the whole empire's full confidence and did so splendidly. My poor Georgie boy I am sorry for you indeed. Just on the top of your having lost so many of our precious ships too! … The loss of all those many thousands of brave bluejackets and officers is… so heartbreaking.[113]

"It is a national calamity, for he was a great man," writes David, whose schemes for getting closer to the fighting line have been many times thwarted by Kitchener, "and the nation owes him as big a debt of gratitude as it has ever owed to anyone; not only for his past services but for his work during the war!! Heaven knows what sort of state the army would be in now if it hadn't been for his organisation!!"[114] "Lord K's death upset us all very much here," says Bertie from Scapa."[115] "Papa is awfully upset," Queen Mary replies to her son. "But we must not be downhearted and must [steel] ourselves to go on the end with this dreadful war."[116]

Some of Kitchener's army comrades are beside themselves. "I am simply overwhelmed and feel for the moment that I am left alone in this world," writes General Birdwood, to Wigram.

107   Warner: *Kitchener: The Man Behind the Legend,* pp.201-202.
108   RA GV/PRIV/GVD/1916 (6/6).
109   RA ADDL/MSS/A/15/6596.
110   RA GV/PRIV/AA60/126.
111   RA PS/PSO/GV/C/P/284a/22.
112   Pope-Hennessy: *Queen Mary, 1867-1953,* p.503.
113   RA GV/PRIV/AA34/54.
114   RA EDW/PRIV/DIARY/1916 (6/6).
115   RA QM/PRIV/CC10/228.
116   RA GVI/PRIV/RF/II/228.

I was with him for nine years… I was writing to him only last week telling him what we thought of the yapping curs in the House of Commons round the old lion. I know well how fond the King was of him and how much he will feel his terribly tragic loss. Even in the midst of the loss of so many other heroic and valuable lives at sea… to my beloved old chief I owe all and everything and just feel that for me the world has come to an end.[117]

His death sends shock waves around the world. The French have not forgotten that he had served in their ranks 46 years ago. Esher has lunch with the Prime Minister in Paris. "He felt the blow quite as much as any of K's colleagues who will shed crocodile tears."[118] Even the Chief of the Basuto sends a message of condolence to King George. "We cry with the King, we cry with you… and all His Majesty's servants."[119]

The King sends but one telegram of his own, to Lord Kitchener's sister. "While the whole nation mourns the death of a great soldier, I have personally lost in Lord Kitchener an old and valued friend, upon whose devotion I ever relied with utmost confidence… I desire to express my heartfelt sympathy in the loss which has befallen you under such sudden and tragic circumstances."[120]

Lord Esher writes that:

His faults were obvious, but his supreme might was, that by night and day, since August 1914, he never had but one thought: how to win this war. I am sorry for the King, who has lost a great subject, but the King has the supreme satisfaction, at this juncture, of knowing that he never wavered in the support that he gave to K, or allowed himself to be swayed by the jealousies and ineptitudes of K's colleagues.[121]

Whilst reeling from the loss of Kitchener, the King has been attempting to collect accounts of the naval action at Jutland. 72 hours after the battle, Commander Dannreuther, one of only half a dozen to survive the catastrophic explosion that ripped the *Invincible* to pieces and took 1,000 men with her, is at the palace. "He is a splendid fellow and seems certain that we did great damage to the German ships, but of course they won't admit it,"[122] says His Majesty. Both Robertson and Louis Battenburg journey to Scotland and back before reporting to the King; and two Captains are at Buckingham Palace on 10th to relate their tales. Jellicoe waits nearly two weeks, until he has gathered as complete a narrative from scattered ships and crews as possible to write to His Majesty, but the account the King and Queen are desperate for is that of their son.

Beatty and his force were already at their guns when news of the battle filtered through to HMS *Collingwood*. Her crew went to their action stations, which for Bertie meant getting off of his sickbed and going up into 'A Turret' at the bow. At first he sat atop the turret for a better view. He could see the battle-cruisers in action ahead of him on the starboard bow; HMS *Lion* was on fire. The view lofty view was all well and good; but suddenly a German ship started firing at *Collingwood*, "and one salvo 'straddled' us. We at once returned the fire. I was distinctly startled and jumped down the hole in the top of the turret like a shot rabbit!! I didn't try the experience again." Bertie watched the rest of the proceedings through a telescope inside his turret. His men were in fine fettle, laughing and joking "in the best of spirits as their heart's desire had at last been granted,

117   RA PS/PS/GV/C/Q/2521/II/56.
118   RA PS/PS/GV/C/Q/724/77.
119   RA PS/PSO/GV/C/P/474/35.
120   TNA: PRO 30/57/115.
121   RA PS/PS/GV/C/Q/724/77.
122   RA GV/PRIV/GVD/1916 (4/6).

which was to be in action with the Germans." The fleet deployed and at 5:37 Collingwood began firing on enemy light cruisers; her second salvo setting one on fire. Then they moved onto another and helped to sink her too. "Our next target was a battle cruiser, we think the *Derfflinger* or *Lutzow*, and one of the *Collingwood's* salvoes hit her abaft the after turret, which burst into a fierce flame." Then their prize turned away and vanished into the mist. "By this time it was too dark to fire." A glance down and Bertie realised that: "the ship was in a fine state on the main deck, inches of water sluicing about to prevent fires from getting a hold on the deck;" but she is unscathed. One torpedo had passed ahead of the *Collingwood* and another astern, there are many close shaves. "We had no casualties and no damage done to us, though we were 'straddled' several times."[123]

The Prince remains disappointed that his ship has no scars to show for her part in the battle. But he has seen what has happened to those men who were not so lucky. "The cruiser *Defence* was concentrated on by the German battlecruisers, and was hit by several salvoes at once. She blew up in a huge sheet of flame and smoke, and when this sank down she had utterly disappeared."[124] Bertie's Captain finds the sight equally as moving:

> Three salvoes hit her and put her heavily on fire, but she continued firing with every gun until the third salvo found the magazine and she was immediately enveloped in an enormous column of white smoke and steam 600 feet high out of which she never reappeared… The appearance of the wreck of the *Invincible,* which was passed on the disengaged side was most extraordinary. The two halves of the ship were some 500 feet apart. No one knew, though I had my suspicions, that it was one of our ships until after we got back.[125]

As for the German High Seas Fleet, she made off when it got dark; "followed by our light cruisers and destroyers which attacked them during the night." HMS *Collingwood* reached Scapa Flow at noon on 2nd June and immediately began replenishing her ammunition and coal. The battle isn't at all what Bertie expected. "I saw visions of the masts going over the sides and funnels hurtling through the air, etc." In reality, he can hardly see a thing for fog and smoke. "No one would know to look at the ship that we had been in action. It was certainly a great experience to have been through and it shows that we are at war and that the Germans can fight if they like."[126] The King is much interested in his son's account of the battle. "So you are sorry *Collingwood* was not hit as you wanted to have some wounds to show you had been in the action? But you had the next thing to it, as you were straddled," he says by way of commiseration. He thinks that if this is what the Germans consider a great victory, then they are welcome to many more of them. "I am delighted to think you have seen action at last and that you are safe… I am afraid you have lost many friends in the fleet, but that was inevitable, alas!"[127]

The void left by the death of Kitchener within the ranks of the Cabinet is glaring, and almost immediately men begin trying to fill it. "All this canvassing and wire-pulling about the succession, while poor K's body is still tossing about in the North Sea, seems to me to be in the highest degree indecent," Asquith writes to Stamfordham as he temporarily takes over at the War Office again.[128]

123   RA PS/PSO/GV/C/Q/832/366.
124   Ibid.
125   RA PS/PSO/GV/C/Q/832/435.
126   RA PS/PSO/GV/C/Q/832/366.
127   RA GV/PRIV/AA60/126.
128   RA PS/PSO/GV/C/K/951/13.

Lloyd George wants the job, and the Prime Minister is anxious. That has he has proven himself passionate and resourceful at the Ministry of Munitions is not in doubt, but his methods are unnerving. One trip to Boulogne to meet with his French munitions counterpart had seen him try and make private enquiries about the work of GHQ, which threw the army into a panic. "Thanks to the effort" of one thoughtful officer, who thought that private communication with French behind Lord Kitchener's back would cause trouble, Lloyd George's efforts were waylaid when this officer threw himself into the path of the Welshman's schemes. A fuming Lloyd George accused him of being "a red tape obstructinist."[129] Most of the conservatives in the Coalition are against the concept of this move, along with almost everyone at the War Office. Some view the prospect as potentially disastrous. What Asquith fears, Stamfordham writes to the King:

> Is interference in appointments, in which as Secretary of State he would have a <u>right</u> to interfere. It is known, for instance, that he has no opinion of Haig or Rawlinson though his judgement can only be a result of tittle tattle gossip… it would be disastrous to the army and indeed might have fatal results on the war if a civilian war minister were to attempt to tamper with the <u>personnel</u>.[130]

The King agrees with his Prime Minister. He admires the relentless energy of Lloyd George, but, much as with Fisher, and Churchill, the King is not wholly trusting of the sly tendencies or of the methods sometimes employed. He would rather have Austen Chamberlain, current Secretary of State for India, replace Kitchener; and failing that he advocates the suggestion of Asquith remaining in charge at the War Office, assisted by Lord Derby. Maurice Hankey, secretary of the Cabinet War Committee, sees His Majesty on 10th June "The King went into a violent diatribe against Lloyd George, as I thought he would. I kept trying to stand up for [him] and reminded the King of all he had done and how useful he is on the War Committee… but the King would hardly listen."[131]

Not only does Lloyd George want the War Office, but he wants the role of Secretary of State for War restored to its former powers, which would be unthinkable to the staff already there; especially Robertson, who had been granted special authority to enable him to work effectively with Kitchener. Stamfordham goes into the matter in detail with Asquith whilst the King is out of London and says that "although [Lloyd George] declares that he has no wish to interfere with the general military policy of the war, there can be no doubt that in possession of the powers he demands, he would assert his authority in matters now entirely controlled by the CIGS." The Prime Minister is aware that several people have suggested that he continue in the role, "though he quite realised that he had his hands tolerably full and did not <u>want</u> to undertake more responsibilities. Derby had already put himself at his disposal, and asked for no pay, not even a definite office, so long as he could help."[132]

But Derby is not perceived as strong enough. Doubtless Lloyd George's concern over the conduct of the war is genuine, but to say that this play for the most important of Cabinet roles isn't tied richly to his own personal ambitions would be unforgivably naive. Asquith attempts to get Bonar Law to take the post, but when he refuses, he has little choice. On 7th July His Majesty holds a Council at Buckingham Palace and gives Lloyd George the seals of the War Office. "Few doubted that he would remain at the War Office only long enough to seize the highest place of all." On the

129 RA Q832/23.
130 RA PS/PSO/GV/C/K/951/14.
131 Rose: *King George V,* pp.194-196.
132 RA PS/PSO/GV/C/K/951/17.

day his new post is announced, Margot Asquith writes in her diary: "We are out: it can only be a question of time now when we shall have to leave Downing Street."[133]

It remains for the King to mark the catastrophic loss of life at sea in the early summer of 1916. On 13th June he breaks with protocol and attends a memorial service to one of his subjects. Their Majesties set off in a carriage drawn by four horses for St. Paul's to honour Lord Kitchener. The crowds have begun gathering before sunrise for a place near the cathedral, they stand amidst showers, "that fell at intervals from grey, murky clouds."[134] The royal carriage passes endless, solemn multitudes wearing tokens of mourning, abnormally quiet; grieving behind lines of policemen and special constables in their dark blue overcoats and matching peaked caps.

"Tears and the 'sadness of farewell' there must needs be a St Paul's today," writes one newspaper. "But in the vast congregation of mourners pride will still be uppermost that Kitchener was one of our race and time."[135] The city's warehouses and shops are closed. At St. Paul's, flowers and wreaths threaten to engulf the cathedral. A cluster of Australian wounded are collected at the base of Queen Anne's statue; New Zealanders and Canadians line southern side of the cathedral steps. "There was no pomp and no display; but the feeling of very deep grief was evident on every hand. It was unmistakeable and unforgettable."[136]

The cathedral is gloomy, there is no natural light at all. One single wreath has been permitted. A three foot arrangement of white lilies and red carnations laid on the tomb of General Gordon, a simple touch linking the deceased with the man that he avenged. *A tribute of respect and remembrance from the women workers at the War Office. In memory of Lord Kitchener.*[137] The King sits between his mother and his wife. Almost the entire Cabinet is present, and allied countries have sent ambassadors and ministers. As 4,000 mourners take their seats, the band of the Royal Engineers, with whom Kitchener's army career began, plays funeral marches under the dome. The service begins with *Abide with Me*, one of Kitchener's favourite hymns. The lack of a body makes the service eerie for the congregation; "the haunting sense of the intangible and mysterious became all the more poignant."[138] Buglers from the Irish Guards, hidden from sight, play the Last Post and the mourners sing the National Anthem. There is such a demand for a way for the capital's population to vent their grief that a second service has to be held at Westminster Abbey. It is full with hours to spare. "No one could say what the course of the war would have been if there had been no Lord Kitchener for the British nation to turn to in the hour of its great peril," reads one of the endless eulogies to the great man.

> For our own part, we believe it to be true that, if he had not been within immediate call, the Secretaryship of State for War must have been filled by a politician, and that no politician could have carried the country with him as did Lord Kitchener in the colossal task of raising the army from a few hundreds of thousands to millions. There have been many greater soldiers that Lord Kitchener, where there is so much to praise there is no need to exaggerate... But for the combined quality of soldier-administrator we know no one [better] in British history... His grave is beneath the bleak northern waters and his monument is an army, millions strong, imbued with his deathless spirit.[139]

133 Rose: *King George V,* pp.194-196.
134 *Morning Post* 14/6/16.
135 *Daily Telegraph* 13/6/16.
136 *Daily Express* 13/6/16.
137 *Daily News* 14/6.
138 *Daily Graphic* 14/6/16.
139 *Daily Telegraph* 13/6/16.

The King pauses in the afternoon to receive Kitchener's nephew, a naval man, then he boards a train and departs for Scotland. He wakes up to the sight of a beautiful bright morning, with snow visible on high peaks. From Invergordon he steams down lines of ships and inspects the *Malaya* in a floating dock as repairs are made to the shell damage she received at Jutland. Then it is on to Thurso, where Bertie is amongst the naval party ready to greet his father. The sail for Scapa with a large escort of sixteen destroyers in high winds. The whole fleet is ready to be reviewed, and their crews cheer loudly as the King steams by. He greets men and officers from each ship and makes the same short speech; congratulating them on their part in the naval action. Then he returns to the Thurso in order to move south to Rosyth, where Admiral Beatty awaits him. "It was a great joy and a surprise to have seen Papa again when he came up here for a day and a night," Bertie tells his mother. "I thought him looking very well… I think he enjoyed his visit."[140]

From under the shadow of the Forth Bridge the King sails for the dockyard with Beatty. Under a glorious blue sky in blazing sunshine, the King stands in front of the battle-scarred *Warspite* and surveys thousands of men assembled that have survived the Battle of Jutland. "I made them a short speech and then they marched past, including their officers." He sees the 28 holes in *Warspite* caused by enemy shells, more on *Southampton*, and Beatty's ship *Lion* with her missing turret. "I am rather proud of the feat which I have performed," the King writes to Queen Mary. "I have visited, inspected, and have been seen by the whole of the officers and men of the Grand Fleet in three days… The spirit… is even better than it was last year when I saw them." A last, harrowing day completes the King's homage to the heroes of Jutland. Beatty accompanies him to South Queensferry to see men wounded during the battle. Then the party moves on to the Royal Infirmary in Edinburgh where the 68 severely wounded men are mostly from Beatty's own *Lion* and *Princess Royal*. "Some of them were terribly injured from shellfire."[141] For David he describes the harrowing extent of some of their injuries: "most of them burnt by the explosion of shells or else by the cordite catching fire in their battery."[142]

The battle is best construed as a draw, but that does not stop the Kaiser from claiming otherwise. "I have already seen several captains of the ships that took part in the battle and they are convinced that the German fleet suffered more than our ships and that their losses are just as heavy," the King tells the Duke of Connaught. "I suppose we shall never know what their losses really were, but they lie so in their official statements that it is impossible to believe anything they say… William's speech to his fleet after the battle is extraordinary as he calls it a great victory which he must know it is not."[143]

"King George in the Big Push"

After a month of naval matters and waterborne tragedy, the focus of Britain's war is about to shift sharply back to matters on land, and onto Kitchener's legacy: his volunteer armies. The day before the Field Marshal's memorial service, the King writes to his uncle in Canada and tells him that "the Russians during the last week have made a splendid advance and have driven the Austrians back for many miles and have taken over 70,000 prisoners besides guns etc. This ought to relieve the pressure on the Italian Front and compel the Austrians to withdraw some of their divisions and send them to Galicia."[144] "Thank God our advance in Galicia and in our Western Provinces is developing

140   RA QM/PRIV/CC10/228.
141   RA PRIV/GVD/1916 (17/6).
142   RA EDW/PRIV/MAIN/A/1892.
143   RA ADDL/MSS/A/15/6596.
144   Ibid.

successfully," Tsar Nicholas writes to the King.[145]

But on the Western Front at the end of June 1916, professional soldiers are lining up to go into battle alongside miners, farmers, labourers, clerks, accountants; men drawn from every walk of life. Gathered from the length and breadth of Britain, tens of thousands are assembled in Picardy to embark upon the most ambitious campaign Britain has ever undertaken. But many of these men have never seen offensive action, and any experience that they have is of holding trenches. Some have had less than adequate training and one division's artillery only has three days of live practise before leaving for France.

It is clear in 1916 that the Allies need to organise and mount a coherent, joint attack against the Central Powers. By mid-February it had been agreed that a combined offensive would proceed in the summer, but all Allied planning is thrown into disarray at the end of that month when the Germans begin their own brutal offensive against the French at Verdun. Casualties grow towards a quarter of a million, and thus the British Army have, by circumstance, now assumed the greater part of the responsibility for the offensive campaign on the Somme, a battleground chosen by the French, where the Germans have had plenty of time to strengthen their positions by digging deep, extensive systems of trenches, fortifying villages in their path. The preliminary bombardment begins on the 24th June and more than a million shells are fired, attempting to silence German resistance and flatten all that lay in the path of the infantry in time for zero hour. By 30th June the scene has been set for the British Army to attempt to make a decisive breakthrough in the German line in three enthusiastically planned stages, with the hope that the enemy's line would cave and Haig could have the cavalry sent through the breach to wreak decisive havoc upon the Kaiser's men. The relative peace of Picardy is about to be shattered as the Allies attempt to win the war by the years' end.

The modern concept of public relations is emerging rapidly by 1916. Through a combination of sound advice, hard work, common sense, and a few sacrifices he didn't necessarily want to make, the King's public image has been steadily improving since the outbreak of war. The press appreciate that when he speaks, there is nothing in any of his public utterances "to compare with the flamboyant verbiage"[146] which characterises his cousin Wilhelm's speeches. The public appreciates that his approach to work is the complete opposite; very understated, very *British*. The nature of the monarchy means that His Majesty is distanced from politicians; "making shreds and tatters of each others' reputations in their public quarrels." His closeness to his subjects has had an overwhelmingly positive effect; public access to the King "which before the war would have seemed hardly feasible, since it has meant the removal of many artificial barriers."[147] Because of his dislike of showing off, His Majesty does not always get the credit that he deserves. "The extent of the King's conscientious labours in connection with the war will one day be more fully realised by the country than they are at present," writes one newspaper in 1915. Security must be considered too. "In many instances it is inadvisable to give details of His Majesty's activities, and the public is therefore largely unaware of the splendid work he is doing in a hundred different ways."[148]

But public tolerance for such privacy when it comes to the Sovereign is waning with the explosion of coverage of the war in newspapers, pictorial magazines and with the advent of moving pictures. There is a feeling of ownership emerging, a sense of entitlement in knowing about the King. His visit to the front in 1914 had been a complete secret. In 1915, the *Daily Sketch* had published a

145   RA PS/PSO/GV/C/Q/2551/6.
146   *The Standard* 28/1/16.
147   *Daily Express* 24/8/15.
148   *Daily Star* 24/8/15.

selection of photographs of His Majesty's visit with a rather stroppy caption that read: "We should like to give the names of these gallant regiments but the censor will not allow us to publish anything but the bare inscription under the pictures."[149] To their fury, prevented from accompanying the royal party, they were left to cobble together stories of this visit from the French press. It caused angry correspondence between the War Office, the palace and the press, who were outraged that they were gagged by the censor when reporters from other nations were not.

In 1916 the King pays a visit to the front that is wholly new in two respects. Firstly, the press will be allowed to accompany His Majesty, and secondly, he will visit in the middle of an offensive, instead of waiting for fighting to die down in the winter months. Haig has no objection to this, but it is made very clear to him in advance, that "His Majesty does not wish to upset [his] arrangements in any way, and that he must not feel bound to be always in attendance on the King."[150] Once again the little tin royal standard is brought out, a metal case of medals and ribbons assembled. With a battle in full flow, the King is anxious that nobody at Haig's headquarters should waste time arranging programmes for him. It is his intention "to motor out every day to see what is to be seen of troops on the march, billets, etc." However, a local expert would be handy. "Someone attached to us who would know all the country, and be able to tell us more or less where troops were located."[151] Haig quickly provides one of his aides, a Major "Gerry" Thompson for this purpose, who can lay claim to being the first battlefield guide on the Western Front.

Because the situation at the front could rapidly change during the King's stay, for the first time there will be an escape plan and emergency protocols for the royal party too: a telephone orderly, a "safe cellar to which *important personages* can be taken for safety." A motor car will be on hand and a chauffeur billeted nearby. If fleeing becomes necessary, the rendezvous point will be an RFC headquarters over a nearby hill. Ladders are ready to be placed against the windows of each VIP by men of the guard, and a ban is imposed on lights being shown from windows during the night. There is even a plan to "muddy the water" with misinformation so that no enemy submarine will be "spurred to special exercises" should word get out about the His Majesty's return date.[152]

After the catastrophe that befell the King in 1915, and given that he will be in closer proximity to danger than ever before, Queen Mary wants a nightly telegram from Wigram outlining the chief events of the day. And His Majesty will not be mounting any horses. "May God be with him and protect him,"[153] the Queen writes in her diary. "I felt very sad at taking leave of you last evening as I hate being away from you," she writes to her husband, "especially at the present moment of anxiety when there is so much to occupy our minds and thoughts. However I comfort myself with knowledge that your visit will give the greatest pleasure in France and I hope you will have an interesting and not too tiring a time."[154] She has promised to look after his little dog Jacky and his parrot, Charlotte, for the King is most preoccupied with whether or not his pets miss him when he is away. "I… hated leaving you," he writes from the front. "In these anxious times it is essential that I should have your help and love and sympathy in all my worries and that we should not be separated."[155]

Despite all of the enthusiasm and preparation on the Somme, the opening day of the battle is the darkest in the history of the British Army. The country suffers a catastrophic 60,000 casualties, and

149   *Daily Sketch* 1/11/1915.
150   RA PS/PSO/GV/PS/WAR/QQ6/4503.
151   Ibid.
152   Ibid.
153   RA PRIV/QMD/1916 (7/8).
154   RA QM/PRIV/CC08/202.
155   RA QM/PRIV/CC04/151.

there is no stunning victory. The King first speaks to wounded men from the battle on 15th July; 59 new arrivals at Hampstead. Three days later at Epsom there are over 1,000 of them for His Majesty to probe for information. General Robertson brings news to the palace, letters and telegrams from the front continue to arrive and the King stays as up to speed as he possibly can as the offensive develops. Throughout July, troops have become bogged down in ill-organised, small-scale attacks at locations like Longeuval and Delville Wood. By the onset of August, though gains have been made, the grand offensive on the Somme is far from the path to imminent victory that had been envisaged.

The King, Stamfordham and Wigram make an early voyage across the Channel aboard *Invicta* on 7th August. "The passage… was a perfect one, flat calm with bright sun."[156] First and foremost, His Majesty swiftly reports to Queen Mary that he is surprised to find that David is "looking the picture of health and really eats much more at meals than he used to." The Prince is just as pleased to see his father. "Papa looks well and isn't at all lame now, and he gave me all the home news while I was sitting with him in the car!! It is a great thing that he has come out now."[157] The King is also immediately pleased with his guide, Thompson; "a charming companion."[158] The feeling is mutual. "I gave you a good chit as a bandobast-wala," Wigram tells the Major. "It is a great pleasure to collaborate with you."[159]

His Majesty's stops in to see Haig, who writes in his diary that he was in the act of fretting over what he considers over-optimistic assessments of the situation on the Somme from General Rawlinson, who is commanding the battle. He updates the King on unfolding events, then they catch up on gossip:

[His Majesty] spoke a great deal about a paper which [Churchill] had written and given to the Cabinet, criticising the operations in France, and arriving at the conclusion that nothing had been achieved! [The King] also said that Viscount French had been very nasty and that he was 'the most jealous man he had ever come across.' I said that these were trifles and that we must not allow them to divert our thoughts from our main objective, namely 'beating the Germans!'[160]

The 1916 tour begins on a hundred miles of very dry roads, dust clouds rising as His Majesty's motor car rumbles along. "The weather is glorious," the King reports to Queen Mary, "with bright sun and not too hot." Having made two visits to the region in the depths of winter, he is charmed by the French countryside. "The crops are splendid and are being cut now all by women and old men… Certainly in summer this country gives one an entirely different impression."[161] The rapid expansion of the British front means that there is always something new to see, and since his visit in 1915, a number of educational establishments have been struck up. The King visits a machine-gun school, a trench mortar school where they have even established a museum; "a collection of all the German trench mortars and hand bombs which have been captured." Even David finds it all extremely interesting, "as ordinarily I never move out of the corps area."[162] Covered in dust, His Majesty inspects drafts at one training camp in the grounds of an old French chateau. "Some of the men were practising bayonet exercises, others doing physical drill. The cooks were busy with the

156   Ibid.
157   RA EDW/PRIV/DIARY/1916 (8/8).
158   RA PS/PSO/GV/C/O/2148/217.
159   RA PS/PSO/GV/PS/WAR/QQ6/4503.
160   (ed.) Sheffield & Bourne: *Douglas Haig: War Diaries and Letters 1914-1918,* pp.216-217.
161   RA QM/PRIV/CC04/151.
162   RA EDW/PRIV/DIARY/1916 (9/8).

next meal of the day. All the life of the camp was in full swing, and not interrupted when the King came through, watching it all, and chatting with the officers and men."[163] And then he comes across a hospital train waiting to depart for the coast with 400 men aboard, casualty clearing stations closer to the front lines, like one at Lapugnoy that His Majesty describes as beautifully tidy and spotlessly clean.

Whilst battle rages on the Somme, the King visits the rest of the front. Mont St. Eloi is:

A sinister place, very weird and awesome at dusk, when owls were hooting in the broken brickwork, and when the light struck through the great rents in the walls of ancient barns and the broken rafters of roofless houses. Weeds and wild flowers had grown in a tangled way over some of these ruins, and there was the scarlet flame of poppies in old shell holes.

The King passes through, silently taking it all in. In the background the sounds of guns goes on, "and the vibration of their fire shook the crumbling walls of the village and brought down some of the loose stones."[164] A sentry salutes His Majesty. The King and his heir clamber up to an observation post for a view of Souchez and Neuville St Vaast. It is a position of solitude, and His Majesty surveys the battlefield by a ruined house, through a large hole in the wall; ground on which tens of thousands of young Frenchmen have already fallen. "Papa got a grand view,"[165] writes David. Shells are bursting on Vimy Ridge, and the King watches the results through field glasses. "Now and again a German 'crump' flung up a great column of earth and smoke not far away, and the blue sky was flecked with the puffs of shrapnel smoke… Flashes of fire jabbed out the panorama of the fields where our batteries were hidden."[166] His Majesty listens to the war going on about him. "We were firing trench mortars besides guns," he writes later, "and besides smoke a tremendous amount of dust was caused by the explosions of different colours."[167]

The King has no intention of swerving the Somme. It rains on the morning of 10th August, for just long enough to temporarily suppress the incessant dust on the roads. His Majesty is joined by General Rawlinson, and they motor out to see General Congreve, who was by far the most successful corps commander on 1st July. He is in pieces, for his beloved son has been dead for a little over a fortnight; killed under his own command just six weeks after his wedding. The General's health is suffering, but he takes the King to the original German front line from 1st July. He sees what is left of former occupation; "cartridge clips, scraps of letters from home, bits of clothing, the odds and ends of trench life."[168] David watches as his father collects a few souvenirs.

His Majesty smiles slightly. "Now I will climb over the parapet."

"It is not so easy as it looks, Sir," answered one of the officers, but the King refused the helping hand held out to him by the Prince of Wales, and scrambled up alone."

Led by a sapper of the Royal Engineers, His Majesty walks across no man's land. He follows the same path as his troops five weeks before. On his left is Fricourt, "and he looked down upon the white ghastliness of its ruin with its broken stumps of trees and the upturned trenches and the broken brickwork of houses that had become but dust and ashes in this refuse heap fouled with corruption." Straight ahead is Contalmaison, "with the ruins of the château, standing among charred tree-trunks." The battle can be heard further forward: "the rush of shells went through the

163   (ed.) Gibbs, Sir Philip: *George the Faithful*, p.248.
164   Ibid.
165   RA EDW/PRIV/DIARY/1916 (9/8).
166   (ed.) Gibbs, Sir Philip: *George the Faithful*, p.248.
167   RA GV/PRIV/GVD/1916 (9/8).
168   (ed.) Gibbs, Sir Philip: *George the Faithful*, p.249.

sky… the shrill singing note of a bit of flying steel, the knock-knock-knockings of the field guns, the humming of aeroplanes." It is not a safe spot. "There was no reason at any moment there should not have been a black puff of German shrapnel over the King's head."[169] After taking in the view towards Pozières and of Mametz Wood,[170] His Majesty crosses into the vacated German lines after his sapper guide, dodging shell holes and barbed wire, discarded sandbags. Then for a little while he stands above one of the old minefields looking into the deep mouths of craters, both enthralled and horrified by what he is shown. He says that he cannot believed that human beings could have lived through it.

The King surveys the German standard of living. He sees the effect of British guns, enemy lines "churned up as thought by a gigantic steel plough," but he can also see how comfortable they have made themselves. He regards a bed with a spring mattress sitting in front of him, then peeks into German dugouts; sees "fine wooden staircases, the well-arranged suites of rooms, the elaborate ventilating apparatus."[171] "They evidently thought they were going to make a long stay," he says, venturing towards one enemy dugout which goes thirty feet underground.

"I should not go right down, Sir" said one of the Generals. "We have not had time to clean them out yet, and they are not very wholesome."[172]

The King agrees, and does not venture all the way inside, "as I think there was a German still in it and [he] was distinctly high."[173] The Prince of Wales thinks that men have been using it as a latrine too.

On his travels the King sees an unknown British grave. It is marked by a little pile of dirt in the middle of a shell-crater, with a wooden cross that reads: *"Here lies the body of an unknown British soldier."* His Majesty salutes the grave with a sad look. "Some gallant fellow lies there," he says. "It is a pity he has not been identified." He sees another marker, this one for two men of the Border Regiment and marked by a steel helmet. The King reads the inscription on their wooden cross. *"RIP Privates Goulde and Pennington of the Border Regiment, killed in action 1/7/16"*[174] There is a hole right through the latter's helmet. The King asks whether they are really any good as protection, and David points out the final resting place of a German, too hastily buried with his boots still sticking out of the ground.

Soldiers passing back and forth across the area are astonished to see the King in their midst. Word spreads. Hundreds of soldiers gather to see him at one stop; most of them Northamptons. Amongst their number he spies a small boy. Joseph Lefèvre is twelve. His father is a prisoner of war and his mother, it is said, was foully done to death by the enemy. His Majesty is told that some men of the Black Watch found him helplessly wandering near Ypres, and this battalion have adopted him. They say he is enrolled on their strength, and he stands before the King in a little khaki uniform.

"I believe," said His Majesty, "I have found at last my youngest soldier. How old are you, my boy?"

The men explain that the boy speaks only French, and so the King speaks to him in his own tongue.

"Do you like being a soldier?" he asked.

"Oui, Monsieur le Roi," the boy replied.

169   Ibid., p.248.
170   RA GV/PRIV/GVD/1916 (10/8).
171   Hammerton: *Our King & Queen: A Pictorial Record of Their Lives,* p.28.
172   (ed.) Gibbs, Sir Philip: *George the Faithful,* p.248.
173   RA GV/PRIV/AA60/149.
174   *Daily Express* 16/8/16.

"And do you think you will like being a soldier when you are grown up?"

"Ah, but yes, Sir,' was the answer in French. 'I want to fight the Boches."

"You are getting on," the King said. "I see they have made you a lance-corporal already. You will soon be a general."

As he leaves His Majesty feels compelled to just double check that the boy is not a fully functioning member of the battalion.

"He is quite willing to go anywhere, Your Majesty," one of them said, "but we don't let him. When we are in the trenches we leave him with the transport."[175]

Throughout his visit, the Kings sees thousands of troops making their way in and out of battle on the Somme. "It is most interesting seeing men from all parts of the Empire,"[176] he tells Queen Mary. He had reviewed more than 3,000 men of the South African Brigade before their departure for France. They have been reduced from more than 3,000 men to something like 700 able soldiers in just a few days in Delville Wood; and yet from somewhere these harrowed young men summon a Zulu war cry for His Majesty when they are drawn up in front of a hedge to meet him. The King sees the 17th Manchesters have been ripped to pieces, the 11th and 12th Royal Scots have also been decimated. And the 38th Division, a formation of Welshmen. It is no longer able to fight since most of their number were sacrificed in the bloody battle for Mametz Wood. The 8th Norfolks have lost a huge percentage of their fighting strength at Trônes Wood, and the King goes through the survivors asking for clarification about the deaths of two of his footmen, Sergeants Kennedy and Church, who have been recently lost on the Somme.

His Majesty is angered and disgusted by the wanton destruction he finds throughout France and Flanders. He goes out of his way to add the town of Bethune to his itinerary and sabotages his schedule as a result, but the town was wrecked by massive shells just the week before and the King wants to see it for himself: "huge holes and several houses destroyed in [the] market square."[177] There is a military policeman, Roberts, on duty nearby, "directing traffic… though the sky above him was very sinister, and the place in which he stood was registered by hostile guns." His Majesty pauses to talk with the man, walks into the road to examine a large shell crater and to stare down into its depths with David in tow. "Some of us standing there were nervous because the King lingered so long. At any second another shell might have come and another shell crater as big as this might have opened the earth at his feet. You can never tell. But the King was extremely interested, and stayed several minutes in this danger spot."[178] Officers and newspaper men grow more and more anxious as His Majesty and the Prince of Wales stand and debate the diameter of the hole in the ground.

The King spends his evenings attending to his boxes and writing to the Queen; a cacophony of shellfire in the background as the enemy attacks the Australian contingent about Pozieres. "The guns are making a great row tonight, one can hear them quite plainly here."[179] There is no special treatment for the royal vehicle. His Majesty stops at every checkpoint, and makes way for troops and valuable guns alike. "Traffic: stop start, stop start. Field guns and Howitzers swung past him, the gunners with their helmets strapped well down, jolting on the carriages… half an inch to spare between the axles of the gun wheels and the panels of the King's car." Battalions squeeze by too. "Manchester men on the march, powdered with white dust from head to foot, with sweat dripping

175   (ed.) Gibbs, Sir Philip: *George the Faithful,* p.248.
176   RA QM/PRIV/CC04/ 155.
177   RA GV/PRIV/GVD/1916 (11/8).
178   (ed.) Gibbs, Sir Philip: *George the Faithful,* p.255.
179   RA QM/PRIV/CC04/155.

down their bronzed faces, with their steel hats on the back of their heads, with rifles and packs weighing heavily… in a blaze of sun, their bodies pressed close to the King's car." His Majesty can hear their deep breathing and the trudge of their exhausted footsteps as they kick the dust up alongside him. They may be tired, but they soon catch on. "They turned their heads at the sight of the Royal Standard, stared into the car, and came on with a look of astonishment, for one and all they all recognise the King, and they swung on talking of him, while mounted officers in their saddles turned and stared back."[180] His Majesty is indulging his preference to surprise the men on this visit; see them in a genuine setting and not awkwardly and inconveniently, for them, drawn up in lines on his behalf. One afternoon he enters some billets in a farmyard where machine gunners from a Lancashire regiment have just collapsed having left the line; dimly lit, "crooked old beams, plaster walls and a litter of straw." One man is snoring loudly, stretched out in a wheelbarrow. He is soon awake. "The sound of footsteps coming across the cobble-stones disturbed him and he stretched his arms and sat up, blinking, and then saw with utter disbelief in the truth of what his eyes revealed, the King and the Prince of Wales and a glitter of brass hats and red tabs. But everybody sees the funny side. "The expression on his face was inexpressibly comic. But the King was wise in going to these places without warning, for he saw the everyday life of his troops. Without any special preparation or tidying up."[181]

Of course His Majesty must pay homage to the French whilst he is in their country. On Saturday lunchtime he motors to Haig's headquarters for lunch with the Commander in Chief, the President and senior French officers. They are late, and Lloyd George is so far behind schedule that they do not wait for him. It is a terribly hot afternoon and jumping out of his motor car outside the chateau gates, the King passes along a gravel path, "overshadowed on one side by fine old trees. On the other side was a smooth expanse of lawn with… a sumptuous bed of scarlet begonias in a blaze of blossom, and beyond, the tall white spike of a yucca in flower."[182] His Majesty sits between Haig and General Joffre as the distinguished group endure a heavy meal. "We had fifteen at lunch," recalled Haig, "and by the King's desire, only water of various kinds was served. Many of us will long remember General Joffre's book of abhorrence… when Shadock handed him a glass of lemonade and a bottle of ginger beer, and asked him which he preferred!"[183] Afterwards the President asks for ten minutes of private conversation with His Majesty, and Haig provides a room. "Affairs of state and Anglo French war policy were discussed, while the rest of us hung about in the hall!! Then Papa was cloistered with Haig till we eventually shoved off."[184] With Haig present, Poincare points out the importance of continuing to press the enemy vigorously; and, in his opinion, "a general attack on a wide front should be made as soon as possible." The French premier thinks that things look bright for the Allies, "but was most anxious, before the approach of winter, that we should have made some decisive advance in order to keep the people of France and England from grumbling."[185] Haig responds that there are weeks of good weather left, and that he believes much can be achieved in that time. Then the party adjourns outside to the gates to greet the press and pose for photographs.

For the latter, northern part of his tour, the King relocates to Cassel, to the busy Rue de Lille. "Have got quite a nice house with lovely view as we are on top of a hill."[186] The town is quaint; "hardly changed since the days when Marlborough and his troopers fought through the neighbouring country and made their headquarters there. Many of the houses, richly carved in

180   *Daily Star* 17/8/16.
181   *Daily Mirror* 17/8/16.
182   *The Times* 17/8/16.
183   (ed.) Sheffield & Bourne: *Douglas Haig: War Diaries and Letters 1914-1918,* pp.218-219.
184   RA EDW/PRIV/DIARY/1916 (12/8).
185   (ed.) Sheffield & Bourne: *Douglas Haig: War Diaries and Letters 1914-1918,* pp.218-219.
186   RA GV/PRIV/GVD/1916 (12/8).

the style of the Renaissance, or with timbered walls and high gables, belong to the sixteenth and seventeenth centuries."[187] His Majesty pays his visit to King Albert of the Belgians and his family on the coast; stopping his motor car to get out and converse with British troops on the way. He reaches La Panne for lunch with the King and Queen and three of their children. After they have eaten, feeling rather sorry for the Belgian royals, who are suspended out here away from everything and bored; the King takes them out for the afternoon. They visit a rest camp for naval troops; review a large gun that has been pointed of late towards the enemy stronghold of Ostend; hidden in a camouflage barn. Then it is on to St. Pol aerodrome to see men of the Royal Naval Air Service. They put on stunt flights for their visitors to entertain them. "I think they were interested in what they saw," the King writes in his diary. "Poor things, they see so little now and feel rather out of it, so I wanted to do something for them."[188] But now he is excited about returning home. "To that happy moment I am anxiously looking forward. Love to all the children and Charlotte who I hope is missing me."[189] After a morning spent dispensing gifts and decorations, His Majesty departs, leaving behind a message for his troops as their trials continue:

> It has been a great pleasure and satisfaction to me to be with my Armies during the past week… The offensive recently begun has since been resolutely maintained by day and by night. I have had opportunities of visiting some of the scenes of the later desperate struggles, and of appreciating to a slight extent the demands made upon your courage and physical endurance in order to assail and capture positions prepared during the past two years and stoutly defended to the last… I return home more than ever proud of you.[190]

"I was greatly interested in all I saw," the King writes to Bertie. "I motored… 687 miles, so you see I did not let the grass grow under my feet."[191] Perhaps just as important for the monarchy is the extent to which the press have been interested in all that *they* have been allowed to see of His Majesty's visit on their maiden royal tour of the front and, given that their voices will inform the rest of his subjects; what they have made of his doings. The notion that the King went to the front for his image would have disgusted him, but the result of this press coverage, when his Majesty is safely home and they are free to describe his visit in detail, is almost as good as if the King had shouldered a rifle on the Somme himself. "He has visited battlefields where our guns were roaring," reports *The Times*, "and over which the enemy throws shells every day. He has climbed in and out of trenches which saw desperate fighting in the early days of the Battle of the Somme, has gone into German dugouts and picked up relics of the battle with his own hands."[192] Not only has His Majesty sacrificed his own safety to do this, not only has he taken his son with him on this mission, but once again his genuine concern for the common soldier and what he must endure has done wonders for his peoples' perception of him.

And it is not only the written word that carries home evidence of His Majesty at the front now. By early September, footage of his tour has been incorporated into a cinematic piece. The producers have received an unprecedented number of orders for *The King's Visit to France* from all over the country. The Royal Family are given a preview at Windsor, and they are delighted to see moving pictures of His Majesty at Fricourt and Mametz. "While the battlefield is being

187   RA GV/PRIV/GVD/1916 (13/8).
188   RA PS/PSO/GV/PS/WAR/QQ6/4503.
189   RA GV/PRIV/AA60/149.
190   *The Times* 16/8/16.
191   RA GV/PRIV/AA60/149.
192   *The Times* 16/8/16.

inspected German shellfire is going on, and the bursting of explosives in the air can be seen in the distance… through field glasses and a telescope supported on the branch of a tree shattered by shell fire the King watches the bombardment of Pozieres."[193] As His Majesty looks on, there are frequent exclamations of surprise from him, as when he recalls that he was completely unaware at the time that these actions were being captured. The production is a huge success. "Always we see him cheerful, smiling, confident. If there is anywhere a Briton who feels at times a passing despondency about the war he cannot do better than go and see this film."[194]

"Foolish and Extravagant Hopes"

Shortly before the King left for France, Britain entered the third year of the Great War. "On this day, the second anniversary of the commencement of the great conflict in which my country and her gallant armies are engaged," says His Majesty's message to the Allies, "I desire to convey to you my steadfast resolution to prosecute the war until our united efforts have attained the objects for which we have in common taken up arms."[195] Asquith refers to a "growing confidence in the final success of the allied cause." There is, declares one editorial, "an exhilarating sense of victory in the air. Only let us heed not to nurse foolish and extravagant hopes of too immediate a success… The enemy is still very strong. He is shaken, not broken."[196]

And this means more sacrifice, more work for everybody. "The King's motto is 'do it now.' He is what the Americans call a 'clean desk man'; he allows no unfinished paperwork to accumulate."[197] And so he is exhausted. In the summer of 1916, Ambassador Page reports that His Majesty looks "ten years older."[198] And yet the scale of work that the war has now placed on the King's shoulders is only increasing with each passing month. The court was originally to have removed to Windsor for at least a short period in the summer, but His Majesty abandons this plan. "The King has now expressed his wish not to leave town until the many pressing questions demanding his constant presence are settled."[199]

There is no such narrow focus on His Majesty's visits as there was when he was pointedly reviewing shipyards and factories in order to help assail labour problems in 1915. Throughout 1916 he concentrates on new establishments, and there is plenty to keep him occupied on the coast. There is a day at an experimental station in Shoeburyness. The King journeys out to Frinton in Essex to review defences, then on to Clacton where after reviewing troops he eats his lunch at the Grand Hotel. Then he is off again, to Wivenhoe. He visits Shoreham on "a beastly day blowing hard with a good deal of rain;" accompanied by Princess Mary. There they attend a convalescent depot housing almost 5,000 men. "Saw them all, everything is also done to amuse them and make them happy and forget what they have been through. A splendid camp and very well run."[200] There are similar establishments waiting for His Majesty at Eastbourne and Summerdown. At Lowestoft the King looks over ships, at Fort Blackhouse in Gosport he is a spectator at the docks in May, watching ships as they are loaded with horses, heavy artillery, stores, drafts of men. He watches three vessels depart

193   *The Times* 5/10/16.
194   *Daily Telegraph* 17/10/16.
195   *Daily Chronicle* 5/4/16.
196   *Daily Telegraph* 5/8/16.
197   Hammerton: *Our King & Queen: A Pictorial Record of Their Lives*, p.11.
198   Nicolson: *King George V,* p.316.
199   *Daily Mirror* 21/7/16.
200   RA GV/PRIV/GVD/1916 (3/11).

for Havre with their cargoes, before the hospital ship *Asturias* arrives with a former shipmate of His Majesty's aboard whom he joins him for tea. The King inspects hospital trains waiting to receive her patients, sees the wounded brought from the ship. "Everything wonderfully well arranged and works most smoothly, does great credit to those who have worked without ceasing since the war began."[201] There are still factories to be seen, so that the King and quite often the Queen alongside him can acknowledge munitions workers engaged on all manner of tasks: St. Peters in Slough where they make munitions and cookers for the army; Perivale to see a fuse inspection department. At Park Royal there is an ammunition inspection depot piled high with 400 million rounds of rifle ammunition.

His Majesty's men keep a watchful eye on the hardship and grief caused by the conflict. When the Trinity Yacht *Irene* is lost he extends his condolences to the families of her crew and acknowledges services she rendered he and his ancestors. There is a nod to William Pillar, captain of a trawler who rushed to the scene of a sinking battleship and assisted a lifeboat in trouble. Along with the entire country, His Majesty is disgusted by the murder of Captain Fryatt; a merchant mariner executed by the Germans when he tried to fight back against a U-boat by ramming it with his passenger ferry. He offers his heartfelt sympathy to his widow, "with feelings of the deepest indignation."[202] A teenage dancer who helped wounded soldiers during the Easter Rising is invited to the palace so that she might receive an award. "The King was very kind to me… he gave me a very hearty shake of the hand,"[203] she tells reporters. He says: "You are a very brave girl. I have great pleasure and great pride in presenting you with this medal."[204]

But one does not have to snatch headlines to gain His Majesty's attention. A 90 year old subject living in an alms house receives a letter from the King. She has lost one son and has fourteen grandsons in the forces. Thomas Houlton, who sweeps the crossing outside East Croydon station has five sons, four grandsons and two nephews in the services. "I am commanded," writs Fritz Ponsonby, "to express to you the King's congratulations, and to assure you that His Majesty much appreciates the spirit of patriotism which prompted the example in one family of loyalty and devotion to the Sovereign and Empire."[205] Mr Knight, the Headmaster of a school in Burton-on-Trent who had lost his three sons in two months receives another letter that informs him that the King 'is grieved to hear of the terrible sorrow which you are thus called upon to bear."[206] One man even uses a letter from His Majesty to plead his way out of a charge for drunkenness, saying that he had been more jubilant than intoxicated after receiving a letter of congratulation on having four sons in the army. He produced it for the authorities and had to promise not to get quite so over-excited again. There are many, many gestures of appreciation made to various subjects. John Hassall, the poster artist, is one of the Special Constables that form the special night watch at Buckingham Palace. One evening the King ventures down to see how they are getting on. He does his rounds and thanks them for his voluntary service:

"I hope you get properly looked after when on duty," he says.

Hassall quips "Well Your Majesty, if I may say so I think the quality of the hot coffee has been a little poor lately."

"Has it?" says the King "We must see about that: I expect they've been going to the wrong shop for it."

201   RA GV/PRIV/GVD/1916 (29/5).
202   *The Times* 4/8/16.
203   *Daily Chronicle* 26/2/16.
204   *Daily News* 24/2/17.
205   *Morning Post* 3/4.16.
206   *Daily Telegraph* 2/3/15.

Crowds stretch across the Thames throughout the night as King George V lies in state, January 1936. (Authors' Collection)

The King, dressed in German army uniform, in conversation with his cousin the Kaiser during his 1913 visit to Berlin. (Authors' Collection)

His Majesty's wartime Prime Ministers: Herbert Asquith. (Authors' Collection)

and David Lloyd George. (Authors' Collection)

A publicity portrait designed to stimulate recruitment in India, October 1914. (Authors' Collection)

Winston Churchill, First Lord of the Admiralty on the outbreak of war. (Authors' Collection)

Admiral Sir John Fisher, recalled as First Sea Lord against the express wish of the King in October 1914. (Authors' Collection)

Prince Maurice of Battenburg, Queen Victoria's youngest grandchild, killed during the First Battle of Ypres in 1914. (Authors' Collection)

His Majesty's cousin, Prince Louis of Battenburg, who was driven from office on account of his origins. (Authors' Collection)

The King's mother, Queen Alexandra looks over a donated ambulance. (Authors' Collection)

The Duke of Connaught, Governor General of Canada at the onset of war. (Authors' Collection)

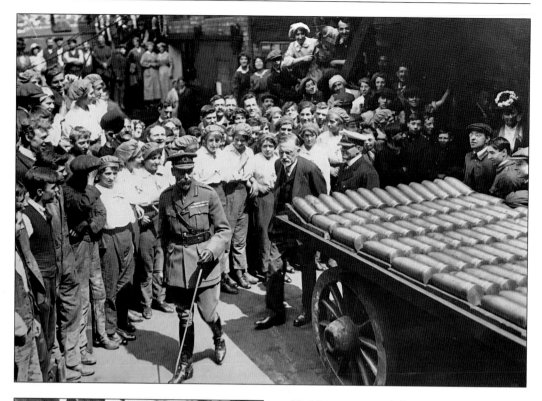

His Majesty inspects shells in a munitions factory.
(Authors' Collection)

The King quizzes John Cassidy, a shipyard worker in
Sunderland who claimed to be 17 years old. (Authors'
Collection)

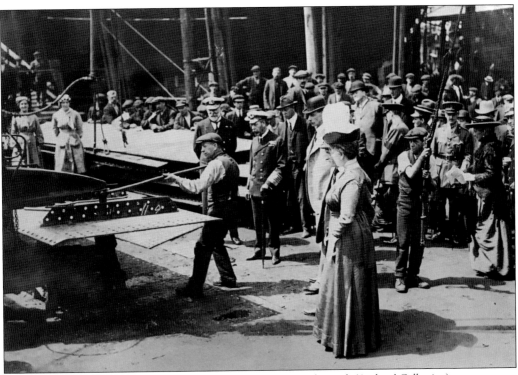

Watching a demonstation by a worker in a northeast shipyard. (Authors' Collection)

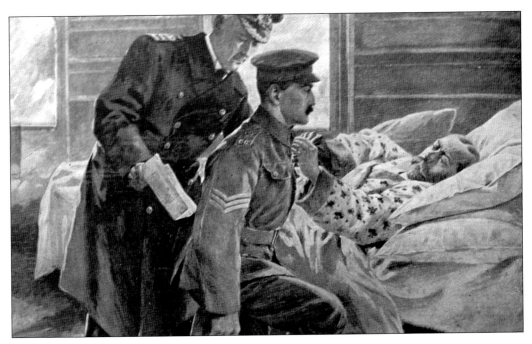

Artist impression of the King's presentation of the Victoria Cross to Sergeant Oliver Brooks after his accident.
(Authors' Collection)

Field Marshal Lord Kitchener, Secretary of State for War from August 1914. (Authors' Collection)

Field Marshal Sir John French, initial commander of the British Expeditionary Force. (Authors' Collection)

And his successor, Field Marshal Sir Douglas Haig. (Authors' Collection)

General Sir William Robertson, Chief of the Imperial General Staff and a favourite of the King. (Authors' Collection)

Wounded men relax during one of Their Majesties' tea parties at Buckingham Palace, March 1916. (Authors' Collection)

The most painful of tasks: Presenting gallantry awards to the next of kin. (Authors' Collection)

Queen Mary on hand to support His Majesty as he presents the VC to the widow and son of Captain Harold Ackroyd. (Authors' Collection)

Prince Albert as a Midshipman in the
Royal Navy. (Authors' Collection)

The Prince of Wales inspects troops in Egypt, spring
1916. (Authors' Collection)

His Majesty works with Lord Stamfordham in
his tent in the gardens of Buckingham Palace,
June 1918. (Authors' Collection)

Major Clive Wigram, the King's Assistant Private
Secretary. (Private Collection)

A post-lunch photo call during the King's 1916 visit to the front. (L-R General Joffre, President Poincaré, the King, General Foch and Haig). (Authors' Collection)

The King inspects battlefield debris and clutter at Messines, July 1917. (Authors' Collection)

His Majesty pays his respects to a Private Pennington on the Somme, August 1916. (Authors' Collection)

The King smiles his way through a picnic lunch in France during a visit to the battlefields. (Authors' Collection)

His Majesty travelled thousands of miles by road in France and Flanders during his visits to the front. (Authors' Collection)

Watching the firing of a heavy gun in France, August 1916. (Authors' Collection)

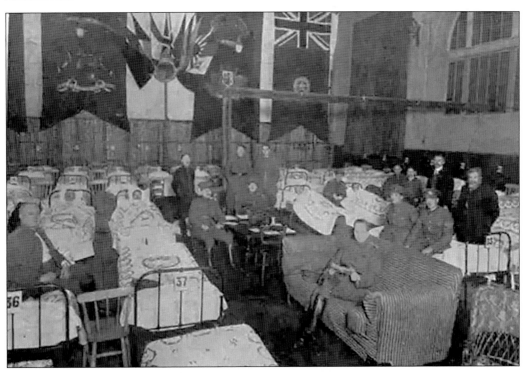

The Riding School at Buckingham Palace fitted out as a hostel for servicemen. (Authors' Collection)

Anti-aircraft detachment at Sandringham 1915. (Authors' Collection)

The King quizzes an airmen on the instruments in his cockpit. (Authors' Collection)

His Majesty emerges from a tank after an excursion in Lincolnshire, 1918. (Authors' Collection)

An amputee serviceman gives the King a demonstration of his new limb. (Authors' Collection)

His Majesty in conversation with a wounded officer. The King made numerous enquiries as to his health, but he died in 1919. (Authors' Collection)

Australian troops line up with their mascot for an inspection by the King, 1915. (Authors' Collection)

The King inspects a native South African Labour Company in France, July 1917. (Authors' Collection)

Less than two years after breaking his pelvis, the
King climbs from a submarine on a visit to the
Grand Fleet, 1917. (Authors' Collection)

Sharing a joke with Admiral Sir David Beatty
during a visit to the Grand Fleet. (Authors'
Collection)

The King pauses to watch Queen Mary during
one of many afternoons spent planting potatoes at
Frogmore, 1917. (Royal Archives/©Her Majesty
Queen Elizabeth II 2018)

Their Majesties are introduced to the residents at a
Wimbledon piggery, 1918. (Authors' Collection)

The King inspects equipment at a laboratory during one of his visits. (Authors' Collection)

His Majesty tries his hand at cutting out a soldier's tunic. (Author's Collection)

The Royal Family watch an Independence Day baseball game between American forces from the stands at Stamford Bridge, 1918. (Royal Archives/©Her Majesty Queen Elizabeth II 2018)

Portraits of the King in army and naval uniform.
(Authors' Collection)

Victims of the submarine menace: The King speaks to stewardesses who have survived the sinking of the *Lusitania*.
(Authors' Collection)

Women war workers fill the Quadrangle at Buckingham Palace to deliver an address for Their Majesties Silver
Wedding Anniversary. (Authors' Collection)

A Silver Wedding Anniversary portrait of the King and Queen, 1918. (Authors' Collection)

Their Majesties children, c.1916 Bertie, David and Harry, Johnnie, Mary and Georgie. (Authors' Collection)

Nicky and his family (L-R) Olga, Marie, The Tsar, The Empress Alexandra, Anastasia, Alexei and Tatiana.
(Authors' Collection)

Former-Tsar Nicholas II in captivity at Tobolsk. (Authors' Collection)

Jubilant crowds in front of Buckingham Palace on 11th November 1918. (Authors' Collection)

Members of the crowd scale the Victoria Memorial outside the palace on 11th November 1918. (Authors' Collection)

Silver War Badge men swarm the King and his horse
to shake hands in Hyde Park, November 1918.
(Authors' Collection)

His Majesty with President Wilson, Christmas 1918.
(Authors' Collection)

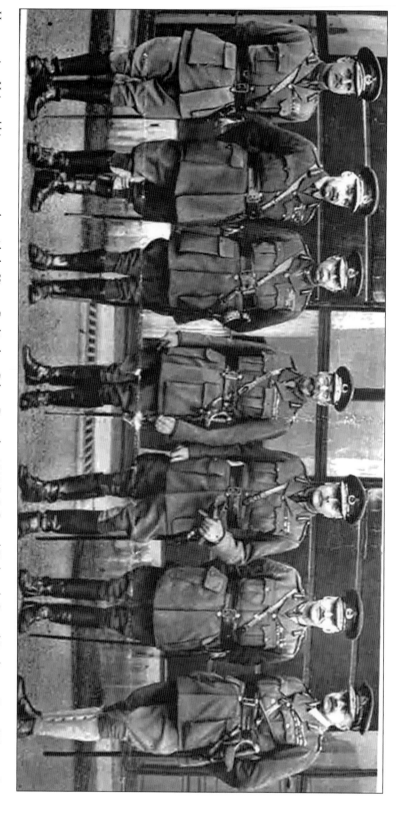

Homecoming: Haig and his army commanders with the King at Buckingham Palace, December 1918 (L–R General Birdwood, General Rawlinson, General Plumer, the King, General Haig, General Horne, General Byng). (Author's Collection)

A final portrait of Prince John and his beloved Lalla Bill, December 1918. (Royal Archives/©Her Majesty Queen Elizabeth II 2018)

The King watches the approach of Sir David Beatty and the naval contingent, Peace Day 1919. (Authors' Collection)

The King acknowledges the two minute silence during the unveiling of the Cenotaph as Bertie watches on, 1920.
(Authors' Collection)

A visit to a shell shock hospital at Hampstead after the war. (Authors' Collection)

The King's Pilgrimage, 1922: Mrs Matthew of Devizes wrote to the Queen and asked if she would lay forget me nots on the grave of her son during the royal visit to the former battlefields. (Authors' Collection)

The Queen was not present, but His Majesty honoured her request. (Authors' Collection)

The King surveys Tyne Cot Cemetery from the top of the bunker that was to form the base of the cross of sacrifice. (Authors' Collection)

Soon the Specials are receiving the same coffee as is taken by the Royal Family inside the palace.[207]

On another occasion there is a visit to a little fishing boat that has been plying the North Sea as a minesweeper.

"I got to know the King was coming," says the Captain,

So we made the boat look a bit smart; and presently, who should come along but His Majesty and Prince Albert, a Lord and an Admiral, and some more. I never saw so much gold lace before. I was all of a shake when they came alongside the quay, and the Admiral said, Your Majesty, this is the ship, and that is the skipper.

Then the King steps aboard.

Skipper, says he quite nice and friendly, I am very pleased to meet you. I am very proud of you. You are a brave man, and so are all your crew. Then he shook hands… He put his hand on my shoulder and walked with me forward, congratulating the crew and having a look round."[208]

One matter in which the King is deeply interested throughout the war is that of medals available for his troops, sailors and civilians as a reward for their service. The awards available in 1914 are hardly adequate in scope as the war grows in scale and comprehension. It had already been decided at the turn of the century that the Victoria Cross could be awarded posthumously, but now more adjustments are made to the availability of existing decorations. Early in the war the King had suggested that a committee consisting of the Prime Minister and a representative of both the Admiralty and the War Office should form and debate the various recommendations that are being put forward for newly acknowledging meritorious service. The King sets Fritz Ponsonby the task of overseeing his input.

The first new medal of the war is created by royal warrant at the end of 1914, when the King happily approves of the Military Cross's creation; an award meant for junior officers for bravery that did not quite warrant the VC. "Kitchener was in a great hurry to get this new cross out and summoned a committee to work out the details," explained Ponsonby, who thought the matter was being rushed. He therefore revelled in being a thorn in Kitchener's side and asking awkward questions about precedence and who would be eligible and why. "When we came to the design I suggested we should have something really good, but Kitchener said it would take too long and there was no need to have anything damned artistic." The committee could at least agree that they should have as many designs as possible for the War Secretary to choose from. "I longed to say that not one of the committee had the slightest knowledge of silver work… but I felt it would not do to say so, more specially as Kitchener seemed to fancy himself as an artist, and was constantly engaged in drawing pathetic designs on the blotting paper." Ponsonby didn't much like any of the original sketches, but one member of the group had asked a leading Herald to draw designs. "To my mind they were very second rate, but considerable trouble had been taken with them and silver paint had been used which I was afraid would captivate Kitchener. Sure enough… he refused even to look at the rough sketches, and at once selected the design with the silver paint." The committee man

207   *Daily Mirror* 4/4/16.
208   *Daily News* 31/1/16.

who had preferred the winning design was smug. "I retorted that so far from being the best it was probably the worst, as Kitchener knew as much about silver work as a Hindoo did about skates."[209]

Choosing the colours for the ribbon was even more traumatic. Ponsonby sat joyfully like a veritable Poobah with a picture book showing all the medal ribbons of Europe, shooting everybody down in flames. "Kitchener began by describing a ribbon which he thought would be attractive, but I told him this was the Emperor of Austria's Jubilee Medal and, although this was not a serious objection, it was a pity to have a ribbon that was worn by nearly everyone in Austria." And so it went on. "His second attempt produced the ribbon of the Conspicuous Gallantry medal of the Navy, and a third proved to be the Black Eagle of Germany... as soon as anything was produced I was able to see whether it was the ribbon of any existing medal of decoration." Kitchener grew more and more exasperated and said: "This damned fellow contradicts me whenever I say anything. We'll have no nonsense; I've got it, plain black and white, simple and dignified," to which I remarked that that happened to be the Iron Cross. That broke up the meeting, and Kitchener said he would choose the ribbon with the King." Ponsonby gladly left Kitchener with a basket of coloured ribbons that his wife had put together for him and the book. Victory was his when the King and Kitchener picked the white and mauve concoction that she had put together on a card which he had left in a suitably prominent position.[210]

The King then next attends to a lack of available awards for the rank and file in the scheme of this monstrous war. The Victoria Cross is for exceptional gallantry, the Distinguished Conduct Medal carries the element of a monetary award for it is prohibitive to give it out exhaustively. His Majesty discusses the matter with Wigram, who writes to Haig at the beginning of 1916. "What strikes one is that the percentage of rewards to the men is a great deal lower than the officers" since the introduction of the Military Cross. Wigram agrees with the King, that a new medal is needed for the men. "The question was raised a short time ago, but I believe that Lord Kitchener sat heavily upon it, and it was entirely squashed."[211] But by the middle of February, the palace have got their way, and His Majesty is immensely proud of his part in instigating the award. A man could win it more than once, and could receive the Military Medal, as it was to be known, as well as the Distinguished Conduct Medal. It carried no gratuity, and "I want it to be given freely," the King writes to his brother-in-law at the front.[212] The medal was instituted in March 1916, and would be available to women before the war's end. By the end of September, almost 1,000 have been bestowed already, including almost 300 to imperial troops, and four men had already been awarded the medal twice. 1916 also sees the introduction of *The King's Silver Badge for the wounded and otherwise incapacitated during the war.*[213] A circular pin, engraved with the words: *For King and Empire, service rendered,* it is to be worn on the right breast or right lapel of civilian clothes so that men no longer fit to serve can be recognised immediately and left alone by vigilant busybodies with a dislike of men out of uniform.

With so many more medals being awarded, the scale of His Majesty's commitment to investitures increases accordingly in 1916. Instead of people visiting the palace in an ad hoc manner to receive their reward from the King whenever they happen to be in London; as of the beginning of the year there are two slots set aside per week. His Majesty holds investitures on Wednesday and Saturday mornings, at which he decorates anyone who happens to be in town; no matter how many or how

209   Syonsby, Lord: *Recollections of Three Reigns*, pp.310-313.
210   Ibid.
211   RA PS/PSO/GV/C/Q/860/2/3.
212   RA GV/PRIV/CC50/1212.
213   *Pall Mall Gazette* 5/9/16.

few care to attend. By the end of 1916 he will have approved of a scheme emanating from the Army Council that also takes into consideration the bereaved families whose loved ones have died in carrying out the courageous acts for which they have been rewarded since August 1914. From now on, the man's next of kin will be eligible to receive the insignia in a public presentation. That is, they will be invited to come to any of the King's investitures. They will be given a railway warrant or other transportation, as well as a list of dates and locations where His Majesty will be distributing decorations. Even if the medal has already been issued by post, a family can still attend and have it formally presented.

The King supports the notion of this new initiative, and he willingly carries out, but he finds it extremely distressing from the outset. He sees two widows on separate occasions to hand them the Victoria Crosses won by their late husbands. One had only been married to her doctor husband a mere six months when 27 year old John Green was killed at Loos whilst rescuing a wounded man caught on barbed wire. His Majesty describes the little ceremony as "very painful."[214] Major Billy Congreve had become the first officer to receive the VC, the DSO and the MC and the King presents his widow, now some five months pregnant, with all of his medals too; but these two tearful ceremonies prove only a small induction to what is now to be a feature of the royal investitures.

On 16th November the King carries out the first bulk distribution of awards to the families of fallen heroes. In the case of ten Victoria Cross recipients, widows, mothers and fathers are present at Buckingham Palace and His Majesty witnesses the whole spectrum of human emotion in meeting these people for whom no words can alleviate their loss or their suffering. Some are stolid, others cry. Mrs Warner goes through the whole ceremony with a look of sheer anguish on her face, and when she emerges with her husband to face the press gauntlet outside the palace, she looks as if she might crumble. One large, solid looking woman with an unruly mass of dark hair transpires to be Lily Cornwell, mother of Jack, who at sixteen years old has been posthumously awarded the Victoria Cross having died of wounds sustained at Jutland. She has also lost her husband Eli since May. "There was a hint of tears in the clear brown eyes" as she stopped to answer the flood of questions from reporters. "I was very shy when I went into the Palace," she explains. "I had never seen His Majesty before, and when he came he was very different from what I expected. He shook hands with me very warmly, and talked to me, and then all my nervousness flew away, because he seemed like such a nice, homely gentleman." The King's gentleness had done much to relax her. "He was so kind that I almost forgot I was talking to a real King, and I felt quite at home and not a bit shy." The hardest moment was when His Majesty referred to the braveness of her son, "here the voice… trembled for a moment, "he told me how proud he was of my boy Jack and what a fine example he had set to others to do their duty at all costs." The King had been made aware of the circumstances of her husband's death. He was an ex-serviceman who had joined the Defence Corps in his sixties to do his bit. "His Majesty spoke nicely and sympathetically of the double loss I had suffered… The King told me he hoped my sorrow would soon heal, and that it would be some comfort for me to know that those I loved best had bravely done their duty."[215]

Two weeks later the King meets 27 more next of kin at one investiture who have journeyed to receive their loved ones' decorations, and not all of them can hold it together as well as Mrs Cornwell. At one public ceremony, the young widow of a man who had won the Military Medal received it on his behalf and promptly collapsed. "For two other women the ceremony also proved too great an ordeal, and they wept bitterly… The people in the stands became silent and many wiped away a tear."[216] At Hull City's ground the Queen joins her husband for moral support when

214 RA PRIV/GVD/1916 (29/11).
215 *Daily Sketch* 17/11/16.
216 *The Times* 18/6/17.

the time comes to make the awards to next of kin. One poor woman who was receiving the Military Medal for her son broke down and sobbed. Queen Mary takes her hand in her own and holds it until the woman has composed herself. Her Majesty even gently reaches out and straightens a photo of the young man which his mother is wearing as a brooch after it becomes dislodged. Widows often brought with them their young children, and the King finds these encounters the most sorrowful of all. At St. James's Park in Newcastle, the widow of a sergeant who has been killed with a medical unit approaches the King and Queen. His little boy will not look at the Their Majesties, overcome with shyness and clinging to his mother. "The King looked kindly at him… lightly kissed the boys cheek."[217] He presents a Distinguished Conduct Medal awarded to a Sergeant Major Lund to his little boy, Eric. "When His Majesty asked to whom he should give it, he replied: "My medal!"[218] The young son of another doctor awarded the Victoria Cross for his fearless forays into danger to treat wounded men doesn't quite know how to behave when he accompanies his mother to an investiture. "The little chap for a moment seemed either too puzzled or frightened, but His Majesty quickly restored his confidence. He opened the case, showed the boy the decoration lying within, told him how well it had been won by his brave father, and patted his head."[219]

The manner in which the Home Front is drawn increasingly into the conflict continues in 1916. All three of the King's main residences have come under threat from aerial attacks by the end of the year. A wire net has been stretched across the roof at Buckingham Palace and regulations drawn up for the Royal Household in the event of a successful German raid; though the King and Queen still rush outside to observe all that the can of enemy aircraft in the vicinity from the balconies instead of taking cover. At the end of 1915 a Zeppelin had come under fire from anti-aircraft guns at Windsor Castle when it drifted uncomfortably close to the East Terrace, and Sandringham's location near to the east coast is at odds with its usual solicitude. In January 1916, Their Majesties are in residence on "a dark night, very still;"[220] with no moon, when a Zeppelin floats over Hunstanton and passes the estate. They venture outside when they hear it in the distance, but see little as it makes off and drops its bombs throughout Norfolk and Lincolnshire. From France in August the King is furious that Zeppelins have returned. "Thank God those devils did no damage at Sandringham in spite of dropping 26 bombs on Dersingham marshes," he writes to Queen Mary. "I have got a map marked where each one fell."[221] But he has a sensible grip on the capabilities of Zeppelin navigators, and does not want the slight threat of a raid on the estate to stop his mother from going to Norfolk. "I think it was an accident they dropped them there, in their report they said they bombed King's Lynn, which shows they never know where they are."[222] However, Queen Alexandra has already proven her resilience by writing to Fisher at the Admiralty earlier in the war: "Please let me have a lot of *rockets* with spikes or hooks on to defend our Norfolk coast," she had demanded; "I am sure you could invent something of the sort which would bring down a few of those rascals."[223]

In September 1916 bombs do strike some of the King's cottages at Dersingham. "At 10 o'clock that Saturday evening they began," his mother explains. "We were all sitting upstairs in Victoria's room when we suddenly were startled by the awful noise! And lo and behold, there was the awful monster over our heads. Everybody rushed up and wanted us to go downstairs." Queen Alexandra had absolutely no intention of complying. "I must confess I was not a bit afraid - but it was quite

217   *The Times* 18/6/17.
218   *Daily Mirror* 10/11/17.
219   *Nursing Mirror* 6/10/17.
220   RA GV/PRIV/GVD/1916 (31/1).
221   RA QM/PRIV/CC04/155.
222   RA QM/PRIV/CC04/158.
223   Battiscombe: *Queen Alexandra*, p.284.

a most uncanny feeling - poor Victoria was quite white in the face and horror-struck - but we all wanted to see it - the house was pitch dark." She even ventured outside, "but saw nothing and for the time the Zeppelins had flown off somewhere."[224]

The King and Queen continue to visit the victims of various air raids in hospitals, some bearing terrible injuries and others tales of miraculous escapes. At Charing Cross after a particularly bloodthirsty raid, they sit with the mother of a young man who is anxiously keeping vigil by his bedside, and "they were particularly interested in the case of a woman who was sitting on the outside of an omnibus with her child on her lap when she received her injury. Nobody could explain why, but the child had been thrown away from the burst and was picked up unhurt."[225]

Having witnessed so much suffering, His Majesty places himself in the middle of a jurisdictional mess regarding who is responsible for warning the public that a raid is forthcoming. He puts Stamfordham on the case and he composes a memo for the King in February 1916 that, worryingly, reveals that apparently nobody is. The Admiralty do not want to know, as they are about to hand the whole question of aerial defence over to the War Office, who declare that they have not yet inherited the responsibility. The Home Office says that the mayors of local areas have nothing to do with it, that the police are supposed to warn the authorities, who are then supposed to warn the army, but this is not proving a reliable method. It is postulated that the matter falls under the purview of Sir John French as Commander in Chief Home Forces, but his office claims that it is only responsible in so far as protecting buildings guarded by the military is concerned. His Majesty is distinctly unimpressed, but matters evolve and a few months later he meets with the officer in charge of London's anti-aircraft guns, taking French with him. They are shown the War Office's infrastructure for dealing with Zeppelin raids, which has advanced considerably since responsibility has been passed to them by the Royal Navy. "We are getting more and more anti-aircraft guns every week;" notes the King. "When they next come they will get a warm reception."[226] He is always glad when one of the infernal Zeppelins is brought down in flames and destroyed, for he considers their intrusion into civilian life unacceptable.

There are myriad new innovations during the war too, and the King is uniquely placed to see their developments. He is much taken with tanks. After an introduction at Hatfield Park which impresses him very much His Majesty makes a summer visit to Elveden to see "six "caterpillars" which went over the trenches, crates etc. and through woods, knocking down trees." The King is told that 150 have been ordered, and another 50 to carry larger guns. "I think they will be a great success they really are moving forts."[227] The King seizes every opportunity to ride in one as the war progresses. At Lincoln he begins by watching "with much interest the manoeuvres and gambits of half a dozen cumbersome but remarkably agile monsters." But he is not going to go home without a joy ride. With a serious face, the King declares that he wants "to make practical acquaintance with the latest developments in tank construction, and proposed that he should take a trip in one of the machines." He scrambles across a muddy crater to a little hatch in the side of a machine, "and a few seconds later the behemoth with its royal passenger lurched forward, slithered into the mud, nosed a way out of it, and careened over the field." His Majesty does not want a mere cruise. "This is my fourth ride in a tank and I want you to take me over all the most awkward places." Lieutenant Weston obliges the King with the roughest course he can find for fifteen minutes. "At one moment the tank had its nose to the sky, and the next it was tumbling head foremost down a

224   Ibid., pp.291-292.
225   *The Times* 18/10/15.
226   RA GV/PRIV/GVD/1916 (19/5).
227   RA GV/PRIV/GVD/1916 (26/7).

precipitous decline."[228] His Majesty can be seen chuckling away through an aperture in the front of the machine. "Splash it went into a big mud flat, lurching heavily from side to side."[229] The King emerges to cheers at the end of his tank ride saying "Good, very good indeed! ... I told them where to go and I picked out all the steepest places."[230] His Majesty is far less passionate about indulging in air technology. During his 1914 visit to the Front, he motors to a sodden field where he is not only shown the latest set up for British machines, but examples of captured German Taubes. The weaponising of aircraft is in its absolute infancy, and His Majesty is shown bombs that are being simply flung off the side of aeroplanes in the hope that they would cause damage to the enemy. He sees the rapid expansion of manufacture at the Royal Aircraft Factory at Farnborough three months later. He watches pilots being trained to fly, experiments for developing gunnery in the air. By the end of 1916 the King and Queen have visited a new club for Royal Flying Corps officers in London, a special hospital for fliers; acknowledging that what had begun as a tiny arm of the Royal Engineers now had a complete lifeforce of its own. The King does not wholly trust aeroplanes. He will never go up in one. But during the course of the war he dons overalls and climbs into the pilot seat of several machines where he is shown controls and has various instruments explained to him.

The scale of the war has reached such proportions by 1916, and Their Majesties have been gifted so many souvenirs and mementoes on their travels, that there is now a designated space to house their collection. It begins with the presentation of a mounted piece of a German bomb which was dropped at Dover on December 24th 1914; the first to strike Britain, engraved in commemoration of that unfortunate precedent. As the war progresses the King becomes extremely diligent at collecting interesting trinkets and on all fronts people are keen to send him items. His Majesty has huge situation maps, Austrian shells, a piece of carved stonework from the ruins of Ypres Cathedral, a German petrol ejector, gas masks, a box made by plating from a German submarine, a small carving of a Madonna and Child carved out of the bone of an ass by a corporal in Macedonia, an iron knuckle duster, two metal stars; examples of those given to Turkish troops for the defence of Gallipoli, Sinn Fein paraphernalia from Ireland, an ash tray made by a Senegalese soldier being treated in Woolwich, a vase made out of a cartridge case, gifts from Belgian refugees. Eventually, all of these items and hundreds more would be displayed at Windsor Castle; in a designated *Relic Room*, or War Room. Painted in brilliant white and stuffed with drawers and cupboards to form a private museum.

"Pottering Politicians"

The King has some sundry matters in which to intervene with the army in late 1916. The most significant involves Sir John French, who is causing trouble. His peerage has done nothing to comfort him as he comes to terms with a role as Commander in Chief at home after having been at the centre of things on the Western Front. His office "became a clearing house from gossip from France as generals, most of them with their own axes to grind, passed through London."[231] He has joined forces with Churchill, who is smarting since his own fall and Robertson warns Haig that these two and others are trying to make mischief. Haig thinks French is essentially harmless, but he despises him for his efforts to undermine his command nonetheless. At the end of the year His Majesty summons Sir John to the Palace, intending to tell him that if he does not cease his criticisms of the doings of the Army in France, he will be kicked out of the service.

---

228   *Daily Telegraph* 10/4/18.
229   *Daily Mail* 10/4/18.
230   *The Times* 10/4/18.
231   Holmes: *The Little Field Marshal: A Life of Sir John French*, p.327.

But the King's greatest worries at the end of the year are once again political. The King has had concerns about the drifting nature of Asquith's governance for years, despite his support of him, but whilst public appeals in some isolated quarters begin to call for his active intervention, the King has no actual avenue to exploit other than pleading with the Prime Minister to heed his advice. Only if he resigns can the King then send for a potential successor and ask him to form a government. Even then, he must take care to choose someone who will be palatable not only to Asquith's own party, but to the House of Commons in general.

At the end of the year Asquith is in pieces. His son Raymond had spurned the chance of an army staff job in favour of serving with the Grenadier Guards in the front line, where he was killed in action on the Somme in September. "Whatever hope I had for the far future, by much the largest part... was invested in him. Now all that is gone."[232] Personal considerations mattered little to the press. "There are now... very obvious indications that the patience of the nation is exhausted. The question of a national appeal to the King against the bungling of the present Government was seriously discussed in the wake of Kitchener's death. The country is no longer satisfied with the Asquithian mantra of "wait and see," or of "shilly-shallying and traitor-truckling policy," or of "politicians of the ordinary shuffling type, with their own petty personal ambitions to promote at the national expense... City sentiment is now dominated by the firm conviction that this war will never be won by a group of pottering politicians, utterly incapable of vigorous and decisive action."[233]

From his appointment at the War Office, it takes Lloyd George some five months to fulfil Margot Asquith's prophecy and help oust the Prime Minister from Downing Street. By the end of 1916, the Welshman is pressing for a reformation of the War Committee. He wants it to be reduced in numbers, so that it will form a less cumbersome body; and this is a reasonable enough suggestion. It is one that was put forward by His Majesty almost a year before. "The King... cannot help thinking that its number, 12, is too great," wrote Stamfordham, "for practical purposes and prompt action." The King had envisaged Asquith, Grey, Balfour, Kitchener and Lloyd George as an appropriate combination, but recognised "that perhaps Mr Asquith may have difficulties in restricting the numbers even if he were inclined to agree with the King's comments."[234] Esher concurred, and the Foreign Secretary, Sir Edward Grey, had also made a similar comment about the impossibility of conducting the war with such a large body. It isn't the principle of the reduction of the War Committee that the King will object to. Once more it is the reckless methods employed, for Lloyd George is holding his resignation over the head of the Prime Minister lest Asquith comply with his demands. Again. This time, he takes matters further, for on 1st December it transpires at a Cabinet meeting that Lloyd George thinks that the Prime Minister should be left out of the new War Committee. He wants to chair it himself, and the group of his choosing will have complete power to deliberate all matters pertaining to the war. Only then, when they have reached a conclusion, will the information reach the ears of Asquith for his consideration. He would remain as Prime Minister, but he will have to let Lloyd George run the war. It is a set of demands that Asquith cannot possibly accept.

The Prime Minister does try to compromise, for he is not blind to the need for change either. He tells Lloyd George that though he is in "complete agreement as to a critical situation having been reached in the war,"[235] and that he too believes that the War Committee needs to be reconstructed;

232   Bates: *Asquith,* pp.122-123.
233   *Financial Times* 8/6/16.
234   BD: MS Asquith A.1. 4 #149.
235   RA PS/PSO/GV/C/K/1048a/2.

but he insists that as Prime Minister, he must chair the new body. He has other ideas about who should be included too, but he bends as much as to indicate that if Lloyd George was to become a vice-chairman of the committee, he would be content to leave its day to day business to him, whilst managing not to compromise his own role as Prime Minister.

But little does Asquith know that Lloyd George, Bonar Law, the Unionist Leader and Sir Edward Carson, the Leader of the Opposition, have formed a powerful triumvirate and agreed to stick together in opposition to him. Asquith is forced to agree to the Welshman becoming chairman of the newly constituted War Committee; lest he have multiple members of his Cabinet resign and his Government collapse. To soften the blow, it will be announced publicly that Asquith will still have "supreme and effective control of war policy," as well as the right to attend meetings of the War Committee whenever he so wished. At worst, the Prime Minister was going to have to reshuffle the Cabinet slightly. "Humiliating as the outcome was, the crisis, it seemed, was over."[236] The Prime Minister leaves London for a weekend by the sea, but is back almost immediately, "fighting for his ministerial life."[237] On a "cold and gloomy" Saturday morning he visits the King, who is resigned to more Government controversy, at the palace to talk over the situation with him. "He looks tired" observes His Majesty, "and has a cold."[238]

As has happened before when Lloyd George has attempted to hold Asquith to ransom, the matter reaches the press. Lord Northcliffe is suspiciously informed as to what is going on and the Sunday papers carry headlines such as: *"Lloyd George to Resign - Dissatisfied with Dilatory Methods of Government."*[239] "There is another political crisis on,"[240] the King notes in his diary. On Monday the coverage in *The Times*, a Northcliffe production, is savage. Its pages carried a personal attack on the Prime Minister in which the author has clearly had privileged access to detailed information about what is transpiring within the Cabinet. "Mr Lloyd George has finally taken his stand against the present cumbrous methods of directing the war," it states. Lloyd George had not wanted Asquith even as a part time attendee with the War Committee, and the article slams the fact that the he has had to compromise on this point; "the assumption being that the Prime Minister has sufficient cares of a more general character"[241] to concern himself with. Lloyd George denies having even seen the article in *The Times* and adds "that he himself had had to put up with misrepresentations for months."[242] He tells Stamfordham that he has no influence on Northcliffe.

Asquith has reached the end of his tether. After this skulduggerous behaviour in going to the press, he assumes on the part of Lloyd George, he now says that he must be in complete charge of Britain's war policy. He no longer has any interest in the agreement which would see Lloyd George effectively as chairman of the War Committee in all but name. If this causes the resignations of the Welshman and his associates, then so be it. He attends the palace to inform the King of all that is taking place, and His Majesty authorises him to accept the threatened resignations of his colleagues and to attempt to form a new Government, telling his Prime Minister that he has complete confidence in him. The King is alleged to be terribly distressed and to have said, "I shall resign if Asquith does."[243] Lord Stamfordham suggests to the Prime Minister that Lloyd George wants him out of office, but Asquith still cannot believe it.

236   Rose: *King George V*, pp.194-196.
237   Ibid.
238   RA GV/PRIV/GVD/1916 (2/12).
239   *Reynold's Newspaper* 3/12/16.
240   RA GV/PRIV/GVD/1916 (3/12).
241   *The Times* 4/12/16.
242   RA PS/PSO/GV/C/K/1048a/2.
243   Asquith: *Lady Cynthia Asquith Diaries 1915-1918*, pp.241-244.

But whilst His Majesty is meeting with other politicians about the crisis, the Prime Minister is about to receive a shock. The previous weekend, most of the Unionist members of the Coalition had met and drawn up a resolution to ask Asquith to dismantle the Government and start again. If the Prime Minister should refuse, they all intend to resign. Bonar Law says nothing of this resolution to Asquith in the interim, but it is finally delivered on 5th December. Additionally, in the middle of a Downing Street conference that evening, the Prime Minister receives Lloyd George's letter of resignation. At 7:00pm Asquith arrives at the palace and shows the letter to the King. Not only has Lloyd George resigned, but he has announced "his intention to go to the country and let people know the true state of affairs and his views as to the war, and how to win it,"[244] which could be crippling for Britain. His Government has crumbled, and Asquith feels he has no choice but to resign. His Majesty is furious at what he sees as unacceptable behaviour on the part of Lloyd George. "I fear it will cause a panic in the City and in America and will do harm to the Allies. It is a great blow to me and will I fear buck up the Germans."[245] He labels Lloyd George "a black-mailer, whom it is better to tackle and have done with."[246]

Whilst Asquith is morosely puffing on a cigar at Downing Street and talking about going to Honolulu, His Majesty must now call upon the leader of the next largest party in the House of Commons and ask him to form a Government. Bonar Law appears at Buckingham Palace at 9:30pm and the King is ready for him. His Majesty has not forgotten that he considered Bonar Law's sentiments during the battle over Home Rule as tantamount to treason, and he is not in a conciliatory mood. They argue; the King supporting Asquith and Bonar Law defending Lloyd George. Bonar Law insists that the Prime Minister has mismanaged the war and His Majesty scorns this statement. Then they move onto an acrimonious discussion about relations between politicians and the military authorities. The King says that the latter should be left to the conduct of the war, as they are the experts. Bonar Law says that Robertson and the soldiers are all wrong, and blames the fall of Serbia, the collapse of Romania and most probably Greece entirely on those in uniform. His Majesty is not impressed with this civilian appraisal, and stands by his generals.

The King has foreseen that when he invites Bonar Law to form a Government, he is going to agree only if His majesty dissolves Parliament, thus triggering a disastrous General Election. The King has had Stamfordham ask Lord Haldane to outline whether he is constitutionally bound to acquiesce to such a grievous act. "Could His Majesty constitutionally refuse to do so?" Haldane replies promptly that the only Minister whom can properly request such a dissolution is the Prime Minister, whether that be Asquith or a new man who has been properly installed. "The Sovereign cannot, before that event, properly weigh the general situation and the Parliamentary position of the Ministry as formed."[247] And so the King is bullish and refuses to promise to dissolve Parliament at Bonar Law's request. The temperature in the room rises accordingly. The Colonial Secretary says that he hopes His Majesty will reconsider, because otherwise it is likely that only Lloyd George will be able to form a Government, though he does agree to try.

Bonar Law thinks he can only assemble the necessary personnel if Asquith is somewhere in the Cabinet, and the Prime Minister thinks that this arrangement is doomed to fail. Not only will his presence be blamed for every future disaster, but there will be friction. Exasperated, Bonar Law returns to the palace and asks the King to host an afternoon conference; sitting Asquith, Bonar Law, Lloyd George, Balfour as a former Prime Minister and experienced statesman and Arthur Henderson, as a representative of the Labour Party at the same royal table. The debate lasts for an

244   RA PS/PSO/GV/C/K/1048a/1.
245   RA GV/PRIV/GVD/1916 (5/12).
246   Rose: *King George V,* pp.194-196.
247   Ibid.

hour and a half, as the attendees try to thrash out the possibility of a National Government. They take it in tuns to plead with Asquith to concede to patriotism and serve under Bonar Law. Lloyd George tells the room that he has no ambition to be Prime Minister. After threatening to tell the country all that is wrong with the war effort under Asquith's leadership, he now says that he is happy to stand out and support another Asquith Government if need be. This is too much for the Prime Minister. He says that in all his "alleged mismanagement of the war" he cannot recall a single time that Lloyd George has disagreed with one of his decisions, "that he had been subjected to vindictive and merciless attacks by the press." He says his job is hard enough, without having to deal with "daily vindictive, merciless attacks" under a reign of "press tyranny."[248] Exhausted and mourning his son, he has no fight left in him. He says he is grateful for the support of His Majesty, "but that he had awoken that morning to feel thankful to feel he was now a free man."[249] The King sits and listens to this lengthy political exchange and then, "with his habitual common sense," reminds the politicians in the room that they have not yet resolved the matter at hand; namely who will be the next Prime Minister. They get nowhere. Balfour spends the duration making a pretty sketch of a bridge and some hills on a scrap of blotting paper that he then presents to His Majesty, and that evening Bonar Law tells the King that he cannot form a Government. "It has been a long trying day for me,"[250] the King notes, with the realisation that he must next send for Lloyd George and that there is nothing now standing between the Welshman and 10 Downing Street.

His Majesty is sorry to lose the only Prime Minister to have served under him thus far. He offers him the Garter as recognition of his long service, but "it was politely and gratefully refused."[251] The King is feeling rather isolated. He has spoken before of his "responsible and rather lonely position."[252] and the fact that Asquith is able to throw up his hands and depart exacerbates the realisation so familiar to him, that he must endure no matter who falls by the way. "My Ministers come and go and are relieved of their duties, but I am here, always."[253] On 7th December, Lloyd George arrives at Buckingham Palace and reports that he is able to form a Government, though some Liberals have refused to serve under him. Balfour has been asked to succeed Sir Edward Grey as the longest serving Foreign Secretary in Britain's history. "You put a pistol to my head," he remarks. As one historian points out: "There were not enough pistols to go round."[254] Lloyd George kisses hands and becomes Prime Minister. The King tries to dredge up some positive sentiment, and is somewhat placated by the fact that there will be a strong Coalition Cabinet. "He himself is very energetic and full of courage," His Majesty writes to Prince Henry, "And means to go to any extreme to win the war, and I believe the country will be quite willing to follow his lead."[255] When the Welshman dies in 1945, Winston Churchill will deliver the traditional eulogy in the House of Commons. "Presently Lloyd George seized the main power in the state and the headship of the Government," he will state. "Seized?" he will be asked. "Seized," Churchill will repeat. "I think it was Carlyle who said of Oliver Cromwell: *He coveted the place. Perhaps the place was his.*"[256]

1916 had begun with so much promise, but at its end the country is disappointed, depressed. There has been defeat in Mesopotamia, rebellion in Ireland, the loss of thousands of lives at sea, including

248   RA PS/PSO/GV/C/K/1048a/1.
249   Rose: *King George V,* pp.196-199.
250   RA GV/PRIV/GVD/1916 (6/12).
251   Rose: *King George V,* pp.286-293.
252   Rose: *King George V,* p.110.
253   Rose: *King George V ,*p.106.
254   Ibid., pp.286-293.
255   Frankland: *Prince Henry, Duke of Gloucester,* pp.41.
256   Rose: *King George V,* pp.196-199.

Lord Kitchener's. Romania have entered the war on the side of the Allies only to be crushed in a matter of months. There has been endless political drama and when the Battle of the Somme finally grinds to a halt in mid-November. Though gains have been made and the German Army has been badly shaken, no decisive breakthrough has been made. And yet the British people have not given up yet. "These ordeals did not produce a mood of defeatism; in fact, the disquiet which spread in the late autumn of 1916 was increased by rumours that certain members of the Cabinet were in favour of a negotiated peace. The public temper was one rather of baffled pugnacity."[257] The Duke of Connaught writes to his nephew for New Year. "May it bring victory and peace and above all may you be spared many of the anxieties, worries and disappointments of this old year, which has been so sad a one for many - I firmly believe you will bring us peace and a lasting one of our own making. This, I know, no one wishes more than you do."[258]

After the turmoil surrounding the change of Government, and with other concerns weighing heavily on His Majesty's mind; for the first time in decades the Royal Family spends Christmas in London. After lunch they venture out to the King George V Hospital on Stamford Street. The military authorities have commandeered a vast building intended to be the new Stationery Office and transformed it into a war hospital. Each ward is decorated in bright colours, with lights and miniature flags, paper chains, flowers and many extravagantly dressed Christmas trees. The King has insisted that the proceedings be completely informal. Visiting hours have begun and many men have family with them and His Majesty does not want their festivities ruined by officialdom. There are impromptu concerts and tea parties in progress; and the sounds of revelry spill out into the corridors; with popular tunes emanating from pianos and gramophones. The King has taken the fourth floor. He spends time playing with a little boy who has been brought to see his wounded daddy. Two girls are performing a song with gusto when His Majesty appears in the doorway. "Carry on!" He says cheerfully. "The request was made in so kind and obviously sincere a way that the young ladies promptly complied, and the patients resumed their time, keeping tattoos on the floor exactly as if there were no near presence of the Sovereign."[259] There are spontaneous outbursts of the National Anthem. The King is particularly interested in spending time with those suffering from severe injuries; spinal cases. And those who have recently arrived suffering from trench foot in bitterly cold conditions on the Western Front.

The Queen takes the third floor, Princess Mary the first. Prince Harry visits those at the top of the building, and Prince George those on the second floor; both dressed smartly for a nervous outing. They are a little stiff at first, reserved, "but as they warmed to their work they forgot their shyness and became deeply interested in their cases."[260] Harry wins over every man on his ward, all of them cheering him heartily when he leaves. The whole family distributes pale blue books in aid of the Queen's Hospital for Disabled Soldiers, and by the time Their Majesties leave with their children in the early evening, word has got out that they are in the vicinity and people have abandoned their own Christmases to form a crowd outside on the street. "Are we downhearted?" Someone shouts. "No!"[261] is the universal response.

257   Nicolson: *King George V: His Life and Reign*, p.285.
258   RA GV/PRIV/AA42/49.
259   *Daily Telegraph* 26/12/16.
260   *Daily Telegraph* 26/12/16.
261   *The Times* 26/12/16.

1917

Dystopia

"A Difficult Case"

1917 is arguably the most anxious year of the King's life. He is under no illusion that peace is a long way off. Three weeks before Lord Kitchener's death His Majesty had told him that he believed Britain would be at war until at least October 1917; indicating that he never believed that the Battle of the Somme would lead to the collapse of the German army, and that it would take another full year of campaigning to subdue his cousin's forces. But at all times, no matter how depressed the King is, no matter how exhausted or exasperated, he must present a stoic, positive, image of a Sovereign resolved to lead his nation to victory. "The vigorous prosecution of the war," he states in a speech in December, "must be our single endeavour until we have vindicated the rights so ruthlessly violated by our enemies and establish the security of Europe on a secure foundation."[1]

Their Majesties have finally found time to retreat to Sandringham for some rest with their youngest children, and three days after the new year David and Bertie arrive to join the rest of the family. The Prince of Wales has been away for eight long months and the Queen is thrilled to see him looking healthy. "Such a joy to get him back for a little."[2] The whole family braves pouring rain, gales, and sleet to go for walks about the estate. The boys go out shooting with their father and are only forced back inside by the weather once, but then snowstorms begin and it becomes nearly impossible to drive the birds up. The King resolutely trudges through drifts and around trees blown down in a vain attempt to find a pheasant, but in the end he is forced to skate instead. David alone is sorry to be in Norfolk, for he has discovered brothels and dancing girls in France, and he admits that he can think of nothing but women. The family spend the dark evenings in the billiard room around the gramophone, the King and Queen dancing and enjoying themselves immensely. "So good for them to have some music like that which takes their minds off the war!!"[3] Writes David. When their parents have retired for the night, he, Bertie and Mary amuse themselves drinking whisky in his room and talking.

Then one by one the children begin to leave. Bertie returns to Portsmouth, David to France. Harry leaves for Eton and Prince George is miserable when they put him on a train bound for Osborne. "Rather weepy poor boy,"[4] writes his father. "It is needless for me to tell you how much you are missed and how sorry we were to see you go," the Queen writes to Bertie. "Since your departure our weather has become more and more detestable… The roads are in a filthy condition - Papa has been out each day but with the ground and bushes so wet I am afraid it was anything but our enjoyment and sport this year is poor."[5] By the end of January Their Majesties are left with two

1   *The Times* 23/12/16.
2   RA PRIV/QMD/1917 (4/1).
3   RA EDW/PRIV/DIARY/1917 (14/1).
4   RA GV/PRIV/GVD/1917 (19/1).
5   RA GVI/PRIV/RF/II/249.

of their children; Mary and Johnnie, and for the duration of their winter stay at York Cottage, they are much engaged with making arrangements for their youngest son.

Prince John Charles Francis is eleven years old. Born at Sandringham in a blistering hot week in July 1905, the King diligently recorded in his diary that his wife had begun to have pains at lunchtime and that three and a half hours later, their little boy had come into the world weighing a healthy 8lbs. The Prince of Wales, as he then was, was very disappointed, because he had been desperate for another daughter. He thought they had enough boys and he wanted a sister for Princess Mary, but Queen Alexandra did her best to buck him up. "I feel it is a disappointment to you as you wanted a little girl so much, which would also have been so nice, for dear little Mary, but never mind."[6] The Prince had quickly surmounted this setback and spent the next fortnight with his family. He divided his time between sitting in the garden, close at hand whilst his healthy new baby slept in the shade cast by nearby trees; and doting on his wife; barely leaving her side, reading to her, taking her meals up himself. Finally, after nearly two weeks, the Prince had left her long enough to play a round of golf. "Now that I have five sons I feel that I have a great responsibility, may God bless them and may they grow up to be of some use to our great Empire."[7]

Prince John was physically the most impressive of all Their Majesties' children; big for his age, solid. They were obliged to leave their young family behind when they departed for their tour of India at the end of 1905. Charlotte Bill, Johnnie's nurse, sent photographs of the children on to their parents and the Princess asked Bertie to tell her "that we think baby looks rather like a prize pig, he has grown so terribly fat!"[8] The extended Royal Family was much impressed by the youngest royal baby. "He certainly is a huge child and very good tempered and amiable,"[9] boasted his mother. Every little milestone in his life was diligently recorded. He cut his first tooth in January 1906, his first word was *Tata*. He began to crawl that July and on 21st November 1906 he took his first steps. His mother marked his height and his weight each year on his birthday, and as he grew older he adorned the pages of her scrapbook with his autograph. His first years were spent at Marlborough House with his parents, where he was doted on. The King took him on outings to Olympia to see the Naval and Military Tournament, for the little boy adored soldiers. He was mesmerised by White City, particularly the scenic railway with its steep descents and sharp turns. His birthday parties were elaborate affairs. For his fourth, Queen Alexandra gave a children's party at Buckingham Palace with performing dogs and a monkey in the ballroom, tea and then fireworks in the garden. "It was very amusing, delightful to see all the children enjoying themselves."[10] Four days later his Godmother gave another party at her house for the little Prince, complete with Punch and Judy show, dancing and games. Johnnie adored his cousin Prince Olav, the only son of the King's sister Maud, Queen of Norway. The two spent snatched weeks at Frogmore, where they were insular, happy in their own company, but every now again others were allowed to participate in their games.

In 1909, Prince John was diagnosed with epilepsy; and as time went on it became evident that he was also suffering from severe learning disabilities. There is nothing to suggest that he remained anything but a fully fledged member of the Royal Family. He was still a small boy, and he remained with his family. In fact, when the other children were left behind to continue their lessons, Their Majesties would take him with them as the alternated residences. The way in which

6   RA GV/PRIV/AA33/5.
7   RA GV/PRIV/AA6/515.
8   RA GVI/PRIV/RF/II/014.
9   RA QM/PRIV/CC21/66.
10   RA PRIV/QMD/1917 (12/7).

Their Majesties approached medical care for their son is a reflection of contemporary attitudes and interpretations of his multiple conditions at the turn of the twentieth century. In 1911, the Prince's health declined. The lapse was put down to a change in medicine. His doctors had ceased giving him doses of potassium bromide, a recognised and longstanding treatment for epilepsy and replaced it with a new alternative; probably phenobarbital. The result was increased fitting, and so they decided to maintain a regime of both drugs together to try and combat Johnnie's condition. This traumatic alteration to his treatment had a depressing effect on his parents. "It will take a long time for him to get stronger," wrote the Queen in March. "They beg us not to be <u>too</u> despondent about him, but I feel he has got so much worse during the last three months that the prospect is not very encouraging - It certainly is very sad."[11]

At this stage it was hoped that Johnnie might eventually outgrow his condition, but in the meantime there was no trace of embarrassment, of derision or of anything but love for the youngest child of the King and Queen from his parents. There was sadness, and there was frustration, because he was a strapping boy and so full of life that it seemed cruel that this invisible malady caused him so much suffering. The Queen wrote to Queen Alexandra from Sandringham once to say that he had "arrived looking wonderfully well, and it seems extraordinary to think that the poor dear child has these horrid attacks more often than before."[12] He seemed to get better and then he would be struck down again. In August 1911 after seven weeks without a fit, he suffered two almost on top of each other. "I am sorry he has again had one or two attacks," writes the King to Queen Mary, "but of course one cannot expect them to cease altogether at once."[13] Queen Alexandra, who is devoted to her grandson, wrote: "I think we must have patience and hope for the best."[14]

In the meantime, Johnnie kept much the same schedule as his close siblings. There were spells at Buckingham Palace with their parents, children's holidays in Scotland. Despite increased fitting, Prince Olav was still a treasured companion whenever the Queen of Norway returned to England to be with her family, as was another cousin, Prince Alfonso of Spain, a delicate haemophiliac whose company he enjoyed. Prince John is a cheerful little chatterbox, always asking questions and for the most part full of boundless energy, but it was never to last. From York Cottage at the end of 1912, the King is compelled to write to the Queen, still in London, with worrying news. His Majesty had been talking to Charlotte Bill, affectionately known as Lalla. Still Prince John's nurse, she was devoted to the little boy and he to her. The King and Queen don't view *their people* as mere servants, or staff, but more as extended family, and this was never truer than when speaking of Lalla, whom they genuinely loved. As far as they were concerned, if Johnnie was not with them, he was in the best possible, loving hands. "I saw Lalla last night," His Majesty began, "she says he is no better and has had two or three attacks each day, and that they last sometimes fully ten minutes, she says they are very painful to see, as he struggles so much poor child. She begs that she must take him to London next week as it will never do."[15] The nature of Johnnie's fits had become so severe that for now he would not be able to play with Olav, for all concerned were worried about what effect it would have on him if he were to witness one. The Queen has definite ideas about what to do when her son suffers a lapse in health. "I shall feel happier if I see the doctors myself after they have seen him and discussed symptoms."[16] The King, who was sorry to have agitated his wife with this news, was happy to defer the child's mother when it comes to making decisions about the Prince.

11   RA PS/PSO/GV/C/O/2548/22.
12   RA PS/PSO/GV/C/O/2548/21.
13   RA QM/PRIV/CC04/76.
14   RA QM/PRIV/CC42/89.
15   RA QM/PRIV/CC04/108.
16   RA QM/PRIV/CC08/160.

"Arrange what you like about Johnnie," he tells Queen Mary. "… if it will make you happier for them to see him. I don't mind."[17]

By the New Year, Johnnie was well enough to roam Windsor with Harry, George and Mary, "exploring the castle, seeing the kitchen, plate room etc."[18] But the Prince was getting older. He was no longer a small child and he was reaching the age when ordinarily he would have become a more public figure. His parents did not want to keep Johnnie out of the public eye because they were embarrassed by him; rather, it was how distressing succumbing to a fit in front of an audience, or being exposed to a vast array of people who did not understand his personality quirks and limited development might be to their child. And so by the outbreak of the war he began to be primarily based at Frogmore under Lalla's care. He loves the gardens, grows his own potatoes and cooks them over an open fire. He is a generous, loving boy, sending childlike letters to his family, or paintings; spending the pocket money David gives him on presents for his father. He picks snowdrops and daisies and sends them on to London, and enjoys visits from Harry who is at Eton just a short distance away. He loves animals, his little dog Jack in particular, and he can be seen galloping through Windsor Great Park on his pony. But by 1916, Prince John had suffered another bad spell, and aside from the epilepsy. It is becoming clear to his family and his doctors that Johnnie's learning difficulties might be insurmountable. The King and Queen decide to make a last ditch effort at some form of education and bring in a Mr Lyons to try and approach the supremely difficult task of adopting some kind of regime that might account for his multiple conditions. Queen Mary takes to confiding in Bertie about how matters are progressing. "I should not think it a very pleasant job." he writes to his mother. "I do hope it will do some good."[19]

But the final attempt to introduce Johnnie to the school room upsets him and makes him "more excited than ever," for emotionally and intellectually, he is akin to a highly strung five or six year old. The Queen hopes that Lyons will persevere a little longer, "though he owns it is a difficult case." For the time being, they let him loose in the library at Windsor in his spare time, "in order that he may not be utterly bored with life."[20] The experiment fails; Queen Mary thinks because, "he is too intelligent really for a boy with that weak mental affliction, and cannot teach him in the babyish way which is really needed so to our regret he must go." This marks the end of any hopes that Johnnie might catch up, or reach a sufficient level of development for him to go out into a world that will not notice that there is something different about him. "I feel we must make up our minds to the fact that poor J will never get really "normal" and that the only thing we can do is to make the boy's life as happy as is possible under the circumstances,"[21] says the Queen. The decision is the right one, for the Prince's mood rights itself and a few weeks later Queen Mary tells Bertie: "I am writing this in the garden at Frogmore under the tree, rain is threatening and Johnnie is jabbering and asking incessant questions, so that I can scarcely write!"[22]

But matters have become difficult for Lalla too. It has been painful to relinquish custody to Lyons so that he might try and school the Prince. With his departure, another solution must be found. This little boy that she has loved and cared for for more than a decade is becoming a young man. The King and Queen are settled on the idea of finding "someone more like a male attendant"[23] to look after the physical side of his care, and they have already heard of someone with experience in such cases who might be available. "There is no doubt J has got worse of late," the Queen tells

17   RA QM/PRIV/CC04/109.
18   RA GVI/PRIV/RF/II/133.
19   RA QM/PRIV/CC10/225.
20   RA GVI/PRIV/RF/II/226.
21   RA GVI/PRIV/RF/II/227.
22   RA GVI/PRIV/RF/II/241.
23   RA GVI/PRIV/RF/II/227.

Bertie in the week after the Battle of Jutland, "which is very sad... I thought I would like you to know."[24] Bertie had not realised it was quite so bad. "It is very sad to think that he will always have to lead that life."[25]

By the end of 1916, it is evident that there is no solution that encompasses the best of both worlds. As he faces becoming a young man with obvious disabilities, Johnnie can no longer remain with his family full time whilst retaining his privacy and his independence. The reality of life as a royal child is that when they are out in the world, they are plagued by journalists and photographers. The King attempted to lay down rules about harassment of his children, but they fell on somewhat deaf ears. There are also safety considerations. Just before the war Scotland Yard uncovered a plot by suffragettes to target Prince Henry, who was barely a teenager at the time, whilst he was at school in Eton. "This caused no undue concern but it did result in in 'a competent' police officer, being posted to keep an eye on [him] while keeping out of sight as much as possible."[26] Had such a thing happened to Prince John, he was in no way able to defend himself. Something has got to give, and so therefore it is with much careful thought, and not a little sadness, that it is decided that he will have his own little establishment at Sandringham.

Though separated for much of the year from his family, he will be able to quietly go about his business, indulge his passions, indoors and out, play freely and not have to worry about unwanted attention. If he had a fit, there would be not a camera or a journalist in sight, and his effervescent, quirky personality would not be judged by the public's ordinary sensibilities, or have to be checked for anybody else. This is not to say that he would be shut off from the world, for the Prince will immediately become a much loved figure to all on the Sandringham estate. Buckingham Palace, or Windsor Castle would have constituted a prison, where his life would have been regimented around the necessity to keep him from prying eyes. The very nature of Wood Farm, Sandringham and the surrounding countryside is free-flowing, open, accessible to the public. Once the Prince stepped from the confines of his new house and garden, he might run into all manner of people, just not scores of reporters and photographers. Rather than to incarcerate him at Sandringham, the plan was devised more to set him free; to give him the space to do whatever made him happy, things that he *could* do, and not worry about all the ways in which he fell short.

Whilst the King carries on a relentless schedule of war work, the Queen takes the matter of Johnnie's new household extremely seriously. On 11th November, she goes with Lalla and Fritz Ponsonby to have a second look at Wood Farm and make up her mind finally as to whether it will meet her son's needs. That afternoon, the King meets her there after shooting on the marshes and they decide that it is ideal. "I hope and think we have finally decided on the stud farm house at Wolferton for Johnnie," writes the Queen. "We shall be able to make it quite nice and comfortable, and we can take in a good piece of ground for him to play in and plant vegetables."[27]

The bulk of the preparation work is done over the New Year, and Her Majesty oversees it all. "I have spent most of my mornings at Wood Farm, she records, "which is very nearly finished now and I hope Johnnie will get into it before long."[28] She supervises decoration, arranges the furniture, hangs pictures and takes great care in selecting the perfect bedroom for her son; one with a window over-looking the railway line from which he will be able to see his beloved *puffers*. The Prince of Wales notes the joy with which his mother carries out this work; "superintending the finishing of the house at which... she is so wonderful and [she] enjoys doing it too; she never

24   RA GVI/PRIV/RF/II/228.
25   RA QM/PRIV/CC10/228.
26   Frankland: *Prince Henry Duke of Gloucester*, p.34.
27   RA GVI/PRIV/RF/II/244.
28   RA GVI/PRIV/RF/II/249.

stopped arranging the furniture and giving instructions!"[29] George and Harry look over the work too. The whole family takes an interest in Johnnie's new home. The Queen returns almost daily as the work nears completion. At the same time she is visiting Frank Beck's widow, who they have set aside a house for at Dersingham, but on 20th January she takes Johnnie with her to show him his new home. He has arrived from Frogmore and is waiting at York Cottage to be able to move in. In the evenings he gleefully joins everyone around the gramophone; running about in boisterous mood and demanding various numbers, chattering happily, surrounded by his family. "He seemed awfully pleased but walked round the table the whole time and each time a tune finished wanted to change the records himself, much to David's dismay." It breaks the Queen's heart to see how her son differs from his siblings. "It is very sad to see this great strong boy, with the mind of a child of six and makes one quite unhappy."[30] Two days later she proudly shows the King the end result of her labours at the farm, and he is immensely proud: "it is a very comfortable little house."[31] Prince John is delighted with all of it. "Johnnie went to stay at Wood Farm, his new little home,"[32] Queen Mary writes in her diary on 31st January. "He is quite comfortable,"[33] the King writes, and the Queen is thrilled to observe that he seems very happy, but it is heartbreaking to depart for London and leave him behind. 'Poor child, it is very sad, we are going to take leave of him this afternoon."[34]

"I Leave Myself in Your Majesty's Hands"

Their Majesties return sadly to London on 3rd February and are flung back into the thick of it immediately. In 1917, the war seeps into every facet of home life, there is no escape from it; and before the King can even begin to address innumerable anxieties, both foreign and domestic, he must get used to only the second Prime Minister of his reign. Given the His Majesty's own nature; his lack of regard for showing off, talking oneself up and for self-aggrandisement, it is little wonder that David Lloyd George frequently sets his teeth on edge. He did admire his vitality, but they agree on little; and the King has been distinctly unimpressed with the politician's methods of late. For his part, in 1911 the new Prime Minister had said: "The King is a very jolly chap but thank God there is not much in his head. They're simple, very, very ordinary people, and perhaps on the whole that's how it should be." A year later he was complaining about court life: "I detest it... Everybody [is] very civil to me as they would be to a dangerous wild animal whom they fear and perhaps just a little admire for its suppleness and strength." Unfairly, he added that the King was "hostile to the bone to all who are working to lift the workmen out of the mire. So is the Queen."[35]

The situation is not helped by the Welshman's complete lack of respect and even contempt for practices and courtesies involving the Sovereign that he could have quite harmlessly taken into consideration. For a brief period, relations are cordial between Monarch and Prime Minister. An early exchange saw Lloyd George write that he was "profoundly impressed by the wisdom of the course suggested"[36] by the King on some matter. The two were mostly able to find common ground when it came to reconstructing the Government after Asquith's demise, but the more comfortably Lloyd George settled into the premiership, the less regard he showed for His Majesty. He had thrown a tantrum in 1915 when the King dared to make a visit to factories at Coventry and Birmingham

29   RA EDW/PRIV/DIARY/1917 (11/1).
30   RA GVI/PRIV/RF/II/249.
31   RA GV/PRIV/GVD/1917 (22/1).
32   RA PRIV/QMD/1917 (31/1).
33   RA GV/PRIV/GVD/1917 (2/2).
34   RA GVI/PRIV/RF/II/251.
35   Rose: King George V, p.92.
36   RA PS/PS/GV/C/R/199-203.

without informing him as Minister of Munitions. Someone simply took their instructions a little too seriously when they were told to regard the trip as secret, but throughout the course of 1917 this reaction would assume more and more irony. In the words of one historian, he discharges his duty to the King "only when it suited him. A myopic radicalism blinded him to the virtues of an hereditary sovereign who views he found obstructive. In spite of his attachment to the mystical traditions of Wales (though he had, as it happened, been born in Manchester) he found no merit in the most romantic of all English institutions." His attitude towards the King was "nonchalance not far removed from contempt," and "he gleefully admitted to his secretary that he had treated the King "abominably."[37]

Lloyd George begins his tenure by refusing to send the King the traditional daily letter from his Prime Minister summarising the Cabinet's business. This letter will be replaced by daily, official minutes which will be an overall improvement on the lapse system of recording Government business in the past, but the lack of courtesy stings His Majesty. From now on he is merely on a list of recipients that will have the minutes forwarded on to them. "It cut at the knees the relationship between the King and his Prime Minister." The flow of these minutes also grows more and more sporadic. "His Majesty is deeply pained," writes Stamfordham in April, "at what he regards as not only a want of respect, but as ignoring his very existence."[38] In January, King and Minister clash over the granting of honours. Stamfordham sends a strong rebuke to Whitehall that reminds Lloyd George, who has been promising them to various men, that "the Crown is the fountain of honour and grants of honours can only be made by the King acting with the advice of his Ministers." The palace was not going to stand for it. "In effect it amounts to a pledge by a minister that the prerogative of the Crown should be exercised in a particular way before His Majesty has approved the proposal or even been consulted thereupon."[39] The King is prepared to be flexible, but he will not be bypassed. Then in March, one of the Cabinet summaries received by His Majesty simply states that "the War Cabinet had a discussion on the Irish Question." The King is not impressed with the lack of an explanatory documents and once again Stamfordham picks up his pen. "As none have been published regarding the above meeting on the very important question of Ireland, His Majesty hopes that you will inform him in generous terms as to what transpired and whether any decisions were arrived at."[40] In April, the Prime Minister fails to inform the King that Arthur Balfour is about to leave the Foreign Office and go on a special mission to Washington. The King thinks that the 68 year-old has enough on his plate at home, and in May His Majesty is disturbed about the outcome of the Mesopotamia Commission.

When it comes to the conduct of the war, they were never going to agree, given Lloyd George's low opinion of the military hierarchy. His insistence in 1916 that military questions be a matter for military experts is, less than a year later, no longer of any use to his cause. For the rest of the war, Britain's key generals will be fighting their own politicians as well as the enemy. There is a huge gulf between the Cabinet and the Generals as the conflict goes on. For his part, Lloyd George has no empathy at all with men in uniform. Even when Chancellor of the Exchequer, and then as Minister of Munitions he has found cause to clash with them and even after taking over at the War Office he had made little attempt to better his relations with the army. For all his political courage, the Prime Minister is, physically, a self-confessed coward and he does not understand what makes these men tick. And they don't trust him. They rally against his meddlesome influence in which he takes the words of their subordinates and his own strategic opinions above their own counsel. And

37   Rose: *King George V,* pp.199-203.
38   Ibid.
39   PA: F/29/1/6: Lloyd George.
40   PA: F/29/1/28: Lloyd George.

in sentiment they have the backing of their King. Like his father, he takes incredibly seriously his position as titular head of the army. His support is not blind, but if His Majesty sees a case when his officers are being compromised in their ability to carry out their duties, he wants to defend them. He might have played a large role in deposing Sir John French, but that was a case based on the merits of one individual's ability; not any doubt about the competency of the army as a whole.

Lloyd George is in a tricky position at the onset of his premiership. His intention is to curb the war on the Western Front. He thinks Haig fritters away British lives. He wants to win the war, but his own, frankly nonsense opinion that this could be done mostly by Italian troops, or in the Balkans instead, only appeals to a tiny minority that does not include the Generals, the King or the Conservative party, whose support he will be depending on. He is going to have to employ all of his guile at this stage if he wants to press his own agenda, and the Prime Minister sets out to do just that. At a conference in Rome at the beginning of the year, Robertson paints a worrying picture of Lloyd George in action. The Prime Minister had brought up the idea of sending more divisions to Italy. Robertson claims to have warned him bluntly that he would never sign off on such a move, at which point the Prime Minister accused the army officer of holding a pistol to his head. When the conference began, Robertson found that he was left outside the room whilst politicians debated military matters. As a civilian, Lloyd George had drawn up a paper on his own strategy, which involves putting the brunt of the responsibility for fighting on the Italian Army. Little headway is made towards getting the Prime Minister's Italian offensive off the ground, and Robertson, whose word is valued by the King, has characterised him as a man who is easily swept up by the opinion of those advocating swift action. It is not easy to dispute this, and Lloyd George cannot dominate the army yet, so he will resort to more underhand methods, which include flouting the constitution, and conspire to put them underneath an entity that can: The French.

General Joffre has been replaced by an odd choice by his Government at the head of the French Army on the Western Front. Robert Nivelle had made a name for himself the year before at Verdun, but his achievements on a limited front hardly qualify him to take control of the French war effort with a promise to use the same methods to bring a swift end to the war. But this he does, and his Government cannot resist.

Until now, the working relationship that Haig has exercised with French command has been one of planning strategy together, correlating their endeavours, and then sorting out their own tactical business before attacking on the agreed date. What Lloyd George now attempts to do behind the army's back, is to put Haig and his force directly under a French Commander in Chief, indefinitely. British soldiers would be following the orders of General Nivelle. On 15th February, the very day that an interview with Haig was published, in which he said he lacked guns, Lloyd George, interpreting this as criticism of his tenure at the Ministry of Munitions, began scheming to have him under French control by suggesting the idea to the assistant French military attaché in London, so that he might raise it with his superiors. On 24th, the Prime Minister holds a War Cabinet to which he invites neither Robertson, the Governments chief military adviser, nor Lord Derby who has taken over the War Office. The King is not told of this meeting either. The list of those excluded speaks volumes as to what is transpiring behind closed doors.

Two days later the Prime Minister has arrived in Calais for an Allied conference. Haig had begun his relations with Lloyd George by trying to play devil's advocate. Robertson despaired when the Welshman succeeded Kitchener at the War Office. 'I suggested to him that he should try and humour Lloyd George a little bit," wrote Haig. "As long as the latter is Secretary of State we must make the best of him."[41] The Commander in Chief arrives at Calais with a representative of transportation, because he is under the distinct impression that this conference has been primarily convened to discuss all manner of difficulties that the Allies are currently experiencing with railways at the front. This was discussed in a cursory manner, but then the Prime Minister has the transportation men leave the room and the conversation turns to matters of strategy. After a brief outline of the forthcoming campaign from the French, for which Haig was prepared, Lloyd George prompts Nivelle, saying that the Frenchman has something further he wants to add. The latter suddenly produces a scheme to reorganise the Western Front under an Allied GHQ in France, headed by a Frenchman and his staff. Under said plan, Haig would be retained only in name as Commander in Chief. He would remain responsible for things like matters of logistics for British troops, but he will have no say in operations. According to two more French representatives present, they had only seen this scheme on the train to Calais, so they didn't draw it up. That, to the likes of Haig and Robertson, left a distinct suggestion that Lloyd George was responsible.

Haig is understandably flustered, as is Robertson, who has heard nothing about this previously either. After some discussion, which apparently didn't seem to go the way Lloyd George had hoped, the French are told to put 'their' proposal in writing. The conference adjourns for lunch, which takes approximately two hours. Suspiciously, although the French officers supposed to be orchestrating this document are sitting alongside their British counterparts, eating for most of it, when the meeting reconvenes they immediately produced a lengthy typed outline. Subsequently, Haig and his staff were having none of this. "It was produced so rapidly that it is hardly possible to believe it had not been prepared and typed beforehand."[42] "Indeed," writes Haig to the King, "this must have been the case because later in the evening, Lloyd George told General Robertson and myself that the British Cabinet had discussed the French proposal which has been made." That evening, Haig tells the Prime Minister and Robertson that he will have no part in placing the British Army under a French commander. "I gave a few reasons and spoke plainly." Lloyd George apparently then agrees that the French proposal goes too far, but states that the British Cabinet have decided that for the forthcoming operations, the British army shall be directly under General Nivelle and take his orders.[43] Lloyd George has been caught out, and as a result, Nivelle's control of Britain's forces is limited to his first offensive in the spring. Haig is given the power to appeal to his Government if he feels that the Frenchman's orders are endangering his force, yet the fact remains that Britain's fortunes on the Western Front; the praise for their success or the blame for their failure at this juncture lies with Nivelle, and with Britain's Prime Minister.

The King has not so much as been sent the minutes of the War Cabinet meeting of the 24th which went into the question of French command, let alone heard anything of the subject of the Calais conference, the manipulation of both of which have completely denied him the right to state his opinion, as well as ensuring that the subject matter would not have become known to Haig or Robertson in advance. Haig has written a detailed account of the conference for the King, "in order that Your Majesty may be watchful, and prevent any steps being taken which will result in our army being broken up and incorporated into French corps. General Nivelle… assured me that the present change and the system of command had been urged by the British Cabinet."[44]

To the likes of Haig and his staff at GHQ, this move is entirely unjustified. They consider that excepting for some tactical clashes and trying not to assume more of the line than they were comfortable with, they have done their utmost to comply with everything that the French have

41   RA PS/PS/GV/C/Q/2521/V/145.
42   RA PS/PSO/GV/C/Q/1591/5.
43   RA PS/PSO/GV/C/Q/832/130.
44   RA PS/PSO/GV/C/Q/832/130.

asked, "often at considerable inconvenience to the British Commander in Chief's plans and to the British armies. The plot brought to light at the Calais conference, therefore, could not be justified... and must be attributed to other causes."[45] They find it astonishing that a British Government would try and divest itself of responsibility for the army by putting it under French orders, especially under the orders of Nivelle, whom they did not consider to have an adequate knowledge of the condition of the French Army as a whole. Haig suggests to the palace that he might give up command of the BEF. "Your Majesty will observe in my dealings with Mr Lloyd George over this question I have never suggested that I would like to resign my command, but on the contrary I have done my utmost to meet the views of my Government, as any change of command at this time might be a disadvantage to the Army in the field. It is possible, however that the present War Cabinet may think otherwise, and deem it best to replace me... If this is so, I recommend that the change be made as soon as possible because of the proximity of the date fixed for the commencement of operations. At this great crisis in our history, my sole object is to serve my King and country wherever I can be of most use, and with full confidence. I leave myself in Your Majesty's hands to decide what is best for me to do at this juncture."[46]

With Lloyd George chipping away at the King's prerogative, the best that he can do is beg Haig not to go. His Majesty has already supported him publicly, with honours and awards towards the end of the Battle of the Somme, and he is terrified at the thought of Haig's resignation. "Such a step would never have His Majesty's consent," writes Stamfordham to Haig. "I am to say from His Majesty that you are not to worry: you may be certain that he will do his utmost to protect your interests."[47] In a meeting with Haig, the King tells him that he will stick by him "through thick and thin."[48] His Majesty is furious with Lloyd George. In withholding information about Cabinet proceedings from the palace, his actions can be interpreted as a challenge to the Sovereign himself. The Welshman has attempted to put the King's army under the control of a foreigner without His Majesty's consent. Wigram goes further than this. He thinks that the Prime Minister wants not only to discredit the monarchy, but to destroy it. Lloyd George is summoned to the palace, where when the King mentions that he has conferred a huge amount of power of General Nivelle, the Prime Minister coyly replies that Haig and Robertson concurred with him. The King had two complaints. He observed "with surprise and pain" that he had never been informed of the War Cabinet decision to place British troops under foreign command. Secondly, he said that the arrangement entered into with the French was offensive. "The King told the Prime Minister that if he were an officer serving in the British Army and realised that he was under the command of a foreign general, he would most strongly resent it... If this fact too were known in the country it would be equally condemned. The Prime Minister said that in the event of any such public expression of feeling, he would go to the country and would explain matters and very soon have the whole country on his side."[49] It is a bold threat, but one that he could well have executed to discredit both the army and the palace. The King already feared such a threat, believing before this meeting that if Haig were to resign, he would be held to blame by the country to some extent and that the Welshman would push for a general election, citing His Majesty as the cause.

Lloyd George wrote war memoirs that ran to well over a thousand pages. He barely mentioned the Calais Conference, making a short reference to the fact that it was occupied with discussing

45   RA PS/PSO/GV/C/Q1591/5.
46   RA PS/PSO/GV/C/Q/832/130.
47   Rose: *King George V,* pp.199-203.
48   NLS: Haig Diary, 11/3/1917 Acc.3155.
49   Rose: *King George V,* pp.199-203.

transportation. This is not the end of the King's concerns about his new Prime Minister's interference in military affairs. He has numerous meetings with Robertson and Derby to discuss "various matters connected with the Army and the Prime Minster." Wigram even makes a trip to France to meet with Haig. All that His Majesty hears disturbs him and causes his distrust of Lloyd George to mount. "I am very worried about it all."[50]

"Slow Drops of Poison"

The King has numerous ways of keeping up with events in Russia. Visitors returning to London visit the palace to tell him about all they have seen, and there are back channels for private correspondence. On the odd occasion that an appropriate courier was travelling in either direction, His Majesty and the Tsar exchanged private letters too; sending familial love, birthday wishes; commiserations and congratulations about various war happenings. "You, my dear Nicky are always much in my thoughts," the King writes in 1915.[51] He sympathised much with his cousin over Russia's lack of munitions, hoping that the Dardanelles could be forced as a way to ship supplies in. I can assure you that in England we are now straining every nerve to produce the required ammunition and guns and also rifles… I only wish we could help you more."[52] Writing to Nicky gave him a rare opportunity to confide in someone who shared the lofty pressures of a crown. "England has made up her mind to <u>fight this awful war out to an end</u>, whatever out sacrifices may be, our very existence is at stake. I am so glad to see by your letter that Russia also means to <u>fight</u> to the end and I know France is of the same opinion, so I feel with God's help, we Allies will be victorious, but this horrible war will last a long time yet."[53] "Please God these dark days may soon pass and that brighter ones are in store for us,"[54] are some of the last words that His Majesty ever penned to his cousin.

One of the main sources of information in Russia is General Sir Hanbury-Williams, who is Britain's representative at Russian GHQ at Mogliev, where the Tsar spends most of his time having taken command of his armies personally in 1915. Hanbury-Williams expected to find secrecy and difficulties at every turn, "and an Imperial Family weighed down with anxieties and the fear of an anarchist's bomb or an assassin's knife." He was to be pleasantly surprised. "My acquaintance with the Emperor, Empress and their children revealed quite another aspect. It was that of an apparently happy, and certainly a devoted family."[55] And the Tsar appreciates the General's straightforward approach. "He suddenly turned round to me at lunch and said: I do like people who look you straight in the face, and no one would accuse you of doing otherwise."[56] At a lunch for the senior officers that make up the Allied mission the Tsar drinks to the health of his cousin the King. Later on, in his kind, quiet way he turns to the British General and says: "Sir Hanbury, I drink to you too."[57]

The Tsar speaks often to Hanbury-Williams about his children. "He is evidently very devoted to them, and said that sometimes he forgot he was their father, as he enjoyed everything so much with them that he felt more like an elder brother to them."[58] His little heir, Alexei is a regular

---

50   RA GV/PRIV/GVD/1917 (2/3).
51   GV/ADD/COPY/175.
52   GV/ADD/COPY/176.
53   Ibid.
54   RA GV/ADD/COPY/176.
55   Hanbury-Williams: *The Emperor Nicholas II As I Knew Him*, p.2.
56   Ibid., pp.44–45.
57   Ibid., p.82.
58   Ibid., p.94.

feature at GHQ. He is full of mischief, "a most happy-natured, attractive little fellow,"[59] and the Allied representatives adore him. Alexei had different games for different Generals. "With me," wrote Hanbury-Williams, "it was to make sure that each button on my coat was properly fastened, a habit which naturally made me take great care to have one or two unbuttoned… he used to stop and tell me I was 'untidy again,' give a sigh at my lack of attention to these details, and carefully button me all up again." The Belgian General he calls *Papa de Ricquel*. He is a big man, "giving great opportunities for attack… fast and furious till either the Emperor or his tutor carried him off."[60] When news arrives of the death of Hanbury-Williams's son in December 1916, he receives unexpected comfort. "I was in the ante-room next the Emperor's before dinner, when the little Tsarevitch came out of his father's room, ran up to me and sat next to me, saying: "Papa told me to come to sit with you as he thought you would feel lonely tonight."[61]

But whilst the Tsar's heir finds a place in the heart of the Russian people, the same cannot be said of his mother. Born in Darmstadt, she was the daughter of Queen Victoria's third child, Princess Alice and thus the Empress Alexandra is the King's first cousin. A cheerful little girl nicknamed 'Sunny,' everything changed when she was six years old and diphtheria carried off her young mother and a sister. She became quiet and withdrawn, though she was bright, a talented pianist and keenly interested in politics. Her first visits to Russia saw her labelled as clumsy, awkward, badly dressed; but the future Tsar was besotted by her. Much like Queen Mary, Alix, or Alicky, is shy and this comes off as aloof, but in the Russian Empress's case the negative perception of her has, over the years, taken on much more sinister proportions. From the outset she was terrified in Russian society, having ascended far too rapidly to the head of it. Everything she said and did screamed awkwardness; every gesture, every encounter. Her determination to help and support her beloved husband in his burdens as Tsar made the country believe that she influenced all he did, and by the time the war began, Alexandra was viewed as a physical barrier between the people and their little father. Any early, gradual acceptance into public life was delayed constantly by pregnancies when it could have been of most use. Her first four children were girls: Olga, Tatiana, Marie and Anastasia, before finally in 1904 she gave birth to Alexei and secured the succession. But when he was six months old, fate struck a cruel blow when it became clear that something was wrong with her son. For more than ten years, the Empress has carried the weight of not only her son's haemophilia, but trying to keep it a secret from the world.

She believes that she is helped through all of this by Grigori Rasputin, a perennially unwashed, semi-literate Siberian monk, who nonetheless is shrewd enough to have claimed a place in the inner sanctum of the Imperial Family and convinced the Empress that he had the power to alleviate her son's suffering. Hanbury-Williams thought he was "an unscrupulous blackguard, posing as a saint," who preyed on the vulnerable Empress, "whose love for her son and naturally nervous temperament made her an easy prey." All sorts of sordid rumours about the Mad Monk and the Empress circulated throughout Russia, and even the extended European network of Royals was dubious about the relationship; at the very least concerned about Alix's influence on political affairs. This unconventional advisor and his exalted position spelled trouble for Nicholas in the eyes of his people, especially "for all those intriguers and place-seekers who had their own axes to grind." Hanbury-Williams called his influence on the autocracy "slow drops of poison,"[62] which would ruin Russia.

German by birth, supposedly dragging down the monarchy, there is no doubt that the Empress is viewed, unfairly, as an enemy of Russia. "The picture representing her as being pro-German is

---

59   Ibid., p.94.
60   Ibid., p.239.
61   Ibid., p.139.
62   Ibid., pp.139-143.

an entirely false one," wrote one royal acquaintance years later. "She was passionately Russian. Her one idea was to preserve the autocracy."[63] Hanbury-Williams is charmed on her visits to GHQ. "I found the Empress much easier to get on with than I expected... It is probable that her own shyness, which gives the impression of aloofness, prevents people from talking to her and freezes up conversation. The moment one began to laugh over things she brightened up and talk became easy and unaffected."[64] Alexandra chats to him about her hospitals, about her love for her gardens in the Crimea, and she asks incessant questions about her uncle, the Duke of Connaught. She sends Hanbury-Williams her own message of sympathy on the death of Lord Kitchener; he returns to his room today after their conversation about flowers to find his room full of roses, sweet-peas, orchids. "Very refreshing in this place where one hardly ever sees a flower."[65] It is a gesture that Alexandra repeats again and again. She confides with the British General about her nerves, her troubles with her heart; she seems overwrought and though she is always kind, hers, he remarks, is the only sad face in the family. The last time Hanbury-Williams sees the Empress, she mentions a trip Petrograd he is to make. "Promise me if you go that you will not believe all the wicked stories that are being gossiped about there."[66] It was hard to know what to say. "At present she stands alone. It is a sad business, and when one looks at those pretty daughters one wonders what will happen to them all."[67]

By 1917, the Russian war effort is faltering. Whilst she brings unparalleled manpower to the table, she lacks the money and the infrastructure to keep fighting on this scale in motion. Her allies do their best by shipping in huge quantities of supplies, and more are purchased from neutrals, but like Britain, Russia suffers from a prolonged shortage of munitions, which as in Britain led to public outcry. In addition, there are rumours of pro-Germanism at court, and whispers of the evil influence of Rasputin fills the air; "and so the undercurrent of growls and grumbles began to assume a more threatening form... The country was disturbed and anxious, advance and success gave way to retreat and failure."[68] Then the Tsar took command of his armies himself. "The change in command seems to be passing in more or less smooth waters," wrote Hanbury-Williams, "but the waves may kick up at any moment."[69] He did not envy the Tsar the impossible twin burden of his military business and all the work of government and diplomatic affairs on top. They find him frank in conversation at GHQ, and he allows them a window into his thoughts. He firmly believes in the need for a monarchy in Russia. "In this country, many as were the problems and the difficulties, their sense of imagination, their intense religious feeling and their habits and customs generally make a crown necessary, and he believed this must be so for a very long time." That is not to say that he thinks things should go on exactly as they are. The Tsar tells them "that a certain amount of decentralisation of authority was, of course, necessary, but that the great and decisive power must rest with the Crown. The powers of the Duma must go slowly, because of the difficulties of pushing on education at any reasonably fast rate among all these masses of his subjects."[70] He has generous ideas about parts of his Empire. "He said that he liked the Poles and appreciated all they had done and how much their country had suffered during the war. He said he would grant them a measure of self-government with which he thinks they will be content, but it

63   Marie Louise, Princess: *My Memories of Six Reigns*, p.62.
64   Hanbury-Williams: *The Emperor Nicholas II As I Knew Him*, pp.93-94.
65   Ibid., p.104.
66   Ibid., pp.117-178.
67   Ibid., pp.145-54.
68   Ibid., pp.5-7.
69   Ibid., p.53.
70   Ibid., p.76.

is going to be a difficult and delicate matter to carry through, a somewhat similar one to our Irish question."[71] But Hanbury-Williams believed that too many of the reports the Tsar receives about the war "are too rosy coloured." If only Kitchener had made it to Russia. "His wide experience of these matters would have been invaluable, as he would have come with an unbiased mind and given a very authoritative and straight opinion."[72] But Lord Kitchener is dead. And by the end of 1916 Hanbury-Williams hears of constant discontent. "A good crop of rumours about - unrest in the country, trouble in the Duma, ministers accused of being pro-German, and… one of the Generals who was in command of a corps last year told me that in the retreat before the Germans his men had only five cartridges apiece."[73] As he sees it, by the time the Tsar took full command of his armies, "the roots of revolution were too deeply planted."[74]

Prince Felix Yusopov is young, handsome, almost the richest man in Russia, and married to the Tsar's niece. The King had met him briefly when he delivered a pile of decorations and medals to Buckingham Palace for Nicholas at the beginning of 1915. Nearly two years later, Prince Felix is not the only man who wants Rasputin dead, by any means, but he is the one ready to do something about it. At the end of December 1916 he lured the holy man to him one night with the promise of a party. He poisoned his food, he lived. He poisoned his drink, he lived. He shot him in the back, and when that didn't work, Rasputin was shot again. As he ran, he was clubbed to the ground, rolled in a blue curtain, dumped in the River Neva and pushed under the ice. Finally, he drowned. Queen Alexandra is not sorry to see the back of him, and astute when she suggests that it is too late to save Imperial Russia. "The wretched Russian monk caused a tremendous sensation in the world," she writes to the King, "but [is] only regretted by poor dear Alicky who might have ruined the whole future of Russia through his influence."[75]

At the beginning of 1917 all Russia hums with talk of the death of the Mad Monk, but there are other factors dragging her to the brink. The King copies a set of notes he has been given on the situation in Russia on 4th January. Nicky has made an unpopular ministerial appointment. "It is regarded as a direct challenge to the Duma and His Majesty's answer to those who plotted Rasputin's death… I do not wish to be alarmist but if Emperor continues present course it seems probable other assassinations will follow that of Rasputin, danger of anti-dynastic movement is by no means excluded." The subject of assassinating the Empress was common, as is that of replacing the Tsar; and crucially, such talk has spread to the army. "I confess that even with the disappearance of the most important 'factor in the drama' I see no light ahead yet," wrote Hanbury-Williams, "and the situation may develop into anything… one feels so anxious, kind as they have both been to me throughout, lest some still more serious trouble be in store for them. The crowned heads of this country are so far from their people."[76] At the end of February the King is strongly in favour of a Danish mission to Petrograd to try and help. He corresponds with the King Christian, who has mooted the idea of two particular men as ambassadors, and writes: "I consider that necessity of their going to Petrograd is as urgent as ever; but you will be able to judge when you can spare them."[77] The Danish King decides that he cannot, and nothing more comes of the suggestion.

By the beginning of March riots have broken out in Petrograd over food shortages and added to existing unrest. Tramways are wrecked, shops sacked. There are large crowds in the street. Men

71   Ibid., p.79.
72   Ibid., pp.105-106.
73   Ibid., p.130.
74   Ibid., pp.5-7.
75   Battiscombe,: *Queen Alexandra*, pp.290-291.
76   Hanbury-Williams: *The Emperor Nicholas II As I Knew Him*, pp.144-145.
77   RA PS/PSO/GV/C/M/1067/8.

from the suburbs are marching into the city and imploring factory workers along their route to stop work. People have begun dying in the chaos. Shots have been fired on the Nevski Prospect. The crowds are singing revolutionary songs and occasionally waving red flags, but the general opinion is that they have done nothing to warrant being gunned down. A report the King receives several days later claims that "by this time the movement had become anti-government; but it was not directed against the war, in fact there appeared to be general dissatisfaction among the workmen at the slackness with which the Government was waging war."[78]

On 12th March, at the Tsar's headquarters anxiety is in the air, but the gravity of the situation has not set in. Nicholas's army commander tries to persuade him to give his Government license to deal gently with soldiers refusing to arrest those taking part in strikes, "but his persuasions were useless, as the Emperor, it is said, was determined to keep matters in his own hands." Hanbury-Williams despairs. "If only one felt that he had someone with him who was strong enough to influence him, one would feel more at ease."[79] In the meantime matters have grown much worse in the capital. One of the army's elite regiments has mutinied after being ordered to fire on the crowds and both the Winter Palace and the Fortress of St Peter and Paul are stormed. The following day there is "a fearful atmosphere of gloom"[80] at Buckingham Palace. "Bad news from Russia," the King writes in his diary. "Practically a revolution has broken out in Petrograd and some of the Guards regiments have mutinied and killed their officers."[81]

For Britain, the notion of Russia dropping out of the war is horrific. Should the Eastern Front fold, then Germany will be able to remove thousands of men and transfer them across Europe to bolster their force in the west. Hanbury-Williams is in frantic communication with Robertson at the War Office over a number of issues brought about by the revolution. Munitions work is thoroughly disorganised, nobody was concentrating on future operations, "the socialist anti-war party must be stopped in the bud."[82] There is, says Hanbury-Williams, no time to waste on diplomatic nonsense. Germany must see that Russia intends to continue the war. He even suggests that the Labour Party should send messages to the socialists and women's unions in Petrograd, "urging them not to forget for one instant in the excitement of present levels, that the enemy is still at the gates."[83] Whilst Hanbury-Williams has seized the initiative at Mogilev, in Petrograd, the British ambassador is "dreadfully depressed at the turn which things have taken." He tells Stamfordham that "the country is not ripe for a republic, but the whole dynasty is so discredited that, though the majority of the nation would prefer a constitutional monarch, there is a not a single acceptable candidate among all the members of the Imperial Family."[84]

On 15th March, the Tsar abdicates on behalf of both himself and of his son, who he will not be parted from. The crown devolves onto the head of his brother, Michael, who hardly wants it. After much talking he agrees "to place his services at the disposal of the new Government, declaring that he would not accept the throne unless called to it by the voice of the people expressed in a constituent assembly."[85] In London, the King and Queen hear of these monumental events the same day. "I fear Alicky is the cause of it all and Nicky has been weak, the King writes in his diary. "Heard from Buchanan that the Duma had forced Nicky to sign his abdication and Misha had

78   RA PS/PSO/GV/C/M/1067/31.
79   Hanbury-Williams: *The Emperor Nicholas II As I Knew Him*, pp.148-149.
80   RA EDW/PRIV/DIARY/1917 [check that POW is at BP] (13/3).
81   RA GV/PRIV/GVD/1917 (13/3).
82   RA PS/PSO/GV/C/M/1067/13.
83   RA PS/PSO/GV/C/M/1067/15.
84   RA PS/PSO/GV/C/M/1067/64.
85   RA PS/PSO/GV/C/M/1067/31.

been appointed regent, and after he has been 23 years Emperor. I am in despair.[86] Queen Mary later says that the collapse of the Romanov dynasty had come as no surprise to her, "since she had never conceived how an order so stiff and hierarchal, and so totally detached from the people of those countries, could possible survive in a free and modern world."[87] David is more blunt with regard to the Tsar. "It seems he has made a hopeless balls of everything of late and is entirely under the thumb of his wife who is a religious bitch!!"[88]

"Courageous Severance"

"What a tragedy has been and continues to be enacted in Russia," writes Stamfordham.[89] A 300 year old dynasty lies in tatters, a country is both at war and in turmoil, but already there is the problem of what to do with the man now to be known as Nicholas Romanov. The former Tsar arrives back at his army headquarters on 17th March; but is only concerned with returning to his palace just outside Petrograd, where the Empress is with their children, who are sick with the measles. His Chief of Staff, General Alexiev, Hanbury-Williams and the rest of the Allied military mission are determined to do all that they can to keep him safe. A day or so later. Nicholas invites the British General to go and see him. "I walked down through the gathering darkness and through the gloomy, dirty streets… Except for a small crowd of loafers outside the entrance gates, there was no one about." When Hanbury-Williams comes face to face with the deposed Tsar he is overcome. "I had no time for a set or stilted speech, and all I could say when I saw that familiar face again was: 'I am so sorry." The rooms have been packed up, all of the flowers and his photographs gone. "But he was sitting at the table in his khaki uniform, just as he used to sit when I went in to see him. He looked tired and white, with big black lines under his eyes, but smiled as he shook hands with me." As Hanbury-Williams makes to leave, The Tsar asks if the General might have a photograph of himself that he can give him, in exchange for one of his own. Before he departs finally to be placed under some form of arrest with his family, he says to the Englishman: "Remember, nothing matters but beating Germany."[90] The farewells at Mogilev are gut-wrenching for the foreign officers that have become part of his inner circle. "I was followed by my other colleagues of the military missions, all distressed and sad. He bid them each goodbye, and we all doubt if we shall ever see him again."[91]

The question of what to do with Russia's fallen Imperial Family in the long term was a complicated issue. In 1983, the most recent of King George V's biographers wrote that "The British Government would willingly have offered them asylum but for the fears expressed by Buckingham Palace; and at the most critical moment in their fortunes they were deserted not by a radical Prime Minister seeking to appease his supporters, but by their ever affectionate Cousin Georgie."[92] This statement lacks the application of any appropriate context. As the King established with his advisers long before his Ministers arrived at the same conclusion, to offer the former Tsar asylum was the wrong decision for the country. Additionally, there would only, in fact, be a tiny window of opportunity in which the British Government *might* have been able to get the Imperial Family out of Russia. The fact that they did not at that juncture has nothing to do with the King.

86   RA/PRIV/GVD/1917 (15/3).
87   Pope-Hennessy: *Queen Mary, 1867-1953*, pp.386-387.
88   RA EDW/PRIV/DIARY/1917 (15/3).
89   RA PS/PSO/GV/C/M/1067/18.
90   Hanbury-Williams: *The Emperor Nicholas II As I Knew Him*, pp.167-171.
91   Ibid., pp.171-172.
92   Rose: *King George V,* pp.209-215.

His Majesty's first act following Nicky's abdication is to draft a message for his cousin and send it to Hanbury-Williams for delivery:

> Events of last week have deeply distressed me. My thoughts are constantly with you and I shall always remain your true and devoted friend as you know I have been in the past.[93]

It arrives at Mogilev after his cousin has departed, and so it is sent on to Britain's ambassador, Sir George Buchanan, in Petrograd. A day later the new Provisional Government say that it ought not to be sent, that it "might be misinterpreted." When this bit of information arrives in front of the Cabinet via a Foreign Office document, Lloyd George is put out. His secretary telephones the palace asking for the original text of His Majesty's message. The King does not feel obliged to give his Prime Minister this information, as it was a private communication. As it seems to be causing such a stir, His Majesty says that they should just cancel it. The King felt that this message "as from one friend to another" had lost its point after the delay in its transmission."[94] But he is not happy. "The King has been greatly perturbed about all the fuss with regard to what was intended to be a private message to the Emperor."[95]

This anxiety is over a simple telegram, and yet despite the fact that the King simply wanted to comfort his cousin, it has threatened to cause embarrassment for Russia's Provisional Government and had the potential to cause friction between the King and his Ministers. What then, would happen if the deposed Tsar was suddenly invited to come and live in Britain?

For a start, there is some haziness when it comes to whether or not any such invitations being speculated about would include the rest of the Imperial Family. "Of course the fact that the Emperor will not be separated from his wife and children is the crux of the situation and the difficulty."[96] Because there is no chance that, given a choice, Nicholas will leave them. In terms of where he *wants* to go, he does not want to leave Russia. He tells Hanbury-Williams that he cannot see why anyone would object to his wishes, which are to eventually go with his family to the Crimea. If he *has* to leave, then the British General claims that Nicky says that "he would sooner go to England than anywhere."[97] In terms of where he *can* go, Germany is, unsurprisingly, not an option. Germany is the enemy and as far as Wilhelm is concerned: "England was behind the Russian Revolution and the abdication of the Tsar, whom she had also let down personally. England must now be held responsible for guaranteeing the personal safety of the Tsar and his wife."[98] Nicholas's mother is afraid of her son having to make any journey by sea. She seems to have a preference for his going to her homeland, Denmark. Other suggestions flung into the mix are Venice, Corfu, and Switzerland.

The events which lead to an offer of assistance from the His Majesty's Government are in full flow on 19th March, the same day that the King sends his telegram of support to his cousin. The British Ambassador had been told to instruct Pavel Milyukov, the Provisional Government's new Foreign Minister that "any violence done to the Emperor or his family would have a most deplorable effect and would deeply shock public opinion in this country."[99] Milyukov's response is to suggest that the Imperial Family should come to England. He does not want them in the Crimea and assumes that the British Government will send a ship to collect them. Buchanan forwards the suggestion on

93   RA PS/PSO/GV/C/M/1067/20.
94   RA PS/PSO/GV/C/M/1067/37.
95   RA PS/PSO/GV/C/M/1067/38.
96   RA PS/PSO/GV/C/M/1067/21.
97   Hanbury-Williams: *The Emperor Nicholas II As I Knew Him*, pp.167-171.
98   Stibbe, Matthew: *Kaiser Wilhelm II: The Hohenzollerns at War*, pp.275.
99   Nicolson: *King George V: His Life and Reign*, pp.300-301.

to the Foreign Office. Two days later the Provisional Government are pressing again and a message arrives from Buchanan to say that the Russians are anxious, on account of extremist agitation, to get the ex-Tsar out of the country as quickly as possible. In spite of any obvious objections, the Ambassador hopes that his Government will make an offer of asylum in England and a guarantee that Nicholas will remain there for the duration of the war. From Hanbury-Williams at Mogilev comes a similar plea from General Alexiev that "absolute safe conduct should be given to whole Imperial Family to… England as soon as possible."[100]

Lloyd George's initial reaction is that which can be expected from a Prime Minister. Whilst the King has sent his cousin a telegram offering his sympathy, Lloyd George has issued a message to Prince Lvov, at the head of the Provisional Government, which is aimed at solidifying ties with the new regime. On 22nd March, he then invites Stamfordham to Downing Street to discuss the former Tsar's future. The subject of Milyukov's asylum request is raised. The King's Private Secretary raises several reservations about the idea of such an offer, in a classic display of Stamfordham's determination and guile when it came to acting in the interests of the monarchy. He points out that quite naturally the King will want to be consulted before any offer is made to the Imperial Family.

Denmark is postured as an alternative, but Lloyd George pours cold water on idea, for Denmark is too close to Germany. He thinks there would be a very credible risk of the former Tsar becoming embroiled in intrigue; other entities may seek to help him form a counter-revolution to reinstate him. If Britain's Government was still undecided about whether she wanted Nicholas and his family on her soil, they have already decided that they definitely do not want him falling into the hands of the Germans. And so despite Stamfordham's arguments against an offer of asylum, the upshot of the gathering is the assertion that Britain cannot deny a request such as this made by an ally. A telegram is to be sent to Buchanan to the effect that the King and his Government "would be prepared to give effect to Milyukov's request that the Emperor and his family should be received in this country."[101] It is to be made clear that the idea originated in Petrograd, not London and that the British Government are honouring to a request from an ally.

From the very beginning, the King and his advisers are thinking this through on a more complex level than his Ministers. What appears at first to be a simple suggestion is actually a powder keg in both a military and political sense, as well as in a constitutional one, that could have massive, worldwide repercussions. It could decide who wins the war.

For a start, is it safe for the Imperial Family to get to England? The Tsar's mother certainly doesn't think so, and the King is reticent too. To make the journey as short as possible the idea of transporting them overland as far as Bergen, on Norway's west coast before they embark on a ship is put forward. But the Provisional Government will not allow this. The Under Secretary of State at the Foreign Office, Lord Hardinge, thinks that this is because once the family crossed the Russian frontier into Sweden, Nicholas would essentially be a free man. Who is going to pay? Stamfordham raises this logical question in his meeting with the Prime Minister, and nobody appears to have thought it through. A man who has been Tsar of all the Russias cannot now occupy a house in Surbiton. To have a former Emperor and, of course, a granddaughter of Queen Victoria living in poverty on British soil would be unthinkable. Balmoral is suggested, but it is thought to be a thoroughly unsuitable residence for most of the year. Then is it suggested that the British Government might make Nicholas an allowance, but any further consideration raises the very real issue of what the public's reaction would be if they find out that they are funding his stay.

100   RA PS/PSO/GV/C/M/1067/30.
101   RA PS/PSO/GV/C/M/1067/29.

And so they decide that Buchanan should "throw out a hint that the Russian Government should settle upon His Imperial Majesty sufficient means to enable him to live with suitable dignity"[102] and then hope that they agree.

"I do feel very strongly that for our own King's welfare," writes one MP to Stamfordham, "and in order to maintain and increase our present influence in Russia we ought to be very careful how we move in this matter. Otherwise you might find our royal family placed to say the least of it, in a very difficult… position."[103] The King has two issues to take into consideration when contemplating Nicholas's asylum offer. The preservation of the monarchy is, of course, self serving; but not entirely. Even regarding the matter completely dispassionately the last thing that Britain needs in the midst of 1917 is for the Monarchy to be overhauled and all of the unrest that this would entail. There are three recent, worrying precedents for the King to examine in terms of how his people react to the proximity of Russian royalty. All out hysteria had broken out in the national press over the matter of a brief meeting between Edward VII and his nephew, the Tsar in 1908. A full state visit to Russia was deemed inappropriate on account of the political climate, and so all the King wanted to do was meet with him on the Baltic coast. "Radical and Labour Members of Parliament thought that the idea was thoroughly inappropriate. The Labour leader called for a resolution asking the King to cancel his engagement to meet the Tsar and to refrain from injuring the feelings of the people."[104] There was even a parliamentary debate on the matter, but King Edward went ahead with the meeting anyway. Tensions flared again in 1909 when the Royal Family met Nicholas at Cowes. The Labour party issued a declaration saying that receiving him on British soil was "an insult to the good name of the nation." On the day of the Tsar's arrival, the press carried complaints and an "influentially signed letter" to the Foreign Secretary, protesting against the official welcome of the Tsar; signed by 70 Liberal and Labour MPs, three peers and a number of church officials.[105] And so the King has obvious concerns, given that this brief meeting and this short stop on British soil caused so much rancour, about inviting his cousin to come and live in Britain. More recently, His Majesty has the example of the public reaction to the Greek Royal Family to consider. King Constantine of Greece is decidedly unpopular in Britain and in France, for among other things he is married to Wilhelm's sister. Various members of his family have been in London thus far in the war, and it has not gone down well. There has been a backlash in the press about His Majesty greeting them; a feeling that Britain has not done all she could in supporting the Greek Prime Minister against Tino; "and that the King of Greece was being supported by Royal influence here."[106] The arrival of the Russian Imperial Family in Britain will put the King's own throne at more risk than his associations with the minor Greek house.

Equally as important as the preservation of the monarchy in the King's mind is the continuing participation of Russia in the war. Should the Provisional Government make a separate peace with the Central Powers, it could very well spell disaster for the Western Front. In the days after the Tsar's abdication Buchanan watches the red flag fluttering over the Winter Palace, sees men hauling pictures of Emperors out of the Ministry of Foreign Affairs. When the Provisional Government issue a manifesto detailing their policy in eight principles, only the last of them mentions the war, and it stops far short of guaranteeing the continued involvement of Russia. It is hardly a joy to read for her Allies. Individual ministers such as Kerensky assure Buchanan that Russia intends to fight on, but as Buchanan says, nobody knows much at all about the new government, or even how

102   Ibid.
103   RA PS/PSO/GV/C/M/1067/27.
104   Lee: *Edward VII, A Biography.* Vol II, pp.691-693.
105   Ibid.
106   TNA: CAB 23/40/9.

long it will survive. Even if the Provisional Government pledges to continue to fight, the reality of convincing soldiers to do so is an entirely different matter. The country has been in a state of anarchy, officers have committed suicide. The Russian Army needs to be reigned back in. In the Navy an Admiral has been murdered, and all of this in the alleged face of German intrigue in the country trying to disrupt the ailing war effort in factories and warehouses.

But Russia has been a good ally thus far. Britain has exercised great influence over her and she has acted in Britain's interests as well as her own. The likelihood of this continuing is fragile enough in the spring of 1917, without adding to the complex situation by inviting Nicholas and just as importantly, someone as reviled as Alexandra to come and live in the country. The Tsar has been swept from his throne because his people no longer wanted him on it. They no longer wanted to be under his influence. Kerensky has already raised the concern that once in England, the Tsar might be free to mount a counter-revolution. Should he go to England, then will they want to listen to Lloyd George and his Government any longer? At least perceiving that Nicholas and his wife have the ear of the King's Ministers? It is also reasonable to think that if asylum is granted to Nicholas, that a flood of other relatives will follow him. And who knows the full scope of the intrigue that will be generated on British soil as a result. There is a very real possibility that an Imperial presence in Britain could distort or even destroy Britain's alliance with this fragile new incarnation of Russia which has divorced itself from the Tsar. If his presence were to have a catastrophic effect on the British war effort, then the King will not be safe from blame, regardless of who extended the original invitation.

Despite Stamfordham's insistence that the King be consulted, and despite all of these obvious concerns, the offer of asylum has been made by Lloyd George and his Government. The palace have not been able to counsel otherwise. This is the fatal turning point in the whole affair; the most likely point, the only point, at which the British Government could have perhaps removed the former Tsar from Russia and brought him to England. The reasons that he does not arrive are entirely Russian. The Imperial children are suffering from measles, and the Tsar refuses to be parted from his family, but, more importantly, the Provisional Government, which might well have been able to make him depart against his will, does not respond to the offer of asylum that they have asked for. Although they have repeatedly stated that they wish no harm to come to the Imperial Family, they are not the only group scrambling for power in the new Russia, and should they relinquish their hold on Nicholas and let him flee to safety, they may completely undermine their own position. Extremists are demanding that he remain in the country. Kerensky later claims that the Provisional Government begged the British not to publish details of the offer, that would have revealed that the requested came from Petrograd, lest it be seen by their political opponents.

Eight days after the offer has been made, nothing has been settled, and the clearest opportunity for swiftly removing the Imperial Family from Russia before the question becomes bogged down in her fluctuating politics has passed. At the palace, the King's sympathy for his cousin has been at odds with his commitment to Britain's interests and his duty as Sovereign. With Stamfordham's counsel, he decides that he will take the opportunity to raise his concerns again, as nothing in the way of a departure has come to pass. He has Stamfordham write to Balfour at the Foreign Office on 30th March:

> The King has been thinking much about the Government's proposal that the Emperor Nicholas and his family should come to England. As you are doubtless aware, the King has a strong personal friendship for the Emperor and therefore would be glad to do anything to

help him in the crisis. But His Majesty cannot help doubting, not only on account of the dangers of the voyage, but on general grounds of expediency, whether it is advisable that the Imperial Family should take up residency in this country.[107]

Balfour is firm. "His Majesty's Ministers quite realise the difficulties to which you refer in your letter, but they do not think, unless the position changes, that it is now possible to withdraw the invitation."[108] Stamfordham is reminded politely that it is trusted that the King will not fight his Ministers on the matter, after all, it is their job to advise him. It is an experienced statesman's way of telling his Sovereign to sit down and be quiet. Stamfordham's reply is predictably terse, but accepting. The offer of asylum has been made and there is nothing that the King can do about it. In the meantime, His Majesty has to attend to his mother, who is frantic about her sister and her Russian relatives. Telegrams are given to him so that he may break news of Aunt Minny's movements to her himself. As predicted, requests have started to arrive from other members of the Imperial Family wishing to come to England. The King is in despair, the position of the monarchy is under threat through the actions of others. Abusive mail is arriving at Buckingham Palace assuming that the asylum offer has been forced through at his hands. Stamfordham has not given up. He writes to Balfour's Private Secretary pointing out that the Government's actions will have harsh consequences for His Majesty. Then he sits down to put the whole weight of the throne behind another missive to the Foreign Secretary in an attempt to convince him that the offer of asylum should be withdrawn:

> Every day the King is becoming more concerned about the question of the Emperor and Empress of Russia coming to this country… As you know from the first the King has thought the presence of the Imperial Family (especially of the Empress) in this country would raise all sorts of difficulties, and I feel sure that you appreciate how awkward it will be for our Royal Family who are closely connected both with the Emperor and Empress. You probably also are aware that the subject has become more or less public property, and that people are either assuming that it has been initiated by the King or deprecating the very unfair position in which His Majesty will be placed. The King desires me to ask you whether after consulting the Prime Minister, Sir George Buchanan should not be communicated with a view to approaching the Russian Government to make some other plan for the future residence of Their Imperial Majesties.[109]

One former Under Secretary of State for India has written to the palace: "If the ex-Tsar and Tsarina come to live here we shall have a revolution and remember that I warned you."[110] Desperation causes Stamfordham to send another letter that afternoon, reaffirming his argument. Whilst all of this is going on, Buchanan is reporting to the Foreign Office that Kerensky is stalling for time, that Nicholas will not be able to leave the country for another month. "It was difficult to allow him to go until the examination of documents seized had been completed."[111] And in that moment, Balfour finally wavers. "I think the King _is_ placed in an awkward position," he writes to Lloyd George. There are diplomatic concerns about saying where the invitation originated from. "I still think that we may have to suggest Spain or the south of France as a more sensible residence than England."[112]

107   RA PS/PSO/GV/C/M/1067/39.
108   RA PS/PSO/GV/C/M/1067/44.
109   RA PS/PSO/GV/C/M/1067/51.
110   RA PS/PSO/GV/C/M/1067/59.
111   RA PS/PSO/GV/C/M/1067/80.
112   RA PS/PSO/GV/C/M/1067/55.

Stamfordham turns his attentions to the Prime Minister. He arrives at Downing Street determined "to impress upon him the King's strong opinion that the Emperor and Empress of Russia should not come to this country, and that the Government ought to inform Milyukov that since they had agreed to his proposal… public opinion had become so stoutly opposed to the idea that His Majesty's Government must withdraw the consent previously given." Again Stamfordham attempts to impress just how unfair it is that this asylum be forced upon the King. "I reminded the Prime Minister," he records, "about what had been said as to the King's attitude regarding the King of Greece, and the exception taken to His Majesty having received the brothers of King Constantine when they were in London." Finally, he succeeds in convincing the Prime Minister of the danger of Nicholas's presence and Lloyd George agrees that the south of France will be a more suitable destination.

Britain isn't abandoning the concern of the Tsar's safety, just the advisability of hosting him. The French War Minister happens to be in London, and the Prime Minister invites him into the room to discuss whether his countrymen might raise similar objections. "He said no, that French people had a personal regard for the Emperor who had been their ally for some years… He did not anticipate any difficulty from the public point of view; thought the Government no doubt would recognise a certain responsibility in guarding the Emperor, and exercising vigilance as to His Imperial Majesty's actions."[113] The Frenchman quite appreciates the specific difficulties raised by the question of the Tsar's asylum in a country with a monarchy, and one where he is so closely related to the Royal Family. Lloyd George agrees to take the matter in hand with the French.

A telegram is despatched to Buchanan on 13th April: "There are indications that a considerable anti-monarchical movement is developing including personal attacks on the King… It is thought that if the Emperor comes here it may dangerously increase this movement. It is also worth consideration whether the presence of the Emperor might not weaken us in or our dealings with the new Russian Government. For these reasons it would perhaps be preferable that the Emperor should go to France when he is allowed to leave Russia. Please let me have your views and in the meantime say nothing further to the Russian Government on the subject unless they themselves raise the question."[114] Buchanan entirely concurs that if it presents any danger to the British monarchy, Nicholas should not come to England. He has asked why the Provisional Government will not let the former Tsar go to the Crimea as he wishes. He is told that the journey presents too much of a risk. As the weeks pass by, the notion of the Nicholas, Alexandra and their five children leaving Russia evaporates completely.

Throughout the three week spell in spring 1917 when the future of Nicholas Romanov seemingly hung in the balance, the King's sympathy for his cousin was at odds with what he knew to be the right course for his country. Despite his huge affection for the ex-Tsar, the King carries out the single most definitive action of his reign that illustrates how seriously he takes his role as Sovereign. Not without a considerable amount of pain, he places the interests of his country above those of his family. In making the initial offer of asylum, the Government has acted with a knee-jerk reaction that might be expected from a concerned family member, whilst the King has behaved like a Minister dispassionately weighing the situation from all angles and considering the effects on the nation.

It was written in 1983 that: "What does remain certain is that by persuading his Government to withdraw their original offer of asylum, [the King] deprived the Imperial Family of their best, perhaps their only, means of escape."[115] Ignoring for a moment the fact that His Majesty's reasoning

---

113   RA PS/PSO/GV/C/M/1067/61.
114   RA PS/PSO/GV/C/M/1067/62.
115   Rose: *King George V,* pp.209-215.

for wanting to block the arrival of the Imperial Family on his shores was sound, during the only window in which it *might* have been possible for them to make the journey, the obstacles in their path have nothing to do with the King. When the asylum offer is made in the third week of March, Britain is committed to receiving Nicky, Alix and their children. The King has failed to convince his Ministers to deviate from this course of action and has been put in his place with a reminder about the limit of his constitutional powers by Balfour. It is the new Russian Government that fails to either accept or reject the offer of asylum. There is an element of blame to be placed on the former Tsar himself too. Multiple sources have referred to the fact that his situation is complicated by his refusal to be even temporarily separated from his family, and that he displayed a failure to accept the reality of his position. It is not until well into April that Stamfordham is able to bring the King's influence to fruition. It is by then highly doubtful that the Provisional Government, who have been wavering for weeks by that point, under constantly increasing pressure in Russia not to let Nicholas leave, would have handed him over.

"Ties of Blood"

Throughout 1917 the King continues to pay diligent attention to the contribution made by troops from across his Empire. "What a fantastic picture it was that Prussian militarism made for itself before the outbreak of this war!" Says the Canadian Prime Minister on a visit to Europe in 1915. "It pictured Canada, Australia, and New Zealand standing aloof and indifferent or seeking an opportunity to cut themselves off from this Empire." But, he asks, "What is the actual picture today? You are bound to the Empire by stronger ties than ever before, and are prepared to fight to the death for the maintenance of its integrity and for the preservation of our common civilisation throughout the world."[116]

The King has searched exhaustively for ways in which to show his gratitude since the arrival of Imperial troops in Europe. His inspections continue, including huge assemblies of Australians and New Zealanders. He makes a point of inspecting a Canadian division on Dominion Day too, a gesture which is hugely appreciated. The wounded are still at the front of his mind too. After handing Bushey Park to the Canadians for use as a convalescent hospital, the King and Queen are visitors on numerous occasions and the same attention is paid to a much smaller outfit in Richmond Park that looks after South Africans. The royal tea party format from the previous spring is used at Windsor Castle in 1917 to entertain Dominion troops on brilliantly sunny afternoons, when taxi drivers donate their time in their hundreds to bring guests and the entertainment is provided by Oswald Stoll and a concert party from the Coliseum. Near Cumberland Lodge the Canadian Forestry Corps have set up shop in Windsor Great Park. The King goes to visit them in April 1917 and finds a hut town on Smith's Lawn that thoroughly impresses him with "splendid roadways, an electric power station, baths, telephones and other conveniences." There are log huts "with blazing fireplaces, stag heads mounted on the wall and fitted with electric lighting and settees they made themselves."[117] There is even a YMCA hut with billiards room. And of course, the King never forgets India. As well as hospital visits and troop inspections, the King listens to individual petitions, receives delegations of wounded Indian troops at Buckingham Palace and thanks them for their contribution to the war effort in person; and in 1917 the Queen has reproductions made from a coronation portrait which are sent to Indian widows with an autograph message:

---

116 (ed.) Hammerton & Wilson: *The Great War Vol.XII*, pp.296-297.
117 RA GV/PRIV/GVD/1917 (16/4).

In sorrow and sympathy my thoughts fly across the seas to my sisters in India, that beautiful lands which I have twice visited, and love so well. I send you this to do honour to a very brave soldier of the Empire who died for you and for us in the glorious fight for truth and freedom against tyranny and broken faith.[118]

The King expends much effort fussing over the welfare and the image of his Imperial troops. He delves into the issue of whether or not adequate religious services are being held for Indians; he has Haig examine claims that French locals, on the assumption that Dominion men are rich, are charging them exorbitant prices for goods. Nobody doubts the commitment or the bravery of the Australians, but they have earned criticism for themselves after some appalling behaviour in Egypt. The King is keen to keep a lid on such escapades when they are transferred to the Western Front and provides Haig with some detailed instructions. Haig confirms that he fully grasps the issue. "The front on which the Australians are to be employed is one offering few temptations!"[119] He assures the palace that the new Australian troops arriving on his front appear to be excellent, and that several of the officers had experience having served in South Africa at the turn of the century. Perhaps, he suggests, the issues encountered in the Mediterranean have even been exaggerated.

As the war expands and the scale of the Dominion contribution grows accordingly, the King is on hand to acknowledge it. On 25th April 1916 he is present for the commemoration of the first *Anzac Day*. Newspapers had latched onto the name earlier in the month and over the ensuing decades it will remain. "I went to London by train at 10:30 and was present at the memorial service in Westminster Abbey for those that fell a year ago today landing at Anzac in Gallipoli,"[120] writes His Majesty in his diary. The reception for hundreds of these Dominion men as they march to the abbey is astonishing. At Aldwych people hang from hotel and shop windows, along the Strand to Charing Cross and Whitehall, as they pass Trafalgar Square, the crowd is immense. There is a complete lack of restraint. Women throw flowers and press forward to grip the men by the hands. "A wave of emotion seemed to sweep over the multitude and they poured out on overflowing tribute of their joy and pride in these men from the Dominions." Outside Westminster Abbey it is thought to be the biggest gathering since the King's coronation. The crowd chants: "Bravo Anzacs!" Giants they looked, almost all of them, and dandies, too, to be particular with their jaunty hats." They stride along "with that free, swinging gait that characterises them,"[121] with the sound of the bands in their ears.

When the King and Queen arrive, the press of the crowd is so great that the police are carried off their feet and the people nearly reach the royal carriages. Mr Hughes, the Australian Prime Minister, gives a speech worthy of the occasion to his contingent.

On this day called Anzac, one short year ago the Australasian soldier leapt unheralded into the arena of war, and by a display of matchless courage, dash, endurance, and tenacity of purpose and resource, proved himself worthy of kinship with these heroic men who, throughout the history of our race, have walked unafraid into the jaws of death thinking it a glorious thing to die for their country. I cannot put into words how proud Australia and New Zealand are of you... I feel myself struggling between grief for the fallen, sympathy for those who have suffered, and pride of your glorious actions... I feel that the sprits of those

118   *The Telegraph* 22/3/14.
119   RA GV/PRIV/GVD/1917 (16/4).
120   *The Times* 12/5/17.
121   RA PS/PS/GV/C/Q/2521/V/143.

faintless ones whose bodies now lie on the peninsula near to us on this day of Anzac urging us to press on, and ever on, to victory.[122]

There are over 2,000 Australians and New Zealanders in the abbey for an impressive and yet simple service that coincides with others in Melbourne, Sydney and Wellington. General Birdwood, their commander at Gallipoli, welcomes his old men in person before taking his seat next to Robertson. Hanging from the chancel rails is a large wreath of tulips and ferns from New Zealanders, dedicated to men of the 29th Division, so as not to forget the British who died on that day too. Hundreds of survivors are present, many of them attended by nurses. It is not significant only as the first commemoration of Anzac Day, but also because it is the first time such honouring of a self-governing Dominion has taken place in England. To his representative in Australia, the King telegraphs: "Tell my people… that today I am joining with them in their solemn tribute to the memory of their heroes who died in Gallipoli… May those who know their loss find comfort in the conviction that they did not die in vain, but that their sacrifice has drawn our peoples more closely together, and added strength and glory to the Empire."[123]

Canada's turn for such recognition comes in July 1917. "May and I were present at Westminster Abbey at a service to celebrate the 50th anniversary of the confederation of the Dominion of Canada and for those Canadians who have fallen in the war."[124] But the King does not restrict himself to large scale spectacles. In 1917 he will also visit a contingent of native South African labourers. The Dominion has asked for strong hands at the front, and thus far 14,000 men have volunteered and been sent to work. It will be a unique ceremony, for never before has such a representative body of native South Africans been assembled for royalty. The little group are said to be extremely excited; comprising Sesutos from Basutoland, Sixasa from Cape Province, Sepedi from Transvaal, and Zulus. Interpreters will be present to repeat His Majesty's words in a variety of necessary dialects at the conclusion of his address. The King walks along the line. He says: "Without munitions of war my armies cannot fight; without food they cannot live. You are helping to send these things to them each day, and in doing so, you are hurling your spears at the enemy, and hastening the destruction that awaits him."[125] At the conclusion of the ceremony the men are interviewed by a journalist and a spokesperson announces that

> It is a day which will never be forgotten in my lifetime… I always desired to see the King, but when he appeared, it seemed as if it were a dream. I thought of the war and his great responsibilities. My heart was grieved, but I comforted him with the knowledge that I have come here to help him, and with the prayer that the Lord may give him victory.[126]

When Wigram relates this account to the King he is delighted.

But as the war develops, His Majesty also takes every opportunity to meet Dominion leaders who are in Britain. He particularly likes Mr Hughes, the Australian Prime Minister, who is very plain spoken, and enjoys a lengthy, frank after-dinner discussion with him at Windsor; His Majesty has "since expressed the great pleasure it gave him."[127] He greets 33 overseas members of the

122   RA GV/PRIV/GVD/1917 (25/4).
123   *The Times* 26/4/16.
124   *The Times* 26/5/16.
125   RA PS/PSO/GV/PS/WAR/QQ18/05707.
126   Ibid.
127   *Daily Mirror* 13/5/16.

Empire Parliamentary Association who are in the country to see munitions work and meet their counterparts in the House of Commons. At the end of 1916 concerns are raised about the number of knighthoods assigned for distribution to the Dominions and Crown Colonies. "At the present moment our maximum allotment is ten and it has been very hard indeed to keep the number down to that figure."[128] The King agrees. "His Majesty is in favour of an increased distribution of honours in the colonies," writes Stamfordham, but the King is obviously mindful of the Sam Hughes debacle and adds: *"so long as they are bestowed upon the right people."*[129]

Although acknowledgement is necessary, it cannot make up the deficit between the position of the Dominions and their lack of proportional representation in making decisions about the conduct of the war. In the summer of 1916, the King had been utilised by his Government during the visit by representatives of Dominion parliaments, and India were invited too; a big step. For what speaks better than a royal reception; kingly attention and praise. The endeavour was referred to as representing "ties of blood,"[130] and sought to give these politicians a much needed insight into the machinations of the war and what it is that their people are actually contributing to. "I trust that your stay here will be both pleasant and instructive," says His Majesty, "and that opportunity will be given you to estimate the efforts being made to keep the Navy and Army efficient in both men and equipment, and to bring the war to a victorious end." His speech is carefully worded so as this does not appear as if Britain are lecturing the self-governing Dominions. "We can learn much from each other, and so it is my earnest hope that such visits as this will be both frequent and fruitful."[131]

But the situation is doing real harm after two and a half years of war. "The Dominion Governments chafed under the feeling that they were not trusted. Their efforts were handicapped because they did not know the mind of the British Government. They found it difficult to shape their own policy."[132] The scale of participation from the Dominions has reached a level that surely warrants a seat at the table when decisions made concerning tens of thousands of their subjects fighting abroad, and given the ceaseless contribution and sacrifice of their people at home. This is finally recognised in the Spring of 1917 with the arrival of Dominion leaders to attend an Imperial War Cabinet, "an executive authority for the war purposes of the Empire while leaving the constitutional issue in abeyance." Lloyd George has gone to great lengths to affirm that all of this effort is not for a mere conversation. "I wish to explain that what His Majesty's Government contemplate is not a session of the ordinary Imperial Conference, but a special War Conference of the Empire. They therefore invite your Prime Minister to attend a series of special and continuous meetings of the War Cabinet."[133] The presence of the Prime Ministers, he states, renders them members of the said Cabinet whilst they are there. "It is a change which we very heartily welcome, says *The Times,* "and which we are confident that the nation no less heartily welcomes with us. The King's speech utters the hope that this step will conduce to the establishment of closer relations between all parts of the Empire."[134]

Anything that involves the Empire is of huge interest to His Majesty, and both he and the Queen are on hand to do all that they can to make the Imperial gathering go as smoothly as possible. It is not constitutionally appropriate that the King take part in any discussions, but there are other ways he can show his support. Away from the sittings he endeavours to meet with and host the different Dominion and Indian representatives. Some members are invited to spend the weekend at Windsor

128   BD: MS Asquith A.1. 4 #240.
129   BD: MS Asquith A.1. 4 #239.
130   *Daily Telegraph* 8/7/17.
131   (ed.) Hammerton & Wilson: *The Great War Vol.XII,* pp.296-297.
132   Ibid.
133   Ibid., pp.296-297.
134   *The Times* 8/2/17.

Castle so that he might get to know them better and find out what issues they feel affect them most. As with everything he is always learning, always looking for more information. At the conclusion of their business, His Majesty invites all of the delegates to a reception at Windsor. The day is fine and warm, the castle looking its best. The conference has come up with four main resolutions, which include preference within the Empire, in particular "making the Empire independent of other countries in respect of food, supplies, raw materials and essential industries." India is to be represented along with the self-governing Dominions at all future conferences. There will be no attempt to more broadly define this new Imperial way of doing business, which is "too important and too intricate,"[135] until after the war. In all 36 sit down to lunch to celebrate the conclusion of a highly successful enterprise. And these are no mere platitudes on behalf of the King, for he is passionate about what has taken place and what it means for the future of his Empire. In particular it gives him "utmost satisfaction"[136] that Indians have sat on an equal footing with representatives of the Dominions. A few days after the end of the Imperial gathering, His Majesty speaks at the opening of a war photography exhibition at the V&A and he mentions eleven allies. Then he corrects himself, "because we could no longer look upon the great Commonwealth and Dominions as simply dependencies of Great Britain. They were allies, and the firmest allies that any country could have."[137]

"Unknown Becomes the Dog"

Round about the second anniversary of the outbreak of war in 1916, things had looked stable for the King and for the monarchy in general. Whilst the Tsar's eventual demise had already begun, the Kaiser's popularity was on the wane. And yet crowds flocked to Buckingham Palace to mark the date. "Every minute the crowd grew, until the space in front of the Palace was black with people. Someone started *Rule Britannia*; and the crowd took up the refrain and sang it again and again."[138]

The reaction to the declaration of the Third French Republic across the Channel in 1870 was as close a precedent as could be found for what might follow the Russian Revolution. Republican rallies had attracted thousands, whilst Trafalgar Square, just half a mile from Buckingham Palace, was awash with red flags, caps and ribbons and witnessed an estimated 10,000 demonstrators sing the *Marseillaise*. The King and his advisers brace themselves for a similar reaction. Like his ancestors he is familiar with opposition. Keir Hardie provides some of the most colourful discourse, referring to the King as "a street corner loafer" and "destitute of even ordinary ability."[139] In return His Majesty labels him a beast. Stamfordham gathers as much intelligence as he can in the wake of the Revolution, and as usual he means to shield the King from nothing. In June he writes that:

Even at the risk of being egotistical, I unhesitatingly say that I do not believe that there is any sovereign in the world to whom the truth is more fearlessly told by those in his immediate service, and who receives it with such good will, and even gratitude, as King George. There is no socialistic newspaper, no libellous rag, that is not read and marked and show to the King if they contain any criticisms friendly or unfriendly of His Majesty and the Royal Family.[140]

135   *Morning Post* 4/5/17.
136   *Daily Mail* 4/5/17.
137   *Morning Post* 11/5/17.
138   *The Times* 3/8/17.
139   Prochaska: *The Republic of Britain, 1760-2000*, p.154.
140   RA PS/PSO/GV/C/O/1106/40.

On 31st March, as Britain was awaiting a Russian response to their offer of asylum for the Tsar, a large rally is held at the Royal Albert Hall to celebrate Nicholas's demise. The speeches are not that inflammatory. They pass a resolution to congratulate the people of Russia on throwing off the yoke of imperialism, and ask for free speech, free press and freedom of religion, as well as social equality. "Sentiments which," said an undercover policeman present, who made a report that was later forwarded to Stamfordham, "I interpreted as applying to Germany and Austria."[141]

But whilst this meeting turns out to be innocuous, an increase of anti-monarchical feeling and rhetoric causes alarm at the palace and coincides exactly with the Stamfordham's attempts to convince the Government to retract their offer of asylum for the Tsar. The piece that garners the most attention is published in *Justice,* which proffers itself as "the organ of the social-democracy" on 5th April. Titled: *The Need for a British Republic,* it says that:

> Our Royal Family… has never been anything more than a convenient semi-monarchical compromise with men and women of German origin, continuously fortified by German intermarriage… Certainly at this moment, if the King and Queen have invited their discrowned Russian cousins to come here, they are misinterpreting entirely the feelings of us common Englishmen. Then there is that ugly Greek business. It is the general opinion that King George and Queen Mary acted with the ejected Romanovs in upholding the despot King Constantine of Greece against the Greek people and their leader… The influence of the court is also nearly always injurious in domestic affairs…Happily, it would be very easy to establish a British Republic. There is no enthusiasm whatever for monarchy in the United Kingdom today: there will probably be less tomorrow. The old objections to Republicanism have quite died down. I cannot imagine anyone sacrificing himself or herself to safeguard the crown.[142]

"The Kingly caste is in greater danger in 1917 than in 1849, when thrones tottered like towers in an earthquake,"[143] says *The Referee.* Another piece mocks the mainstream press, in particular *The Times.* "It devotes a column and a half… even in these stirring times, to proving how absurd a Republic must be… how the colonies all adore our little George V… and how 315,000,000 Indians put up prayers night and morning for the successor of Akbar the Great, resident in Buckingham Palace."[144] The same publication printed a letter reported to have been written by a serving artilleryman. "Is Tommy Atkins loyal? Well, in barrack rooms it is always — the King, — — the King… ask any Tommy to fill in the blanks and he will find its vulgar vernacular."[145] A leading trade unionist exclaims: "My Army, my navy, my colonies, my Empire." Where is the difference between such proclamations and the bombastic vapourings of William of Germany?"[146]

In June 1917, King Constantine of Greece joins the Tsar in losing his crown, temporarily, at least. The French High Commissioner there helpfully suggests that Tino should come and live on the Isle of Wight. His fall from grace was much celebrated in Britain and there is not a chance, as far as his cousin the King is concerned, that he will be allowed on English soil. His Majesty is under huge pressure in early summer, and his mood is dragged down further by the worry he expends on republicanism movements in Britain. Lloyd George continues to marginalise him. "Very glad

141   RA PS/PSO/GV/C/O/1106/10.
142   RA PS/PSO/GV/C/O/1106/1.
143   RA PS/PSO/GV/C/O/1106/18.
144   RA PS/PSO/GV/C/O/1106/27.
145   *Justice* 3/5/17.
146   *The Clarion* 4/5/1917.

Government are going to grant amnesty to Irish prisoners as it ought to help convention," he writes in mid-June. "I see it is to be announced in [the] House today and I have never been asked for my approval. Usual way things are done in present day."[147] The King is also angered by minutes from the Imperial War Conference that advocated communications with America that completely bypassed both his input and his inclusion. Stamfordham appeals to Balfour as a former Prime Minister, a seasoned Cabinet member "and also if I may presume to say so, as an old friend"[148] to approach the matter with the Prime Minister. "Briefly I may tell you that His Majesty is deeply pained at what he regards as not only a wont of respect, but as ignoring his very existence. The country may wish to have a Republic, but so long as they elect for a monarchy there are certain traditional observances and duties which the Government cannot disregard with reference to the Sovereign [and] surely one of these is the recognition that all messages of the nature of the above to the chief of state should emanate from the <u>Sovereign.</u>"[149] Away on a visit to the fleet, the King quips in a letter to Stamfordham that he: "better join the King of Greece in Exile. You might inform PM that whenever I am in train I am connected to London by wire and have my own telegraphist."[150]

Republican scaremongering continues into July. The founder of Britain's *Vanity Fair* writes to the King of the very worst of rumours; that "the hindrance of our blockade, the alleged inadequate restriction and insufficient internment of Germans, the long defiance of the Allied Powers by King Constantine, and even the alleged leakage of secret information, are represented as being all due to Your Majesty, or members of the Royal Family."[151] Queen Alexandra was not helping matters. In 1917 Tino's sister Marie, who had married into the Russian Imperial Family, fled to England and spends much of her time with the King's mother. "Great was Queen Alexandra's indignation when she was told that 'little Minny's' continued presence at Marlborough House and Sandringham had aroused suspicions that she was intriguing there on behalf of her brother. "I will do my best not to be seen in public with the poor child," the Queen wrote in righteous anger, "but I will not give her up or [refuse to] see her in private here as that would indeed be too cruel and hard."[152] However, she plagues her son with what was tantamount to an obsession with their Greek relatives, despite the antagonism any dealings with them created for His Majesty. She repeatedly insisted that he "interfere personally on behalf of 'poor, excellent, honest Tino." In vain did the King point out to her that it was not in his power to do anything. "I am not prepared now on account of the strong feeling which certainly exists in this country against him, to do anything , in fact no would would listen to me if I did." Queen Alexandra was not to be convinced. Time and again after visiting her at 'the Big House' King George would return to York Cottage exclaiming in despair, "I simply cannot make Motherdear hear, much less understand, anything at all about Greece."[153] People are whispering that the King should abdicate. Other rumours say that he is seriously considering it. Stamfordham tells one conduit of this information, that despite all of the changes that the His Majesty faces, despite "a strenuous time" at the palace, "really it was difficult to regard or speak with seriousness on a matter which anybody acquainted with the King could only regard in the light of grotesque absurdity."[154]

Stamfordham remains relatively relaxed about such utterances. "Every sort of charge is being conjured up against the King in regard to other monarchies," he tells a friend. "These are the natural

147   RA PS/PSO/GV/C/O/1153/XXII/425.
148   RA PS/PSO/GV/C/Q/1102/9.
149   Ibid.
150   RA PS/PSO/GV/C/O/1153/XXII/425.
151   RA PS/PSO/GV/C/O/1106/47.
152   Battiscombe, pp.289-290.
153   Ibid.
154   RA PS/PSO/GV/C/O/1106/58.

outcome of war and the Russian Revolution. I feel disposed to ignore more or less this irresponsible talk. [His Majesty] meanwhile is following those strictly constitutional lines from which he has not diverged during the seven exceptionally difficult, and indeed critical, years which the world have passed through since his accession."[155]

But a recurring theme raised by palace correspondents is that the King could still be more visible to his people. "There seems to be a strong feeling among some classes that Their Majesties do not show sufficiently in public," Stamfordham writes to one correspondent. "What do you think? No one has any idea how much the King has done in inspecting troops, visiting munition works all over the country, and going to hospitals etc." Frustrating this was, once the censor stepped in, only a fraction of His Majesty's endeavours are allowed to be made public. Stamfordham was willing to entertain the most esoteric ideas in order to raise the King's profile. "Personally I believe if the King would place himself at the head of the Venereal Disease movement it would be highly appreciated by his subjects. It is non-political, and yet concerns the health of the present, and the very existence of the future generations."[156] In response to this, a friend says: "I think, in a word, that we ought to observe the valuable principle of "cane ignotum pro magnifico:" *unknown becomes the dog.*[157]

For all the bluster, the incidents of anti-monarchical behaviour that physically manifest themselves are quite tame. A clergyman from Derbyshire describes a variant of republicanism that has broken out amongst local colliers. "A neighbouring village has started a club, whose members ordinarily wear no hats, but carry caps, in their pockets, which the ostentatiously put on whenever the National Anthem is sung."[158] He goes on to describe one man's beliefs that the Royal Family will do all they can to shield Wilhelm and his dynasty from the consequences of their crimes.

The *Manchester Guardian* epitomises what turns out to be the reality, that the monarchy is that entrenched in British national life, that with everything else the country has to face, "we shall probably find that the issue between republicanism and monarchy is not a vital one."[159] *The Herald* opines that "it would not benefit the masses to be governed as the masses are governed in France and America… to exchange a man of the type of the <u>King</u> George for a man of the type of <u>Lloyd George</u>."[160] Why destroy an age old system when there is no need to? When people ask, why do we need a King? The response is, why do we need a President? "In practice we do not find Republicanism an improvement upon limited monarchy," writes *The Clarion*. It appears to be "a sheer waste of energy to whip up a revolt against a King who is no more a Kaiser than Old King Cole."[161]

In hindsight the threat to the crown in 1917 may not appear particularly terrifying, but at the time; when his cousin had lost his throne, his country was being crushed under the weight of the war in its third year, with labour growing unsettled, the republican threat is, to the King, very real. The world as he knows it is caving in on itself. Nothing is sacred, and nothing is beyond destruction.

"A Very Novel and Delicate Business"

The palace gradually takes on advice about the visibility of the King, but one thing that the Monarchy can do immediately is distance itself as much as possible from its Germanic heritage.

---

155   RA PS/PSO/GV/C/Q/1104/8.
156   PA: S/13/15/32: Strachey.
157   Ibid.
158   RA PS/PSO/GV/C/Q/1104/11.
159   *The Times* 21/4/17.
160   *The Herald* 28/4/17.
161   *The Clarion* 29/6/17.

Stamping out the House of Hohenzollern is one thing, but across the country people latch onto the idea that any traces of Teutonic blood can be bred out of the British Royal Family. Germany has been an endless font of spouses, labelled *The Royal Marriage Maker*. This could clearly not go on. "So far as Britain is concerned the German royal matrimonial emporium is henceforth a bankrupt and discredited concern." One had only to review, it is said, the impact of those German brides; the Empress Alexandra and the Kaiser's sister, Sophie of Greece, to see the danger of this tradition. "History, with few exceptions, typifies them as scolding, fretful, neurotic, and narrow-minded women, disdainful of the people"[162] One can only imagine what the King would make of such a declaration, given that his beloved wife, in her origins, essentially fitted the criteria of this group.

Nonetheless His Majesty is a fretful man, and has previously proved himself to be highly sensitive to accusations about being German in origin; not a proper Englishman. "Not many centuries ago kings often chose close mates for themselves or for their sons from among the daughters of their own nobility," points out one publication. "Thus the Royal House became truly a part of the nation." Time and time again, the idea that the King's children should find spouses amongst the nobility at home is raised; specifically that David should take an English bride. "If the monarchy is to survive in the British Empire, it must speedily undergo the profoundest modification," says the *Penny Pictorial*. "The old state of affairs cannot continue... The British crown is not like other crowns. It may conceivably take a line of its own, and emerge rejuvenated from trials that may destroy every other monarchical system in the world."[163]

But David is certainly not ready for marriage, and His Majesty is anxious. He wants to do something now and is prepared to take a much more drastic step. In May 1917 he is told of the specific jibe that one only has to look at the name of the royal house: Saxe-Coburg and Gotha, to understand that he is quite obviously German. When he heard this "he started and grew pale."[164] It is incredible hurtful for both the King and Queen to hear such things given their dedication to the war effort. His subjects were never privy to the full extent of the King's anger towards Germany after the outbreak of the Great War. He had already removed the Garter banners for German or Austrian members from St George's Chapel at Windsor in 1915, with some reticence, but in 1917 the Titles Deprivation Act is introduced to strip British titles from those who had allied themselves with the enemy, despite their close blood ties to the Crown. But the King still has to address the problem of the German titles and names carried by the extended Royal Family. The King, backed unreservedly by Stamfordham intends to make some sweeping changes.

As Ponsonby explained it, His Majesty came to the conclusion that something must be done about the names of the Royal Family. He sends for Prince Louis of Battenburg and takes him into his confidence with regard to a drastic scheme that will involve members of the Royal Family being rechristened. Prince Louis concurs. "He said of course it is absurd that I should be a Prince of Battenburg, but when the war broke out I did not want to be like Schmidt who became Smith." He feels no tie to his existing title. "I have been educated in England and have been in England all my life. I am absolutely English."[165]

Whilst the King is away on engagements, Stamfordham takes the matter on and confides in Lord Rosebery. "For heavens sake keep it absolutely and sacredly private as excepting the Duke of Connaught the matter has not been mooted to those whom we propose to 'alter' - though not veterinarily!"[166] Rosebery's reply does not inspire him with confidence. He feels that "this is a very

162   *Weekly Dispatch* 8/4/17.
163   RA PS/PSO/GV/CO/1106/52.
164   Nicolson: *King George V: His Life and Reign*, p.309.
165   Rose: *King George V*, pp.174-175.
166   RA PS/PSO/GV/C/O/1153/XVI/345a.

novel and delicate business," and he is not particularly qualified to delve fully into the question, but he thinks "the country would stomach it if it was explained that it was to get rid of Teutonism, and the press was properly inspired."[167]

It is clear that the King will have to compel his relations to resign their own titles, rather take them from them forcibly, for it will save an awful lot of bother. The titles were, after all, conferred by ruling sovereigns on those who bear them. If, however, they are willing to dispense with their Germanic titles, His Majesty will compensate them with British ones. One surely cannot refuse a King, but that is not to say that His Majesty faces no familial opposition in carrying out this scheme; the worst of it from Queen Mary's brothers. Alge, styled as Alexander of Teck "was furious, as he thought that kind of camouflage stupid and petty."[168] As for Dolly, Adolphus of Teck, he provides only unsuitable names which would only be suitable for the Sovereign; and he drags his feet then complains when he doesn't like the one selected for him. As the King's shield against such awkward confrontation, Stamfordham makes the situation very clear for his disgruntled brother-in-law. "His Majesty says that it was chosen after you had failed to suggest any alternative... Then, if you remember, it was proposed that you might... invent a name from a translation of Hohenstein, but this did not appeal to you." After that, it had been "suggested that by purchasing a place the name of which you liked you could assume that as your family name." The King is adamant that the blame for Dolly having a name conferred upon him is his own. "In these circumstances His Majesty cannot now go back upon his decision and give the undertaking you ask for that you shall again make a change when the war is over. The King is confident that you will soon get accustomed to the name and the longer the family bears it, the better you will like it."[169]

Thus Dolly became a somewhat disgruntled Marquess of Cambridge. He asked for a Dukedom, but the King was only willing to confer those on his children. Alge, inwardly put out, almost became the Earl of Kendal but eventually opts for Athlone as his title instead. Louis of Battenburg willingly becomes Mountbatten and as for his two sons, both of whom are serving in the Royal Navy, George is given the courtesy title of the Earl of Medina and Louis jr. will eventually become Earl Mountbatten of Burma. Princess Beatrice's son becomes the Marquess of Carisbrooke.

More importantly, the King is not going to inflict upon his relatives that which he is not willing to do himself. He intends to change his family name and dispense with the House of Saxe-Coburg and Gotha. Firstly, experts need to be consulted as to what the King's surname is. The Royal College of Heralds is consulted, and even they are not quite sure. Queen Victoria once wrote that it was 'Guelph d'Este.' The College thinks that it is more likely Wepper, or Wettin which comes from Prince Albert. All of which sound thoroughly Teutonic and defeat the object of the exercise.

The matter is thrashed out for weeks, with multiple sources throwing their favourite choices into the mix. D'Este is a royal name that originally comes from the Duke of Medina, the second father in law of James II, but has more recently been used by George III's morganatic grandson by his 6th son, the Duke of Sussex. It doesn't sound English enough, so all involved start assessing possible names from royal dynasties of the past. The King squashes the idea of Plantagenet immediately, because though it will clarify the line of descent back to the Middle Ages, is thought too theatrical. Stamfordham's friend Lytton Strachey at *The Spectator* thinks that there can be no objection to Lancaster but the suggestion gains little traction. His Majesty doesn't care for Tudor at all, with its ties to Henry VIII and his headless wives; not to mention his daughter Bloody

167 RA PS/PSO/GV/C/O/1153//XVI/348.
168 Athlone: *For My Grandchildren*, p.160.
169 RA GV/PRIV/CC50/1377.

Mary. The Duke of Connaught suggests 'Tudor-Stewart' but the King and Queen "strongly"[170] disapprove. The suggestion of Plantaganet-Tudor-Stewart with a claim that it "would embody the principal Royal descents and could not fail to be popular with the two Kingdoms and the principality"[171] is all but ignored.

Having almost exhausted dynasties, Lord Rosebery comes up with what he thinks is a masterstroke: Fitzroy. It has royal precedence, having been the name given to Henry VIII's illegitimate son with Bessie Blount before he was made Duke of Richmond. It had also been used for some of Charles II's extra-marital offspring. And that is the key to its downfall. The Royal Family should not be named Fitz-anything, as it is traditionally a prefix used for illegitimate children (including by, at some ancient point, a rather unimaginative medieval noble who named their child "FitzOther") Stamfordham agrees that it is nice sounding, and short, but though two centuries have elapsed and Rosebery will champion his suggestion until he is blue in the face, the King and Queen will never be able to see past the connotations of the name being conferred upon royal bastards.

The most promising suggestion by far appears to be Stewart. The King's claim to the throne descends from that house on the one hand, so His Majesty could certainly be entitled to use it. The Queen wanted it, and so His Majesty; but there is opposition, including from the speaker of the House of Lords. Asquith points out that one Stuart was beheaded and another run out of the country. He dines with Rosebery and the Archbishop of Canterbury to discuss the matter and both agree that it is not ideal, and so Stewart is discarded. "It is disastrous," cries Stamfordham to Rosebery, "that [we] cannot produce a name which is the foundation upon which the new fabric must be raised."[172]

Then there is an epiphany in the middle of June. The suggestion is Windsor, and Stamfordham is delighted with it, if only it was not already taken as the family name of Lord Plymouth. In fact, the name has been used liberally throughout history. The Governor of Windsor Castle had adopted it in Norman times and it had been in use until Henry VIII made the bearer of the title give up the name and his lands so that he might then exchange the latter for much larger swathes of territory freed up by the dissolution of the monasteries further from London. But as for Lord Plymouth, Windsor is in fact merely a second courtesy title, and hasn't been used in over 200 years, so far as Stamfordham or anyone else can make out.

None of these facts need stop a determined King from adopting the name if he so wishes, and he does. After discussing it with numerous, trustworthy confidants, he remains extremely keen. "I am quite sure Windsor is the best for my family name."[173] By the first week in July His Majesty is busy with finalising the wording of the proclamation that will make him the first reigning sovereign of the House of Windsor. "Do you realise that you have christened a dynasty?" Rosebery writes to Stamfordham. "There are few people in the world who have done this, none I think. It is really something to be historically proud of. I admire and envy you."[174] "At 10:30," the King writes in his diary on 17th July 1917, "I declared that my house should have the name of Windsor and that I relinquished all my German titles for myself and family. I also informed the council that May and I had decided some time ago that our children would be allowed to marry into British families. It was quite an historical occasion."[175]

170   RA PS/PSO/GV/C/O/1153/XVI/347.
171   RA PS/PSO/GV/C/O/1153/XIV/251.
172   RA PS/PSO/GV/C/O/1153/XVI/348a.
173   RA PS/PSO/GV/C/O/1153/XXII/425.
174   RA PS/PSO/GV/C/O/1153/XVI/354.
175   RA GV/PRIV/GVD/1917 (17/7).

In Germany, Wilhelm mocks his cousin. "The Kaiser let it be known that he would be delighted to attend a performance of that well-known opera, "The Merry Wives of Saxe Coburg Gotha." And a Bavarian nobleman says: "The true royal tradition died on that day in 1917 when, for a mere war, King George V changed his name."[176] But in fact a Government memo records that severing all ties "has infuriated them, however much they may pretend to ridicule it in the press."[177] And however bitter Wilhelm was, or how funny his people found the move, in Britain, the creation of the House of Windsor rebranded the Royal Family for the 20th Century; into something quintessentially English, and as a side effect proved to be a stunning piece of PR by the King and his advisers. His Majesty's proclamation prompted an outbreak of patriotic fervour that reinvigorated a country exhausted by war. Credit for the move is showered upon the King. Once again it is said that he "has the happy faculty of doing the right thing at the right time and in the right way."[178] His Majesty is perceived as having drawn the British monarchy closer to its people. "King George's decision marks another step in his democratic progress. It takes him further along that path of nationalism in which his feet have been set ever since he came to the throne… He has been steadily and more and more proving himself the representative and the expression, so to say, of the people. He is no figurehead of a monarchical government, no mere dummy on a throne set far above those in whose hands are really the mechanism of our prosperity and peace and glory. But he more and more evinces his aim and his power to show forth in its highest form that which is the real spirit of the nation."[179]

"373 to 50"

In the midst of all of the anxiety in the opening months of 1917, there are reasons to be positive. On 11th March, General "Stanley" Maude achieves the incredible feat of conquering Baghdad. Telegrams of congratulation pour into the palace from Allies. "It is with the greatest satisfaction that I have received the good news," says the King in a telegram to Maude. "I heartily congratulate you and your troops on this success achieved under so many difficulties."[180] But by far the most significant improvement in war affairs comes when the United States finally joins the war on the side of the Allies. Even after the sinking of the *Lusitania*, America had remained divided. This was unsurprising when one considered the disparate interests of all of the recent immigrants who had sailed there. Reports from the British Ambassador in Washington D.C. are a muddle of problematic issues which it seems impossible to circumvent. "The country… turns away from all national questions, and still more from all world questions." But he cannot see an American alliance with Germany and Turkey, more that she will remain neutral, because "still the old cry of "down with England!" has… great weight, and the characteristic tone of the press, however hostile to Germany; is constantly and invariably unfriendly to England."[181]

In February 1916 Colonel House meets with Stamfordham on his return from Germany, bursting with impressions; gossip about the court and political intrigue. The country was, he said, convinced "that victory will be found in the submarine and mine - the sole object of Germany today is the destruction of England. They do not renounce the hope of a separate peace with Russia, the same with Italy. They will try to do the same with France. It is only with England that they will never

176   Rose: *King George V,* pp.174-175.
177   RA PS/PSO/GV/C/Q/1552/8a.
178   *The Record* 19/7/17.
179   *Ladies Pictorial* 23/6/17.
180   *The Times* 5/3/17.
181   RA PS/PSO/GV/C/Q/1110/3.

attempt to make a separate peace: they want to destroy her."[182] House had revised his predictions and thought that in a years' time, America will have joined the Allies. By that summer, the whole question was being skewed by the upcoming presidential election, thanks to huge blocks of German and Irish voters that no candidate wanted to alienate by cozying up to the Allies. "The simple facts are that this country has, in the course of past years protested on behalf of Greece, of Hungary, of Poland, of Italy and of the Jews in Romania and Russia… But no measure has been introduced in congress on behalf of Belgium, or of the French or of the Armenians." The British Ambassador cynically points out why. "The reason of this is not a desire to abstain from interference, or a disbelief in the hideous stories most abundantly proved, but simply and solely a fear of abstaining proved, but simply and solely a fear of alienating a certain number of votes."[183] In November Woodrow Wilson carried 30 states using slogans like *He Keeps Us Out of War,* and *America First.* But he manages to keep his country out of the Great War for no more than five months.

At the beginning of February 1917, Germany's renewed determination to starve Britain towards defeat using unrestricted submarine warfare finally breaks the dam. It is a calculated decision. The Germans know that America might enter the war against them as a result, but they are banking on being able to win it before the United States can send enough proficiently trained troops into battle to tip the balance in the Allies' favour. Two days after the Germans announce their naval policy, Wilson severs diplomatic relations. Then on 26th February, British Intelligence intercepts a message on the way to a German representative in Mexico City, telling him that he is to offer the Mexican Government New Mexico, Texas and Arizona in exchange for an alliance against the United States. With fresh losses of American lives at the hands of German submarines, Wilson goes to Congress, and on 7th April the King notes in his diary that "the United States of America declared war against Germany yesterday by a large majority in the Congress; 373 to 50."[184] It is an immense relief to the Allied war effort. There are immediate diplomatic functions for the King to perform, beginning with the obligatory telegram from one head of state to another. "I desire on behalf of my Empire to offer my heartfelt congratulations to you on the entry of the United States of America into war for the great ideals so nobly set forth in your speech."[185] A week later the American Ambassador came to Windsor Castle with his wife. The King has a long talk with Mr Page, who assures him that his country will do anything they can for the war effort.

A gathering is quickly organised at St. Paul's: "A service of dedication at which Americans in London will consecrate themselves, their lives, their fortunes, everything they are and have, to the war of democracy against Hohenzollernism." Mr Page, who has referred to America joining the Allies as "the supreme political event of all history,"[186] is to attend, as are as many Americans in London as can be squeezed under the cathedrals famous dome. The press quickly dub it "America Day," and similar services are quickly organised at Manchester, Hull and Birmingham. The King and Queen will be making the journey from Windsor Castle especially; accompanied by the Duke of Connaught, Princess Mary and other members of the Royal Family.

Their Majesties climb into a horse drawn carriage at Paddington, encouraged by a group of female porters and carriage cleaners who "raise a lusty feminine cheer," and receive the King's salute. The weather is unseasonably kind, and the crowds pegged back behind besieged barriers shout: "Bravo

182   RA PS/PS/GV/C/Q/839/7.
183   RA PS/PSO/GV/C/Q/1110/7.
184   RA GV/PRIV/GVD/1917 (7/4).
185   *The Times* 8/4/17.
186   *The Times* 21/4/17.

America!"[187] London's streets are awash with red, white and blue; a seamless blend of Union Jacks and the Stars and Stripes; Selfridges and other West End shops have done a roaring trade in the latter and there are no more to be had. Trafalgar Square is encircled with both, with Nelson's Column as a centre piece; "bathed in the sunlight of a perfect spring morning."[188] For the first time in history a foreign flag is hoisted alongside the Union Flag on the Victoria Tower at Westminster. "No other flag other than the Royal Standard or the Union Jack has ever been run up the parliamentary flagstaff."[189] The two are hoisted at 8:00 am and flutter lazily together in a light breeze until sunset. Nearly two dozen veterans of the American Civil War, proudly wearing their medals and carrying Union Jacks, march to the cathedral just ahead of the King and Queen. Packed with over 3,000 worshippers, the cathedral is "washed in a vivid grey-olive light." An American, Bishop Brent, preaches a solemn sermon, a "service to almighty God on the occasion of the entry of the United States of America into the Great War for freedom." *God Save the King* is sung along with *the Star Spangled Banner* and *the Battle Hymn of the Republic.* Sitting beside his mother, the King is impressed.

But it will be months before America is ready to put troops into the field, and a full year at least before she can start doing so in large numbers. Balfour, as a recognisable statesmen; though "in his 69th year and a bad sailor"[190] has been sent west and having been met at the Canadian border he travels to Washington to find that there is a crushing amount of work to do: in munitions and war material, how to render naval assistance to the Allies, the departure and arrival in Europe of the American Expeditionary Force, recruitment, hospital ships, export restrictions for the enemy and finance. A British Admiral on site early reports directly to the King that "It is evident... that they are very unready, this however they fully realise, and there was an entire absence of false pride and jealousy in acknowledging their short comings, and asking us frankly for advice and assistance."[191] And a War Office memo received at the palace says that America is better off than Britain was in August 1914.

The plan as it stands is to get a division to Europe as quickly as possible. In the meantime the King dutifully entertains the advance guard; the commander of the American fleet who comes to settle matters with Jellicoe, American military attaches, commissioners of the American Red Cross. Colonel House is soon in London at the head of a mission and the King is on hand to visit an American Officers' Club that has immediately sprung up in Chesterfield Gardens. The Canadian Pacific Line have donated the furniture, the Office of Works has helped and there is a library filled with American journals, a billiards room, bedrooms which Queen Mary thinks look very bright and comfortable.

At the end of May, 25 doctors and 68 nurses bound for British hospitals to start gaining experience immediately arrive in London. From Cleveland, they are given a reception in the gardens at Buckingham Palace; with "white lilies in full bloom, masses of Rhododendron, crimson and mauve."[192] Two weeks later the King receives General Pershing and his staff, who have just arrived in Britain and are set to go to France to make arrangements for the arrival of the first troops. There are no speeches. His Majesty shakes Pershing warmly by the hand and finds the General utterly charming. They engage in a long conversation. "The General is struck by the "charm and simplicity" of his reception, but somewhat embarrassed when the King, explaining he was 'not a politician and

187 *Daily Telegraph* 19/4/17.
188 *The Telegraph* 21/4/17.
189 *The Times* 21/4/17.
190 *Daily Telegraph* 11/6/17.
191 RA PS/PSO/GV/C/Q/832/380.
192 *Daily Telegraph* 24/5/17.

did not see things from their point of view', expressed the hope that as many as possible of the American troops would serve with the British Army." Pershing doesn't quite understand what he means and replies "that America was determined to create an army of her own."[193]

In August the first large bodies of troops march through London via Trafalgar Square and Piccadilly to where Mr Page is waiting for them on the balcony of the embassy in Grosvenor Square. Then it is on to Buckingham Palace. Whilst he is waiting, the King looks out from his window at the palace and sees that the steps of the Victoria Memorial are empty. He sends an order downstairs, and hundreds of wounded men in blue, women and children are picked out of the crowd and given this prime spot to watch the march past. Queen Mary is ill, so Queen Alexandra joins her son, dressed all in black with an arrangement of pink carnations at her waist to see the first ever body of American troops march through London; "fine, muscular, athletic men."[194]

The King is proving popular with Britain's new Allies already. "What impressed them the most about England? "The King!" They tell a representative of the *Daily Mail*. These particular soldiers were inspected by His Majesty at their camp soon after their arrival:

> We thought before the King came there would be a lot of fuss. Some of our boys expected to see him strutting about with a golden crown on his head, and most of us thought there would be a good deal of ceremony. We expected him to be surrounded by a big staff and hedged in and very much on his dignity. But what happened was quite different. He came along just like you or me. There wasn't any crowd… He didn't strut, but just behaved like a straight common sense kind of man. He was wearing no frills and was right down to his job. He knew all about us. He knew many of our names. He talked with the boys who were around just like anyone else might have done.[195]

In France, enthusiasm for impending American participation in the war trumped anything seen in England. Suddenly, much to the consternation of the King's subjects living in Paris, such as Lord Esher; it is as if Britain no longer existed at all. Jealousy over the very sudden and complete transfer of French affections is prevalent for the rest of the war. "Paris is awash with American flags and you want a strong field glass to find a Union Jack," Esher tells Stamfordham at the end of April. He wryly refers to the short memories of the French and notes, "our position in France is becoming a secondary one."[196]

More importantly, Esher deprecates the immediate effect that the promise of tens of thousands of American soldiers arriving in the distant future will have on France's motivation. Following the failure of Nivelle's offensive Esher admits to Stamfordham that they have been "going through somewhat agitated moments here. The failure of French hopes about their offensive, hopes that were pitched too high by Nivelle's florid talk when first appointed to command," has been depressing to watch. The Government is reeling. Rather than wishing to press forward in the quest for victory, "the French view of the whole position is that having lost one million <u>dead.</u> They cannot afford to lose another million. This would mean to them an atrophic existence hereafter."[197] He rather thinks that it is going to be hard work to get France to do much. "The entry of America into the war makes our position more and not less, difficult. The temptation to procrastinate, the mirage of countless millions of men… are likely to prove fatal, unless the mode of handling the people changes and

193   Syonsby, Lord: *Recollections of Three Reigns*, p.317.
194   *Daily Telegraph* 16/8/17.
195   *Daily Mail* 17/9/17.
196   RA PS/PS/GV/C/Q/724/93.
197   Ibid.

improves."[198] His fears are not unfounded at all. In fact in the same week Repington of *The Times* is apparently told by Nivelle's replacement that "his role would be to 'hold on' by an 'aggressive defensive and await the advent of American armies.' These he proposes should be trained by French officers and <u>commanded</u> by them. The plan has already been sent to the United States. How will the most conceited people in the world receive it?"[199] Esher is an astute man, and as he has already told Lloyd George that "England alone can direct this war to a satisfactory ending."[200] Plans are already in existence for the summer campaign that will follow the Nivelle debacle. Attention will turn north to Belgium and the bulk of responsibility for trying to end the war in 1917 will fall to Haig and his force east of Ypres. Esher's guess about a French unwillingness to proceed and the information apparently given to Repington appear to hold water. At the beginning of May, Haig gathers his subordinates and tells them that the objective of the British and French armies will be to try and wear down the German Army before striking a decisive blow on the Ypres front, which will hopefully press through and secure the Belgian coast.

"No Eyewash"

At home, the war effort is taking its toll on the British people, including the King and Queen; but with recommendations about becoming as publicly visible as possible coming into the palace from all quarters, there can be no let up. And, pulled in multiple directions, Their Majesties are about to embark on a harrowing summer schedule to try and help publicly drive the country to victory. "Never in the records of the British monarchy had King and Queen striven so systematically and so thoroughly to bring themselves into direct touch with the people of the land, not by taking part in spectacular displays or presiding over big functions, but by going down among them and mixing freely together."[201] During the latter part of the war, the modern concept of public relations continues to be shaped and expanded at the palace. It not always a smooth path, for there is much to be learned and new boundaries to be established, but at least Stamfordham is displaying a sense of humour about this unavoidable encroachment into royal life. "I met Lord Stamfordham yesterday outside Buckingham Palace," says one newspaper man while the King is away visiting factories. "He seemed quite hilarious, and when I asked him what was the source of his amusement he replied; "the newspapers."[202]

Though the King is having to come to terms with the idea of making himself more visible to this subjects in the work that he already does, he is still utterly repulsed by the idea of doing anything merely for the benefits of publicity. At one point David refers to something his father had done as "good propaganda". His father retorts: "I do things because they are my duty, not as propaganda."[203] But even if the King hates to dwell on it, the benefits of proper public relations are now apparent. Stamfordham, in truth, has more important things on his plate than forging relations with the press. Ponsonby has still got one foot in the reign of Queen Victoria: "I think there is a risk in your making yourself too accessible," he tells David. "The Monarchy must always retain an element of mystery... must always remain on a pedestal."[204] Of all the King's advisers and confidants, it is Clive Wigram that is the trailblazer at the palace. "I think that in the past there has been a tendency to

198   RA PS/PS/GV/C/Q/724/95.
199   RA PS/PS/GV/C/Q/724/93.
200   RA PS/PS/GV/C/Q/724/95.
201   Hammerton: *Our King & Queen: A Pictorial Record of Their Lives*, pp.34-39.
202   *Daily Mirror* 18/5/17.
203   Rose: *King George V,* p.170.
204   Ibid., pp.226-268.

despise and ignore, if not insult the press, which is a powerful weapon in the 20th century," he tells a friend in 1917. "I have been working very hard to try and get Their Majesties a good press, and have been to the Press Bureau and other places. I hope you may have noticed that the movements of the King have been better chronicled lately."[205] He fully realises that such work is an assault on any republican whisperings. He tells Haig that His Majesty must put himself out there for the public to see. To encourage the cooperation of newspapers, he wants a full time representative of the press working from Buckingham Palace to this end, "and sufficient sums for propaganda purposes would be forthcoming."[206] It may not sound like he is asking for a lot, but it is radical at the time.

In the meantime, the War Cabinet agreed in May 1917 that "the present restrictions on the publication of His Majesty's movements were unreasonable, and that much wider publicity should be given."[207] There follows a relaxation the rules concerning the King's movements at home. In addition, His Majesty approves that as long as the Press Bureau checked to make sure they did not compromise royal security, they will be allowed to print prospective announcements. They are provided with full programmes of where the King is going and what he is doing and in the main, the royal willingness to try and move with the times on the point of public relations begins to pay off immediately in terms of the country's impression of the King and Queen's war work.

Labour is restless. There is a feeling that employers will use war conditions to exploit the working man; that they are banking huge profits. But perhaps worst of all is the widely spread suspicion that speculators are forcing the price of supplies up, and that they are making their fortunes out of the hard-earned money of the working-classes. Lloyd George and is Government are worried, and so they ask the King to go back out on the road to munition production centres, shipyards and factories to try and imbue the workers with some patriotic enthusiasm. After sundry visits to Ponders End, Hayes, Watford and Woking, the real hard work begins. It is a bold move. "Timid employers and directors whispered to themselves that there might be hostile demonstrations,"[208] and everything has been thrown together at comparatively short notice. Nonetheless in the face of republican rumblings, some eight weeks after the Russian revolution, the King sets out for Cheshire with Queen Mary, who is determined to share in this work with him. Once there, their programmes will diverge in order to cover more ground. Since His Majesty's last expedition out into the world of war labour, industry has expanded greatly and so there are infinite new institutions and facilities on which they can spend their time. Throughout this new spell of visits there are very distinctive stops in each locality: the workers, the wounded, an investiture and a meeting with local trade unionists so that His Majesty might discuss with them their current concerns.

The King visits a vast new explosives factory employing 8,000 men and women. His Majesty is challenged at the entrance to declare any contraband he carries. He thinks this is great sport and surrenders a gold cigarette and match case and removes his spurs, putting on rubber overshoes to inspect TNT and gun cotton processes. At a chain and anchor works, the men continue about their business as the King moves through. He watches men at workbenches streaking with sweat as they beat links into shape with their hammers and makes remarks how hard they are working. Across the Mersey, His Majesty meets a group of Merchant Mariners that have been torpedoed thus far in the war, before he stops at a shipyard which employs 13,000 hands. In the building berths the King falls behind schedule on account of his incessant questions. "Amidst cheers a grey headed little man was brought from the bowels of one of the ships and presented to the King. His name is McKinley,

---

205   PP CW May 1917.
206   Rose: *King George V,* p.159.
207   TNA: CAB 23/2/54.
208   Hammerton: *Our King & Queen: A Pictorial Record of Their Lives,* pp.34-39.

and he has 32 relatives serving with the colours." The King is astonished.

"I think I have heard of you before," he says. "I sent you a letter last December." "Yes, Your Majesty," says the old hand. The King smiles. "I think we may call your family *The Fighting Macs*."

His Majesty sees another man missing a leg. Knowing a little something of the advances in artificial limbs through his visits, the King asks him if he has one. William Astbury, wounded at Gallipoli, replies that it is too sore for him to wear one.

"What kind of job have you in the works?" Asks His Majesty.

"Oh a soft one," was the answer.

"I hope it will always remain so, enjoined the King with a smile."[209]

There is no time for rest as he heads inland. Manchester and Didsbury are even more enthusiastic to see Their Majesties. The King and Queen motor through the city for dense, cheering crowds. Veterans of the Indian Mutiny and even the Crimean War are singled out to meet His Majesty. He clocks in at the Westinghouse Factory as worker #10,001, where one man tells the King that he has done 26 years in the army, and being no good anymore for soldiering, is glad to do his bit at the bench. "I am very proud of you and all like you," says His Majesty.[210]

At Warrington the King is mesmerised by the blast furnaces, he stands staring into a great fountain of sparks spraying from the Bessemer converter; turning industrial amounts of molten pig iron into steel. At Barrow, 12,000 school children line the route. His Majesty saw the Vickers works two years previously, but they are almost beyond recognition; now employing 35,000 people. He spends three hours going over them in minute detail, and the rolling mills. "At every town, village, or cluster of cottages by which the royal train passed, men, women and children were waiting beside the railway. Even among the hills, miles from any village, small knots of people stood on the embankment to cheer and wave a loyal greeting." In Cumberland, the boys of St Bees College left their cricket and tennis and lined the railway fence, "a picturesque guard in flannels, while hundreds of young children grouped on the cricket pitch waved and shouted."[211] By the King's desire the train moves past them slowly so that he will have time to wave a greeting.

Throughout the tour His Majesty is taking every opportunity to ask workers about their welfare and current labour issues. More lengthy discussions are held with labour leaders and trade union secretaries. There are nine at Barrow alone, including a lady from the National Federation of Women Workers. "What do you think of the recent labour trouble?" he asks one. The secretary replies: "We came out as a protest against what we considered the real grievance of other workmen, but having registered our protest we resumed operations." The King evidently appreciates the man's frankness, shakes him cordially by the hand. "I hope you will now remain at your work, for the nation needs all the service that every one of us can give."[212] 3,000 engineers had come out on strike the morning of his visit to the Mersey shipyards, and the directors held their breath; "but we got an excellent reception at every one, very civil." The fact is even more gratifying given that His Majesty has passed through neighbourhoods densely populated by Irish communities. At another location, a firm telegraphs ahead to London that his men are coming out on strike; earnestly advising that the King should think about postponing his visit. His Majesty replies that he is going to visit the place, strike or no strike; and he did.

Then the King and Queen press further north, where the wind becomes more frigid and the spring sunshine disappears. Everyone is told that there is to be "no eyewash."[213] His Majesty wants

209   *Daily Telegraph* 17/5/17.
210   Ibid.
211   *The Times* 18/5/17.
212   *Morning Post* 17/5/17.
213   *Daily Graphic* 2/6/17.

no ceremony, no expenditure on decorations, no red carpet. He motors to Gretna for a long visit to the new Government explosives outfit; "it covers ten square miles and over 16,000 men and women are employed there. A wonderful place,"[214] says the King. The newspapers nickname it *Cordite Town*. There are 85 hostels for 6,200 workers, married quarters for 550 families, bungalows, a central kitchen, a bakery, two laundries, a private police force and a postal service, two schools, cinema halls, recreation rooms, banks, shops, and three canteens. There is even a factory railway service to bring people in and out.

His Majesty's "week with the workers" has been a success with the press. By rail, car and foot, the days have been strenuous, and the amount of information thrown at the King and the trail of journalists behind them is bewildering, "but among all the confused impressions of the happenings of the week one is clear... From first to the last the tour has been the occasion of a wonderful demonstration of affectionate loyalty by the King's subjects of all ages and all classes... Workers everywhere have welcomed them with a heartiness which was convincingly real."[215]

Their Majesties arrive back to a London "of sunshine and brilliance with dancing daffodils in the grassy border outside the palace gardens, and bushes bursting into bloom in the park beyond."[216] His Majesty has also begun to take on board recommendations to sit and talk with the leading representatives of labour and unions and the depth of The King's interest and empathy is beginning to be revealed. Will Thorne, the MP and activist, stops in at Buckingham Palace following a visit to Russia. He speaks to a journalist about his impressions. His visit "was marked by an entire absence of formality or convention." He has never been to see His Majesty before.

> During my conversation with the King we passed from the narrative of my experiences in Russia to talk of labour matters at home, and during the half hours' conversation we had together I told His Majesty some solid homely truths... The King, I thought, showed considerable knowledge of many matters affecting the workers generally, and his pointed references to them showed that he understood keenly and appreciatively some of the causes of unrest in the labour world. Certainly he had no misgivings about my own point of view.[217]

Another labour representative was just as surprised.

> Frank himself, [His Majesty] encourages frankness in others... as the King in an easy lounge suit sat back in his chair held forth in an animated strain, with vivid movements and gestures and an occasional burst of hearty laughter, or turned upon me a Lewis gun of questions as to the state of feeling in a belligerent country from which I have just returned, or expounded earnestly his view of the kingly office, I realised how little I had known him and how many were the gaps in my preconception of his personality. The King is proud of his Kingship, proud of his country and the Empire, proud of his stock, but there is no swagger in his pride, it acts upon him simply as a call to spend all he has of energy and devotion in the service of his peoples. The ruler of the state, he is also its first and hardest working servant.[218]

214   *Morning Post 2/6/18.*
215   *The Times 19/5/17.*
216   *The Queen 19/5/17.*
217   *The Times 31/5/17.*
218   Ibid.

"We Really Can't Take It All Lying Down"

The Home Front has been swallowed whole by the war by 1917, and the King cannot avoid an interest in the air war conducted over British skies, for it reaches new and frightening levels of destruction. He monitors technical advancements and what their impact might be, reading in one operational summary that the Germans had produced new aeroplanes. "His Majesty read in the account that the Germans had a useful new three seater," writes Wigram to the authorities. "Would you be so kind as to let me know for His Majesty's information whether you think these aeroplanes are in any way equal to ours, and whether they are likely to cause us much trouble?"[219] He is still determined to press the authorities on the matter of anti-aircraft defences too. In June 1917 the King goes out after dinner to see the Observation Room in Spring Gardens. "They explained exactly what happens in a Zeppelin raid on London, which was most interesting."[220] He visits the victims, and if neither he nor the Queen can get to them, they send telegrams and gifts of sympathy. They are not necessarily prompt, because it takes time to gather information, but secret air reports are sent to His Majesty for him to read too. He sees detailed descriptions of the progress of each airship, miles covered, bombs dropped, damage caused, action taken against them.

The first reference to a new menace comes in the King's diary on the 28th November 1916. "An aeroplane came over London at 12 today and dropped six bombs, did very little damage, a few people were slightly wounded."[221] He is told that the German was later brought down at Dunkirk; and goes out with Queen Mary to see the damage where a bomb has hit the roof of a mews in Eton Square. But six months later London falls victim to a new concept in aerial raids. It marks one of several that are an "entirely new phase of German aerial attacks against this country. Previous air raids had either taken the form of night raids carried out by rigid airships, or of daylight raids by single aeroplanes or seaplane. On a few occasions a group of the smaller aircraft reached these shores, but made off again."[222] The intelligence fed to the King is that new types of aeroplanes have been specially designed for flying at greater heights, and for carrying a heavy load of bombs. These aircraft begin to travel in large formations, almost twenty at a time so far as can be made out, and are deeply distressing for the authorities.

They have been twice before. sweeping across the coast behind a flight leader coordinating their movements. On the first occasion they found Folkestone: rest camps and the railway stations. They had cast shadows over Medway on their second visit, but they got tied up in knots. Then on 13th June they make straight for London and find the City. It is the most devastating raid of the war on the King's capital. This raid is like nothing the people of London have ever seen before. The concentration of bombs exceeds anything attempted by airships. The city has not yet been bombed by more than a couple of those at a time, and now there are more than a dozen planes dropping as many bombs as thirty of those could have done. They come from a greater height too, meaning that "their penetrating capacity and, in the case of the small bomb, the adoption of a delay action fuse has rendered the aeroplanes for more deadly than the airships."[223]

Opposite the Tower of London, the scene at the Royal Mint is terrifying. Four are killed and nearly 50 wounded as thousands of panes of glass exploded from their frames and showered onto the workforce, and into the machinery. Casualties are dispersed to hospitals across the area; the walking wounded being treated as far afield as King's College, the German Hospital and the Great

219   RA PS/PSO/GV/C/Q/978/1.
220   RA GV/PRIV/GVD/1917 (11/6).
221   RA GV/PRIV/GVD/1916 (28/11).
222   RA PS/PSO/GV/C/Q/776/20.
223   RA PS/PSO/GV/C/Q/776/20.

Northern. The Metropolitan takes nearly sixty casualties, five of whom do not survive their injuries but the two main depositories are St. Bart's and the London, the latter of which receives 200 victims, with more than two dozen succumbing to their wounds.

His Majesty has been having lunch with his mother, but he immediately wants to go out and see what he can do. He visits both of the main hospitals. They are supposed to receive warnings of air raids in order to get ready to receive casualties, but on this occasion the rattling of the windows and the blasts of the anti-aircraft guns are all the notice they have had. Dying civilians are on the doorstep of St. Bart's within minutes. When the King arrives off duty staff are rushing in to help, ambulances are arriving, Londoners are dragging and carrying the worst cases in on improvised stretchers made out of shop shutters; wrapped in blankets and even tablecloths. Passengers have jumped from buses at the scene and helped to reload them with the wounded, and bulk casualties screech to a halt outside the hospital doors with female conductors and drivers doing all they can to help. Many are cases of shock, and His Majesty watches doctors administer morphine to women with the hair singed from their heads. The hospital is in chaos, there is blood everywhere. Many patients require emergency operations and the King watches surgeons attempting to save a man whose knee has been blown away. "All very sad, these damned Germans are indeed beasts dropping bombs on London."[224]

And then there are the bodies, many of them unidentifiable. "Some were black, as if they had passed through a furnace." One man's watch still, ticks on his wrist. "Another who lost her life was a handsome young woman of 20 odd. She had a refined face, which had not been disfigured like others that were injured beyond recognition. And then there are tiny, lacerated bodies of children killed in the blast."[225] His Majesty does not want to obstruct the work of the hospital, and so he keeps out of the way, passing through four or five wards and talking quietly to those who are conscious. They cannot quite believe that they are talking to the King, that he has rushed to their sides in the midst of the carnage.

The saddest effect of the German raid on 13th June is the loss of nearly twenty children in Poplar whose school received a direct hit. Almost all of them were five years old. The local authority has received the parents' consent to bury them together in a special grave in East London. At the funeral service the Bishop of London reads a message from His Majesty:

> The King asks that you will assure the parents of those children who were killed… how His Majesty and the Queen are thinking of them in their saddened homes, especially today, when the bodies of their little ones are laid to rest. The early ending of young, innocent lives, at all times pathetic, is made more so than ever in these cruel and tragic circumstances. Their Majesties pray that the mourners may be blessed with God's help and comfort in their sorrow.[226]

In the meantime, the perpetrators of this tragedy have got away, but most of the discussion in the weeks following the 13th June bombing raid is not about making the Germans pay for their actions. The King gives orders for the Military Wing at St. Bart's to keep him updated on the progress of the victims, but he wants to know how the authorities intend to make sure that there is no repeat of this outrage. Stamfordham is informed that "the King wishes you to find out what the Government proposes to do as regards future air raids in London. His Majesty says that he is against reprisals on principle, but at the same time he thinks that we should warn the Germans that we will

224   RA GV/PRIV/GVD/1917 (3/6).
225   *Daily Telegraph* 14/6/17.
226   RA PSO/GV/C/QQ13/WAR/5547.

bombard their... towns if they continue any further attacks on [ours]."[227] *The Times* reports that expanded innovations are to be introduced at train stations; including illuminated signs, buzzers. A conference of teachers resolves to introduce air warnings to schools, and to dismiss their pupils when they are sounded. Throughout the remainder of the war the threat of raids and the sound of gunfire in London becomes a not infrequent occurrence. On a personal level the King abhors the "beastly noise,"[228] but anti-aircraft fire causes injury too. The Architect of Public Works visits the palace to inspect Their Majesties' rooms with a view to protecting them more extensively than the simple wire net across the roof, and there are evacuation plans in place for the Royal Family.

The King grows progressively more angry as the war goes on with regard to the threat of German airmen to civilians. "I am glad today on the way back to Germany the French brought down four of them and perhaps another,"[229] he says after a raid on Piccadilly Circus in October. After another attack in December, he refers to the instigators as "those brutal Huns,"[230] the first time he has referred to enemy using that term in in his diary. By the end of the year he has advocated at least threatening Germany with reprisals. And he has allegedly said to a local vicar at one area of devastation: "I wish the people who are against retaliation could see this wreckage."[231] His Majesty has abandoned his original stance, which was that Britain should not lower herself to the same level as the Germans and that she could then emerge from the war with her morality intact. "If the Germans go on with these raids in London," he writes to Stamfordham two days after the June raid on London, "we ought certainly to bomb their towns. I am against reprisals, but we really can't take it all lying down."[232] The image of George VI walking in the ruins of London during the Second World War is far better known than the precedent, the work of his father. As well as a royal determination on the part of Their Majesties to share in the sufferings of their city, one thing that continues to emerge after the raid in London in June 1917 is the spirit that will come to symbolise the capital during the Blitz a quarter of a century later. Visiting one destroyed street, the Queen is "greatly amused at the spirit of the woman claiming to be bomb proof, who told him she had eaten nothing but dust and plaster since Friday night."[233] "We are proud of the people of London!" Declares *The Telegraph*. "They were suddenly reminded, under conditions somewhat unnerving, that they were not outside the war area, as defined by the Germans. They heard the engine pulsing above them; the noises of the street traffic were drowned by the explosion of bombs, many people saw their fellow creatures struck down before their eyes. In such circumstances, face to face with the fruits of Kultur,"[234] they stood resolved to carry on. That evening flowers began to arrive from the Queen for victims in hospitals across the city, and in the days that follow, with Princess Mary she visits three hospitals, taking gifts of bags of clothing, tobacco for the men, decorative items like teapots or chintz boxes for the women.

"A Splendid Reception Everywhere"

Their Majesties are forced to leave the victims of the air raid in order to get to King's Cross. In a stuffy carriage they eat dinner as the engine pulls out of the station and gets underway. The royal train reaches Picton, where it has conspired to be a cool summer evening, much appreciated after

227 RA PS/PSO/GV/C/Q/989/17.
228 RA GV/PRIV/GVD/1917 (1/11).
229 RA GV/PRIV/GVD/1917 (20/10).
230 RA GV/PRIV/GVD/1917 (6/12).
231 *Daily Mail* 22/10/17.
232 RA PS/PSO/GV/C/O/1153/XXII/425.
233 *Daily Mail* 22/10/17.
234 *Daily Telegraph* 14/6/17.

the heat of the train. Yorkshire could have been a dicey location for a Kingly visit given the gentle undercurrent of republican talk, but after the first day of work His Majesty proudly states: "Had a most successful day, glorious weather, hot sun and got a splendid reception everywhere."[235]

At Stockton, in the midst of a huge crowd there is a carriage for the King and Queen. "Children in bright clean pinafores strained their voices to swell the volume of their greeting. On the pavements, in the doorways and at upper windows women cheered heartily."[236] It is only half a mile to their destination, and Their Majesties decide to walk, "the same as you and me."[237] They wind through narrow, old fashioned streets, the locals giving them a rousing reception and children waving tiny flags. Women crowd on their doorsteps in surprise to see what all the commotion is about. "Hundreds of people fell in behind the official party and cheered and cheered again as they went along. The incident was immensely popular."[238]

In one day the King and Queen visit eleven establishments at Stockton, Middlesbrough and West Hartlepool; travelling between them by boat, meeting sweating, grimy workers toiling in shipyards. Firms have attached bunting to masts, streamers upon every pole and railing. For miles on the Tees there is little to see but blast furnaces, towering slag heaps and slipways. "Smoke pouring from a hundred stacks, glimpses of fierce light where furnaces blazed, piles of pig iron, weather beaten ships in dock, new ships clearly painted and the gaunt skeletons of ships recently begun."[239] Drifting smoke sometimes blocks out the sun. At one point the boat passes an internment camp for German prisoners, who stop their work on the slag heaps, removing material suitable to make roads and they gaze curiously at the passing spectacle. Most are stony faced and silent, several stand to attention. One even waves. At the end of each long day His Majesty climbs back aboard his train and as it races off to the next town he begins work on his boxes, delivered by messenger. The King is much gratified by the crowds, for he worries still about the spectre of republicanism. "Our visits here have so far gone off most successfully," he tells Stamfordham from Wearside, "glorious weather but the heat rather adds to the fatigue. The people here are most enthusiastic"[240]

"Another beautiful hot day with a breeze,"[241] his Majesty reports the following morning, with his naval penchant for keeping an eye on the weather. He is to visit all of the Wear's principal shipyards in the morning. At Sunderland he enters one premises where the workers have scratched 'We will deliver the ships' in yellow chalk on the partly built hull of a cargo ship. At Sir James Laing and Sons' yard he spies on the edge of a crowd a tiny boy in a greasy cap, "his face was smutted and his clothes were well worn." His Majesty asks for him to be brought over. He presents himself as John Cassidy and the King bends right down to look him in the eye so that they may talk properly.

"How old are you?" Asks His Majesty.

"Seventeen!"

"Are you sure you haven't made a mistake?" The King asks in surprise, for he looks less than twelve. "The boy held to his story and added that he left school three years ago and was a good scholar."[242]

At Newcastle, following overnight thunderstorms, His Majesty spends a steamy Sunday afternoon under threatening clouds at St. James's Park, distributing 118 decorations. "Behind the

235   RA GV/PRIV/GVD/1917 (14/6).
236   (ed.) Hammerton & Wilson: *The Great War Vol.XVIII*, p.130.
237   *Daily Telegraph* 15/6/17.
238   (ed.) Hammerton & Wilson: *The Great War Vol.XVIII*, p.130.
239   *The Times* 15/6/17.
240   RA PS/PSO/GV/C/O/1153/XXII/425.
241   RA GV/PRIV/GVD/1917 (15/6).
242   *The Times* 16/6/17.

men in uniform spread a small irregular bank of women and men who wore mourning, widows and fathers of dead heroes." The cheering is deafening and prolonged when recipients step up. "Half a dozen limped and several could not walk without the aid of sticks. For these soldiers the King had the greatest solicitude and he watched in each case to see that the decorated man got down from the dais without mishap."[243] "Ah he's right good all through is George, and so is his missus," says one witness.[244]

His Majesty's efforts in the sphere of labour continue in mid-September with a return visit to the Clyde and another investiture, this time at Ibrox. His parting act is an inspection at Glasgow's Central Station of over 200 men and women of the merchant service, representing 68 torpedoed ships, "one of the outstanding ceremonies of the whole tour." Three men have been torpedoed twice and there are four stewardesses who survived the sinking of the *Lusitania*, one by clinging to an overturned boat and the other to a deck chair in in the water. Thus with the exception of some local visits, the bulk of the King and Queen's effort to promote and encourage war labour and industry in 1917 comes to a close. The press have nothing but praise for their efforts; His Majesty is declared a "working monarch."[245] "The King's visit to the northern dockyards and shipbuilding ought to and must have served to impress a vital truth on public attention," says another publication. "It is that nothing, absolutely nothing, is of such pressing interest as are the present state and future prospects of our shipping."[246]

"Naval Interests"

Hours after returning from his labour tour of the northeast, his Majesty sets off from Euston again for the most in depth yet visit yet that he has made to the Grand Fleet. It is going to be notable because accompanying the royal party north are journalists and a photographer. "They are to be given as much freedom as possible compatible with naval interests."[247] There is even going to be moving picture footage of the visit that will be broadcast throughout the country. It is a bold move for a service that is used to operating behind a veil of privacy.

"Safely arrived after good journey. Alas, weather very bad, raining and blowing hard," the King telegraphs to Queen Mary. "Old Bertie looking extremely well."[248] Conditions are atrocious: a force eight gale, then squalls, thunderstorms and tropical rain. "The lightning flickered about the topmast and the wireless aerials."[249] His Majesty is to stay aboard *Queen Elizabeth* with Beatty, who has succeeded Jellicoe in command of the Grand Fleet, and there is a demonstration of methods of treating the wounded. Inert actors are brought up, "on bamboo stretchers from below on canvas and cane, and they wrap a man tightly round until he looks like a large and more neatly bound edition of an Indian porpoise." There are rope loops on the sides for stretcher bearers. One after another the 'wounded' men are "rushed along the mess deck and into the reading room, hastily... now a very efficient dressing station when they were placed on whoever side of the ship was safest from enemy fire."[250]

The weather clears suddenly at noon. "First the masts were visible: tripod masts, straight masts... and stubby masts and then the grey, serried ranks of ships of war as far as the eye could reach

243   *The Times* 17/6/17.
244   *The Times* 18/7/17.
245   *The Times* 17/9/17.
246   *The Field* 29/9/17.
247   RA PS/PSO/GV/PS/WAR/QQ21.
248   RA PS/PSO/GV/PS/WAR/QQ21.
249   *Daily Telegraph* 27/6/17.
250   *The Times* 27/6/17.

loomed up out of the murk."[251] His Majesty makes tours of various vessels before *Queen Elizabeth* and four other ships sail out to Pentland Firth. "We were able to do our firing which was most interesting."[252] There is the scurrying of feet. "Between decks there was the rush and bustle of hundreds of men moving to their accustomed places. One heard the swish of canvas hoses being run through the flats, the clang of copper nozzles in the iron floor, and the hissing of compressed air. The King wanted to see them at this work." To an outsider, it is "a weird and uncanny sight, for the gun members did not bear the semblance of men. They wore anti flash clothing... and the hooded caps of cotton, chemically treated... give them the look of nuns." Each man has a thick white suit on, gloves, helmet. He also has a respirator strapped to him, "with a flexible rubber tube and two reservoirs. At the end of the tube is a rubber grip to be kept inside the lips and gripped by the teeth. There are goggles too, to protect the eyes." His Majesty watches as men toss the stiff powder bags to one another. "To the left of the breech another man stands with hose pipes to his ears as well as his mouth. He is the telephonist who gets the orders from the fire station." The King is impressed with all he sees. They return to Scapa and the rain descends again. From behind the veil of a purple sky come crashes, "that filled the sky with a splendour of sound... the tossing seas turned through dark green to black."[253]

"Never has the British Navy stood higher in the estimation of friend or foe," says His Majesty in his public telegram to Beatty at the conclusion of his visit. "You can assure all ranks and ratings under your command that their brothers throughout the Empire rely upon them with pride and confidence to defend our shores and commerce."[254]

Set free on their return to London, journalists fill their columns with details of all that the King has seen and done. His Majesty first has the opportunity to see the cinematograph of himself in Scotland at the Scala Theatre before its wider release. He watches the footage of various ships. There he is knighting Vice Admiral Pakenham aboard *Princess Royal*, the first shipboard investiture since 1794. There are guns, the ships and their crews and then a farewell picture of 2,000 cheering seamen. For the King, though, the thing that means most to him during his visit is his time spent with Bertie. "Papa brought me such a good account of you which has given me great pleasure," Queen Mary told their son. "He was so glad to have seen something of you those days while he was at Scapa."[255]

The Other Side of the Looking Glass

Having received her husband back in critical condition after his Western Front visit in 1915, and having kept close tabs on him via special reports the following year, the main feature of His Majesty's 1917 visit is that Queen Mary decides to go with him. GHQ would rather see the Duke of Connaught accompany His Majesty, but for reasons that Wigram refuses to put in writing he does not concur. It is likely that he thinks that with Connaught being a Field Marshal; an army man, he might steal the King's thunder. And besides, from the outset of planning, the Queen is utterly determined to make the trip. His Majesty also has an idea that this time, he would rather live in a train and use it to move around, as he wasted a lot of time driving too and from the Chateau Bryas in 1916. But from a military point of view, the idea is concerning on account of a vast increase in German bombing activity behind the lines in 1917. A train is an easy mark, and sidings are not healthy places near forward areas. There is less logic now in assuming the King's safety if he

---

251   *Daily Telegraph* 27/6/17.
252   RA GV/PRIV/GVD/1917 (23/6).
253   *Daily Telegraph* 27/6/17.
254   Ibid 28/6/17.
255   RA GVI/PRIV/RF/II/26.

kept away from the front line. He will always be in some semblance of danger now whilst at the front, as will the Queen. His Majesty will now have to be protected by airmen in the immediate area of wherever he is staying, and ideally spend no longer than two nights in the same locality.

The King returns from his Clydeside visit on 27th June to find 20 boxes waiting for him, but five days later he departs with the Queen for France. He is more belligerent than on previous occasions about being tied down to any formal activities; after all once again the size of the force on the Western Front has swollen and every second is, to His Majesty, precious time he wants to spend seeing as many troops as possible. The Queen will be sticking to base hospitals and support areas behind the lines; travelling separately. For her protection, a new man has been found. Sergeant Brown of Scotland Yard had only just returned to the police force after serving in the Intelligence Corps since the beginning of the war. They depart for Havre and Rouen, leaving the King to motor to his first residence; "a town of old houses, narrow streets with high, steeped roofs of red tiles and grey slates...a beautiful harmony of colour, rising between a labyrinth of fantastic chimneys."[256]

His Majesty's staff, which includes the attachment of Major Thompson again, are given a list of items of interest in the area he is to visit on the preceding evening. They will select the locations where they would like to take him and then the plans would be given to the local army commander so that he might know of the King's presence. His first day is spent at Messines, where General Plumer has just achieved a stunning victory and seized the town back for the first time since 1914 in a preparatory attack for the summer offensive. He is much looking forward to seeing the battlefield and the men that have fought for this costly but efficient win. The area is far from safe, and the palace is asked if His Majesty has his own protective headwear. "They are vile things to wear but just as well to have them," writes a member of Plumer's staff. "I fear that we are not in the possession of steel helmets as they are not yet the fashion in London against air raids," says Wigram. "Will you therefore be so kind as to provide these articles of headgear for us; although you will have trouble to get His Majesty to wear them,"[257] he warns. Plumer collects the King after breakfast and they set off, crossing the border and beginning to pass Belgian corn and hop fields, the little Royal Standard stuck on the front of the motor car as it bumps along. The road is leading them up towards the recently vacated British front line; new shoots of grass coming up "across a desolate, dead-brown slope, mottled by masses of blackened tree trunks... against a leaden sky."[258]

Whenever His Majesty sees a group, or even a solitary soldier going about his business, he wants to stop and talk to them about their part in the battle. A group of high ranking officers in the Second Army have assembled in a nearby orchard to meet the King, but he is far more interested in a woman who lives in the attached cottage. Right there, in the middle of the war, she is mechanically turning the handle on a mangle as she does her washing, a little child about her skirts. She refuses to stay away. Her husband is with the French Army and she lives alone there. She has nowhere else to go. Her home "shakes almost every hour of the day and night to the thunder of the guns."[259] The party crosses no man's land on foot, His Majesty taking it all in. On this terrain, walking a mile on foot feels like five. There are bits of kilts and skeletons lying discarded on the ground. There are enormous mine craters. "The silence and emptiness of the battlefield impressed the King." A few labourers are quietly working in the distance. A "dull, light rain,"[260] beings to fall and His Majesty refuses to don a coat then sets off to meet them; the thud of the guns striking uncomfortably close to the ground they have just left behind. When they reach the recent German line the King

256   *Daily Telegraph* 16/7/17.
257   RA PS/PSO/GV/PS/WAR/QQ18/05707.
258   *Morning Post* 16/7/17.
259   *The Times* 16/7/17.
260   *Morning Post* 16/7/17.

is startled to find a YMCA outfit occupying an enemy dugout and dispensing comforts to troops nearby, such as cocoa, on nightly marches. In charge is a Cambridge man who says that 48 hours after the Germans moved out, they moved in. It is a tight fit inside, a gramophone is playing. "His Majesty showed himself much interested in the work going on there, inquired how the organisation managed to obtain such a good stock of supplies, asked whether they were often shelled, and was glad to observe that the place was at least splinter proof."[261] As he leaves he thanks them for all the hard work they are doing, and says that he is sure that it is appreciated by the men. When His Majesty leaves, a sign is put up. "Patronised by HM the King."[262]

It hardly seems possible that the ridge running between Wytschaete and Messines is back in British hands after nearly three years. It is still being shelled regularly, and so His Majesty's staff are nervous. There are guns going off somewhere to the left, the

constant coming and going of aircraft with the bursting of shell fire at them from their anti-aircraft guns and the occasional rattle of machine gun fire. Tommies came out of dugouts and craters, and stood pointing and staring. One of our batteries opened fire not too far from where the King walked... [He] was in the centre of the real thing.[263]

His Majesty manages to appear very cool. He walks slowly, stopping every now and again to examine things that take his interest. He points to the tattered, field-grey remains of German uniforms.

The King spies an officer of the Gordon Highlanders overseeing a party recovering timber and tells him to be careful of unexploded shells. The man grimly replies that he's already had one man severely wounded by putting the edge of a shovel straight into one. Other officers approach and His Majesty stands amongst them, "making them all laugh at some of his remarks, and the men stood about listening to his words, astounded to find him in such a place, and grinning at his jokes."[264] Descending the ridge just a little the royal party leaves the old German front line behind and approaches a little train on a light railway, ready to be drawn by a petrol engine along a narrow-gauge track. The royal carriage is an ammunition truck with a makeshift roof and rudimentary benches and a chair lining the inside. This will be the King's transport to examine the villages in the vicinity. It moves at a fair speed, with its passengers squashed together inside to the amusement of a nearby Labour Corps unit.

"Lord love a duck. Blessed if that ain't the King," one man apparently says.

"The King?" says another as they approach Wytschaete. "Good Lord, so it is. Well... Good on him to come this old way. I hope he doesn't get copped by a shell."[265]

David is with his father, and they can't quite believe how close to danger the Sovereign and his heir have ventured. "I can tell you he ran a greater risk than I would have ever dreamed of to come right up to the firing line," says one soldier. "He came right by where we buried three of our chaps only last night and if you ever hear anyone say the King only goes to base you can give them the lie direct." He has seen His Majesty before, and is surprised at the toll being exacted by the war. "He has aged considerably since I last saw him... God bless him. I am a patriot and he has had some worry; you can see it in his face.... I don't think it right for him and the Prince of Wales to take such risks, but I can assure you he had a hearty welcome."[266]

261   *Morning Post* 17/7/17.
262   *The Red Triangle* 20/7/17.
263   *Daily Telegraph* 16/7/17.
264   Ibid.
265   Ibid.
266   *Morning Post* 17/7/17.

Ruined houses are the first sign that he has arrived. Then there are "sinister notice boards, sandbag shelters, deep dugouts besides road side banks, bits of old ruin... and tattered stumps of trees." The group drives slowly through the dusty ruins of the village, for if the dry surfaces are disturbed too much it attracts shellfire. There is a gas alert on. "Heavy shells came whistling from Long range guns, the note rising high as each shell came nearer, then ending in a big smash. The King stood still and looked across and listened."[267] As they move through the ruins Plumer points out landmarks. "Among the shell holes the King stopped now and again to examine some grisly relic of the fighting. There were bits of German uniforms and equipment, broken rifles, unexploded bombs, and such things as a pack of cards."[268] They descend into a dugout where someone fishes out an electric torch that reveals a half-eaten meal on the table.

In the days that follow the sight of that little Royal Standard brings French and the Flemish peasants to their cottage doors, "and made British soldiers start, running across fields, ambulance men sauntering on the road side, sitting on lorries and wagons shaving themselves look up suddenly."[269] His Majesty is always behind schedule, always wants to stop and see everything, discuss all he can and meet as many of his troops as possible. He can always find time for tanks, and their owners oblige the King with a demonstration. At first they cannot be seen. Then "the thick underbrush swayed and cracked... suddenly thrusting into open country, with broken branches and leaves garlanding its ungainly head... [it] blew a cloud of unpleasant blue vapour into the sunshine and lurched clear of the ruin it had created." It is a terrifying sight, as it comes lurching and puffing out, "first the hideous huge snout and then the ponderous shoulder lifting through the bushes. Close beside it came its brother... Together the twin primordial monsters rolled out in the open, grunting and searching round for something to destroy." His Majesty watches another. "From the other side a behemoth came lumbering up the slope, and there it rested, peering down the abyss below. While the spectators held their breath, the gigantic thing slowly lowered its blunt nose into space, and then headlong it plunged." The King is fascinated. As it slows to a halt his Majesty runs up to meet it, and smiles as a face appears low down at a hatchway and bursts out into the open.

"Are you hurt?" he asks as the young commander as he scrambles to his feet.

"No sir."

The King laughs. "Let's see the rest of them. Get them all out."

One by one the rest of the crew come tumbling out onto the grass like a team of acrobats, and His Majesty laughs again and again.

"You don't see to be any the worse for it," he says "with twinkling eyes."[270]

The King sees plenty of preparation for the Third Battle of Ypres, which is set to commence at the end of the month. He watches the Guards practice their attack. At Herzeele they advance against a strongpoint. Drums simulate the roar of the guns; and men on horseback with flags move slowly forward to mark the artillery barrage that will protect them. "The slow advance, the sudden dash into the trench, the check till the barrage moved on again, the tumbled appearance of prisoners from trench and stronghold running with their hands held high, everything was true to life, and it made a really thrilling spectacle," says one journalist. His Majesty is rather more thinking that before long, all of these men will be facing bullets that are real; and that flags will be replaced with high explosive shells. He also sees an attack from another perspective. "Instead of being immediately behind our own front line watching the backs of our advancing men, he was now, in theory, in a German trench, and he saw what a British attack looks like to the enemy...

267   *Daily Telegraph* 16/7/17.
268   *The Times* 16/7/17.
269   *Daily Telegraph* 16/7/17.
270   *Morning Post* 17/7/17.

He saw the barrage come slowly creeping towards him… Nearer the barrage crept and again the line came on." It is the closest His Majesty will ever come to battle. "Suddenly, flinging stones for bombs, the wave was upon him, and the trench in which he stood was captured. And still ruthlessly on the barrage crept, and on behind it to the third line went the men."[271]

As always, the King is most interested in visiting medical units, looking at a variety of different outfits representing the chain of evacuation for wounded men. At a dressing station for the Ulster Division, he quizzes doctors about the ratio of compound fractures arriving during the Battle of Messines. At a casualty clearing station His Majesty is not satisfied until he has seen the inside of almost every hut; and this includes stopping in one to watch a man who has received shrapnel wounds in both arms being operation on. There are advances in technology and innovation happening right before his eyes. He visits a special park on the road to Wormhoudt where men are pioneering advancements in the art of hiding things in plain site; "home of the high priests of the great mysteries of *camouflage,* a magicians' palace in a Belgian farm, where nothing is what it seems to be. It is a bewildering place… a land on the other side of the looking glass."[272] Local women work busily on nets that are used to conceal artillery. "'ip, ip, Ooray,"[273] they cheer as the King passes.

There is novelty in camouflage, but horror in a visit to see the Director of Gas services, who orchestrates a monstrous demonstration of chemical abominations for His Majesty. There are gas shells, and the King watches a thick greenish vapour roll sluggishly over some trenches. There is the latest type of flame-projector "flung out across the slope of an open field its evil red tongue of scorching, tearing flame, which consumes and stirs up whatever is in its path. Then he saw the operation of so-called 'boiling oil' or oil-projectors, which tossed great floods of flaming lighting to char or devour whatever it touches."[274]

Throughout his ten day tour, His Majesty finds himself in some surreal situations. He takes tea outside one afternoon as the weather improves, with the Earl of Cavan, entertained by the band of the Coldstream Guards. "German aeroplanes passed over us and we watched the shells bursting from our anti-aircraft guns…several of our machines were after them."[275] Reconciling the warm summer evenings with the massive endeavour shortly to come, and with the fickleness of life at the front is difficult. On one evening the King sits in his garden at Cassel working on his boxes. "A great bombardment going on tonight and you could see the flashes of the guns and shells bursting."[276] When he wakes up the following morning he is told that the noise comprised a two hour German attack on the town of Bailleul. At first he is told that hardly any damage has been caused, but the true tragedy soon comes to light. "I regret to say this is not correct as 7 bombs fell on [a] Casualty Clearing Station" writes His Majesty in his diary. "25 patients were killed and 65 wounded, and three staff killed and four wounded."[277] The Germans were looking for the railway, but instead have managed to drop nearly 100 bombs on the town and hardly damaged this target at all.

The King transfers his base further south to Bavrincourt, but is feeling "very seedy,"[278] and 48 hours are subsequently wiped off of his schedule by a bout of enteritis. Dawson is summoned from where he is working at Boulogne and he promptly sends His Majesty to bed. "I feel so weak and wretched," he says on 8th July. "Slept nearly all day. Blowing hard, some rain and much colder."[279]

271   *The Times* 16/7/17.
272   *The Times* 16/7/17.
273   *Daily Telegraph* 16/7/17.
274   *The Times* 17/7/17.
275   RA GV/PRIV/GVD/1917 (6/7).
276   Ibid.
277   RA GV/PRIV/GVD/1917 (7/7).
278   Ibid.
279   RA GV/PRIV/GVD/1917 (8/7).

All he can do is sleep and lie awake listening to thunderstorms until 10th, when a meeting with French dignitaries aggravates the need for the King to get back to work. Once he is back on his feet again, His Majesty concentrates on the southern part of the British front. He makes sure to stop near Arras to see the scene of the successful fighting in April. He cannot enter the town, as it has just been shelled, but he can walk up to Vimy Ridge, which with its commanding view of the countryside is a prize so proudly wrestled from the enemy. Officers are watching to make sure that the King is not too exposed, but there is an appreciable danger in his position. His Majesty can't quite get over just how good the view is from top of the ridge. "You see how completely for the last two years [the enemy] has overlooked all our positions and could watch our movements, He looks down on Lens, France's black country, "with its cathedral and churches still seemingly intact, and the uncouth marks of the mine structures, silent now, and the black, smokeless chimneys rising against the sky all around the city." The King has become distracted by nearby scattered graves dotted about, where a cross marks the resting place of one of his soldiers. He cannot pass one without stopping to look, and to salute. Here he finds an unknown Canadian,

> a grave well tended and with cornflowers… a broken trench helmet with which the cross is anointed. *"It is hard that any one of these brave fellows should be unknown,"* he said, the world ought to know every one of them… More than once he expressed his appreciation of the careful and reverent way in which our dead are buried, and in which all possible data are collected and preserved.[280]

His Majesty is keen to revisit the Somme too, where he was present in the midst of battle eleven months before. "It is quiet now, and the flame has burnt out, and there is only a great memory dwelling in this loneliness."[281] General Byng points out to the King "all the places and the valley of Ancre where all the terrible fighting took place last year."[282] The change is incredible. "It is not merely that the guns have ceased to roar and the tide of battle has flowed away since the Germans have retreated, but this country, which last year was hideous and brown and shell torn is all green grass and waving flowers." Nobody yet lives here again, amidst this "endless tapestry of brilliant colours woven on a background of green. The face of the ridge, which was soaked with blood last year, is scarlet now with poppies."

At the Butte, near Warlencourt, a tiny piece of high ground that was fiercely contested the previous year, His Majesty gets out to climb to the top. It is barren "Not even the weeds will grow on that hillock of evil memory." There are three wooden crosses on top; the graves of Durhams killed near the end of the battle. "The King spoke about these crosses, and hoped they would be replaced by a permanent memorial, giving the names and details of the men who fell."[283] He travels by light railway again, "and saw all the country where such desperate fighting had taken place," wrote his Majesty later on. "Every tree is dead having been destroyed by shellfire."[284] These places are only villages in name; "no more than names painted on bits of board above some rubbish heaps."[285] An Australian flag flies over the ruins of Martinpuich; both Bazentins are nothing but dust and rubble. "Delville Wood still remains terrible. While all the country round us is clothed in green, nature herself seems to have shrunk back shuddering from the devil's wood, as if there was a

280   *The Times* 17/7/17.
281   *The Times* 18/7/17.
282   RA GV/PRIV/GVD/1917 (12/7).
283   Ibid.
284   RA GV/PRIV/GVD/1917 (13/7).
285   *The Times* 18/7/17.

place too awful even for her to attempt to transform." Shoots have just about begun to spring from the battered foliage and blackened tree stump, and there is "grass sprouting reluctantly among the ridges and furrows of shell holes, but that is it".[286]

Queen Mary has been just as busy as the King. So far as the press men can make out, this is the first time that a Queen of England has visited an army in the field since the Wars of the Roses in the fifteenth century. To find an instance of a King and Queen together visiting the seat of war, they think that you have to go back to 1304, when Queen Margaret accompanied Edward I to Stirling Castle. Her Majesty has pottered back and forth relentlessly in a Rolls Royce at a steady speed of 25mph. She has been keen not to be overwhelmed by hospital visits, not only because she is a bright, inquisitive woman who wants to see the work of an army behind the lines too; but because it is too much for her. Frequently reduced to tears at the bedside of troops, she cannot bear the emotion of it without respite. "I strongly advise you not to try to work the Queen too hard and to vary the items as much as possible and not let hospitals crowd in one on top of the other," Wigram clarifies with GHQ.[287] Queen Mary also visits Haig, who is not sure what to make of such a momentous event in history. "This is the first lady to have a meal at my headquarters since War began!"[288] She writes to the King from across the front on their 24th Wedding Anniversary: "I am very sorry we cannot spend it together which we generally do... You cannot think how glad I am that I came out here, it is all too interesting for words and one fells so proud of all that our people have accomplished out here in the way of organisation."[289] "It was terribly tiring but awfully interesting" the Queen tells Bertie. "My brain is still in a whirl with all I have seen."[290]

The Fog of War

Three months of ceaseless activity have taken their toll. In May, June and July the King alone has covered some five and half thousand miles. "George and I are feeling dreadfully tired,"[291] writes Her Majesty. By the height of summer, consultants have told both the King and Queen to slow down and relent from the strain of an incessant programme of travelling. From Scotland, His Majesty had written to Queen Mary about how exhausted and depressed he felt. The notion of being a permanent source of enthusiasm and motivation for other people has him under incredible strain. "I can't ever sufficiently express my deep gratitude to you darling May for the splendid way in which you are helping me during these terrible, strenuous and anxious times. Very often I feel in despair and if it wasn't for you I should break down. Everybody seems to give one extra worries these days... I miss you now abominably."[292] One relative remarks to His Majesty that his troops are doing well, and his response is glum. "Yes, it is all very well: the news from France and the advance of our troops may be satisfactory, but then there are the losses at sea and in the air. The public may only get one report, but I have to know everything."[293] Queen Alexandra knows how hard her son is working, and warns him of taking on too much. "I am not too tired," the King assures her. "In these days I must go about and see as many people as possible and so encourage them in their work. They appreciate

286   Ibid.
287   RA PS/PSO/GV/PS/WAR/QQ18/05707.
288   Rose: *King George V,* p.182.
289   RA QM/PRIV/CC08/211.
290   RA GVI/PRIV/RF/II/267.
291   RA GV/PRIV/CC50/1384.
292   Pope-Hennessy: *Queen Mary, 1867-1953,* p.505.
293   Marie Louise, Princess: *My Memories of Six Reigns,* p.185.

it, I believe, and I am quite ready to sacrifice myself if necessary, as long we win this war."[294] A few times a week he manages to sit down with his beloved stamp albums. "He used to declare that they had saved his life in the War; for during such intervals as he could spare from his anxious duties he would obtain complete relaxation by pouring over some rare issue with the aid of a magnifying glass."[295] Queen Mary is just as fraught. "What a pulp one's brain becomes when one is over-worked as we often are,"[296] she writes to His Majesty. Her efforts are becoming fabled. "Even the men in the Royal party show signs of fatigue much sooner than the Queen, who trudges cheerfully along miles of cinder tracks, of rubbish, of railway sleepers and contrives to look cool by furnaces," writes one magazine. "It is a saying among her entourage that the Queen will go on until she drops, and her smile is a genial at the end of a day as at the beginning."[297] But there is a price to pay. "The length of this war is depressing," The King had written in 1916, "I really think it gets worse the longer it lasts." The Queen's hair is now flecked with grey, and she is suffering from neuritis in one arm. Of the doctors' instructions to rest, she is matter of fact. "As usual there is plenty to do," she writes, "so that the 'rest' idea has not been carried out, though I confess once or twice I have not accompanied Papa on his inspections."[298] Matters finally come to a head in August, when Princess Mary tells a friend that a bad cold has resulted in her mother suffering a mild collapse.

By August, the anniversary of the outbreak of war has come around again and there will be yet another service at Westminster Abbey. London is in a glum mood, for everybody from the King down to the working classes now, it is as if there is no facet of life that is not in some way ruined or made harder by this unceasing war to which there is no end in sight. The *Fog of War* hangs not only on the battlefields but oppresses the Home Front too. "Under its sombre cloak, enthusiasm tends to languish and doleful creatures… are prone to multiply. The people feel the privations, and see some of the havoc of war; they begin to lose sight of the great purpose and sense of the splendours that redeem in some degree the horrors of the conflict."[299]

Spending the summer on the road has created a backlog in the King's determined endeavours to present as many decorations as possible in person. The number of gallantry awards is swelling in accordance with the scale of the war. Victoria Crosses are even being selected by ballot. In the last half of 1916, 526 men were gazetted to the Distinguished Service Order; 3,605 Military Crosses were awarded, 2,101 Distinguished Conduct Medals, and, thanks to the Battle of the Somme, an astonishing 19,791 Military Medals.[300] In line with measures to make His Majesty more visible, the palace have realised the huge public interest roused by the King's investitures. Unless the weather has been fine and special measures have been taken, until now, the bestowal of awards at Buckingham Palace have been private affairs. Crowds have gathered outside, many of them friends and relatives of the recipients, watched men disappear inside and then gawped through the railings until they emerge again with their medals. The Archbishop of Canterbury has written to Stamfordham urging that "it would make a huge difference if more of the things which *are* done, giving decorations etc… were done in public. Even those who don't go would read about what happened."[301] Similar appeals have been made by Lord Rosebery and other eminent correspondents. It has been ordained that His Majesty will carry out investitures in the forecourt at Buckingham Palace, but the first and

294   Nicolson: *King George V: His Life and Reign*, p.316.
295   (ed.) The Times: *Hail and Farewell: The Passing of King George V*, p158.
296   Pope-Hennessy: *Queen Mary, 1867-1953*, p.506.
297   *The Ladies Field* 21/9/17.
298   Pope-Hennessy: *Queen Mary, 1867-1953*, p.505.
299   *Daily Telegraph* 3/8/17.
300   *The Times* 2/1/17.
301   Prochaska: *The Republic of Britain, 1760-2000*, pp.165-166.

largest affair of the summer is accommodated in Hyde Park; where on one Saturday afternoon at the beginning of June, the King decorates nearly 400 officers, men and nurses.

"The idea of such a ceremony is so simple and so obvious that one wonders that nobody even through of it before,"[302] but the only precedent for such a gathering is a summer morning six decades ago when Queen Victoria conferred 62 of the first Victoria Crosses for the Crimean War; "a day of plumes and cuirasses, brass helmets and gorgeous uniforms, the Queen on horseback wearing a red jacket and a Field Marshal's sash."[303] In 1917, thousands turn out to watch, and the whole event is structured to be as entertaining a spectacle as possible. "It was an ideal summer day and Hyde Park had never looked finer. The flowering trees were a blaze of colour, and massed beds of flowers glowed in the sunlight... Tens of thousands of people crowded the public spaces... Here was a group of American nurses... here were children from an orphanage; here was a group of distinguished soldiers."[304] They stand forty deep and have been gathering since dawn. Young boys hang from the branches of trees, where flats and houses overlook the park, people have crowded together on windowsills, massed bands play military airs. High overhead a group of aeroplanes fly in lazy, wide circles, disappearing in and out of fluffy clouds; guarding the park against a sudden enemy raid. The humming of their engines is audible on the ground, where activity swarms around a dais erected on the grass, on which His Majesty will stand with his extended family. It is flanked by blocks of seats which have been reserved for 500 wounded men, and more recline on the grass in front of them. Members of Parliament and those relations whose loved ones are to be decorated also sit expectantly.

An open landau drawn by four bays leaves Buckingham Palace. The whole route is overflowing with people, the King and Queen are cheered all the way up Constitution Hill, and as they enter the park through the gates at Hyde Park Corner the crowd surges excitedly. As His Majesty arrives with his royal entourage, "the National Anthem crashed forth and the Royal Standard broke from the flag post. There was one great burst of enthusiastic cheering from all the onlookers." The two hour ceremony begins, members of the crowd without a clear view holding mirrors aloft and craning their necks to see what is happening. Like everything else the King tries to do, the ceremony is simple and unostentatious; a scene of restrained pathos that touched every heart." Officers and men are brought before His Majesty; "some stricken men, some maimed, some lacking a limb, one sightless who had to be led up by one of his comrades."[305]

But though there are heart breaking scenes, this is supposed to be a day of celebration, not of sorrow. "There were Britons, Canadians... men of the sea and men of the land." First to come up was Major Murray, of the Australian Infantry, whose valour had won him the DSO twice and a VC. Next came Major Forbes Robertson of the Border Regiment, given the DSO and a Military Cross. "Men wanted fresh voices to cheer when the next two came, for they were the Captains of the *Swift* and *Broke*, who had attacked a fleet of six German destroyers in the Channel, sunk two of them, and put the other four to precipitate flight. Do you wonder that the people shouted as though they would rend the skies?"[306] The bands play favourite popular tunes, the noise level is raised every time the King presents a medal, and the biggest ovations are naturally reserved for the recipients of the Victoria Cross; and for the relatives of four men who have died in the act of winning the medal. There is a Scottish mother who took a VC that had been earned by her son when he shielded the

302   *Evening News 2/6/17.*
303   *Daily Telegraph 2/6/17.*
304   Hammerton: *Our King & Queen: A Pictorial Record of Their Lives,* pp.39-40.
305   Ibid.
306   Ibid.

body of his officer with his own. Then came a widow, whose husband died of burns after bringing back his blazing aeroplane and saving the life of his observer.

The palace begins to have certain investitures filmed. The dramatic increase in scale of his investitures does not stop His Majesty from taking a personal interest in those that come to receive their awards. This was no mere production line in which medals were affixed and men shooed on their way. "King George V was a remarkable man," recalled one soldier who was presented with a Victoria Cross in 1917 after heroics near Arras. "He had a wonderful memory… There were quite a lot of us at this investiture… about a dozen VCs altogether he invested. But when he spoke to us he spoke to us about the battalion chiefly and it was astounding his knowledge of the battalion and the officers in it. He enquired after individual people." He met the King on subsequent occasions and found that he had never forgotten the detail. "He never forgot a thing. He never missed a trick that man."[307]

In August, 1917 the King receives a letter from his uncle that suggests that the time has already come to commemorate those initial members of the BEF who originally went to war and so dramatically held the line at Ypres. "At the risk of being thought a great bore by you," writes the Duke, "It has often been brought to my notice… that nothing has been done specially to thank the great services of the old British Expeditionary Force of 1914 that went out to France under Lord French… It is undeniable that, but for their indomitable pluck… the German army would have got through to Paris and Calais and both France and Britain would have been at their mercy… May I ask you to give this matter your kind consideration? Believe me it is worth it."[308] His Majesty is immediately determined to follow up his uncle's suggestion, and in just a few weeks *The Times* announces that the King wishes to give special recognition to the men of 1914 in the form of a decoration, a star, for the first troops "which put up the most decisive resistance known in history."[309]

But on a much larger scale, the Order of the British Empire is a measure of just how much the war has infiltrated the life of the entire nation. At the palace, thanks to the prompting of Lord Esher, by 1917 just how the tireless effort by expended on the home front by ordinary men and women could be acknowledged is under investigation. The answer is the creation of a new order; the OBE. But this move is not greeted without scepticism. Fritz Ponsonby believes that the timing has to be completely right. "A new decoration is a delicate thing, and unless it is launched under favourable circumstances it may be looked upon with suspicion, and even ridicule."[310] "One fears that any new order will go to those already occupying public positions," writes one publication. "It is not the noisy public man, or woman, who deserves most recognition, but he or she will get it, unless steps are taken in time the real workers will in many cases be overlooked. Unless something is done we fear that any whose work should be recognised will be forgotten."[311] His Majesty immediately tasks a committee with drawing up statutes and discussing matters of precedence; a long and arduous process; as is the job of drawing up the first list of recipients. An allowance is allotted to each Dominion and each Colony. Should civil servants be eligible? On what principle should the order be distributed to the Allied countries? Should officers of the army and navy be eligible? Should neutrals be eligible or only allies? Details also have to be thrashed out that specify various levels of recipients; including commanders and knights of the order. Though the order is to be open to

307   IWM Sound: Reginald Haine VC Catalogue # 33, Reel 5 1973.
308   RA GV/PRIV/AA42/52.
309   *The Times* 10/9/17.
310   PA: F/46/7/9: Lloyd George.
311   *The World* 9/1/17.

all, the press emphasis is naturally on the fact that women are to be included. "To all women the recognition implied in the several degrees that may be created will be a most gratifying tribute."[312]

There are 268 appointments on the list when it is finally published in the middle of the month, and "by far the most popular and most human feature" are the names and citations for medallists of the OBE. 52 of them are being given for acts "of great courage, self-sacrifice, or high example; of initiative or perseverance, or skill, resource or invention." Jenny Elgar is to receive one for her conduct after an explosion at a shell filling factory; so is Maude Bryce, a firewoman. A Miss Golding has been awarded a medal for devotion to duty after going straight back to work after losing a finger and thumb in an accident making detonators. Miss Mary Williams will receive one "for intelligence and courage in securing the arrest of many who had gained entry into a shell filling factory in suspicious circumstances." One of the oldest recipients is to be Thomas Harper, 74, who had gone to Australia, yet immediately returned home to his old firm. "He came over at his own expense, and for over two years has put in an average of 54 hours a week, and has actually done the work of two men. Sometimes he has fainted at his work, and has then refused to go home, stating that he could not rest whilst he thought his country wanted shells."[313]

The OBE is perhaps overused for the remainder of the war. According to *The Times,* in the first 18 months there are almost 6,000 appointments already. But arguably appointing too many people is not possible. With suffrage in the minds of politicians at that moment, as well as minor republican agitation, the introduction of a new honour which sought to level the balance in acknowledging the effort of women in the war, as well as men who would not have received an honour in the existing system, was a timely installation by the King and his advisers. In late September His Majesty holds his first large ceremony in the 1844 Room at Buckingham Palace. The Queen had already been invested in private by her husband, so that she might stand at his side wearing the purple sash and star and welcome 130 others into the new order.

"Poor Fellows"

As the war went on, as with everything else, the scale of His Majesty's hospital visits reaches proportions that were unthinkable in 1914. He sees every sort of building being utilised: the Government Stationery Office, one of the stands at Ascot, a convent school in Slough, workhouse buildings up and down the country, lunatic asylums, schools; all received royal visits after they had been converted in facilities to deal with the mounting number of broken victims of war. The King and Queen also witness many a fad come and go. At the beginning of 1915 there is a craze for treating men out of doors. At Cambridge, His Majesty sees over a thousand men being exposed to the elements as much as is possible to try and surmount their various conditions. The same was true at Cliveden, where he sees that "the patients practically live out of doors."[314] Another establishment goes through a phase of taking patients with dangerous wounds and leaving them immersed in baths of tepid water, and an establishment at Bethnal Green favours ambrine treatment for trench foot; submerging patients in melted paraffin wax boosted by substances like eucalyptus and olive oils.

The King, despite the huge increase in the amount of men he has to see, retains that personal touch. The more patients that there are, the longer both he and Queen Mary spend visiting them. His Majesty sits on the end of one patient's bed playing with the man's kitten; he comforts a Maori

312   *Daily Telegraph* 2/6/17.
313   *The Times* 25/8/17.
314   Ibid 20/7/15.

soldier suffering from TB who was mortified that his tribe would despise him when they saw he had no physical wound. One man shows the King x-rays that illustrate a foreign object moving in time with his heart beat. Corporal Peach, who lost his left arm at Loos, marvels as His Majesty sits down on his bed and asks him to tell him all about his experiences, while the Queen, sympathetically listens nearby. When they are done chatting to him, Their Majesties delight the corporal by signing their names in his autograph book with his own fountain pen. On another occasion, the King meets a Kent soldier who has been hit with an explosive bullet in Trônes Wood, and quizzes him about the damage done. The corporal happily offers to have his dressing removed so that the His Majesty might see for himself. And the King and Queen do not forget these men as soon as they leave their bedsides. Constant enquiries about whether they have everything they want are followed up; whether it be deliveries of cigarettes, flowers. One man who has been in hospital for ten months with no visitors tells the Queen he quite fancies some chocolate, and by the very next post an array of confectionery arrives.

With the vast growth in wounds, various establishments begin to specialise in particular injuries and conditions, and Their Majesties are in a prime position to witness all manner of innovation. There is even a special facility in Rochester Row for the treatment of venereal disease which unnerves the King slightly. "Everything possible is being done for these poor fellows."[315] Queen Mary in particular cannot deal with the helplessness of looking upon a man for whom there is no hope. The hospital for officers of the Royal Flying Corps that opens in Eaton Square is particularly painful, because it houses some horribly maimed young men who have fallen from great heights in aerial accidents or have been involved in terrible, even fiery crashes. On one of His Majesty's visits to the Star and Garter establishment at Richmond, he greatly admires the arrangements for the 64 permanently disabled men there, but is saddened by the results of them all having been hit in either the spine or the head. At the Empire Hospital in Vincent Square there are men who have suffered permanent and horrific wounds; "all very bad either spinal or head cases," notes the King. "I fear several will never recover."[316] Queen Mary is spotted trying to retain her composure with tears silently rolling down her cheeks at the bedsides of such cases, and on this occasion, a huge pile of flowers from the gardens of Buckingham Palace arrived following the visit, courtesy of Her Majesty; with instructions that they be distributed to the loneliest of men first.

The King and Queen are therefore immensely fond of an array of institutions that provide hope, training, and a second chance at life; a path by which a man may regain his independence after suffering at the hands of war. They approve heartily of the work they observe being carried out at the Lord Roberts Memorial Workshops for Disabled Soldiers and Sailors in Fulham. His Majesty is so impressed with St. Dunstan's in Regent's Park, which looks after blinded servicemen, that he writes them a cheque for £500. "They have all had their eyes shot out during the war... poor things."[317] On one visit he and the Queen remain for nearly two hours: "Their first visit was to the workshops where carpentry, boot repairing, basket making and hat making is carried on." Elsewhere on site, men demonstrate their new prowess at reading using Braille and writing from dictations.[318] Their Majesties talk to each man that they encounter and congratulate them on their progress. On a return trip, the King declares himself "much impressed by the great developments which had taken place since he was last there." Cobblers and joiners are in training by 1917; and wherever he goes, His Majesty insists that the men should continue their work as usual so that he might be able

315   Ibid 23/2/17.
316   RA GV/PRIV/GVD/1917 (28/5).
317   RA GV/PRIV/GVD/1915 (26/4).
318   *The Times* 27/4/17.

to judge the skill and proficiency with which they were mastering their various trades."[319] There is even a poultry farm, marked out by an ingenious system of enclosures that enable the men to find their way about. The King wanders down to the farthest corner, and finds an officer holding a bird. He asks what he is doing and the officer says: "I was trying to discover what kind of hen this is, Sir, and I have just made out that it is a cock!"[320] His Majesty is highly amused. Massage therapies are being utilised at a converted workhouse in Shepherd's Bush that has become the Hammersmith Military Hospital. Specialising in orthopaedics, they are using not only massage but electricity to try and advance men's recoveries. In the Croydon War Hospital establishments at Thornton Heath and Norbury, massage treatment is being utilised for jaw injuries and by February 1917, the King is able to visit the Almeric Paget Military Massage Corps in Portland Place; "very interesting,"[321] where men are sent specifically for courses of treatment involving this as a primary therapy.

His Majesty is also a key observer in the development of the nation's understanding of invisible wounds during the Great War. At the beginning of 1915 he describes going to a new establishment at Queen's Square, Kensington, for officers who "are all suffering from shock and concussion from the shells."[322] This is typical of the thinking at the time and His Majesty's terminology and his descriptions of sufferers develops in line with medical comprehension. The King has a long talk one day with one very obviously young man who has been serving in the ranks. He is coherent but not right. He calls himself Leonard, and he lies to His Majesty and says he is 19. When the King quizzes him not about his *military age* but the true figure, all he says is that he is anxious to get back to the war again as soon as possible. He says that he is not sorry that he joined the army under age. He truly meant to go to the front. His Majesty wants to know if he had any trouble getting into the army, and what his father made of it. "No Your Majesty, my father said he wouldn't stop any boy of his who was plucky enough and lucky enough to get into the army in time of war."[323] He is considered a severe case, and the King is informed that in fact, the boy had enlisted in the South Staffordshire Regiment at the age of 15. By 1916 His Majesty refers to the officers at Queen's Square as "nerve cases"[324] and a few months later, when he visits a special section of a London military hospital establishment at Denmark Hill, the King has begun to use the phrase *shell-shock*. In 1917, hospitals dealing with this unseen affliction, especially when concerning officers, are given tactful names that mirror a better comprehension of a genuine issue and not one that had at least in part been previously connected to shirking. "In [the] afternoon May and I went to Golders Green where we visited the *Home of Recovery*," His Majesty wrote one day in October. "There are 100 soldiers suffering from shell shock and nerves, the treatment seems very good and they teach them trades."[325]

Queen Mary in particular is fascinated by pioneering works in plastic surgery and facial reconstruction. Much of this work is down to Dr. Gillies, a New Zealander and a Mr King, a dentist and the King and Queen witness the beginnings of their work at the Cambridge Hospital before a move to Sidcup to an enlarged facility. The Queen is so taken with the miraculous results of their endeavours that she lends her name to their hospital. It is unsurprising that Their Majesties are so impressed. "It may often be necessary to continue the treatment for one to two years, if the features are to fully built up and restored. Sometimes the disfigurements are so great that the men refuse to return to their home and friends." As far as the King and Queen are concerned, this is the least of

319   Ibid 21/3/17.
320   *Morning Advertiser* 21/3/17.
321   RA GV/PRIV/GVD/1917 (20/2).
322   Ibid.
323   *The Times* 18/2/17.
324   RA GV/PRIV/GVD/1916 (17/2).
325   RA GV/PRIV/GVD/1917 (25/10).

what these disfigured sailors and soldiers deserve, and the press complies. "No effort, it is obvious, should be spared to give these men, many of them mere lads, a fresh interest and a new start in life to make them, 'presentable' citizens, and lead them to realise that they are not useless wrecks."[326]

Another of Their Majesties' favourite establishments is located at Roehampton House, which becomes a specialist hospital for wounded men who have lost limbs in the war. The old custom has been to discharge such men from hospital when their wounds were healed and then post a generic artificial limb after them. "Of course, not being fitted, they were generally misfits and often useless."[327] By the winter of 1914 it was already evident that this method would no longer suffice, and funding had been obtained. The King and Queen also gave generous donations from private funds. The facility has greatly expanded by July 1917, and with Princess Mary, Their Majesties see 700 men. "They are fitted with artificial limbs all made there in the workshops and it was wonderful to see what they could do in spite of their losses. It is extremely well run."[328] One thousand men have been treated already, and there is a waiting list of another 2,000 waiting to be summoned. The King is told that 100 are leaving with a renewed capacity to earn their own living every month. Private Keighley had lost both of his legs at Loos and was about to receive his brand new, state of the art artificial ones. He is full of enthusiasm for the future, and jokes that his lot "could have been worse."[329] His Majesty is not a stupid man. He knows that the cheerful faces that he sees and the stiff upper lips on display have a lot to do with his presence. He sits with one man at Epsom who tries to convince him that having his arm taken off is nothing to get upset about. The King looks at him and says that, nonetheless, he hopes that he will not miss it too much, and that his recovery will be speedy. Every wounded man missing a limb that Their Majesties subsequently encounter on their travels is keenly interrogated about whether they are soon to go to Roehampton. In April 1916, the King and Queen are passing through the rooms at the Victory League Club when Her Majesty spies a young Australian missing an arm as a result of the fighting at Gallipoli. She begins chatting with him quite informally, learning when and where he obtained his wound. The King arrives too and joins the conversation and asks if he is to get an artificial limb. The young man appears to be a little confused about the process by which this might happen and says that well, he wouldn't be able to afford one. The Queen immediately declares that she is going to have him sent to Roehampton and if necessary she will buy one for him. No, says His Majesty, it will be from both of them.

As 1917 develops, there is a fully fledged campaign taking place under General Allenby, with a British force pressing out from defending the Suez Canal and advancing into Ottoman territory. Gaza and Beersheba form the gateway to Palestine just inland from the Mediterranean. For the King, matters take a personal turn when the surviving members of the Sandringham Company take part in the first battle for Gaza at the end of March. A messy failure, Allenby's force is bolstered and the second attempt was more in keeping with the sort of advance one might see on the Western Front. The 5th Norfolks began their journey into battle on the 17th April and were part of a solid effort that nonetheless is a costly defeat. 6,444 casualties "cast a gloom on the whole army"[330]

As well as the sheer weight of information and worry that the King has no choice to assume with regard to the war, he also continues to burden himself with an astonishing amount of esoteric

---

326   *Morning Post* 19/1/17.
327   *Daily Express* 24/8/15.
328   RA GV/PRIV/GVD/1917 (30/7).
329   *Daily Telegraph* 13/3/16.
330   Bruce: *The Last Crusade*, p.41.

interests and preoccupations. Some of the issues His Majesty is drawn to refer to special interest groups, one of which are conscientious objectors. In February 1917 it transpires that a work force of nearly 1,000 of these men are to be employed in the vicinity of Dartmoor prison, on land belonging to the Duchy of Cornwall, now David's possession. With only a few prisoners currently housed there, it is not proving possible to keep up the farm attached to the place or land close by. The Duchy has said that they will hand over the whole prison to the Home Office on the condition that they could keep the prison buildings clean and in good order and cover their manpower requirements. The men in question are not bona fide objectors in the eyes of the law, they have either had their appeals refused, or they have not applied, so by law should be on the strength of the army. "They have committed offences against military discipline, which they allege were prompted by a conscientious objection to military service and have been sentenced to imprisonment." They have however, on being caught, been offered a conditional release if they agree to undertake work of national importance for the rest of the war. "They are working in camps in various parts of the country, some on the making of roads, some on waterworks and other public services, some on timber cutting and some on land."[331]

Putting aside the connection to the Duchy and the fact that the King admires this innovation in putting men to work, he is not keen on the image projected of them living in prison cells. His Majesty has to be placated with assurances that there will be no warden to speak of, but a manager, that there will be perfect freedom of association, that the men will eat roughly the same as a soldier in the army and that they will be provided with a canteen, recreation rooms; that none of the doors will be locked and they will wear their own clothes and be able to go into the village at their leisure. But after all these men have made an agreement with the Government to avoid prison, so "the manager will have certain powers of punishment in case of idleness or insubordination." Persistent offenders would find themselves being sent to prison to complete their sentence or compelled to serve in the army. His Majesty is placated for now, but in October rumours reach the national press about conditions at Dartmoor and he sets Wigram on a mission to find out the truth. "The King has asked me to draw your attention to two letters in todays *Times* about conscientious objectors," he writes to the War Office. "Would you be so kind as to let me know for His Majesty's information what truth is there in [their] complaints of ill treatment? It seems a pity that these allegations should be allowed to be published in the press, and they can do no good when people's nerves are strained and overwrought after three years of war."[332] Aside from the issue of adequate treatment, the thought of housing political offenders under one roof does not sit well with the King. He believes that there is a possible "danger of allowing political conscientious objectors to live together, with a view to the organising a revolution."[333] The palace also raises the point that religious and political conscientious objectors ought perhaps to be treated differently.

His Majesty also maintains his interest in individual events. "I most deeply regret the loss of the Vanguard with practically all hands," he tells Bertie when the ship explodes and sinks in the middle of the night, taking almost 850 of her crew with her. "It is terrible that so many valuable lives of officers and men should have been taken in this sudden way, although to die in your sleep is a most merciful death."[334] There is time for the King to make sure a letter is sent to a crippled woman in Harlesden who has lost four sons already and has a husband serving in the Royal Defence Corps having closed his business to join the war effort. His Majesty reads about one solitary soldier killed in 1914 and is moved by the tale of how he returned again and again to rescue comrades who had

331   RA PSO/GV/C/QQ10/WAR5125/1.
332   RA PSO/GV/C/QQ10/WAR5125/1.
333   RA PSO/GV/C/QQ10/WAR/5910/4.
334   RA GV/PRIV/AA60/242.

been left behind on the retreat. On his fourth run, he was killed, but even then he managed to throw the man he was carrying to safety, and he was discovered alive the next morning. The King writes to the young man's mother despite the lapse in time, in the sincere hope that his public acknowledgement of her son's brave deed might console her at least a little in her bereavement.

"Virtuous Enthusiasm"

In 1917, it is not only people's nerves that are stretched. The Royal Household has been on an austerity footing since the beginning of the war, as a result of which Their Majesties have exercised frugality on a militant scale that far exceeds their friends. The King has dined at a restaurant or club once since August 1914, he only attends the theatre if there is some charitable cause to be supported and ceremonial occasions are dialled down. In 1917 His Majesty uses as a precedent the semi-state, sombre precedent for the state opening of Parliament set by his grandmother following the death of Prince Albert some half a century ago. The affair is a "study in drab khaki."[335] There are no gilt carriages, only black landaus, the horses drawing them are bays, not the usual white steeds covered in decorative garb. There is no lace or bearskins for the military bands. When the Duchess of Connaught dies in March 1917 her funeral is a muted affair at Windsor. "The pomp and pageantry of a royal funeral were modified to war-time conditions. Officers and men of the Guards who lined the processional route through the precincts of the castle wore service khaki instead of blazing scarlet and gold. Within the chapel the assembled dignitaries made no dazzling display of the emblems of their offices."[336]

Queen Mary's youth was spent counting pounds, if not pennies, and she excels at being thrifty; rooting out extravagance "with virtuous enthusiasm." Anywhere that she could save money or material for the war effort, she would have it done and set an example for the nation. There is no longer even a clean napkin at every meal for the Royal Family. When the King whispers a complaint about this to Clive Wigram's wife, he is roundly chastised by his wife who has heard the remark from the other end of the table and puts him in his place by bellowing down that he ought to be more supportive of her war economies. With the exception of the elderly Queen Alexandra, when the Royal Family venture out, if they take a motor car at all instead of saving petrol needed for the war with horse and plain carriage, the usual three are discarded and up to seven people squash into one vehicle. Most of them have been locked up until after the war, but His Majesty sends his own private motor to hospitals so that wounded men might be taken for a drive. At Sandringham, long wet afternoons are spent by the Queen and her conscripts picking up horse chestnuts, which were needed for munitions factories, while schoolchildren on the estate and in the neighbouring Norfolk villages are set to work collecting scrap iron, jam jars and old glass bottles, Her Majesty afterwards inspecting the results.[337]

But in 1917, the biggest concern faced on the Home Front is the nation's supply of food. Germany had abandoned a campaign of unrestricted submarine warfare at the beginning of 1916, under political pressure both at home and abroad. But by January 1917 even the Kaiser, who had previously held a moderate opinion on the matter, begins to support its resumption: "first and foremost because Hindenburg threatened to resign unless restrictions against sinking unarmed or neutral merchant ships were lifted." He advocates his support for this drastic policy after his advisors tell him that,

---

335   *Daily Telegraph* 8/2/17.
336   Ibid., 20/3/17.
337   Pope-Hennessy: *Queen Mary, 1867-1953*, p.508.

starved of supplies, England will be "forced to her knees within four to six months."[338] The Chief of the Admiralty Staff in Berlin sends out secret instructions to the effect that as of 1st February, "every enemy merchant vessel encountered within the barred area is to be attacked without delay." This included not only neutral vessels in the prescribed area, but hospital ships. The bringing in of prizes is urgently desired, especially if they have large quantities of gold, platinum, nickel, steel and iron wire, chrome, copper, barbed wire, quicksilver, rubber; anything that could be utilised for the German war effort. "This form of warfare is to force England to make peace and thereby to decide the whole war. <u>Energetic</u> action is required, but above all <u>rapidity</u> of action." The instructions go on. "The sole aim is, that each boat shall fire her entire supply of ammunition as often as possible."[339] Nothing is allowed to interfere, special orders for the suppression of venereal disease are even issued to maintain crews at their optimum strengths for the prosecution of the submarine campaign.

In mid-April, Admiral Beatty reports to the King that, in command of the Grand Fleet, his time is greatly taken up with combating this determined German menace. At best, he thinks they may be able to account for having destroyed four enemy submarines. "The weather had been greatly against us as we have experienced for the last two months nothing but blizzards and very heavy gales of wind which has made active operations almost impossible."[340] His primary aim, acknowledging that he cannot prevent all losses, is to enable passage of the Scandinavian traffic to be continued as well as possible, and to this end he is operating a convoy system. Much faith is being placed in this innovation, introduced firstly in bringing coal backwards and forwards across the Channel. By May, convoys will be used in the Atlantic too. Nonetheless the losses in British shipping claimed by German submarines after 1st February are astounding. Information delivered to His Majesty at the palace from the Netherlands reports "that no power of inventiveness on our part has been able to prevent it." This disturbing document informs the King that the enemy claims to have accounted for the sinking of 6,975,000 tons of shipping. "No wonder she shrinks and calls us pirates!…" they gloat. "To beat her with every imaginable weapon, to wear her down till the iron claws by which she binds our enemies together are bust asunder must be our incessant work till peace comes, for not before England's will is broken will the world be right for peace."[341]

During the first two years of the war "it may be said that scarcity of food was not felt at all. The working classes, with higher wages, actually enjoyed far better and more substantial meals than they had been able to obtain in normal times." There were issues with a supply of sugar, but aside from that, the people of Britain marvelled at how normal the food situation remained. "The plenty which prevailed surprised many people who had been taught to fear that famine would follow war in a country which relied on the production of others for the greater part of its food, and some of whom in 1914, indulged in panic buying to stock their larders against the hungry days which they believed to be imminent." But the losses in food supplies coming into the country at the hands of submarines in 1917 is exacerbated by a poor harvest the year before. In the last part of 1916, in certain official quarters there are growing concerns about the amount of foodstuffs available. Ministers begin preaching publicly about restraint and economy; "but their appeal was too vague in form to secure an effective response. It was difficult, too, to persuade people whose eating habits were not extravagant that they must eat less when in hotels and restaurants the most elaborate and expensive meals could be served to all who could pay for them." In mid-November, the "standard" loaf of bread is implemented; the size and weight regulated, and by the beginning of December, the

338   RA GV/PRIV/AA60/242.
339   RA PS/PSO/GV/C/Q/1145/10.
340   RA PS/PSO/GV/C/Q/832/373.
341   RA PS/PSO/GV/C/Q/1552/8.

Board of Trade, who have been granted "wide powers… for the control of the manufacture, sale and use of food," have met repeatedly with hotel and restaurant managers and a limit has been imposed on the number of courses which can be served at luncheon and dinner in public eateries. This "plan to curb the appetite of the gourmand" limited meals to "a nominal two courses at the midday meal and a nominal three at any meal taken between 6 and 9:30pm."[342] But it is not taken that seriously. Patrons simply ask for seconds and restaurants make the courses bigger.

The King has been aware of heightening concerns since talks began in November 1916 and the President of the Board of Trade has visited him to talk at some length about food supplies. Shortly after that meeting, His Majesty had issued a proclamation that reinforced the Government's decision to place food regulations under the all-encompassing Defence of the Realm Act; by now not so popularly referred to by the public as a killjoy of sorts named Dora. The Ministry of Food is founded to combat rising prices and the concerns over a lack of available supplies. Lord Devonport took on the role of Food Controller. "A good deal was expected by the public from [him] - probably much more than it was in his power to accomplish." The chief complaints are that he shows "a hesitation amounting almost to timidity in forming decisions, and that by handling this problem in a piecemeal way which involved the issue of a multiplicity of Orders he confused the public and left many opportunities of evasion open to the unscrupulous."[343]

In February, Devonport works out a system that gauges the total quantities of meat, flour, bread and sugar used in any week should not exceed certain projections based on a specific allowance for each person at each meal. There is also a day factored in on which people are expected to go meat free. None of this is yet compulsory, and the projections are referred to as "honour rations"[344] by one publication; but the scale is adopted with vigour at the palace. In fact, the His Majesty is so determined to adhere to this scale, that all of the food is laid out on a first come, first served basis, "and at breakfast those who were late got nothing," explained Fritz Ponsonby. "Lord Marcus Beresford, who came to stay, quickly got the hang of this and dogged the Queen's footsteps into the dining room. The point was that there was just enough and no more for everyone; but as most people helped themselves too generously, there was nothing left for the person who came last." On one occasion, a courtier finds himself delayed on the telephone at the start of breakfast and arrives to find that everything has been claimed. "He rang the bell and asked for a boiled egg. "If he had ordered a dozen turkeys he could not have made a bigger stir. The King accused him of being a slave to his inside, of unpatriotic behaviour, and even went so far as to hint that we should lose the war on account of his gluttony."[345]

In Germany, the Kaiser lives in a state of luxury that is "hardly distinguishable from peacetime court life."[346] In total contrast, the restraint shown at the royal table in London by the beginning of 1917 far exceeds that shown by most of His Majesty's subjects who have the means to pay for whatever food they desire, and the lengths that the King and Queen go to set an example to the public as concerns rise over food levels reach sometimes comical proportions. One Minister jokes about courtiers returning to duty at Buckingham Palace and dreading the "change from the ample luxury and service of his own table to the spartan regime of the Royal Household." In addition to the ban on alcohol still in effect, the wife of His Majesty's librarian describes one meal as comprising mulligatawny soup, vegetable cutlets, green peas, new potatoes, and cold baked custard in china cups. In 1917 a dinner given by the King for 32 guests consisted of soup, fish, chicken

342 (ed.) Hammerton & Wilson: *The Great War Vol.XII*, pp.435-444.
343 Ibid.
344 *Daily Sketch* 14/4/17.
345 Syonsby: *Recollections of Three Reigns*, p.329.
346 Stibbe: *Kaiser Wilhelm II: The Hohenzollerns at War*, p.275.

and macaroni. By comparison, the French President provided his dinner companions on a similar date with "caviar, turbot, saddle of lamb, roast partridge and roast pheasant, salad, Neapolitan ice, strawberries, gateaux, grapes, peaches and pears."[347]

In May His Majesty appeals to the public based on a proclamation issued by George III in 1800. "We are authorised to state that the King is not asking his subjects to do anything which he is not prepared to do himself," reports *The Morning Post.* "Very early in February strict rationing was introduced into the Royal Household and has been steadily adhered to." The Master of the Household has taken an unprecedented step in discussing the matter with the press, and has "stated emphatically that the King would never ask, and had never asked, his people to make sacrifices in which he was unprepared to share."[348] His Majesty is risking a repeat of the abstention fiasco in 1915, when he was left high and literally dry by Lloyd George; but this time there are shortages to consider and it is considered worth the chance. Essentially, what the King is asking his people to do if they are in a financial position not to have to rely on bread as a staple part of their diets, is to conform with what is already in practice in the Royal Household and has been for weeks: "To reduce the consumption of bread in their respective families by at least one-fourth of the quantity consumed in ordinary times. To abstain from the use of flour in pastry and moreover carefully to restrict or wherever possible to abandon the use thereof in all other articles than bread."[349]

The proclamation is well received by the mainstream press. "The King is practicing what he preaches, and preaches in words of fine dignity... His Majesty's words breathe the spirit which brought us into the war 1,000 days ago, and which has since sustained us in efforts for exceeding in character and extent anything the most sanguine amongst us ever dared to hope."[350] *The Times* thinks that this can only be considered an interim measure. Any appeals for voluntary rationing have not succeeded and the only thing that can possibly avert serious deficiency in food supplies is compulsory rationing. "If the King's proclamation convinces the country during the interval that every day's waste brings real want nearer it will have done all that anyone has a right to expect it to do."[351] Thanks to this campaign for economy, led by His Majesty's example; bread consumption was lowered to an appreciable extent. Metal badges are produced for those who have taken *The King's Pledge*, but they cannot be manufactured quickly enough. Purple ribbons are handed out instead. Lord Cecil tells his constituents that if they are eating the same amount of bread, sugar, and potatoes as they did before the war, "he or she is guilty of disloyalty to the country and to those fighting for us."[352] And for those that are unwilling to exercise restraint, they are named and shamed. *The Daily Graphic* identifies levels of success in voluntary rationing such as Portsmouth and Colchester, and tells the entire country that Birmingham is consuming more since the publication of the King's proclamation in early May.

Public kitchens are opened; to help those in need obtain a decent meal at a cheap price in times of high prices. Queen Mary is particularly invested in these and opens the first one on Westminster Bridge Road in May 1917. After a thorough inspection, Her Majesty stands behind the counter, 'and with much grace and kindliness helped to supply a long string of poor people with dinner... "The Queen, her peoples' waitress," says *The Evening Standard.* Wearing a grey outfit and a large

---

347   Rose: *King George V,* pp.177-178.
348   *Morning Post* 3/5/17.
349   Hammerton: *Our King & Queen: A Pictorial Record of Their Lives,* pp.32-33.
350   *Daily Telegraph* 3/5/17.
351   *The Times* 3/5/17.
352   *Daily Telegraph* 12/5/17.

hat trimmed with ostrich feathers, the Queen, assisted by Princess Mary who keeps track of what is served, provides dinner anyone who cares to take their place in the queue.

"Rice Pudding?" She asks as a plate is handed up by a tiny little girl.

A brimming supply was loaded onto it. "My dear, do take care" cries the Queen. "Don't upset it!" The communal kitchen quickly runs out of plates, for a building crowd has flocked to see the royal workers. "The Queen sympathised with those who came without altogether, but when a woman asked for a rhubarb jelly mould on the same plate with hot roast beef Her Majesty made a little protest before complying."[353]

Of course, as well as eating less, the people of Britain can try and produce more for themselves, and once again the King and Queen are determined to set an example. They have an allotment at Windsor and they plant potatoes, sweating alongside members of the household who have been put to work. They spend nearly a full week at it. A portion of the grounds at Buckingham Palace are also set aside for cultivating potatoes, the Queen picks up apples that have been blown down at Windsor so as they do not go to waste and there is a drive led by Their Majesties to cultivate herbs used for medicinal purposes which had previously been obtained from Germany and Austria.

The King does all he can to promote cultivation, economy and food production. The first visit he makes is to a margarine factory. Butter is now at two shillings a pound, and even the purists who scorn margarine, of which the King privately admits he is one, cannot afford to be as fussy. His Majesty's tour is to try and help down "the last brick in the crumbling wall of prejudice against the universal use of margarine."[354] At the Maypole factory at Southall the King spends 45 minutes watching margarine and chemicals being pumped through a mass of pipes before looking in on the factory's recreation room and dining hall; both of which have been converted into hospitals. In the following months there are visits to biscuit factories, a seed distribution establishment and even fishing towns like Grimsby, "where they saw fish being slung in baskets from trawlers to the quay, and long lines of cod, plaice, whiting and turbot exposed for auction in the sheds. As they walked through the docks the King and Queen were almost hemmed in by crowds of cheering fish workers, but they took the buffeting and inconvenience with the greatest humour."[355]

His Majesty also gives his approval for Royal parks to be utilised. Many of London's do not have suitable soil to yield good crops, and the city atmosphere is thought too dirty but at Hyde Park a "West End Allotment" is created. A member of the park's staff will always be on hand to talk to the public about how to grow food and what they might be able to accomplish should they be looking for advice. Portions of Richmond and Bushey Parks are brought under the plough too and sections of the gardens at Osborne House on the Isle of Wight are planted with vegetables. Plots that were "a blaze of harmonious colour throughout the whole of summer"[355] are now planted full of potatoes.

But *The Times* is correct. His Majesty's proclamation and the drive for voluntary economy in food consumption proves to be an interim measure. By the end of 1917 compulsory rationing is being brought into effect. Two meatless days are to be factored into the supply to each person; and everyone from the King to his poorest subjects will be entitled to buy for themselves no more than four pounds of bread and two and a half of meat in a week. His Majesty's subjects have until the beginning of October to apply for their ration cards and the King and Queen will be issued with them just like everybody else. Jam, meat, sugar, cheese and of course bread are all

353   *Evening News* 21/5/17.
354   *Daily Graphic* 30/11.
355   (ed.) Hammerton & Wilson: *The Great War Vol.XVIII*, p.132.
356   *Evening Standard* 4/1/17.

under Government control. And for his part, His Majesty continued to press his Government on the intricacies of satisfying the nation's stomach in the long term. At the end of the year he has Stamfordham pen a letter to Lloyd George's secretary after a drive through London.

> The King desires me to write to you to beg that you may express to the Prime Minister how seriously His Majesty regards the system which compels the poorer classes to submit to the inconvenience and discomfort of waiting, sometimes for hours, in long queues in order to purchase the necessaries of life. This morning The King and Queen in going to and from Deptford saw instances of these queues, and it brings home to Their Majesties the hardship experienced by the poor, while the richer portion of the community do not suffer in this respect. It means in many cases women having to absent themselves from their homes taking their children with them, to wait no matter what the weather may be, wasting valuable time, and not infrequently the women are obliged to stay away from work thereby losing pay. The old cry of "one law for the rich and another for the poor" is often raised unfairly, but in this instance one could hardly deny that it is justifiable.[357]

"A Flame of Patriotism and Self-Sacrifice"

It is as well that his interest in all facets of the nation's plight are sustained. For there is no question by this point that the war will continue into 1918. After the events of the Calais Conference, the army had followed the Germans as they staged a retreat back to an impressive new position; the Hindenburg Line. In April the Battle of Arras began; Britain's subsidiary effort attached to General Nivelle's grand offensive. The Canadians surged forward and seized the commanding Vimy Ridge that the King had viewed enviously from afar the previous summer. Along the line British troops advanced as far as three and a half miles. "This news bucks one up"[358] writes the King, but although this was an impressive achievement, that is where success expired. The coveted breakthrough of the German line does not follow and once again the advance disintegrates into scrappy, attritional warfare. Part of the reason that the battle ambles on is to shore up the French. To the south of the Aisne, having promised to end the war swiftly, Nivelle's spectacular plan is a spectacular failure. The direct consequences include *collective disobedience* (mutinies) amongst French troops. In Britain, Lloyd George faces humiliation. He had bought into Nivelle's ridiculously optimistic plan for the spring "with reckless enthusiasm"[359] and relegated Haig to serving under him. To say that he has egg on his face is putting it lightly. As Stamfordham says to the Governor General of Australia: "Nivelle was for the moment to be their saviour, and in an evil moment the powers that be here agreed practically to put Haig under Nivelle. Within a few weeks Nivelle was 'degommed' and Petain put in his place and Haig once more a free agent, if not indeed top dog as he ought to be."[360]

Lloyd George is chastened after his attempts to place the BEF entirely under French command. As his private secretary and lover noted in her diary on 12th May: "Nivelle has fallen into disgrace, and let [him] down badly... Haig has come out on top in this fight between the two chiefs, and I fear [the Prime Minister] will have to be very careful in future as to his backings of the French against the English."[361] This is something he is evidently aware of, for when Haig sees the French Government reeling in the face of their enormous setback, thoroughly despondent, he credits Lloyd

357   PA: F/29/1/50: Lloyd George.
358   RA GV/PRIV/GVD/1917 (10/4).
359   Prior & Wilson: *Passchendaele: The Untold Story,* p.30.
360   RA/PS/PSO/GV/C/P/284/104.
361   Prior & Wilson: *Passchendaele: The Untold Story,* p.31.

George with bucking them up in mid-May. "There is no doubt that he is very popular with the French and they seem to believe in him," wrote the Commander in Chief to His Majesty. Rather than reel at the apparent hypocrisy on display, Haig was willing to believe that the change in the Prime Minister might be permanent. "I must say that he appeared in quite a new light at this last conference, and spoke out as the champion of the British Army and British interests in a way that delighted my heart. In fact it is the only conference at which I have been present at which Your Majesty's representations have taken their rightful place. So all this seems to look hopeful for the future."[362] Robertson, too, gave a positive appraisal of Lloyd George at this conference.

> The Prime Minister was very firm indeed with the French Government and insisted that they should say really what they meant and that he would not have our men killed unless the French also fought to the full extent… He spoke very well and very strongly on the necessity for keeping up pressure on the Germans… On the whole I think it is the best conference we have had… The Prime Minister did his part very well and I feel that we have once more pulled the French together and got them going.[363]

Given his new strengthened position, it was predictable what Haig would want to do when the emphasis for the rest of the year's campaigning on the Western Front fell on the shoulders of his troops after the fall of Nivelle. He had long been hankering after the launch of an offensive around Ypres. The lofty ambitions that Haig holds for his campaign are to completely expel the Germans from Belgian soil by advancing out of the dreaded Ypres salient and seizing the Belgian coast too as part of the bargain. At the Admiralty, Jellicoe was vocalising loudly about the submarine campaign, and a victory along the coast would take the bases from which this menace operated.

But as a commander on the Western Front, Haig can do nothing without the consent of His Majesty's Government. And it was not an easy job to convince them as summer arrived. Despite the fact that he had been humiliated earlier in the year, and despite his posturing about leaving military matters to military professionals, Lloyd George is reticent about the scale of Haig's campaign in Flanders. But his own suggestions once again revolve around distant theatres and when these prove unrealistic he proves remarkably docile when it comes to finding a different, viable path. There is a difference between taking the advice of the military authorities to make an informed decision, and the Government accepting it as the last word without question, but this nuance is lost in the run up to the Third Battle of Ypres. What Lloyd George does do, is attach a caveat to the campaign. As it stood on the eve of battle, the Third Battle of Ypres would either achieve all it set out to in the opening throes, and Haig would receive sanction to carry on; or it would not meet expectations, in which case the Government would call it off.

The King's message to Haig reveals just how effective the pre-emptive strike in Flanders at Messines is at the beginning of June: "I rejoice that, thanks to thorough preparation and splendid co-operation of all arms, the important Messines Ridge, which has been the scene of so many memorable struggles, is again in our hands. Tell General Plumer and the Second Army how proud we are of this achievement, by which in a few hours the enemy was driven out of strongly entrenched positions held by him for two and a half years."[364] "The Boche got 450,000 tons of ammunition on the top of him, almost a million pounds of explosive under him and the intervals filled up with gas and boiling oil!"[365] Writes an officer on Plumer's staff to the palace.

362   RA PS/PSO/GV/C/Q/832/138.
363   RA PS/PSO/GV/C/Q/1114/21
364   *Daily Telegraph* 11/6/17.
365   RA PS/PSO/GV/PS/WAR/QQ18/05707.

But the course of this sort of limited, meticulous attack was not to be repeated to sufficient effect. What was becoming apparent, namely at Vimy Ridge and at Messines, was that bite and hold was a better way to make progress into the enemy line, but by the time the campaign begins, this knowledge has been ignored. The Third Battle of Ypres is launched on 31st July 1917, and on the following day the heavens open and hampers progress. "The most beastly day I ever saw," writes the King in London. "Never stopped raining all day."[366] Throughout the beginning of August, as his troops struggle to drag themselves through the mire in Flanders to no conclusive avail, there are endless downpours. It improves by the time the court adjourns to Windsor Castle for a well earned rest after the frantic activity of summer, but the Earl of Cavan, commanding his corps on the Western Front, reports to His Majesty that it will take more than a few days to improve conditions in Belgium. "Langemarck is still on a quaking bog; if the surface is dry you can just get over it, if not, you sink in to the armpits."[367]

The truth is, that like the Battle of the Somme, the impetus has gone out of the fighting in Belgium and what began as a vast endeavour to sweep the enemy from the battlefield has become another attritional disaster aimed at edging forward at huge cost to the country's manpower. David Lloyd George and his Government show no signs of ordering a halt to the campaign, despite having prepared themselves for this eventuality, and the army fights on. Haig changes the personnel in command of the battle. Out goes General Gough, the kind of bullish individual better suited to try and ram the enemy off the field, and in comes Plumer, the victor of Messines. He is to employ the same tactics now to the main summer offensive as proved so successful in this preparatory endeavour. He will be making smaller, clinical advances a step at a time to try and overcome areas of the battlefield that have proved particularly traumatic to try and conquer. At the conclusion of each, only when his men are fully prepared and his guns brought up, will he set off again.

And this he does, but as the weeks wear on, the Third Battle of Ypres descends into chaos. In declining conditions, in which tens of thousands of men are added to Britain's depressing casualty lists, it is not until the beginning of November that the symbolic village of Passchendaele is seized. By this time it makes little difference to the outcome of the war at large. The army has failed, but Britain's politicians, who hold the constitutional key to calling off this ailing offensive, have been mute observers. Much blame will devolve onto the King's officers in the aftermath of a battle that has become synonymous with the wasteful attrition of the Great War, but the Prime Minister must take his share of it as well. "He too wanted a sudden, smashing victory, preferably carried out by non-British troops on a battlefield far distant from the Western Front. But while he sought such a scenario, he sanctioned Passchendaele and so allowed the British army to be diminished by some 200,000 men over a period of only four months."[368] This will not be considered, least of all by Lloyd George himself, at the turn of the year when it comes to planning the continuance of the war and replacing huge losses.

In 1917, the conduct of the war and its progression has forced the Home Front to the top of the King's agenda. Constant pressures and shortages have left the country exhausted and miserable. "Labour was growing increasingly restless. The number of working days lost to strikes in 1917 was well up on the previous year... In the deteriorating economic and social climate, the left-wing press... began to see the capitalist social order, and with it the Monarchy, as increasingly vulnerable."[369] And yet sheer, relentless hard work, coupled with an awakening to the importance

366   RA GV/PRIV/GVD/1917 (1/8).
367   RA PS/PSO/GV/C/Q/832/58.
368   Prior & Wilson: *Passchendaele: The Untold Story*, p.xiv.
369   Prochaska: *The Republic of Britain, 1760-2000*, p.156.

of modern public relations has paid dividends for His Majesty. In the latter part of the year the mainstream press lauds royal efforts. Editorials heap fresh praise on the King as a result of his endeavours in 1917. "Nor," says a Northcliffe paper of all publications, has he been treated fairly. "He has sometimes had very much the reverse from the politicians."[370] In fact, when the war began it was clear under Asquith's Liberal Government, that "there existed a marked tendency to belittle the influence of the crown."[371] Had not all of the recruiting done in his name been focused on Kitchener as opposed to the Head of State?

But however hard he works, it is nothing if people cannot see his efforts. It is stated that at the beginning of the war His Majesty was kept in the background, "and the incalculable advantages which the possession of our ancient monarchy provides almost foolishly thrown away."[372] But now, the role that he has shaped for himself, with the help of Stamfordham, Wigram and Ponsonby; as well as many trusted and vocal correspondents, is praised relentlessly. The King has emerged as a patriotic figurehead for the nation; filling the immense void left by the death of his friend, Lord Kitchener. *The Daily Graphic* calls His Majesty a "Pioneer National Service Worker" on his 52nd birthday. "The Most English of Englishmen."[373] The country realises that no other British sovereign has ever come into closer touch with his people, with the average man and woman. Because of this the King is no "inaccessible being, remote from the common run of interests and emotions, one minutes contact with his steady humanity and a kindliness that is instantly felt to be free from the least trace of condescension is enough to change their minds." Common by the end of 1917 is the impression that the King "loathes anything that smacks of self-advertisement," and that nothing he does is contrived for the sake of publicity above all other considerations. "It has taken time for the British people to pierce through to the man behind this Sovereign, behind the trappings of royalty, behind, too, the stupidity of the censorship, and to know King George as he really is." For every subject that has not had the chance to meet His Majesty, they have the public accounts of those that have to inform their opinion of the King. "I have served under many men, says one anonymous official, "but I would sooner serve under King George than any of them." He describes His Majesty as diligence itself, consideration itself, and "absolutely loyal to his subordinates, whether they are Cabinet Ministers or on his personal staff or employed on one of his estates." He leads by example. "One cannot be even a few minutes in the King's company without realising that here is a man whose life pivots on his sense of duty and devotion to his country and to the Empire that he knows so well."[374]

"I think one's first impression of the King," says a correspondent, "and also one's last, is that he is genuine all through. There is not an atom of pose about him." This is a sentiment expressed repeatedly by those who come into contact with His Majesty. "They find themselves speaking and spoken to by a man who quite obviously means what he says, whose manner has the unmistakeable stamp of an honest human kindliness, who asks questions because he wants them answered, and who never has to pump up an interest he does not feel."[375] The King often vanishes on his tours. "You may take it from me that there is no 'conducting' the King round… There is always a little party going round… but very often you will look round and find the King is missing, and then you will find that he has slipped away round one of the machines… and is busy talking to some of the workmen."[376] The difference between the King of England and his German cousin is not lost on his

370   *Daily Mail* 13/9/17.
371   *The Globe* 12/10/17.
372   Ibid.
373   RA GV/PRIV/GVD/1917 (2/6).
374   *Daily Chronicle* 23/10/17.
375   Ibid.
376   *Lloyds Weekly News* 18/11/17.

people. There is not a trace in His Majesty of "the restless… vapouring, egotistical temperament of the Kaiser." But as the King says, you can never keep everybody happy. "Dear King," writes Enid Pritchard of Kensington. "Please will you not put quite such hard words in your speeches, because at my school we have them for dictation. Your speeces [sic] a very interesting but there are hard words in them."[377]

At the end of the year, the King and Queen manage a three week break at Sandringham. As soon as they arrive they go to Wolferton to see Johnnie in his little house. But in order to get this semblance of a rest, the war has to go with them. His Majesty's worries and concerns follow him, as do troops requiring medals. Visits have to be made to convalescent officers and the war encroaches more on royal life in Norfolk than ever before. His good wishes to all ranks in both the Royal Navy and the Army are published. "I realise your hardships… and rejoice in the successes you have won so nobly. The nation stands faithful to its pledges, resolute to fulfil them. May God bless your efforts and give us victory." There is a separate one too for those who have been maimed by this endless, miserable war, jointly issued by the King and Queen. "Our Christmas thoughts are with the sick and wounded sailors and soldiers… We wish all a speedy restoration to health, a restful Christmastide and brighter days to come."[378]

"Scarcely a family in the land today is without intimate and anxious interest in the fortunes of the soldier or the sailor, if not of the prisoner of war, or the sick or wounded man," writes *The Daily Telegraph* as 1918 approached. "The nation stands faithful… If in all things we act in the spirit of the King's assurance, we shall have nothing with which to reproach ourselves in the coming year."

The nation feels that it has lived to fight on after a year of abject misery and hardship. "We have entered the final stage of the war,"[379] it is proclaimed. But nobody is quick to assume victory, there is still all to play for. "So ends a busy and very anxious year," writes Queen Mary on New Year's Eve. "May God grant us a happier one in 1918, with a lasting peace for the whole world."[380]

377   PA: F/29/4/4: Lloyd George.
378   *Daily Telegraph* 26/12/17.
379   Ibid.
380   RA PRIV/QMD/1917 (31/12).

1918

Disrepair

"It is the Last Battle that Wins the War"

The strain of being the central character in Britain's war effort, of projecting confidence and positivity every time he leaves the palace, continues to take its toll on His Majesty. The King's beard is turning white, the lines about his eyes increasing. The war has entered its fourth year. "The atmosphere here has been decidedly low," writes Wigram, "and I have been endeavouring to assure the King that it is the last battle that wins the war."[1] Sometimes it feels as if nothing he does is enough. "It was disheartening for His Majesty to practice virtue yet to be identified with tyranny; to live austerely… and drive himself to the limit of endurance with State papers and public appearances, yet to be reminded by Ramsay MacDonald that "it is the Red Flag which now floats over the Imperial Palace in Petrograd."[2] In 1918 a committee is appointed by the Government that suggests that no person not born of natural British subjects should be employed in a Government office during the war unless they can provide a justifiable reason why the nation needs them in their post. Lord Justice Bankes is to report to Bonar Law on the advisability of a continuance of their appointment. His Majesty is not buoyed to find out that he is of extraction that might theoretically require him to justify his role as King of England to such a committee.

Their Majesties are forced to stay in Norfolk for a prolonged period of time at the beginning of the year; only coming down to London for urgent business because there is structural work at Buckingham Palace that can be deferred no longer on account of the war. "The quadrangle is like a builder's yard, and scaffolding covers that part of the palace usually occupied by the King."[3] It is their longest stay out of London since 1914. His Majesty has strained his hand and cannot shoot, so he ice-skates in between dealing with boxes. The Royal Family clear nine inches of snow surrounding York Cottage themselves. "Hard work but very good exercise,"[4] and Sundays are reserved for long family walks after church and going to see the horses.

On his first day back in London after repairs are concluded at the palace, the King resumes hospital visits before plunging into a schedule of informal discussions with ministers, receptions, visits to Harwich and Deal and investitures that includes welcoming large contingents of recipients of the new OBE. His Majesty's speech at the opening of Parliament is less than three minutes long and to the point. "It is our duty," he concludes, "to prosecute the war with all the vigour that we possess."[5] It is the King's duty to be bullish, but it is not a sentiment that comes easily at this juncture. "Looking at the whole progress of the war as straight as possible," writes Lord Esher to the Queen, "there is no great satisfaction to be got out of the results of the past few months…

---

1   PP: CW 2/1/18.
2   Rose: *King George V*, pp.221-222.
3   *Daily Sketch* 5/1/18.
4   RA GV/PRIV/GVD/1918 (17/1).
5   Ibid 8/2/18.

The position of the Germans has improved and ours has become less satisfactory."[6] And so it will remain until the Americans begin to arrive in force. It is believed that the enemy are planning a significant offensive before that can occur, and there are worrisome issues everywhere His Majesty turns. A shortage of manpower, threats to the Home Front in the shape of both enemy attacks and shortages of supplies; the list goes on. And the King and Queen are about to sacrifice a third son to the war effort. Prince Henry is to go to Sandhurst. As heir to the throne, David is quite purposefully protected from a full experience at the front. Bertie's health has conspired to keep him mostly out of harm's way, but neither will apply so much to Harry should he find himself ready for active service, for how can a King preach to his subjects about the need for every available man if he holds his third son back from the line of fire?

Personal considerations aside, the world as he knows it is crumbling. In 1918 it feels like civilisation is under threat, and Russia is one of the most deeply concerning matters for His Majesty at the turn of the year. The revolution is a puzzle for the rest of Europe. The otherthrow of the Romanov dynasty was the first such displacement of such a regime since 1789, and in the midst of it there is a war to win that Russia herself helped to start. Much to their allies' surprise and relief, the Provisional Government had managed to mount an offensive in July 1917. "Whether it is only a flash in the pan or this effort will be supported all along the front," postulated Stamfordham, "remains to be seen, but the political situation still remains very uncertain, and the Government are by no means safe in their saddle."[7] The Russian Army launched itself against the Austro-Hungarians in Galicia towards Lemberg. Initially it was a success, but much like on the Western Front, the advance soon ground to a halt and amassed heavy casualties. Mutinies occurred. Soldiers' committees were formed where they discussed what they wanted to do next. Orders were not obeyed, if they ever were, until they had been debated by the men. With German intervention, the Austrians hit back and the Russian offensive collapsed. In a matter of days they fell back some 150 miles. Riga was captured and the Russian Army disintegrated. "Units disappeared, fought each other, ransacked towns burned manor houses"[8] or simply went home. By the end of the year anything up to 370,000 men had deserted. A report in August from Petrograd that arrived at Buckingham Palace told of chaos on Russian railways, and the country's financial position was described as "impossible." Nobody was paying any taxes, and the Provisional Government was printing more and more money. Security is apparently laughable and Minister-Chairman Kerensky and his colleagues live in terror at the thought of a counter-revolution. He is "still the only individual that has any hold on the people, but the nation is doomed if its 180 millions cannot produce a bigger man. He has got the theatrical qualities of a Napoleon but none of his moral courage or useful ruthlessness." He sits in the Emperor's sitting room at the Winter Palace, and sleeps in a Tsar's bed. He drives in Nicholas's Rolls Royce and stills dreams childishly of peace with Germany by consent. "The editor of the official military paper told me the other day," wrote Buchanan, "that he wanted to publish some reports from two returned Russian doctors, illustrative of the treatment of Russian prisoners in Germany. Kerensky said he was not to "worry the Germans too much."[9]

None of this inspires the King with any confidence, but there is worse to come. On Easter Sunday 1917, while the King and Stamfordham were wrangling over the Tsar's potential asylum, Vladimir Ilyich Ulyanov, his wife, and thirty of their closest friends had left Zurich for Germany. History knows him better as Lenin. It is German policy to support revolution and unrest in enemy

---

6   RA PS/PS/GV/C/Q/724/99.
7   RA PS/PSO/GV/C/P/284/104.
8   Gerwarth: *The Vanquished: Why the First World War Failed to End 1917-1923*, p.32.
9   RA PS/PS/GV/C/Q/722/55.

countries, and they had facilitated his return to Russia with the hope that he would rally the Bolshevik movement against the Provisional Government, to try and replace it with something wholly more radical, before taking Russia out of the war. On 16th April 1917, Lenin arrived in Petrograd to a rapturous reception, with supporters waving red flags, throwing flowers and singing the *Marseillaise*.

From the very beginning of their seizure of power, the Provisional Government, aiming for liberal reform, had to make allowances to appease the far Left, including the Bolsheviks, who had a vastly different outlook; including on the matter of the Tsar and his future. As 1917 progressed, Kerensky promised to continue with the war, which undermined his Government's position, and struggled to effect the changes that they had promised. All of this was to Lenin's advantage. He declared that the war was an imperialist venture and needed to be ended, which was exactly what exhausted, hungry Russians wanted to hear.

Lenin's plans are made easier by the fact that someone else has dispensed with the Tsar. He missed his chance to steer a revolution to his own ends in 1905, and he was not about to make that mistake again. With the collapse of the military offensive in 1917 and the chaos that ensued in the army, the Provisional Government found itself in peril. An attempt at a coup was made in July, which failed, but disorder reigned throughout Russia by the time of the Bolshevik revolution, which was in fact a relatively low key coup that took place at the end of October. "The Provisional Government has been deposed," declared Lenin. "The task for which the people have been struggling has been assured… Long live the revolution of soldiers, workers and peasants."[10] At the end of October General Gourko, the Provisional Government's former Chief of Staff, by then in exile in London, told the King that there would have to be much blood spent before any lasting Government was established in Russia. He was not wrong.

Even with the change in leadership, the over-riding concern was still that Russia may make a separate peace, but in mid-November news arriving from Stockholm is promising. A report seen by the King says that "it would be folly for Bolsheviks to make a peace that would release millions of German soldiers to crush British and French democracies and saddle Europe with German Imperialism."[11] What the Bolsheviks want is more revolutions like their own all over the continent, not a resounding victory for the Kaiser. But in his declaration, Lenin pledged peace, and in order to keep his grip on the country intact, he had to deliver. On 15th December 1917, the Bolsheviks signed an armistice with the Central Powers, and this is ratified by the Treaty of Brest-Litovsk in March 1918. At the cost of a third of the population of the Tsar's Empire, not to mention 89% of Russia's coal; which he blamed on his predecessors, Lenin was free to concentrate on stabilising Bolshevik power.

"Encouraging Mutiny"

Every now and again, Stamfordham attends one of His Majesty's conferences and it startles him that much, or that he believes is so crucial that he deems it necessary to record the conversation in its entirety for future reference.

In October 1917, the Prime Minister had arrived at the palace to espouse on the future of the war with His Majesty, and it was quite a performance. Lloyd George began by outlining the fact that much of the recent fighting had fallen to Britain, and that none of her allies looked set to take anything on of an offensive nature in the near future. This was a reasonable point, and the

10   Gerwath: *The Vanquished: Why the First World War Failed to End 1917-1923*, pp.34-35.
11   RA PS/PS/GV/C/Q/1552/16.

Prime Minister's logic was that in that case, once again, in 1918, the brunt of the offensive would rest with Britain and that she would suffer huge casualties as a result. Therefore when peace came, the country would be "unable to assert herself and to make her voice heard and her will prevail in the momentous decisions to be come in the council of peace." The Prime Minister declares that it is his duty "to ensure that whenever the climax is reached England is at the zenith of her military strength and in a position more than to hold her own among the nations of the world." He does not appear, however, to have considered that if Britain were not to fight, and the Allies were to lose the war, that Britain's military strength would be decimated, not simply find itself in a weakened position. Britain would be a defeated power and would hold no cards at all when it came to any council of peace. "We must meet in conference," he said of the Allies, "and... consider the wisdom of contenting ourselves with remaining on the defensive in Flanders, curtailing our subsidiary campaigns." The Prime Minister advocated sending every available man home in that case for employment in agriculture, shipbuilding, aircraft construction and so forth. "In this way we could hold the enemy on the Western Front until such time as our Allies consented to cooperate in a general offensive: meanwhile our numbers would be increasing and the training of the army perfected." This plan did not seem to have taken into account the idea that Germany might launch an offensive, which was very much on the cards, or what the consequences would be if everyone had been sent home to tend fields and work in shipyards. Naturally the King was highly disturbed, and must have stated once again his belief that the military authorities should be attending to military matters as the experts, because despite the fact that on 25th September 1917, Lloyd George had once again assured the French Minister of War that he would assist in putting all the armies on the Western Front under a French Commander in Chief, he assures His Majesty "that he did <u>not</u> wish to interfere with the military authorities or their strategy. He only wants to win the war - and win it well." One can only imagine the expressions of both His Majesty and Stamfordham when they heard this, but then the Prime Minister also stated that "the politicians would lay down when they thought the climax would come and their general outline of the plan to be adopted. The general staffs would then have to confer without the politicians and work out the details."[12]

At the beginning of 1918 the King has fresh reason to fume in Lloyd George's direction as the erosion of his political influence continues at the hands of his Prime Minister. He had already bullishly refused to make Max Aiken a peer at his friend Lloyd George's behest. It takes all the guile of Lloyd George and Bonar Law to convince him to consent to an honour for this businessman with a controlling stake in the *Daily Express*. Now, the Prime Minister has appointed the Canadian as Minister of Information, and insists that he should also hold the Cabinet office of Chancellor of Duchy of Lancaster. Stamfordham points out that the Duchy is the personal property of the Sovereign, entailing closer relations between the King and its Chancellor than with many of his ministers, and yet once again the King is forced into accepting an appointment of which he does not approve in an historic crown office. Only weeks later, the *Daily Express* is attacking His Majesty over a visit David has made to the Pope. A visit that the King was against anyway. "To be attacked so unfairly, and by a newspaper belonging to a member of the Government, was a double humiliation - and one without redress."[13]

Towards the end of January 1918, once again Lloyd George arrives at Buckingham Palace in animated mood. He remains for over an hour, and in his own words "opened his heart" on the present military situation.

12   RA PS/PSO/GV/C/K/1340/1.
13   Rose: *King George V,* pp.204-208.

Stamfordham is primed like a boxer to address a number issues of concern to the palace, and lands the first punch when he demands to know the meanings of recent attacks on the military authorities, namely Haig and Robertson, in the Northcliffe press. The Palace are not the only ones questioning this sudden, unpatriotic fervour. *The Morning Advertiser* points out that the *Daily Mail* has the cheek to flog the army's hierarchy on one hand, whilst claiming to be *"The Soldier's Friend"* on the other. Another refers to Lloyd George's *"Press-Gang,"* and refers to the swelling in criticism of the conduct of the war away from his own doorstep as "his usual devices." At Westminster one MP has said "that attacks in the press on Admirals and Generals are cowardly. The men who make them, he remarked, are acting in a way in which gentlemen should not act at any time." He warns the Government, and particular the Prime Minister, "that they will never stand clear in the estimate of the public until they sever their connections with the newspapers."[14] Stamfordham also wants an explanation for the Prime Minister's own calls for "less secrecy and more open speaking on the part of the Government," namely feeding the press his complaints about the conduct of the war. Infuriatingly, Lloyd George merely says that the public wish to know the truth about what is transpiring at the front, and says that in that case it might be necessary for him "to publish some of his written opinion and forecasts which had been ignored or rejected by the military experts." Moving away from denying culpability for any press campaign against the generals, he proceeds to personally attack them. He says that the army has nobody who can dictate strategy. "Haig is a good fighter but not a strategist, not a big man, and I never thought he was." Later on he also says "Haig is no judge of men." As for Robertson, he says that he is no strategist either. He dismisses him on the basis of a lack of experience in the field and says that he

> Knows nothing of the fighting of this war and yet comes to the War Cabinet with all the airs of a great general. He has never originated any strategic plan and though I have frequently asked him in what manner he expects us to win the war he has never given me a reply, he is almost always wrong in his forecasts.

The Prime Minister also says that Robertson is "in with the press," which although it may have had a ring of truth to it was nonetheless a rich accusation coming from Lloyd George, especially when one of the papers in question belongs to Northcliffe. The Prime Minister complains that whenever he has "ventured to make suggestions or to question the soldiers' policy or strategy," he has been ignored. The fact that his strategic suggestions have generally been ridiculous does not occur to him. He says that "not only in the case of Romania but in that of Turkey and indeed the Western Front he had made in writing representations, suggestions, forecasts as to the proper strategy to be adopted only to have them rejected by the military experts: but he has been proved right, they wrong." This is a dubious interpretation of events if ever there was one.

From then on, Stamfordham is merely an observer as Lloyd George begins to rant, showing the sheer extent of his apathy and resentment for the military hierarchy. He claims that Haig told him that "when the big attack against Poelcappelle was made we should push through to Ostend," and that he himself had told the General, "never and you will only lose men."[15] If this is the case, then this attack was made in October, at a point when the Prime Minister had long since told Haig that the Government would call off any wasteful advances being made as part of the campaign on the Western Front. Having never made any attempt to use the prerogative he had secured for his

Government as casualties mounted the previous autumn, Lloyd George is heaping the full blame for the cost of Passchendaele on the army.

The Prime Minister has a frustrating tendency to pour contempt on the military authorities and instead look for answers from more junior officers. On this occasion, he declares that he has spoken to a very able Colonel, so someone who is by definition several ranks below any of the army commanders, "who has been for some time at the front, who said that with the exception of the brigadiers no general officers were even seen near the front line: they know nothing of the front and gave orders which it was impossible to carry out." Not only would a Colonel be in no position to make such a sweeping statement, but the claim is sheer nonsense. Lloyd George claims that only Plumer is remotely regarded by the men, again dubious, and says that the army has lost all respect for their commanders.

"Can you find any better generals to replace those now in command?" Stamfordham asks.

"I'm not at all sure that I can't" replies the Prime Minister.

His contempt for the army's hierarchy does not stop on the Western Front either. Lloyd George thinks that the War Office "is rotten and extravagant in men, money, material." This is the same War Office that Lloyd George himself assumed control of for months after Kitchener's demise. His Colonel informant has told him that "in every Battalion there are upwards of 100 men at "Headquarters" doing nothing. Even the army's horses, he claims, are overfed. Their oat allowance might be cut by 75%. "Altogether the Prime Minister's attitude was one of profound dissatisfaction and distrust of the army and of the conduct of the war. He said he sometimes felt things could not go on as they are and that he should have to come to the King and say so."[16]

With this in mind then, it is unsurprising when the Prime Minister launches a sting to get rid of Sir William Robertson. "It is a thousand pities that [they] cannot work in unison," General Rawlinson had written, "for it makes things very difficult."[17] The disruption caused by the enmity between Downing Street and the War Office is not lost on those that had to live with the fallout. "We must have complete confidence in each other, if we are to stand the strain," writes Hubert Gough, commanding Fifth Army in January.

> The action of the Government has not been above serious criticism during the last two months, and the press, with their veiled attacks on the CIGS and the Chief and the Army generally, and in consequence that great necessity of the moment, mutual trust and confidence, has been considerably shaken... We are no longer forced to attack carefully prepared positions, as we were in the past three years, we can afford now to wait, because the Bosch can't afford to wait. If we don't attack, he must. What is essential now is to stop all this crabbing, all these attacks on the Army, whatever their sources may be and restore complete and <u>mutual</u> confidence.[18]

For the King, the whole affair is frightening confirmation of how limited his influence has become. Politics and politicians of the time worry His Majesty to distraction.

> His whole heart was set on national unity in the supreme effort to win the war at this most crucial stage, and day by day he was made aware of quarrels and intrigue within the Cabinet

---

16   Ibid.
17   RA PS/PSO/GV/C/Q/2522/2/16.
18   RA PS/PSO/GV/C/Q/832/300.

and in the army which outraged his loyal spirit… He could not adjust his principles to an era of constant replacements and uncertainty of tenure in key positions.[19]

In November, following a humiliating reverse for the Italian Army at Caporetto, at an international conference Lloyd George proposed the formation of a Supreme War Council that would coordinate Allied policy. The body, which was opposed by General Robertson, was established under Foch, the new French commander, at Versailles, and Sir Henry Wilson, who along with Sir John French has the ear of the Prime Minister, is appointed as the Government's representative.

Just a few weeks later, Lloyd George persuades the French that the Supreme War Council should include an executive committee that would have a reserve of thirty Allied divisions, hundreds of thousands of men at its disposal. The Prime Minister, at a time when all expect a German offensive on the Western Front in the near future, was attempting to deny Haig access to British reserves unless their use was sanctioned by the council at Versailles. At the same time, Sir William Robertson was to be given the impossible choice of either switching places with Wilson and going to the "Versailles Soviet,"[20] as he refers to it, or remaining as CIGS but with his power curtailed. "What a dilemma for Robertson!" wrote Lord Beaverbrook. "What a desperate confusion of all his hopes and aspirations. Either way he was done for."[21] Lloyd George, of course, will support whichever post Robertson rejects. Unsurprisingly, he wants neither role. Even if it means an end to his military career of some four decades, as he says to Stamfordham, he believes that "the ridiculous system of setting up, practically two CIGS must result in failure and destruction of confidence amongst the troops as to who really is their commander. Men will not die for committees."[22]

Once again, Lloyd George has said nothing of this change to His Majesty. When Stamfordham reproaches him for this, the Prime Minister insists that Lord Derby, at the War Office, was supposed to have informed the King and that he forgot to do so. As Robertson has hoped, His Majesty is profoundly disturbed at the thought of his removal. Stamfordham assures the General that the King "considers that your retirement from office, especially at this critical period of the war, will entail an incalculable loss alone upon the army and upon the nation generally." It is added that personally, the King does not want to lose an advisor with whom he has an established relationship and "in whom His Majesty has he most implicit confidence."[23]

After the opening of Parliament, Robertson calls on the King at Buckingham Palace. "The Prime Minister wants to get rid of him, it would be a national calamity."[24] His Majesty holds little hope of trying to overcome Lloyd George, so attempts to convince Robertson to accept the Versailles posting. Robertson outlines for the King why he cannot commit to either job. He thinks that the system would be unworkable, and he would rather retire than work in it. And so the following day Stamfordham is sent to do battle with the Prime Minister once again. He arrives at 10 Downing Street mid-afternoon and expresses surprise on the King's behalf as to what is transpiring at the head of the army; as had His Majesty not happened to send for Lord Derby he would not have found out about the proposed changes. "I told him that the King strongly deprecated the idea of Robertson being removed from the office of CIGS, that his loss in that capacity would be an incalculable one to the army, would be resented in the country, rejoiced in by the enemy… and the King considered that Sir William had enjoyed the absolute confidence of the army officers and men."

19   Gore: *King George V, A Personal Memoir,* p.304.
20   RA PS/PS/GV/C/F1259/13.
21   Nicolson: *King George V: His Life and Reign,* pp.204-208.
22   RA PS/PS/GV/C/F/1259/15.
23   RA PS/PS/GV/C/F/1259/17.
24   RA GV/PRIV/GVD/1917 (12/2).

Lloyd George retorts that he doesn't share the King's favourable impression of Robertson, "who had never fought at the front, hardly ever visited the trenches, and was not known by the rank and file." He then tells Stamfordham that the opinions that were relied on by the palace were obviously manufactured for the King, a quip which goes insultingly against the very grain of everything the His Majesty's Private Secretary stands for. He repeats what he said on 22nd January, "that Robertson had displayed no capacity as a strategist, and asked where anyone could put their finger on the map and say that this or that is due to Robertson's advice. In fact," he claims, "his forecasts had generally been wrong."[25] Ministers are apparently ready to resign if Robertson remains in his current role with the special powers given to him to work alongside Kitchener. But if Robertson were to resign, Lord Curzon and Derby would apparently quit their posts. Once again the King is looking at the ruination of his Government. Stamfordham resorts to begging Robertson not to resign, but to record his disapproval of the system, his belief that it was unworkable, and might even cost us the war, but for the sake of the King, the army and the country, to remain on and do his best to carry out the new arrangement. Robertson agrees to consider this, and Stamfordham sits down with His Majesty to explain the day's events. "I am much worried as the Prime Minister is trying to get rid of Robertson," His Majesty writes afterwards. "If he doesn't look out his Government will fall. It is in deep water now."[26] But more pleading on the part of the King's Private Secretary is to no avail, for Robertson will not remain in his post with diminished powers. He cannot, he says, even do it for His Majesty when he believes that the scheme is disastrous, "and he could not look anyone in the face were he to do as I asked." Added to this conviction, support for him is his waning. "I have reported to the King the gist of what you told me, Stamfordham writes. "Needless for me to say with what deep regret His Majesty learnt of the conclusion of which you have arrived."[27] At one final meeting the King sits down with Lloyd George, who has already told Stamfordham that if His Majesty persists in trying to maintain Robertson's current position for him, "the Government could not carry on, and the King would have to find other ministers." His Majesty reiterates again that he believes the loss of Robertson to be a serious setback for the army, and in a time of war, the nation. "This, however the Prime Minister would not admit,"[28]

Marginalised by Lloyd George and at the end of his constitutional tether, later that day the King writes with regret that Wilson is to succeed Robertson as Chief of the Imperial General Staff. "I don't trust him,"[29] he writes. Wilson is the complete opposite of his predecessor, whom the King regards so highly. Whimsy or flippancy is not something that His Majesty expects from a senior official either. "Sir," Wilson writes at one stage, "the Boche has been very naughty, very naughty indeed. Sir; we must give him a whipping."[30] Esher, who has seen much of Wilson in France, is even more scathing when he warns the palace that: "Wilson... thinks that where Buddha and Christ have failed, he can succeed. You will see plenty of signs of this anon."[31] On 19th February, Robertson visits the palace for the last time as CIGS.

> It was with something more than mere regret that I took leave of the King... Indeed I felt so moved that I fear His Majesty thought me indifferent and callous. Quite the reverse was the case, and in fact I scarcely knew how to get through the interview. I have for many years experienced nothing but the kindest consideration from His Majesty, and at this particular

25   RA PS/PS/GV/C/F/1259/32.
26   RA GV/PRIV/GVD/1918 (13/2).
27   RA PS/PS/GV/C/F/1259/25.
28   RA PS/PS/GV/C/F/1259/32.
29   RA GV/PRIV/GVD/1918 (16/2).
30   Rose: *King George V* p.205.
31   RA PS/PSO/GV/C/Q/724/97

time to be prevented from carrying on the important and difficult work to be done, for the welfare and safety of country and the throne, is to me a real great sorrow.[32]

Stamfordham assures Robertson that His Majesty is consoled by the thought that he will be close at hand with counsel and advice whenever he may seek it. "I much regret his going," writes the King, "as I have absolute confidence in his judgement."[33]

Mere weeks later, His Majesty learns of another high profile departure through the medium of the press, as opposed to his Prime Minister. Hugh Trenchard, Chief of Air Staff is widely regarded as the *Father of the Royal Air Force,* he is a complex man, who somehow combines being stubborn, incoherent and clumsy with an obvious regard for the men serving under him and a coherent vision of the rapid development in his field. The sheer magnitude of his contribution to the Royal Flying Corps in the field is impossible to deny. The RFC had expanded and progressed beyond anyone's wildest dreams in the years since 1914. Initially left at home whilst others commanded the fledgling force in the field, Trenchard was a competent chief at home, until expansion divided the RFC into wings and he was given one of them, supporting Haig's First Army. The two got on well, and in August 1915 he became commander of the RFC in France. During his time in this post, given free reign by Haig to go about his work, he established the [crux] of Britain's air policy.

The Royal Air Force comes into being on 1st April 1918, with a separate air ministry having been formed at the beginning of the year. Trenchard returns home as chief, the Government's main advisor on the business of air fighting. He does not want to leave the front, and he knows that he is not suited to office work, but he is the only real candidate for the post in London and so he is recalled. Within a month he is completely disillusioned. "I am still on the brink of stopping," he writes to a confidant, "I am certain that I could get this show running perfectly if I only became a dictator at home, but of course this is impossible."[34] The King has complete faith in Trenchard, and his loss will be another blow, but the military man cannot live with the interference of Lord Rothermere, the new Air Minister. At the behest of Lloyd George, Rothermere is out to curb Haig's control over the air war on the Western Front. Trenchard resigns, and having pleaded with him to stay on, Rothermere suddenly accepts his letter in mid-April. When the Minister visits the palace to inform His Majesty, the King is miserable, and considers it "a great misfortune,"[35] not only because another trusted advisor has been dispensed with, or because it constitutes more ugly political manoeuvring when there is a war to be won, but also because it once again highlights how futile His Majesty feels that his own position has become. The following day, with the RAF having only been in existence for a fortnight, the situation worsens when another visitor informs the King that two members of the Air Board are going to resign because they cannot stomach Trenchard's replacement. 'The situation has been brought about by Rothermere who is impossible," writes His Majesty. "Wish he would go, but suppose Prime Minister won't let him."[36] In response to the King's objections about Trenchard's removal, Lloyd George tells Stamfordham that the King is "encouraging mutiny by taking up the cause of these officers whom the Government had decided to get rid of."[37]

But his Majesty is not the only one reeling from the removal of the man who has done so much to bring Britain's fledgling air force into being. Rothermere survives Trenchard by less than two

32   RA PS/PS/GV/C/F/1259/37.
33   RA GV/PRIV/GVD/1918 (19/2).
34   Jordan: *The Battle for the Skies,* pp.68-85.
35   RA GV/PRIV/GVD/1918 (13/4).
36   RA GV/PRIV/GVD/1918 (14/4).
37   Becket: *King George V and His Generals,* pp.259-260.

weeks. Questions are asked in Parliament, demands are made to give Trenchard a suitable role in the Royal Air Force, but nonetheless the new Chief of Air Staff offers Trenchard one of a number of sundry roles that are an insult to his position or require him to answer to Sykes. In the end, Trenchard assumes command of the Independent Air Force, the creation of which he had opposed as unnecessary. It is a come down, to say the least, and merely comprises a unit separate from the RAF command structure that is to concentrate its attentions fully on bombing Germany. He "spent the rest of the war attempting to effect a policy he believed in under the auspices of a command he didn't believe in." The day that the Armistice is signed he writes: "Thus the Independent Air Force comes to an end. A more gigantic waste of effort and personnel there has never been in any war."[38]

Amidst all of this upheaval, all of this bickering and transience in the upper echelons of the army, Sir Douglas Haig is aware that he is about to be attacked by the Germans on a vast scale. For there is a window of opportunity open to the enemy in which to win the war, to make all of the additional men who have come over from the Eastern Front after the signing of the Treaty of Brest-Litovsk and Russia's exit from the war count. If they have not won the war by the middle of the year, when the seemingly limitless influx of American troops begins to arrive in France to oppose them, Germany will be doomed.

And Britain's front line fighting forces are weaker than at the beginning of 1917. The Prime Minister denies this. At a conference he produces a list of calculations and says that Britain has "always been over-insured on the Western Front." But, as Haig and his staff later argue, "it is to be noted that he took no account of the relative fighting value of the various categories of the numbers he quoted."[39] At the beginning of 1918, Haig is having to operate in full knowledge that he does not have the support of his Prime Minister. More than once during 1917, when affairs on the Western Front were being discussed," wrote Robertson,

> "there is no doubt in my mind that a recommendation from me… to appoint a new Commander in Chief would have met with [Lloyd George's] instant approval. Without such a recommendation, which could, if necessary be publicly quoted in support of the appointment, [he] was not prepared to act and therefore no change was made.[40]

In January 1918 the Prime Minister goes so far as to actually send advisors to the Western Front to seek out an alternative to Haig. They can find nobody sufficiently qualified.

As well as being numerically worse off, thanks to the machinations of the Supreme War Council, the British Army is also holding a longer line. Haig has known since the beginning of November that enemy strength was building opposite his force. On 2nd January he sees the King at Buckingham Palace and His Majesty agrees that "the country and the army must be prepared for a very hard time, for severe losses, and to be obliged to relinquish certain points and positions on our front."[41] Less than a week later Haig tells members of the War Cabinet that any decision to extend the front must take into account the fact that they were facing a considerable German onslaught. "We must expect to be attacked, to be pressed back and lose ground and guns… We must prepare for 100,000 casualties a month. Possibly there will be surprise attacks against us and the French, followed if successful by other attacks."[42] General Rawlinson concurs, because he writes to Clive

---

38   Jordan: *The Battle for the Skies*, pp.68-85.
39   RA PS/PSO/GV/C/Q1591/5.
40   Gerwath, Robert: *The Vanquished: Why the First World War Failed to End 1917-1923*, p.34.
41   (ed.) Sheffield & Bourne: *Douglas Haig: War Diaries and Letters 1914-1918*, pp.369-370.
42   RA PS/PSO/GV/C/Q1591/5.

Wigram that month: "We must… concentrate all of our efforts on preparing to meet a series of violent attacks by the enemy."[43] And yet despite this, it is being proposed that the British line be extended to 130 miles long. To man this line, Haig has 57 divisions, of which all but ten, he later claims, were under strength. Up and down the line his army commanders are begging for men, and he cannot meet all of their demands. In a letter to Wigram, Rawlinson claims that unless significant reinforcements were received, the fighting efficiency of the army will be compromised.

Lloyd George is not necessarily guilty of withholding men on the eve of the battle, but must bear responsibility for constraining throughout 1917 the amount of men available to Haig, and for the strength of the army at the onset of 1918; because he had denied the BEF new recruits. What the Prime Minister and the War Cabinet have been trying to do is implement an indirect policy whereby they can exercise control over how the war is conducted on the Western Front by dictating the troops available to the army. In an April memorandum Maurice Hankey, the Secretary to the War Cabinet, conceded that the War Cabinet's policy when it came to recruitment was designed to keep "the War Office short [of men] to compel the soldiers to adopt tactics that will reduce the waste of man-power."[44] This he writes, is dangerously mortgaging Britain's future.

When the last of the fighting died down on the Western Front at the beginning of December 1917, the Army Council, on the orders of Lloyd George, reviewed the manpower situation after the year's costly fighting. Their subsequent memorandum emphasised the need for immediately replacing Haig's losses. If this was not done, they said, the war may well be lost. But the troops were not forthcoming in large enough numbers. The Royal Navy, Air Force, shipbuilding, food production and even forestry was regarded as a higher priority for available manpower than Haig's need for fighting men. Lloyd George tells Esher that Haig "had eaten his cake, in spite of warnings."[45] At Versailles in January, it was mooted that American troops might be filtered into British units to fill the void, but General Pershing will not hear of it. And so without enough men to maintain Haig's divisions, the structure must change. In February and March the number of British battalions has to be reduced from 741 to 600. The number of men under each divisional general changes, as does the layout of their force. These units have been honed throughout the war, tried and tested, and now they are separated and shuffled, with all of the logistical and tactical changes that this will entail for them to operate properly.

"A Very Much Finer Chap Than I Imagined"

Throughout all of this political strife and upheaval, the King is not idle. There is a concerted effort by both His Majesty and the Queen to widen their perspective, to seek out the more esoteric, the less glamorous aspects of war work and acknowledge the contributions of those employed on them. There is a visit to the postal censorship buildings, where "4,000 men and women are employed; they read through 25 tons of letters every day, we saw the museum where every conceivable thing has come through the post for Germans… We also saw the laboratory where messages in secret ink are discovered. Many spies have been found out through this." In the West Country, Palmer and MacKay's cloth factory is inspected, where the army's famous khaki is produced. Their Majesties watch dyeing, spinning, weaving and finishing. At a tobacco factory in Bristol, they witness mountains of woodbines, and at another cigarette manufacturer in Bedminster "one saw pouring

43   RA/PS/PS/GV/C/Q/2522/2/114.
44   TNA: CAB 63/20.
45   CC: ESHR 1 1/12/1917.

out of the machines 600 to the minute." Cigarettes cascade out of a tube "like water in a continuous stream,"[46] and in another room 500 girls make them by hand.

The King tastes the waters at Bath too. The Pump Room has been given over for war use. By 1918, over 25,000 military treatments alone have been given to wounded and invalided officers and men. The swimming baths have been used by soldiers to vary their exercise and the Royal Mineral Water Hospital, which was supplied by the hot springs, has treated well over 2,000 patients. Their Majesties are deeply interested by all that they see. "First they were shown a deep bath, the oldest and one of the most important forms of treatment... The patient is immersed to the neck in several hundred gallons of the radioactive water, every part of the body being submitted to its influence, while a powerful under-current douche is applied to the specifically affected part." Other baths are fitted with chairs operated by hydraulic power that lowers crippled and helpless patients into the water. It has proved beneficial in treating cases of shell shock. "Next the King and Queen inspected the douche massage treatment, in which the patient is subject to massage under douches of the natural hot mineral water. This is employed in practically all stiffened joint conditions where there is any acute inflammation."[47]

In Walthamstow Their Majesties look over the motor lorry works of the Associate Equipment Company. The establishment has doubled in size throughout the duration of the war so far, and it now employs 3,000 people and makes nothing but military lorries, of which it turns out 125 per week. His Majesty is particularly intrigued by tests which check the integrity of a new chassis. He tracks down a shop steward with strong socialist views for a frank discussion. "He had a few plain words to say, and concluded that 'we engineers are not the sort of people we are painted by some of the newspapers. We are prepared to a man to do our bit for our country'... The King was much pleased and shook hands very cordially at parting." As soon as the royal party have left, the steward is asked what he thought of His Majesty. "I found him a very much finer chap than I imagined. He's all right."[48]

Another day is spent looking over a chemical works, those of the Thermo-Electric Core Reduction Co., which is working as part of the armaments industry, "where they make tungsten and chrome etc. for hardening steel... very interesting but difficult to follow not being a chemist."[49] At a laboratory at Teddington, the King sees rooms used for the careful testing of fuses, and aeroplane parts. He watches them setting up gauges and remarks that it looks like extremely delicate work. "You talk of the millionth of an inch. It seems almost impossible to image such minute divisions." His Majesty is even more fascinated by an enormous wind tunnel where aeroplane parts are tested. An electric apparatus generates a gale of 50 mph so that they might carry out their experiments. "The test was accompanied by an almost deafening roar, which have some idea of the conditions under which flying men carry out their duties."[50] The King sees boot stores at White City with over four million pairs stacked ready for use. Tents, 120 of them a day, are manufactured alongside gas hoods and haversacks. Galleries are stuffed with bales and rolls of proofed canvas, heavy fabrics and sail cloth for hangars. His Majesty talks to the men about supply.

Descending to the main aisle of the establishment the King overtook a very animated scene... The work here proceeding was chiefly that of sharing up the linings for tents to be used in tropical climates, and the most effective protection against the rays is given by yellow and

46   *Morning Post* 9/11/17.
47   *Daily Telegraph* 10/11/17.
48   *The Times* 5/4/17.
49   RA GV/PRIV/GVD/1918 (13/11).
50   *Daily Telegraph* 24/11/17.

red colourings. Masses of canvas in the most vivid of these tones enveloped tables, machines and made a gay setting" gave the huge room a circus aspect.[51]

In West London His Majesty, with the Queen, visits an establishment than manufactures aeroplane engines. The King watches a steam hammer operator shaping parts, and in the yard the royal visitors watch complete aeroplane engines being tested.

> Each engine made a great noise on its own account, but the climax was reached when, at a signal from the foreman, all the engines were set going together, and the workers at the same time indulged in hearty cheers for the King and Queen. The noise was deafening but Their Majesties were evidently greatly pleased by the compliment paid to them.[52]

This display was to have ended the visit, but the King and Queen have seen the elementary parts and the finished engines, and they want to go back and see the middle stage, the components being fitted together.

They have even found time to visit schools and talk to pupils in the capital. Venturing into Bermondsey they visit one boy's establishment where more than 100 former pupils have already been killed in the war. "You all know what patriotism is," His Majesty says to the little faces in front of him.

> Patriotism as I understand it is a love of your country, a love so great that you are prepared to give up your own interests, and even to sacrifice your lives, if necessary... During this terrible war I can say that the whole nation has shown its patriotism in a remarkable manner. I feel sure that when you leave school you will never forget what you have been taught here and that you will show the same patriotism as those who have gone before you, and keep bright the high traditions of this old school.[53]

Everywhere there is a feeling that Britons will have to draw on their last reserves in pursuit of victory, not only in the matter of manpower on the Western Front. The King encourages fundraising for the war effort. In March 1918 Tank Banks spring up all over London: one at Trafalgar Square, another behind the Royal Exchange. As they rumble into position huge crowds gather, and here people can contribute to the war effort over a makeshift counter in the side of the machine. His Majesty issues letters in support of the scheme: "I am confident that my people are willing to contribute both now and in the future whatever money may be necessary to secure victory."[54] Organised by Bonar Law, the target is to gain £100 million in bonds and savings certificates. One elderly lady appears with £200 in a bag, claiming that she has heard that King is "hard up."[55] It is placed to her credit in war bonds.

His Majesty also continues to offer his own residences at every opportunity. If the authorities think that they can use Balmoral as a resort for wounded men, then they can have it. The Government have made no response. Neither have they expressed any desire to take the King up on offers to use Buckingham or Kensington Palaces as offices. In February 1918, an MP puts questions to the Commissioner of Works, "to ask whether any public announcement will be made

51   *Daily Telegraph* 10/12/17.
52   *Daily Telegraph* 15/3/18.
53   *Daily Telegraph* 16/2/18.
54   *Daily Telegraph* 4/3/18.
55   *Daily Chronicle* 15/4/18.

as to the King's gracious offer, and what use will be made of it."[56] his Majesty has not withdrawn his offer for Buckingham Palace to be used as a hospital either, for there is always a shortage of beds in London. The Palace has always felt too grand. The King once said that he would have no objection to demolishing it, turning the gardens into a public park and relocating to the palace at Kensington, which was a fraction of the size. At the beginning of 1916 the question was asked by His Majesty if there was any way that the state rooms could be used by the Red Cross. Lengthy discussions were held, but the drainage was simply not sufficient to facilitate a hospital and there are security concerns that would provoke an inconvenient issue around needing a separate entrance for any hospital. Much construction work would have to be carried out, and the King came to the conclusion that rather than take on that expense, he would simply make a larger than usual, £10,000 donation to the Red Cross in 1916.

However, after the success of the Royal Tea Parties in 1916, the Riding School was given over to the Church Army. Accomodation for soldiers is scarce around Victoria Station, the main rail terminus in London for men returning on leave. By the time they arrive in the city, sometimes in the middle of the night, invariably they can get no further until public transport resumes and so a hostel is opened at Buckingham palace. Floors are laid, bathrooms fitted out, stores collected and beds installed. There is no charge for either a bed or the food provided. "The coffee furnished in the riding school is actually made in the Palace itself," reports one newspaper "and it already has the reputation of being by far the best cup of coffee obtainable by any soldier in any west end resort."[57] In the mornings transport is on hand to after the men have eaten their fill to take them across to Euston, Paddington and King's Cross so that they might continue their onward journeys across the country if necessary. Imperial soldiers are encouraged to extend their stay further if they have no English homes to go to and want to do a spot of sight-seeing in the capital. The King is a constant visitor. "He never announces his coming, but goes quietly up to the balcony where Queen Victoria used to sit watching her sons learn to ride. Then he comes down, and, passing among the men, has a word for each."[58] In the course of the war 27,500 men were given a place to sleep at Buckingham Palace on their way to and from the various fronts. The King also hears that the Irish Women's Association is in need of accomodation for continuing its good work in aid of Irish prisoners of war and Irish regiments at the front, and so he provides a suite of rooms at Kensington Palace. "Stores of food and comforts are collected, and several thousand parcels are being despatched each week." [59]

Away from London, at Windsor the riding school is used to entertain hundreds of limbless men from Roehampton, hosted by the Mayor and people of the town, and in 1916, even Balmoral is offered for the war effort, first of all as a hospital, and secondly as a convalescent home, "but the fact that it could only be used for eight months of the year, and the great distance from London proved insuperable objections to His Majesty's offer being accepted."[60] The grounds at Buckingham Palace and Windsor Castle, such as they are since turnips have replaced flowers, are still utilised by wounded soldiers being treated in nearby hospitals.

In the meantime Queen Mary continues to oversee a stringent regime of economy at the palace. The market garden in the grounds is now in full swing, with the produce being sent to hospitals and the refuse collected from it used for fuel. The palace laundry list has been obliterated and the net economy of the constant austerity measures is that the Royal Household uses less than 75% of the ration allowed to it by the fuel overseers by the end of 1917. His Majesty is said to have given strict

56   *Daily News* 14/2/18.
57   *The World* 25/4/16.
58   *Daily Mirror* 28/3/17.
59   *Times* 28/2/17.
60   *The Globe* 14/2/18.

orders that no central heating is to be used in Windsor Castle or in Buckingham Palace before a certain winter date. "No fuel is to be used in any of the hothouses in the Frogmore gardens and the plants effected will be sent next month to hospitals. There is to be rigid economy in the matter of coal in all the palaces and also at Sandringham."[61] The more acute the fuel crisis gets, the more the Royal Household cuts back; halving the lighting in the passages, corridors, ante rooms and private apartments of the royal residences. The King's residences are recycling too: empty pots and tins, waste paper, worn oil, linen and wool. Some of it is sent out to agencies, the ashes are then sifted and used for fire-banking and fuel. The Queen is even diligently making the entire household retain their fruit stones, for they can be made into charcoal for use in respirators.

So far as food is concerned, compulsory rationing is now in effect. Everyone living in London and the counties of Kent, Surrey, Sussex, Essex, Hertfordshire and Middlesex will be rationed for meat, butter and margarine. People will only be able to buy these items at the shops at which they are registered, and every adult will be entitled to a weekly amount of a quarter pound of butter or margarine, and one and a quarter pounds of meat. Ration cards have arrived at Buckingham Palace from the Westminster Food Control Committee too, for the entire household, including Their Majesties, will be adhering to the new allowances. Sir Derek Keppel, the Master of the Household, gives an interview to the *Daily Express*.

> We are all in line here with the rations, and I am saying no more than what is true when I tell you that I never knew any people so thoroughly conscientious in this matter as the King and Queen... The Royal Household is a large and varying one. Its changing character causes some difficulty in their rationing but if any error is ever made in the calculation it is generally in the direction of less rather than more... Of this be certain, the royal table suffers in common with the servants hall.[62]

Royal stocks are also used to alleviate other shortages. Eton College is having trouble getting hold of enough meat, and so the King has arranged to send venison weekly from his own estates. Proceeds are going to go to the Red Cross, and a number of bucks in the large herd at Windsor Great Park are to be slaughtered until the period of scarcity is overcome. Eventually more than £400 is raised for charity. With the meat shortage, freshwater fish is becoming a staple article of food for the nation too, "and again the King has set the example by allowing fish to be taken from the lakes in the royal ground adjoining Windsor Castle, the stream of Home Park, and the pond at Frogmore. Several consignments of the fish have already been despatched to various parts of the country."[63] The King has invited South Wales fishermen to come and do the work, and all proceeds will, again, go to the Red Cross.

His Majesty also continues to take every opportunity to publicly support food economy and production. The number of allotments being worked by members of the public have boomed, and the King and Queen make numerous visits, including an extensive tour in South London. At the Merton Park School Allotments "a practical gardener gives instructions, and the industry is carried out on business lines under the supervision of the Headmaster." The produce is sold chiefly to the parents of the boys. There are also extensive allotments on the north side of Clapham Common, on land provided by the local council. Wimbledon has excelled itself in the matter of food production. His Majesty is so impressed by the work being done here that he calls it to the attention of the Food Produce Department at the Board of Agriculture. Workers from the London and South Western

61   *Truth* 25/9/18.
62   *The Gentlewoman* 23/2/18.
63   *Daily Telegraph* 6/3/18.

Railway have plots by the company's power station in Durnsford Road and Wimbledon Park now has a cooperative piggery attached to it on what used to be the Guards' polo ground. The King is much interested in the livestock but the Queen is completely taken with the rabbits.

A little girl presents Her Majesty with a pig named Daisy, wrapped in a Union Jack and decorated with red, white and blue streamers and sat in a basket. She is promptly donated to the Red Cross. In the London Borough of Wandsworth there had been 30 acres of allotments before the war. Now there are 509, held by 7,500 people. "Saturday is a busy day on the ground and many of the plot holders were at work, their wives and children helping." One woman gets so over-excited at the sight of His Majesty in their midst that she grabs the King's hand. Then she notices Queen Mary and says, "you are not jealous, are you?" The Queen laughs loudly. "Oh dear no, not at all!"[64]

"Fifty Hours in France"

In getting ready to launch an astonishing offensive to try and win the war before American troops started arriving in force later in the year, it is clear to the enemy that the impetus for the Allied war effort in 1918 is going to come from the British, and it is on Haig's front that the German Army intends to strike.

Thanks to the policy of limiting the flow of troops to the front, the Commander in Chief simply does not have the men he needs to defend in depth along the entirety of the line they are now manning. Haig is forced to make decisions that will endanger some of his force, but there is no shying away from them. The priority is staying in the war in the event of a large-scale enemy offensive, and he clinically assesses the most important areas. He cannot leave the northern end of the British line weak, around Ypres. The major rail junction at Hazebrouck which enables supply and transport along the whole front must be protected, as must the Channel ports, else Britain will be finished, invaded even. To the south, General Horne and his men protect the Vimy Ridge and more important high ground, and below them General Byng and the Third Army stand in front of Arras before General Gough takes over the line. His Fifth Army holds the Somme sector, and unfortunately for him, and the thousands of men under him, any strategic objectives that might appeal to the enemy are nearly 50 miles behind his front line. If Haig is going to risk being attacked anywhere with a minimum of disastrous consequences, it is here. It is a cruel call to make, but he just cannot acquiesce to Gough's appeals for men. If the Fifth Army is attacked with everything that the German army can throw at them, they will not be able to hold out. They will have to retreat to an emergency line sketched out for them to the rear and try and stem the tide while British and French reinforcements are found to reinforce them.

And by mid-February it is emerging that the likelihood is that this is exactly where the German Army intends to strike. Preparations are clearly in hand against the British front held by Gough and Byng. Operation George, northern operations, have been ruled out because in March, the low-lying ground is still too cumbersome. Operation Mars was discarded as a front runner because the defences at Arras are too daunting to begin operations with. And so it is that Operation Michael is chosen; a devastating effort on the line south of Arras and on the Somme, at the southernmost tip of which, the Kaiser's forces can try and sever the bond linking the British line to the French beside them. Then they will turn north and try and roll up the British line all the way to the Channel coast, as further operations are launched to rout the British Army. This is Germany's last chance to win the war, and they intend to give it everything.

64   *Daily Telegraph* 22/7/18.

On 21st March, Operation Michael is launched at 4:40 am with a massive artillery bombardment, an apocalyptic concert by some 10,000 guns, building in power for a number of hours. German troops burst out of a thick fog and overrun the British forward area. By the end of the day the BEF has suffered some 38,500 casualties. The King has been holding meetings on various war matters, and spends the afternoon visiting hospitals with the Queen. It is not until the following day that the severity of events on the Western Front begins to emerge fully for him. "Saw the Chief of Staff," His Majesty writes, for he doesn't often deign to refer to Wilson by name, "who told me that the fighting in France continued to be very heavy, we have lost ground at several places, especially west of Cambrai. We have asked the French to help us with some of their divisions, it is an anxious time for us all."[65]

The Kaiser's men carry on their progress and Gough's army begin falling back on the emergency line, most of which is along the River Somme. The Third Army has begun to fall back too. The King goes about his work, presenting VCs and entertaining a Prince of Serbia, but he is fraught. "Our troops have had to fall back on Peronne," he writes on 23rd March. "These are very anxious days."[66] The emergency line does not hold. German troops begin crossing the river. Haig is desperately trying to secure French reinforcements, but his ally is hell bent on protecting Paris at all costs, and on being ready to defend themselves against any possible German attack on their sector. In command, General Petain will not move his reserves to support the British and weaken his own line. This is ludicrous to Haig, who highlights for them the fact that the enemy clearly intends to prise the British and French forces apart. With all the men that the Germans are currently putting into the field on the Somme, how can the French argue that another offensive is about to be launched against them? Who will make it?

"Terrifying events unfolding in France," the King writes on the 24th. "Please God we shall be able to check them."[67] Wilson has gone to France with Lord Milner, the new War Minister. With Haig they agree that if they are to get the French to participate in this unfolding disaster to the proper extent, they must give Foch command of the whole line. Putting British troops under French command is no political manoeuvre this time, it is a move made out of desperation in the midst of a huge reverse on the battlefield, and Haig does not object to this resolution. At a meeting the following day, he gets his way. It is agreed that Amiens, that strategic point which had been some 40 miles beyond German reach just a few days ago, must be covered at all costs. The French draft a resolution appointing General Foch to coordinate the Allied troops about the town, but Haig agrees that it should be extended to all French and British troops on the Western Front. Hang pride, Britain's future is in the balance.

In the meantime the King is still frantic. He arrives back at Buckingham Palace mid-afternoon on the 26th to some better news. "Things are a little more satisfactory and the French are helping us in the south,"[68] but Wigram has received a letter from Rawlinson that outlines just how serious the situation is. "The enemy's intention is clearly to separate us from the French and then to turn the whole of his strength on to one or other of us with a view to smashing us irretrievably and then forcing a German peace on the allies," he says. "He has so far succeeded in crushing our Fifth Army and in rough handling our Third Army and in doing so has driven a wedge into the Somme area."[69] By now the BEF has suffered some 75,000 casualties. Troops are being released that the

65   RA GV/PRIV/GVD/1918 (22/3).
66   RA GV/PRIV/GVD/1918 (23/3).
67   Ibid., (24/3).
68   Ibid., 26/3.
69   RA PS/PS/GV/C/Q/2522/118.

Government have been holding back. There is no more debate with regard to keeping them safe or using them on other fronts. There is only one that matters.

On 27th March the King bids goodbye to David, who has left for the Italian front. By now the court should have adjourned to Windsor for Easter, but he will not leave the capital. That evening Wilson, newly returned from France, visits the palace and the upshot of his report about the present situation on the Western Front is that His Majesty can stand it no more. Providing that it will not interfere with the work of his armies, and will not upset any arrangements, he intends to cross to France himself the very next morning to see what he can do to help.

Within a couple of hours the Master of the Household is already on his way to the front to try and find somewhere for the King to sleep. Nobody at GHQ is to be burdened with making any arrangements. All that is asked is that one or two of their motorcars be made available on His Majesty's arrival. There is to be no air protection, no escort, no policemen to guard the King's person. Safety and comfort is chucked out of the window. The whole trip, which ordinarily would have needed a month or so to arrange, is improvised in less than twelve hours.

Operation Michael continues to the south, where the tired German attackers have begun meeting resistance from a line newly bolstered with French troops. That day, the German Army launches Operation Mars too, in front of Arras. Again proceeded by a terrifying bombardment, this time they are not helped by a veil of fog, and as they well knew, the defences at Arras are formidable.

Admiral Keyes collects His Majesty, who has only Stamfordham and Wigram in attendance, from Dover just before lunch on the 28th. The crossing is terrible, rough seas and a south westerly gale. "I was nearly sick."[70] But the King is determined to carry on, green or not. GHQ have sent Major Thompson to meet him, and General Plumer, whose army is not embroiled in any of the fighting, has made the short journey from Flanders. The Queen supports His Majesty's decision to rush to the front, dangerous as it may be. She herself is distraught. "I have never suffered so much _mentally_ as I am suffering _now_," she tells her husband across the Channel, "and I know you are feeling the _same._ We must just have faith and believe that God cannot allow those Huns to win and that our brave and gallant troops will be able to withstand the onslaughts in spite of the overwhelming numbers of the enemy."[71]

Though Thompson is present to act as a guide, His Majesty has refused to let any sort of programme be put together. He will end up where he ends up, congratulating those coming out of the line on their efforts, consoling those who need it and spending as much time as he can with those who have been wounded, in the hope that the sight of their King amongst them during this great trial will have some kind of galvanising effect on men who have been battered by the enemy. One of the suite has remembered the little tin Royal Standard. It is fixed to the front of a car and off they go. That night the rain cascades down and the wind outside howls and rattles the windows in their frames.

29th March is Good Friday and the King sets off to Haig's headquarters for a quick greeting before the Commander in Chief hurries off to a conference with Foch. It will be their only contact on this visit. General Cox, who heads up the intelligence department, has a little time to talk His Majesty through the current situation, then the King gets out on the road, ready to smile and encourage and put on a brave face for his army. He finds a battalion of Gordon Highlanders who have just come out of the line. Officers and men occupy a field, sitting and lying sprawled out after their ordeal. The visit is such a surprise that their commander is off having lunch in a nearby village.

70   RA GV/PRIV/GVD/1918 (28/3).
71   RA QM/PRIV/CC08/213.

Not everyone on the King's travels has the energy or the inclination to get excited after what they have been subjected to, but when the Scotsmen realise who has drawn up at the roadside, large numbers of them rush over and swarm around His Majesty's car excitedly. They cheer loudly when the King emerges from inside. He shakes hands with them, asks them how they are doing after their part in the battle. He passes New Zealanders on their way to the front and the remnants of a Machine Gun Battalion who have lost 20 officers and 300 men. Their steel hats are crusted with mud as they rest in a little village. His Majesty joins them and asks a first man how he had fared. "Another, who kept firing until the enemy was within 25 yards, was asked how he managed to get away." He does not have a heroic or exciting answer. The men he didn't kill simply went away. A sergeant, who had stuck to his gun until the enemy knocked it out, had then joined some passing infantry and for want of any other weapon was seen killing a German with a pick axe. These men have been through hell.

After lunch the King meets the locals, who are doing all that they can for his Majesty's troops when they appear exhausted after having been pursued for days by the German Army. Nearby, the remains of an entire brigade, hundreds of men, had arrived in the middle of the night and the occupants of a nearby chateau mobilised everyone in the locality. "Fires were lit, coffee was prepared, hot water was put out in great tubs and when the battalions marched in in the darkness they found the whole population waiting to receive them."[72] His Majesty spends the afternoon with the wounded, which requires even more of a performance on his part. He finds two ambulance trains being loaded, and the King walks through the trains, "opening the doors of compartments containing sitting or walking cases." He sits himself down, as cheerfully as he can and begins to chat with them, attempt to make them feel better. "He smiled and engaged, asking the men who they were, listening to their stories, especially the machine gunners who spoke of exacting a gruesome toll on the advancing Germans."[73] The men are stunned when the King of England suddenly appears in their midst. "A strapping soldier, obviously born in the colonies, leaned forward in his seat as His Majesty opened the door, looking critically at him a moment, then, painfully extended his hand, said, "I've often heard of you. Put it right there!! The King gave him a hearty handshake."[74] He even has time for the driver, talking to him about his efforts to take load after load of maimed men to base hospitals.

In places, the entire chain of evacuation is in disarray because units have retired so quickly. His Majesty gets out of his car at a huge makeshift casualty clearing station which has recently fled to this location. The first thing he does is tell the commanding officer to carry on, to make no acknowledgment of his presences. There are over 2,000 men there, most of whom have not yet been treated. The gruesome suffering on display is gut-wrenching. "Saw some very sad and dreadful sights, operations of every kind going on."[75] The King has nothing but praise for the medical officers, nurses and men operating such facilities in impossible conditions. He walks among the stretchers "bearing huddled figures, from which arose many groans and gaspings, and here and there the sobbings and wheezings of men so exhausted that slumber had overcome pain." His Majesty stops for any patient who wishes to engage with him. "A deeply human side of the King came out in his solicitude and compassion, as he moved softly amid this scene, pausing often to speak to those who smiled recognition or to inquire about those who seemed in sad plight." One Canadian chaplain is so overcome by His Majesty's visit that he can barely hold back tears. "This will buck the boys up more than anything I can think of… That poor lad over there has just asked

72   *Morning Post* 5/4/18.
73   *Daily Telegraph* 1/4/18.
74   Anon: *The Life of King George V: The Life and Work of a Monarch Beloved of his Peoples,* pp.113-114.
75   RA GVPRIV/GVD/1918 (29/3).

me what is going on, and when I told him the King had come over to visit us, he said, 'God bless his old heart.'" Though he is keeping up a positive show, the veneer of positivity that His Majesty projects almost slips once or twice. "Although the King kept a uniformly cheering air, one could see that he was sensibly affected by this spectacle. I heard him say in a low aside to one of his suite: "This brings home the meaning of the offensive indeed."[76]

On Saturday morning the King begins another gruelling ten hour tour by paying homage to the Royal Flying Corps, who have spent an exhausting amount of time in the air. They have "done splendidly since the 21st March, they have brought down over 300 enemy machines besides having inflicted great damage with bombs and machine gun fire. They are awfully proud of themselves and well they might be."[77] Then his Majesty continues on his travels, stopping to see all kinds of units in the Third Army sector. "The little flag that alone marked his car brought strength and comfort to the battle-tired soldiers whom he met as they rested by the road side."[78]

One Welsh battalion's officers decide that their men should get up and cheer as the King flies past in his car. "The fellas didn't, the officers did... after a period up in the front line, you weren't in any mood to cheer anybody, you wanted to get back, clean up and have a few days rest."[79] The King knows how exhausted these men are, he knows that they are all that stands between Britain and defeat, and he knows that they have little to be cheerful about after what they have so recently endured. It is why he instructs that they should just be left to go about their business, why he does not want officers dragging people to their feet to acknowledge him. But this is not a wasted journey, for many men are buoyed by his appearance. This is showbusiness, to some extent and the King knows how to play his role to. He comes across more resting troops, lounging in a field that has been torn asunder at some point by shellfire. They spy his car and make a rush for it, surrounding him.

His Majesty jumps down and laughingly asks: "Who are you?"

They scream out their response.

"Oh we all know you!" Replies the King.

He gets a thunderous roar in response. As his car pulls away, His Majesty leans from the window and calls out: "Are we downhearted?"

The mens' roar of "No!" is so loud, "that the cattle peaceably grazing half a mile off stopped munching and raised their heads to see whence the noise came."[80]

On 30th March General Ludendorff calls a halt to the German offensives while he considers his options. The Fifth Army has ceased to exist. 178,000 British casualties have been suffered and 92,000 French. But Germany have suffered almost a quarter of a million losses themselves. For all the damage they have done to the allies, German troops have failed to sweep the British Army from the battlefield. No terrifying gap has opened up between Haig's force and his French allies. The enemy has gained a massive 1,200 square miles of ground, but it is ground that is worth little from a military point of view. It is also ground that to a large extent they had given up themselves when they retreated to the Hindenburg Line in early 1917.

After 122 miles on the road, the King is at work early again on Sunday morning. He tours the First Army area and meets yet more troops who have just emerged from the battle to the south, after he stops to commend a unit of bus drivers for their indefatigable efforts. These men tell them that the worst hardship has been the lack of sleep as they were so relentlessly pursued by the enemy.

76   *Daily Telegraph* 1/4/18.
77   RA GV/PRIV/AA60/296.
78   *The Church Family Newspaper* 5/4/18.
79   IWM Sound: Taylor Catalogue #11113, Reel12&13,1990.
80   *The Times* 1/4/18.

"Have you had enough sleep now?" Asks His Majesty.

"Oh yes Sir, more than enough," they assure him.

"Thats right," he says, "always make up the leeway when you get the chance, and remember not to give the Boches the same chance."[81]

The Royal party reaches Calais in the middle of the afternoon and the King departs France in the midst of another storm. He arrives back at the palace that Easter Sunday to find three days worth of boxes waiting for his attention and feeling dead tired, but once again His Majesty is lauded for his contribution to the war effort. "Once again at a moment of crisis the King has done the right thing in the right way, and given to all the assurance of his devotion to the Empire."[82] Conversely, Lloyd George and his Government were under attack in some quarters of the press over the reduction in the size of divisions. "We believe, if the army on the western line were asked today what was its chief want, it would reply in two words: more men. For see how it stands with them. …Everyone can understand that the deprivation of a fourth battalion throws a frightful strain on the other three, whch must do the work of four… We at home praise our men, and we mean it. But if we would really serve them, we would give them more men.[83]

But this is Germany's last ditch attempt to win the war, and they can't just give up and go home. Successive offensives are going to break like waves on the Allied line in the west. The ground further north is now firmer, and Operation George has been reformatted and renamed: *Georgette*. Ludendorff imagines his armies smashing through the line south of Ypres and walking over the BEF in huge force until they reach Dunkirk and Calais and knock Britain out of the war. On the first day, they will attack Horne and Plumer's men in the Lys Valley about Armentieres. 24 hours later they will strike for the Messines Ridge, aiming for the high ground in the area, threatening to encircle Ypres. "This was the attack Haig had feared, and the reason why Gough had been forced to stand alone for so long while the safety of Flanders was ensured. But even so, of the 56 British divisions, 46 had already been sucked into the fighting in repelling the German assaults on the Somme and at Arras."[84]

After a four and a half hour barrage the German infantry come forth at 8:45am on 9th April. Fog helps them on their way on low lying ground and they advance up to five and a half miles in places, though they have still failed to cause a wholesale British collapse. That day, Haig has begged Foch to take some pressure off the British line, which has now been under sustained attack for more than two weeks. He refuses, but says that he has four divisions which can move north if necessary. "This arrangement was quite inadequate."[85] On the following day Operation Georgette's second blow is delivered at Messines after yet another terrifying barrage. Won so conclusively the summer before, Plumer's men are forced to abandon the Messines Ridge. Yet again the Germans had not quite broken through, but there is hardly any space here in which to manoeuvre. Hazebrouck is tantalisingly within the enemy's grasp, and if they take it and get to the Channel, the war is over for Britain. Haig has again written to Foch and insisted that the French must take a more active part in defending the Allies from oblivion. The French commander visits that evening "and said that he had at last made up his mind that the main German attack was being delivered against the British Army, and that he would move a large French force to take part in what he called the 'bataille

81   *Daily Telegraph* 1/4/18.
82   *The Church Family Newspaper* 5/4/18
83   *Morning Post* 2/4.
84   Hart: *The Great War,* p.428.
85   RA PS/PSO/GV/C/Q/1591/5.

d'Arras' Nothing, however, was done."[86] On 11th Sir Douglas Haig issues a special order of the day throughout the BEF:

> Many amongst us now are tired. To those I would say that victory will belong to the side which holds out the longest. … There is no other course open to us but to fight it out. Every position must be held to the last man; there must be no retirement. With our backs to the wall and believing in the justice of our cause each one of us must fight on to the end. The safety of our homes and the freedom of mankind alike depend upon the conduct of each one of us at this critical moment.[87]

He writes again to Foch on 11th and 14th April "pointing out that the British troops were getting fast worn out, that the French were practically not engaged, and that it was urgently necessary… to take some of our line."[88] But somehow, the British Army holds on. French troops finally began to arrive in Plumer's sector and are placed under his command. With reinforcements, the German tide is eventually stemmed and Hazebrouck held. Just. "Desperate fighting is going on in France," recorded the King on the 18th, "but we are holding our own." After a pause to reorganise his exhausted formations, Ludendorff relaunches the German offensives on 17th April. He suffers frightening casualty figures for all but no gain. Though more localised attempts are made at the end of the month, "for a period of 21 days," Haig was keen to record in the face of a frustrating spell dealing with his allies, "the British armies sustained the whole weight of the German attack."[89] And they are already rebuilding. On 19th April Churchill, as Minister of Munitions, visits the palace and boasts to His Majesty that every single one of the 1,300 guns lost in the German advance has already been replaced.

"Putting New Heart Into The Nation"

Throughout the spring, as Germany tried to win the war, the King carried on. For it is not only the army that needs a figurehead, a projection of such confidence and surety and calm that they cannot believe in anything but victory.

> He was here, there and everywhere putting new heart into the nation, and attending to the smallest detail concerning the equipment and comfort of his men overseas. Once he was seen among the crowd watching the arrival of an ambulance train and enquiring into the arrangements made for the reception of the wounded. Then he went over to the free buffet for service men and took refreshment at the counter with them.[90]

The victims of Operation Michael have begun to arrive at hospitals in the capital and within 48 hours of his return from the front, His Majesty has begun to visit them.

On 6th April, after a large investiture attended by more than 300 recipients, the Royal Family finally depart for Windsor; but it is far from a holiday. The King and Queen have barely been in residence at the castle for 24 hours when he departs north for a scheduled visit to Lincolnshire. As the German offensive against the Ypres sector is launched, His Majesty puts on a brave face

86   Ibid.
87   Hart: *The Great War,* p.430.
88   RA PS/PSO/GV/C/Q/1591/5, pp.62-63.
89   Ibid.
90   Anon: *The Life of King George V: The Life and Work of a Monarch Beloved of his Peoples,* p.115.

as he tours aircraft factories, tank establishments, hospitals. He spends time with naval men at Immingham in the sick quarters, presenting medals, inspecting torpedo stores, trawlers. The Allies have not lost the war, but they have not won it either, and the King is determined to leave no stone unturned when it comes to crediting the nation for weathering the German storm, and urging his subjects to press on with their efforts. On the anniversary of his father's death, suffering from fatigue, speculates in his diary that he cannot believe that "any sovereign of these realms has had a more difficult or troublous eight years than I have had."[91] Within three weeks, Sir Henry Wilson arrives at the Palace to report that the Germans have mounted another offensive; "attacked this morning between Reims and Soissons and drove us and the French back to the River Aisne about five or six miles which is unfortunate."[92] The advance continues, up to 13 miles in places. "There is a possibility," writes Wilson, "perhaps a probability, of the French Army being beaten."[93]

In the midst of this new turmoil, Their Majesties have a planned tour of Yorkshire to carry out, to areas that have not yet had any royal attention during the war. They cannot cancel it, and set off from St. Pancras the day after the launch of the latest German attack. At Bradford and Keighley thousands await Their Majesties in glorious sunshine as they prepare to investigate the textile industry. Before the war the army had used less than 1% of the wool manufactured at Bradford, Leeds and the surrounding area. Since August 1914, however, the War Office have purchased an astounding 1,600,000,000 pounds weight, valued at more than a hundred million sterling; much of it coming from this corner of Yorkshire. It has to be said, too, that if any strain of republicanism is gaining speed in Britain, the King might expect to see a hint of it here. But he spends a day with workers amongst their looms, and travels past extensive crowds, waving flags and cheering Their Majesties on their progress at extremely short notice.

The following day is even more strenuous as the royal tour moves on to Dewsbury, Batley, Heckmondwicke and Huddersfield. All districts are "a blaze of colour" and the people have lined the streets and countryside in thousands to greet the King and Queen as they are shown the breaking down and recycling of uniforms which has saved £2.5 million pounds since 1916. "Everywhere looms and workshops were decorated with flags and royal greetings." The tour is rounded off at Leeds, where Their Majesties are greeted by the Lord Mayor and a pile of officials who present prominent war workers. The reception from the city's population is almost overwhelming. Having spent two days looking at the production of cloth, at Leeds, the King and Queen follow the process through to the end, watching the manufacture of clothing for the war and affordable civilian wear. "The purpose of the scheme is to make adequate provision at controlled prices of ready to wear clothing for those who are accustomed to use it." The King looks over the samples of cloth in the exhibition and makes a purchase for himself from the most affordable grade. After an outdoor investiture at Beckett's Park and a visit to the local hospital Their Majesties depart for London "after three very strenuous but successful days."[94] They are thrilled with the reception that they have received.

The day after the King's 53rd birthday he notes that "the Germans are still gaining ground, but the French reserves are coming up fast."[95] Battle has raged for nearly two weeks on the Aisne as the Germans try to execute Operation Blücher. A fissure 35 miles wide and some twelve miles

91   RA GV/PRIV/GVD/1918 (6/5).
92   Ibid., 27/5.
93   Nicolson, Harold: *King George V: His Life and Reign*, p.323.
94   *Daily Telegraph* 31/5/18.
95   RA GV/PRIV/GVD/1918 (31/5).

deep had been torn in the Allied line, but luckily for the British and French armies, Ludendorff begins to deviate from his original plan, committing reserves to the battle that had been ear-marked for use elsewhere. American troops help the French stabilise their line at Chateau-Thierry on the River Marne. "Retreat?" One U.S. Marine officer was heard to say, "Hell, we only just got here!"[96] But on 9th June it is Wilson's turn to break news of yet another German offensive to the King. Attacking between Noyon and Montdidier, Operation Gneisenau originally surged into the Allied forward positions, seizing up to four miles of ground before once again the French managed to steel themselves. One the 11th they even managed to strike back at the enemy, and Ludendorff is forced to suspend his offensive action.

The King's schedule has now assumed an aspect of ad hoc work again, for he does anything and everything he can think of, no matter how small, to try and encourage the war effort on the Home Front. There is a tour of both the Army Clothing Depot in Pimlico and Glenfield's Clothing Factory in Brick Lane; a visit to the Clanfield's Boat Repairing Company in Old Kent Road. On one afternoon at Buckingham Palace His Majesty, the Queen and Princess Mary simply down what they are doing and drive to Waterloo Station to receive a hospital train from Southampton carrying 106 wounded officers and men. It takes merely half an hour to unload all of the patients, furnish them with tea and something to eat and then send them on their way to London's hospitals.

In France Ludendorff is desperate. He has reached a point where he can either defend his positions for as long as he possibly can, attempting to drag the length of the war out; or he can make one last attempt to win it. Wilson is once again a harbinger of doom, for he arrives at the palace to inform the King that the Germans have attacked the French on both sides of Reims. Dubbed the German Peace Offensive, it has been unleashed on the French and the Americans. Ludendorff's plan is to defeat them both and then turn again to deal with Britain once and for all.

And still His Majesty ploughs on with his work. Now that the Royal Air Force is an entity of its own, the King must pay due attention to the service as he would the army or the navy. He has a hand in the matter of the new uniform that will be issued to its members. He is "much interested"[97] at a visit to a balloon training wing. He enters the instruction huts and sees classes of officers and men engaged on the construction of model balloons and learning telegraphy and ship recognition. In the machine shop, winches and cables for the manipulation of captive balloons are seen. His Majesty is surprised to learn that a thin cable can take a strain of seven tons. Outside he sees one run out and a balloon rise to 1,200 feet. "The King asked what would happen to the officer in the car if the balloon were stuck at that height, and at a signal a dummy figure of a man dressed in khaki came tumbling through the air and fell with a thud on the grass."[98]

London's air defences are scrutinised too. By now Sir William Robertson has been appointed Commander in Chief Home Forces and with the officer in charge of protecting the capital from the German aerial menace, he arrives at the palace. They show His Majesty plans for defending the city and afterwards the King and Queen embark on a tour in order to see them for themselves; "a very interesting morning"[99] at North Weald Bassett, Hainault Farm and Wanstead Flatts where there are balloons, searchlights sound indicators and a gun station. "Their Majesties were greatly impressed by the extent and variety of the various defensive measures available and an excellent idea of giving effect to them in practice was obtained."[100]

96   Hart: *The Great War*, pp.440-441.
97   RA GV/PRIV/GVD/1918 (16/7).
98   *The Times* 17/7/18.
99   RA GV/PRIV/GVD/1918 (26/7).
100   *Daily Telegraph* 27/7/18.

All of this work is being documented in line with the palace's new awareness of public relations, led doggedly by Clive Wigram. All of the summer's investitures are being carried out in the quadrangle at Buckingham Palace. Anyone in uniform can pass through the gates to observe, as well as anyone in civilian dress who can provide "a reasonable excuse to pass within." *The Telegraph* describes one Saturday morning investiture in May. "The relatives of those about to be honoured had a small enclosure with chairs; and one of the gentlemen ushers was present to receive them, while some half-dozen much be-ribboned and badged boy scouts lent useful assistance."[101] A dais has been erected in front of the glass covered shelter over the entrance to the palace, "with a crimson carpet; a crimson and white-striped canopy." A British airship ponders overhead. "While I seemed to hear King Edward's ghost chuckling with pleasure at the sight of the real people," writes a correspondent for the *Pall Mall Gazette*, "I was afraid to listen to what Queen Victoria was saying." One interested observer passes the palace, wonders what the commotion is and asks a policeman. They are told that the King is holding an investiture. "You can go in if you like."[102]

A Frenchwoman, a correspondent for the *Petit Parisien*, is absolutely astonished. "There is no difficulty about getting in," she writes.

> It is unnecessary to use any influence or provide oneself with a letter of introduction or even a ticket of admission. The King of England is to be seen by everybody. I note the simplicity of his costume. There is nothing outwardly to distinguish him from all the others. While *God Save the King* is being played he stands at the salute, holding himself quite straight, his grave, firm countenance full at once of dignity and kindliness. I look all around me. There is no hysterical enthusiasm; more of that open-mouthed wonder which doubtless is accorded to every step and every histrionic gesture of the Imperial Kaiser, but in all eyes may be seen a kind of trust and esteem and affectionate pleasure with which one looks upon a kinsman or a friend of whom one is proud. We have here a truly democratic sovereign, one who instead of imposing his will upon the people feels that he incarnates their sentiments and wishes, who associates himself with their labours, and shares their anxieties and ordeals, who fulfils his difficult role simply and conscientiously. When the American labour representatives said that with him they had no impression of being in the presence of a King, they bestowed the highest praise in one who is quite content to be, the first gentleman of his Kingdom.[103]

The new Ministry of Information is playing its part in getting across the royal message, but the King still wishes to have his own, direct contact with the press. In particular, he is keen to pay his own acknowledgement to newspapermen from the Dominions and so he has the ministry organise tours for collections of various newspaper affiliates from all corners of the Empire. Canadian editors are received on a Saturday afternoon at Buckingham Palace." When they later meet a representative of the *Telegraph*, they declare "that they were delighted by their reception, and what struck them most was the King's knowledge of every part of the dominion, his appreciation of Canada's services in the war."[104] Two months later it is the turn of India's press men. His Majesty receives them one at a time, appropriately in the Indian Room at the palace, and they "were gratified to find that the King and Queen knew something of them individually."[105]

101   *Daily Telegraph* 27/5/18.
102   *Pall Mall Gazette* 27/5/18.
103   *Daily Telegraph* 10/6/18.
104   *Daily Telegraph* 5/8/18.
105   *The Times* 21/10/18.

The Americans are afforded special treatment because their visit coincides with when the Royal Family wish to be at Sandringham. They are taken by special train to Norfolk and given a tour of the estate, shown a famous racehorse in the stables. The Royal Family spend nearly three hours with them. "The King was greatly interested in America, it was very gratifying to us to find how keen he was to know all about us." There are 25 representatives in total and some of them are old hands, not easy to impress. They quickly realise that this is no holiday for His Majesty, for there is evidence of his work everywhere. I have known all our Presidents for the last 40 years," one tells *The Times,*

> and have been at numerous receptions at the White House … I have never seen more graciousness, courtesy and perfect power of making guests feel at home than was shown by His Majesty today… We were all charmed with his personality and the keen intelligence he took in current affairs.[106]

It is in 1918 that the Press Office is established at Buckingham Palace. It owed its birth to events the year before, when Lord Derby had mentioned to Stamfordham that there was an idea of attaching a press reporter to the Royal Household to assist them in producing reports about Their Majesties' war work. Twelve months later the first camera crew arrives at the palace to "film" the King. His Majesty is to send a message of congratulation to the Italian Army in the field and it has been decided that it would be extremely novel if it was not only conveyed in a traditional manner to Victor Emmanuel's troops, but if they could then witness its having been handed to the King's messenger at the beginning of its journey. Thus the King's handing of his message to Colonel Bromhead and his four officers is committed to posterity. "The intention is that the film shall be reproduced in various military picturedromes through Italy, so that the soldiers may witness the handing over of the message, and may subsequently see upon the screen the text of the document reproduced."[107]

"New Heart and New Spirit"

The King pays as much interest to the role of America in the war as he does to one of his own Dominions or Colonies, with good reason. The Allies desperately need the colossal weight of industry and manpower that the United States can put into the field. And the war is still not uniting people across the Atlantic. "In many parts of the country there is absolute indifference, and in many parts there is positive hostility." German and Irish interests, the latter in particular, "have distinguished themselves here by the extreme violence of the language of the press."[108] And so gratitude is everything, and royal gratitude trumps all other forms. As far as His Majesty is concerned, any encouragement he can show American troops will help balance out the hard truths that must be overcome at the front. In April 1918, each and every man arriving in Europe from the United States are handed a facsimile of a message to them all from the King:

> Soldiers of the United States, the people of the British Isles welcome you on your way to take your stand beside the armies of many nations now fighting in the old world… The Allies will gain new heart and spirit in your company. I wish that I could shake the hand of each one of you and bid you God speed on your mission.[109]

106   *Ibid* 14/10/18.
107   *Morning Advertiser* 6/5/18.
108   RA PS/PSO/GV/C/Q/1110/20.
109   RA GV/PRIV/GVD/1918 (21/7).

There are a constant flow of dignitaries liaising with their British counterparts passing through London and the King meets them all. They include two future Presidents; Franklin Roosevelt in his capacity as Assistant Secretary of the Navy, "a charming man, he came to see me and told me everything his navy is doing to help in the war, which is most satisfactory."[110] and Herbert Hoover as Food Controller, "a very interesting man."[111] Other men represent the Industries and Priorities board, the Treasury and the State Departments. In March His Majesty hosts Mr Henry Dawson, head of the American Red Cross. "He has already raised over 20 million pounds in America and is just going to ask for the same sum again."[112] Labour is the hot topic in 1918, and of course Their Majesties make sure that this is not neglected too. In September Mr Gompers, the President of the American Federation of Labour, is received at the palace. "Had a long talk with him and he appears to have sound views about most things," remarks the King.[113]

His Majesty inspects troops and the King and Queen also visit various establishments popping up in London to accommodate U.S. servicemen. The Washington Inn in St James's Square is an American YMCA hut for officers, and there is a corresponding Eagles Hut at Aldwych for the men. "Both are comfortable and well arranged and they are much used."[114] They also receive men of the American Aviation Corps who are camped at Ascot. His Majesty even grants land at Englefield Creek for a hospital for American wounded with a 500 bed capacity. The authorities are thrilled to be housed on one of the King's estates. "Will you please convey to His Majesty," writes the Chairman of the U.S. Red Cross, "No country whose people are so thoughtful and generous as to provide such care for American soldiers and sailors can be considered as a foreign land."[115]

The King gets the opportunity to see American ships that have crossed the Atlantic and joined forces with the Royal Navy off the Scottish coast. Even the sailors do not know that he is coming until a few hours before his arrival in mid-July. The morning is bright and warm, "rays of the sun playing on the immaculate white caps of officers and men who assembled on deck. As far as the eye could see the white ensign was being unfolded by a breeze."[116] After an inspection of his own ships and an investiture, His Majesty boards the U.S. flagship *New York*. The King stands on a searchlight platform above the bridge with Beatty to survey her crew and is given a tour. His Majesty is much impressed with everything he has seen. "A most beautifully clean ship and they are most efficient."[117]

A San Francisco editor who had been part of the contingent invited to Sandringham was just as impressed with his royal encounter. "The King is better looking man than indicated by photographs, which fail at... reflecting the vivacity and charm of a cordial habit... not an imposing personality, but are of definite dignity. He has the rather husky voice of one who smokes over much." He tells them of an encounter with American troops at the front. His Majesty says that he was in the midst of a group of officers, when he "heard one of your chaps ask, pointing to me, who is that bug? Told that I was the King of England, he sneered, King of England, hell! Where's his crown?"[118] The labour delegation were astonished that once their little formal reception was concluded at Buckingham Palace, The King, Queen and Princess Mary all remained in informal conversation with the various representatives for over an hour.

110   Ibid., (29/7).
111   Ibid., (29/7).
112   RA GV/PRIV/GVD/1918 (15/3).
113   Ibid., 23/9.
114   Ibid., 25/6.
115   *Daily Telegraph* 5/6/18.
116   *Daily Telegraph* 24/7/18.
117   RA GV/PRIV/GVD/1918 (22/7).
118   *Western Evening Herald* 2/1/19.

The King moved freely from group to group, discussing various phases of the war and surprising the members of the mission by his intimate knowledge of industrial problems and of the leaders in the industrial movement both in Great Britain and abroad. His personal attitude, his wide range of knowledge, coupled with his sound and statesmanlike grasp of industrial questions and national and international problems, made the event one of extraordinary interest and value, apart from the fact that we were being so highly honoured.[119]

There are, of course wounded Americans to visit. A large hospital is established for them at Dartford, staffed by personnel from the King's County Hospital in Brooklyn, whose population fund their endeavours. The King and Queen make a tour of the wards and spend a good length of time in the shock wards. One man is convinced that he has been killed three times, and "gravely assured His Majesty that he was once drowned in the Mississippi. "I am glad you are getting over it now," said the King, with a sympathetic smile." The Americans have their own approach to these cases. "Their Majesties were interested to notice the variety of maps, pictures and ornaments such as are not usually seen in hospitals. The officer in charge informed them that the cases treated here have seldom required [physical treatment] and, every effort was made to claim their attention and take them out of themselves." The patients read excerpts of poetry that they have been writing, and the King is informed that so far the results have been most satisfactory. The medical officer says that he is "astonished to find how much practical knowledge the King possessed of surgical cases and of hospital work and equipment. For example, he seemed to be quite familiar with the bone and skin grafts."[120]

But by far the showpiece of the King attempts to show solidarity with Britain's new ally occurs on Independence Day 1918 at Chelsea Football Club. The press are keen to point out that it will be the first time in history that a Sovereign celebrates the Fourth of July, for His Majesty promises some weeks in advance to attend a baseball game contested by the U.S. Army and the U.S. Navy at Stamford Bridge.

"Remarkable scenes at Chelsea" reads one headline. It should be said that none of the British spectators have a clue what they were watching, but it is the spectacle that counts, for it is sheer pandemonium. "It took us completely away to those distant times when we could rejoice under a blue sky without looking for Zeppelins and Gothas."[121] A silver airship bobs overhead; circles round and about, "at times descending so low that the expressions on the faces of its crew could be plainly distinguished."[122] There are flags everywhere, Old Glory and the Union Jack predominate, but the rest of the allies have not been forgotten. The King and Queen arrive. Princess Mary accompanies her parents, and Bertie and the Duke of Connaught arrive after completing another engagement. As they pass piles of flowers adorning the grandstand the airship unveils two enormous flags, the Stars and Stripes and the Union Jack. The crowd includes peers, politicians, generals. Almost 50,000 are present; soldiers and sailors from both nations and the Dominions, lady friends, nurses, wounded men in light blue and Chelsea Pensioners in their red coats here and there. The teams emerge, the U.S. Army in green with blue caps and the U.S. Navy in blue trimmed with red. They assemble in front of the Royal Box and the King comes down to meet them. It has been rumoured that he will pitch the first ball, but in the event he has signed one, which he hands across.

The atmosphere is raucous all afternoon. The crowd "rollicked and roared and screamed and yelled and sang." Each contingent brings fanatics: "zealots who assemble in companies to howl their

119   *The Times* 31/7/18.
120   *The Times* 18/10/18.
121   *The Times* 5/7/18.
122   *The Field* 13/7/18.

respective sides to victory. There were boards at the entrance to the ground directing army 'rooters' to go one way, navy rooters another." Aided by megaphones, it soon becomes apparent to the neutral that "the army rooter is tame and inarticulate compared with him of the navy, whose voice is that of ocean storms."[123] One journalist is fortunate enough to be sitting next to a man from Pittsburgh, "who kindly explained what was happening… If you think I understand his explanation of the game, or the brilliant strategy of the players who wore jockey caps, long stockings, boxing gloves and fencing helmets and swing Indian clubs, gentle reader, you are in error."[124] The Brits enjoy the afternoon thoroughly, but can make head nor tail of it. "Many present yesterday made no secret of their innocence [and] persisted in calling the pitcher the bowler, the catcher the wicket keeper and the striker as the batsman," but the Americans were chivalrous about it. Baseball hasn't the dignity of cricket, in fact it makes football look like the "recreation of well mannered mice by comparison to it." For the two groups of supporters constantly abuse one another. The navy chide the army "unmercifully and in language stranger and peculiar. And the army… were subdued and voiceless. From this point it was plain that the navy were at the highway to victory." The entertainment lasts some two hours. "We should not care to say who was the better side, because frankly we do not know, but the navy won by 2 to 1." Megaphones, hooters and trumpets go berserk and spark a pitch invasion by the Americans. "The uproar was tremendous, and then suddenly on some unknown signal it died and the Welsh Guards plays the first strains of the Star Spangled banner."[125] Hats come off and they stand to attention, saluting. The King and Queen have surprised all by remaining until the end. "Quite exciting, only got home at six,"[126] writes His Majesty in his diary.

"Daughters of Britain"

His Majesty is a feminist, of sorts. Women's suffrage was a contentious issue before the war and in January 1913 the Franchise and Registration Bill was introduced into the House of Commons. But it was held up by bureaucracy and the finer points of parliamentary procedure. Mrs Pankhurst and her followers were frustrated; "they concluded that Mr Asquith had escaped, whether from cunning or stupidity, from his own assurances; the ardour of their militancy was much inflamed."[127] In seeking attention for their cause, campaigners have dragged the King into many a stunt or protest, some of them violent. At Tattenham Corner in 1913, Emily Davison threw herself under the King's horse during the Derby. That same year, protesters had also tried to set fire to the Royal Academy, and bombs had been found near the Bank of England and St. Paul's. The opening months of 1914 saw a surge in extremist activity. "Eminent personages" were attacked and an attempt was made to petition the King at Buckingham Palace. During a performance at Her Majesty's Theatre "unruly women'" shouted at him. Later, protestors were responsible for the explosion of a bomb in Westminster Abbey which slightly damaged the Coronation Chair, and on a pre-war trip to Scotland, the King found more than one suffragette hanging from the front of his motor car as he was trying to progress about the country. And so His Majesty's patience had, on a personal level, been sorely tried, but he is just as appalled at the accounts he hears about methods of forced feeding which were being carried out on women using hunger strikes as a means of protest in prisons. Stamfordham was instructed to approach the Home Secretary: "His Majesty cannot help feeling

123   *Daily Telegraph* 5/7/18.
124   *Daily Chronicle* 5/7/18.
125   *The Times* 5/7/18.
126   RA GV/PRIV/GVD/1918 (4/7).
127   Nicolson: *King George V: His Life and Reign,* p.211.

that there is something shocking, if not almost cruel, in the operation to which these insensate women are subjected through their refusal to take necessary nourishment."[128]

But there is a difference between the King's opinion of a small faction of militant protestors, terrorists even, and what he thinks of womankind as a whole. He lives and works side by side with a strong willed, independent woman, and he adores her. He is immensely proud of Queen Mary's contribution to the war effort and time and time again reminds her that without her at his side, he would not be able to manage all that is asked of him. His Majesty is content to have his wife act in any way she sees fit when it comes to administering to the specialist needs of Prince John, he never holds her back from any aspect of war work she chooses to carry out, including a visit to the front, to the extent that he was perfectly happy to see her wield a machine gun. On a visit to a rifle range in 1915, Their Majesties were watching men practice their gunnery when the King was invited to fire the weapon himself. He did so with dignity and politely. Then it is set up again for Queen Mary and she is invited to take a turn. When the first few rounds go off she draws back and giggles, but then instantly resumes her grip on the trigger and empties the entire magazine with glee. His Majesty sees the accurate results of his wife's shooting and smiles broadly.

After the births of David and Bertie the King spends each of the Queen's pregnancies praying for daughters, and just as he is proud of the women in his own family, the King is proud of his female subjects and all that they have contributed to the war.

The very aspects of the women one meets in the streets as they turn out from their various places of employment for an hours' rest, or when the days work is done, is strangely different from what it used to be," writes one journalist. "The girls are more alert; they bear on their faces the look of those who are self-reliant and who have discovered unsuspected stores of energy… The great central fact remains is that here in the 20th century, and in the midst of a vast war, …women have emphatically come into their own. When the call came they were ready and eager to respond and the history of our times will chronicle no more superb achievement than the brilliant success of women's work in these stern times of difficulty and crisis.[129]

The King has been advocating for their capable inclusion in the nation's plight all along. Early on in the munitions crisis in 1915 he suggested that women might be brought in to manufacture shells in larger numbers, and that Mrs Pankhurst might be employed as a successful recruiting agent. When conscription is being fought over, His Majesty also advocates a poll tax on all male employees in shops where their work could be carried out by women instead. In 1916, he also spoke out in favour of the employment of women gardeners, setting the example by bringing three London girls up to work at Sandringham. By 1918 women are not only eligible for the OBE, but the first of them are legally entitled to vote, and in some quarters Their Majesties are credited with helping this to happen. "It is an open secret that the pride of the King and Queen in the war work that the women of England have undertaken knows no bounds… Our broad-minded King, encouraged we feel sure, by his sympathetic Queen, had made it possible for good services rendered by women to be recognised in the same way that men receive reward."[130]

In the course of nearly four years of war, His Majesty has seen thousands of female workers and their passion, their dedication and their vivacity at the exciting new world opening up for them gives him no end of pleasure. He bombarded working girls with questions: How long had they been

128   Ibid., p.212.
129   *Daily Telegraph* 1/7/18.
130   *Ladies Pictorial* 30/6/17.

employed? Did they llike their work? And what of their brothers at the front? He has a fatherly soft spot for a girl in uniform, and these war-girls have infiltrated almost every establishment that the King visits. He meets smartly turned out members of the Women's Auxiliary Army Corps working as clerks, typists, telegraphists at home and abroad. During 1918 His Majesty engages a female chauffeur for the first time. Miss Irene Stephen of the Army Service Corps drove the King about Brighton in a Daimler limousine for nearly three hours. "His Majesty, on alighting, asked her many questions: how long had she been driving, how she liked the work, and what car she generally drove. He also complimented her on her good driving."[131] As a sailor, the King has a special place in his heart for the Wrens, their naval equivalent. He inspects one contingent during his trip to Lincolnshire. At Immingham he meets a contingent of girls in their own naval uniform. "The morning was grey and raw, and a thin mist of rain drifted over from the brown waters of the Humber."[132] His Majesty walked up and down their ranks "commenting on their utility and smart appearances."[133]

But it is by far in factory settings that His Majesty meets the most female war workers. At one of The Government's new facilities on the Welsh border the King sees 3,000 women producing TNT and gun cotton.

> The welcome given to the King and Queen was spontaneous and exuberant. Hundreds of trousered young women, some in brown, with brown or scarlet caps and belts, some in cream with white caps, some in Khaki, surged along in the wake of the royal visitors as they passed through the chain of buildings, and an attempt by works officials to stem the merry rush was quite unavailing.[134]

Neither of Their Majesties are in the least perturbed by the sight of women in trousers. "The King said they looked very real, handy girls."[135]

His Majesty is so thrilled with all that he has seen of women workers on his second labour tour in 1917, that he decides he wants to get out and see London's girls in action; and so he descends upon a fuse factory immediately on his return. At first the girls are shy, "but the King quickly put them at their ease... The girls were charmed with the King; the King was delighted with the girls."[136] At Leeds Their Majesties are immensely flattered to learn that hundreds of smiling faces that greet them at one factory belong to girls who have finished their night shifts, yet remained at work to get a look at the King and Queen. Just as with the men that he comes into contact, the King is keen to hear their stories, so it is with women. At Barrow, His Majesty had spied a woman wearing a medal and regimental badge and asked why this was. She replied that they were here husbands, "whom she lost two years ago, and as he could no longer serve his country she was anxious to do what she could in his stead and so entered a munition factory."[137] When he starts visiting schools to in late 1917, the King does not only have messages for the boys. He addresses groups of little girls too, for they can have a role to play as well. "I know the boys will be loyal subjects, and that whatever walk of life they may enter, they will do their best to serve their country... I know the girls will do the same, and will follow the example of their older sisters who are doing such splendid work in this war."[138]

131   *The Gentlewoman* 1/6/18.
132   *The Times* 11/4/18.
133   *Daily Telegraph* 11/4/18.
134   (ed.) Hammerton & Wilson: *The Great War Vol.XVIII*, pp.128-129.
135   *Ladies Pictorial* 2/6/17.
136   *Daily Mail* 23/5/17.
137   *The Times* 18/5/17.
138   *The Times* 19/10/17.

In July 1918, the King and Queen are set to mark their silver wedding anniversary. "Quite early in the year it became manifest that there would be a widespread desire" on the part of the country to present gifts and hold commemorative events. "But the King and Queen, as soon as they realised that these efforts were likely to assume considerable proportions; and might therefore have diverted money both from the organisations which in one way or another are striving to help and restore the wounded; caused it to be made known that they would accept nothing for themselves."[139] The only gifts that they will be prepared to accept will be a silver cup from the City of London, who also present Their Majesties with a collection for £53,000 for the charities of their choice.

As far as events are concerned, they will only permit one. "The King and Queen have consented to receive from women war workers an address of loyalty and homage on the occasion of their silver wedding."[140] On a Saturday afternoon a great procession organised by the Ministry of Labour will be staged representing all facets of women's service. 2,500 women form up in Hyde Park after lunch on a perfect, almost cloudless day; sunny with just the faintest of breezes. The park is "glowing with colour and charged with the enthusiasm of a London crowd."[141] To the beat of Guards bands, the women of Britain march along The Mall, through Admiralty Arch, up along Pall Mall, Lower Regent Street, and Hyde Park Corner, to Buckingham Palace where weekend crowds dangle from vantage points upon the Victoria Memorial.

The King stands bareheaded on the balcony, watching them assemble with his daughter alongside him and a number of female relatives present. The windows are crowded with members of the Royal Household who want to see the spectacle for themselves and they watch soldiers with little flags indicating to each group where they should arrange themselves. Wounded men have been invited to form a little line of hospital blue, who are joined by a small group from King George's hospital. They are wheeling a reclining couch on which one of their numbers rests, suffering from a severe spinal injury. "For ten months he has lain recumbent, and his pale face lighted up with pleasure as a very favoured position was given him."[142]

A spokeswoman from the Ministry of Labour reads a celebratory address from the "Daughters of Britain":

> It is with feelings of profound loyalty and devotion that we avail ourselves of this opportunity of placing before Your Majesties a record of our respect and homage on this occasion of [your] silver wedding. For four anxious years it has been our dearest wish and earnest endeavour to devote ourselves, mind and body, to the service of our country and our allies in their conflict of our common foe... It is our dearest hope that before the next anniversary of this day, the dark cloud of war may be dispersed, and we earnestly pray that in the years succeeding we may share with Your Majesties the return of peaceful happiness and prosperity in our beloved country.[143]

The King comes to the end of the platform to issue his reply and a "sea of upturned faces followed every word," as His Majesty speaks for a little longer than is his usual preference.

> In our visits to various centres we have had opportunities of seeing and appreciating the great part which the women of our land are taking in all branches of war service, and everywhere

139   *Daily Telegraph* 6/7/18.
140   *Morning Post* 19/6/18.
141   *The Times* 1/7/18.
142   Ibid.
143   *The Times* 29/6/18.

we have been filled with admiration at their achievements, an admiration which I believe to be shared by the whole nation…The range of war work undertaken by women is well exemplified in your imposing procession… When the history of our country's share in the war is written no chapter will be more remarkable than that relating to the range and extent of women's participation. The Queen and I heartily thank you… we are touched by the thought that the first expression of loyalty and devotion on this occasion of our silver wedding should come from this representative body of women.[144]

The most exciting part of the afternoon comes with a march past. "Window breaking, arrests by the police, prohibited meetings, disorderly gatherings, acrimonious attacks - all these things are incidents of an era wholly superseded and forgotten;"[145] for this much larger representation of Britain's women exude an eagerness is infectious and they are dedicated to doing their bit for their country as much as any man; "uniformed, disciplined, capable, crowned with health and determination… It was a pageant of triumph, for the persistence, the adaptability, and the sacrifice expressed in the various uniforms proved beyond all argument that woman is worthy of the citizenship that has lately become hers."[146]

The Irish Guards play the opening bars of Land of Hope and Glory and they break into sections with the efficiency of soldiers. The Voluntary Aid Detachment girls come first given pride of place at the head: three hundred of them in grey cotton dresses and aprons. Princess Mary's detail is there, as are representatives of the Dominions. "Then came the Women's Legion, Lady Londonderry's gallant, khaki-clad women, who were the first to help the army in substitution work. Next were the WAACs to whom London has grown accustomed. The crowd are fascinated by the smartness of the WRENs, who have never appeared as a public body such as this in London: "marching well in their neat uniforms with blue jean sailor collars and white covered navy hats." Then come the Land Girls in their holland tunics and high boots. They are followed by "foresters with green caps, and the Women's National Land Service Corps. Munition girls wear a vast array of outfits; "one regiment in white linen coats and trousers and caps, another group in brown holland."[147] But the sensation of the day was the section from the anti-gas department, dressed head to toe in bright red with matching caps. The procession continues. "Women police, omnibus girls, railway girls marching in a great moving picture gave way presently to the fine group of nurses representative of the metropolitan asylums board, ambulance drivers, splendid looking women in navy uniforms;" the first women to be employed in any public service. "After them came four drivers with their smart Royal Mail uniforms and coaching whips, and behind them the post girls with their GPO bags. Then came the tramway girls in their linen coats… and most feminine of all, with brown veils fluttering in the wind. The military nurses from Endell Street Hospital,"[148] who turn their heads to the left as they take the King's salute. Before they depart the King and Queen chat informally the head of each contingent. "It was a most imposing sight" writes His Majesty, "and extremely well arranged."[149]

It was altogether a day that has made history on the evolution of women's position in the service of the Empire. Had anyone four years ago witnessed Saturday's scene, how he must

144   TNA: CAB 24/68/6.
145   *Daily Graphic* 1/7/18.
146   *Daily Express* 1/7/18.
147   *The Times* 1/7/18.
148   Ibid.
149   RA GV/PRIV/GVD/1918 (29/6).

have rubbed his eyes!…The abuse heaped even in 1915 on the mere notion of women replacing men on the land… they are already as familiar as cabbages in the parks, or a Handley Page turning somersaults.

These 3,000 women stand for a million and more.

These are changed days from those of sentimental refrain: how men must work and women must weep. There was nothing in the very least weepy about the companies, remarkably fit and remarkably picturesque, who swung down Constitution Hill to the playing of the Guards' bands… They had the resolute air of women who will work while men must fight, and the King paid a high and serious tribute to their spirit.[150]

"A Brutal Murder"

From Petrograd in July 1917, Sir George Buchanan reported arrangements made to move the Tsar to Tobolsk in Siberia. Nicholas was still declaring a preference for the Crimea, but apparently had "seemed quite pleased with [the] proposed change of residence." It seems to Buchanan, too, that this might be a plausible solution to the problem of what to do with the Imperial Family. "I expressed hope that when he was in Siberia, [the] Emperor's movements would not be so restricted. In spite of many faults which he had committed and his weak character, the Emperor was not a criminal and deserved to be treated with as much consideration as possible."[151] That, and from the Provisional Government's point of view, socialist agitation was building and there were fears of a counter-revolution. They'd like their former Tsar far away from the seat of any such uprising.

The Royal Archive's file on the Tsar ends dramatically in April 1917 and does not properly begin again, discounting reference to the Siberian move, until May 1918. It is evident that material was either destroyed at the time and never filed, or removed early on, for its absence has not affected cataloguing, and there is documented correspondence from several years later.[152] discussing the lack of any papers relating to the Tsar's situation for that that period. The most plausible explanation is that whatever this correspondence dealt with in regard to Nicholas Romanov and his family, for correspondence there surely was, expounded upon the existing evidence that the King was involved in attempts to try and secure the removal of the former Tsar from Russia.

In the months following the collapse of British asylum offer in 1917, His Majesty was deeply concerned about the safety of his cousin. Once again it is important to realise the difference between not wanting to grant the Nicholas asylum in Britain and washing his hands of his cousin's fate entirely. In June 1917, the King's worries revolved around the likelihood that the Tsar's house arrest at his palace at Tsarskoe Selo, just outside Petrograd, might be exchanged for something more severe. "I own that I feel very anxious for the safety of the Emperor," he wrote to his former Private Secretary. "If he gets inside the walls of the prison of St Peter and Paul, I doubt he will ever come out alive."[153] All accounts that he received about Russian affairs as the year progressed added to his concerns. Hanbury-Williams arrived home following the revolution and at the palace "gives a lamentable account of the situation there."[154] General Gourko, the Tsar's Chief of Staff prior to his abdication, "is so disgusted with the state of affairs in Russia that he is going to France

150   *Morning Post* 1/7/18.
151   RA PSO/PS/GV/C/M/1067/70.
152   RA PSO/PS/GV/C/M/1067/82.
153   Nicolson: *King George V: His Life and Reign,* pp.214-218.
154   RA GV/PRIV/GVD/1917 (10/6).

with his wife."[155] A prominent ex-pat who had been in Russia for two decades convinces the King that "things could not be worse there and there must be further bloodshed before they can get a proper government."[156]

Unlike the Bolshevik grab for power in Petrograd, which resulted in just half a dozen deaths, the Russian civil war that followed was bloody in the extreme. In 1918 Russia is a land without law or order, with "a whole series of overlapping and mutually reinforcing conflicts,"[157] dominated by a rapidly escalating struggle between the armed forces of Lenin's Bolshevik Government and its 'counter-revolutionary' opponents, there were also attempts by certain regions to break away from Petrograd, and violence escalated further in the spring and early summer of 1918 with the establishment of a monopoly on food distribution which saw poor peasants in rural areas sent out to seize all surplus food at gunpoint if necessary. They were threatened with death, family members were taken hostage and villages burned. It was estimated that a quarter of a million people had been killed in these "bread wars."[158]

In May 1918, the Czechoslovak Legion revolted. Formed out of men working in Russia before the war, who wanted to wage war on the Hapsburg Empire and claim their independence, the majority of them had tried to get out via Vladivostock after the Treaty of Brest-Litovsk and go to join Allied forces in France. Concerned that the Bolshevik Government wouldn't let them get there, they systematically began taking control of the eastern reaches of Russia's railways before moving further into Siberia. They refused to stand down, and took up the same violent philosophy as every other interest group in the country at that time; committing numerous atrocities that included burning Bolshevik soldiers alive. By the Summer of 1918, rumours have spread that anti-Bolshevik troops are marching on Ekaterinburg. Lenin had made no decision on the fate of the Imperial Family, but there was terror at the thought of a counter-revolution bearing him as a figurehead. In the third week of July 1918, a statement appeared in the press.

Ex-Tsar shot. Local Soviet Decision.

It is now announced by the Bolshevik Government that the ex-Tsar has been shot by the order of the Ural Regional Council, who state that they decided upon the course owing to the threat of the Czech-Slovaks against the capital of the Red Ural, and their discovery of a counter-revolutionary plot in which the former monarch was involved.[159]

At first London doesn't know what to make of the news. As of 23rd July, the Foreign Office could not confirm reports of Nicholas's execution. "I saw Mr Balfour this morning," writes Stamfordham, "and while accepting the view that the news is not official he fears that the announcement made by the Soviet is almost certain to be correct, as there would be no object in publishing what was not true."[160] The Royal Family is plunged into despair. The ex-Tsar's death is being celebrated in many quarters, but on the other hand, many feel that the late Emperor had been a faithful ally and friend of this country.

Russians in London have immediately started to organise a memorial service and there is the question of whether or not the Royal Family can attend. For a start, Stamfordham is concerned

---

155 Ibid., (25/10).
156 RA GV/PRIV/GVD/1918 (3/11).
157 Gerwath, Robert: *The Vanquished: Why the First World War Failed to End 1917-1923,* p.77.
158 Ibid., p.82.
159 *Manchester Guardian* 22/7/18.
160 RA PSO/PS/GV/C/M/1344A/2.

that the claim has not yet been held up as official. "If the news is taken as authentic, and the service announced in *The Times* of today for Thursday next takes place, this news was no more official yesterday when the Queen, Princess Mary Queen Alexandra and Princess Victoria were present at a matinee and presumably will be no more official on Wednesday when Their Majesties will attend [a wedding]." Stamfordham is inclined to think that the whole affair should be postponed "until such a time as the Government can state officially that the Ex-Emperor is dead, otherwise, if it is assumed that the news is not true, and the King does not send a representative to Thursday's service, and afterwards we are informed officially that the Emperor is dead, it would be impossible to have a second memorial service."[161] In normal circumstances, if the King did not attend himself, he would at least have sent a representative. Balfour has been looking at precedents and the palace are taking their own steps; sending telegrams to both the Danish and Swedish courts; but it appears that there is no news to be had beyond the Bolshevik statement in the newspapers.

On the following day, the Queen writes in her diary that "the news was confirmed of poor Nicky of Russia having been shot by those brutes of Bolsheviks last week... It is too horrible and heartless." Queen Alexandra and Toria come to tea, a tearful episode with everyone "terribly upset at the news."[162] The King decides to hell with precedents, he is going to attend the memorial service at the Russian embassy's pretty little chapel in Welbeck Street himself, though he still can't quite believe that his cousin is dead; "Dear Nicky... We can get no details, it is (or was) a most foul murder. I was devoted to Nicky, the kindest of men, a thorough gentlemen, loved his country and his people."[163] The memorial service is a crowded affair. The King is present in his Field Marshal's uniform, accompanied by a large group of relatives. The rest of the congregation is made up of civil servants, members of the diplomatic corps, prominent Anglo-Russians and Several Russian military and naval officers. There are no attendees from His Majesty's Government so far as Stamfordham can fathom and he is incensed. "Surely not from fear of offending the Bolshevists!" Perhaps, he suggests, they are covering their own backs with a General Election in mind.

> I really am aghast at the callous indifference of the public and the press with regard to this... "sickening horror" ...The Emperor no doubt was a weak man, but there are plenty of them in places high and low in the world. Whatever he was he was a true friend to this country and as long as he was on the throne his army fought, which is more than be said for it under a republic![164]

On 28th July, the King receives confirmation from the Foreign Office beyond all doubt via a British agent in Moscow, which states that "we have little doubt that the Emperor has in fact been murdered."[165] "Dear Nicky was shot by the local Soviet at Ekaterinburg on night of July 16th," His Majesty writes in his diary. "It was nothing more than a brutal murder."[166] Finger pointing when about the fate of the Tsar predictably occurs through German channels. England is accused of causing the Russian Revolution and inciting unrest there. "If England now fulfils the kindred duty of her court by wearing mourning for the murdered Tsar, she ought to have fulfilled her duty of granting at least personal protection... Therefore, they have killed the Tsar. England must have foreseen this result." It is ludicrously claimed that even in the weeks before his death,

161   Ibid.
162   Pope-Hennessy: *Queen Mary, 1867-1953*, pp.506-507.
163   RA GV/PRIV/GVD/1918 (25/7).
164   RA PSO/PS/GV/C/M/1344A/9.
165   RA PSO/PS/GV/C/M/1344A/11.
166   RA GV/PRIV/GVD/1918 (28/7).

the Government might have saved him if they had cared to, though this claim was void of any supporting evidence. "The Tsar has been sacrificed to British policy, just like everything else that comes in its way. This political brutality is known throughout the world... The English court makes use of his death, which was welcome to them and or which England herself is partly responsible, in order to make of it before the world a melodramatic spectacle."[167] Stamfordham wryly makes a key point, that Wilhelm and his Government could have attempted to make the Tsar's release a clause of the Treaty of Brest-Litovsk, and that this constituted "probably the strongest leeway under Bolshevik rule for getting them out of the country." Whether Nicholas would have accepted any such offer from his enemies will forever remain unanswered."[168]

In the many courts across Europe which are populated by the relations of the Imperial Family, concerns have quickly moved on to ascertaining or securing the safety of the rest of their Russian kin. There are a plethora of Grand Dukes under arrest in Petrograd whose fate is a source of constant anxiety and the Danish Minister there is constantly active in trying to obtain information about them. It soon transpires that the Grand Dukes in prison are, at least for now, the most significant issue as August dawns, as is the safety of the Empress and her five children.

The faintest of rumours suggest that the Tsarevich has also been murdered and here the evidence of British involvement in trying to rescue them from imprisonment in Siberia survives. King Alfonso of Spain, His Majesty's cousin by marriage has stated that he will take the Empress, her children and the Tsar's mother, and apparently even approaches the Germans for their help in getting them out. After all the matter now excludes a deposed Emperor, and concerns the fate of women and children. He has the full support of the King, who has just returned from his visit to the front. "I shall be most grateful," he telegraphs to Spain, "if you will exert all your influence in whatever direction you think best to secure the Imperial Family of Russia from the present pitiable position."[169] This is clearly the main avenue being explored for the evacuation of the Tsar's family. "One only hopes that some good may come from the representations of the King of Spain," writes Stamfordham, and that the unhappy Royal Family of Russia may be liberated from their present cruel position."[170] But Britain is no mere bystander. The Director of Military Intelligence at the War Office tells General Poole, in the Baltic: "If you have a chance of helping and saving them then Mr Balfour desires that you do so."[171] Four days later his orders are firmly reaffirmed: "To render any and all assistance possible in evacuating the Empress, her children and the Tsar's mother from Russia."[172]

But it is all for nothing. On 31st August Stamfordham receives a telegram from the War Office:

> I think I ought to let you know at once for His Majesty's information that we have just received a very distressing telegram from the intelligence officer serving under General Poole at Murmansk to the effect that there is every probability that the Empress of Russia, her four daughters, and the Tsarevich were all murdered at the same time as the late Tsar. This information reached the Foreign Office from a source which he had no reason to doubt. I am very much afraid, therefore, that the news is only too likely to prove true.[173]

167   RA PSO/PS/GV/C/M/1344A/13A.
168   Hanbury-Williams: *The Emperor Nicholas II As I Knew Him,* pp.225-226.
169   RA PSO/PS/GV/C/M/1344A/22.
170   RA PSO/PS/GV/C/M/1344A/29.
171   RA PSO/PS/GV/C/M/1344A/20.
172   RA PSO/PS/GV/C/M/1344A/19.
173   RA PSO/PS/GV/C/M/1344A/30.

Stamfordham informs His Majesty immediately. "I hear from Russia that there is every probability that Alicky and four daughters and little boy were murdered at the same time as Nicky," writes the King. "It is too horrible and shows what fiends these Bolshevists are. For poor Alicky, perhaps it was best so," "But those poor innocent children!" Stamfordham is in shock too. "Naturally the King is deeply grieved of the ghastly fate which has befallen his relatives, and it is almost incredible that the innocent children shouldn't of have been spared."[174]

Information continues to filter through and by mid-September, His Majesty has a reasonably accurate idea of the events that have supposedly led to the death of the Imperial Family. In the spring of 1918, the Imperial Family had been transferred from Tobolsk to Ekaterinburg. When troops opposed to Lenin's Government began an advance from Chelyabinsk, the local Bolsheviks, a particularly virulent strain, had become resigned to the fact that they must evacuate the town. As far as the King is told, they had then asked what they should do with the Tsar, and were told "do whatever you think fit." Thus on 16th July at a meeting of delegates belonging to the Ural Provisional Government of Soldiers and Workmen, it was decided to shoot him. Nicholas was informed and his sentence carried out same night by Lettish soldiers." But. No trace of any bodies have been found, and though ugly rumours persist that the Empress and her children have been burned alive, British officials in the area insist that the entire family might have been removed from Ekaterinburg alive by the Bolsheviks as they fled north.[175] It would be many months before accurate evidence was amassed detailing what had happened to Nicholas and his family. During this period, unsurprisingly the Duke of Connaught noted that he found the King miserable and depressed.

The fate of the Tsar haunted those that knew him. For those select few who were close to him, who felt that they might possibly have done something more to save him, the fate of the Imperial Family was something that they never fully recovered from. "Everyone, I suppose," wrote General Hanbury Williams, "has shadows which pass before them at times… To me one of the darkest of these shadows is that of the late Emperor of Russia and those who belonged to him. The sunbeams that light them up are the unfailing kindness which he always showed me in times of personal or other trouble, his sunny and cheerful nature, and his unfailing courage when things seemed to be going badly. His loyalty to the Allied cause was only equalled by his determination to fight out the war to the bitter end… My happy memories of him are darkened by the tragedy of his end and the regret that I could do no more to save him and his family in the days when their fate may still have been said to hang in the balance."[176] None were more stunned by his loss than his cousin. At the end of the year when he received a group of American journalists at Sandringham, reference was made in the King's study at York Cottage to his cousin the Tsar. He walked across to a desk and picked up a photograph, and holding it up with a burst of obvious feeling, he says, "poor chap, poor chap, poor chap."[177]

"The Ball Has Begun to Roll"

In mid-July the palace begins to plan what has become His Majesty's annual tour of the Western Front. Wigram has begun to dub Major Thompson "Thomas Cook," and the King's designated travel agent thinks this rather funny. "Thomas Cook will be pleased to render any services possible to His Majesty… I will parade at any place and time you give me, my toothbrush, razor and blankets all ready for a life in the open." The King begins work as soon as he disembarks on the

174   RA PSO/PS/GV/C/M/1344A/31.
175   RA PSO/PS/GV/C/M/1344A/35.
176   HW, p.8-9.
177   Ibid.

continent; watching tanks and even a locomotive being unloaded from onto the docks. The little Royal Standard comes out once again and His Majesty begins his tour with it affixed to his car, determined to visit each of the separate army areas. On his way to meet Haig, he is intrigued at the sight of German prisoners at work behind the British lines, building railways alongside Canadians and Chinamen. At Crecy a forestry unit cuts down thousands of trees, "sawing the great trunks into planks for military purposes,"[178] and once again much of the labour is carried out by captured enemy troops. The Commander in Chief is pleased to see a change in the King's mood. "His Majesty looked well and very cheery. So different to his frame of mind on the occasion of his last visit in March." The pair have a chuckle over a "message" from Lloyd George, for the Prime Minister, the King says, "now talks about 'poor Haig' and the excessive length of line which he had to hold... The Government is now determined to support us," writes Haig. "Lloyd George wishes me to insist strongly on having our front reduced before autumn comes."[179]

His Majesty is feeling particularly homesick on this visit. "As you know I am never happy when away from you,"[180] he tells the Queen. But he is already buoyed by a changed atmosphere at the front, and by Haig's enthusiasm for the army's prospects. There is positivity, "an atmosphere of victory."[181] The King's schedule is somewhat erratic and with good reason, for the British Army is to launch an offensive and His Majesty will not just be at the front in the course of an advance, but at zero hour.

Whilst the events of June and July were playing themselves out on the French sector, the BEF had been regrouping after the exhausting spring offensives and incorporating reinforcements into their ranks. The Somme area has passed into the hands of General Rawlinson and his Fourth Army, and in front of his battalions he can see that the Germans no longer seem to have the stomach for the war. Their zeal for entrenching themselves in impregnable positions is lacking. Many of the best troops have been flung into action against the French to the south and those that are left have not the doggedness of units that Rawlinson or any other British commander has grown used to facing on the Western Front. Having failed at every turn to break the Allies, to end the war, German morale is in the gutter, not only at the front but at home where there is significant unrest in the face of prolonged shortages.

Rawlinson decides to test the water, and the Australians make a successful attack on a limited scale at Hamel on 4th July. He thinks that all of this points towards a bright future on his front. "With this experience before us, and in view of the open country behind the Boche lines," he tells the palace, "which was especially suitable to the employment of the cavalry and tanks, we came to the concussion that a much more ambitious scheme than that of Hamel might be undertaken in the area with good prospects of success."[182] The essence of this new approach is complete secrecy. Rawlinson has set into motion a method of attacking that combines everything that has been garnered thus far in the war; all that the British had learnt since the Battle of Neuve Chapelle. "It was a collegiate effort... fully integrating all the new weapons into one ferocious methodology of modern war."[183] Whilst Sir Henry Wilson is preaching caution in London, putting off the idea of a conclusion of the war to 1919, or even 1920, plans gather pace on the Western Front. More than 2,000 guns are covertly assembled and ammunition piled high. The RAF have combined with new

178   RA GV/PRIV/GVD/1918 (14/8).
179   (ed.) Sheffield & Bourne: *Douglas Haig: War Diaries and Letters 1914-1918*, pp.438.
180   RA/QM/PRIV/CC04/170.
181   *Morning Post* 15/8/18.
182   RA/PS/PS/GV/C/Q/2522/2/136.
183   Hart: *The Great War*, p.447.

artillery specialities; flash spotting and sound ranging, to locate almost all of the German guns in the area. More than 500 tanks are assembled and the infantry are armed with machine guns, mortars, grenades, and a wealth of technological advances all developed since 1915.

The Battle of Amiens begins at 4:20am on 8th August. The King spends the day with General Horne, chatting with troops, and he presents the first Military Medal awarded to an American who had rushed an enemy machine gun with two Australians and seized both the weapon and eight prisoners. His Majesty also spends a prolonged spell with the officers and men in charge of a super heavy gun named *Boche Buster*. To a large extent, they are a law unto themselves; rampaging about the countryside with their gun mounted on a train, often concealing their movements from superior officers. They are put through the mill by the King. "He asked so many questions which were very technical, revealing what a vast knowledge he had."

His Majesty asks; "What are you allowing for loss of muzzle velocity?"

Surprised at such a specialist question, the officer replies: "one and half feet per second, Sir."

The King thinks for a moment and then says, "Well I think you may be about correct, but don't be surprised if the day comes when you have to allow two and a half feet per second." His prediction proves uncanny in the following weeks. Then His Majesty asks what the predicted life of the gun is, and the men tell him that it is put at 250 rounds.

"Well," says the King, "you mark my words, they always underestimate the lives of these guns. She'll fire not only 350 rounds, before having to be retubed, but at the 300th round she'll be firing as accurately as she is now."

The officer is astonished by His Majesty's knowledge. "He didn't flummox me with a single question, fortunately, but he would have quite a lot of people I think… He walked all over the mounting with me asking all sorts of questions, and then he asked if he could see the gun loaded."

The King is standing on the gun mounting, and is reluctant to get down when told about safety precautions, for he is evidently excited by this demonstration. It takes six men on either side to carry the single shell. With all their might they ram it home.

"Gun ready, Sir."

"Fire the gun, please" he responds, for naval officers say please. Off went the gun, taking the rest of the royal party by such surprise that they all clutch their heads and turned away. "His Majesty stood as still as a statue and seeing all these cowed heads turned around and said in quite a loud voice: "I consider it makes no noise at all, no noise at all," and they all looked very sheepy after that."

But the King still wants more. "Then he said may I look at the map? So we climbed up into the command post wagon and he pored over the railway map of the front line and he was extremely interested."

There then follows possibly the only tactical order given by His Majesty to his troops in the Great War. For, "he turned round and said do you know gentlemen, I have just come from the launch of the Fourth Army attack at Amiens… I see from the railway line that the Germans will have to rush their reinforcements now at Ypres down to resist… and I see from the railway line… that they will have to go through Douai Station to get there as quickly as possible. Why not keep Douai station under harassing fire from now on?" "My heart sank within me," says the officer. "I thought oh dear, what's going to happen?" The gun does not fire at night, for the flash it gives off is too revealing and besides, there are not enough lights to illuminate their work. But whether it is intended to be an order or a helpful suggestion, he is told by his commander afterwards, "I'm afraid you will have to do that, that's an order." He will get them every torch he could find. Douai Station, 18 miles away apparently became a target for them night after night.[184]

---

184   IWM Sound: Stewart Cleeve, Catalogue #7310 Reels 8,15-16,1983.

That night the King receives an update. "[We] have made splendid progress, having advanced six miles in places, taken several thousand prisoners and over 100 guns, tanks and cavalry are also being used. Very good news and it has bucked us all up."[185] This time fog was on the side of the Allies, and it was a catastrophic day for the Kaiser's armies, referred to as a black day for the German Army.. "With its 'All Arms Battle' the British tactical rollercoaster had reached a peak to which the Germans had no counter."[186] These are developments that His Majesty is keenly aware of.

Never has the RAF done better than in this battle," the King is keen to tell Bertie, "their losses have been heavy but… they have done an awful lot of damage by low-flying, destroying bridges, columns of transport, trains, aerodromes and have killed many of the enemy by machine guns. Frequently they have destroyed lines of Hun machines on the ground which is most useful. The Germans have lost very heavily in this last fighting and our tanks have done magnificent work and everybody swears by them. It's really wonderful what they can do now.[187]

His Majesty spends the next two days, as the Battle of Amiens rages, at a musketry school near Etaples and looking extensively at tank manoeuvres; "a demonstration of tanks attacking with infantry using smoke and carriers bringing up stores and ammunition over trenches and shell holes, it was most interesting."[188] That night, the King watches German bombers pass overhead on their way to targets to the rear of the British lines. "The news from the front on the Somme is splendid," he writes to Queen Mary. "Our troops are continuing their advance and have now got 17,000 prisoners and 300 guns." What makes him even prouder is the fact that this battle has been a very British endeavour, "so I am delighted it has all worked out so well. Everyone is in high spirits and the Germans have certainly taken a nasty knock."[189] But now enemy resolve has hardened, and rather than flog a dead horse, the British command realise that it is folly to continue with their advance on the Somme. They had gained up to twelve miles in places and dealt a short, hard blow to the German armies from which it would do well to recover. Its purpose has been served. There is to be no degenerating offensive at huge cost to the BEF, because Haig agrees and on 11th August he orders Rawlinson to stop and regroup before the Allies' next move.

With the fighting at an end, His Majesty heads south the following day. "In the course of the day he went over last weeks' battlefields, and, while pausing at such utterly ruined towns and villages as Villers Bretonneux… was able to judge for himself what the devastation of modern warfare means."[190] The display is humbling. "Passing through Doullens I stopped at [the clearing station] which I had visited last Good Friday, they were bombed some time ago and half the hospital was burnt… since March 21st 46,000 wounded have passed through."[191] The operating theatre that he had so admired during his emergency dash to the front in the spring is a mass of charred ruins. "From the lips of the commanding officer the King heard the story of the outrage, and as he was leaving the royal visitor paid a splendid tribute to the sisters and doctors."[192]

185 RA GV/PRIV/GVD/1918 (8/8).
186 Hart: *The Great War,* p.450.
187 RA GV/PRIV/AA60/341.
188 RA GV/PRIV/GVD/1918 (10/8).
189 RA QM/PRIV/CC04/178.
190 *Daily Telegraph* 14/8/18.
191 RA GV/PRIV/GVD/1918 (12/8).
192 *Daily Telegraph* 26/8/18.

His Majesty travels on to meet with Rawlinson and the commander of the Australian contingent that have acquitted themselves so well; greeting men who have just come out of the line. He congratulates all on their success, and sets off exploring. He sees German guns, machine guns, horses and an ambulance that have been snatched in recent days; motors through Amiens,

> Which has considerably been knocked about by shells and bombs and there have been fires. The inhabitants are not going to be allowed to return yet, as the walls of many houses are still unsafe. We passed several 'cages' in collecting camps full of German prisoners captured in the last two days, several thousands of them. They seemed very hungry and were eating hard.[193]

Throughout the course of his visit the King motors some 800 miles. "I have had a pretty strenuous time, but I think my visit has done good and given pleasure,"[194] he has written to Queen Mary. An escort of destroyers, airships, seaplanes and other sundry vessels escort him home, entertaining His Majesty with a smoke screen demonstration. He alights from his train in London looking "bronzed and happy, though a little tired."[195]

Rawlinson sends a letter appraising the Battle of Amiens to the palace shortly after the King's return to the capital. He ventures to think that it is "one of the cheapest and most important victories that has been won by the British army during the present war." But he explains the reason for stopping.

> It was, however, felt that a general attack against the line held by the enemy along the old Somme battlefields could only be undertaken at considerable cost and a deep and rapid penetration was not to be expected. The Commander in Chief decided, therefore, not to make a general attack on this line and ordered the Fourth Army to push on by means of strong patrols without risking heavy losses... To sum up, the Battle of Amiens has shown that our Imperial and Dominion forces have lost none of the fighting qualities of the Anglo-Saxon race owing to the set-backs which they suffered earlier in the year... the ball has begun to roll, it is rolling the right way and we intend to keep it on the move.

But Rawlinson at least will not allow himself to be carried away.

> It is perhaps rash to make prophecies... I have great hopes that within the next month we may drive him back over the Hindenburg line. Had we another fifteen or twenty good fresh divisions available we could hunt him out of France before the campaign of 1918 is brought to an end by the approach of winter. But these resources are not available except in the American army and these Pershing jealously keeps under his own command.[196]

The Duke of Connaught writes to His Majesty shortly afterwards, again with no thoughts of victory, but confident that the Germans are in no fit state to make an offensive, at least. Things are better than anyone dare hope, and open warfare has returned to the Western Front.

---

193   RA GV/PRIV/GVD/1918 (2/8).
194   RA QM/PRIV/CC04/183.
195   *Daily Telegraph* 14/8/18.
196   RA PS/PS/GV/C/Q/2522/2/140.

"Family Business"

For now, there is nothing to do but carry on investing everything in the war effort, and the contribution of the members of the fledgling House of Windsor and its near relatives has become so all-encompassing that attempting to lead the nation through Great War has become the family business.

All of Queen Victoria's surviving children have taken their share of responsibility since 1914. The King has given his Aunt Helena the honour of publicly looking over her "beautiful hospital train for which she collected £25,000 and is now sending to France for our wounded. There are eight coaches and they take 175 lying down cases, it is most up to date in all its fittings and arrangements."[197] At Windsor she is also at the centre of an array of hospitals, children's nurseries, and enterprises that assist the disabled and brighten the lives of their families. Her daughters, the Princesses Helena Victoria and Marie Louise have followed her example, and the former had done valuable work in connection with the YMCA, even visiting France. Louise, Duchess of Argyll has concentrated on the west of Scotland and Kensington. Her business ability is useful on many committees, as is her public speaking ability, and although Princess Beatrice is hampered by gout, in addition to her little hospital she devotes hours to charity work every week.

But of all his aunts and uncles, the King grows more and more indebted as the war goes on to Arthur, Duke of Connaught.

But of all his aunts and uncles, the King grows more and more indebted as the war goes on to Prince Arthur, Duke of Connaught. He returned home from his post in Ottawa at the end of 1916; spritely and active for all of his 66 years and with no intention of slowing down after half a century in the service of his country. He was a regular fixture at the Palace on his return to London, but his endeavours took on a new impetus after the death of his wife at the beginning of 1917, the day after their 37th wedding anniversary. Bereft, he threw himself into his work as a distraction from his grief.

He was interested in the revival of the post of Inspector-General of Overseas Forces, particularly in order to watch over Imperial troops in training, but this was not to be. The role had been whittled down to one of little importance by the time it was plausible as a job, and Prince Arthur wanted to do something meaningful. A widower for not even a fortnight, he was without a job but took very seriously the notion that a Field Marshal never retires. He travelled extensively, and was back on the continent shortly before his nephew's own visit in July 1917. In October, he returned to look at support work, but by 1918 he had begun to deputise for the King in key areas. A visit to the Middle East was never a possibility for His Majesty, and so in 1918 his uncle sets out on a royal visit to eastern theatres of war, despite being extremely ill. The King's own doctor, still in France, manages to convince Prince Arthur to pause, albeit briefly in Monte Carlo but then he passes through Cairo and on to Khartoum. Then it is Allenby's HQ at Beit-Mabala on the Palestine front; meeting with troops at Gaza, Jerusalem. He thinks that England does not realise what these men are having to endure; the conditions, the great difficulties in bringing up supplies. "Palestine, he writes to His Majesty "was unlike an other country in the world. The various factions there were liable to make political issues from any event and he took care to restrict his activities to British and military functions, which he hoped could be done without controversy."[198]

---

197   RA GV/PRIV/GVD/1915 (7/4).
198   Frankland: Witness of a Century, pp.359-360.

The Prince's trip to Athens immediately afterwards is even more sensitive in the wake of Tino's abdication. The King's troublesome cousin has left his son, Alexander on the throne, and he has declared his intention to marry a commoner. Prince Arthur is nearly torpedoed on the way to Greece, and when he gets there the Greeks assume that he will arrange his own daughter, Princess Patricia's marriage to the Alexander, or worse, so far as the British Royal Family is concerned, promise the hand of Princess Mary. Prince Arthur knows that his nephew will not have his only daughter sent to such a volatile country, and his own is too old for the King. The Prince winds his way through this treacerous situation with grace and charm. Alexander did not marry his love until after the war, and then there was no revolution, and Greece will remain on the side of the Allies until the end of the war. The British minister in Athens was thrilled with his intervention, and tells His Majesty of "his readiness to 'do anything, however tiresome, which Lord Granville ventured to suggest.' But though disaster has been averted, the King's uncle departs for him with reservations. "Though he though the King was a nice boy, he found that he was thoroughly ignorant of anything connected with his role as a constitutional sovereign and he was afraid that he hated being King, hated the government… and missed the liberty he had had when his father was ing and his elder brother heir to the throne… Prince Arthur felt that he was still devotd to his father and he believed that he ws probaby really pro-German himself. If he was not allowed to marry Mademoiselle Manos, he would most probably abdicate."[199]

But of all his aunts and uncles, the King grows more and more indebted as the war goes on to Prince Arthur, Duke of Connaught. He returned home from his post in Ottawa at the end of 1916; spritely and active for all of his 66 years and with no intention of slowing down after half a century in the service of his country. He was a regular fixture at the Palace on his return to London, but his endeavours took on a new impetus after the death of his wife at the beginning of 1917, the day after their 37th wedding anniversary. Bereft, he threw himself into his work as a distraction from his grief.

He was interested in the revival of the post of Inspector-General of Overseas Forces, particularly in order to watch over Imperial troops in training, but this was not to be. The role had been whittled down to one of little importance by the time it was plausible as a job, and Prince Arthur wanted to do something meaningful. A widower for not even a fortnight, he was without a job but took very seriously the notion that a Field Marshal never retires. He travelled extensively, and was back on the continent shortly before his nephew's own visit in July 1917. In October, he returned to look at support work, but by 1918 he had begun to deputise for the King in key areas. A visit to the Middle East was never a possibility for His Majesty, and so in 1918 his uncle sets out on a royal visit to eastern theatres of war, despite being extremely ill. The King's own doctor, still in France, manages to convince Prince Arthur to pause, albeit briefly in Monte Carlo but then he passes through Cairo and on to Khartoum. Then it is Allenby's HQ at Beit-Mabala on the Palestine front; meeting with troops at Gaza, Jerusalem. He thinks that England does not realise what these men are having to endure; the conditions, the great difficulties in bringing up supplies. "Palestine, he writes to His Majesty "was unlike an other country in the world. The various factions there were liable to make political issues from any event and he took care to restrict his activities to British and military functions, which he hoped could be done without controversy."[200]

The Prince's trip to Athens immediately afterwards is even more sensitive in the wake of Tino's abdication. The King's troublesome cousin has left his son, Alexander on the throne, and he has

---

199   Frankland: Witness of a Century, p.361.
200   Frankland: Witness of a Century, pp.359-360.

declared his intention to marry a commoner. Prince Arthur is nearly torpedoed on the way to Greece, and when he gets there the Greeks assume that he will arrange his own daughter, Princess Patricia's marriage to the Alexander, or worse, so far as the British Royal Family is concerned, promise the hand of Princess Mary. Prince Arthur knows that his nephew will not have his only daughter sent to such a volatile country, and his own is too old for the King. The Prince winds his way through this treacerous situation with grace and charm. Alexander did not marry his love until after the war, and then there was no revolution, and Greece will remain on the side of the Allies until the end of the war. The British minister in Athens was thrilled with his intervention, and tells His Majesty of "his readiness to 'do anything, however tiresome, which Lord Granville ventured to suggest.' But though disaster has been averted, the King's uncle departs for him with reservations. "Though he though the King was a nice boy, he found that he was thoroughly ignorant of anything connected with his role as a constitutional sovereign and he was afraid that he hated being King, hated the government… and missed the liberty he had had when his father was ing and his elder brother heir to the throne… Prince Arthur felt that he was still devotd to his father and he believed that he ws probaby really pro-German himself. If he was not allowed to marry Mademoiselle Manos, he would most probably abdicate."[201]

Scattered across Europe as they are, some members of the Royal Family manage to render useful service for others. The Duke of Connaught's daughter Margaret, known as Daisy to the family, is the Crown Princess of Sweden. "I would like to put on record the wonderful work she did during the war," wrote Princess Marie Louise.

> Daisy was unique; she possessed the most beautiful character… [She] had her own office in the palace, where, assisted by some of her friends, she founded and organised the important work of tracing the British wounded, missing and prisoners of war. The work she did was in no way connected with any official organisation. She was what I might describe as our 'liaison' officer. Through her we were able to have news of my brother Albert, as she could communicate with him, which, of course, we were unable to do.[202]

Daisy was also the conduit through which Queen Mary was able to communicate with her beloved Aunt Augusta, who had been like a mother to her, in Germany up until her death in 1916 at the age of 94.

Queen Alexandra bit off more than she could chew when it came to war service. Constantly helped by the King's unmarried sister Toria, she proved as charming and as sympathetic as her son on her many visits. At the bedside of one soldier with a wounded knee, she swung her leg up on his bed and compared his plight with her own joint pain, but the war is a particular strain on someone of her generation. She finds it difficult to comprehend the scale or the horror of modern, industrial warfare and as the war progresses she fails to maintain the pace of work that she had set for herself.

For a short period at the end of August 1918, all of the King and Queen's children are together for the first time in many months. It is a quiet week at Windsor Castle, and there is barely any contact with the outside world. Assembling the entirety of His Majesty's family in one place has become like herding cats, as for the King's children, the Great War is significant because it coincides with the coming of age of his eldest children and because it is in the midst of the conflict that they take

201   Frankland: *Witness of a Century*, p.361.
202   Marie Louise, Princess: *My Memories of Six Reigns*, pp.179-181.

their first steps into the working life of a member of the Royal Family. By 1918, Prince John is the only one of His Majesty's children not in uniform. Prince George has begun his journey into the Royal Navy, making several official visits in the company of his parents. Prince Henry finished his first term at Sandhurst in the summer. With his mother and sister, he had visited a projectile factory just after his 18th birthday; before spending Easter Monday with workers too, those at Vickers who have given up their Bank Holiday. "He took on no airs and assumed no privileges, he remained, in fact, entirely modest."[203]

But Princess Mary has been perhaps the most surprising revelation so far; taking advantage of all of the leaps and bounds made by the nation's young women as a result of the war. She had not long turned 17 when the war commenced and was immensely shy. Her role was limited to being her mother's right hand in Queen Mary's war work. She did, however, suggest the idea of a Christmas present for all soldiers and sailors on active service in 1914 and make an appeal to help fund it. For the first half of the war, as was appropriate, Mary's appearances were in the company of one or both of her parents. She soon began training as a nurse, and as a probationer at Great Ormond Street asked that she receive no special consideration at all.

On what should have been a highlight of the social calendar in 1918, thanks to the war there is a birthday lunch in the State Ballroom to mark the occasion of her coming of age, and nothing more by way of festivities. The Princess works for two mornings a week at Great Ormond Street. The Queen has seen her in action and proudly tells the King that she is an exemplary nurse, "which I am delighted to hear," he replies, "but she is a curious girl, always so reticent and never tells one anything. I expect she has much more in her than one thinks."[204] For another three mornings, Mary does clerical work at the headquarters of the Voluntary Aid Detachment at Devonshire House. She has her own special little unit, identifiable by special shoulder straps on their uniforms and recruited from amongst the daughters of palace officials. It is a proud little group, efficient in their shorthand and typing, which deals specifically with appointments for the various members.

Princess Mary's afternoons are filled with visits and tours. One takes her to South Lodge for an entertainment in aid of waif and stray societies, on another occasion she is in Oxford to confer badges and stripes on members of the Women's Land Army and various village workers. The Princess conducts prize-giving at the London Orphan School and also opens a new wing at a Windsor hospital named after her grandfather, one that will specifically offer massage treatment for wounded and discharged soldiers. The Princess even starts a craze for rabbits in the summer of 1918. Bunnies are much en vogue after she starts her own initiative in conjunction with the Food Production Department at the Royal Mews. Some visits are still in the company of her parents and the King does all he can to try and bring his daughter out of her shell. During a visit to a Walthamstow motor lorry works, he is conversing with a forewoman when he sees that Mary has become a little detached from the group. He excuses himself briefly and goes to fetch her. Leading the Princess gently by the arm he introduces her with complete informality as "my daughter"[205] and brings her into the conversation. She may be shy, but Princess Mary has her father's memory for faces, and she is bright, very much her mother's daughter. One American delegation declares that: "We all fell in love with Princess Mary, so shy and yet so well informed, and so keen a thinker, with such a pride in the women of her country. It all felt like a meeting of friends."[206]

As for Bertie, by 1918 illness has eventually driven him to shore. He had undertaken his first public engagement, looking over the rifle range under the houses of Parliament in March 1916. The

---

203   Frankland: *Prince Henry, Duke of Gloucester*, p.37.
204   RA QM/PRIV/CC04/183.
205   *The Times* 5/4/18.
206   *Fort Scott Daily Tribune* 19/6/18.

Prince celebrated his 21st birthday in December 1916, and his father invested him with the Order of the Garter. "I cannot thank you enough… I feel very proud to have it, and will always try to live up to it."[207] At this point, though, the palace were doubting his ability to continue a life at sea. Even Bertie himself believed he was not fit for it, but he did not want to disappoint his father. By August 1917, the Prince was in hospital once again, utterly miserable. His Majesty counselled patience, and when Bertie suggested that he move to the Royal Naval Air Service instead, he was surprised to find that the King was unopposed: "Papa jumped at the idea."[208] It has been unfairly stated that the King was "strongly prejudiced"[209] against the air services, but in fact his concerns simply amounted to not wanting to leave the ground himself.

In the meantime, Bertie made his own decision to undergo surgery. "I don't think I can get any better without an operation, and I should like to get it over and done with."[210] Finally, after three years of suffering, he was properly diagnosed. The King spent an anxious day fretting over his son whilst surgery took place. "Rigby operated on Bertie this morning," he recorded. "He found a large duodenal ulcer… and had to short circuit. He bore the operation very well, it took 50 minutes, Saw all the doctors afterwards and they were quite satisfied."[211] His Majesty abandoned a trip to Sandringham and kept vigil at Bertie's bedside for more than two weeks as his temperature flared, subsided and then finally his stitches came out.

By February 1918, Bertie is serving at Cranwell, living in a tiny cubicle and supervising 500 former navy boys. It is a big adjustment from shipboard life, and one that he takes extremely seriously. His father stops in to visit in mid-April, stepping off the train at a little country station to find an excited Prince Albert. "How are you old man?"[212] He asks. Bertie is still in naval uniform, for as yet they haven't merged the identities of the RFC and the RNAS under one uniform, and he gives His Majesty a comprehensive tour. He carries out other engagements of his own now too, including attending a performance at a Lincoln theatre in aid of the National Union of Journalists' War Distress Fund, purchasing a picture at an auction afterwards. In July he makes a proper introduction to public life, giving a "well-delivered"[213] little speech in front of the Lord Mayor at Mansion House, accompanied by his great uncle, the Duke of Connaught, before both joined the rest of the family at Stamford Bridge for the Independence Day baseball game.

Always, though, Bertie is overshadowed by David. The Prince of Wales's relationship with his parents is at a high at the beginning of 1917. He was eating properly, and the King thought him "looking wonderfully well"[214] in the spring. But this domestic pleasantness was at odds with David's misery about his role in the army, in life and his future. The Prince feels like a spare wheel at Cavan's headquarters and is no nearer the front line. He sulks in his room after another rebuff. "I could not face… any company. I wanted to be alone in my misery!! I feel quite ready to commit suicide and would if I didn't think it unfair on Papa."[215]

At the end of 1917, Lord Cavan made the move from the Western Front to the Italian after Victor Emmanuel's troops were routed at Caporetto, and David sailed to join him shortly afterwards. "I… think the experience will be good for him," writes General Rawlinson to Wigram, but it is rather

207   Bradford: *George VI*, p.91.
208   Ibid., p.93.
209   Ibid., p.95.
210   Ibid., p.94.
211   RA GV/PRIV/GVD/1917 29/11.
212   *The Times* 12/4/18.
213   *The World* 9/7/18.
214   RA GV/PRIV/GVD/1918 (11/5).
215   Ziegler: *King Edward VIII: The Official Biography*, p.75.

a long way off and one does not quite know what may happen there."[216] The King thinks that the reward, the boost to morale, the presence of royalty with troops on another front and the experience for his son, outweighs the risk. David is not at all impressed. "It is too fearfully sad and depressing for words."[217] He arrives at Mantua unclear about what they are actually in Italy to do. He is not the only one. "The whole show is the vaguest thing on record and we know nothing of the future… as it all depends on where the Italians stop the Huns." But it is at least more exciting than France, for the Italians are in full retreat through Treviso and Padua. "This is real campaigning not the stale old warfare in Flanders, and it's all a great experience for me."[218]

By the turn of the year, Stamfordham is anxious to have the Prince of Wales back from Italy. "Time is slipping away and these years are valuable and important ones in His Royal Highness's life. He should be mixing with leading men other than soldiers, doing some useful reading and *gradually* getting accustomed to speaking in public."[219] His Majesty agrees, and greets his son in early February when he returns to London, "looking fit and very well."[220] In the spring, the Prince of Wales takes his seat in the House of Lords, and the following day he embarks on his own tour of Wales; "a quite arduous programme; and to visit those parts of his Cornish Duchy." The King is hugely proud of his heir, for David, who is not anti-monarchy, just anti-being-a-monarch-himself, is becoming popular. He wears a convincing mask, and does not give off an air of one stifled and frustrated by the role he is expected to play to those who come into contact with him. "Wherever he went a warm welcome awaited him," claims one publication. "Never before has an heir to our throne gained so rich an experience in his early youth as he. In a word, he's a prince charming and a brave soldier to boot."[221] A missive written by a Canadian officer who witnessed him with Imperial troops also claimed that David: "had been the best force in real Empire building that it was possible for Great Britain to have, because he absolutely won the hearts of the many he came into contact with. As they put it, he was every inch the gentleman and sportsman, so simple, so charming and so genuine"[222]

The plan for the Prince in the latter part of 1918 is to have him spend three months taking a staff course at Cambridge, but after the chain of events triggered by the Battle of Amiens begins to gain momentum, Haig writes to Stamfordham. "Possibly the King might think it desirable that the Prince of Wales should be in the theatre of war at the present time." He sent Major Thompson over with the letter in person, so that if His Majesty is inclined to agree, he "will be able to answer any questions and take any orders." The Commander in Chief even has a schedule in mind, suggesting that David spend time with the Australian and Canadian Corps in turn, and then join whichever army headquarters happens to be engaged in the most interesting operations at the time. "I should be delighted of course if he would look upon my house as his base during the period, and Major Thompson will be available to accompany the Prince if so desired."[223] The King thinks it a very good idea indeed, but he instructs Stamfordham to write to David at the front, because he does not want him to order him to do it. In fact the Prince had been looking forward to a slack period at home, but when the final decision is left to him, he accepts that this is a clever suggestion, incorporating contact with Imperial troops as it does and says that he wants to go. "The King has told the Prince

216   RA PS/PS/GV/C/Q/2522/2/110.
217   (ed.) Godfrey: *Letters from a Prince*, p.9.
218   Ziegler: *King Edward VIII: The Official Biography*, pp.80-82.
219   Ziegler: *King Edward VIII: The Official Biography*, pp.80-82.
220   *The Gentlewoman* 2/3/18.
221   Ibid.
222   Ibid.
223   RA PS/PSO/GV/C/Q/1382/7.

that he ought to be at least one month with each of these corps,"[224] writes Stamfordham to Haig, but once again this is left up to his son.

"Victory is Within Our Reach"

The British Army may have delivered a stunning blow to the enemy at the beginning of August, but there is much costly, difficult fighting still to be done. The Germans are down, but most certainly not out. Yet. For the Battle of Amiens marks the start of a three month campaign to systematically destroy any resistance that the Kaiser's men have left. "The fighting ranged from full-on assaults on layered defensive positions to bloody ambushes and the resulting frantic skirmishes. There are few more stressful military operations than an advance to contact through unknown country against a concealed enemy. The war was in its last stages but the casualty lists were mushrooming fast. The war had never seemed more painful."[225] The German Army is not going to be allowed to rest, and if everything goes to plan, they will not know where the ensuing blows are to come from. On 20th August the French attack south of the Somme, before on the next morning, Byng's Third Army launch the Battle of Albert, hitting the enemy in between the Ancre and Scarpe Rivers south of Arras. The Allies spend the rest of the month grinding their way forwards as the enemy frantically throws in their reserves. On the 26th, the First Army under General Horne attacks in the Arras sector. The Germans are falling back along the line, and the Australians take the opportunity to strike again on the Somme.

On His Majesty's return from the front, the Court adjourns to Windsor. "The news from France continues good," writes the King. "We and the French gain ground every day." On 30th he is at St. Leonards on Sea to see Bertie and the local contingent of RAF Cadets under his command. As ever, for a man who doesn't entirely trust aeroplanes, the King is proud of the new flying service. His pride is now augmented thanks to the Prince having become part of the new RAF, and he sends any anecdote he can muster about the air war to Bertie with enthusiasm. Of course he is particularly enamoured by anything that is connected to his son. "Bertie commands the Fifth Squadron. I also saw them at physical drill, boxing etc. and some of the houses in town where they live. They are extraordinarily smart."[226]

At the beginning of September it is the turn of the Canadians to drive another nail into the German military coffin; forcing them back onto the Canal du Nord and the intimidating Hindenburg Line. As ever, His Majesty is kept fully appraised. "Got the good news that we had taken Queant (a most important point in the Hindenburg Line) and the Germans are retreating on that part of the line and that we had captured 10,000 prisoners."[227] Yet still, nobody is getting carried away. Keeping the Allied war machine in harmony is a temperamental business.

Adversity has forced the allies into each other arms," Rawlinson explains in a letter to the palace. "What we have now to fear is that prosperity and success may breed dissension. We have only to stick together and the war is won, but Lloyd George is a cantankerous person and always personal prospects are involved. Pray goodness Henry Wilson will keep him within bounds. I have warned him several times."[228]

224   RA PS/PSO/GV/C/Q/1382/17.
225   Hart: *The Great War,* p.452.
226   Ibid., 30/8.
227   Ibid., 3/9.
228   RA PS/PS/GV/C/Q/2522/2/142.

Windsor remains "hot and damp like Turkish bath."[229] The King walks alone by the river with his little dog, Jack; watches the Coldstream Guards training in the park. For all of the news that is coming in of success at the front, there are worries and anxieties at home. On 4th September he is compelled to hold a council in order to prevent a strike in Yorkshire, and later in the month civil unrest effects the operation of railways in Wales. On 11th September, Haig, who is home for a brief 48 hours, meets His Majesty at Buckingham Palace for lunch. He finds the King in good spirits, as well as full of hatred for Germany; "but I saw that he had not yet realised the magnitude of our recent victory. He is determined to continue the war till the Germans are completely broken."[230]

In mid-September, intelligence arrives at the palace from The Hague. A Dutch courier had just returned from Berlin, where he was "astounded at change in conditions in Germany since his last visit three weeks ago. "[The] whole country is in a ferment and process of decomposition has set in."[231] There are outlandish rumours: that the Kaiser has told his entourage that he can no longer bear his responsibilities and is prone to fits of weeping, that his wife has suffered a collapse, that women have been gunned down during food riots, that German officers are being shot by their own men.

The Allies have dreamt up even more misery for the enemy on the Western Front. Attacks are scheduled up and down the line to brilliantly co-ordinate with each other and cause catastrophic damage to German positions. On the first day, the 26th September, the French and Americans start an attack on the Meuse-Argonne sector. The scale is incredible, the front nearly 50 miles long. Though they paid heavily themselves, the Allies wipe up to 120,000 men from the strength of the enemy's dilapidated armies as he is forced back. The next day, Britain's First and Third Armies attack the Hindenburg Line in the direction of Cambrai, across the dry Canal du Nord. It was part of a formidable defensive system. With nothing to do but wait for events to play themselves out, His Majesty travels to Sandringham the following morning, whilst Plumer's Second Army launches yet another attack in Flanders in conjunction with Belgian and French troops. In a single day, combining everything that they have learned in four years of war, they surge across the Ypres battlefields and come up on the Passchendaele Ridge. On 29th, it is the turn of the Fourth Army under Rawlinson to attack the Hindenburg line on the Somme, along with American troops temporarily put under British command. The German line is breached, and the Allies are on their way to the Rhine. By constantly switching and attacking on a number of fronts they have overwhelmed the fragile German line. The enemy cannot rest, cannot focus on where the danger is at its most threatening. They cannot win the war, but they have not yet quite lost it either.

But events on other fronts are conspiring against them. After seizing Jerusalem in the latter part of 1917, Allenby routs the Turks in the Battle of the Megiddo in September 1918. On 23rd, His Majesty writes that his General has won "a great victory over the Turks, driving them back. His cavalry got into Nazareth and cut of their retreat north, by yesterday morning he had captured 120 guns and 18,000 prisoners, he will probably capture all their transport and the Turkish army in Palestine will be wiped out, I hope."[232] Allenby's collection of British, Indian, and Allied troops sets out for Damascus, chasing the retreating Turks and linking up with Arab forces. They seize the city on 1st October. The Imperial connotations of his victory are significant; "I am confident that this success, which has effect the liberating of Palestine from Turkish Rule," the King publishes in the press in suitably grand language, "will rank as a great exploit in the history of the British Empire, and will stand for all time as a memorable testimony to British leadership and to the fighting

229   RA GV/PRIV/GVD/1918 (6/9).
230   Sheffield & Bourne: *Douglas Haig: War Diaries and Letters 1914-1918*, p.459.
231   RA PS/PSO/GV/C/Q/1552/8.
232   RA GV/PRIV/GVD/1918 (23/9).

qualities of British and Indian troops."[233] Bulgaria formally surrenders on 30th September. "This is splendid news," writes the King, "and will help the Allies greatly to defeat the Germans."[234] His Majesty has begun to believe that the end is in sight. The writing is on the wall for Germany. The relentless march of the Allies on the Western Front is a depressing view, as is the news of defeats for their Allies. At home the economy is in tatters and society is beginning to come apart at the seams. "The combination of defeat at the front, political division at home, and no hope for the future was a potent brew that unsettled the troops in the line."[235]

For France and for Belgium, the forward momentum is hugely symbolic, for with every advance, towns and villages that have lived under German occupation for more than four years are being liberated. Saint-Quentin is reclaimed on 1st October, followed by the liberation of Armentieres and Cambrai. Still at Sandringham, the King works through his boxes, receives Victoria Cross winners and keeps up to date with the Allied advance; making time for shooting whenever he can. The German and Austro-Hungarian Governments have approached President Wilson on the subject of an Armistice, but His Majesty is unconvinced. "At the same time the Germans continue to burn the houses in towns and villages as they retreat. Curious ideas of peace."[236] He wants the enemy destroyed. Allied gains continue on 10th October, including the liberation of Le Cateau. "The Boche is obviously getting tired," Rawlinson writes to the palace. "Some of his divisions are fighting very badly, but he still has a few good ones in hand and these we shall have to smash before we can break through. Things on the whole are going very well and I feel very proud of my army - they have fought magnificently."[237]

For King Albert of the Belgians, who has refused to leave his country and personally commanded his troops in battle, the liberation of his country is especially poignant. On 14th October Roulers is retaken. His Majesty travels down to London. "Saw Henry Wilson who gave me the latest news from the front which is good and the Germans are being driven back. The Prime Minister came to luncheon alone with me and we had a good talk about everything and he thinks Germany will be ready for peace very soon."[238] Convinced now that victory is not far away, the King decides that he should be in London. Menin falls back into Belgian hands, and within two days the Germans are also expelled from Lille, Douai and Ostend[e]. By 20th October, the whole of the Belgian coast, the towns of Zeebrugge and Bruges are free once again too. The Mayor of Lille despatches a telegram to His Majesty: "At the moment when the British troops made their solemn entry into the town of Lille, saluted by the enthusiastic acclamations of its people at last liberated, I desire to associate the name of Your Majesty with the glory of your valiant soldiers, and with the gratitude of my fellow citizens."[239] The King is touched. "Please convey my thanks to the Mayor of Lille for the sentiments of heartfelt gratitude to which his message has given expression," he asks of Haig, "and assure him of the gratification it is to me and my people to know that the valiant citizens of Lille have been delivered from the hands of the enemy, and also that the British troops played so prominent a part in the historic event."[240]

His Majesty addresses inter-parliamentary delegates representing the Allies in French. The last time he had seen them was in the midst of the Battle of Verdun in 1916. "Now the armies of France, and Italy of Belgium and the United States, side by side with ours are driving the enemy

233   RA GV/PRIV/GVD/1918 (30/10).
234   Hart: *The Great War,* p.460.
235   .
236   RA GV/PRIV/GVD/1918 (8/10).
237   RA PS/PS/GV/C/Q/2522/2/146.
238   RA GV/PRIV/GVD/1918 (14/10).
239   *Daily Telegraph* 1/11/18.
240   *Daily Telegraph* 4/11/18.

before us, his forces shattered, his people clamorous for peace, victory is within our reach and we are all agreed that it must be a complete and decisive victory."[241] The speech is well received by the press in terms of this last sentiment. "It may safely be said that on this issue the whole nation is nearer to unanimity than it has ever been before on any single issue in all our long history. And the reason is, as the King pointed out, that in other wars… both sides have in the main fought chivalrously… Consequently when the fight was over we could shake hands with mutual respect." His Majesty is not alone when he fails to see such evidence in 1918. "The distinguishing features of the present war is the deliberate disregard by the Germans of every code of law, every feeling of human kindliness, which might stand in the way of their ambitions. A people who have thus behaved must be punished if the world is to be freed from the danger of a repetition of the atrocities which they have committed and applauded. That is why we cannot cease fighting until our victory is complete."[242]

General Allenby has not stopped at Damascus. Since the end of September his force has marched north on Aleppo, and on 26th October he seizes it from the Turks. It is the end for the Ottoman Empire, and not just in terms of the war. Four days later they sign an armistice at Mudros and bow out of the Great War. Within hours they are followed by Austria-Hungary. The Germans had demanded an offensive of them in 1918 and it had commenced in June. In opposition, supported by both French troops and the British contingent, the Italians managed to hold their line. Austrian morale plummets along with the realisation that the German victory they have been holding out for is not going to happen. The death blow comes when the Allies launch their own attack on 24th October. The Austro-Hungarians do not have the stomach for the Battle of Vittorio Veneto. The line collapses. "The Italians have taken 80,000 prisoners and 1,600 guns,"[243] writes the King. "The Austrians are now asking for an armistice and their Empire appears to be going to pieces." He is not wrong. The Hapsburg Empire, like the Ottoman, is about to be consigned to history.

"We Live in a Kind of Merry-Go-Round"

Germany stands alone and the Allies march on. But this was no cheap advance to victory. The methods employed to get them to this point and to keep bludgeoning the German Army are unforgiving, brutal. Of 1.2 million men serving in the BEF between August and November in 1918, in the region of 360,000 become casualties in a matter of weeks. If it went on for too long, there would be no army left, so it is as well that the end is in sight. General Ludendorff is suffering a breakdown, and Germany is now resolved to an exit strategy, to pull back to their own territory and rely on the population to rise like one impregnable force and defend their homeland.

The final Allied offensives commence on 4th November. The wet conditions are much as should be expected for this time of year. In addition to the bloody advance, the Germans are laying traps and mines as they retreat and destroying whatever they must to hamper the progress of the Allies and cause more casualties. Preparations are already being made with regard to declarations and messages that he King will have to issue in the event of an armistice. The Allied Supreme War Council offers Germany peace and four days later Prince Max von Baden, the new Chancellor, despatches personnel to discuss the terms of an armistice with the Allies. Civil war looks imminent. The King had limited power, and the Tsar had had so much that he didn't know what to do with it. As for Wilhelm, he has been demonstrating for some time now that he no longer wants the

241   *The Times* 21/10/18.
242   *Daily Graphic* 22/10/18.
243   RA GV/PRIV/GVD/1918 (24/10).

power he has; that he is woefully out of his depth. His response has been to gradually withdraw from his responsibilities. Ultimate power over the army still resides in his hands, but Wilhelm has been willing to let others assume the burden of command, has even become openly deferential to his generals.

When it looked like Germany might win the war in the spring, Wilhelm was suddenly enthused. "He celebrated the first successes of the new German campaign on the Western Front with the words: "The battle is won, the English have been utterly defeated." Three days later, champagne was ordered at headquarters and he declared that 'if an English delegation comes to sue for peace it must kneel before the German standard, for it is a question here of the victory of monarchy over democracy." His triumphant mood does not last. In July, the Kaiser refers to himself as a defeated warlord and claims to have had a nightmare; "visions of all my English and Russian relatives and all the ministers and generals of my own reign marching past and mocking me."[244] With the onset of the Battle of Amiens on 8th August, Wilhelm gave up all hope of victory.

When the German Government begins sounding out the Allies with regard to a possible armistice in the autumn of 1918, it becomes apparent that they regard "the Kaiser's very presence as the chief obstacle in the way of immediate negotiations." Thus von Baden suggests he abdicate. If he nominated one of his grandchildren as his successor, as a constitutional monarch, his dynasty may survive."[245] It is even suggested to the Kaiser at his army headquarters, that he go forth and die at the head of his armies. In the meantime, the King meets with Haig's Chief of Staff. "This morning the German delegates came in under the white flag and were received by Foch and Rosy Wemyss and the terms of the Armistice read to them, they were given 72 hours to refuse or accept them." His Majesty is confident that they will accept. "Apparently, revolutions are breaking out in many places in Germany, including Munich where they have declared a republic. The navy has mutinied at Kiel and other ports."[246] Wilhelm has been told in no uncertain terms that he will end up like the Tsar if he does not go into exile. On 9th, Germany is declared a republic by a majority and the Hohenzollern dynasty is toppled. The Kaiser characteristically insisted later on that he was still contemplating what to do when von Baden announced his abdication for him, that that he "went through a fearful struggle [then] consciously sacrificed"[247] himself for the fatherland. The King and Queen were careful never to crow over Wilhelm publicly, but His Majesty held so much anger in his heart for his cousin, that he poured forth his feelings in his diary as he learned the news. "How the mighty have fallen. He has been Emperor just over thirty years. He did great things for his country; but his ambition was so great that he wished to dominate the world and created his military machine for that object. No one man can dominate the world, it has been tried before and now he has utterly ruined his country and himself, and I look upon him as the greatest criminal known for having plunged the world into this ghastly war, which has lasted over four years and three months with all its misery."[248]

"Big and Little Willie have bolted into Holland," writes Wigram on 10th November. "I doubt whether we shall find anyone to treat with and to carry out the terms of the Armistice. Supposing the Socialists refuse to give up the ships, locomotives, wagons we demand? I suppose we shall have to take them by force, but this may mean some months more."[249] That day Arthur Balfour visits the palace to sit down with the King and talk him through what is happening with regard to peace

244   RA PS/PSO/GV/C/O/1637/1.
245   Ibid.
246   RA /GV/PRIV/GVD/1918 (8/11).
247   Hohenzollern, Wilhelm of: *The Kaiser's Memoirs,* p.290.
248   RA GV/PRIV/GVD/1918 (9/11).
249   PP: CW 10/11/18.

negotiations and with many different logistical issues that will come into play the moment that an armistice is signed. Wigram has been in conclave with the Queen, "who understands thoroughly the problems we have to face." Her Majesty is "full of ideas, and we discussed Their Majesties going down to see the first batches of returned Prisoners of War."[250] Clive Wigram is completely occupied by the myriad complications and logistical issues that will be thrown up as soon as rifles are downed and the world tries to return to peace. "Events pass very quickly and we live in a kind of merry-go-round," he tells his wife. "I am trying to get my master to have some captured guns and aeroplanes inside the railings here. [Stamfordham] was rather startled at the idea, but I pointed out that Clemenceau and the French ministers had been enquiring last week whether the King and the Royal Family over here were really trying to shelter the Kaiser and to let him down light. These rumours are probably made in Germany, but there they are. These trophies in front of Buckingham Palace might help to balance the minds of the people."[251]

The resettlement of labour in the midst of a Bolshevik storm sweeping the continent is a terrifying prospect, as is the imminent shift in industry away from the wholesale business of waging war to peacetime manufacture.

> Employers cannot go on giving these high wages," says Wigram. "When the price of raw material comes down the price of articles produced will drop and the high profits of the employer will fall too. I understand that the price of articles will not drop quick enough and that there will be a period when wages are reduced but prices for the consumer remain high and not in proportion to drop of wages. This is the rub.[252]

The King jumps at his suggestion that he should sit down with the Minster of Labour about resettlement.

> They are none too happy about the civilian side of resettlement. We have been rather caught with our breeches down. The War Cabinet have not had time really to thrash out these questions and to sanction the necessary legislation... We all came to the conclusion that everything must be done to keep the nation engaged during demobilisation - start racing, let loose some more beer - bring back jockeys, clowns, football players as pivotal men.[253]

On the night of 10th November Their Majesties sit up late talking with Wigram. He arrives after 11 o'clock to announce that a wireless message had been intercepted indicating that German GHQ have been authorised to sign the armistice.

> Certainly yesterday evening it looked as if there might be no-one in authority to sign. Rumours reached us that a very advanced socialist had seized the reins of Government. Big and Little Willie with Hindenburg and several officers of the great imperial general staff had been sitting in the train since morning and the Dutch Government were scratching their heads to know what to do.

His Majesty is furious that Wilhelm has fled. "The King felt very deeply that the finish of the war had come about in this way and that he should not be able to bring to book the Kaiser and others,

250   PP: CW 5/11/18.
251   PP: CW 7/11/18.
252   Ibid.
253   PP: CW 10/11/18.

who have by their behaviour proved to be the enemies of civilisation and humanity. I think His Majesty would have liked to try the Kaiser by court martial. Then people say that His Majesty is pro-Boche."[254]

"At dawn the Canadians took Mons," writes the King on 11th November 1918, "which was the place where we first came into contact with the Germans over four years ago and from where the retreat began."[255] At about the time of the recapture of the town, a meeting between the Allies and the German delegation takes place in a railway carriage in the Forest of Compiegne. "The Germans were brought during the night... and had no idea where they were." Admiral Wemyss tells the palace "that the Prussians were very dejected and cringing without any dignity."[256] The German armies have been given fourteen days to withdraw back beyond their own borders and surrender massive quantities of war material, and even locomotives that they could otherwise use to move it should fighting break out again. They were to surrender ships, submarines, the rest of the High Seas Fleet is to be interned; and Allied armies are to occupy the west bank of the Rhine.

At Buckingham Palace, the day has begun inauspiciously. The Duke of Connaught joins His Majesty for breakfast and Wigram visits the King at 9:30 to congratulate him, but events do not quite appear to have dawned on him yet. "He was still murmuring about the Kaiser not being there to sign the armistice, and to have his guilt brought home to him." Queen Mary is in a far better mood. "The Queen flew at me and shook both my hands."[257] At quarter to 11 there are still no signs of what is about to transpire outside. "We had prepared four large placards with the news and were about to hang these on the railings outside when the press bureau said we were to stand fast as Mr Lloyd George thought that the news should be kept for him to announce in the House of Commons in the afternoon. Did you ever hear anything so monstrous?" Fumes Wigram.[258] And so outside the crowd is still ignorant. People with time to spare stroll about The Mall looking at the captured German guns. Against the palace rails a small crowd had gathered to watch the changing of the guard, and the only flag in sight was the Royal Standard, which flew tautly on the breeze above the palace façade. Just before the hour people begin to whisper. Some can't believe what they are hearing; others begin to cheer immediately. Nonsense notions about placards are abandoned, and they are put up. Passers-by join the crowd; until men and women are running down The Mall toward the palace, from Constitution Hill and from the direction of Victoria Station. From somewhere, many of the burgeoning crowd have already obtained flags. They begin to cheer as the guard that has been mounted at the palace for the duration of the war marches off.

At 11:00am on the eleventh day, of the eleventh month, the sound of the guns died and the Great War ended.

The swarm of excited people outside Buckingham Palace ebbs and flows around the Victoria memorial like a tide and stretches all the way down The Mall. Men are perching like birds on the knees and shoulders of statues. A New Zealander clinging to an angel's wing facing Constitution Hill starts to chant: *We Want King George* and in their thousands people join him. They sing *Auld Lang Syne,* the *Marseillaise* and the National Anthem until finally the Their Majesties emerge onto the balcony.

254   PP: CW 11/11/18.
255   RA GV/PRIV/GVD/1918 (11/11).
256   PP: CW 15/11/18.
257   PP: CW 11/11/18.
258   Ibid.

The cheering that greeted them was like the roaring of a mighty ocean. Hats, flags, umbrellas, handkerchiefs, scarves, even neck-ties and jackets - anything that lent itself to the occasion were waved in an ecstasy of jubilation. Then, the Guards struck up the National Anthem. Never, in the history of the Empire, had the anthem been rendered with such fervour, such sheer abandonment to relief and exultation, by the great British public.[259]

The fact that the King is moved is obvious to all.

He had acknowledged his people's greetings with a military salute, but now he took off his service cap and waved it back to the waving multitude below him. That was indeed the climax of an unforgettable scene; unforgettable in the depth and spontaneously of its emotion. With the cheers still thundering up to them, the King and Queen, as if reluctant to go, still looked back and smiled their farewells as they withdrew.[260]

But the crowd has no intention of going anywhere. More people are arriving. Through Green Park "came a procession of munition girls in their overalls with a tremendous Union Jack. Men with flags tied to sticks and umbrellas, women who had weaved their hats in the national colours, Dominion soldiers, officers and men of British regiments, troops from the United States, men of the Royal Air Force, Wrens… girls from Government officers and children poured into the wide open space before the palace railings. Motor lorries brought along cheering loads of passengers, some in uniform and some civilians. Motor cars carried three and four times their normal number of people. Every taxi held a dozen men and girls on the roof." By noon the throng "had become a wonderful, surging multitude, stretching far up The Mall." Servants appear on the balcony at the palace, hanging festoons of crimson velvet over the balcony,

But the crowd had to suffer a long wait. Merry incidents enlivened the interval. A rollocking band of subalterns, carrying flags and blowing police whistles, rushed into the massed people, cleared a circle and romped hand in hand round a teddy bear on wheels decorated with flags. An American officer from the top of a taxi cab entertained the crowd with a demonstration of college yells. Insistently and loudly, however, the cry *We Want King George* punctuated the songs and cheers and laughter. The crowd had gathered with a fixed purpose and as the minutes sped they became more determined to have their way.[261]

Inside the palace there is work to be done. The the Army Council, led by the Secretary of State for War, arrive at the palace wishing to pay their respects to His Majesty on this auspicious day. The King meets them in the dining room immediately. Then Sir William Robertson arrives alone. This is particularly poignant for His Majesty and for Clive Wigram too, who counts the former CIGS as a friend. The Board of the Admiralty arrive, then the Air Board, and the King's aunts and family friends descend on Buckingham Palace too. Outside the crowd still clamours for more. "We once again went on the balcony, there was an enormous crowd who gave us a wonderful reception, the Guards massed bands played all the national anthems of the Allies and a few popular airs, it was an extraordinary sight."[262] His Majesty is accompanied by his family, including the Queen and Princess Mary.

259   (ed.) Gibbs: *George the Faithful: The Life & Times of George V "The People's King" 1865-1936*, p.281.
260   *The Times* 12/11/18.
261   (ed.) Hammerton & Wilson: *The Great War Vol.XVIII*, p.143.
262   RA GV/PRIV/GVD/1918 (11/11).

"A roar of cheering went up such as London had not heard during the period of the war, and above the upturned faces, handkerchiefs fluttered, hats waved, and thousands of flags, the flags of all the Allies, flapped and shook. The strains of the National Anthem, played by the Guards, at first were scarcely heard against the cheering, but gradually the people caught the music, and with the third line of the hymn the voices took up the words. Came once more *Rule Britannia*, and then another tremendous note of cheering, led by the King, while the Queen waved a flag above her head… after this 10,000 people took up *Tipperary.*"

Afterwards, though it has begun to rain, the King and Queen go for a drive with Princess Mary. "By the Strand to Mansion House and home by Piccadilly, there was a vast crowd, most good humoured, in some place it was hardly possible to get along." The drizzle mars the enthusiasm of the crowd not one bit, and the small police escort hastily brought together can barely keep them off the open carriage; which has to crawl along Fleet Street, Ludgate Hill; Holborn and Trafalgar Square. "There was no announcement of his coming; no troops, no fanfares. The frenzied mob swept right up to the carriage cheering His Majesty, shouting his name, and trying to shake him by the hand."[263] Flags became soaked, but wet and with colours running they were waved. Late in the afternoon some 1,000 women war workers had marched into the forecourt headed by a band of pipers and begun to lead the singing. Their leader had arrived, breathless, "full of zeal and wanting to organise something" that morning in Wigram's office. "I took her round to Derek who nearly fainted when I said that [she] be allowed to march into the forecourt of the palace with detachments of the womens organisations to sing."[264]

They are still there when the Royal family emerge again. "Two powerful lights flanking the balcony were turned on, and searchlights from the direction of the Admiralty helped to light up the scene and throw the figures of Their Majesties into strong relief. There they stood, regardless of the rain, bowing and smiling to the sea of faces before them. The spectators… cheered and sung and cheered again."[265] Clive Wigram has been scanning the crowds every time the King and Queen present themselves, "and I can assert that there was no Bolshevism in the crowds."[266]

Big Ben and St Paul's Cathedral clock have begun to chime again throughout the course of the day. All the Defence of the Realm Act regulations are gleefully abandoned. Dora be damned. The light in the tower at Westminster is switched back on, theatres and hotels are ablaze. The Strand is brightly lit for the first time in years and illuminates "a boisterous crowd; dancing, singing, blowing tin trumpets and riding on top of motor cars. With perfect synchronicity the fleet switched on their lights, sirens of every note, star shells, fireworks, searchlights, making all sorts of patterns on the sky for a full hour. Then at nine of clock, the sirens suddenly ceased, the lights snapped out and in the chill November might the fleet resumed its silent watch."[267]

At the palace the Royal Household has taken great pleasure in breaking into the cellars and liberating bottles of champagne. David has spent the day with the Canadian Corps. "I feel it can't be more than a marvellous dream and I sill feel in a sort of trance," he tells the Queen. "But I suppose I shall soon wake up to the fact that it is really true."[268] For the King, after untold months of anxiety and fear, of watching his people suffer and dreading the worst, he is euphoric. "Today has indeed been a wonderful day, the greatest in the history of this country."[269]

263   Anon: *The Life of King George V: The Life and Work of a Monarch Beloved of his Peoples,* pp.116-117.
264   PP: CW 11/11/18.
265   *The Times* 12/11/18.
266   PP: CW 11/11/18.
267   *Morning Post* 13/11/18.
268   Ziegler: *King Edward VIII: The Official Biography,* pp.84-85.
269   RA GV/PRIV/GVD/1918 (11/11).

At this moment, the Kaiser is without a country, the Tsar is dead. "The Emperor of Austria-Hungary had renounced his rights… King George of England was the only Emperor of a white race left in the world."[270] And his people know why.

On King George's services during the Great War it is not yet the time to speak at length," wrote one newspaper the following morning. "It is enough to remember today, that from first to last the King has never spared himself, night or day; that he has never failed to express, as only a King can express, the true national sentiment towards our fighting men; that he has gone about among his people in shop and factory, and shown them by his kindly sympathy that he is one of them and with their work: that he has constantly visited the Royal Navy and the British armies abroad; and that in the matter of personal sacrifice, and personal austerity the King has ever been the first.[271]

270   Anon: *The Life of King George V: The Life and Work of a Monarch Beloved of his Peoples*, pp.116-117.
271   *Morning Post* 12/11/18.

1919-1922

Disengagement

Victory

"The Change in the World"

The Great War and all that it had inflicted on the world's population did not simply come to an end. For now at least, Europe has downed its weapons; with luck the fighting is at an end, but peace negotiations will take months. What the terms of the armistice do is make it next to impossible for the Germans to take up arms against the Allies again anytime soon. "It is indeed a great relief after four years and three months and we have won a great victory over a cruel and barbarous enemy," writes His Majesty to Prince George. "It will be some time before peace is signed, but there can be no more fighting."[1] The King and Queen depart in a carriage for St. Paul's just before lunch for a simple service of thanksgiving. The cathedral is full by 11:00am; the police gently turning away a pressing crowd still trying to get inside. In the nave, aisles, and transepts there is barely room to stand. Amidst the "joyful clangour of the great bells," Their Majesties arrived to cheering from excited crowds. Once again, with just a little less ardour than the previous day, the people of London "gave themselves up to the joyous enthusiasm, the loudest roar of cheers went up whenever the King and Queen were seen in public, and again the palace was the chief centre of attraction." On the Strand, at Trafalgar Square and at Piccadilly the traffic is immovable all day. Medical Students from St Mary's are driving round elsewhere "clinging to the outside of a lorry with a complete skeleton perched on the bonnet; all including the skeleton wearing women's clothes."[2]

A visit to church is an obvious reaction to the end of a cataclysmic war; but as for everything else, chaos reigns at Buckingham Palace. For now nobody quite knows what to expect next. "There seems to be a lull," writes Clive Wigram on 12th November. "It is difficult to realise the change in the world."[3] Everyone has a different idea about what His Majesty should be doing. "We must not lose our heads with this tremendous wave of loyalty and enthusiasm." writes Wigram. "Bad times are ahead."[4] Their Majesties have cancelled a tour of Catterick, Ripon, Sheffield and Leicester with the signing of the armistice, because His Majesty thinks it more important that he stay in London and close to his Ministers. He is rather overwhelmed with all of the proposals. One courtier thinks that it is imperative that the King should go now on a tour of Britain's major cities. "I say no," says Clive Wigram. "The army is the nation of tomorrow and these are the people to be with and to visit first."[5] Tempers are frayed and petty confrontations abound. Invitations are coming in from,

1   RA GV/PRIV/AA60/374.
2   *Daily Telegraph* 13/11/18.
3   RA GV/PRIV/GVD/1918 (12/11).
4   1 PP: CW 2/11/18 2/11.
5   PP: CW 15/11/18 15/11.

it seems, every city, town and village. All want a visit from His Majesty. Wigram has even written that he is "not sure Their Majesties will not have to visit the Dominions. We have to be several fields ahead."[6]

Isn't it rather notable, writes *The Times*. "The War Lord of Prussia slinks furtively across the border… Not a vestige remains of the bombastic assumption, set out in a hundred speeches, that the Kaiser and his house are the most essential of all the elements in the German nation." And yet in Britain the first impulse of the populace, it is pointed out, is to share their victory with the Royal Family. In the days that follow there are demonstrations all over the capital. The King and Queen spend more than a week making journeys to the far corners of London to celebrate victory with their subjects. In the East End they climb into a carriage at the Tower of London and journey through Mile End, Whitechapel, Commercial Road. The procession, "if it can be called, was probably the most simple ever seen on an historic occasion. Two mounted policemen in front to clear the road. Two more policemen right in front of the carriage." The crowd is so dense, and so close that they almost tread on the hooves of the policeman's mounts. "There was a nondescript vehicle, something between a tradesmen's van and a costermonger's barrow, which kept so close as to seem part of the procession; it held several soldiers in khaki, cheering, waving caps and flags."[7] There has been no intricate planning. "The smallest possible interference was made with the normal appearance of the East End. The tramway cars ran, the drays lumbered, and the butcher' s and baker's carts careered very much as usual." There are children everywhere. "Hanging out of windows, clustered on the kerb [they] did their utmost… to get their brains dashed out by the horse's hooves."[8] Outside Aldgate station an enthusiastic soldier breaks from the crowd and jumps onto the back of the royal carriage, "whence he hung on while he extended his right to His Majesty. Neither the King nor the Queen noticed the man at first, but when the King did so he burst out laughing." East London is hosting an impromptu street party. "Women in khaki jackets and soldiers in millinery, girls fully rigged out in officers kit, and flocks of children blowing tin trumpets and squeakers, formed an amazing amalgam of the human species."[9]

In South London, Their Majesties drive along the Old Kent Road, where a makeshift Guard of Honour is formed by girls wearing gas masks. Through Kennington the crowd bursts into *Rule Britannia*. At Oval spectators throw flowers to the royal carriage; and on Camberwell Green the King and Queen are greeted by wounded soldiers from King's College Hospital. His Majesty is moved. "The demonstrations of the people are indeed most touching."[10] North of the river scenes are ecstatic too. At Kentish Town, Holloway Road, Islington, Pentonville Road and down towards Euston there are people dancing in the streets; an epidemic of clothes swapping. A golden brown mist hangs over the northern edges of the city, for thousands of bonfires have been lit up on Hampstead Heath. The King and Queen set out from Kensington Palace Gardens into a dry easterly breeze to see more crowds in Notting Hill, Ladbroke Grove, Willesden, Kilburn, Maida Vale and down to Paddington Green; before a final trip down the King's Road, past Stamford Bridge, across the river through Putney and Wandsworth.

On 14th November the King has his first night out on the town since the war began. "May, Mary and I went to the Alhambra and saw *"The Bing Boys on Broadway,"* very pretty music."[11] The

6   Ibid.
7   *The Times* 14/11/18.
8   Ibid.
9   *Daily Telegraph* 14/11/18.
10   RA GV/PRIV/GVD/1918 (14/11).
11   Ibid.

house is full, decorated with an array of Allied flags dominated by the Union Jack. Every night the theatre has to replace them in full, because the audience abscond onto the streets to celebrate with them in hand. A vast array of pink and white roses adorn the fronts of circles and the stage. The orchestra look as if they are sitting in a garden. "The enthusiasm and rejoicing during the last week has surpassed everything I have ever seen," His Majesty tells Bertie. The King has decided that his second son will remain at the front so that he might take part in King Albert's triumphant reentry to his capital. "I should have sent for you… to come home, but I was anxious for you to go to Brussels and you were in France."[12] "We have shown ourselves to the balcony several times each day and have driven every day in an open carriage through miles of cheering crowds. I should think in the last week we have seen quite four million people.[13] "The rejoicing in London has been wonderful and has gone on for a whole week," he tells Prince George "The demonstrations of loyalty by the people outside the palace and during our many long drives through London has been quite remarkable, a pity you were not here to see it."[14]

By the 19th, Dominion representatives have assembled in London and the King rides to Westminster to present an address in the Royal Gallery in front of Parliament. At 24 minutes long, with an audience of some 900 people, it is a trial for His Majesty, but he is accompanied by a large family contingent; including David who is newly arrived from the front to take part in the prolonged ceremonial of victory. While the King congratulates the Royal Navy, Army, Royal Air Force, the Dominions, India, Colonies, and Protectorates, civilians, in particular women, His Majesty is keen to point out that nobody should forget those who have not survived.

> While we find… cause for joy and pride, our hearts go out in sorrowful sympathy to the parents, the wives, and the children who have lost those who were the light and stay of their lives… May they find consolation in the thought that their sacrifice has not been made in vain. These brave men died for right and for humanity. Both have been vindicated.

The overwhelming theme of the King's message to the nation is the future, and the immense work that all face in returning to peace:

> Now that the clouds of war are being swept from the sky, new tasks arrive before us. We see more clearly some duties that have been neglected, liberal provisions must be made for those whose exertions by land and sea have saved us. We have to create a better Britain; to bestow more care on the health and wellbeing of the people… In these years Britain and her traditions have come to mean more to us than they had ever meant before. It became a privilege to serve her in whatever way we could… The sacrifices made; the sufferings endured, the memory of the heroes who have died that Britain may live, ought surely to ennoble our thoughts and attune our heats to a higher sense of individual and national duty… May the morning star of peace which is now rising over a war-worn world be here and everywhere the herald of a better day, in which the storms of strife shall have died down and the rays of an enduring peace be shed upon all the nations.[15]

Back in London Wigram has fought tooth and nail for the King to attend a gathering of the Silver War Badge men; those presented with a marker to wear that signified that they were no longer able

---

12   RA GV/PRIV/AA60/371.
13   RA GV/PRIV/AA60/371.
14   RA GV/PRIV/AA60/374.
15   RA Speeches and Replies to Addresses by HM King George V.

to serve as a result of their wounds. His Majesty was concerned about a lack of turnout, but he need not have worried. Up to 35,000 people converge on Hyde Park; entertained by nearly twenty bands. An open invitation had been issued to all recipients of the badge, and dense crowds have formed to show these men their appreciation. The King issues a message for each of them.

> I am glad to have met you today, and to have looked into the faces of those who for defence of home and Empire... have sacrificed limbs, sight, hearing and health. Your wounds... inspire reverence in your fellow countrymen. May Almighty God mitigate your sufferings, and give you strength to bear them. The welfare of the disabled in the war is the first claim on the country's gratitude, and I trust that the wonderful achievements of medical science combined with national and voluntary supported institutions, may assist you to return to civil life as useful and respected citizens.[16]

His Majesty rides down the lines on horseback, Queen Mary and Queen Alexandra in an open landau behind. Excitement is running so high that discipline evaporates and the men crowd the carriage carrying the two queens; wanting to shake hands with Their Majesties. They wave and smile, though they are a more than a little perturbed. As for His Majesty he and his horse have vanished into a large crowd attempting to get to the King. "They broke through and came round me to shake hands and I was nearly pulled off my horse."[17]

"This Last Fortnight Has Been a Heavy One"

His Majesty had expressed a desire to congratulate Haig and his troops in person even before the signing of the armistice. He wants to see as many men as possible, but "not to have them out lining the roads for miles while he flits past in a motor car, which the King does not at all appreciate." It is also made clear that he does not want a single man, down to the lowest rank, to be stopped from going on planned leave because he is to be present at the front. He will see whoever is there, wherever they have come to rest. After 11th November the palace are also intent on getting His Majesty to Paris, before President Wilson can arrive from America and claim all of the gratitude and enthusiasm that the French population has to expound on their allies. This means two nights in Paris at the beginning of the trip, but the King is expecting them. However, the embassy in Paris are warned: "That this is in no sense a state visit, and that therefore there will be no necessity for His Majesty to see the Corps Diplomatic or do the various functions which are usually undertaken on such occasions."[18] For this reason too, the Queen will remain at home, but Thompson will have to make sure there is sufficient room, for the King not only wants the Prince of Wales to accompany him, but Prince Albert too. "We shall have a lot of interesting things to see besides the troops,"[19] His Majesty assures his second son.

Just before the royal party starts for France, they hear that Lloyd George and certain colleagues are planning for a massed victory parade; receiving both Foch and Haig in London during His Majesty's absence. "Nice people,"[20] remarks Wigram. The first hint of the royal party's arrival on the French coast comes when shortly half past twelve in the afternoon, six airships and aeroplanes emerge out of the haze. HMS *Broke*, the Royal Standard fluttering in the breeze, docks at the mail

16   *Western Gazette* 23/3/19.
17   RA GV/PRIV/GVD/1918 (23/11).
18   RA PS/PSO/WAR/QQ20/07484/1.
19   RA GV/PRIV/AA60/371.
20   RA GV/PRIV/GVD/1918 (27/11).

packet quay in front of cheering crowds, ships sirens, a band playing the National Anthem and aircraft circling round and round the ship, their engines buzzing. Haig and his staff are waiting to greet the King and, the French press are delighted to see His Majesty, bar two Socialist papers which ignore his visit. One newspaper sees it as "consecration henceforth of the unshakeable alliance between England and France." Also, "it will be to King George's eternal honour that he has been the incarnation of the English people during this moving hour. The part which he has played since outbreak of war has been of admirable lucidity and straightforwardness." Another notes regrettable favouritism that has emerged since April 1917 when it comes to France's allies and hopes that this will rectify such a notion.

> Paris today is given the opportunity of repairing, by its warmth of reception of King George, a species of injustice which it commits towards the British people and soldiers when it seems to forget and neglect them since the entry of America into the war. France will be unworthy if they do not seize every opportunity of telling their British friends that they know what they owe to them.[21]

First, Paris, for an afternoon carriage ride for both French and British dignitaries from the Gare du Bois Boulogne, past elaborate decorations; gigantic shields bearing British colours and arms, and banners stretched across the streets that read: *Welcome.* The procession passes along the Champs Elysees and to the Palace of Foreign Affairs. It is a miserable, wet day, and the crowds are soaked, but the drizzle holds off for the duration of the drive. "The streets were lined with troops," writes His Majesty, "all the houses decorated with flags and there were enormous crowds in spite of the weather who cheered most enthusiastically and gave us a wonderful reception, a great demonstration of gratitude to England for what she has done for France." The King is astounded at the ardour of the crowd, which he tells the Queen surpasses anything that they saw during their state visit in 1914. Wigram is riding in his army uniform, feeling rather silly and inadequate. Part of him regrets remaining at the palace for the duration of the war, though his family tell him he has more than done his duty there. Charles Cust is alongside him in navy garb. They are subjected to endless shouts of *Vive la marine anglaise; Vive l'armee anglaise,* "Rather anomalous considering neither of us had seen a shot fired,"[22] he rues. The carriages pass outside the Arc de Triomphe, as the centre arch is reserved for troops returning from the front. Above, people have been selling a view from their windows for 4000 francs, another 450 if one wanted a seat. Ponsonby is seated in a carriage with the French Minister for Foreign Affairs. "There is no doubt that the tremendous emotion of the crowd was something quite out of the ordinary. Monsieur Pichon… was so overcome that he broke down and cried like a child."[23]

The royal suite returns to the Elysee for a State Banquet in the evening. The King is required to shake hands with 150 people and to nervously respond to a most eloquent speech by the President, in French. The rooms are stifling and his is relieved to escape by 10:30. The following morning Prince George of Greece, despite Stamfordham's best efforts, is determined to have an audience with His Majesty. They manage to get him in for breakfast with the King unseen. After a visit to the British Embassy, and lunch with the tearful French Foreign Minister, the King has one more dinner to survive. He is beginning to feel the strain of the relentless schedule that he has maintained since the armistice. "This last fortnight has been a heavy one," he confides in the Queen, "I have never

21   RA PS/PSO/WAR/QQ20/07484/1.
22   PP: CW 28/11/18.
23   Syonsby: *Recollections of Three Reigns,* pp.330-331.

done so much in such a short time and I own that I am tired, but still I shall try and struggle on."[24] He is homesick, too, and missing his wife. He has the same rooms as during their 1914 visit and everything reminds him of Queen Mary. "I am sending you a few chocolates, they are very difficult to get, I miss you of course dreadfully and hate to be away from you." He is thrilled that David and Bertie are present. "It is everything having the two boys with me."[25] But the boys are young men now and being with their father cramps their style. "It is very funny how the Prince of Wales and Prince Albert try to go off on their own, and escape from Papa,"[26] writes Wigram. But by doing so they can widen the scope of the royal visit, and their excursions to towns, villages, officers' clubs and the like when they break away from the men are engaging and cheerful.

The royal party is met by Major Thompson at Arras and the bulk of the King's visit begins. On Haig's recommendation they will be staying at Valenciennes, and Thompson has secured the Chateau de Sebourg, which until three weeks ago was a German artillery school. The owner, Baron de la Grange, receives the King and introduces himself as a royalist. "He has lived in the house during the whole of war although it was occupied by Germans, they were not too civil to him."[27] The people in the village suspect him of being pro-German, but, "anyhow he is full of interesting tales,"[28] notes Wigram. The whole area is devastated. "We have made the roads pretty good," His Majesty tells Queen Mary, but it is awful to see the destruction of whole towns and villages from shellfire, hardly a house remains for miles."[29] The royal suite is amused to learn that Haig has refused to attend Lloyd George's procession back in London. "They wish to put him in the fourth carriage and practically to play no part," writes Wigram. "The skunks."[30] In the event, Queen Mary is on hand to at least receive the French dignitaries.

I quite approve," the King tells her, "as when I am away you represent me and it would not have done if the whole show was run by the Prime Minister alone and he did all the entertaining. I am sorry that they should have coming in this official way in my absence, but I should not be surprised if the Prime Minister had arranged it so entirely because we knew I was away.[31]

As an army man, Wigram is proud at Haig's non-attendance, his refusal to "lower the military prestige of Great Britain by driving at the tag end… and then Lloyd George is reported to have said that he wished Haig to be present to show how much he appreciated Haig's services! Funny bloke."[32]

The short days at the front are full of activity. The King has a claim on being the first battlefield tourist on the Western Front, with a unique experience of combing them with not only the Generals that conquered them, but junior officers and men too who describe their experiences. The royal party feel quite breathless at Avesnes, where Hindenburg had had his headquarters for some time. Battle had been orchestrated from here, the Kaiser and his heir had walked the streets. At Landrecies His Majesty finds himself almost where the war began for the BEF. A General who had been but a

24   RA QM/PRIV/CC04/192.
25   Ibid.
26   PP: CW 15/11/18 15/11.
27   RA GV/PRIV/GVD/1918 (30/11).
28   PP: CW 30/11/18 30/11.
29   RA QM/PRIV/CC04/192.
30   PP: CW 30/11/18 30/11.
31   RA QM/PRIV/CC04/194.
32   RA GV/PRIV/GVD/1918 (1/12).

Major in 1914 shows the King a fork in the road. With the help of a man who was a Sergeant on that day they explain to the King how the Coldstream Guards attempted to hold up the German advance; the latter even pointing out where he lay in the road to fire at the enemy. Rawlinson is on top form as he guides the royal party over the battlefields of the Sambre, the Oise and the St. Quentin Canal; showing His Majesty where the Fourth Army had broken through the Hindenburg Line. At Riqueval Bridge, which was saved from being blown up on the initiative of a Captain in the North Staffordshire Regiment, the officer in question who is there to regale all with his tale. The King stops in a vast array of places throughout the week for alfresco lunches, unpacking sandwiches in a ruined farm, in fields, and in an empty dwelling from which the enemy had made off with all of the furniture with a string band of the Lincoln Regiment playing in the background. On another day even a little mess hut belonging to the men of the Chinese Labour Corps; with its usual inhabitants "dressed in an extraordinary medley of costumes," having "made great efforts to decorate their hut tastefully for this occasion."[33]

His Majesty has the car stopped whenever anything attracts his attention; jumps out to examine things more closely and then he is off again. At Bony he finds the American cemetery, and walks up and down the lines of neat little wooden crosses, bending down to read the nameplates; a day with General Byng's Chief of Staff reveals all kinds of behind the scenes stories about the later stages of the Allied advance and the logistics or dangers of victory. He tells the royal party that when the armistice was signed the Third Army were nearly at the end of their tether as regards transport and feeding the troops. They are having trouble with the local inhabitants when it comes to billeting the men. "The French in these areas are not at all pleased to see them as they are trying to resettle and get their land again under cultivation. In fact all the YMCA huts and other places of meeting erected by us before have been pulled down." At dinner one night the Assistant Provost Marshal says that they have caught four German secret service men in the villages nearby in the last two days. "There are hundreds of German spies trying to spread Bolshevik literature among our men."[34] Everywhere there is evidence of the French arriving home to begin to try and rebuild their lives. In one village there is a lone elderly woman, newly arrived back in her village and poking through the rubble that used to be her home with a stick. At Maroiles, which had been the centre of a thriving cheese industry before the war, they have returned to find that as well as their cows, all of their machinery has been taken by the enemy. "Along the road a pitiable feature was seen in the civilian population which, in twos and threes… as well as in many of the army lorries were making their way back to their homes uncertain of whether they would find their houses standing at the journey's end. It is estimated that the British are feeding nearly three quarters of a million of the civil population in France and Belgium."[35]

At Le Quesnoy the commander of the New Zealand Division shows the King where his men took the ancient, fortified town. As soon as he passes, troops crowd around for a chat or follow on his heels through quaint narrow streets. At Neuilly the King walks along the railway embankment, scene of heavy fighting in October. He can pick up remnants of the battle. "The whole place is still littered with equipment of various kinds, cartridges, innumerable helmets, bayonets, knapsacks, grenades and so forth. The railway line here had been thoroughly and scientifically put out of action by the explosion of a small charge at every rail joint."[36] Cambrai is much larger, and the reception from the locals and the troops stationed within is rousing. Everywhere there are German signs written up with directions showing the way to aircraft shelters, cinemas and the like. His Majesty's quick eye finds

33 *Daily Telegraph* 9/12/18.
34 PP: CW 1/12/18 CW1/12.
35 RA PS/PSO/WAR/QQ20/07484/1.
36 *Daily Telegraph* 6/12/18.

a blinded French soldier wearing both the Croix de Guerre and the Military Medal among a line of ribbons on his breast and begins chatting with him. More than anything the King is stunned and angered by the wanton destruction caused by the enemy on their way out. "The whole of the centre of the town has been burnt, many hundreds of houses set on fire on purpose by the Germans, they generally set light to the beds the day they leave; they will have a nice bill to pay later on."[37]

Halfway through the trip, thanks to the cold weather His Majesty has caught a cold. Powered on by an array of nasal douches, condiments and lozenges supplied by Wigram, he carries on to Mons, another location full of sentiment for the British Army; site of their first engagement in 1914. The locals have lavishly decorated the town in anticipation of the visit. "The difference of the treatment meted out to the French and Belgians is very marked," writes Wigram. "The Belgian houses and roads are quite normal."[38] Back across the border, Gavrelle is "all overgrown with weeds and rank grass pitted with shell holes, and littered with fragments of equipment, shells, cartridges, belts of machine guns, and other rubbish of battle. The long rows of trees that used to line most of the main roads in this district are mostly gone now."[39] Monchy le Preux is nothing but rubble. "From a heap of ruins which was once the church... the General described to us the very successful attack of his army."[40] Neither the King nor Wigram can believe the extent of some of the German positions. "I have never seen such a display of natural positions fortified by every means that human hand and brain could devise,"[41] writes the latter. General Horne describes to them how he broke all the principles of war in the final stages of war to force a victory, and under a bright winter sun the King inspects the battlefields of Flanders. "We... came to Passchendaele which is a mass of shell-holes and nearly every building is obliterated." His Majesty motors past Hell Fire Corner, a bloody site if ever there was one, and climbing the high ground overlooking Ypres the King and his companions can see knocked out tanks from the latter part of 1917 across the landscape. But of all the places on a map that are given form on this trip, one moves His Majesty more than any other. "At last I went into Ypres having seen it since 1914." The town is symbolic for Britain, encompassing more than four years of struggle and bloody attrition on the Western Front. "It is practically flat. The walls of the cathedral, the famous cloth hall are alone standing out of a heap of stones."[42] But even those furnish "about as much standing wall as the ruins of Whitby Abbey."[43] But this is no day of triumph. "A sad day visiting the graves of all ones best pals at Ypres,"[44] writes Wigram. It feels like another lifetime, but finally His Majesty can pay his respects to those friends he lost at Ypres in 1914; for they are buried in the town. Charlie Fitzmaurice and Willie Cadogan, and of course Prince Maurice of Battenberg. The King spends time at his cousin's grave, and is moved to find flowers left there by his daughter on her recent visit to the front. The rain is cascading down by the time His Majesty arrives at Calais for a rough, delayed crossing home; but three hours after leaving French shores the King is exchanging salutes with his uncle at Victoria Station.

"At the Birth of Victory"

There is much royal toing and froing from rail termini in the wake of the armistice, for after nearly five years, freedom of movement is restored. Princess Beatrice's daughter Ena, the Queen of Spain

37   RA QM/PRIV/CC04/200.
38   PP: CW 7/12/18.
39   *Morning Post* 9/12/18.
40   RA GV/PRIV/GVD/1918 (7/12).
41   PP: CW 9/12/18.
42   RA GV/PRIV/GVD/1918 (8/12).
43   *The Times* 10/12/18.
44   PP: CW 9/12/18.

is able to see her mother for the first time since Prince Maurice was killed. "Though far away from you all my heart and thoughts have constantly been in England," she tells the King. "You can understand how trying my position has often been among the many conflicting interests of a neutral court and how hard to disguise one's true feelings, as the news was good or bad for the allies. But now in this wonderful moment of England's great victory, when your feelings of pride and relief must be almost too big for words, I wish by one short line to tell you how truly I rejoice with you in this supreme hour… I have felt these five years of separation very deeply."[45] Marie of Romania, another of Queen Victoria's grandchildren, arrives to stay at the palace, Daisy is able to travel from Sweden to see her father, the Duke of Connaught for the first time in years. The first to arrive the the King's favourite sister, Maud, Queen of Norway with her son Olav, to Prince John's delight. Landing at Rosyth they entrain for London and for the first time since the onset of the war, she will spend Christmas at home. There is an emotional family reunion at Euston Station on a specially laid carpet of red baize, underneath a mass of Norwegian flags suspended from iron girders. The King, Queen, Bertie, Mary, Queen Alexandra, Toria and the Duke of Connaught all having come to greet Queen Maud and her son.

The endless stream of visitors to the palace will continue for months, those with stories to recount from all over the world; officers from Romania, Mesopotamia and Palestine. The King meets the Chaplain of the English Church in Berlin, who has been there since before 1914 and Emir Faisal, son of the King of the Hejaz arrives in the company of Colonel Lawrence. There are many farewells to partake in too. General Cowans, who has served as Quartermaster General for the duration of the war is to step down; His Majesty knights Superintendent Quinn of Scotland Yard for long service. Generals from Canada, Australia and New Zealand bid goodbye on their returns home, as does Sister Tremaine, who nursed the King after his accident in 1915. General Plumer is to leave for Malta to take up the post of Governor, and a Japanese liaison presents the King with "a beautiful old Japanese sword in remembrance of our victory."[46]

There is much gratitude to be meted out from Buckingham Palace, for acknowledgement from His Majesty for work done is high praise. There are separate messages for the Salvation Army, for Ulster troops, and for the Swiss President and for the Queen of the Netherlands for their care of British prisoners of war. The King and Queen attend a command performance at the Coliseum to show their appreciation "for the good work which members of the variety professions have done during the war."[47] At His Majesty's request the proceeds are to go to the Artists' Benevolent Fund. Closer to home the King gives a dinner at Sandringham for all of the men on the estate who had serviced in the war; more than 400 attended. There is another, too, for detachment of Special Constables who have formed a guard for the palace throughout the war. "I am deeply sensible of the valuable service given during the war by these gentlemen in guarding Buckingham Palace and its surroundings besides other special duties," says His Majesty. "I heartily thank them for this proof of their patriotism, their high sense of duty and of loyalty to me and my family."[48]

But it is not just individuals and small interest group that are acknowledged by the King. He makes a speech for the Mercantile Marine at Guildhall, recognition of their work in the face of the German submarine menace; that "they had to bear the brunt of… his most deadly blow… without any of the glamour cast by the pomp and circumstance of war." His Majesty reminds all in

45   RA GV/PRIV/AA/43.
46   RA GV/PRIV/GVD/1919 (19/5).
47   *The Times* 28/7/19.
48   *Morning Post* 16/5/19.

attendance that "even when the submarine peril was at its height, no single British crew ever refused to sail. "It is a grand and stainless record."[49]

The march past is the favoured method of recognising large bodies of men and women for their war contribution as it comes to an end. His Majesty takes up a position on a dais on the forecourt outside the palace as they proceed past him and he shows his appreciation. The Guards Division is to be broken up, but before this occurs, on the same spot from which his grandmother welcomed back three battalions of Guards from the Crimea the King says: "As your Commander in Chief I wish to thank you one and all for faithful and devoted services and to bid you God speed. May you ever retain the same mutual feelings of true comradeship which animated and ennobled the life of the Guards Division."[50] It takes over an hour for all of the men to pass and this parade has particular resonance for His Majesty, as the Guards constitute the first regiments of the British Army and David road as part of the procession. "It was a splendid sight and there were great crowds to see them who have them a most hearty reception."[51] A month later it is the turn of a three mile line of London battalions to march past the palace; then almost immediately afterwards Dominion troops. There are more than 12,000 of them, and the march in a "festival air… a perfect spring day, of golden sunshine with intervals of pearl grey shade."[52] A flight of aeroplanes passes over as well as an airship which dips her flag in salute. The King's speech is suitably grand for the departure of the Empire men.

> We and the future generations will never forget the part played by the Canadian in the second battle of Ypres an on the Vimy Ridge, by the Australians and New Zealanders at Gallipoli and in the advance in France in the spirit of 1917 by the troops of all three Dominions in the breaking of the Hindenburg line last year, by the South Africans in Delville Wood, and by the Royal Newfoundland Regiment at Monchy le Preux… I wish you God Speed on your homewards journey, with the hope that the outcome of his world struggle may assure peace to your children and to your children's children.[53]

The processional route along The Mall to Buckingham Palace, then on to Westminster Abbey and the Houses of Parliament via Victoria Station before taking to the Strand is being referred to as the *"Triumphant Way of the British Empire."*[54]

The most popular and exuberant parade in front of the King is that of the Special Constables; men unfit or too advanced in age to serve abroad that have tirelessly poured their energies and their enthusiasm into the Home Front. Nearly 18,000 of them pass in front of His Majesty before they are all demobilised, followed by members of the City of London Police Reserve. Last but not least would come the Boy Scouts, Sea Scouts and Sea Cadets who had been sent out as buglers during air raids, and had carried out many a useful messenger task or turned their hand to any other contribution they could make, including unloading newly arrived ambulance trains. Having assembled in Hyde Park, the Specials march off to the memorable 'All Clear' call of the Boy Scouts' bugles. In brilliant sunshine the men march eight abreast past the King, as crowds of friends and relatives swarm the route to get a glimpse of this last hurrah.

49   *The Times* 30/7/19.
50   *The Times* 23/3/19.
51   RA GV/PRIV/GVD/1919 (22/3).
52   *Daily Telegraph* 17/4/19.
53   *Morning Post* 5/5/19.
54   *The Times* 19/3/19.

The end of the Great War also brings about a revolutionary new way of thanking those who have provided loyal public service which has flourished ever since. Official receptions; the presentation of brides and debutantes at court and so on, have been completely neglected during the war, and there are huge arrears as nothing of this sort has taken place since 1914. But these are stuffy functions and do not represent what the King and Queen Mary stand for at all. In the immediate aftermath of the Great War the royal garden party is born; buoyed by the reception of such outdoor functions as the large-scale investiture in Hyde Park. The war has helped the nation to realise, "as it never realised before, the value of the services of its less exalted sons and daughters." Ever astute when it comes to public feeling, the King and Queen agree to make "the way less difficult and less costly for those deserving of recognition to be received,"[55] for the dress code will be not nearly so stiflingly expensive. The innovation is greeted with joy by female quarters of the press.

> This summer… is the first for five years in which we can enjoy the English countryside… with hearts untroubled by thoughts of the not far distant death and desolation wrought by the fury of the guns across the Channel. At the birth of victory, what more perfect setting could be found in which to pay homage to our King and Queen than that of a lovely old English garden?[56]

The dressmakers of London are thrilled "at the thought of beautiful light dresses devoid of stuffy and labour intensive velvet and brocade for trains." Many such organisations are starved of labour which has gone off to war, so all benefit. "New fabrics are being prepared, and will be jealously kept for the garden parties… There are whispers of soft silks, giving wholly new effects of shading and lovely embroidered muslins, of fine lace just tinted to the most delightful suggestions of soft shades. That is to say nothing of the possibilities of parasols, gloves and hats."[57]

The gardens of Buckingham Palace can accommodate thousands, with the 360 foot west front as a backdrop, acres of spacious lawns, trees for shades and even an ornamental lake, the water for which is piped underground from the Serpentine. The first garden party is so successful that the King and Queen decide to hold one for war workers. They are not exclusively for women, but it is here that numerous organisations receive their due acknowledgement from their King and Queen for all they have done for their country. 10,000 invitations to tea had gone out for the first events, and Princess Mary in her VAD uniform stands alongside her parents and many of His Majesty's aunts, cousins, his sister in law to welcome men and women; doctors, nurses in blue, white, crimson and slate, women from the Ministry of Labour, Queen Mary's Army Auxiliary Corps, the Wrens, the Women's RAF, the YMCA, Church Army representatives, charities, the Queen's War Work for Women Fund and the Women's Land Army. There are Boy Scouts, Girl Guides, members of the Serbian Relief Fund; even the Vegetable Products Committee which had sent fruit and vegetables to the fleet. As they enter the gardens many of the guests are speechless, as one nurse describes:

> It would be difficult to believe that such extensive grounds were on the other side, and when there London seemed so far away. What sights awaited all those who recd the command to attend. Everyone on entering was handed a card with the letter on it of the tent where to go for tea, and what a tea! The tables, decorated with massed of malmaison carnations, were lovely.[58]

55 *Daily Telegraph* 24/5/19.
56 *The Gentlewoman* 31/5/19.
57 *Daily Telegraph* 24/5/19.
58 RA GV/PRIV/GVD/1919 (9/8).

It is characteristic of the King too, that he does not overlook those who have served, but who have come out of the war having fallen from grace in their respective professions. He finds it incredibly distasteful that some men have been thrown under the bus by those who have climbed above them since 1914, and is sympathetic with those who have failed in their endeavours, but done so whilst being loyal to the King and country. Louis of Battenberg, now Mountbatten, he is seen with many times in public after 1914. In November 1918, His Majesty has Stamfordham write to Lord Haldane: "The King directs me to tell you how deeply he appreciates all you have done to make our victory possible and how silly he thought the outcry against you."[59] His Majesty he has also inspected New Zealand troops with General Hamilton at his side after his failure at Gallipoli, had Asquith to stay at Windsor Castle. He even presses Lloyd George to include the former Prime Minister in peace talks, for his experience is invaluable. General Townshend is received at the palace despite having surrendered Kut and remaining in Turkish captivity for the second half of the war; General Trenchard is a visitor to Buckingham Palace after departing the Air Ministry, and Sir William Robertson is frequently in royal company. Wigram is furious when his attendance at the palace on armistice day is missed from the court circular and with the King insists that this is rectified the day afterwards. He is also insistent that His Majesty see General Gough, who commanded the Fifth Army during its hardships in March 1918. "I am putting up a note to Stamfordham to point out that His Majesty saw Nixon, Johnny Hamilton and Duff after their failures." For of course although his army was decimated, it was put in danger by a lack of available personnel, through no fault of Gough. "It is monstrous that the Prime Minister and others should persecute him."[60] The King's benevolence only stretched so far. Though he has conducted a number of public functions on amiable terms with Sir John French at his side after he had resigned as Commander in Chief of the BEF, he is not invited to the palace. And there is no sign whatsoever of Admiral Fisher.

When it comes to one particular homecoming the King is willing to stick his neck out. In November 1918, the King sent his personal congratulatons to Haig on the achievement of his victory, but, when Haig wished to publish the telegram, permission was denied in case Lloyd George regarded it as unconstitutional. Haig has resisted the cheek of Lloyd George when it came to riding in a victorious parade of Frenchmen. He thought the suggestion "impertinent." He never had any intention in taking part "in a triumphant procession with a lot of foreigners through the streets of London on a Sunday! This too after all I have done to keep the peace with Foch and the other French supreme commanders during three years." He has his own plan. Having not been home for Christmas since the onset of the war, he wants to reach Dover on 20th December, he has invited his entire staff and his army commanders too, "so that they… may not only share the welcome with me, but can also spend Christmas with their people." He makes it very clear that he will not submit to anything along the lines of Lloyd George's first plan. "As you know, I hate ovations and nothing will induce me to receive a welcome in combination with a pack of foreigners. The welcome must be purely British."[61] The King supports this plan wholeheartedly, but Wigram begs him to expand it, inviting Haig and his fellow officers into London, for His Majesty to go and meet them at the station; "to receive a welcome from the capital of the empire."[62] This is not the Generals' triumphant entry. That cannot occur until peace has actually been signed, but it is a rare and significant occasion for London to welcome home the men who have led the British Army to victory. His Majesty allows himself to be convinced by his advisors with ease. It will be in small measure revenge, for Haig was

59   Nicolson: *King George V: His Life and Reign*, pp.263-264.
60   PP: CW 6/11/18.
61   RA PS/PSO/GV/C/K/1387/7.
62   PP: CW 3/12/18.

prevented from publishing a message from the King personally congratulating him on winning the war, lest it offend the Prime Minister. They may only be coming home for Christmas with their families, but both at Dover and in London the population will get to show their appreciation for the leaders of the BEF with no interference from political quarters.

Dover: *'Guardian of the Narrow Seas.'* There is dazzling sunshine, but a high, cold wind is sweeping the harbour, and heavy seas break against the piers, tossing up "glittering showers of spray" that highlight the white cliffs. The weather means that at the last minute, the Generals have to sail home under the Belgian flag. The town has put up banners to welcome the heroes home, but wind has wrapped them and tangled them around their ropes. At Charing Cross Station a red carpet has been unfurled and the platform sits under a canopy of flags. More are wrapped around the iron pillars supporting the glass roof, entwined with laurel and with palms. Stands have been built to seat ticket holders, soldiers have climbed on top of a nearby train to watch and at lunchtime the train arrives. "Up to this point, there had been no unrestrained cheering, but as the Generals move further along the platform to the gate and take their places in five open royal carriages, the crowds massed inside the station raise their voices. Outside, in the forecourt of the station, larger and denser masses of people took up the shouting as the carriages swung through the archway into the street."[63] From Charing Cross the military convoy traverses Trafalgar Square, where the crowd is thickest and twists up Pall Mall, along Piccadilly, round Hyde Park and down Constitution Hill to Buckingham Palace. Wigram is ecstatic. "The Field Marshal received a right royal British welcome with no foreign touch about it, I am feeling quite happy, as the King initiated and carried through this scheme in spite of a certain amount of opposition."[64] 48 sit down to lunch with the King and Queen, with scarcely a politician in sight.

The final royal engagement of 1918, however, garners much less enthusiasm from His Majesty. "I fear we shall not be able to get down to Sandringham for Christmas,"[65] the King writes in his diary on 18th December. It is a heartbreaking prospect, for it will be the first family gathering involving his sister Maud for years, not to mention the fact that it would have been a private celebration of the end of the war after weeks of strain following the armistice. The King has been sparring with Lloyd George again, for the Government have invited President Wilson to England. The President defers, saying that he must go to Paris first, which lays his State Visit to Britain's shores right across the Christmas holiday; starting on Boxing Day. Stamfordham protests, telling Lloyd George that His Majesty is "surprised and hurt" at not being consulted about the arrangement... Lloyd George brusquely replied that the King's objections had been put to the Imperial War Cabinet and that they had "overruled the King."[66]

"Tiresome,"[67] is the King's measured response; for now he must be on duty, must receive Wilson and his wife and hold a state banquet. It is the first time that a President of the United States has been a royal guest in England. Christmas morning is sharp, frosty, the "ground quite white."[68] It is a working day, and the Royal Family attend the service at Westminster Abbey. The following afternoon the President arrives from France. A dull sunlight penetrates the smoke stained glass roof at Charing Cross; barrels of holly and mistletoe hang from the girders with flags. The distant sound of cheering heralds the arrival of the King, Queen and Princess Mary, and a tiny silk version

63   *The Times* 20/12/18.
64   PP: CW 20/12/18.
65   RA GV/PRIV/GVD/1918 (18/11).
66   Rose: *King George V,* p.232.
67   RA GV/PRIV/GVD/1918 (18/12).
68   RA GV/PRIV/GVD/1918 (25/12).

of the stars and stripes flutters on the front of the engine as it pulls into the station. His Majesty walks alongside Wilson down the platform, the pair chatting. Large crowds have emerged to roar the progress of the royal carriages along to the palace. In Trafalgar Square, the National Gallery is smothered in bunting, venetian masts strung with flags, more hanging out of window; the main carriage is showered in red, white and blue confetti. "London was looking its best for a winter's day," the King writes proudly, "and all the streets were beautifully decorated, we passed through Trafalgar Square, Pall Mall, St. James's Street. Piccadilly and Constitution Hill to the palace and the very large crowds have him a splendid welcome."[69]

The King and Queen take the President out onto the balcony at the behest of the crowd and Wilson makes a short speech. "He seemed very gratified with his reception. he paid visits to Mama and the family… Mr and Mrs Wilson and Uncle Arthur dined with us and the children downstairs in the Carnarvon Room. He is quite easy to get on with and I had a talk with him after dinner."[70] His Majesty's good mood doesn't last. The President and his wife are given the Belgian suite at Buckingham Palace, overlooking the gardens and where most of anything decorative is still in boxes where it had been packed away owing to air raids. At a state banquet the following evening Wilson makes a terrible impression. In front of nearly 120 guests, when he replies to a toast to his health he fails to mention anything at all about Britain's part, or her sacrifices in the war. "Not a word of appreciation, let alone gratitude came from his lips," writes Lloyd George. To Prince Henry, the Queen describes the President as "an autocrat if ever there was one."[71] The King is just as appalled. "I could not bear him, an entirely cold academical professor; an odious man."[72] According to gossip gleaned by David, his wife made no more of an impression. "Mrs" is of doubtful origin and has a strange past and that there are some priceless stories of her stay at Buckhouse."[73]

Wilson and his wife depart for Manchester for a brief tour, leaving the King and Queen to kick their heels for 48 hours until their return to London for a public departure. When the King escorts Wilson back to Victoria Station, he climbs into his carriage, the crowd cheers, a band strikes up with the American National Anthem, and as the train pulls out of the station the President is still politely bowing to his audience. Duty done, after the quick presentation of a Victoria Cross to a young soldier about to depart for Canada, finally, the Royal Family depart for Sandringham in time to celebrate New Year's Eve in Norfolk.

"Darling Johnnie"

Amongst the family members thrilled with the arrival of the King and Queen at York Cottage is Prince John, who in some ways has been thriving since his move to Sandringham. He is much grown, in fact, he is already as tall as his father. His sailor suit has been left behind since his move to Norfolk, in favour of neat blue serge suits, but whilst he is a young man in body, in mind, he is still a little boy. Lalla takes him to the seaside at Heacham, and when the King are not in residence, he receives lots of visits from his Grannie and auntie Toria. He is always asking after Princess Mary, and she in turn adores her youngest brother. Johnnie's disposition is one of complete innocence. He talks to everyone he meets, asking them incessant questions about their thoughts about various subjects and what they do for a living. He has become extremely popular in the local villages; especially the children, and drives to and fro delivering apples to people on the estate in his little

69   Ibid., 26/12.
70   Ibid.
71   Frankland: *Prince Henry, Duke of Gloucester*, p.46.
72   Rose: *King George V,* p.232.
73   (ed.) Godfrey: Letters from a Prince, p.163.

cart. He is also a prankster, playing incessant jokes on his personal servants; for Lalla has been joined by a more appropriate body man, Mr May, who can better help him with any physical assistance he needs now that he is maturing.

He does miss his family when they are not in Norfolk, but his privacy is assured and he is constant contact with them. He wants to know if his Papa has been reviewing soldiers, to send his love from his little dog to Princess Mary's pet. He wants to know if his parents have been to Windsor; he sends his father presents, wants to know what David is doing. "I am very busy here," he signs off in one. "Best love from your devoted son."[74] Queen Alexandra adores her Grandson, loves to baby him and coddle him. She has never really grown up and neither can he. She provides one update in the summer of 1917 for Queen Mary. She tells Her Majesty that "your darling Johnnie… is looking the picture of health and had tea with me at my cottage by the sea, where he was full of fun and talked incessantly, telling me about… his new house which he is very proud of. Next day I could see him [outside his] house playing football with… Charlotte and the other three women of his household!! He was so hot, but he came rushing to me and showed me his garden and all over the house which certainly is very nice and comfortable and he seemed quite happy."[75] The only thing that Johnnie has lacked since 1917 is a companion, for as far as Prince Olav and Prince Alfonso are concerned, he has been robbed of them for the duration of the war. That and his fits have been growing more frequent.

"I never saw so much water on account of all the rain we have had,"[76] the King writes in mid-January. Prince John has been having a busy week. He and Olav are inseparable; he spends an afternoon with his Grannie at the big house, and on Saturday morning, 18th January, he gets up early and goes for a brisk walk with Princess Mary. The Queen had been with Queen Maud to see some new tenants on the estate. She returns and has begun writing a letter to Bertie at RAF Headquarters in Belgium, when at 5:30pm the telephone rings. It is Lalla at Wood Farm. Distraught she tells the Queen that Johnnie has suffered a severe attack and passed away in his sleep afterwards. Queen Mary breaks the news to the King, and together, in complete shock they motor down to Wood Farm. Lalla is heartbroken, but in a way resigned, as if she knew she would lose her beloved charge in this way one day. The Prince looks peaceful lying in his bed. The Queen tries to finish her letter. "I feel rather stunned so excuse more," she tells Bertie. "Poor Mary and Georgie awfully upset. Their first *real* sorrow."[77]

Queen Alexandra is devastated. In addition to the loss of a grandson, she herself lost a baby boy named John, who is buried at Sandringham. He had lived for just a few hours, and this fresh loss brings the memories flooding back. Bertie is crushed. "It must have been a great shock to you coming at a time like this… And your being down at Sandringham too makes it easier for you I expect. I can see from your letter that it has upset you very much I don't wonder either. When I received the telegram from Papa it upset me too, especially as I had not seen him since this time last year."[78] He does, at least, have David with him. He had arrived at Spa just after the telegram and they comfort each other. The Prince of Wales is not oblivious to grief for his brother, but his response on the whole is callous. He hopes that the funeral will summon him home and enable him to see his latest lady friend, but the King blocks a return for he and Bertie because they will not make it in time.

74   RA GV/PRIV/AA60/313.
75   RA QM/PRIV/CC42/127.
76   RA GV/PRIV/GVD/1919 (13/1).
77   RA GVI/PRIV/RF/II/305.
78   RA GV/PRIV/CC11/4.

His death is the greatest relief imaginable… but to be plunged into mourning for this is the limit just as the war is over which cuts parties etc. right out!!… No one would be more cut up if any of my other three brothers were to die… but this poor boy had become more of an animal than anything else, and was only a brother in the flesh and nothing else!![79]

David writes something in a similar vein to his mother; a letter of "chilling insensitivity."[80] She is too distraught to answer, and he later apologises profusely.

The family return again to Wood Farm the following day to sit with Johnnie, before a long walk in the afternoon. The bell in the Curfew Tower at Windsor begins to toll as soon as the news is received. The court goes into full mourning, and flags have been lowered to half mast in London, Paris, Belgium, even Casablanca. The news comes as a great shock to the public. Prince John had not yet reached the age when he would have expected to have been seen a lot in public; but nobody thought he was so poorly. It is known that he is not entirely healthy, but the statement issued to the press is a revelation. "As is now publicly announced, he had suffered from that most distressing and mysterious of all maladies."[81]

His Royal Highness the Prince John, who has since his infancy suffered from epileptic fits, which have lately become more frequent and severe, passed away in the sleep following an attack at 5:30 this afternoon at Sandringham. The complaint from which he died was of almost life long duration.[82]

Their Majesty's loss, it is pointed out, is all the more cruel when after so many years of toil, the King and Queen have so recently celebrated victory with their people.

The King who has for more than four years suffered at heart over the bereavements of his people, brought to grief by war, is now himself stricken and sorrowing, and the Queen whose sympathies had gone to so many thousands of mothers is now a heart-broken mother herself… Few of us knew that during these years of war-born anxiety King George and Queen Mary carried in their hearts a great private and personal burden.[83]

In the meantime, at Sandringham His Majesty has had to carry out a singular engagement in the midst of his grief. Seventeen year old Thomas Ricketts is about to depart for Newfoundland and the King presents him with his Victoria Cross. The youngest army combatant to receive the award, he had taken a leading role in capturing an entire German battery of field guns in mid-October. But the King cannot bring himself to do anything else. Aside from a walk with two of his sisters, in the aftermath of his youngest son's death, His Majesty's time is consumed in reading hundreds of telegrams and letters of condolence that will continue to arrive at Sandringham for weeks.

In Spain, Ena has only learned of Johnnie's death from the newspapers. It is so hard after all you have gone through these last terrible years to have now to hear this fresh shock and grief," she writes.[84] Haakon, King of Norway has not made the trip to England with his wife and son.

79   (ed.) Godfrey: *Letters from a Prince*, p.158.
80   Ziegler: *King Edward VIII: The Official Biography*, p.80.
81   *The Times* 20/1/19.
82   Ibid.
83   *Eastern Morning News* 20/1/19.
84   RA QM/PRIV/CC45/563.

"I am sure little Olav has taken it very much to heart." He has had a letter from Maud that describes how crestfallen their boy is at the loss of his cousin. "He does not say much but he grieves and ponders over it all by himself for a long time and his last letter to me he just told me how pleased he was to have seen Johnnie again."[85] Lady Eva Dugdale, one of Queen Mary's companions is stricken too, but she feels that his parents could not have done more for him. "It must be such a comfort to you to feel you had done all you could to make his life bright and happy, and I am so glad to have seen his little home and one feels it must have been such a joy and interest to him."[86]

Universally, the extended Royal Family find that their stoicism is aided, just a little, by the notion that his suffering is at an end. "One likes to feel he was taken from it really at the right moment," writes Eva Dugdale, "before he could realise there was any difference in his life to that of others, or feel any disappointment, hard as it seems now to lose him."[87] "Of course the poor boy has been in such bad health for so long," the Duke of Connaught says, "and was likely never to get better, that it is perhaps a mercy for him to have passed away quietly and to be saved from a sad life… But it is hard for you to lose one of your sons and he was such a fine boy."[88] Queen Mary puts her grief into her own words a fortnight later.

> For him it is a great release, as his malady was becoming worse as he grew older and he has thus been spared much suffering. I cannot say how grateful we feel to God for having taken him in such a peaceful way, he just slept quietly into his heavenly house, no pain, no struggle, just peace for the poor little troubled spirit which had been a great anxiety to us for many years, ever since he was four years old. The first break in the family circle is hard to bear.[89]

On 21st January, Prince John is laid to rest at Sandringham. The Prince's little rough-haired terrier Spot is bereft, estate carpenters act as pall bearers, carrying his oak coffin to the church in a downpour. It is very much a family service, and for the King and Queen the estate is family. Her Majesty tells Bertie that St. Mary's was "crammed with our own people, who love poor little Johnnie, who was so kind hearted, and polite to them all."[90] "It must have been very trying for you," Bertie writes to his mother, "but at the same time a great relief to know that all those present had known him all his life and had the same feelings as you."[91] The service is simple, but emotionally charged, the congregation visibly effected by their loss. They sing two of Johnnie's favourite hymns, and his father has chosen *Peace, Perfect Peace*.

Afterwards the Prince is carried outside, where grey skies are threatening, to under the east window of the church. The graveside is swathed in flowers. The King and Queen have chosen a cross of pale red carnations, lilies and violets. '*For our darling little Johnnie, from his sorrowing parents,*' Queen Mary has written on the card. Queen Alexandra has left him orchids, lilies and chrysanthemums with a note for her '*precious grandson, whose memory will never fade… We shall ever miss him sorely here on earth.* There is a token marked from the Prince's *devoted brothers and sister*' and more gifts from the servants at York Cottage, those at the big house and from local schoolchildren. The King and Queen stand close to the open grave, lined with moss, evergreens and flowers; with Harry and George immediately behind them and a devastated Princess Mary at their

85   RA QM/PRIV/CC45/564.
86   RA QM/PRIV/CC47/619.
87   Ibid.
88   RA QM/PRIV/CC45/562.
89   RA QM/PRIV/CC44/16.
90   RA GV/PRIV/RF/II/306.
91   RA GV/PRIV/CC11/5.

side. "It was an awfully trying moment when the coffin was lowered, and we were terribly upset," Queen Mary tells Bertie.[92] At the conclusion of proceedings Their Majesties and Queen Alexandra drop flowers onto the coffin.

"We are inundated with wonderfully kind letters of sympathy from all classes,"[93] writes Her Majesty, and the King and Queen spend a sad afternoon answering them. Later they meet with Johnnie's servants from Wood Farm and thank them all for their good and faithful care of their son. The King and Queen don't quite know what to do with themselves. In the days that follow they return to their son's grave to look at the flowers. Queen Mary has taken some to press, along with a lock of her son's hair. They with Lalla and Mr May at Wood Farm and just spend time in the rooms there with Johnnie's things, and in the garden that he so loved. "Miss the dear child there very much indeed,"[94] the Queen writes in her diary. Both she and Queen Alexandra find something comforting in the fact that their two boys, their two Johns, "should be lying close together in our own little churchyard. I thank God my poor little boy is at rest,"[95] Queen Mary adds. "We have been over twice to Wood Farm," she tells Bertie, who is most upset at having missed the funeral, on 24th.

> The little house looks so desolate without the occupant, and all his things, his garden etc. bring him so vividly to one's mind. The servants are so touching too in their grief. Harry came for two nights, was much upset of course, Both he and now Georgie have returned to their respective colleges so the cottage feels very empty and is <u>very</u> silent.

She has at least managed to get the King out of the house, for he had put down his gun on news of his son's death and remained inside, which is completely unheard of. "I am thankful to say Papa resumed shooting… It is so good for him and gets him out."[96] There is nothing more to do but clear away her son's things. "This week I had to help Lalla to pack up Johnnie's little belongings at Wood Farm," she tells Bertie. "Rather a sad affair. I have put a clock of his aside for you." The last task is to take care of her son's little household. Nobody is to lose their place. "Wood Farm will probably be let, Mr May will be pensioned and the servants dispersed, and Lalla will, I hope, come and live with us at Buckingham Palace for the present."[97]

"Moments in History"

And so the business of victory is cruelly marred for His Majesty. On his return to London he takes up work again, whilst in the background complicated peace deliberations take place at Versailles. The King's input is minimal. In November he had attempted to advise Lloyd George on who to take to the Peace Conference with him. "You served for many years in Mr Asquith's Government and know his worth as a lawyer, a statesman and a man of clear, dispassionate judgement, and the fact of his having been Prime Minister at the outbreak of the war invests him with an especial authority valuable to you in council, and I feel that your selection of him as a member of the conference would be applauded both at home, in the Dominions and abroad." He asked at the time, that Lloyd George "postpone any definite decision in the matter until we have had the opportunity

92   RA GV/PRIV/RF/II/306.
93   Ibid.
94   RA PRIV/QMD/1919 (22/1).
95   RA PS/PSO/GV/C/O/2548/33.
96   RA GV/PRIV/RF/II/306.
97   RA GV/PRIV/RF/II/307.

of talking it over together."[98] Ultimately there is no room for Asquith, but negotiations begin in January 1919. The King receives a verbal daily report on proceedings, augmented by the odd letter from the Prime Minister that contains general observations and details of particular debates. Marrying the interests of a large number of nations with the guarantee that fighting would not again break out is an intricate task, and it is not until the early summer that it is finally achieved. Shortly after half past four on Saturday 28th June 1919, word arrives at Buckingham Palace that the Treaty of Versailles had been signed. The Home Office put together a statement swiftly for His Majesty: "The signing of the treaty of peace will be received with deep thankfulness throughout the British Empire. This formal act brings to its concluding stages the terrible war which has devastated Europe... It manifests the victory of the ideals of freedom and liberty for which we have made untold sacrifices. I share my peoples' joy and thanksgiving, and earnestly prey that the coming years of peace may bring to them every increasing happiness and prosperity."[99]

From early in the afternoon the space around the Victoria Memorial has been busy, ostensibly to witness a procession publicising the victory loan down in Trafalgar Square; which, it was said, was going to include "tiny folk dressed as miniature angels of peace." But, this done, "with that sure instinct that the true Londoner displays when something momentous is to be anticipated," the crowds have begun to move down The Mall to the palace. Soon there is no space to be had. Everyone knows why they are gathering, but not really what is about to occur.

> It was a strangely quiet assemblage... tense expectation, a strained eagerness to hear the first boom of the guns. Somewhere in the distance there was the noise of the bursting of a tyre, at which everyone jumped to momentary attention. But half-past five passed and still there was silence. No one, however, showed the slightest inclination to go away. These were moments in history and everyone wished to see what manifestations they held.[100]

Not a few had been present in August 1914.

"A few minutes after six the roar of the first gun crashed out sharp and reverberant. The effect was electrifying. A mighty cheer went up, with, as it seemed, the lifting of the whole load that has been borne for well-nigh five years."[101] By the time the third round has been fired, His Majesty has emerged. "May and I and the children went out on the centre balcony and there was a great demonstration of loyalty."[102] A cheer rolls back down The Mall like a wave, and soon the noise of the crowd emerges coherently as the National Anthem, sung with gusto. The King and his family remain for nearly an hour.

After dinner official word arrives from Lloyd George in Paris, brought by aeroplane no less. "Mr Lloyd George with his humble duty to Your Majesty has the honour to announce that the long and terrible war in which the British Empire has been engaged with the German Empire for more than four years and which has caused much suffering to mankind has been brought to an end this afternoon by the Treaty of Peace just signed in the hall."[103] Outside the crowd has swelled. At 9:00pm cheers are being raised again and again, '*We want King George*'. The King returns dressed in uniform; the Queen beside him in cerise with a gold wrap. Once again they are joined by their

98   *Daily Telegraph* 30/6.
99   *Daily Telegraph* 30/6/19.
100   Ibid.
101   Ibid.
102   RA GV/PRIV/GVD/1919 (28/6).
103   RA PS/PSO/GV/C/Q/1556/1.

children. David wears a Guards uniform, Bertie that of the RAF. The King puts a high estimate on the number of people now celebrating outside his windows, "probably 100,000."[104]

London's searchlights play across the darkening sky. "Their Majesties repeatedly acknowledged the salutations of the crowd, the band meantime playing marching tunes and a number of lively national airs." The masses want another speech, and this time the Royal Family are prepared. Those at the Victoria Memorial claim that they hear the Kings words: "The Queen and I thank you most sincerely for this demonstration of loyalty to us. We are deeply touched by it, and we thank you for your kindness from our hearts." There are then demands for a speech from David. He moves to the front of the balcony and says: "I join with the King and Queen in thanking you for your magnificent reception tonight. I am very proud to have served with so many of you who are here." The band leaves, but the crowd shows no inclination to go home. The searchlights are still pointed at the palace. "The upper portions were brilliantly illuminated and for a few moments the Royal Family was held by the concentration of light from various directions."[105] The crowd are singing *For He's a Jolly Good Fellow* as the King steps forwards, salutes and bids them goodnight. Inside he sits down to write his diary entry for the day. He notes that it is five years to the day since the Arch Duke and his wife were assassinated in Sarajevo. "Today is a great one in history and please God, this dear old country will now settle down and work in unity."[106]

The Government decides to have one, nationwide celebration to conclude Britain's achievement. The whole country will celebrate victory and have the opportunity to acknowledge those who led, those who fought and those who worked to make it happen. Saturday 19th July is to be 'Peace Day.'

The authorities have had to turn Kensington Gardens into a military encampment. As well as the huge British contingent, representing multiple parts of the services and even including two guns and four tanks, there are troops from Belgium, France, Italy, America, China, Greece, Japan, Poland, Portugal, Romania, Serbia, Siam and Slovakia. The camp warrants its own hospital, with more beds set by at local hospitals in case they were needed, and its own post office to collect mail, sell stamps and issue or cash postal orders. Security and discipline are maintained by a special detachment of military police. The only prolific absentees are the Russians, for Britain is at war with Soviet Russia and the Indians, who devastatingly have had to be quarantined at Hampton Court after an outbreak of influenza.

"The morning was fine and warm, but overcast and not too hot,"[107] the King writes in his diary. The extended Royal Family have all gathered at Buckingham Palace. At noon they take their places outside. His Majesty leads them out in the uniform of a Field Marshal to a green and gold pavilion, decked with a royal cipher has been erected below the Victoria Memorial by the Office of Works. Here they stand in front of the Prime Minister, who is surrounded by politicians and statesmen. The crowd outside Buckingham Palace is immense, many having camped the night in Green Park. "The fervour was intense, and the whole scene, enhanced by a sudden burst of sunshine, was brilliant. Gold and purple drapery and flags of the Allies decorated the facade of Buckingham Palace."[108] A colonnade of trellis pillars is festooned with laurel, and fifty foot masts are surmounted by gilded crowns and bear 30 foot streamers. Lines of men, 800 of them standing or seated in blue uniforms, wounded and disabled are given pride of place in the picturesque crescent gardens. There are also reserved places for the Silver War Badge men, widows and grieving

104   RA GV/PRIV/GVD/1919 (28/6).
105   *Daily Telegraph* 30/6/19.
106   RA GV/PRIV/GVD/1919 (28/6).
107   RA GV/PRIV/GVD/1919 (19/7).
108   *Daily Telegraph* 21/7/19.

mothers. Cinematographers are poised at the Cenotaph, the royal pavilion and at a point on Hyde Park Corner where they might capture troops emerging through the Wellington Arch. "If the Kaiser had won," says an American officer, he would have had captured flags carried down the Unter den Linden as the captives of his bow and spear, "and my! What a day he would have had."[109] But that is not very British at all, and London will do things her own way. She may have had many a moment of spontaneous joy and celebration since the armistice was declared, but the time has finally come for Britain's ceremonial triumph.

The Victory March of the Allies takes more than two hours to pass the palace façade and the King is stunned. "It was one of the most impressive sights I ever saw, and so well arranged."[110] Each unit is led past by a man with a placard naming it. First come the Americans, with General Pershing riding at their head; bands playing *Over There*. Pershing salutes the King and then dismounts for the leading representative of the group is to join His Majesty so that he might too take the salute of his men, and then remain in the royal pavilion to observe the rest of the parade. "With a quicker step came the Belgians, the sharp rhythm of their music stimulating enthusiasm. Chinese officers and Czechoslovaks were disappearing when a wonderful volume of sound surged down The Mall."[111] Foch is leading the French contingent towards the palace to the sound of French trumpeters. The King shakes him warmly by the hand, and the grave expression on the old man's face is replaced by a broad smile as he joins His Majesty and engages in animated conversation with Queen Mary and Queen Alexandra. Having greeted the Prince of Wales and Lloyd George, he stands to the right of the King and returns the salute of his men, smartly wearing their steel helmets and many of them with miniature Union Jacks tied to their bayonets.

Then come Italy, Japan, and Serbia, who receive special recognition. "Suddenly the Guards band changed their melody to *A life on the Ocean Wave*. The music gave fresh inspiration. "The crowd was in an ecstasy of delight."[112] The Royal Navy contingent, nearly 5,000 of them, are passing beneath the gaze of Nelson in Trafalgar Square and entering The Mall through Admiralty Arch. All eyes are on them, and the King watches proudly as his friend, Admiral Beatty, and his fellow officers approach on foot. The crowd cheers loudly as he joins his Majesty to watch a formidable procession of sailors pass by. Minesweepers, with their special flag, gain an extra loud cheer, as do the Wrens and the Mercantile Marine representatives, many of them in civvies, who cheer the King and wave their hats on their way past.

There is a brief pause, and the wounded and maimed begin to get restless, many of them are wheeled closer to the pavilion. "Disabilities were forgotten in the excitement of the moment that they prepared to greet their regiments," to look for their friends as the army contingent is led down The Mall by their Commander in Chief. Camera operators and photographers have rushed forward too. Haig's reception is deafening, and he joins His Majesty as the Household Cavalry begin to pass, followed by the Guards. Regiments march proudly past, one by one to a raucous ovation from the crowd. The Royal Army Medical Corps brings up the rear, before it is the turn of all of the female army contingents. Last but not least, Britain's new service, the Royal Air Force receives the salute of the King. "The march was 7.5 miles long," writes His Majesty, "there were enormous crowds in the street and their enthusiasm was marvellous... About 20,000 took part in the procession."[113] With the parade at an end, the Royal Family adjourn to give a luncheon in the State Dining Room,

109   *Morning Post* 21/7/19.
110   RA GV/PRIV/GVD/1919 (19/7).
111   *Daily Telegraph* 21/7/19.
112   Ibid.
113   RA GV/PRIV/GVD/1918 (21/7).

elegantly decorated with red carnations and roses, for all of the leading Generals and Admirals congregated for the occasion, almost 50 people sitting down to eat.

In the meantime the vast crowd outside has been entertained. There are parties for children through the royal parks, country dancing and performances of fairy scenes from a Midsummer Night's Dream. Whole families have turned out; parents, grandparents, children. "Proud, indeed was that family party that could bring its very own sailor or soldier with it into Hyde Park on Saturday… and if that man wore the rainbow ribbon… or the new general service ribbon, the domestic pride was complete." Late in the afternoon the King, Queen, Princess Mary and Prince George enter the park at Apsley Gate to a tremendous ovation. "Had they not toiled and suffered with their people? So it is only right that they should celebrate with them too? It was a happy inspiration on the part of Their Majesties to come and join in the popular rejoicings in this way." The King is much amused watching the boisterous, spontaneous celebrations. The happiness on his face is apparent. Children are climbing rails, refreshment tents are "packed beyond hope of entrance," people share their picnics with others. There are little girls in fancy dress costumes fashioned out of the flags of the Allies, little boys stripping down to bathing pants and leaping into the Serpentine. After the Royal Family have left again, it begins to rain. Britons do not give in to rain, and few leave. "Light summer frocks might be ruined, hats of gauze reduced to pulp, but there would never be another day like this so what did it matter?"[114]

An estimated 200,000 brave the weather to watch a patriotic open air concert in Hyde Park, that features a choir of 10,000, "the Imperial Choir of Peace and Thanksgiving." The conductor "looked like a ragged beaver, the rain trickling down his neck," by the end of the performance, but there is a huge ovation for *Rule Britannia* as the concert comes to a close. Thousands know that they will not find a way home until the morning, and they don't care. And the policemen on duty are largely redundant. "The crowd was trusted to behave itself and it did. Perhaps the drizzle had something to do with it. It is difficult to give reign to one's wildest impulses while the water is squelching in one's boots."[115] Bowing to the demands of the crowd, His Majesty has twice been out on the balcony with his family. But in Hyde Park, "the great bulk of the people waited patiently for nearly three hours, with the water collecting in puddles at their feet." For few want to depart before the evening's showpiece, a decadent and imaginative firework display in the park by Messrs. C.T. Brock and Co. And it is worth it, for it is widely held to be the most impressive entertainment that the company has ever produced.

The King takes to the roof of his palace to watch with the rest of the Royal Family and for an hour long past their bedtimes, children scream with delight down below. His Majesty is as mesmerised as everyone else. The show begins with *Victory, Thanks to the Boys* spelled out in fireworks, then come batteries of gold comets, shooting stars, garlands of roses and forget me nots and swarms of silver fireflies. This is elementary work, for it is followed by two colossal fire portraits of the King and Queen rendered on the night sky. There are blazing revolving suns, iridescent peacock flumes, jewel headed cobras, a great flight of 100 celebration rockets. Then come more fire portraits: Beatty, Haig, Foch, followed by an aerial Field of the Cloth of Gold, an interpretation of Niagara Falls by moonlight, and a token of silver fire falling from a height in silence with blinding brilliance. There are whirling snakes, special shells which burst with a terrific bang, the bursting of them lighting up half a million faces. Comets, showers, sprays, a giant opalescent bubble, a terrace of golden fountains, roman candles, hissing scorpions, aerial golden wheatsheafs, and a "fairyland glimpse producing a magical moonlight illumination." Finally comes the word *Peace* spelled out across the

114   *Daily Telegraph* 21/7/19.
115   Ibid.

skies over London, followed by *God Save the King*, sprayed out in a "barrage of dazzling flashes."[116] Weary, wet, the crowds are singing *The End of a Perfect Day* as they stream out of Hyde Park in search of a way home, or a place to lay their heads.

On 11th January 1920, the King receives a telegram from his Prime Minister in Paris. "Mr Lloyd George with his humble duty to Your Majesty has the honour to say that the final exchange of the ratifications of peace between the allies and Germany took place this afternoon at the Quai d'Orsay, and that after five and a half years a state of peace now exists once more."[117] The King is less than convinced that this is an end to European conflict. "So after five years and five months," he writes, "we are once more at peace with Germany, but for some time our relations with her will be very different to what they used to be."[118] He is not wrong, and for His Majesty in the aftermath of the Armistice and the signing of the Treaty of Versailles, it feels that he many never be free of the war and all of the trouble that it has caused.

Rehabilitation

"Living on a Volcano"

Still in mourning for their son, the King and Queen return to London in February 1919 conscious of the fact that Britons need to move on with their lives. A Royal Wedding occurs at the end of February when the Duke of Connaught's popular daughter Patsy, having once been linked with kings across the continent, marries a naval officer and relinquishes her royal titles. London is enthused, and though Their Majesties do not attend the subsequent celebrations on account of their mourning for Prince John, they give a party for 1,000 guests at St. James's Palace. The state apartments are reopened to the public at Windsor, and at the beginning of the year the King returns to civilian work, patronising the arts and visiting a foundry in Whitechapel to watch new bells being cast for Westminster Abbey. The Trooping of the Colour takes place for the first time in six years, though it has to be moved to Hyde Park because of the temporary offices still on Horse Guards Parade. The Prince of Wales turns 25 in 1919 and there is much work to be done to settle him properly into his royal role; deciding on all of the different institutions he is to become patron or president of. He moves out of Buckingham Palace and into his own home at St. James's, and in the summer he will depart for Canada to carry out his own tour of the Dominion.

But Britain, and in turn the Royal Family, also has time to try and enjoy itself again. for His Majesty, this means racing. The day after the King's 55th birthday he boards a special and heads south of London for the Derby at Epsom. Five years after the race had last been run, the press declare that is like "the renewal of an old friendship. Everything was familiar."[119] There is much satisfaction, for "the size of the gathering... furnished evidence that the heart of this country after five years of over-pressure... is beginning to beat once more rhythmically and regularly."[120]

A fortnight later it is Ascot's turn to take centre stage. "Whatever else we have learnt or forgotten in the last five years, we still know our way to Ascot." Since the beginning of the year the course has been restored, having been used as an RAF encampment for more than a thousand men; strewn with sheds for lorries and bits of aeroplane. The grandstand had been a hospital equipped with 80

116   RA MRH/MISC/048/1.
117   RA PS/PSO/GV/C/Q/1556/3.
118   RA GV/PRIV/GVD/1919 (11/1).
119   *Morning Post* 4/6/19.
120   *Daily Telegraph* 5/6/19.

beds. There is something timeless about Ascot, "the royal procession, the scarlet coated out-riders, the old world carriages, the teams of four horses and their bewigged postillions."[121] "Everyone wore a high hat like old days,"[122] remarks the King afterwards.

In 1919, the Royal Family returns to Balmoral, and the trip is billed by the press as "Their Majesties' first real holiday for five years."[123] The King and Queen, with all of their children bar David, are waved off from Euston Station by a considerable crowd in a train decked with pink carnations. By the time the royal train draws up at a junction just outside Aberdeen, His Majesty wears a kilt of the Royal Stewart hunting tartan. The staff at Balmoral are thrilled to see them, assembling to cheer the motor cars as they arrive. Deeside is crowded, for the King is not the only notable personage to have missed his Highland sojourns. Princess Beatrice is at Mar Lodge with her daughter, The Connaughts are to come north too. Lord and Lady Sandhurst at Abergeldie, Braemar Castle is sublet and there is not a room to be had in hotels or lodgings. "Delighted to be in this dear place again after six years and to see all our nice people,"[124] the King writes in his diary. Unsurprisingly, His Majesty throws himself ecstatically into sport: shooting and deer-stalking; claiming a stag on his first day. His outings are all the more special because Bertie is at his side, keeping "impressive pace with his father."[125]

But though there is time to relax, to resume everything that has had to be set aside for the duration of the war; life, though it goes on, will never be the same again. Britain is restless in 1919, perceived by her people at the time as being under threat from multiple entities within and without.

The Great War has brought about the dawn of a new, confusing world, and the uncertainty of life moving towards the 1920s is something that His Majesty is acutely aware of. Parliament convenes again in mid-February; the gallery full of wounded soldiers. The King's speech is unusually long, and far less formal than his usual endeavour. Britain, he says, must be reborn. From the ruins of the Great War she must revive herself with the same determination that has won the war. "We must stop at no sacrifice of interest or prejudice to stamp out unmerited poverty, to diminish unemployment and mitigate its sufferings to provide decent homes, to improve the nation's health, and to raise the standard of well-being throughout the country."[126]

But the euphoria of victory has worn off, and there is nothing but a long, difficult road ahead. His Majesty's realm is grieving, impoverished and terrified at what the future might bring. As he did during the war, His Majesty sees his role as one of example, that as a constitutional monarch he can stand at the head of the nation and hold up a light for his subjects to follow. Throughout the year he continues to encourage and attempt to cajole his people into action. "With the end of the war a great chapter in the history of our country is closed," he says at the Guildhall on the signing of the Treaty of Versailles. "The new era which is opening before us brings its own tasks, and the same qualities which have carried us to victory will be needed in full measure for the work of reconstruction. The spirit of union, self-sacrifice and patience, which our people displayed during the years of fighting will still be required if we are to reap the benefit of the peace which we have won." And in a speech to London County Council The King declares that "it rests with us to show ourselves worthy of the sacrifice others have made and to build up a new world to replace the shattered fabric of the old."[127] The Press seizes on these speeches as a rallying call for the nation,

121   *Daily Telegraph* 18/6/19.
122   RA GV/PRIV/GVD/1919 (17/6).
123   *Daily Graphic* 18/8/19.
124   RA GV/PRIV/GVD/1919 (19/8).
125   *The Queen* 23/8/19.
126   *Southwestern Echo* 11/2/19.
127   *Daily Telegraph* 31/7/19.

The King's Lead. "Mobilisation for war is far easier than mobilisation for peace," reads an editorial in the *Telegraph*, "because organisation for peace lacks glamour, makes a less contagious appeal to patriotism and must be undertaken amid the confusion of thought and exhaustion of effort which war inevitably produces. And this has been no ordinary war...We are at a crossroads of our destiny, and His Majesty could not have rendered more timely, more kingly service to the subjects he serves."[128]

While the world is trying to emerge from the spectre of the most destructive conflict it has ever seen, agitation and disorder threatens to tear it apart again already, and the Royal Household is alive to the danger. In the midst of the outpouring of joy after the armistice, Stamfordham commented to a friend that the scenes of loyalty to the King were indeed, "both remarkable and gratifying," but that they should not get too carried away. They needed to show all classes that His Majesty is no mere figurehead, but "a living power for good... and ready not only to sympathise... but... to further their solution."[129] Even before the end of the war, there are republican rumblings across British society. "A short act might be run through Parliament in 24 hours," claimed *The Nation*. "The palace in London could be Government House... The Royal Family would be compensated, it would be glad to go on pleasant terms. The change would be popular in all our colonies... The Royal caste of Europe has no friends left in the world." The editor was not so convinced. "Perhaps," he added, "but we think we prefer George V to Lloyd George I."[130]

In the week running up to the armistice a huge event was held at the Royal Albert Hall, technically under the auspices of the National Union of Railwaymen, but in reality a republican rally. From Scotland Yard, Superintendent Quinn sent a sergeant and a constable undercover to observe and provide a report for the palace. The main speaker steered clear of openly threatening the King, but it ran pretty close to the mark. The attendees cheered the Bolsheviks, celebrated revolutions in other countries and sang *The Red Flag*. The speakers were inflammatory to say the least. One said that "a wave was sweeping over Europe and crowns and titles were falling like dead leaves." The crowd cheered. "I say God Speed the revolution. (Hear. hear) God speed the day when there will be a notice 'to let' outside Buckingham Palace... The radical politician, George Lansbury, sealed proceedings by declaring: "We have heard plenty of frankly displayed revolutionary sentiments tonight. I wish to goodness you would get on with it."[131] Stamfordham is of the opinion that it is useless to try and suppress such action, and that the perpetrators would just be allowed to vent until they ran out of steam. "There seems to have been some pretty hot stuff let loose... Let's hope it was all gas."[132] But the King is not so able to shrug off such things. They fester in his mind, and at the same time, the Prime Minister has decided that he wants a General Election.

On 2nd December 1918 Lloyd George wrote to Bonar Law. "The more I think of it, the more convinced I become that there ought to be a General Election, and that the sooner it can be arranged, subject to the exigencies of the military position, the better." Notwithstanding, of course, that such an election was likely to keep him in power, or that the resumption of party politics might spell the end of his spell as Prime Minister, he writes that he thinks "it would be right that it should be a coalition election that is to say, that the country should be definitely invited to return candidates who undertake to support the present Government not only to prosecute the war to

128   Ibid., 30/7/19.
129   RA PS/PSO/GV/C/O/1106/65.
130   *The Nation* 26/10/1918.
131   RA PS/PSO/GV/C/O/1220/30.
132   RA PS/PSO/GV/C/O/1220/31.

its final end and negotiate the peace, but to deal with the problems of reconstruction which must immediately arise directly an armistice is signed."[133]

It is a move that mirrors that made by the Government in the Khaki Election of 1900. The Prime Minister's desire for such a swift election is no secret. At the end of September the idea had already been criticised in the mainstream press. It would require Lloyd George asking the King to dissolve the current Parliament, for which there appeared to be little good reason. "It certainly cannot be based on the customary ground of inability to govern with the present parliament, for Mr Lloyd George enjoys a House of Commons which is submissive to the verge of obsequiousness." Clearly, they said what he wanted was "unfettered play for his policy for a further period of five years." There are admittedly plausible arguments for such an election, "we do not deny, but the objections gravely outweigh them, and it is to the King alone that we can look to balance the reasons for and against it and to decide as the permanent interests of the country dictate."[134]

His Majesty thinks that a General Election at this juncture is a criminally irresponsible idea. On 5th November, Lloyd George arrives at the palace and asks for a dissolution, in the knowledge that the King would be against such a suggestion, so that he might get a General Election before Christmas. "We discussed the question from all sides and at last I agreed to his proposal, being against it before,"[135] the King wrote in his diary. What he neglected to record was that he only backed down after exercising his right to try and advise his minister to the absolute limit in the form of a savage row with Lloyd George. Whilst it is extremely unlikely that Britain's sovereign would ever dissolve Parliament against the will of his Prime Minister, this is a different story. Lloyd George is essentially asking for a new Parliament in the interests of party and personal consideration, which the King, as a neutral should not be moved by. His concern should be the needs of the nation, and the evidence that this dissolution benefits his realm as a whole is scant.

The King lists every reason he can think of against a General Election at the exact instant that Europe is downing weapons. Lloyd George, he argues, does not need a new Government. He already has the support of the House of Commons with regard to restoring peace, and the leader of the Opposition, Asquith, has pledged that his party will continue to support the Government. There is also, His Majesty points out, considerable risk in how soldiers might vote, and indeed the women who were now enfranchised. In fact, the King has been told that a large percentage of servicemen would not be able to vote because logistically, there would not be enough time to disperse their voting papers, which was certainly not a fair way of doing things. His Majesty reminds Lloyd George that whilst he may be all but guaranteed a sweeping victory on the coat tails of victory, he is risking his own long term political future. There is precedent. In the Khaki Election that the Prime Minister is trying to mirror from the turn of the century, yes, the sitting Government had enjoyed a huge victory, but it wasn't a properly reflective vote, "and ended in ruining them and keeping them out of office ever since." The population would also be asked to vote in the midst of winter, when coal and food were lacking and their subsequent reaction unpredictable. It is a gamble. Why risk the country kicking the Government out of office at such a critical time and leaving the country in disarray? The Prime Minister is not deaf to such protestations, but they do not dissuade him. "He seemed inclined to discount the danger of disfranchising the soldiers, and thought the women were more likely to vote 'sanely' now than after on when there might be discontent." Unconvinced, the King bitterly gives his assent and agreed to dissolve Parliament.[136] Lloyd George wavers in his resolve. On 25th November he notes in his diary that the Prime Minister has paid a visit to the

133   RA PS/PSO/GV/C/K/1348/2.
134   *The Globe* 29/8/18.
135   RA GV/PRIV/GVD/1919 (5/11).
136   RA PS/PSO/GV/C/K/1348/11.

palace. "I think he is rather nervous about the election and that the high percentage of soldiers votes will not be realised. He was getting ready to put the fault on the military for not making the necessary arrangements.[137] Lloyd George proves prepared to risk long term disaster to seize upon the enthusiasm for his Government in the midst of victory and gets the desired result, with 526 out of 707 seats won in the Commons. Asquith's Independent Liberals are trounced, with the former Prime Minister, much to His Majesty's regret, losing his own seat in Parliament after more than 30 years. The King's warning about Lloyd George's political future, however, proved to be prophetic, for he would be turned out of 10 Downing Street in 1922, never to return.

Throughout 1919 Britain is rife with industrial unrest. "The working classes are loyal... but their nerves are all on edge," says one peer to the palace. "The losses by death, the anxiety, the strain. They are in such a state that anything might happen."[138] The country is viewed as a bonfire ready to ignite. At the beginning of the year the King's eye rests warily on the Clyde and on South Wales; a worst case scenario running through his mind. "The People grow discontented and agitators seize their opportunities; marches are organised, the police interfere; resistance ensues; troops are called out and riot begets revolt and possibly revolution."[139] Throughout February and March His Majesty meets with numerous labour and union men, and they "had all come away impressed with the desire for improved social and industrial conditions, and his anxiety to learn the truth first hand."[140] But whilst the King's genuine interest and concern in the plight of labour is commendable, it alone cannot bring an end to disorder. In the course of the year, some two and a half million workers are involved in strike action, a figure that surpasses even Germany, who have lost the war. On railways, at docks, amongst other transport workers there are strikes. There is even a strike of bakers nationwide. And disorder descends into violence. There are race riots in the Northwest and at Cardiff. At the latter gangs of out of work, white ex-servicemen clash with black workers and sailors. Lynch mobs take to the streets and terrorise black communities in a week of violence that cost three lives and injures dozens more. Strikes persisted throughout the early 1920s, culminating in the General Strike of 1926. "Strikes and threats of strikes all over England are not pleasant," the Queen writes to Bertie at the beginning of 1919. "One feels one is living on a volcano."[141]

Nationalism causes His Majesty no end of anxiety too. As of January, Irish entities wage a War of Independence against Britain, having formed a breakaway government. The 1919 Government of India Act did little to calm nationalist sentiment there; Egypt and the Sudan were embroiled in revolution against British occupation throughout the year, and there is even rioting in Malta. But the spectre that terrifies the King more than anything is the red shadow of Bolshevism, or communism. In His Majesty's mind, the two were largely the same thing. By no means was every revolt or violent spree in Europe in 1919 caused by Bolshevism, but what the King observes, with his people, is a demonstration that in order to be reborn, a defeated nation first wants to violently cleanse itself of those who caused its ruin in the first place. Lenin's dream is a worldwide revolution, Bolshevism spreading to every corner of the globe. In the aftermath of the armistice, there are high hopes that this will happen in Germany, whilst Vienna has been engulfed in violence. A March intelligence report by the Foreign Office pointed to Hungary as the "storm centre" of Bolshevism, but also stated that "an even graver danger to the world would be a Bolshevik wave over the Far East,"

137   RA GV/PRIV/GVD/1918 (25/11).
138   RA PS/PSO/GV/C/O/1106/64.
139   Gerwath: *The Vanquished: Why the First World War Failed to End 1917-1923*, pp.229-231.
140   *Morning Post* 19/3/1919.
141   RA GV/PRIV/RF/II/306.

and India.[142] It is likened to the spread of a disease, and if it wasn't the harbinger of enough unease, a habit has also sprung up of blaming Jews for the spread of Bolshevism beyond Russia, resulting in violent anti-Semitism. It is not just defeated nations at risk of this contagion either. European representatives are allegedly provoking unrest amongst Mexican workers, and neutral Spain comes close to civil war. There is even a perceived threat of Bolshevism in Canada, orchestrated by a man with a sinister record as the leader of an anarchist wing of Russian Bolshevists in New York.

The world viewed Bolshevism with fear, augmented by the horrific tales told by those fleeing it. Stories of atrocities know no bounds: industrial guillotines, women of higher classes being nationalised for rape by any worker that chose to carry it out, Chinese torture experts hired to carry out gruesome interrogations, prisoners of the Chekas with their heads rammed into cages of hungry rats until they talk.[143] The murder of the Tsar has done nothing to subdue such talk. At the end of 1918 Churchill said at Dundee, that the Hun had been replaced by a new enemy. "Bolsheviks, he says "hop and caper like troops of ferocious baboons amid the ruins of cities and the corpses of their victims." And now Lloyd George has written a memorandum that says: "The greatest danger that I see in the present situation is that Germany may throw in her lot with Bolshevism and place her resources, her brains, her vast organising power at the disposal of the revolutionary fanatics who dream it is to conquer the world for Bolshevism by force of arms."[144]

"If Bolshevism really threatens to become the most deadly enemy of European civilisation," writes the Political Intelligence Department at the Foreign Office at the end of 1918. "Not only is it an urgent task... [that] Bolsheviks in Russia should be overthrown, but that its dangerous influence in other countries should be extirpated not by theoretical arguments but by shedding full light upon the disastrous results of such a policy of tyranny and violence."[145] And Britain is actively opposing Bolshevik rule in Russia, where the chaos following the revolution in October 1918 which put Lenin in power further complicates a complete tangle of violence and crossed purposes. By the end of 1919, the Allies will have sent nearly 200,000 men to the likes of Murmansk, Archangel, Vladivostock and Odessa to provide logistical and fighting support to anti-Bolsheviks, known as the "Whites" against the "Red" forces of Lenin and his Communist Party.

The King is fully exposed to the continuing bloodshed affecting his relatives in Russia. It is little wonder that he is terrified of Bolshevism gaining traction in his own realm. In March 1919 a report arrives at Buckingham palace claiming that there are in Berlin, 26 million roubles in gold, pre-revolutionary Russian coinage, which is to be used for propaganda in England. It is also claimed that at a recent meeting it has been resolved that all efforts at spreading the Bolshevik revolution "must be concentrated on England which they regard as the only safe country and backbone of the present system of civilisation."[146] If they can bring Britain to her knees, it seems that they believe that anything is possible. The King is told of a journalist caught trying to bring a letter into the country from Lenin to the British people. He is "more or less" detained on a warship,"[147] but whilst the authorities can remove any such propaganda, he is British and so there is nothing that they can do to stop him entering the country. His Majesty is horrified at such tales, and asks for reassurance that the Government is doing all in its power to prevent dangerous propaganda being brought into the country.

142   TNA: CAB 24/68/6.
143   Gerwath: *The Vanquished: Why the First World War Failed to End 1917-1923*, p.97.
144   Ibid., p.156.
145   TNA: CAB 24/68/6.
146   RA PS/PSO/GV/C/Q/1552/8.
147   RA PS/PSO/GV/C/O/1220/47.

A Limerick Soviet is established in Ireland in April 1919, but it is motivated more by republicanism than any Bolshevik sensibilities. The British Army put it down inside a fortnight. The founding of the British Communist Party in 1920 does nothing to allay the King's fears, formed as it is to help facilitate the spread of communism around the world. Buckingham Palace will keep a close eye on it with the aid of the Metropolitan Police and less likely spies, the most vocal of whom would be Sir Henry Thornton, a friend to Their Majesties' who manages the Great Eastern Railway. One of his staff, nicknamed the 'Bolshevik railwayman," a former communist and union man, turns informant and furnishes a number of detailed reports on this new party. The threat of Bolshevism is less severe in Britain and in France than in the rest of Europe, but at the time, the King characterises what is a very real fear, a national obsession even, with the spread of Bolshevism to British shores and the threat that such contagion would entail.

"Crash of Thrones"

It is unsurprising that in this political climate, to be a head of state or a recognisable politician is not necessarily a healthy occupation. Sidónio Pais, the President of Portugal is a divisive figure. An attempt was made on his life on 5th December 1918 and the King sent him a telegram exuding his "warmest congratulations"[148] on having been preserved from such an end. Just nine days later, however, Pais was on his way to catch a train to Porto when just before midnight, though surrounded by extra security personnel, he died after being shot twice by an assassin. Then in Paris, Clemenceau, the French Prime Minister is on his way to a meeting with Balfour and Colonel House during the Peace Conference in February 1919 when he is shot in the back by a would be assassin. "I am shocked to hear of the dastardly attack made upon you this morning," the King says. He is worried, for Clemenceau is nearly 80. "I earnestly trust that the injuries received are not serious, and that, thanks to your splendid energy and courage, you may soon be restored in health, to continue your great and lauded efforts for France and the Allies."[149]

But it is another thing altogether to be a Sovereign in these troubled times. Asquith had referred to a crash of thrones. "In the days that are to come after the war," said *The Times* as far back as 1916, "when the dreadful reckoning will be presented to the people of Europe, it is possible that more than one throne may be shaken to the ground."[150] As a victor, and in this royal respect, a survivor, it is not surprising that other monarchs reach out to Britain's Sovereign to try and steady themselves against a wave of unrest and possible revolution. In the wake of the armistice, Holland is facing a bout of republicanism and Queen Wilhelmina contacts His Majesty whilst he is visiting his troops at the front immediately after the armistice. "If Your Majesty would have the kindness to come and see me before going back to England," reads her telegram, "it would give me great pleasure to welcome you here."[151] The King is categorically not impressed with this "extraordinary proposal."[152] "I have sent a civil refusal," he tells Queen Mary. Not three weeks before Queen Wilhelmina had provided Wilhelm with asylum, not to mention there is the danger of the political state of affairs in her country, "which was on the verge of a revolution only last week and is hardly out of the woods yet." His Majesty has no intention at all of carrying out such an engagement. "I am not going to be used to bolster up monarchies which are sham, that is not my metier."[153] The

148 *The Times* 11/12/18.
149 *Daily Telegraph* 20/2/19.
150 *Sunday Times* 9/4/16.
151 RA PS/PSO/GV/C/M/1049a/1.
152 RA QM/PRIV/CC04/200.
153 RA QM/PRIV/CC04/194.

King has rendered some distant assistance to the deposed Austrian Emperor though, and in May 1919 an intermediary asks him to renew his support. The Vatican have been told that Charles and his relatives are living in "very strained circumstances, owing to confiscation of their properties." His Majesty's representations are requested to try and coerce the Czechoslovak Government into restoring some of them in Bohemia. This, they say, will "complete his work of charity and justice."[154]

For the King, though, the most emotional of his royal attachments is to the Romanovs, for though the Tsar and his immediate family have been murdered there are multiple family members unaccounted for and others that have been tossed into prison. Most importantly for His Majesty, he has his mother to consider. Queen Alexandra is beside herself with worry for her sister, the Dowager Empress Marie, who remains in the country. Lenin was almost assassinated just after Nicholas's murder and it sparked a "Red Terror" in Russia, the scale and brutality of which was astonishing and bloodthirsty. The execution of the Tsar has done the Bolshevik's few favours and for a while the future looks uncertain. Though they have rallied since, the situation remains unfathomable and the longer the civil war goes on the more depraved it becomes.

In the midst of this, Europe's remaining royal houses try to extract or discover the fate of their extended families. Queen Olga of Greece, a granddaughter of Tsar Nicholas I, submits a letter for His Majesty through a British representative in Switzerland. She is trying to secure the release of a number of her brothers from Bolshevik captivity, and in the event of a British naval or military expedition landing at some Russian port, she wants to know if they can render assistance. Some members of the family have fled, but a number of Grand Dukes; cousins and uncles of the Tsar have been imprisoned for some time at the Peter and Paul Fortress in Petrograd. British, Danish and Romanian royal representatives combine to not only share information about their health and living conditions, but also to try and secure their release. The brother of two of them has long been resident in Britain, as is the wife of Grand Duke George, so the King plays a concerned and active role in trying to secure their safety. "We are constantly on the watch for any opportunity of ameliorating their position," the Foreign Office assures the palace, "but... fear that any overt act with that object would make matters worse rather than improve them."[155] The strength of three royal houses is not enough to save them, for the five Romanov Grand Dukes in question are executed outside the fortress by a Bolshevik firing squad on 28th January 1919.

The Tsar's brother and brief successor, Michael, has been executed at Perm in Siberia. At Alapaevsk, more Romanovs were thrown alive into a mineshaft and then shot from above as they writhed in agony. So far as his aunt, the Dowager Empress Marie is concerned, the King spends nearly half a year attempting to extract the Tsar's mother from Russia. For a diminutive, elderly woman, she proves difficult to move. By the end of 1918 she is in the Ukraine, at the southern tip of the Crimea, where a strong nationalist movement stands in opposition to Bolshevism. Along with several surviving Romanovs, including two of her daughters, she is guarded by members of the Russian Volunteer Army. The peninsula is a stronghold of the Whites, and the Crimea is geographically favourable, only accessible by a narrow strip of land; but the Ukraine is by no means a peaceful spot. The Bolsheviks want it, and it is rife with anti-Semitism at the turn of the year too. In February 1919 Cossacks representing the Ukrainian National Republic slaughtered 2,000 Jews in a pogrom at Proskurov; during which people were hacked to pieces with sabres.

Following the fate of the Tsar, his wife and children, His Majesty is in no mood to be passive.

---

154   RA PS/PSO/GV/C/Q/1552/17.
155   RA PS/PSO/GV/C/M/1344A/59.

He wants Aunt Minny removed to safety. In the week following the signing of the armistice the threat of the imminent removal of the German garrison on the peninsula escalates the threat to her safety and the King asks the Royal Navy to go and see the Dowager Empress on his behalf. An official visit is not viable because Britain has not recognised the Crimean Republic, and so ships are despatched there, whence a Commander with a trustworthy Russian counterpart land covertly on a nearby beach in the early hours. They manage to obtain an audience with Marie and find her in good health. "His Majesty the King of England is very anxious as to your safety and that of your family who are with you in the Crimea," reads the letter from the Admiral in command of the Royal Navy in the Mediterranean. "I have therefore been instructed by the British Admiralty to make arrangements if possible to enable you to leave the Crimea secretly and to convey you in the first place to Constantinople in a very fast vessel." The Dowager Empress is assured that she can trust the man bearing this letter, and is pressed to make the trip to Turkey, "where a British battleship is at Your Majesty's disposal, and from where you will be able to communicate directly with the King."[156]

But His Majesty's aunt brushes off the danger to her person, though it is clear that her family do not share her confidence. Her guards believe that she is not safe, but that she is probably not in any immediate danger. She engages both men for some time, and has lots of questions about current affairs, but most importantly, she believes that her son, the Tsar, is still alive and she has no intention of leaving the country. She says she has "reason to hope."[157] They could not remove her by force, and until more ships arrive at Sevastopol, HMS *Shark* is left off the coast of the Crimea, to answer rumours that Britain and French fleets have mutinied and are no force in the region. The covert party return with a letter for Queen Alexandra and a telegram to be sent ahead that simply read: "Hurrah. Delighted at last to wire."[158]

But the King is being continually pressed by his mother, and another attempt is made two weeks later to dislodge Aunt Minny from her stronghold at Alupka. This time the naval men ply her with papers and cigarettes and more messages from England. The King of Italy has now joined His Majesty in trying to remove her to safety, and says that he will place any palace in the country at her disposal if she would only go there. Additionally, she tells the naval representatives that the King of Romania has sent a yacht for her. "She asserted that <u>nothing</u> would induce her to go to Romania in that little ship, but with His Majesty the King of Italy's special offer and a battleship, the question was quite different." But she still believes that she is in no danger. She remarks that the Bolsheviks are cowards. And she has spent the last five years encouraging Russians to be strong and to remain, so how could she now leave? "To this I replied that the present time when things were quiet was the very time to take advantage of the King of Italy's offer, as it could be announced as a visit only, and the departure could be made openly and easily from Yalta Harbour." But still the sticking point is her beloved son. "Her Majesty stated that she would never believe that the Tsar was dead, and therefore did not like the idea of going away." She remains resolutely determined to stay put. Nothing her family can say has convinced her otherwise, and after pleading with her for nearly an hour, Captain Royds is no better than convinced that she might be wavering a little.[159] Not even a plea from Queen Alexandra works. "Though I long to see you awfully," Marie telegraphs for Christmas, "see no real necessity to leave now for the moment. Have written today loving

156   RA PS/PSO/GV/C/M/1344A/48.
157   RA PS/PSO/GV/C/M/1344A/47.
158   RA PS/PSO/GV/C/M/1344A/46.
159   RA PS/PSO/GV/C/M/1344A/55.

Christmas wishes to you all."[160] "No one can fail to admire Her Majesty's courage in remaining where she is,"[161] remarks Stamfordham.

The idea of giving sanctuary to an elderly woman, who was in fact Danish, Tsar's mother or not, is acceptable to the Government because few can see it as a political move; especially when she is the sister of the King's mother. She is harmless, surely. In mid-January Michael's wife and daughter arrive at Malta aboard HMS Agamemnon. They have fled from the Ukraine where they had pleaded for protection in England, where they have made their home before.[162] The Government baulks at the idea of a constant stream of displaced Romanovs arriving in Britain, and the Foreign Office demands to be consulted before any more are put aboard navy ships; pointing out "that the presence of these persons is most embarrassing in the present circumstances."[163] More pointedly, Grand Dukes will not be welcome, for the threat of their political manoeuvring could be harmful to Britain. There is no issue with removing them and helping them away from their current predicaments, but the Government does not want them residing in the country. A tactful conversation has to take place with at least one in Paris. His Majesty despatches Lord Hardinge to speak to the Grand Duke Alexander. "He said that he quite understood and did not seem to be in the least bit perturbed by what I had said, and expressed the hope that the time was not far off when all such objections would be removed, and he would be able to travel freely to England and elsewhere."[164]

As spring 1919 approaches, the Dowager Empress still refuses to move, but in April, the suggestion of a Bolshevik occupation of the Crimea emerges via Paris and the Admiral on hand in the Black Sea is put on notice to remove Marie and her suite. The King has now expressed his huge concern for the safety of the Romanovs remaining in the Crimea. The Admiralty deem the situation critical enough to tell the naval men on the spot "that they should be embarked whatever may be their personal desires and removed to a place of safety as soon as preparations can be made. Their eventual destination will be communicated later."[165]

The King's aunt still has no inclination to move on the 8th, even though the French, whose sphere of influence now includes the Crimea, are preparing to evacuate Odessa. Finally, on 11th April a telegram arrives at the palace from the Commander in Chief in the Mediterranean to say that HMS *Marlborough* is en route to Constantinople, stuffed with a large contingent of Romanovs and their entourage. To a large extent the passengers are practically destitute, lacking both money and clothes, but His Majesty is immensely relieved to have finally removed his aunt from Russia. "I am thankful to know you and yours are safe on board the Marlborough," he wires through to the ship, "but I realise what leaving meant to you and I sympathise with you most heartily. I know Lord Methuen will do everything he can for you at Malta, and I hope later on you will let me know your wishes regarding the future."[166]

The Dowager Empress, her daughter Xenia and her family are to carry on to Malta, from where another ship will take them to England as the guests of the King and Queen. "Much looking forward to seeing you soon," His Majesty telegraphs to Malta, "best love George."[167] *Lord Nelson* will put in at Portsmouth, at his insistence, and the only people allowed to greet the Russian royals will be their relatives. The Press are banned from the railway's jetty, and ditto at Victoria Station.

160   RA PS/PSO/GV/C/M1344A/69.
161   RA PS/PSO/GV/C/M/1344A/72.
162   RA PS/PSO/GV/C/M/1344A/74.
163   RA PS/PSO/GV/C/M/1344A/76.
164   RA PS/PSO/GV/C/M/1344A/79.
165   RA PS/PSO/GV/C/M/1344A/90.
166   RA PS/PSO/GV/C/M/1344A/101.
167   RA PS/PSO/GV/C/M/1344A/114.

It is made clear to newspapers, photographers and all of the relevant authorities that this will be a family affair. The Tsar's diminutive mother steps onto English soil dressed in black with a small bunch of pink carnations at her breast; her sister Alexandra's favourite flowers. She departs straight for Marlborough House to be with her, whilst Xenia and her children settle at Buckingham Palace. The next two days are spent grieving, exchanging information and coming to terms with all that has happened to the family in the last two years.

There is one final, painful task that falls to the King in respect of the fate of the Romanovs. In February 1919 it is reported that some eight tons of personal items belonging to Nicholas, Alexandra and their children are being sent to Vladivostock. "Some of these things are of great national as well as of material value. On the body of the Grand Duchess Elizabeth, for instance… was found the holy picture before which the Emperor prayed when about to abdicate. This is studded with precious stones and is valued at several hundred thousand roubles."[168] It is suggested that the twenty cases are placed aboard HMS *Kent,* which is on hand, and His Majesty approves. They arrived by the end of March and are submitted to the keeping of the senior naval officer present "until further instructions are given as to their disposal."[169]

In October the cases arrive in England, and the King asks Fritz Ponsonby to receive them and store them at the palace. They are brought up to the Throne Room, all gold and red damask, with chandeliers; the throne at the end of the room with canopy above and curtains at the side; dust sheets laid over the carpet and fifteen huge packing-cases corded and sealed." But Ponsonby finds them void of their once valuable contents. "The first one, about four feet high and eight feet long, contained nothing but pokers, shovels and tongs… The second contained harness and saddlery, most of which had perished. The third, labelled 'Books from the Empress's Library', was full of trash, old Russian railway guides, and children's books and novels. So one by one the packing-cases were opened and nothing but absolutely worthless trash was found.[170] After lunch one afternoon the King and Queen sit down with Xenia to go through the contents of the cases. It is a torrid experience, though the exercise yields nothing of any value. These items, the King surmises, have been pinched by the Bolsheviks.

The King remains instrumental in the lives of Nicholas's close relatives. Xenia has nothing to her name, and eventually he settles Wilderness House on her, in the grounds of Hampton Court. He also allocates a large sum of money to her, which nonetheless is too great a task to manage for one who has grown up in the decadence of the Russian Imperial Court. Ponsonby places it in the hands of a clerk, "who did the park's accounts to pay everybody and gave her the balance each month." Even then, she spends nothing on herself. At one point Ponsonby finds that she "practically starved herself, and never spent a penny on her clothes, in order to give more to her sons."[171]

The Dowager Empress stays in England for a time, but eventually settles in Denmark. The King and Queen, Queen Alexandra and Princess Victoria between them settle £10,000 a year on her, but over the course of time His Majesty assumed responsibility for the whole amount. "She was… used to being infinitely wealthy and didn't know the value of anything."[172] A Danish Naval Captain was enlisted to manage her finances. In 1928 when Marie died, although the King was recovering from a life-threatening illness himself, he went to great pains, as did Ponsonby, to make sure that her

168   RA PS/PSO/GV/C/M/1344A/82.
169   RA PS/PSO/GV/C/M/1344A/85.
170   Syonsby: *Recollections of Three Reigns,* p.335.
171   Ibid., p.336.
172   Ibid., p.337.

jewellery was received intact. When they were eventually sold the jewels fetched some £350,000, and His Majesty had the money put in trust for her daughters.

Whilst the fate of the Romanovs caused the King untold pain, it was not the hardest blow to bear as far as his family was concerned as a result of the war. That came when behind his back, David Lloyd George tried to put his cousin Wilhelm on trial, entertaining London as a location for proceedings. For whilst he can use his influence to rescue his aunt and his cousins, over this, he has no control.

The German delegation at Compiegne on 11th November warned the Allies that the terms of the armistice would bring their country to its knees. And they were not wrong. At the beginning of 1919 Germany is in a state of utter, revolutionary chaos. At the beginning of December the previous year, His Majesty had received an update on cousin's situation. "We now know that William fled into Holland to a place called Amerongen (where he still is) on November 10th."[173] The King is in no mood to forgive. A few weeks after the Armistice, Bertie runs into the Kaiser's sister whilst serving with the RAF in Germany. "She asked after you and the family," he tells his father, "and hoped that we should be friends again. I told her politely that I did not think it was possible for a great many years!!!" His Majesty agrees. "Your answer to Cousin Vicky (who of course I have known all my life) was quite correct. The sooner she knows the real feeling of bitterness which exists here against her country the better."[174]

But whilst privately it took time for the the King's anger to subside, he reviles the idea of kicking a defeated foe in public. He will not hear of taking the surrender of the German fleet himself, and a few months after His Majesty hears that the wife of the British representative in the Netherlands had jeered at the Kaiser on his arrival in exile, her husband is given early retirement. The King's Government, however, are thinking along different lines.

As early as 20th November 1918, Lord Curzon, a member of the War Cabinet, has already been to Paris to discuss with Clemenceau what the joint attitude of the Allied Governments should be with regard to the former Kaiser. It is agreed that both Governments hold him responsible for the war, having "committed a great crime against humanity and he ought to pay for this like any other criminal." The French think a trial is the best course of action, but there is a question mark on whether the Dutch would hand him over. "With regard to punishment it might be difficult to proceed as far as execution," says a Cabinet memo, "but, if found guilty, the ex-Kaiser could be treated as a universal outlaw so that there would be no land on which he could set his foot." Emotions run high in the War Cabinet. Curzon wants action taken immediately, because after the Peace Conference it is hardly likely they will be able to seize the Kaiser as a prisoner of war. Lloyd George sees no problem with a death sentence. He "didn't believe in limiting the punishment for a crime which had caused millions of deaths." The same applies for Wilhelm's heir, the Crown Prince. "Rulers who plunged the civilised world into war must be made to pay the penalty, and it was undoubtedly no sufficient punishment for them to retire to some neutral country and enjoy a life of comfort." If necessary, he advocates telling the Netherlands that they will be excluded from any future League of Nations if they refuse to comply. Churchill leads a faction that are not so bloodthirsty. "It would be difficult to say that the ex-Kaiser's guilt was greater than many of his advisers, or greater than that of the Parliament of the nation which supported him in making war." It would be nothing short of ridiculous if Wilhelm were indicted and then the charges did not stick. Churchill councils extreme caution before the Government commits to any form of action. The Prime Minister is bullish. He says "that he regretted to find any hesitation in the [room] with

173   RA GV/PRIV/GVD/1919 2/12.
174   Rose: *King George V,* pp.229-231.

regard to trying the ex-Kaiser for high treason against humanity."[175] He does, however, agree with his colleagues in having the Attorney General form a committee to debate the idea of bringing charges for causing the war and for breaching international laws during the conflict. They are also to examine how a tribunal would be formed to try such charges and to examine with the Foreign Officer how realistic it was to induce the Dutch to hand Wilhelm and his associates over for such a trial.

Given a little over a week to consider "this important difficult and delicate matter," the Committee returns that: "The ex-Kaiser is primarily and personally responsible for the deaths of millions of young men" They do not believe that Wilhelm could be extradited, and so the Dutch would have to surrender him. They think that given the internal situation there at the present moment, this shouldn't be a problem. The makeup of any court, they think, should be solely Allied, no neutrals and no German representation. "As to the charges, making him responsible for the origin of the war would be a never-ending, meticulous and far too general, unless irrefutable evidence could be supplied that would narrow the focus of the trial." They suggest bringing charges in the matter of unrestricted submarine warfare... charged with the murder of thousands of men, women and children who had died whilst sailing on ships that carried no munitions of war." Significantly, "as chief Law Officer of the Crown," the Attorney General doubts the success of any war crimes trial if the Kaiser is not charged."[176] So far as Wilhelm is concerned, the Government have been convinced that he should be held personally responsible for his crimes against international law. "I trust that we shall avoid the blunder of 1649 and emulate the wisdom of 1815,"[177] remarks *The Times*, with reference to Charles I and Napoleon Bonaparte; but nevertheless, it is an election pledge by Lloyd George throughout December that the Kaiser be brought to book.

It is the Canadian Prime Minister, Sir Robert Borden that speaks up with a level solution. "He suggested that the best way of bringing the ex-Kaiser to justice might be by a resolution devised at the peace conference." The weight of the treaty when presented to the Dutch could make all the difference. This is the course that events take, and His Majesty will be dragged personally into the matter soon after the Treaty of Versailles is signed in June 1919. Article 227 of the treaty reads that the Allies will make a request to the Dutch to deliver Wilhelm so that he may stand trial, and that he will be publicly arraigned "for a supreme offence against international morality and the sanctity of treaties."[178]

It takes less than 24 hours for German relatives to begin addressing their concerns to the King, in the name of Wilhelm's mother, his late aunt Vicky, entreating him "to use this influence to save the grandson of the late Queen Victoria from so unheard of a degradation, which must and would be felt by every gentlemen in this country, as a besmirching of their honour, never to be effaced!" These clauses, says Alexander, Count Munster, "must fill any German's heart, who has an atom of self respect left, with untold bitterness." He cannot conceive how this has come to pass. "It seems to me incomprehensible that the British nation can lend her hand to carry the feeling of hatred and revenge so far."[179]

To make matters worse for the King, who deprecates such a trial anyway, he learns not from his Government, but when he reads in the newspaper details of a speech Lloyd George gave at the House of Commons on 3rd July, that it is a possibility that the Kaiser's trial should be held in London. The Press are not too impressed following Lloyd George's speech. "Why London? Why

175   TNA: CAB 23/42/8.
176   TNA: CAB 23/42/12.
177   *The Times* 30/11/18.
178   Oxford University: *The Oxford Handbook of Law & Politics*, p.437.
179   RA PS/PSO/GV/C/Q/1560/7.

the capital of one of the major belligerents?" Asks *The Daily News.* "The prisoner who is about to be brought to London is a grandson of Queen Victoria, the son of a British Princess Royal and a cousin of the reigning monarch… it seems an act of extraordinary thoughtlessness." Has the country not enough concerns in the wake of the greatest war in history?

> We are up against problems of human adjustment, of life and death, of international reconstruction in the presence of which the question of whether the ex-Kaiser shall be put to death or left to a great old age felling trees in a Dutch woodland will seem a matter of incredibly little moment. For most sensible minds it is enough that the despots have gone.[180]

This, more than any other slight by Lloyd George, hurts, for this is a member of His Majesty's family, and this is his capital. The palace leap into action. Stamfordham has been on to Curzon, who claims that he is "in entire agreement with the views expressed by the King,"[181] and has written a lengthy letter on the matter to the Prime Minister. "I am profoundly distressed," writes the Bishop of Chelmsford to the palace. "No other words explain what I feel - concerning the trial of the Kaiser in London. It is more than a blunder. It is a crime… It can do no good. [It] will place the Royal Family in a most difficult position and do intolerable harm."[182] From Paris, Britain's Ambassador, Lord Derby, confidentially tells the palace that the French have no stomach for the trial. "They think it will make him a martyr and that it will consolidate a party in Germany behind him in his favour, which would never be consolidated if we did not have this trial. People say quite openly to me they look upon it simply as a redemption of an election pledge in England."[183] Lord Esher, too is fuming. He cannot help but think of all the documents that will become public property, "if this idiotic Kaiser trial materialises." Does Britain want potentially inflammatory correspondence with France in the public domain? "Ditto with the Boche over Baghdad." What about all of the letters going backwards and forwards before the war between Wilhelm and family members and Admiral Fisher about the Royal Navy? Having fully vented his spleen he muses that "somebody once wrote a play in which Napoleon, instead of being the chained eagle of St Helena ended his days as a waiter at New York."[184]

Meanwhile, the King is still in shock, and for His Majesty, the situation is getting messier by the day. One witness noted that Lloyd George's determination to extradite his cousin "incensed the King." It moved him… to "a violent tirade… on and off for half an hour,"[185] Prince Henry of Prussia has written to his cousin, the King, but openly, publishing in newspapers a missive that says: "In the name of justice, I beg Your Majesty to desist from any demand for the extradition of His Majesty the Emperor Wilhelm." He puts himself at the King's disposal to "refute the calumnies regarding the German Kaiser which have been spread about for years in contradiction to all truth."[186] Other newspapers have printed a rallying call to all former German royalty to unite and stand beside the former Kaiser. Wilhelm's second son is even asking that he be permitted to place himself ready for extradition in place of his father.

But the British Government have actually begun planning for the trial as soon as the Treaty of Versailles is ratified. The Foreign Office will need to liaise with the Dutch for his delivery, transport for Wilhelm and his staff needs to be arranged. An authority must be designated as responsible for

180   *The Daily News* 5/7/19.
181   RA PS/PSO/GV/C/Q/1560/11.
182   RA PS/PSO/GV/C/Q/1560/14.
183   RA PS/PSO/GV/C/P/1273/30.
184   RA PS/PSO/GV/C/Q/1560/12.
185   Rose: George V, pp.229-231.
186   *The Times* 10/7/19.

his person. A residence needs to be arranged, and it is Lloyd George's rather medieval suggestion that he be housed at Syon, the Duke of Northumberland's house on the Thames and sailed along the river each day to stand trial at Westminster. "An alternative plan was to try the Kaiser in… Hampton Court on the outskirts of London; but that would have meant evicting all the courtiers' widows and other old ladies from the apartments which they occupied by the grace and favour of successive sovereigns.[187]

The King has made no reply to Prince Henry's original telegram, and so his cousin once again uses the press to further his cause. In August *Hamburger Nachrichten* publishes an open letter to His Majesty, but one which though farcical includes some distasteful accusations, veiled references to private conversations and more demands that the extradition of the Kaiser be dropped. "Documents as well as facts undoubtedly indicate that it was solely the British Government which for years prepared this world war in order to eliminate Germany as a troublesome competitor from the world market." Germany was overcome, he declares, not by the aims of the Entente, but by silver bullets which lodged in the back of the German people. "The German spirit, which at present seems dead, still lives, and will one day awaken to the full consciousness of the disgrace and shame which has been inflicted by its victors. It will one day demand a reckoning from its fortunes."[188] This letter does not receive an answer either.

With no power to stop the trial, the King's last hope is that the Dutch refuse to hand over his cousin. Rumours had reached Buckingham Palace in July suggesting that they may put up resistance. "This is good news,"[189] Stamfordham tells Lord Rosebery, and Lord Derby thinks that the French will be very glad if he stays put.

As soon as the Treaty of Versailles is ratified in January 1920, the Queen of the Netherlands is issued with a note saying that the Supreme Council of the Allies wish to put Article 227 into effect, and that they insist the Kaiser be handed over pending a trial. International treaties, it says, have been violated as well as the most basic human rights. It lists the violation of neutrality of Belgium, devastation of territory with no military value, unrestricted submarine warfare, loss of life at sea, and "innumerable acts against not combatants committed by German authority in defiance of the laws of war." The moral responsibility, the note claims, lies with the ex-Kaiser, Germany's supreme war chief. "Holland will not fulfil her international duty if she were to refuse to associate herself with other nations as far as she can to pursue, or at least not to hinder the punishment of the crimes that have been committed."[190]

Once again the King receives letters from his German relatives. The first is penned by a collection of German princes. "If the monstrous suggestion is carried out which demands that [the Kaiser] should be delivered up by the neutral countries to vindicate his conduct then the world will witness the spectacle of an independent Monarch… brought before a court of justice composed of his enemies, in every way incompetent to judge him." They plead with the King, and point out that he bears the same German origins as themselves. "We trust to the wisdom of Your Majesty to prevent a crime, the responsibility for which would weigh heavily on Your Majesty's shoulders."[191] The King passes the letter on to the Foreign Office. "While refraining from any comment as to the tone and nature of this letter," says Stamfordham, "His Majesty asks that you should send copies of the translation both to Lord Curzon (who was by now the Foreign Minister) and to the Prime Minister,

---

187   *The Times* 10/7/19
188   *Morning Post* 4/8/19.
189   RA PS/PSO/GV/C/Q/1560/16.
190   RA PS/PSO/GV/C/Q/1560/28.
191   RA PS/PSO/GV/C/Q/1560/24.

and that you should invite an expression of opinion as to the best course of procedure."[192] Curzon says the tone has irritated him, and that the King would be wise not to answer, but that the Foreign Office will help to prepare a reply. His Majesty opts for the latter.

> I would point out that whatever action may be taken by the Allies will be in accordance with the terms of the treaty already concluded and ratified by the German Government," he begins. "…[You] will no doubt appreciate that the responsibility for the decision to proceed with the arraignment of the former German Emperor can in no sense be attributed to me personally, as the constitutional head of a sovereign state, but rests in common with all other responsibilities involved in the treaty.[193]

But thank God for the Dutch, who in the face of no small amount of bullying, refuse to give up Wilhelm of Hohenzollern. At first Queen Wilhelmina's Government are embarrassed and don't know which line to take. "In the meantime there is much resentment against the ex-Emperor for having placed Netherlands in such an embarrassing situation and a widely expressed but somewhat forlorn hope that he may himself come forward and take some course which would extract them from it."[194] At a secret Cabinet meeting at Claridges Hotel, three options are presented. Britain can demand that the Dutch hand over the ex-Kaiser, "That Holland could be told that the Allies would accept a firm note reminding them of the rights of asylum, but that they would allow them to intern him somewhere else."[195] Or the Netherlands could be induced to hand him over absolving themselves by saying they did so in the interests of European peace.

By the beginning of February the King is informed that his Government might waive the idea of a trial if Wilhelm can be packed off to some distant land where he can be forgotten. The Falkland Islands is suggested; "or if the Dutch Government objected to such an arrangement, they should be asked to send the Emperor to one of their colonies, Java or Batavia, in which case, however, we should claim the right of our consul or some such authority to see that the conditions of internment were carried out and prevent any chance of the Emperor's escaping."[196] The Allies must tread carefully, because in the event that Queen Wilhelmina and her Government really do dig their heels in, they are demanding the delivery of an individual who has fled to Dutch territory as an asylum seeker, and as per their constitution, they should not be considering handing him over. The clever argument is made that had not Britain, at least, gone to war over the violation of Belgium; the bullying of a small nation by a powerful one? How then now can the Dutch be pressured into extraditing the ex-Kaiser?

A month later it is reported to the palace that "final settlement of the whole question now depends entirely upon the degree of pressure which Supreme Council is prepared to exercise."[197] Following a refusal to present Wilhelm to the Allies, another note is sent which claims that the Dutch determination not to comply with their request is painful to all involved and increases the pressure.

> The Powers urge upon the Dutch Government in the most solemn and pressing manner the importance attaching to a fresh consideration of the question put before her. They desire

192   RA PS/PSO/GV/C/Q/1560/27.
193   RA PS/PSO/GV/C/Q/1560/35.
194   RA PS/PSO/GV/C/Q/1560/33.
195   TNA: CAB 23/44B/10.
196   RA PS/PSO/GV/C/Q/1560/37.
197   RA PS/PSO/GV/C/Q/1506/46.

that it may be clearly understood how grave the situation might become if the Netherland Government were not in a position to give those assurances which the safety of Europe so imperatively demands.[198]

Once again the Dutch refuse. "The Government of the Queen has by no means forgotten the acts of inhumanity which occurred during the war and against which it protested whenever Dutch nationals were innocent victims of the same, but it considers that the memory of these outrages can in no way influence its attitude in the present case."[199] Thankfully, for the whole of Europe, and in particular His Majesty, this is one battle that the Allies cannot win. All that David Lloyd George can do when the Dutch issue a royal decree naming a definite place of residence for the ex-Kaiser some forty miles from Germany, is write an angry letter to his opposite number, informing him that in this case,

> The Allied Governments are unable to accept any responsibility whatsoever for this decision… Should the continued presence of the ex-Emperor or of his family in the place of residence now assigned to them in Dutch territory, produce at a future date any of the results that are feared, the Netherlands Government cannot escape the exclusive responsibility, both for the event and for its consequences, which they have thus deliberately chosen to assume.[200]

By the advent of the Second World War, British attitudes to Wilhelm have cooled. On three separate occasions before his death in mid-1941, the Government reaffirm their intention to grant asylum to the ex-Kaiser in Britain should he ask for it. He never does. Wilhelm lives out his days at Doorn as a country gentleman. He never changes. He veers from one course of blame as to what has become of him to another. He tries to pursue his own interests through Hitler in the 1930s, and then hates him when it transpires that this will get him nowhere. He never again corresponded with his English cousin, but in 1936, when Wilhelm hears that His Majesty lies dying at Sandringham he will telegraph his sympathy to Queen Mary.

"A Sacred Charge"

For the rest of 1919, the King's war work goes on at a pace not far off that of the previous five years. There are still thousands of war decorations and OBEs to be handed out at a number of large scale investitures, there are still thousands of wounded men in hospitals to visit across the country too, and convalescent Dominion men still enjoy the freedom of the grounds at Windsor Castle. The Prince of Wales has been put to work receiving returning prisoners of war at Dover, and he is also scheduled to spend time with the Australians and with American troops; whilst Bertie is with RAF Headquarters at the front. "It would never do for people to say of course he goes home because the fighting is over," the King tells Queen Mary, "sure you agree with me…In fact our boys ought to set the example to others in these democratic days, it will all be in their favour later on."[201]

At the end of the conflict, and in its aftermath, the King and Queen are fully invested in playing a part in paying the debt that the nation owes to those maimed in the war. There is little about his post-war work that the King takes more seriously than treating and supporting disabled servicemen. "The care of those who have so grievously suffered in the country's cause is a sacred charge," he

198   TNA: CAB 24/98/39.
199   TNA: CAB 24/100/9.
200   TNA: CAB 24/101/71.
201   RA QM/PRIV/CC04/197.

says.[202] Whilst the country is in riotous celebratory mood on Peace Day in June, His Majesty puts out a statement that says:

> Today we are celebrating a victorious peace, and amidst the national rejoicings my thoughts and those of the Queen go out to the men who, in the gallant part they have taken to secure that victory, have suffered and are yet suffering from the cruel hand of war, to these, the sick and wounded who cannot take active part in the festival of victory, I send our greetings and bid them good cheer, assuring them that the wounds and scars so honourable to themselves inspire in the hearts of their fellow countrymen the warmest feelings of gratitude and respect.[203]

Before the end of the war His Majesty attached his name to a scheme for a new fund to assist disabled officers and men discharged from the services; to help them establish themselves in civilian life, or support their wives, widows, families or dependants. Initially dubbed *The King's Disabled Fund for Sailors and Soldiers and the Air Force,* at Mansion House, the Duke of Connaught announced that the whole of Their Majesties Silver Wedding gift from the City of London, some £53,000, would be allocated to this cause. Additionally, the King and Queen decided to make a personal gift of £25,000. The fund had been started by an MP named Hodge who got the idea at a dinner party when he recalled a conversation he had had with a man who had lost a leg at Loos. He was retrained as a boot-maker, but to start a business he needed £25 worth of leather. Mr Hodge happened to tell that story at a dinner, and the guests promptly collected £300 amongst themselves. "It became apparent that there was a great field that was not covered by the state provision of pensions and allowances. The need was urgent. Other applications for help, even for such a small funds as £5 began to pour in... A new set of tools, the purchase of a small business, rent, money for buying a coster's barrow." After he had raised some £115,000 the King stepped in as a patron and the fundraising target was now £3 million. His Majesty and the Queen are thoroughly impressed with Mr Hodge's philosophy. "To be their own master is naturally the ambition of thousands of these disabled men.... The noblest charity that can be offered to these men is to help them to their economic independence."[204] Hodge pledges to stick to *The Three R's*: Restoration, Reeducation and Reinstatement. Pointedly, this new fund is not going to tie itself up in administrative knots. He "hated sealing wax and red tape as the devil hates holy water." He wants instead "an abounding human sympathy for the men who had done so much for us all."[205]

His Majesty also lends his influence to the *King's National Roll of Patriotic Employers.* Said *Employers* are charged by the King with a solemn obligation, to take on as many disabled men as possible, to commit to a certain percentage of their workforce being comprised of maimed heroes. There should be work for them all, "for all those whose lack of employment would offend the general conscience."[206] By the end of the year in excess of 5,000 companies have added their names to the list already. The King also pledges smaller amounts and lends his support to a number of smaller groups. His Majesty, David and Bertie all appear in 'a victory film" in aid of St Dustan's Hospital for blinded servicemen. He interrogates men about the problems they encounter in dealing with the bureaucracy of the pensions system so that he might suggest improvements. The Village Centres Council receive £100. They are to be organised on county lines and their object is

202   *The Times* 22/5/19.
203   *The Times* 19/7/19.
204   *Daily Telegraph* 4/9/18.
205   Ibid., 1/8/18.
206   Ibid., 11/11/19.

to fund, essentially, community centres for disabled ex-servicemen to attend after being discharged from hospital. The first was to be at Enham on 1,000 acres near Andover, which the King would still be visiting in 1922, and at such centres men could continue their treatment and training for new occupations. His Majesty can only do so much, and so he is sure to pay due attention to large scale donors, hoping to encourage more. They include Sir Bruce Ismay, *Titanic* survivor, indeed scion of the family that founded the White Star Line, who pledges a colossal £25,000 to a fund for disabled merchant seamen. His Majesty acknowledges it as a fitting tribute "to the splendid services rendered by the officers and men of the British Mercantile Marine."[207]

It will be decades before Britain has finished paying this debt, and the provision for disabled servicemen and how it is administered is one that will evolve over time, with plenty of stumbling along the way. In June 1919 disabled men went on strike, and from the Leeds Branch of the National Federation of Discharged Sailors and Soldiers a telegram was sent to His Majesty to publicise their case. "Your Majesty, From 1914 onwards we answered the call for King and Country. Today we ask your gracious help in securing a living allowance for those who have been maimed in the King and country's service."[208] In the autumn there are an estimated 800,000 disabled servicemen in Britain, and 100,000 of them are not in employment. *The Times* claims that 5% of Britain's workforce is made of disabled servicemen. In line with these figures, which do not specify how many of these men are permanently unable to work, the King issues another proclamation reaffirming: "A dear obligation upon all who, not least through the efforts of these men… enjoy the blessing of victorious peace to make acknowledgment of what they have suffered on our behalf."[209]

Remembrance

"Silence is More Eloquent Than Words"

Whilst the King's work for disabled servicemen forms a significant part of his post-war work, it is in remembrance that his legacy lies. Whilst the Great War still raged, already Britain was conscious of the need for commemorating hundreds of thousands of men, and indeed women and children who had lost their lives. The first Anzac Day commemorations took place in 1916. The King and Queen, having walked the ruins of South London, support an endeavour to commemorate those in a certain borough who have been killed as a result of enemy air action and there is a service in the summer of 1918 at Westminster Abbey for members of the civil service, of which some 8,000 have fallen so far. Days later there is an evening gathering at St. Paul's for munition workers "and as a memorial of those of the war workers who have given their lives in the cause." Their Majesties drive through the streets with a minimal escort in an open carriage, to be greeted by a large crowd in front of the cathedral that includes swathes of American troops. These services for specific social groups, professions and units prove to be a precedent. In 1919 both Westminster Abbey and St. Paul's host a continuous programme of memorial events and the King is present at them all. In February it is the turn of the Guards, and Bertie accompanies his father to Westminster for another in remembrance of those lost with the RAF and its antecedents. The abbey is filled to capacity; a muted combination of khaki, the new air force blue and widows and parents in black. It is a moving service, "stately,

207   *The Times* 3/1/1919.
208   *Morning Post* 7/6/19.
209   *The Times* 15/9/19.

beautiful and with a note of true patriotic fervour."[210] In April it is the Household Cavalry. "May and I attended a memorial service at Westminster Abbey… Very fine and impressive service and a great number of people."[211] "Now and then the sunshine filtered meagrely in, burnishing a brass chandelier that lay in path of its rays… and making the candle light look dim, but mostly the ancient building remained grey and sombre."[212] On St. George's Day, St. Paul's commemorates some 43,000 men of the Royal Artillery who have fallen; a gun placed 'in action' at the chancel steps, facing the congregation. May sees the turn of the cavalry, the Dominions. Queen Alexandra accompanies His Majesty to St. Paul's to commemorate almost 2,000 railway men. Almost the entire congregation of 4,000 is composed of grieving relatives, some of whom have travelled from as far afield as Aberdeen and Dublin; shown to their seats by guards and inspectors in uniform.

The service for nearly 60,000 men of the Royal Navy is particularly poignant; not only because it is His Majesty's own service, but because so many of them have been committed to the sea. There are no graves, they lay "swept by the tide and current."[213] A large family contingent attends, including the Dowager Empress Marie and Prince Louis of Battenberg. The King and Queen sit beneath the pulpit. "The Cathedral was very full and the Archbishop's address excellent."[214] Marines sit on one side of the nave, sailors on the other; admirals are clustered beneath the dome: Beatty, Sturdee, Jackson and Colville.

In the summer of 1920 the King speaks at the opening of the Imperial War Museum at Crystal Palace.

> We cannot tell with what eyes future generations will regard this museum, nor what ideas it will arouse in their minds. We hope and pray that, realising all we have done and suffered, they will look back upon war, its instruments; and its organisation as belonging to a dead past. But to us, it stands not for a group of trophies won from a beaten enemy, not for a symbol of the side of victory, but as an embodiment and a lasting memorial of common effort and common sacrifice."[215]

The King also played a significant role in the despatch of certificates commemorating the fallen. He fought hard to have the date of the casualty included, but it proved a potentially overwhelming task. The King acquiesced, but he stilled rued the lack of the date of death being added. "It was quite possible that a large European war might break out again in the next ten or twenty years and then there would be the danger of the two wars being confused."[216]

Work is also carried out for war memorials at Balmoral and at Sandringham in memory of members of the Royal Household who have laid down their lives. On 17th October 1920 he unveils a cross at the latter estate; by the side of the road near the public entrance to the estate, so that everyone may see it. Of all the King's residences, that in Norfolk has suffered the worst number of casualties and it records the names of 77 men killed. It is a private function for the local community. "After the singing of a hymn and a short prayer, the King pulled away the union jacks with which the base of the cross had been enshrouded, and dedicated the memorial." His Majesty says: "May their example inspire us to like courage in the greater war against evil, may their memory

210   *The Times* 20/2/19.
211   RA GV/PRIV/GVD/1919 (2/4).
212   *Daily Telegraph* 3/4/19.
213   *Daily Telegraph* 13/6/19.
214   RA GV/PRIV/GVD/1919 (12/5).
215   *The Times* 10/6/20.
216   PPTP/PP/BAL/MAIN/NS/157.

ever burn brightly in those who are here."[217] The last post is sounded by Percy Loose of Dersingham, late of the Sandringham Company. The King lays a victors' wreath of laurel on the memorial and Queen Mary and Queen Alexandra adorn it with chrysanthemums before the royal party walks back to York Cottage.

His Majesty as always taken an interest too in the evolving of the Imperial War Graves Commission. As long ago as October 1915, the palace had been informed by the War Office that the French Government had passed an act "to provide for the acquisition of land by that Government, for the purposes of burial of British soldiers, who are killed or die in consequence of wounds or sickness, occasioned by the presence of the British Army in France."[218] The French Government also asked that the King permit the Prince of Wales to act as President of such a commission and would assume responsibility for liaising with the French about British war graves. His Majesty ponders the matter, and David is allowed to decide for himself. "This kindly thought will never be forgotten by those whose dead we buried on French soil," announces the King to the French President, "and I gladly approve of the suggestion that my dear son, the Prince of Wales should become President of the National Committee to whom the care of the graves will be entrusted.[219] Driven by Fabian Ware, who was instrumental in the organisation of British war graves on the Western Front early on, the Imperial War Graves Commission was born in 1917.

The Royal Family take an active interest in the commission, and will lend their support to the idea of commemorating large numbers of those "lost" on the battlefields on huge memorials along the Western Front. "A society was formed to collect funds, in order that this might go forward without delay… the King and Queen, accompanied by the Prince of Wales, attended a grand concert at the Albert Hall, the object of which was to obtain funds for the erection of the Somme Battlefields Memorial."[220]

In November 1919, as the first anniversary of the end of hostilities approaches, just how it should be marked becomes a source of immense interest across the nation. The concept of the two-minute silence is first brought to the King's attention via Lord Milner, the Colonial Secretary. A South African named Percy Fitzpatrick had put forward the suggestion, hoping that both His Majesty and the Government would take it on board. It was based on something similar he had seen done in South Africa. "Only those who have felt it can understand the overmastering effect in action and reaction of a multitude moved suddenly to one thought and one purpose… The effect is magnetic… Why not perpetuate this and extend it to the whole Empire?" Milner thinks that this suggestion can only be put to the nation by the King himself. Wigram solicits the opinion of the Cabinet, who think it should be carried out so long as the King agrees. Their only mild concern is that if it becomes a precedent, "in remote years, after the passing of the present generation, the idea of the nation downing everything for a short spell in memory of the Great War might prove inconvenient, and annoyance. But the King loves the idea, and wants to do all he can to install this short tribute to the victims of war as a lasting, national tradition. All agree that the pathos of the eleventh hour, or the eleventh day, of the eleventh month would be perfect. Milner leads a Cabinet committee to carry out some feasibility studies; talk to the Dominions and to India. When this is done, the Foreign Secretary visits His Majesty at the palace to talk him over the finer points of the scheme; The thing he likes most about the idea of the silence is the simplicity. He scorned the idea of last posts and anything more elaborate. He thought everyone should just pause where

217   *Daily Telegraph* 16/10/20.
218   RA PS/PSO/GV/PS/WAR/QQ16/3163.
219   Ibid.
220   (ed.) Gibbs: *George the Faithful: The Life & Times of George V "The People's King,"* pp.307-308.

they were" that "if the observance of the 'Eleventh Hour' is to entail upon the sailors or soldiers anything in the form of an extra parade or official duty, much of its significance will be lost and their appreciation of it inevitably impaired." Striking the tone between suggesting the silence, and being seen as trying to force it upon the nation is taken very seriously. Milner and his colleagues think that the Government should have nothing to do with publicising the idea in the press. It has to be a personal appeal by the King, something between he and his subjects, "and that the public should be given clearly to understand that it was left to them to respond spontaneously to His Majesty's express wishes."[221]

With this in mind, on 7th November 1919, a proclamation appears in the newspapers: from Buckingham Palace:

> Tuesday next, November 11th, is the first anniversary of the Armistice, which stayed the world wide carnage of the four preceding years; and marked the victory of right and freedom. I believe that my people in every part of the Empire fervently wish to perpetuate the memory of the great deliverance, and those who laid down their lives to achieve it. To afford an opportunity for the universal expression of this feeling it is my desire, and hope that at the hour when the armistice came into force, the 11th hour, of the eleventh day, of the eleventh month, there may be, for the brief space of two minutes, a complete suspension of all our normal activities... all work, all sound, and all locomotion should cease, so that, in perfect stillness, the thoughts of everyone may be concentrated on reverent remembrance of the glorious dead... I believe that we shall all gladly interrupt our business and pleasure, whatever it may be, and unite in this simple service of silence and remembrance.[222]

The Press embrace the idea wholeheartedly. "It has troubled the minds of many how adequately to express the feelings of the Empire on so momentous an anniversary," says one newspaper. "There is healing in remembrance; says *The Telegraph*. Silence is more eloquent than words... We hope they may know that they are not forgotten, but we who still bear the burden of the flesh stand in need of this commemoration, for the new inspiration which it may convey to each one of us as we confront the conflicting tasks of these unrestful times."[223] "We think of all that moment meant to us a year ago," echoes the *Daily Mail*, "of the crushing load of anxiety lifted from millions of hearts. In all the history of the world the clock struck no more fateful hours, and we shall remember it fittingly as the King desires."[224]

Advice is published as to how the population might behave at the fateful hour. The maroons would be fired from London's fire synchronised-stations and former air raid sirens would be set off by the police. It is suggested that church bells strike in villages to mark the beginning and end of the silence. Police are to stop traffic in London and in other cities and towns officers of the law have been authorised to do the same. Their watches are to be synchronised. Shops and businesses should remain open, "but shopkeepers and their customers will, it is hoped, agree to a pause during the two minutes. People in the streets can best cooperate by simply standing still when the signal sounds."[225] Even express trains have been allotted an extra five minutes to enable them to slow down, stop for two minutes and then build speed again.

221   RA PS/PSO/GV/PS/MAIN/28481.
222   *Morning Post* 7/11/19.
223   *Daily Telegraph* 7/11/19.
224   *Daily Express* 7/11/19.
225   *The Times* 7/11/19.

The first Armistice Day was bright with a cold wind. Amidst a mass of copper-coloured foliage in the parks on either side of Buckingham Palace, crowds have gathered; stretching away down The Mall. From the left of the front façade a detachment of Guards marches into view. The maroons sound, the guards present arms "and from a great babel of noise and confusion arose the greater silence." The sound of motor engines died, men and women stood bareheaded or with handkerchiefs to their faces. It is a complete contrast to the scenes of twelve months ago. Every now and again a pitiful sob or hysterical cry can be heard. That London could fall almost completely silent seems impossible.

Cynics were astonished at how fiercely the King's city adhered to the silence. In front of the Cenotaph, a temporary monument of wood and plaster, "was gathered one of the saddest throngs in London." The base of the memorial was awash with floral tributes; 'from the most costly tributes florists could produce, to the humble bunch of flowers." Wigram fights his way through the crowds to place a wreath from Their Majesties: laurel leaves and yellow immortelles, tied with a broad crimson ribbon adorned a hand written card from the King: 'In memory of the Glorious Dead From the King and Queen November 11 1919.[226] People stand up on the tube, where trains have come to a halt in the tunnels. When they all begin their journeys again they are to run slowly, so as not to overload the power supply at once. The Port of London Authority suspends all works. At London's premier department stores the fire bells are rung to alert customers as to the time. Selfridges is packed, but deathly silent. Men remove their hats and girls bow their heads. Ex-servicemen stand to attention; many of them with tears streaming down their faces. Omnibuses and trams stop in the street, telephone exchanges fall silent.

Throughout London, Britain and the Empire people have rallied to the King's call. "After twelve months of reaction, of fierce effort to forget, we came together, as we came in grief and danger, terror and tribulation, says one newspaper. "Let us at the eleventh hour of the eleventh day of the eleventh month of every year, hold this service of pity and thanksgiving... The year may come when the meaning is obscured, when observance is a sham. But not in our time."[227] The King is thrilled with the response, and with the part he has played. But he cannot, and does not claim all of the credit for the start of this remembrance tradition. When, a few weeks later, Fitzpatrick sails for South Africa; he does so with a note on his person from Buckingham Palace: "The King... desires me to assure you that he ever gratefully remembers that the idea of the two minutes' pause on Armistice Day was due to your initiation, a suggestion which was readily adopted and carried out with heartfelt sympathy throughout the Empire."[228]

"The Dean of Westminster's Project"

In 1920 the existing cenotaph is replaced with a permanent, identical stone version; which is due to be unveiled on Armistice Day that year. By September, people of all classes have come to assume that the King will perform the ceremony, but this quite surprises His Majesty. There was an unveiling when the first version was put up, and therefore this is not a new monument simply a replacement. His people, however, have received the installation of the permanent monument in a different light, and think that it is a national event, and so His Majesty consents to unveil it. If he is going to do it, though, he wants it done properly. He expects Lloyd George to be present, along with a representative of every regiment in the army, also, representatives of the services of the

226   *The Times* 12/11/19.
227   *Daily Express* 12/11/19.
228   RA PS/PSO/GV/C/O/1542/13.

Dominions, India and the Colonies; including the navy, marines and air force, and he wants the two minutes' silence worked into the ceremony.

Then, in October, the plan for the ceremony turns in a new, grander direction. The Dean of Westminster Abbey approaches Stamfordham with a suggestion he would like him to put before His Majesty. With thousands of unknown graves scattered across numerous fronts, his idea is "that one such body... should be exhumed, brought... to England; conducted by military escort from Victoria Station; and interred in Westminster Abbey in the nave with a funeral service attended by the highest in the land and the chiefs of the British forces."[229] Sir Henry Wilson approves, but has said that it first needs to be put before the King. The response is not promising. "His Majesty is inclined to think that nearly two years after the last shot fired on the battlefields of France and Flanders is so long ago that a funeral might now be regarded as belated, and almost, as it were, re-open the war wound, which time is gradually healing."[230] The King decides that he would like to talk to Lloyd George about the idea before he makes a decision. In the meantime, though, Wigram has been to see Wilson at the War Office, and he claims that the generals have shown universal support. "He was very emphatic that the King should initiate it, and that the people would expect such a noble tribute to the rank and file to come from the highest in the land."[231]

From this point on the palace is heavily involved in the concept of burying an unknown warrior. The plan becomes known as *the Dean of Westminster's project*. The Dean has an uncomfortable meeting with the Prime Minister's secretary, who "had sat unmoved without a twitch on his face for ten minutes."[232] The King is still concerned about the belated nature of the burial, and he is not the only one, for the Archbishop of Canterbury is also dubious; but Wigram convinces His Majesty that it is simply in line with war memorials that are currently being unveiled in ceremonies up and down the country, including the new cenotaph. The King is just about sold.

> I know for certain the Prime Minister would agree to the burial of an unknown soldier in Westminster Abbey, that sort of thing appeals to him and will no doubt appeal to the public, so I have nothing more to say, and I suppose Armistice Day is the most suitable day as the Cenotaph is so near the abbey.[233]

His Majesty is, however concerned about the magnitude of the crowds with both events happening at the same time and wants to be fully informed during planning about how the authorities intend to keep everybody safe.

His Majesty thinks that the Cenotaph should be unveiled first, and then the funeral carried out which means that to get from one ceremony to the other he will walk in the funeral procession. By this time, it is nearing the end of October and arrangements must be pressed through. There are difficulties in deciding which of the thousands of requests from grieving relatives whose loved ones have never been found are to be present in the abbey, and most will have to be content with a passage through Westminster to see the grave that could, just might be that of their loved one. His Majesty wants every single one of them that wishes to pass the Cenotaph after the procession has moved on to be facilitated. In the end, a ballot had to be carried out on 5th November for places at the service. Women who have lost a husband and one or more sons are to be accommodated first,

229   RA PS/PSO/GV/C/O/1637/1.
230   RA PS/PSO/GV/C/O/1637/2.
231   RA PS/PSO/GV/C/O/1637/3.
232   RA PS/PSO/GV/C/O/1637/5.
233   RA PS/PSO/GV/C/O/1637/10.

then mothers who have lost their only son, or all sons and finally widows. Relatives of VC winners are also to be considered.

In the meantime, arrangements are being carried out with regard to who will be buried on Armistice Day and how. Great pains have been taken to make sure that there are no clues as to the identity of the Unknown Warrior, for he is to represent all those who have been robbed of the dignity of a known grave. The body of one unidentified and unidentifiable man was exhumed in each of four areas spanning the British front in France and Flanders and brought into Headquarters at St. Pol,

> Where they were placed in the chapel attached to the British hutment there. Every indication of the part of the front from which they had come was removed. Then the general now in command on the Western Front went alone into the chapel and selected one of the bodies which was at once... sent down to Boulogne. The three remaining bodies were then buried.[234]

He could be a soldier, a sailor or an airman, he could be British or from one of the Dominions or India. All those who mourn a loved one missing on the battlefields can harbour the hope that it might be him buried in Westminster Abbey. For some this is not enough, and relatives desperately try to ascertain if by this act of remembrance, their beloved might have been brought home. Mr Nathan of Penge asks: "Is there any possibility of it being my son who was killed... He had a fair complexion and mole on his left shoulder, and [a] daisy stamped on his wrist. Short and stout." And from Norfolk a mother in the best English that she can manage: "Will it be my dearest boy... I cannot get no informashon [sic] were he was buried... he was the only boy I had at home to help me."[235]

The coffin will be of English oak, and it will be shrouded in a tatty, faded Union Jack. The flag in question has survived life at the front, and adorned many a warrior burial amongst his comrades. After arriving at Dover from Calais he will be transferred to a railway carriage waiting to take him to London. The train will arrive quietly at platform eight at Victoria Station, where it will rest overnight being placed on a gun carriage for the final journey to Westminster.

The 11th November is "a perfect late autumn day in London, with a touch of frost in the air, a veiled blue sky, and sun that would soon break through in full splendour." Crowds start to gather along the usual route, but Londoners have grown used to celebration. This is different: "no brightness of colour, no bunting or festoons and scarcely any flags."[236] There is no wind and they hang lifeless at half mast. On Whitehall the female members of the Royal Family take up position at the windows of Government offices to watch proceedings. The rest of these vantage points are filled with relatives of the fallen. Outside thousands await the arrival of the Unknown Warrior.

The King takes up a position on the north side of the Cenotaph facing Trafalgar Square with his three eldest sons. First, distant salutary guns punctuate the silence. Then the solemn, slow, rhythmic sound of drums becomes audible. From the far end of Whitehall, beneath Nelson's Column on the base of which a mass of humanity balances to get a better view, a ripple of movement begins as one by one men begin to remove their hats as the procession approaches. The first sight of it is four mounted policemen. Then come the bands. The sound of the pipers of the Scots Guards join the drums. Behind them there is a space, and then the gun carriage swings slowly into view, the coffin mounted atop and draped in the symbolic Union Jack. A steel helmet and a side arm crown the display. The pall-bearers keep their slow pace with the coffin; Admirals and a representative of the Royal Marines on one side, Generals, including Haig and Wilson on the other. Behind them

234   RA PS/PSO/GV/C/O/1637/16.
235   RA LC/LCO/SPECIAL1920:Unknown Warrior.
236   *The Times* 12/11/20.

stretches a line of representatives of all services.

The new Cenotaph is shrouded in two huge flags. The crowd is silent; "It's like being in church," one woman whispers. The gun carriage draws up alongside His Majesty, who has been watching the procession approach. A naval officer hands him a wreath of laurel, entwined with red flowers which the King lays on top of the coffin. A note drafted by His Majesty reads: *"In proud memory of those warriors who died unknown in the Great War. Unknown, and yet well known; as dying and beyond they live."* It is 11:00am and Big Ben begins to toll. On the last chime, His Majesty unveils the Cenotaph. The flags tremble for the briefest of moments and then they fall away. All are silent. A baby's cry rings out from somewhere on Whitehall. A few seconds before the two minutes have elapsed a woman's cry of agony pierces the silence. The King takes another wreath from an army officer and lays it at the base of the monument; an arrangement of white flowers. The last post rings out, the flags have been removed and the Prime Minister and other dignitaries lay their tributes. "Soon the base was hidden beneath palm leaves and orchids, lilies, roses and laurels."[237]

The procession reforms, this time with the King and his sons behind the coffin as chief mourners. The walk continues, pasts thousands of grieving relatives for whom space has been reserved around Westminster Abbey. "The service was beautiful… everything was most beautifully arranged and carried out"[238] the King writes in his diary. As the coffin is lowered into the floor of the abbey, a Field Marshal's salute is fired on Horse Guards Parade. The soil in which the Unknown Warrior will lie for eternity has been brought from the battlefields of France. The grave is finally filled in on 17th November, but in the interim crowds have filed past to pay their respects; in numbers that rival King Edward VII's lying in state. "All the arrangements and the manner in which the service were conducted were in reverence, beauty and dignity worthy of an event unparalleled and imperishable in the national life and of the abbey's national traditions," Stamfordham writes to the Dean of Westminster. "His Majesty sincerely thanks you and all concerned with the perfect manner in which everything was carried out."[239]

In 1921 the King supports fundraising for *Lord Haig's Fund for the British Legion*. 8,000,000 new poppies are sold at three pence each; every coat seems to be adorned with one. Real poppies sell for £5 each at Smithfield's and the hammer falls 49 times on a full basket of fresh ones at Christie's which sells for £463. "Lord Haig expressed the hope that Poppy Day may be firmly established as a festival every year on the day when we remember the glorious dead."[240] That year the ceremony at the Cenotaph on Armistice Day is carried out by General Horne whilst His Majesty marks the two minute silence at Sandringham. 1922 sees the beginning of the annual ceremony presided over by the Sovereign and attended by members of the Government on 11th November. In pouring rain His Majesty is in attendance with the Prince of Wales and Prince Albert. "The true dignity of his bearing was never seen to better advantage than during those moving ceremonies. In the memory of thousands this view of the King will, perhaps, survive all other recollections of him."[241]

"The King's Pilgrimage"

In 1922 the King makes a state visit to Belgium. As soon as his business in Brussels with King Albert is concluded, His Majesty means to make his own, private pilgrimage and return to the Western Front. He has been very careful not to order them to accompany him, but Haig is immediately keen

237   *Daily Telegraph* 12/11/20.
238   RA GV/PRIV/GVD/1920 (11/11).
239   RA PS/PSO/GV/C/O/1637/13.
240   *The Times* 12/11/21.
241   (ed.) The Times: *Hail and Farewell: The Passing of King George V,* p.180.

and Beatty can tie his presence in with business he has to attend to in Paris.

The King sails from Dover on his yacht *Alexandra*. It will be the last time he uses her, for she is to be sold to raise some much needed funds for His Majesty. The Instone Airline are pioneering a daily passenger service to Brussels and have been granted permission to make a pass over the yacht to take photographs. Wigram is just praying that crew don't open fire with their anti-aircraft guns. Haig entertains everyone with war yarns as they cross a flat Channel and gets onto the subject of the collection of letters in his possession. "The most curious was one from Petain saying that Paris must be saved at all risks, and that there was nothing for it but to order the French Army to break away from the British Army and form up round Paris. This was in 1917. The situation was saved by Antoine, who finally induced Petain to cancel the order." The party ponder what would happen if such correspondence, were published now. This is something that His Majesty has long feared. This single letter would show "that the French at one time seriously considered leaving us in the lurch." Ponsonby finds the conversation enlightening. "He told us a great many interesting things, and when I asked him if these would one day be made public he merely said not by him."[242]

In Brussels there are private dinners with King Albert and Queen Elizabeth, receptions for the Corps Diplomatique, a luncheon at the British Embassy. And of course a State Banquet. The King's speech recalls how far they have come since 1918. "I more than once was your guest or a few hours in your post of heroic vigil at Furnes or La Panne," [243] he says, but expresses his happiness that once more the Belgian Royal Family are home. His Majesty is rather perturbed by the size of the palace and the distance that separates him from the Queen, but he fares better than some. Ponsonby ends up wandering the corridors with Haig and Beatty. "As I told the King next day, quite a simple thing like getting back to one's room becomes a matter of great difficulty when one is led first by a man who has commanded the British Fleet and secondly by a man who has led the biggest Army we have ever had in the field."[244] Forays into Brussels include paying homage to Edith Cavell.

> We… went to the Tir National, where the Germans shot 35 Belgians, [and] Nurse Cavell, it was a cold blooded murder and will never be forgotten, one saw the spot where the chair stood in which she sat when they shot her, she was not dead after a volley fired by twelve soldiers and they finished her with a revolver, the dirty brutes.[245]

His ceremonial duties complete, His Majesty departs for his tour of battlefield cemeteries by train with only Haig, Ponsonby, Wigram and one or two others for company. All that he wants to do is pay homage to his troops, in as private a manner as possible. The programme is crowded, with so much that the King wants to see, so he will not be able to see the southern end of the British front.

The party heads inland to Tyne Cot Cemetery near Passchendaele; to where nearly 10,000 men currently lie, more than half of them unidentified. Ponsonby finds the scale of death utterly bewildering. The head gardener walks the lines of graves with His Majesty, a former soldier himself. His Majesty is informed that some 2,000 ex-servicemen are living out on the Western Front, that some have married French and Belgian women. In the middle of the site, a sea of wooden crosses, sits the concrete pill-box that has given this immense burial ground its name. It is going to form the base of a huge cross of sacrifice. The King says that it "should never be moved, it should remain

---

242   Syonsby: *Recollections of Three Reigns*, pp.342-343.
243   RA Speeches and Replies to Addresses by HM King George V.
244   Ibid, pp.347-349.
245   RA GV/PRIV/GVD/1922 (10/5).

always as a monument to the heroes whose graves stood thickly around."[246] As the party continues on, His Majesty is immensely interested in seeing how the land has changed.

It was of course extremely interesting for me going over the battlefields again," he writes to David, "which I knew so well during the war and where I had not been since 1918, just after the Armistice. It is extraordinary how rapidly they have built and are building the houses again. I could hardly recognise some of the places again, they are so changed… But the fields are all cultivated and sheds and huts have been put up everywhere for the people to live in.[247]

The devastation was so comprehensive at Ypres, that though work has begun, the town still heavily bears her scars. His first port of call is the cemetery in which his cousin, Prince Maurice of Battenberg and his friends, Charlie Nairne and Willy Cadogan lie. He is satisfied to see how well they are taken care of. In the centre of the town, work has begun on rebuilding the tragic medieval cloth hall, the interior columns rising from the ashes. Rows of houses have already been completed. The King is taken to the Menin Gate, one of the entrances to the town to meet with Belgian representatives. Those working on the reconstruction of the town put down their tools for an hour and rush up to see His Majesty, the crowd pressing in on him densely at times. He presents a Belgian General with a chaplet of palms and bay leaves with a spray of red roses in memory of the country's dead; then he congratulates the Burgomaster on how swiftly the town is being rebuilt.

But on this spot in particular is to be one of the memorials to the missing that the King has been advocating. The architect, Sir Reginald Blomfield, shows His Majesty the plans for an immense 45 foot arch to span the entrance to Ypres. On top, there will be a sculpture of a lion facing where the German Army sat at Menin, in an alert and defensive position. It has not yet decided what will occupy the other side. Three holes have been incorporated into the design of the roof so that light may flood the interior of the memorial. So many men have been lost in the mud of Flanders that vast panels of Portland stone will cover all sides of the arch in order to facilitate all of their names. The King notices how high some will be, and urges that the names will be clear enough for all to read.

Vlamertinghe Cemetery has been chosen as a stop because it will show His Majesty the aspect of a completed cemetery. Here, the IWGC have finished removing the original wooden crosses and have replaced them with identical headstones, all two and a half feet high and just over a foot wide.

Fabian Ware, who is accompanying the King explains that there has not been any effort at uniformity, all of the commission's cemeteries are individual, and The Director of Kew Gardens has acted as a horticultural advisor, giving valuable advice as to what trees, shrubs and flowers should be selected for the various regions. His Majesty is quite taken with the sight of the matching headstones, simple and the same for both officers and men. "He agreed that this was the only possible way."[248]

The Royal Party is ready to cross the border into France by early evening. "The sun was shining … the concrete forts lying like the bleached skeletons of strange monsters in the fields."[249] The train continues on to Vimy, where the party will rest for the night. Before setting off the following day, His Majesty sends a telegram to General Byng, who conquered the ridge in 1917 at the head of Canadian troops and who is now Governor-General of Canada: 'I have just spent the night at Vimy. My thoughts are with you.'[250] Four years of peace has done nothing to temper the King's attitude

246   Fox: *The King's Pilgrimage*, p.10.
247   RA EDW/PRIV/MAIN/A/2452.
248   Fox: *The King's Pilgrimage*, p.33.
249   Ibid., p.32.
250   Ibid., p.51.

when it comes to having French dignitaries trail him around the battlefields. He was determined that the time he wanted to spend quietly paying tribute to his soldiers will not become a ceremonial procession along the old Western Front. Unfortunately for His Majesty, Lord Hardinge, Britain's ambassador to France, had pointed out that it was problematic landing at Calais and then going on to Brussels for the state visit without a reception, never mind touring the battlefields of France clandestinely. Hardinge is left to be firm with the French. His Majesty has, however devised his own plan to be able to see Foch without getting involved in politics. The planned route will take the Royal Party past the significant French cemetery of Notre Dame de Lorette, and so he has Ponsonby write to the General. "His Majesty does not feel that he can possible pass by this spot so full of sad and glorious memories without there paying a personal tribute to our French comrades in arms."[251] It is casually suggested to Foch that the King will leave his train and that he might like to stop by.

It is a "beastly day, cold with strong north wind and rain off and on"[252] when his Majesty leaves for the French cemetery. Situated on high ground, it was crucial in the Allies defensive line and tens of thousands of France's troops had been sacrificed on its slopes. The site had been one of pilgrimage for centuries before the war. The conflict had obliterated the beautiful old chapel, but since, the hillside has become home to a huge French war cemetery. There is a little temporary chapel of iron, but it is intended to rebuild it. An enormous amount of labour has already gone into levelling the ground. 6,000 graves have been finished, but its intended to bring in 12,000 more.

At 10 o' clock the King arrives in a little procession of motor cars which tackle the steep incline leading up the hill. "On the outskirts of the cemetery the face of the earth is still pitted with shell holes, cumbered with barbed wire, broken iron and the debris of war." Inside, His Majesty is extremely pleased to see Foch again, and shakes him warmly by the hand. Haig and his French counterpart immediately begin to renew their acquaintance, chattering excitedly, "and as soon as the French officers and their guests walked towards the cemetery Lord Haig was seen to slip his arm affectionally through that of the great Marshal."[253] On a mound over which flew the French flag he placed his chaplet of red roses, palm and bay, bearing the simple inscription. On the spur of the moment His Majesty decides to hold a two minute silence on the weather beaten hillside. And he is the King of England so nobody will interrupt him. Ponsonby thinks it strikes the perfect tone.

With Haig and Foch, the King walks on a little way. "We got a wonderful view; in spite of the weather, of the battle ground all round."[254] The two commanders struggle to hold a map between them in the biting wind and point out makers. Loos, Lens, the piles of coal in the surrounding countryside. Then there is the Vimy Ridge, Neuville St Vaast, St Eloi, Bapaume. The King listened with keen interest and was clearly delighted at the cordial comradeship of the two great soldiers. He turned to them at one point with the confident query: "Toujours bons amis, n'est ce pas?" Foch replied with fervour: "Toujours, toujours, pour les mêmes causes et les mêmes raisons," and grasped Earl Haig's hand. As the two clasped hands in the grip of comradeship the King placed his hand over theirs."[255]

The motorcade descends onto the Somme. The rain begins to fall heavily but His Majesty is unmoved. He means to carry on. The King meets a travelling party of IWGC gardeners. He is most interested to learn how they work travelling with their little convoy from cemetery to

251   RA PS/PSO/GV/PS/SV/056080.
252   RA GV/PRIV/GVD/1922 (12/5).
253   *The Times* 13/5/22.
254   RA GV/PRIV/GVD/1922 (12/5.
255   *The Times* 14/5/1922.

cemetery. At Warloy-Baillon he sees a pretty burial ground set in an orchard still filled with blossom. His Majesty thinks that Forceville, to the west of the village of the same name is "a very nice cemetery."[256] Here one gardener amongst the fragrant lime trees wears eight medals, and the King calls Haig back to meet him. After visiting another four cemeteries the party departs for Albert. A stop here has not been scheduled, but His Majesty gets out anyway to see the town, still in ruins, the cathedral tower with its golden statue of the Virgin and Child hanging precariously above the remains of the church.

Everywhere that the King goes, though there are not formal ceremonies, the locals turn out to greet him. "The smaller cemeteries were surrounded by the villagers, five or six deep, the children standing on the low walls, the King as he inspected the graves passing close to them."[257] The children edge forward, to see if they can touch him and His Majesty is charmed by them, but they do not follow him as he walks amongst the graves of his soldiers. For the most part the locals remain outside the cemetery, and reverent as he pays his respects. In some cases little girls are sent in with their own floral tributes, to show solidarity with the British soldiers that lie so near their homes. "The difficulty," says Ponsonby, "was the prefects and Mayors, who always wanted to make long speeches. This is where Colonel Oudrey, our French officer came in; when a man looked like making a speech we whispered 'Discours!' to Oudrey, who at once tackled the man and tactfully stopped it."[258]

That evening the royal train comes to a stop on the coast at Etaples, a fishing port at the mouth of the River Canche. During the war it had been the largest of the hospital centres, and so there are thousands of nearby graves. First thing the following morning His Majesty visits a vast cemetery where 6,000 graves are already situated. In the years to come that number will double. "It was early when the King arrived at Etaples Cemetery. The sea was a soft flood of silver grey in the morning light, and its salt breath, which is the very vigour of our British blood, came up sharp and strong to meet the smell of the pines." This visit will be slightly more formal, for it is here, where the graves of British meet Dominion and those of the Colonies, that His Majesty has asked representatives of the Empire to meet him so that they might visit the graves of his countrymen together. The High Commissioners for Canada, New Zealand, Newfoundland and representatives from Australia and South Africa have turned out.

Throughout the duration of this pilgrimage the King has been painfully aware of the financial and logistical concerns that will prevent many a bereaved relative from following in his footsteps. As soon as news of His Majesty's impending visit had been published, letters began to pour into the palace with requests from such families. Applications for the King to visit graves were tragic. Mr Paul who had lost both sons and was now childless; Mrs Webb who grieved for her only son, Mrs Giles couldn't afford to go herself, Mr Halford, who had rejoined his regiment at 49 and whose sixteen year old boy had been killed at Ypres. His Majesty is told about all of the schemes to aid trips to the battlefields. Many of his subjects do not own passports, and the issue of cost had been raised. It was decided to work out a scheme whereby in lieu of a passport, a battlefield pass could be granted instead, which would allow the bearer to spend time on the Western Front. The War Graves Commission could not cope with it, and MI5 had volunteered to administer the scheme using their existing equipment and infrastructure. The first passes were issued in September 1921, and in 1922 it is anticipated that the number of passes will exceed 20,000. A pass has been mocked up for His Majesty as a souvenir, and he is suitably impressed, but he is also informed that hostels all over the former British front have taken in 15,000 visitors so far, and that in conjunction with the

256   *Daily Telegraph* 13/5/22.
257   Fox: *The King's Pilgrimage*, p.59.
258   Syonsby: *Recollections of Three Reigns*, pp.349-350.

War Office, 2,500 visits had been subsided by April 1922. The Red Cross are even bringing people over from Canada and New Zealand. The season for visits has already begun during the King's pilgrimage, and he meets Australian parents at Picquigny who are there to see their boy courtesy of the Salvation Army. In almost all cases, the King's path has not crossed with those men whose loved ones have asked him to stop in and see their loved ones, but he is able to honour one request at Etaples. A West Country mother had written to the Queen "as one mother to another, begging that she might lay on the tomb of her dead son... a spray of forget-me-nots."[259] With the Queen not present, the King goes in search of her son with the foreman gardener and dutifully lays the flowers on her behalf. He is accompanied by Sir James Allen, the High Commissioner for New Zealand, who had lost a son at Gallipoli.

A compromise has been found with regard to the French Government. The only formal ceremony of any kind will be carried out in sight of the sea at Terlincthun Cemetery near Boulogne. On a clear day white cliffs are visible across the Channel. For the duration of the King's pilgrimage the Queen has remained close to Brussels, but she arrives after lunch to carry out this engagement with His Majesty. Already waiting nearby is HMS *Alexandra* and a squadron of French destroyers waiting to escort them out of French waters.

Outside crowds have gathered from amongst the citizens of Boulogne, and the staff of the War Graves Commission. They watch as Their Majesties are greeted at the gates by French dignitaries and make their way through the graves to the Cross of Sacrifice at the opposite end of the cemetery. The King has also asked to meet Herbert Baker, who has designed the cemetery and representatives of the commission and of the French Government's equivalent body. At the cross His majesty lays a wreath, before a period of silence is observed. "His solemn pilgrimage has been crowned," writes one British newspaper, "by this stately requiem... by one of these tender deeds which forge the unbreakable bond between throne and people."[260]

Before the Last Post, and before Their Majesties depart for home, the King gives a lengthy speech. Underneath the Cross of Sacrifice, His Majesty turns to face the crowd, "and, his voice vibrant with emotion, but under rigid control, delivered his message:

> Standing beneath this Cross of Sacrifice, facing the great Stone of Remembrance, and compassed by these sternly simple headstones, we remember, and must charge our children to remember, that, as our dead were equal in sacrifice, so are they equal in honour, for the greatest and the least of them have proved that sacrifice and honour are no vain things, but truths by which the world lives. Many of the cemeteries I have visited in the remoter and still desolate districts of this sorely stricken land, where it has not yet been possible to replace the wooden crosses by headstones, have been made into beautiful gardens which are lovingly cared for by comrades of the war. I rejoice I was fortunate enough to see these in the spring, when the returning pulse of the year tells of unbroken life that goes forward in the face of apparent loss and wreckage; and I fervently pray that, both as nations and individuals, we may so order our lives after the ideals for which our brethren died, that we may be able to meet their gallant souls once more, humbly but unashamed... Never before in history have people thus dedicated and maintained individual memorials to their fallen, and, in the course of my pilgrimage, I have many times asked myself whether there can be more potent advocates of peace upon earth through the years to come, than this massed multitude of silent witnesses to the desolation of war.[261]

259   Fox: *The King's Pilgrimage*, p.87.
260   *Daily Graphic* 15/5/22.
261   Fox: *The King's Pilgrimage*, p.92.

Postscript

The astonishing thing about the reign of King George V is not how long he occupied the throne, it is that whilst he did, the world changed beyond all recognition. In the twenty or so years that remained to him, His Majesty received no respite. He oversaw momentous changes in Ireland with the establishment of the Irish Free State and the Parliament of Northern Ireland. He sees the first Labour Government, and in 1930 the first Round-Table Conference on Indian Constitutional Reform was opened. His Majesty was a tower of strength to his ministers. Despite being alarmed by the rapid acceleration of the pace of life in the 1920s and '30s, he did his best to stay current. "Whilst visiting the wireless section of the British Industries Fair at the White City, the King informed a salesman that on his own set, he could never 'cut' London, and could get neither Germany nor Paris at Buckingham Palace; but at Sandringham he could get other countries quite easily. The salesman said afterwards to a Press representative that the King's knowledge of wireless was almost that of an expert."[1] The first Christmas message from the Sovereign was broadcast in 1932.

His Majesty, much to his own surprise, had achieved mass popularity. Never was this more evident that in 1935, when he celebrated his Silver Jubilee.

> The love and devotion this simple, honest, God-fearing man had inspired in the multitude of his people came pouring out in a mighty cataract of unrestrained rejoicing... The nations outside the British Empire were astounded that such feelings could be shown for a representative of monarchy in the twentieth century. The King himself, too, was amazed at the warmth and sincerity of the affection shown for him.

"All this for me!" he was heard to exclaim.

> When, with the Queen, he made unannounced and unexpected tours of the back streets in some of the less fashionable streets of London, he was deeply touched by the devotion of his people. In these streets, far removed from any processional route, the decorations and loyal messages were just as abundant, just as effective as those along the great main highways of the capital. I did not realise that they felt like this towards me,[2] he said.

In fact, the appreciation of the people moved the King to tears. "I am sure I cannot understand it, for, after all, I am only a very ordinary sort of fellow." After a service of thanksgiving on May 6th, His Majesty broadcast a message of gratitude to his people:

> At the close of this memorable day I must speak to my people everywhere. Yet how can I express what is in my heart?... How could I feel to be most deeply moved? Words cannot express my thoughts and feelings. I can only say to you, my very dear people, that the Queen and I thank you from the depth of our hearts for all the loyalty, may I say, the love with

1   (ed.) Gibbs: *George the Faithful: The Life & Times of George V "The People's King" 1865-1936,* pp.305-306.
2   Anon: *The Life of King George V: The Life and Work of a Monarch Beloved of his Peoples,* pp.5-6.

which this day and always you have surrounded us. I dedicate myself anew to your service for the years that may still be given to me... To the children I would like to send a special message. Let me say this to each of them whom my words may reach: The King is speaking to *you*. I ask you to remember that in days to come you will be the citizens of a great Empire. As you grow up always keep this thought before you; and when the time comes be ready and proud to give to your country the service of your work, you mind, and your heart.[3]

On Christmas Day, 1935, His Majesty made his last broadcast to the nation.

It is [the] personal link between me and my people which I value more than I can say. It binds us together in all our common joys and sorrows... I feel the link now as I speak to you... Once again as I close I send to you all, and not least to the children who may be listening to me, my truest Christmas wishes, and those of my dear wife, my children and my grandchildren who are with me today. I add a heartfelt prayer that, wherever you are, God may bless you and keep you always.[4]

A little over three weeks later, he died. Clement Atlee, Leader of the Labour Party, delivered a eulogy in the House of Commons:

The responsibility which rests on the shoulders of a ruler of a great nation must always be heavy, even in times of tranquillity, but when a man is called upon to rule not over one nation but over a Commonwealth of nations, not in peace only but during the greatest war in history, not in a period of slow development but when the tide of change is running strongly and old landmarks are being swept away, the burden must be almost intolerable.

    Yet this was the lot of King George. He reigned during a period of transition... Even without a world war I think those years must have been years of stress. The advance of science, the spread of education, the progress of ideas of self-government at home and oversea, the pressure of economic forces... The World War came and accelerated all these developments. It was a forcing house of change. The old world passed away and a new one was born.

    Two things, I think, were required from the Sovereign of a great State in those conditions. The first was sympathy with the new ideas, and readiness to accept change and to adapt himself to altered conditions; and the second was the power to give to society, bewildered by the rapid progress of events, a rallying point of stability. These things were found in King George in full measure.[5]

His Majesty died just before his troops returned to that corner of northwest Europe so blighted by war to do it all again. Queen Mary, however would live to see it. Shortly before his death, the King had remarked that his heir would ruin himself. He was not wrong. The Queen witnessed David's abdication. In the years following the war, Edward VIII's relationship with his father had deteriorated. The throne was the elephant in the room. Their son didn't want it, and he did not share his father's pragmatism, nor his willingness to adapt and accept the hand that life had dealt him. For his part, the King could not come to terms with his son's unwillingness to embrace his future, or to put his role ahead of his own wishes as he had had to do. When he gave up the throne,

---

3   Ibid., pp.2-3.
4   Ibid., pp.152-153.
5   Pope-Hennessy: *Queen Mary, 1867-1953*, p.573.

his mother was angry, and she was hurt. "To other members of the Family she declared both at that time and subsequently that no single event in the whole of her life… had caused her so much distress or left her with so deep a feeling of humiliation." In hindsight, the Monarchy was better off. "I will do my best to clear up the inevitable mess," Bertie wrote to his mother as he stepped into the breach, "if the whole fabric does not crumble under the shock and strain of it all."[6] He did much more than that.

To her disgust, Queen Mary was sent to the West Country by her second son when war broke out again. "For her to leave London in war-time was not, she declared, "at all the thing," for she looked upon it as a dereliction of duty."[7] The King was ultimately able to talk her round, and she withdrew to a relative's house at Badminton in Gloucestershire. Now in her 70s she rode about in a farm cart, accompanied by the men assigned to protect her in the event of invasion or in case of a Nazi attempt to kidnap her by aeroplane. The Queen Mother busied herself salvaging for scrap iron and bottles for the dump operating out of Slaites Quarry. Her Majesty had ever had a particular bond with Prince George, by then the Duke of Kent. In August 1942, the telephone rang at Badminton to tell her that her Georgie was dead, killed in an air crash at the age of 39 when it collided with a hillside in Scotland and caught fire.

And in 1952 she would lose a third of her sons. Bertie, who reigned as George VI, had had an operation to try and cure him of lung cancer. He was well enough to spend Christmas at Sandringham with his family, and by the end of January, the doctors pronounced themselves delighted with the state of his health. But at 9:30am on Wednesday 6th February she was told that a telephone message had just arrived from Sandringham. His Majesty had been found dead that morning by his valet. At 85, "from this last great emotional shock of her life," Queen Mary never recovered. "To a lifelong friend, Lady Shaftesbury, who came to visit her about this time, Queen Mary made one of her rare references to the likelihood of her own death. 'I suppose,' she said suddenly, 'one must force oneself to go on until the end?' 'I am sure,' replied Lady Shaftesbury, 'that Your Majesty will.'"[8] As 1953 began Her Majesty watched keenly the preparations for her granddaughter's coronation. She ordered that if she did not live to see it, events "must on no account of mourning be postponed." Queen Mary passed away on the evening of 24th March, 1953, some five weeks before the ceremony.

George V was a bundle of contradictions. A country squire with humble tastes, he nonetheless understood his role at the head of one of the world's dominant powers. Tolerant of those of different race and colour in a time when few of his contemporaries would have even considered that they should be, he was also pragmatic about the future of the Empire as its figurehead, whether he personally dreaded developments or not. The same was true of domestic politics. Throughout his reign George V was more successful than not when it came to separating his personal opinions and feelings from his responsibilities as King. Likewise, though in private he could be tactless and bolshy, not once after he was crowned did these traits penetrate his public life and cause his realm embarrassment. Loth to perform public speeches, George V's reign nonetheless pioneered the new concept of public relations and the Royal Family. He understood that to survive, the monarchy could not sit apart from the people, behind closed doors, but had to take its place more effectively among them. He went out amongst his subjects in a manner that would have fully astounded his predecessors. He was loved for it by those that met him because it was clear that he did this, not because of how benevolent it would make him look, but because he genuinely cared, because he

6   Ibid., p.583.
7   Ibid., p.596.
8   Ibid., p.619.

considered that it was part of his job and because he believed that it was something that a King who represented an entire nation, not just the upper echelons of its people, needed to do to fulfil his role. In this, his Queen was his constant companion, because she not only understood this concept, but because since childhood her mother had raised her to passionately believe in it too. In short, King George and Queen Mary were good people, decent people. They led by example and without being aloof or unapproachable. Their subjects knew all of this and not only respected, but loved them for it. The Great War both highlighted all of these traits, bringing them to the attention of the world under a microscope for nearly five years, and accelerated their adaptation and development. His Majesty amassed 450 troop visits, 300 more to hospitals, the same again to munitions factories and shipyards; and with his own hands conferring more than 50,000 awards. The King presented 95% of all of the Great War Victoria Cross's to the recipients or their next of kin.

Amidst the fall of empires, demands for Home Rule in Ireland, self-government in India, the decline of the House of Lords, the rise of the Labour Party; the cataclysmic event that stood out above all others and with which, as they mourned him, the nation associated their King was this war. In total contrast to his Russian cousin, George V was precisely the right man: industrious to a fault; a man who truly cared about those he came into contact with, what they endured, and how either with broad strokes or finite interference he might try to help to make their lot easier. Unlike Nicholas II, His Majesty was also in the right place, Britain, which dictated that he be a constitutional monarch not weighed down by the perils of practical leadership in either a military or political sense, which held him at a safe distance from the mistakes of those who were. And in that case, he was free to wholly dedicate himself to the role that was then left for him to fulfil. And unlike his cousin, for whom the war would prove the culmination of his failed reign, for the King, the Great War was precisely the right time. What Britain needed was a supreme patriot, with a love for his people and an unshakeable belief in them, in his role and in a sense of duty that he believed should see him work every bit as hard as they did towards victory when such an effort was required of everyone who valued Britain's future. His Majesty believed that it was something that all Britons must achieve together. The war might have aged him, but unlike numbers of crowned heads who fell during and in the years following 1918, it did not break him. Instead, the Great War was instrumental in shaping the modern monarchy and formed a legacy upheld not only by the King himself, but then faithfully by his son, George VI and by his beloved granddaughter, Elizabeth II.

Bibliography

Archives

RA: Royal Archives, Windsor Castle.
TNA: The National Archives, Kew
NLS: National Library of Scotland, Edinburgh
PA: Parliamentary Archives, Westminster
BD: Bodleian Library, Oxford
CC: Churchill College, Cambridge
PP: Private Papers of Lord Wigram

Newspapers

The Times
Daily Telegraph
Morning Post
Morning Advertiser
Daily Graphic
Daily Sketch
Westminster Gazette
Pall Mall Gazette
Daily Mirror
Daily Express
*See individual references for additional publications

Biographies of George V

Gore, John: *King George V, A Personal Memoir.* John Murray, London, 1941.
Nicolson, Harold: *King George V: His Life and Reign.* Constable & Co. Ltd. London, 1952
Rose, Kenneth: *King George V.* Weidenfeld & Nicolson, London 1983.

Other Printed Sources

Anon: *The Life of King George V: The Life and Work of a Monarch Beloved of his Peoples.* Associated
    Newspapers, London, 1936.
Anon: 'The Royal Family and the War' *(The Times History of the War, Vol. XVIII).* London, 1919.
Asquith, Cynthia: *Lady Cynthia Asquith Diaries 1915-1918.* Hutchinson, London, 1968.
Asquith, Earl of Oxford: *Memories and Reflections. Vol. II.* Cassell & Company Ltd. London, 1928.
Asquith, Margot: *The Autobiography of Margot Asquith.* Methuen, London, 1985.
Athlone, HRH Prince Alice of: *For My Grandchildren.* Evans Brothers Ltd, London, 1979

Bates, Stephen: *Asquith*. Haus Publishing Ltd. London, 2006

Battiscombe, Georgina: *Queen Alexandra*. Constable, London, 1969.

Beaverbrook, Lord: *Politicians & the War 1914-1916*. Thornton Butterworth Ltd. London, 1928.

Becket, Ian F.W: *King George V and His Generals*. In *Leadership in Conflict, 1914-1918*. Leo Cooper, Barnsley, 2000.

Birdwood, Lord: *Khaki and Gown*. Ward, Lock & Co. Ltd. London, 1941.

Bogdanor, Vernon: *The Monarchy and the Constitution*. Clarendon Press, Oxford, 1995.

Bonham Carter, Violet: *Winston Churchill As I Knew Him*. Wiedenfeld & Nicolson, London, 1995.

Bradford, Sarah: *George VI*. Penguin Books, London, 2011.

(ed.) Brock, Michael & Eleanor: *H.H. Asquith: Letters to Venetia Stanley*. Oxford University Press, Oxford, 1982.

(ed.) Brock, Michael & Eleanor: *Margot Asquith's Great War Diary 1914-1916, The View from Downing Street*. Oxford University Press, Oxford, 2014.

Bruce, Anthony: *The Last Crusade: The Palestine Campaign in the First World War*. John Murray, London, 2002.

Cassar, George: *Kitchener: Architect of Victory*. William Kimber & Co. Ltd. London, 1977.

(ab.) Cathcart, Michael: *Manning Clark's History of Australia*. Chatto & Windus, London **[??]**

Chalmers, W.S.: *The Life & Letters of David Beatty, Admiral of the Fleet*. Hodder & Stoughton, London, 1951.

Churchill, Sir Winston: *Great Contemporaries*. The Reprint Society, London, 1941.

Churchill, Sir Winston: *The World Crisis 1911-1918*. Penguin, London, 2007.

Clark, Christopher: *Iron Kingdom: The Rise and Downfall of Prussia 1600-1947*. Penguin, London, 2007.

Clark, Christopher: *Kaiser Wilhelm II, A Life in Power*. Penguin Books, London, 2009.

Cooper, Duff: *Haig*. Faber & Faber, London, 1935.

(ed.) David, Edward: *Inside Asquith's Cabinet, From the Diaries of Charles Hobhouse*. John Murray, London, 1977.

Fox, Frank: *The King's Pilgrimage*. Hodder & Stoughton, London, 1922.

Frankland, Noble: *Prince Henry, Duke of Gloucester*. Weidenfeld & Nicolson, 1980.

Frankland, Noble: *Witness of a Century*. Sheheard-Walwyn, London, 1993.

Gerwath, Robert: *The Vanquished: Why the First World War Failed to End 1917-1923*. Allen Lane, London, 2016.

(ed.) Gibbs, Sir Philip: *George the Faithful: The Life & Times of George V "The People's King" 1865-1936*. Hutchinson & Co. Ltd. London, 1936.

(ed.) Godfrey, Rupert: *Letters from a Prince: Edward, Prince of Wales to Mrs Freda Dudley Ward, March 1918-January 1921*. Warner, London, 1999

Grigg, John: *Lloyd George, From Peace to War 1912-1916*. Methuen Ltd., London, 1985.

(ed.) Hammerton, J. A. & Wilson, H.W: *The Great War: The Standard History of the World-Wide Conflict, Vol. X*. Amalgamated Press, London, 1918.

Hammerton, John Alexander: *Our King & Queen: A Pictorial Record of Their Lives*. Amalgamated Press, London, 1935.

Hanbury-Williams, Sir John: *The Emperor Nicholas II As I Knew Him.* Arthur L Humphreys, London, 1922.

Hardinge, Lady: *Loyal to Three Kings.* Kimber, London, 1967.

Hart, Peter: *The Great War.* Profile Books, London, 2013.

Healey, Edna: *The Queen's House: A Social History of Buckingham Palace.* Michael Joseph, London, 1997.

Hohenzollern, Wilhelm of: *The Kaiser's Memoirs.* H.Fertig, New York, 1975.

Holmes, Richard: *The Little Field Marshal: A Life of Sir John French.* Cassell, London, 1981.

James, Lawrence: *The Rise and Fall of the British Empire.* St. Martin's Griffin, New York, 1997.

Jenkins, Roy: *Churchill.* Pan Books, London, 2001.

Jordan, David: *The Battle for the Skies: Sir Hugh Trenchard as Commander of the Royal Flying Corps'.* In *Leadership in Conflict, 1914-1918.* Leo Cooper, Barnsley, 2000.

Judd, Denis: *The Lion and the Tiger; The Rise and Fall of the British Raj, 1600-1947.* OUP, Oxford, 2004.

Lee, Sir Sidney: *Edward VII, A Biography.* MacMillian and Co Ltd, London, 1927.

[ed.] Longford, Elizabeth: *Darling Loos: Letters to Princess Louise 1856-1939.* Wiedenfeld & Nicolson, London, 1991.

MacKenzie, Donald A: *Lord Kitchener: The Story of his Life and Work.* Blackie & Son Ltd., London, 1916.

Mason, John W: *The Dissolution of the Austro-Hungarian Empire 1867-1918.* Longman, London, 1985.

Massie, Robert Kinloch: *Nicholas and Alexandra.* Dell, New York, 1968.

Marie Louise, Princess: *My Memories of Six Reigns.* Evans Brothers, London, 1956.

McCrery, NIgel: *All the King's Men.* Pocket, London, 1999.

Palmer, Alan: *Twilight of the Hapsburgs: The Life and Times of Emperor Francis Joseph.* Avalon, London, 1997.

Parker, Nigel J.: *Gott Strafe England, The German Air Assault Against Great Britain 1914-18 Vol. I. 1914-1916* Helion, Solihull, 2015.

Parker, Nigel J.: *Gott Strafe England, The German Air Assault Against Great Britain 1914-18 Vol. II. 1917-1918.* Helion, Solihull, 2015.

Pope-Hennessy, James: *Queen Mary, 1867-1953.* George Allen & Unwin Ltd. London, 1959.

Prior, Robin & Wilson, Trevor: *Passchendaele: The Untold Story.* Yale University Press, New Haven, 2002.

Prochaska, Frank: *The Republic of Britain, 1760-2000.* Penguin Books, London, 2000.

Purcell, Hugh: *Lloyd George.* Haus Publishing Ltd. London 2006.

Rawlinson, Cdr A.: *The Defence of London, 1915-1918.* Andrew Melrose Ltd. London, 1923.

Ridley, Jane: *Bertie: A Life of Edward VII.* Chatto & Windus, London, 2012.

Robertson, Sir William: *From Private to Field Marshal.* Constable & Co. Ltd, London, 1921.

Rose, Kenneth: *Kings, Queens & Courtiers: Intimate Portraits of the Royal House of Windsor from its Foundation to the Present Day.* Weidenfeld & Nicolson, London, 1985.

St. Aubyn, Giles: *Edward VII: Prince and King.* Collins, London, 1979.

(ed.) Sheffield, Gary & Bourne, John: *Douglas Haig: War Diaries and Letters 1914-1918.* Weidenfeld & Nicolson, London, 2005.

Simkins, Peter: *Kitchener's Army: The Raising of the New Armies 1914-1916.* Pen & Sword, Barnsley, 2014.

Stibbe, Matthew: *Kaiser Wilhelm II: The Hohenzollerns at War.* In *Leadership in Conflict, 1914-1918.* Leo Cooper, Barnsley, 2000.

Syonsby, Lord: *Recollections of Three Reigns.* Eyre & Spottiswoode, London, 1951.

(ed.) The Times: *Hail and Farewell: The Passing of King George V.* The Times Publishing Co. Ltd. London, 1936

Thompson, Leonard: *A History of South Africa.* Yale University Press, London, 1992.

Wake, Jehanne: *Princess Louise: Queen Victoria's Unconventional daughter.* Collins, London, 1988

Warner, Philip: *Kitchener: The Man Behind the Legend.* Cassell, London, 2006.

Watson, Francis: *Dawson of Penn.* Chatto and Windus, London, 1950.

Windsor, Duke of: *A King's Story: The Memoirs of the Duke of Windsor.* Prion Books Ltd. London, 1951.

Ziegler, Philip: *King Edward VIII: The Official Biography.* William Collins & Sons, Glasgow, 1990.

Index